T0417676

STUDIES IN THE TRANSMISSION OF TEXTS & IDEAS

11

EDITOR IN CHIEF

Wim DECOCK

EDITORIAL BOARD

Anthony DUPONT
Michèle GOYENS
Marleen REYNDERS
Stefan SCHORN

SUBMISSIONS
SHOULD BE SENT TO

Marleen REYNDERS
marleen.reynders@kuleuven.be

Questioning the World

Greek Patristic and Byzantine Question-and-Answer Literature

edited by

Bram DEMULDER

Peter VAN DEUN

BREPOLS

D/2021/0095/70

DOI 10.1484/M.LECTIO-EB.5.121071

ISBN 978-2-503-59075-2

e-ISBN 978-2-503-59076-9

ISSN 2565-8506

e-ISSN 2565-9626

Printed in the EU on acid-free paper.

TABLE OF CONTENTS

BRAM DEMULDER & PETER VAN DEUN

INTRODUCTION:
QUESTIONS AND *KOSMOI*

Ἐπιζητεῖ δὲ ὁ λόγος, εἰ συγκατεσκευάσθη τῷ κόσμῳ τὸ σκότος, καὶ εἰ ἀρχαιότερον τοῦ φωτός, καὶ διὰ τί τὸ χεῖρον πρεσβύτερον; Λέγομεν τοίνυν καὶ τοῦτο τὸ σκότος μὴ κατ᾽ οὐσίαν ὑφεστηκέναι, ἀλλὰ πάθος εἶναι περὶ τὸν ἀέρα στερήσει φωτὸς ἐπιγινόμενον. Ποίου τοίνυν φωτὸς ἄμοιρος αἰφνιδίως ὁ ἐν τῷ κόσμῳ τόπος εὑρέθη, ὥστε τὸ σκότος ἐπάνω εἶναι τοῦ ὕδατος; Λογιζόμεθα τοίνυν ὅτι, εἴπερ τι ἦν πρὸ τῆς τοῦ αἰσθητοῦ τούτου καὶ φθαρτοῦ κόσμου συστάσεως, ἐν φωτὶ ἂν ἦν δηλονότι. Οὔτε γὰρ αἱ τῶν ἀγγέλων ἀξίαι, οὔτε πᾶσαι αἱ ἐπουράνιοι στρατιαί, οὔτε ὅλως εἴ τι ἐστὶν ὠνομασμένον ἢ ἀκατονόμαστον τῶν λογικῶν φύσεων, καὶ τῶν λειτουργικῶν πνευμάτων ἐν σκότῳ διῆγεν, ἀλλ᾽ ἐν φωτὶ καὶ πάσῃ εὐφροσύνῃ πνευματικῇ τὴν πρέπουσαν ἑαυτοῖς κατάστασιν εἶχε. Καὶ τούτοις οὐδεὶς ἀντερεῖ, οὔκουν ὅστις γε τὸ ὑπερουράνιον φῶς ἐν ταῖς τῶν ἀγαθῶν ἐπαγγελίαις ἐκδέχεται, περὶ οὗ Σολομών φησι· Φῶς δικαίοις διὰ παντός.

(Basil of Caesarea, *Hom. in Hexaem.* 2.5; ed. SC 26bis)

But reason asks, was darkness created with the world? Is it older than light? Why in spite of its inferiority has it preceded it? Darkness, we reply, did not exist in essence; it is a condition produced in the air by the withdrawal of light. What then is that light which disappeared suddenly from the world, so that darkness should cover the face of the deep? If anything had existed before the formation of this sensible and perishable world, no doubt we conclude it would have been in light. The orders of angels, the heavenly hosts, all intellectual natures named or unnamed, all the ministering spirits, did not live in darkness, but enjoyed a condition fitted for them in light and spiritual joy. No one will contradict

Questioning the World, Greek Patristic and Byzantine Question-and-Answer Literature, ed. by Bram Demulder and Peter Van Deun,
Turnhout, 2021 (*LECTIO*, 11), pp. 9-19   © BREPOLS🐝PUBLISHERS   DOI 10.1484/M.LECTIO-EB.5.121500

this; least of all he who looks for celestial light as one of the rewards promised to virtue, the light which, as Solomon says, is always a light to the righteous [...]. (trans. NPNF)

This volume brings together studies on Greek Patristic and Byzantine texts which question the world. In a narrow sense this means that this book is about cosmological *erōtapokriseis* – about question-and-answer literature which discusses the nature of the universe – and this is indeed the case for a large part of the volume.[1] One of the aims of the work, however, is to make it clear that 'question-and-answer literature' and 'cosmology' cannot always be defined quite so narrowly. Basil of Caesarea's homilies on the Bible's creation narrative, as quoted above, readily illustrate this.

While, strictly speaking, the literary genre of *erōtapokriseis* is formally marked by a series of questions followed by answers, the questioning attitude which defines this genre cannot be confined to such a formal criterion. The spirit of inquiry, of *zētēsis*, behind question-and-answer literature can only be brought out by considering a wide array of texts (see Papadogiannakis in this volume). Hence the need to inquire into questions and answers as they play an important role in and interact with genres such as anthology (Roosen, Ceulemans, Van Deun in this volume), exegesis (Cvetković, Tollefsen, Mueller-Jourdan), capita literature (Tollefsen), dialogue (Meeusen), philosophical treatise (Boeri), or – as in the passage from Basil – homily (also Ceulemans in this volume).[2] After calling for a questioning attitude (ἐπιζητεῖ), Basil indeed goes on to show his audience how questioning the creation narrative should proceed.

More specifically, Basil's questions and answers concern the connection between darkness and the cosmos from a theological standpoint and quickly spill into decidedly ethical issues concerning the inferiority of darkness and the righteousness of light.

---

[1] On the literary genre of *erōtapokriseis* in general see, apart from Papadogiannakis' chapter in this volume, e.g. Papadoyannakis 2006; Efthymiadis 2017; Perrone 2019. Earlier collective volumes include Volgers & Zamagni 2004 and Bussières 2013.

[2] See also Papadoyannakis 2006, p. 99–100; Efthymiadis 2017, p. 47–50; Rigolio 2019, p. 22–24 on the connection between question-and-answer literature and dialogue.

This brings us to a second problem of demarcation which will be confronted by the authors in this volume: cosmology, which is a modern label anyway, cannot be understood here as an investigation into the structure of the visible universe. As will become clear throughout this volume, 'cosmological' questions and answers include a broad spectrum of issues such as, indeed, light and darkness (Mueller-Jourdan), but also e.g. evil (Papdogiannakis), number (Morlet), divine will (Tollefsen), liturgy (Boudignon), general world view (Roosen, Meeusen), and, of course, God (Papadogiannakis, Boeri).

As Mueller-Jourdan's discussion of the ontological status of light and darkness will show, Basil's answers to his questions about light later occupied John Philoponus. This is but one of many examples to come of how cosmological questions and answers are at the same time fascinating and challenging objects of reception studies. A particular concern of this volume is the two-faced involvement of questions and answers in the dynamics of reception. On the one hand, questions and answers are a fruitful form for receiving earlier knowledge (Boeri, Morlet, Ceulemans). On the other hand, the very format of *erōtapokriseis* also makes them prone to being received and incorporated into later collections of questions and answers or into other genres (Boudignon, Meeusen, Roosen).

The first two parts of the book focus on two important *corpora*: the collections of *erōtapokriseis* wrongly attributed to Justin the Martyr (part 1) and the oeuvre of Maximus the Confessor (part 2). The third and the fourth part of our study of cosmological *erōtapokriseis* are devoted to the theme of cosmology (part 3) and the genre of *erōtapokriseis* respectively (part 4).

1. *Pseudo-Justin*

Yannis Papadogiannakis opens his contribution by pointing out how the process of ζήτησις ('inquiry') gave rise to the literary format of question-and-answer literature and how, from the outset, questions of natural philosophy were central to this endeavour. After having thus indicated the impetus for this volume as a whole, Papadogiannakis offers a *tour d'horizon* of the cosmos as it emerges from Pseudo-Justin's *Quaestiones et responsiones ad* *orthodoxos*.[3] Issues of cosmic macro-structure (God's place in the cosmos, the existence of evil, empirical and scriptural arguments for the flat earth and the firmament) and cosmic micro-structure (the role and persistence of the elements) are discussed in detail along with God's role in the cosmogony. By paying great attention to the philosophical and theological background of Pseudo-Justin's cosmological enquiries, Papadogiannakis gives insight into what will be a concern throughout the present volume: although the texts under scrutiny present us with inquiry of a cosmological nature, the ulterior theological motive of said inquiry should never be ignored.

The next three contributions complete this picture of Pseudo-Justin's cosmological *erōtapokriseis*. **Benjamin Gleede** goes beyond the *Quaestiones et responsiones ad orthodoxos* and undertakes a historical contextualisation of the Pseudo-Justinian corpus of *erōtapokriseis* as a whole. After sketching the *status quaestionis* on these collections of questions and answers, Gleede carefully examines the literary form of the texts under discussion by looking into aspects such as the prefaces, the dialogical character, and the aporetic conclusions. This enables him to argue in favour of the texts' literary integrity and, subsequently, to attribute the collections to a single, Nestorian author. Gleede concludes his contribution by outlining the historical milieu of this author and by proposing a date between 451 and 519 for the emergence of the corpus.

The contributions of Marcelo Boeri and Sébastien Morlet probe further into the philosophical and theological background of the Pseudo-Justinian corpus, which is outlined in Papadogiannakis' contribution, by turning to issues of (polemical) reception. **Marcelo Boeri** focuses on Pseudo-Justin's *Confutatio dogmatum quorundam aristotelicorum*, a work which exemplifies the problems with a strict definition of the *erōtapokriseis* genre: while it is not strictly a work in the question-and-answer format, it breathes the same zetetic spirit and the same philosophical (particularly cosmological) interest as the other Pseudo-Justinian collections.

---

[3] On the Pseudo-Justinian corpus of *erōtapokriseis* and its historical context see also Ritter & Toth 2018, which takes into account early versions of the papers by Papadogiannakis and Gleede which appear in the present volume.

Boeri demonstrates this by considering Pseudo-Justin's arguments against Aristotle's Unmoved Prime Mover, the *pièce de résistance* of Aristotelian cosmology. As Boeri argues, Pseudo-Justin's objections to Aristotle's theory should, surprisingly perhaps, be considered as internal criticism: they are based on Aristotle's own premises and assumptions and would, as such, be acceptable on Aristotle's own terms. While not losing sight of Pseudo-Justin's Christian agenda, which does not allow for the eternity of movement and, hence, an eternal cosmos, Boeri exposes Pseudo-Justin's polemics as a prime example of Byzantine philosophy. Moreover, while the polemical *Confutatio* does not propose an alternative cosmological model and its scientific contributions point to a pre-modern understanding of science as speculative rather than empirical, Pseudo-Justin's work attacks Aristotle by attesting to the ever valid cosmological principle that the laws governing the movements of the terrestrial world govern the heavenly movements as well.

Sébastien Morlet concludes the volume's section on Pseudo-Justinian cosmological questions. Morlet offers a case study of one of the *Quaestiones et responsiones ad orthodoxos*, the collection which was introduced in Papadogiannakis' chapter. Morlet's close reading unveils a polemical reception of Philo of Alexandria in the 69th question of the collection: 'Why is the number 7 indicative of change?' While acknowledging the significance of the number 7 in nature, Pseudo-Justin firmly argues that the number follows nature and not *vice versa*. Hence, this *quaestio* should be read as a rejection of arithmological speculation. More specifically, Morlet points out, it is a critical response to Philo's *De opificio mundi*. As the analysis of this complex instance of Philonian reception shows, Philo is at the same time the (structural and philosophical) source and the target of Pseudo-Justin's text. Morlet goes on to connect the results of his interpretation to the theological milieu in which the Pseudo-Justinian collection arose and argues for an Antiochian, anti-Alexandrian context given its anti-arithmological stance. More specifically, Morlet sympathetically yet with due caution reconsiders the hypothesis that Theodoret was the author of the collection, thus further stimulating the debate on the historical context of the Pseudo-Justinian collections.

2. *Maximus the Confessor*

The four chapters of the second section of this volume shed light on the cosmological questions and answers entertained by Maximus the Confessor.[4] **Vladimir Cvetković** gives a wide-ranging overview of Maximus' cosmology by taking the *Ambigua ad Ioannem* as a starting point. Once again, then, we are confronted with a text which is driven by questions and *aporiai* without being a prototypical example of the *erōtapokriseis* genre. Cvetković traces how, throughout the *Ambigua*, Maximus develops his views on the *logoi* of creation (*Amb.* 7), on the logical structure of the cosmos (*Amb.* 10), and on the five divisions of the creation (*Amb.* 41) in dialogue with his Neoplatonic and Patristic sources. Thus, this chapter yields crucial insight into how, in question-and-answer literature (and related genres), *ad hoc* polemics and influence can occur together with more general and oftentimes original system-building tendencies.

With particular attention to the *Quaestiones ad Thalassium* as well as to *erōtapokriseis*-adjacent texts such as the *Capita de caritate* and the *Ambigua ad Ioannem*, **Torstein Tollefsen** compares Maximus' Christian doctrine of creation with Neoplatonic pagan cosmology. Both *kosmoi* are characterised by divine goodness and find their origin in divine will. Each tradition, however, presents us with a very different conception of this divine will. While, in Neoplatonic cosmology, divine will is non-deliberative (it is the will of the One to be itself rather than a choice between options) and pertains exclusively to the care for the cosmos as a whole, Maximus' cosmology allows for divine will to be deliberative (God contemplated the making of the world) and personal. God's will directs Him to create and care for His indiviual creatures within a temporal horizon which has a definite beginning. In other words: in Maximus' cosmos, as opposed to the Neoplatonic cosmos, divine care for particulars and divine care for universals go hand in hand. Showing once again that, in these matters, cosmology cannot be separated from other, e.g. theological, domains, Tollefsen goes on to connect Maximus' cosmol-

---

[4] See Blowers 1991 and Van Deun 2015 on Maximus' *erōtapokriseis* and on the difficulties with strictly delineating which of his works fall under this genre.

ogy to the mystery of Christ as the mystery of divine love which is manifested cosmologically as well as soteriologically.

While Tollefsen focuses on the (polemical) reception of earlier traditions *within* question-and-answer literature, **Christian Boudignon** turns to Maximus' creative reception *of* earlier questions and answers. In his *Letter of Abamon* (traditionally known as *De mysteriis Aegyptiorum*), the Neoplatonist Iamblichus replied to his teacher Porphyry's objections against religious practices. This Iamblichus did by distilling *aporiai* from Porphyry and tackling these as questions. As Boudignon shows, Maximus' *Mystagogia* reflects Iamblichus' question-and-answer work both structurally and philosophically. More specifically, Maximus' notions of image and figure, which are at the heart of his thinking about liturgy, closely follow Iamblichus' notion of symbol, which stands at the centre of his conception of religious practice. The first part of the *Mystagogia* describes the church as image and figure of the world and, ultimately, of God. This echoes Iamblichus' conviction that cult statues are reflections of the stars and, ultimately, of the gods. The second part of Maximus' work explains the role of the high priest (whose entrance into the church is the image of God's entrance into the world) in terms of Iamblichus' take on the telestic art (the pagan ritual which aims to summon the divine in statues). This ritual depends on the cosmic correspondence between the intelligible and the sensible which is witnessed through 'universal sympathy'.

A third dynamics of reception which complements the previous two chapters is uncovered by **Bram Roosen**, who offers a discussion and critical edition of the remnants of a Maximian question-and-answer collection (*CPG* 7707.38 and *CPG* 7697.26a + 7707.20; the former receives its *editio prima* here). This collection of *erōtapokriseis* probably had Maximus and Theodosius of Gangra as its protagonists, but only two answers, without their respective questions, survive in different versions. Roosen, then, adds an important element to be considered when discussing *erōtapokriseis*: their very nature makes for an often complex textual transmission and for difficulties in determining authenticity and authorship. They are prone to adaptation resulting in different versions; they are often excerpted, which causes their genre characteristics to be adapted to another genre such as the anthology; they were transmitted only fragmentarily, ... Roosen's case study offers insight into these generic challenges while also bringing out the complexities of the thematic focus of this volume: the fragments, which discuss the terms πρόγνωσις, προορισμός, φύσις, οὐσία, ἄτομον, and ὑπόστασις, testify to the need to adopt a broad definition of cosmology, taking into account its relevance to other domains, i.c. Christology.

3. *Cosmologies in Sixth-Century Byzantium*

Both contributions in the third section, like that of Cvetković in the previous one, confront the challenge of extracting or rather reconstructing a systematic cosmological doctrine from question-and-answer literature, i.e. from a text which treats very particular *aporiai*. The works in question here are both sixth-century texts: John Philoponus' *De opificio mundi* and the collection of *erōtapokriseis* which was once incorrectly ascribed to Caesarius of Nazianzus.[5] **Pascal Mueller-Jourdan** takes up the challenge of reconstructing a coherent explanation of light from Philoponus' question-driven comments on the biblical creation narrative. One of Philoponus' main goals is to defend the authority of Scripture over and against other investigations of natural phenomena (most notably by Plato and Aristotle). Of particular concern is the notion, expressed in Genesis, that primitive, incorporeal light was created *before* the creation of corporeal luminaries (i.e. bodies which give light). Maintaining the balance between philosophical systematicity and *aporia*, Mueller-Jourdan gives an overview of the cosmological issues which are evoked by this statement. Most notably, Philoponus' views on the creation of primitive light before the creation of luminaries seem to posit a moment of the cosmogony which ignores the laws of physics which come into effect once the cosmos is created.

Tackling a similar reconstructive endeavour through a different methodological approach, **István Perczel** inquires into the theological background of the author behind the Pseudo-Caesarian collection of *erōtapokriseis*. Building upon his earlier work,

---

[5] For a general overview of sixth-century cosmology see e.g. Tihon 2017.

Perczel identifies this author as the Isochrist Origenist Theodore of Caesarea. The rationale behind this identification is an interpretation of the apparently anti-Origenist Pseudo-Caesarian questions and answers as being composed in a coded language which awaits decoding. Perczel develops a decoding method and applies it to the cosmological sections of the work. This results in a cosmology which allows for a pre-temporal creation of rational beings and an ensuing pre-cosmic fall of these beings.

4. *Questioning Genre in the Middle-Byzantine Period*

While, in the previous section, the contributions took into account matters of genre in order to solve cosmological problems, this section shifts the focus: cosmological issues are taken into account in order to consider questions of genre. The following chapters, not unlike that of Roosen earlier, explore the generic versatility of *erōtapokriseis*. **Michiel Meeusen** studies the reception of Plutarch's *Quaestiones convivales* in Michael Psellus' *De omnifaria doctrina*. As Meeusen's analysis shows, the transfer between two instances of question-and-answer literature can come with drastic generic changes. While Plutarch's questions and answers received the embellishment of dialogue, Psellus strips away this dialogical framework in order to be able to focus on transmission of knowledge rather than on intellectual debate. After an overview of Psellus' interest in the profane physical phenomena discussed in Plutarch's *Quaestiones convivales*, Meeusen turns to a case study which once again challenges the bounds of cosmology as we understand it today: by discussing a question on the workings of the 'evil eye', he reveals changing attitudes towards physical wonders as well as Psellus' contribution to the creation of a Christian world view.

After Meeusen's discussion of the vicissitudes *within* (the broad boundaries of) the *erōtapokriseis* genre, **Reinhart Ceulemans** shows how *erōtapokriseis* can emerge from a *different* genre, i.c. homily. Ceulemans identifies part of MS B 43 of the Great Lavra monastery on Mount Athos as the unique witness of an untitled, twelfth-century anthology of one hundred chapters. After a general discussion of this anthology, Ceulemans offers an edition and translation of the excerpts taken from Severian of Gabala's *Homilies on the Hexaemeron*, which occur in the cosmological section of the anthology and are partly presented as *erōtapokriseis*. A comparison of these excerpts with Severian's text as well as with the catena tradition and other indirect witnesses gives insight into how the homily is, as it were, an *erōtapokriseis*-ready genre: shortly after the publication of Severian's homilies, certain sections were adapted into some form of compilation and, probably from there, made their way into other texts such as the anthology under discussion.

Peter Van Deun sheds further light on the connections between anthology and question-and-answer literature by considering the literary format of *De oeconomia Dei*, a twelfth-century anthology compiled by Nilus Doxapatres. As its title implies, this anthology has divine benevolence as its focus and amply treats issues of cosmogony and cosmology, especially as they pertain to mankind. This chapter shows once again how a great variety of earlier literature, including but not limited to earlier *erōtapokriseis*, can be moulded into new questions and answers. Van Deun's painstaking analysis reveals how this process of reception allows for subtle philosophical and exegetical originality through the intervention of the anthology's composer. Moreover, it shows the difficulty of assigning a genre label to *De oeconomia Dei* and, more generally, the difficulty of distinguishing genres in Byzantine literature.

Like Rome and, at least according to most authors discussed in this volume, the cosmos, this book was not built in a day. It ultimately traces back to a workshop on Pseudo-Justinian *erōtapokriseis* which was held in Leuven on 17 December 2014 and during which early versions of the contributions by Yannis Papadogiannakis and Benjamin Gleede were presented. This event took place within the framework of the KU Leuven GOA (concerted research action) 'From Chaos to Order – the Creation of the World. New Views on the Reception of Platonic Cosmogony in Later Greek Thought, Pagan and Christian' and was supported by Lectio, the Leuven centre for the study of the transmission of texts and ideas in Antiquity, the Middle Ages, and the Renaissance. We thank Peter Toth, who also presented a paper, and the other participants at this workshop for sharing their valuable insights. We thank the other contributors to this volume, who were invited and agreed to come on board some time after this initial workshop and who showed extraordinary patience throughout the process. We thank Sarah Van Pee for editorial support in the early stages and Maxim Venetskov for preparing the *indices*.

Bibliography

P. Blowers (1991), *Exegesis and Spiritual Pedagogy in Maximus Confessor. An Investigation of the Quaestiones ad Thalassium*, Notre Dame: University of Notre Dame Press.

M.-P. Bussières (ed., 2013), *La littérature des questions et réponses dans l'Antiquité profane et chrétienne: de l'enseignement à l'exégèse*, Turnhout: Brepols.

S. Efthymiades (2017), 'Questions and Answers', in A. Kaldellis & N. Siniossoglou (eds), *The Cambridge Intellectual History of Byzantium*, Cambridge: Cambridge University Press, p. 47–62.

Y. Papadoyannakis (2006), 'Instruction by Question and Answer in Late Antiquity: the Case of Late Antique Erotapokriseis', in S. Johnson (ed.), *Greek Literature in Late Antiquity: Dynamism, Didacticism, Classicism*, Aldershot: Ashgate, p. 91–105.

L. Perrone (2019), 'Questions and Answers', in P. M. Blowers & P. W. Martens (eds), *The Oxford Handbook of Early Christian Biblical Interpretation*, Oxford: Oxford University Press, p. 198–209.

A. Rigolio (2019), *Christians in Conversation. A Guide to Late Antique Dialogues in Greek and Syriac*, Oxford: Oxford University Press.

A. M. Ritter & P. Toth (2018), 'Sechs ps.-justinische Traktate', in C. Riedweg et al. (eds), *Die Philosophie der Antike. Band 5: Philosophie der Kaiserzeit und der Spätantike*, Basel: Schwabe, p. 2250–2263.

A. Tihon (2017), 'Astronomy', in A. Kaldellis & N. Siniossoglou (eds), *The Cambridge Intellectual History of Byzantium*, Cambridge: Cambridge University Press, p. 183–197.

P. Van Deun (2015), 'Maximus the Confessor's Use of Literary Genres', in P. Allen & B. Neil (eds), *The Oxford Handbook of Maximus the Confessor*, Oxford: Oxford University Press, p. 274–286.

A. Volgers & C. Zamagni (eds, 2004), *Erotapokriseis. Early Christian Question-and-Answer Literature in Context*, Leuven – Paris – Dudley, MA: Peeters.

PART 1
PSEUDO-JUSTIN

YANNIS PAPADOGIANNAKIS

COSMOLOGY AND ITS 'PROBLEMS' IN PS.-JUSTIN'S *QUAESTIONES ET RESPONSIONES AD ORTHODOXOS**

Cosmology in Late Antiquity was a vigorously contested and debated subject, if the volume of literature in the form of treatises, homilies, exegetical commentaries, and collections of questions and answers devoted to the topic is anything to go by. From this wealth of material, I would like to focus on a rich but neglected vein of enquiry on cosmology as displayed in the collection of questions and answers dating probably from the early sixth century, and attributed to Ps.-Justin: the *Quaestiones et responsiones ad orthodoxos* (hereafter QRO).[1] My intention is to analyse the ways in which cosmological 'problems', objections, and enquiries are addressed and debated as part of the process of ζήτησις ('enquiry'). Debate was an integral part of what drove Christians to address a Christian cosmology, even as it has been noted that 'early Christian thinkers articulating doctrine

* I am grateful to the European Research Council, which funded the research for this contribution with a Starting Grant for the project 'Defining Belief and Identities in the Eastern Mediterranean: The Role of Interreligious Debate and Disputation' and to Richard Sorabji for advice and assistance with that research.

[1] Various suggestions have been made concerning its authorship. Tzamalikos 2012, p. xi–xii has recently attributed the QRO to sixth-century author Cassian the Sabbaite. Toth 2014 re-examined the attribution of the QRO to Theodoret. After a review of the literature on QRO authorship, Gleede, in this volume, argues more plausibly for an as yet unidentified author and for a later date (as late as the first half of the sixth century) for the collection. Voicu 2015, p. 555–557 also argues tentatively for a later date, possibly after the *Henotikon* (482), and for an author who is opposed to the council of Chalcedon. His basis for this argument is QRO's Christological terminology and its references to baptismal practice. Most recently Toth in Ritter & Toth 2018 concurs with the proposed later dating of the collection.

Questioning the World, Greek Patristic and Byzantine Question-and-Answer Literature, ed. by Bram Demulder and Peter Van Deun, Turnhout, 2021 (*LECTIO*, 11), pp. 23-65 © BREPOLS♦PUBLISHERS DOI 10.1484/M.LECTIO-EB.5.121501

about Creator and creation rarely did so for strictly "cosmological" purposes. It is not an exaggeration to say that even in their Hexaemeral commentaries or their treatises addressing questions of cosmology, writers throughout the patristic age rarely, if ever, undertook straightforward expositions of cosmogony, metaphysics, physics, astronomy, etc. in isolation from ulterior theological and didactic concerns'.[2]

The QRO is a mixed bag, without any apparent ordering principle or plan. Questions vary in length and complexity from a couple of lines to 10–15 lines, ranging from linguistic aspects to the interpretation of disputed biblical passages, alongside the discussion of theological, historical, and more abstract philosophical-theological issues.[3] The QRO raises a number of questions about the range and kind of enquiries that it contains, the ways in which they came into the collection, the degree of the author's engagement with the issues in dispute, the purpose of their compilation, the audience for these collections, their reception, and the relationship of this collection to the rest of the Ps.-Justinian corpus where cosmological issues feature prominently. As this contribution hopes to make clear, the QRO are deeply implicated in the continuing debates on cosmology, echoing as they do many of the issues that exercised contemporary Christians in Late Antiquity.

1. *Format*

Before dealing with the particular issues that come up in QRO, it is important to set out the framework of understanding from which these collections and their format need to be approached. Questions and answers as a format originated in Classical Antiquity. Integral to many of these collections is the process of ζήτησις ('enquiry')[4] for the pursuit of which Aristotle laid out rules in his *Topics*.[5] Some of the earliest examples of this format involved enquiries about curiosa, human physiology, and the natural world

---

[2] Blowers 2013, p. 3.
[3] See Gass 1842; Dagron 1992; Papadoyannakis 2008.
[4] Zamagni 2004, p. 3 helpfully distinguishes between format and process.
[5] See the discussion in Mansfeld 1992; Oikonomopoulou 2013.

in the form of the Aristotelian προβλήματα.[6] This set in motion a tradition of using this format to discuss natural phenomena and their religious dimension.[7] This tradition continued well into the Byzantine period and beyond.[8] Built into these ζητήματα is the expectation that they would help their readers make sense of the world.[9] As well as enabling scientific investigation of the natural world, problems were formulated for the sake of facilitating dialectical debate.

In Aristotle's dialectical theory, 'problems are discursive formulations that allow for debate to be initiated on an issue on which there is no consensus among discussants. This is why, in the *Topics*, Aristotle is interested exclusively in a particular type of problem, namely the *dialectical* problem: an interrogative proposition that is put forward for discussion (προβάλλειν), which invites two contrary opinions ("whether x is the case or not" [...])'.[10] Thus Aristotle provided the rules and general template for debating disputed issues and established a tradition in which these προβλήματα were employed for intellectual training and as an exercise in debate.[11] Moreover, in the same tradition '[p]roblems are not formulated solely for the sake of facilitating dialectical debate though: for Aristotle, they also enable scientific investigation of the natural world. In this function they hold a central place in Aristotle's method of organizing scientific enquiry, as we learn from *Posterior Analytics*'.[12] The relevance of this point for analysing the QRO will become apparent later in this contribution.

---

[6] Blair 1999 and Taub 2015 and other contributions in Mayhew 2015.

[7] Williams 2012; Inwood 2002.

[8] On the Byzantine reception see Rey 2004 and contributions in Rigo 2013.

[9] Meeusen 2014; Meeusen 2015.

[10] Oikonomopoulou 2013, p. 43–44. Blair 1999, p. 172, discussing the terminology of πρόβλημα, points to its etymology: 'προβάλλω, "to set out as an obstacle", was probably first used in an intellectual rather than its original military context by Plato when describing the tactics of the Sophists defending themselves. By extension, the *problema* became something difficult to overcome or to solve, a knotty problem'.

[11] Oikonomopoulou 2013, p. 44. See also Quandt 1983. Mansfeld 1992, p. 67–68 notes how the Sceptics used προβλήματα 'to provide counter arguments to the positions supported by others' and 'to produce a deadlock viz. an ἀντιλογία or διαφωνία'.

[12] Oikonomopoulou 2013, p. 44.

Philo of Alexandria was the first to discuss various problems arising from the Bible in a question-and-answer format.[13] The first Christians to use this format were Tatian, Marcion, Apelles, and their students to raise objections against disputed passages in the Bible.[14] Thus the ἐρωταποκρίσεις were not only associated with debate, polemics and apologetics but also with instruction and catechesis.[15]

The language of ζήτησις is all-pervasive not merely in collections of questions and answers but also in homilies and other types of literature, harking back to the earliest examples of this format that dealt with natural phenomena. In the course of one of his *Hexaemeron* homilies, Basil embeds the construction (εἰ + ὑπόθεσις + ἀπόδοσις)[16] which, as will be shown, is the stand-

[13] Niehoff 2011.
[14] Bardy 1932–1933; Perrone 1991 and 1996; Hilhorst 1999; Zamagni 2013.
[15] Papadoyannakis 2006.
[16] *In Hexaem. hom.* 2. 4 (ed. SC 26bis; trans. NPNF vol. 8): Ἀλλὰ καὶ σκότος, φησίν, ἐπάνω τῆς ἀβύσσου· Πάλιν ἄλλαι μύθων ἀφορμαὶ, καὶ πλασμάτων δυσσεβεστέρων ἀρχαὶ πρὸς τὰς ἰδίας ὑπονοίας παρατρεπόντων τὰ ῥήματα. Τὸ γὰρ σκότος οὐχ ὡς πέφυκεν ἐξηγοῦνται ἀέρα τινὰ ἀφώτιστον, ἢ τόπον ἐξ ἀντιφράξεως σώματος σκιαζόμενον, ἢ ὅλως καθ᾽ ὁποιανοῦν αἰτίαν τόπον φωτὸς ἐστερημένον, ἀλλὰ δύναμιν κακὴν, μᾶλλον δὲ αὐτὸ τὸ κακὸν, παρ᾽ ἑαυτοῦ τὴν ἀρχὴν ἔχον, ἀντικείμενον καὶ ἐναντίον τῇ ἀγαθότητι τοῦ Θεοῦ ἐξηγοῦνται τὸ σκότος. Εἰ γὰρ ὁ Θεὸς φῶς ἐστι, δηλονότι ἡ ἀντιστρατευομένη αὐτῷ δύναμις σκότος ἂν εἴη, φησὶ, κατὰ τὸ τῆς διανοίας ἀκόλουθον. Σκότος, οὐ παρ᾽ ἑτέρου τὸ εἶναι ἔχον, ἀλλὰ κακὸν αὐτογέννητον. Σκότος, πολέμιον ψυχῶν, θανάτου ποιητικόν, ἀρετῆς ἐναντίως· ὅπερ καὶ ὑφεστάναι, καὶ μὴ παρὰ Θεοῦ γεγενῆσθαι, ὑπ᾽ αὐτῶν μηνύεσθαι τῶν τοῦ προφήτου λόγων ἐξαπατῶνται. Ἐκ δὴ τούτου τί οὐχὶ συνεπλάσθη τῶν πονηρῶν καὶ ἀθέων δογμάτων; Ποῖοι λύκοι βαρεῖς διασπῶντες τὸ ποίμνιον τοῦ Θεοῦ, οὐχὶ ἀπὸ τῆς μικρᾶς ταύτης φωνῆς τὴν ἀρχὴν λαβόντες ἐπεπόλασαν ταῖς ψυχαῖς; Οὐχὶ Μαρκίωνες· οὐχὶ Οὐαλεντῖνοι ἐντεῦθεν; οὐχ ἡ βδελυκτὴ τῶν Μανιχαίων αἵρεσις, ἣν σηπεδόνα τις τῶν Ἐκκλησιῶν προσειπὼν οὐχ ἁμαρτήσεται τοῦ προσήκοντος; ('Darkness was upon the face of the deep [Gen. 1. 2]. A new source for fables and most impious imaginations if one distorts the sense of these words at the will of one's fancies. By darkness these wicked men do not understand what is meant in reality – air not illumined, the shadow produced by the interposition of a body, or finally a place for some reason deprived of light. For them darkness is an evil power, or rather the personification of evil, having his origin in himself in opposition to, and in perpetual struggle with, the goodness of God. *If God is light, they say, without any doubt the power which struggles against Him must be darkness, Darkness not owing its existence to a foreign origin, but an evil existing by itself. Darkness is the enemy of souls, the primary cause of death, the adversary of virtue.* The words of the Prophet, they say in their error, show that it exists and that it does not proceed from God. From this what perverse and impious dogmas have been imagined! What grievous wolves [Act. 20. 29], tearing the flock of the Lord, have sprung from these words to cast themselves

ard way of constructing a πρόβλημα-objection not in only in Ps.-Justin's QRO but in many other collections too.

The language of ζητήματα and ἀπορίαι comes up in the homilies of Basil of Caesarea, Gregory of Nyssa, Severian of Gabala,[17] and Anastasius of Sinai,[18] where the homilists proceed from solving one ἀπορία to another. In other contemporary collections of ἐρωταποκρίσεις, cosmological issues were examined in the context of the exegesis of the Octateuch by Theodoret[19] and in the *Apocriticus* of Macarius Magnes.[20] Likewise, in the early sixth-century dialogues *Theophrastus* by Aeneas of Gaza and *Ammonius* by Zacharias of Mytilene, ἀπορίαι and ζητήματα are raised, debated, and solved.[21] Cosmological enquiries form a significant part of Ps.-Caesarius's collection of ἐρωταποκρίσεις[22] and are the main subject of *De opificio mundi* by John Philoponus in the sixth century.[23]

2. The Structure of the Cosmos

While disputed issues on cosmology come up in various places in the QRO, to date they have not been the subject of sustained analysis.[24] Some are more philosophical-theological than others,

upon souls! Is it not from hence that have come forth Marcions and Valentini, and the detestable heresy of the Manicheans, which you may without going far wrong call the putrid humour of the churches?').

[17] *De mundi creatione* III; ed. PG 56, col. 449: θέλω ζητῆσαι πῶς ἐποίησεν ὁ Θεὸς τοὺς φωστῆρας; λοιπὸν ζήτημα; col. 452: ζητοῦμεν δὲ ποῦ δύνει ὁ ἥλιος καὶ ποῦ τρέχει τὴν νύκτα; col. 454: ἐρωτάσθωσαν οἱ αἱρετικοὶ ἀπὸ τῶν φαινομένων ἵνα μάθωσιν ἑαυτῶν τὴν ἀπορίαν; col. 455: ὅταν ἀπορήσω, πῶς ἐξ ὑδάτων ὁ οὐρανὸς πέπηκται, λύει μου τὴν ἀπορίαν ὁ μακάριος Δαυῒδ λέγων; col. 460: ἀναγκαῖον δὲ ἐν ἑταίρῳ καιρῷ πάλιν ζητῆσαι; col. 461: ὅτε τὰ ζητήματα προτείνουσιν ἀπὸ τῶν ἀνθρωπίνων λογισμῶν λαλοῦσιν.

[18] This is made clear in the opening of the work, where Anastasius addresses the recipient of the work and states programmatically that he will be offering solutions to his ἀπορίαι: αἰτοῦντα περὶ τῶν ἐν τῇ ἑξαημέρῳ πολλοῖς ἀπορουμένων τὴν λύσιν ποιήσασθαι (*In Hexaem.* 1. 2. 13–14). See Papadogiannakis 2019.

[19] Petruccione 2007.

[20] Ed. Goulet 2003 and ed. Volp 2013.

[21] Sorabji 2015 and Champion 2014.

[22] See Spanu 2016 and Perczel's contribution in this volume.

[23] See Scholten 1996; Gleede 2009; Gleede 2011; Sorabji 2015.

[24] Gass 1842, p. 130–141 was the first to devote a short discussion of some of the cosmological issues in the QRO collection as part of a long article which

whereas others take their cue from the various pronouncements of the Bible focussing on specific verses and others are more abstract. Early on in the collection God's place in the cosmos is at issue in Q. 9: [25]

> Εἰ τὸ περιέχον μεῖζον μέν ἐστι τοῦ περιεχομένου κατ' οὐσίαν, ἧττον δὲ κατ' ἀξίαν, οἷον οὐρανὸς καὶ γῆ ἀγγέλων τε καὶ ἀνθρώπων, οἶκος οἰκούντων σῶμά τε ψυχῆς, περιέχει δὲ τὸ πᾶν ὁ θεός, πῶς οὐκ ἐστιν ἧττων τοῦ παντὸς τῷ λόγῳ τῆς ἀξίας.

> If the container / that which contains is bigger / greater according to its essence than that which is contained but lesser in worth, such as the heaven and earth [compared] to angels and humans, the lived-in house [compared] to those who live in it, the body [compared] to the soul, [and if] God contains everything, how is He not lesser than the universe by measure of worth?

This pithily constructed enquiry challenges the idea of God's transcendence. It goes against the principle of the Creator containing the universe while Himself not being contained by anything. The roots of this problem can be found in an ancient Greek debate over competing 'infinite universe' and 'closed world' paradigms in pre- and post-Socratic Greco-Roman cosmology.[26] Philo, when arguing against the Chaldean (and now Greek) idea that the world is itself God or else that it contains God, appropriated this principle as a basis to argue for the transcendence, freedom, and incomprehensibility of the Creator in relation to the creation. The ultimate goal for both Jewish and Christian authors was to prove that '[t]he Creator is not part of a larger infinite whole; rather, His own nature is alone infinite and unbound, thereby giving definition to the created, finite other.' [27]

---

has been the first and only extended discussion of the contents of the collection. On the importance of the collection in the process of Christian self-definition see Papadogiannakis 2008.

[25] The Greek text of the QRO used throughout is from the forthcoming edition by Toth, which supersedes the edition by Papadopoulos-Kerameus 1895.

[26] See Blowers 2012, p. 80.

[27] Blowers 2012, p. 80.

The earliest Christian use of this idea appears in the *Shepherd of Hermas*, 'but was soon to appear frequently among Christians, both Valentinian Gnostics and orthodox alike':[28]

Πρῶτον πάντων πίστευσον ὅτι εἷς ἐστιν ὁ θεός, ὁ τὰ πάντα κτί-σας καὶ καταρτίσας καὶ ποιήσας ἐκ τοῦ μὴ ὄντος εἰς τὸ εἶναι τὰ πάντα, καὶ πάντα χωρῶν, μόνος δὲ ἀχώρητος ὤν. πίστευσον οὖν αὐτῷ καὶ φοβήθητι αὐτόν, φοβηθεὶς δὲ ἐγκράτευσαι. ταῦτα φύλασσε καὶ ἀποβαλεῖς πᾶσαν πονηρίαν ἀπὸ σεαυτοῦ καὶ ἐνδύσῃ πᾶσαν ἀρετὴν δικαιοσύνης, καὶ ζήσῃ τῷ θεῷ, ἐὰν φυλάξῃς τὴν ἐντολὴν ταύτην.[29]

First of all, believe that God is one, who created all things and set them in order, and made out of what did not exist everything that is, and who contains all things but is Himself alone uncontained. Believe in Him, therefore, and fear Him, and fearing Him, exercise self-control. Observe these things, and you will cast off all evil from yourself and will put on every virtue of righteousness and will live to God, if you observe this commandment.[30]

In his response to Q. 9, Ps.-Justin, before defending the transcendence and freedom of the Creator, castigates the enquirer for not having asked the question according to the proper rules. He then goes on to state the principle on the basis of which the question is flawed and continues:[31]

Ἔστι γάρ τινα περιεχόμενα ἥσσονα ὄντα τῶν περιεχόντων καὶ τῇ οὐσίᾳ καὶ τῇ ἀξίᾳ, ὡς τὰ γίγαρτα τῶν ὀπωρῶν. Ἔτι δὲ τὰ λεχθέ-ντα περιεκτικὰ τῷ εἶναι περιέχει τὰ περιεχόμενα, ὁ δὲ θεὸς τῇ βουλήσει περιέχει τὸ πᾶν. Καὶ τὰ μὲν ἄλλα περιεχόμενα χρῄζουσι καὶ αὐτὰ τοῦ περιέχοντος, ὁ δὲ θεὸς οὐ χρῄζει τοῦ περιέχοντος αὐτόν. Καὶ τοῖς μὲν ἄλλοις περιεχομένοις τὸ εἶναι καὶ τὸ διαμένειν οὐκ ἔστιν ἐκ τῶν περιεχόντων αὐτά, τῷ δὲ παντὶ ἀμφότερα ὑπάρ-χει ἐκ τοῦ θεοῦ. Καὶ τὰ μὲν λεχθέντα περιεκτικὰ διὰ τὰ περιεχό-μενα ὑπάρχουσιν, ὁ δὲ θεὸς οὐ διὰ τὸ πᾶν ὑπάρχει. Διὸ μείζων ὁ θεὸς τοῦ παντός, ὥσπερ τῇ οὐσίᾳ, οὕτω καὶ τῇ ἀξίᾳ.

---

28 Osiek 1999, p. 103–104.
29 *Shep. Herm.* 26. 1–2 (ed. GCS 48).
30 Trans. Holmes 2007.
31 See Schoedel 1979; Blowers 2012, p. 79–80.

For there are things which are contained that are lesser both in worth and in essence to the ones that contain them such as the stones in fruit. Moreover, while the aforementioned containers contain their contents by their existence, God contains everything / the whole with His will. And while other things that are contained need that which contains them, God does not need anything that contains Him. And while other contained things do not owe their existence and permanence to that which contains them, the whole / All owes both of these things to God. And the aforementioned containers exist because of their contents, but God does not exist because of the whole. Therefore, God is greater than the whole / everything, as much in / with regard to the essence as in / with regard to worth.

There still remained, however, the unresolved issues of how God could contain creation without utterly overwhelming or penetrating it with His perfect being, violating its otherness. If, as Gnostics, Marcionites and Manichaeans considered it to be, material creation was defective or vile, how could God contain it? This very worry is refracted in a follow-up question, Q. 10:

Εἰ τὸ περιέχον ἐπὶ φρουρᾷ καὶ συντηρήσει ἐστὶ τοῦ περιεχομένου, πῶς ὁ θεὸς περιέχων τὸ πᾶν οὐκ ἐπὶ φρουρᾷ τοῦ κακοῦ καὶ διαμονῇ περιέχει τὸ πᾶν; καὶ γὰρ ἐν τῷ μέρει τοῦ παντὸς τὸ κακὸν θεωρεῖται.

If that which contains is for the protection and the preservation of that which is contained, how does God, in containing the universe, not contain it for the preservation and continuance of evil? For evil is considered part of the universe.

The response to this enquiry highlights two of the features of these collections: their uneven character (the response runs for two lines only), and their attempt to deflect criticism without veering off towards more extended disquisitions:

Τὸ πᾶν ἔργον ἐστι τοῦ θεοῦ, καὶ τηρῶν ὁ θεὸς τὸ πᾶν, τὸ ἔργον αὐτοῦ τηρεῖ. καὶ ὥσπερ οὐκ ἐποίησεν ὁ θεός τι φύσει κακόν, οὕτως οὐδὲ τηρεῖ τι φύσει κακόν.

The whole [i.e. universe] is God's work and by protecting / preserving the whole, He protects / preserves His work. And as God did not create anything evil by its nature, He does not protect / preserve anything that is evil by its nature.

The concern with the existence of evil comes up elsewhere in the collection too (Q. 85):

Εἰ τότε καλὸν φαίνεται τὸ καλὸν, ὅτε συγκρίνεται τῷ κακῷ, καλὸν δὲ ὁ κόσμος, δῆλον ὅτι κακὸν ὁ μὴ κόσμος, τουτέστι τὸ πρὸ κόσμου. καὶ εἰ μὲν ἀμφότερα ἐκ θεοῦ, τουτέστι τὸ πρὸ κόσμου καὶ ὁ κόσμος, πῶς οὐχ ἑκάτερα ἐξ αὐτοῦ, τουτέστι τὸ καλὸν καὶ τὸ φαῦλον; εἰ δὲ θάτερον μὲν ἐξ αὐτοῦ, ἕτερον δὲ οὐκ ἐξ αὐτοῦ, πῶς οὐκ ἔστιν αὐτόματον καὶ μὴ ὑπ' αὐτὸν τὸ μὴ ἐξ αὐτοῦ; πῶς δὲ ἀλη-θεύει ὁ λέγων, 'ὅτι ἐξ αὐτοῦ τὰ πάντα'; ἐν γὰρ τοῖς πᾶσι καὶ τὰ πρώην οὐκ ὄντα καὶ νῦν ὄντα περιέχεται.

If the good appears good only then, when it is compared with the evil, and [if] the universe is good, then it is obvious that the non-universe is evil, namely that which [exists] before the world / universe. And if both [come] from God, namely that which [exists] before the world and the world, how is it that each one of both [things] – the good and the evil – do not [come] from Him? If, on the other hand the one [is] from Him, and the other not from Him, how can it not be that what does not come from Him happens of its own accord and not under His influence? How can the man who says 'from Him are all things' [allusion to Rom. 11. 36] be telling the truth? For in 'everything' is included both what did not exist formerly and what exists now.

The problem here is how to square two seemingly contradictory / discrepant ideas. If all things are from Him, as Rom. 11. 36 claims, then evil must come from God too. In his reply, Ps.-Justin seeks to dismantle or counter the premise of the enquiry by invoking the early Christian view that had become axiomatic in his time, mainly in response to Gnostic and Manichaean hypostatization of evil that informed a strong dualism: that evil does not have an independent, autonomous existence.[32] While the roots of the idea of the existence of good and evil as primordial principles could be found in classical philosophy, it is in Middle Platonism that both principles are seen as autonomous and pitted against each other producing a radical dualism. For Manichaeans, it became a fundamental tenet of such considerable appeal as to attract Augustine, who invoked their explanation as a reason for

---

[32] Mosshammer 1990.

converting to their religion. 'So obsessed by the problem of evil that they found evil everywhere,' Manichaeans used the question *unde malum?* as a bait in their proselytising.[33] As BeDuhn puts it: '[f]or the Manichaeans, evil is something one suffers, at the hands of either internal or external others. They insisted that the evident pains and injustices of the world were irreconcilable with God's goodness. God could not be omnipotent master of the forces by which innocents suffered and evil often, prevailed in the cosmos. Nor could they accept a God who could only help or instruct people with the crude methods of the switch-yielding schoolmaster. Suffering can only be explained by the presence of something other than and contrary to God with which he is forced to contend'.[34] By the time the QRO was put together, the existence of evil was used as criticism of an imperfect Demiurge by both Marcionites[35] and Manicheans.

In his answer, Ps.-Justin also denies the possibility of the spontaneous (also rendered 'fortuitous', 'automatic', or 'chance') creation of the non-being (τὸ πάντη μὴ ὂν οὔτε ἐκ θεοῦ οὔτε ἐξ ἄλλου οὔτε αὐτόματόν ἐστι).[36] The idea that the world was created by non-intelligent causes and is subsequently governed by causes of the same kind rather than by a Creator was not acceptable to Christians. In his homilies on the *Hexaemeron*, Basil attacks the idea of a spontaneous creation at the outset. A little later, in his first homily, he explains:

> Καὶ καθότι πολλοὶ τῶν φαντασθέντων συνυπάρχειν ἐξ ἀϊδίου
> τῷ Θεῷ τὸν κόσμον, οὐχὶ γεγενῆσθαι παρ' αὐτοῦ συνεχώρησαν,
> ἀλλ' οἱονεὶ ἀποσκίασμα τῆς δυνάμεως αὐτοῦ ὄντα αὐτομάτως

---

[33] Lieu 1992, p. 188.

[34] BeDuhn 2010, p. 272.

[35] See May 1997; Löhr 1998; Löhr 2002.

[36] Τὸ κακὸν οὐδὲν ἕτερόν ἐστι παρὰ τὴν ἐκτροπὴν τοῦ καλοῦ. Διὸ ὕστερον τοῦ καλοῦ τὸ κακόν· ἐκτροπὴ γάρ ἐστι τοῦ καλοῦ· ἀλλ' εἰ τοῦτο, δῆλον ὅτι οὐκ ἐκ τῆς συγκρίσεως τοῦ καλοῦ τὸ κακὸν φαίνεται κακόν, ἀλλ' ἐκ τῆς οἰκείας φύσεως. Τὸ δὲ πρὸ τοῦ κόσμου μὴ ὄν, πάντη οὐκ ὂν ἦν· καὶ τὸ πάντη μὴ ὄν, οὔτε καλόν ἐστιν οὔτε κακόν. Διὸ τῷ οὕτω μὴ ὄντι οὐδὲν συγκρίνεται. ἔτι δὲ τὸ πάντη μὴ ὂν οὔτε ἐκ θεοῦ οὔτε ἐξ ἄλλου οὔτε αὐτόματόν ἐστι. πρὸ τοῦ κόσμου οὖν οὐδὲν ἕτερον ἦν, πλὴν θεοῦ. Τοίνυν τῆς συγκρίσεως τῶν ὄντων οὔσης πρὸς τὰ ὄντα, οὐκ ἄρα συγκρίνεται ὁ κόσμος τῷ μὴ κόσμῳ, οὐδὲ ἐν τῷ κόσμῳ περιέχεται τὸ μὴ κόσμος· τὸ γὰρ μὴ κόσμος οὐδέν ἐστι, τὸ δὲ περιεχόμενον ὄν ἐστι. Καὶ ὅτε λέγομεν ἐκ τοῦ μὴ ὄντος τὸν θεὸν πεποιηκέναι τὰ ὄντα, οὐ θέσιν τοῦ ὄντος δίδομεν τῷ μὴ ὄντι, ἀλλὰ τὴν παντελῆ ἀναίρεσιν τοῦ ὄντος.

παρυποστῆναι· καὶ αἴτιον μὲν αὐτοῦ ὁμολογοῦσι τὸν Θεὸν, αἴτιον δὲ ἀπροαιρέτως, ὡς τῆς σκιᾶς τὸ σῶμα, καὶ τῆς λαμπηδόνος τὸ ἀπαυγάζον·

Among those who have imagined that the world co-existed with God from all eternity, many have denied that it was created by God, but say that it exists spontaneously, as the shadow of this power. God, they say, is the cause of it, but an involuntary cause, as the body is the cause of the shadow and the flame is the cause of the brightness.[37]

This 'ingenious blending of the determinism represented by fate and necessity (ἀνάγκη) with the randomness represented by fortune and chance (τύχη)'[38] was widespread both among intellectual adherents of the classical tradition and among the common people, including sometimes the Christian laity. A variation of the concept of material necessity at work in nature appears in Q. 125, in response to the question of whether God's being as a creator did not suffer diminution when, after the creation, it passed from a state of potentiality to actuality.[39]

---

[37] *Hom. in Hexaem.* 1.7 (ed. SC 26bis, p. 114; trans. NPNF vol. 8). The idea of a fortuitous creation was attributed to the atomists by Aristotle in his *Physics* (196a24–35; ed. Ross 1950; trans. Sedley 2007, p. 192 with discussion of this passage p. 167–204): εἰσὶ δε τινες οἳ καὶ τοὐρανοῦ τοῦδε καὶ τῶν κόσμων πάντων αἰτιῶνται τὸ αὐτόματον. ἀπὸ ταὐτομάτου γὰρ γενέσθαι τὴν δίνην καὶ τὴν κίνησιν τὴν διακρίνασαν καὶ καταστήσασαν εἰς ταύτην τὴν τάξιν τὸ πᾶν. καὶ μάλα τοῦτό γε αὐτὸ θαυμάσαι ἄξιον. λέγοντες γὰρ τὰ μὲν ζῷα καὶ τὰ φυτὰ ἀπὸ τύχης μήτε εἶναι μήτε γίγνεσθαι, ἀλλ' ἤτοι φύσιν ἢ νουν ἤ τι τοιοῦτον ἕτερον εἶναι τὸ αἴτιον (οὐ γὰρ ὅ τι ἔτυχεν ἐκ τοῦ σπέρματος ἑκάστου γίγνεται, ἀλλ' ἐκ μὲν τοῦ τοιουδὶ ἐλαία ἐκ δὲ τοῦ τοιουδὶ ἄνθρωπος), τὸν δ' οὐρανὸν καὶ τὰ θειότατα τῶν φανερῶν ἀπὸ τοῦ αὐτομάτου γενέσθαι, τοιαύτην δ'αἰτίαν μηδεμίαν εἶναι οἵαν τῶν ζῴων καὶ τῶν φυτῶν. ('Some people consider the fortuitous to be the cause of this heaven and of all the worlds, explaining that it was fortuitously that there arose the vortex and the motion which separated things and set the universe in this arrangement. This is itself pretty amazing. For on the one hand they say that animals and plants neither are nor come to be by luck, but that either nature or intelligence or some other such thing is their cause (it not being just anything that arises from each seed, but an olive tree from this one, a man from that one), yet on the other hand they say that the heaven and the most divine of perceptible things came to be fortuitously, without any cause comparable to that of animals and plants'.) On the debate on spontaneous creation see Köckert 2009, p. 133–135; Gleede 2012. A similar question appears in the collection of Ps.-Caesarius: Q. 112 and Q. 113 discussed in Papadogiannakis 2013, p. 275.

[38] Pelikan 1993, p. 155.

[39] Εἰ τὸ εἶναί τι δυνάμει τοῦ εἶναι τοῦτο ἐνεργείᾳ καθέστηκεν ἔλαττον, πῶς ὁ τοῦ κόσμου ποιητής, πρὸ τῆς τοῦ κόσμου δυνάμει καὶ οὐκ ἐνεργείᾳ, τῷ τῆς ἐλαττώσεως

The issue of whether creation was good or not emerged in other guises, too. For the anonymous enquirer the capacity of living creatures (human beings included) to hurt each other was yet another proof of an imperfectly created world. A benevolent creator would surely have never created or allowed such creatures to exist. Q. 149 poses the problem thus:

> Εἰ τὸ ἀναιρούμενον ὑπὸ τοῦ ἀναιροῦντος ἀπόλλυται καὶ τὸ ἀναι-
> ροῦν φαυλότητι τὰ τῆς ἀπωλείας ἐργάζεται (πλεῖστα δὲ τοιαῦτα
> ἐν τοῖς ἐμψύχοις πάντων τῶν ἀλόγων εὑρίσκεται καὶ ἐν αὐτοῖς
> ἐστι θεάσασθαι οὐ μόνον κατ' ἀλλήλων ἀλλὰ καὶ κατὰ τῶν ἀνθρώ-
> πων τὰ τῆς ἐπιβουλῆς ἐπεκτεινόμενα), πῶς ἀληθεύει ὁ λέγων ὅτι
> ὁ θεὸς πάντα καλὰ λίαν ἐποίησεν; εἰ δὲ ἀληθεύει, ἀγαθὰ δὲ καὶ
> φαῦλα ἐν τῇ κτίσει ὑπάρχουσι, πῶς τὰ μὲν ἀγαθὰ ἀγαθοῦ, τὰ δὲ
> φαῦλα φαύλου δημιουργοῦ οὐ γνωρίζονται καὶ δύο ἐναντίαι ἀρχαὶ
> κατὰ Μανιχαίους οὐ δείκνυνται; εἰ δὲ ἡ ἀναίρεσις τῶν ἀναιρουμέ-
> νων ἐπ' ἀγαθῷ γίνεται, καθὼς τοῦτο παρ' ἐνίοις ὑπείληπται, πῶς
> οὐκ ἦν ἀγαθώτερον τὸ ἐν ἀρχῇ ἐκ τοῦ μὴ ὄντος εἰς τὸ εἶναι αὐτῶν
> κωλυθῆναι τὴν πάροδον.

If that which is killed by that which kills it, perishes, and that which kills brings about perdition because of its wickedness (for many are found among the animate from the non-rational beings, and among them it is possible to see them threaten not only each other but humans too), how is he truthful who says that God created everything good?[40] If it is true, and there are good and evil things in the creation / created world, how are the good things not recognized [as coming] from a good creator and the evil things from evil creator, and [how are] not two opposite principles shown accord-

---

οὐχ ὑποπίπτει ὀνόματι; Ἀπόκρισις· Ὧν ἡ δύναμις τῆς ἐνεργείας φυσικῇ τινι ἀνάγκῃ ἀφέστηκε, τούτων ἡ δύναμις ἔλαττον τῆς ἐνεργείας οὐ φυσικῇ ἀνάγκῃ ἀλλ' ἰδίᾳ
βουλῇ ἀφέστηκεν, οὗτος ἀνυπόβλητος τῷ τῆς ἐλαττώσεως ὀνόματι. 'διενοήθης', φησί,
'καὶ πάντα σοι πάρεστι'. On the broader debate see Sorabji 1983, p. 186, 196, 206,
209, 233, 249–252; Sorabji 2015.

[40] According to Titus of Bostra (*Contra Manichaeos* II. 38; ed. CCSG 82),
Mani had used the example of wild animals that kill each other and threaten
people as one of the many proofs that God had not created everything good:
Λοιδορεῖται [ὁ Μάνης] μὲν οὐ τοῦτο μόνον ὁ τῆς κενωτάτης κατὰ Θεοῦ βλασφημίας
εὑρετής, ἀλλὰ καὶ ζώοις τοῖς ἀγρίαν φύσιν παρὰ τοῦ Δημιουργοῦ λαχοῦσι, σαφῶς
δίκην ἐχθροῦ τὰ πάντα φιλαιτίου κατὰ τῶν δημιουργημάτων κινούμενος [...]. Θηρία
γὰρ ἅπαντα τετράποδά τε καὶ ἑρπετὰ κακίζων, παραπλήσιον τι πάσχειν δοκεῖ, ὥσπερ
ἂν εἴ τις φιλαμαρτήμων δοῦλος καὶ λίαν πονηρός, τὰ μὲν ἄλλα τοῦ δεσπότου αὐτοῦ
ἀκαταιτίατα ἀποδέχοιτο, μισοίη δὲ καὶ διαβάλλοι μάστιγά που καὶ μόνον φαινομένην.

ing to the Manichaeans? If the killing of the things that are killed is done for a good cause / reason, as this is thought by some, how is not more benevolent to prevent / stop from the beginning / in the first place their passing from non-existence to existence?

Ps.-Justin begins his refutation by stating that the creator created all living beings so that they can be born, decay and perish. He is also the creator of the distinction between rational and non-rational living beings.[41] And if, the author continues, these non-rational living beings threaten each other and are killed by other non-rational animals, this is allowed to happen by God's providence. For if these non-rational animals are subject to decay and death, while being deified by humans, how much worse would it had been had they been created immune to harm and perdition? Thus, by what they suffer, they are recognised as unworthy of being called and honoured as gods. Non-rational animals were created as a help for humans, some as their food, some as a punishment (education) for them, and their passing or coming into existence cannot be reproached on account of wickedness and due to the fact that they are needed. If this is so, Ps.-Justin concludes, it is obvious that created, non-rational animals come from a benevolent creator.

More concrete challenges to the biblical record of creation involved the issue of a flat or spherical earth (Q. 72):

---

[41] Ὁ ἐκ τῆς δημιουργίας τῶν ἐμψύχων λογικῶν τε καὶ ἀλόγων περὶ τοῦ δημιουργοῦ ἀκόλουθον ποιούμενος τὴν ζήτησιν, πρὸς τὴν φύσιν αὐτῶν ὀφείλει ἀποβλέπειν, τὴν κατὰ τὴν τοῦ δημιουργοῦ ὅρον ἄγουσαν τὰ θνητὰ πάντα, ὥσπερ εἰς γένεσιν, οὕτως καὶ εἰς φθοράν τε καὶ ἀπώλειαν. Εἰ δὲ κατὰ ταῦτα μὲν ζώου πρὸς ζῷον οὐκ ἔστι διαφορά, τῶν δὲ διαφορῶν εἰς καὶ αὐτός ἐστι δημιουργός, δῆλον ἄρα ὅτι πάντων τῶν ζώων λογικῶν τε καὶ ἀλόγων εἰς καὶ ὁ αὐτός ἐστι δημιουργός· ἣν δὲ ἐκ τῆς ὑπ' ἀλλήλων ἐπιβουλῆς ὑπομένουσιν ἀπώλειαν, κατὰ τὴν θείαν πρόνοιαν συγκεχώρηται συμβαίνειν αὐτοῖς· εἰ γάρ, ὑποκειμένων αὐτῶν τῇ τε κατὰ φύσιν καὶ τῇ κατὰ ἐπιβουλὴν φθορᾷ τε καὶ ἀπωλείᾳ, οὐ παρητήσαντό τινες θεοποιῆσαι αὐτά, πόσῳ μᾶλλον ἂν ἐθεοποιοῦντο, εἰ βλάβης τε καὶ ἀπωλείας διὰ παντὸς ἐκτὸς μεμενήκασιν; ἵν' οὖν ἀφ' ὧν ὑπομένουσιν ἃ ὑπομένουσιν. γέγονε δὲ τὰ ἄλογα ζῷα εἰς ὑπουργίαν ἀνθρώπου, τὰ μὲν εἰς τροφήν, τὰ δὲ εἰς παιδείαν, ὡς τὸ 'ὀδόντας θηρίων ἐπαποστελῶ εἰς αὐτούς, μετὰ θυμοῦ συρόντων ἐπὶ γῆς'. Ἀλλ' εἰ ἀγαθόν ἐστι τὸ τρέφεσθαι τὸν ἄνθρωπον ἐκ τῶν ἀλόγων ζώων καὶ ὑπουργεῖσθαι ὑπ' αὐτῶν καὶ παιδεύεσθαι δι' αὐτῶν, ἀγαθὴ ἄρα ἡ εἰς τὸ εἶναι αὐτῶν πάροδος καὶ ἀδιάβλητος ἐπὶ φαυλότητι φύσεως καὶ τῆς ἐξ αὐτῶν χρείας. Εἰ δὲ τοῦτο, δῆλον ὅτι ἑνὸς δημιουργοῦ ἐστι ἀγαθοῦ πάντα τὰ ἄλογα ζῷα δημιουργήματα.

Εἰ ἐν τῇ νυκτὶ ὁ ἥλιος ἀποκρύπτεται, πῶς οὐ σφαῖρα ὁ οὐρανὸς ἀποδείκνυται; ὁ γὰρ ἀπὸ φιλοσόφων ὅσιος ἀνὴρ εἶπεν ὅτι 'ὥσπερ σικύα σώματι, οὕτως ὁ οὐρανὸς ἐπίκειται τῇ γῇ, καὶ ὁ μὲν διὰ τὸ κοῦφον ἀνωφερής, ἡ δὲ διὰ τὸ βαρύ ἐστι κατωφερής· διὸ τῇ ἀνθολκῇ ὑπ' ἀλλήλων συνέχονται'. Εἰ δὲ τοῦτο ἀληθές, ὅλου τοῦ οὐρανίου κύκλου εἰς τὴν γῆν ἐρηρεισμένου, ἔνδον ἀνάγκη ὑπάρχειν τοὺς φωστῆρας καὶ φαίνειν ἀεί. Πῶς οὐ ἀποκρύπτονται;

If during the night the sun is hidden, how is it not proven that the sky is spherical? For the holy man of the philosophers said that 'like gourds on a body, so is the heaven sitting upon / hanging over / lying on the earth and the former [heaven] points upwards because it is light and the latter [earth] points downwards because it is heavy. Therefore, they are held together by this inverted [mutual] attraction'. If this is true that the heavenly disk / vault is fixed firmly upon the earth, the luminaries are by necessity inside [it] and they shine always. How are they not hidden? [42]

The response is based on an empirical observation derived from everyday life. Ps.-Justin does not accept that the earth is spherical.[43] Instead he notes that even on a flat surface objects can be concealed from our view due to the sheer distance that separates us from them. This is the case with ships that cannot see each other because they are too far from each other, separated by the huge expanse of the sea. This expanse does not allow one to see beyond the horizon. The same observation applies to the luminaries. He is willing to accept that heaven and earth are held together by pulling each other in the opposite direction (ἀνθολκῇ), but argues that this applies only to the first heaven and the earth (because they were created simultaneously). It does not apply to the earth and the firmament, for the earth existed before the firmament, holding all the liquid substance without the attraction of the firmament which came into existence later.[44]

---

[42] On the similarities between the QRO and Severian of Gabala's exegesis on the question of the spherical or flat earth see Voicu 2015, p. 549–550. Cf. also Ceulemans' contribution to this volume.

[43] On the background to this debate in Late Antiquity see Scholten 1996, p. 271-419; Inglebert 2001, p. 210–221; Kretschmer 1889, p. 34–59; Krüger 2000, p. 351–446. For the Byzantine reception of Antiochene views see Caudano 2008.

[44] Εἰ ὁμολογουμένως πολλά ἐστιν ἕτερα τὰ ἐν τῷ αὐτῷ καὶ ἴσῳ ἐπιπέδῳ ὄντα καὶ διὰ τὸ μῆκος τοῦ διαστήματος κεκρυμμένα ὄντα τῆς ὄψεως, οἷον τὰ πλοῖα τὰ ἐν τῇ

The idea of a spherical earth in its earliest manifestations can be ascribed to Pythagoreans and also appears in Plato. The main exponent, however, was Aristotle in *De caelo* II. 40.[45] It appears in a popularised version in *De mundo*,[46] which describes 'a terrestrial sphere within a celestial sphere, of which the latter has the same centre as the former and rotates daily from east to west around an axis running through its centre, whereas the former [earth] does not move. The stars are fixed to the celestial sphere and thus follow its rotation'.[47] Against this background, Q. 73 compares and contrasts the idea of a heaven that rotates on a stationary earth with the biblical depiction of a static or stationary heaven that 'has been set as an arch [Is. 40. 22] or stretched as skin [Ps. 103. 2]'.[48] For Ps.-Justin, the obvious point of departure

---

θαλάσσῃ ὑπ' ἀλλήλων μὴ ὁρώμενα, τοῦ πλάτους τῇ τῶν ὑδάτων ἐπιφανείᾳ περιορίζοντος τὴν ὄψιν περαιτέρω μὴ ἀνατείνεσθαι τοῦ ὁρίζοντος, τί θαυμαστόν, εἰ καὶ ἐπὶ τῶν φωστήρων γίνεται ἡ ἐπίκρυψις διὰ τὴν αὐτὴν αἰτίαν; Τὸ δὲ διὰ τὴν ἀνθολκὴν οὐρανοῦ καὶ γῆς ἵστασθαι τὸν οὐρανὸν καὶ τὴν γῆν, ἐπὶ μὲν τοῦ πρώτου οὐρανοῦ καὶ τῆς γῆς ἔνεστι τοῦτο εἰκάσαι διὰ τὸ ἅμα γεγενῆσθαι αὐτά, ἐπὶ δὲ τοῦ στερεώματος καὶ τῆς γῆς οὐκέτι· ἵστατο γὰρ ἡ γῆ πρὸ τοῦ στερεώματος, τὴν ἅπασαν βαστάζουσα ὑγρὰν οὐσίαν, χωρὶς ἀνθολκῆς τοῦ στερεώματος· ὕστερον γὰρ τῆς γῆς γέγονε τὸ στερέωμα.

[45] Pellegrin 2009. The QRO is only one of the works in the Ps.-Justinian corpus that engages with the work of Aristotle. Recent surveys in the history of the reception of Aristotle in Late Antiquity and Byzantium by Bydén 2013 and Criscuolo 2013 touch briefly upon the Ps.-Justinian corpus. Martín 1989, Martín 2000, and Boeri 2009 however, have shown that the influence of Aristotle in Ps.-Justin's polemic against Aristotle and the neoplatonists is more thorough in the *Quaestiones christianorum ad gentiles* and the *Confutatio dogmatum Aristotelis*. On the complex relationship between both works and the QRO see Gleede 2011, p. 76-82. A lot remains to be done on this subject. See also Boeri's contribution to this volume.

[46] While the Aristotelian authorship is disputed, the treatise nevertheless further disseminated and popularised Aristotle's views.

[47] Burri 2014, 95.

[48] Εἰ διὰ τὸ καθ' Ἕλληνας σφαῖραν ὄντα καὶ κινεῖσθαι τὸν οὐρανὸν ἐν τόπῳ ἐστί, πῶς διὰ τὸ ὡς καμάραν πεπῆχθαι ἢ ὡς δέρριν κατὰ τὴν γραφὴν ἐκτετάσθαι ὁ οὐρανὸς οὐκ ἐν τόπῳ ἐστίν; ὥσπερ γὰρ τὸ κινούμενον, οὕτω καὶ τὸ πηγνύμενον ἐν τόπῳ ἀνάγκη νομίζεσθαι. εἰ δὲ τοῦτο, πῶς τὴν ἐπὶ τῇ περιγραφῇ τοῦ οὐρανοῦ παρ' ἀλλήλων κατάγνωσιν δικαίαν οὐκ ἕξομεν; εἰ δὲ ὁ οὐρανὸς κατὰ ἀμφοτέρους ἐν τόπῳ καὶ ἑκατέροις ἡ τοῦ τόπου ποιότης καὶ ποσότης καθέστηκεν ἄγνωστος, τί πλέον θάτεροι θατέρων κεκτῆσθαι δυνάμεθα, τῆς περὶ τῶν προλεχθέντων καταγνώσεώς τε καὶ ἀγνοίας ἑκατέρους ἐπίσης κατεχούσης; A similar question was posed to Augustine by some brothers: 'De motu etiam caeli nonnulli fratres quaestionem movent, utrum stet anne moveatur. Quia, si movetur, inquiunt, quomodo firmamentum est? Si autem stat, quomodo sidera, quae in illo fixa creduntur, ab oriente usque ad occidentem circumeunt septentrionibus breviores gyros iuxta cardinem peragnetibus, ut caelum

is the biblical text. To support the biblical witness of a heaven like
an arch or vault he conjures up the image of a (hemispherical?)
body sitting like a lid afloat on the waters. The negative pressure
creates the suction (the verb πωμασθῇ used here alludes to the
image of suction cups) that keeps this body attached to the water.
The heavenly body sits afloat on the water in a similar manner.[49]
The waters support the heaven and the earth the waters, and the
divine commands the earth. To this end, Iob 26. 7 ('hanging the
earth upon nothing') is pressed into service.[50]

Q. 104 raises another problem with the description and
role of the firmament as it appears in Ps. 148. 4: 'praise Him,
you heavens of heavens and you water above the heavens!' The
question points to contradictions that emerge from differing,
competing depictions of the firmament, the place of the stars /
luminaries (fixed or rotating), and how they affected the theory
that the heaven is spherical.

If the surface of the firmament is laden with water to enable it to withstand the heat of the stars beneath the firmament,
how is the view of those who say that the luminous bodies are
not fixed in the firmament but rotate beneath it, true? For if the
luminaries were fixed on the firmament, how can they move,
the heavens being stationary? If the stars move along with the
heavens, how is the myth that the heaven is spherical not true?
And if the latter argument is inappropriate, that it is right that

---

si est alius nobis occultus cardo ex alio vertice, sicut sphaera, si autem nullus alius
cardo est, velut discus rotari videatur' (*De genesi ad litteram* II. 10. 23).

[49] This idea is not dissimilar to the view held by Thales (as reported by Aristotle) that the earth was floating on the water. On this idea see Heyd 2014,
p. 492–494.

[50] Εἰ μὲν γὰρ ἔλεγον οἱ χριστιανοὶ τὸν οὐρανὸν μὴ εἶναι ἐν τόπῳ, καθάπερ λέγουσιν οἱ Ἕλληνες, ἴση ἂν ἔμελλεν εἶναι ἡ παρ' ἀλλήλων κατάγνωσις, λεγόντων μὴ εἶναι
τὸν οὐρανὸν ἐν τόπῳ·φωναῖς δὲ σημαντικαῖς τοῦ ἐν τόπῳ εἶναι τὸν οὐρανὸν πρὸς ἀλλή-
λους χρησαμένων, παντελῶς ἀνήρηται ἡ τοιαύτη κατάγνωσις. Εἰ δὲ τοῦ μὲν σφαῖραν
εἶναι τὸν οὐρανὸν καὶ σφαιρικῶς κινεῖσθαι ἀδυνάτου ὄντος, τοῦ δὲ ὡς καμάραν εἶναι
αὐτοῦ δυνατοῦ δεικνυμένου, οὐδεμία ἄρα ἡ τῶν χριστιανῶν ἐπὶ τῇ ἀγνοίᾳ κατάγνωσις.
Περὶ δὲ τοῦ τόπου ἐκ τῶν καθ' ἡμᾶς στοχαζόμεθα περὶ αὐτοῦ, ὅτι ὥσπερ παρ' ἡμῖν ὅταν
ᾖ περιφερὲς σῶμα, ὁμαλόν τε καὶ κοῖλον καὶ πανταχόθεν ἰσοπερίμετρον, ἐὰν πωμασθῇ
ἐπὶ τὰ ὕδατα, βαστάζεται ἐπὶ τῶν ὑδάτων, τούτῳ τῷ τρόπῳ βαστάζεται ὁ οὐρανὸς ὑπὸ
τῶν ὑδάτων. ''Ὁ τανύσας', φησί, 'τὸν οὐρανὸν ὡσεὶ καμάραν'· τῷ τῆς καμάρας ὀνόματι τὸ περιφερὲς ἐδήλωσε τοῦ σώματος τοῦ οὐρανοῦ. Βαστάζει οὖν τὸν μὲν οὐρανὸν
τὰ ὕδατα, τὰ δὲ ὕδατα ἡ γῆ, τὴν δὲ γῆν τὸ θεῖον πρόσταγμα· 'ὁ κρεμάσας γὰρ τὴν γῆν',
φησίν, 'ἐπ' οὐδενός'.

the stars rotate along / together with the sky, how is not true the word calling the heaven spherical and how are the waters above it not useless? Rounding off his enquiry, the anonymous author connects the topography of the heavens directly with the recompense of the righteous and the sinners in the Final Judgement. The former will receive their recompense above the firmament, and the latter below it.[51]

For the enquirer, whether the stars move or are static not only has direct implications for the role of the firmament, but also (ultimately) for the judgement of the righteous and the sinners. The idea that the firmament held the waters above was put forward by other Christian authors such as Chrysostom.[52] In the construction of his objection to this point, the enquirer refers to other opinions that claimed the waters above the firmament cooled it down. Severian of Gabala[53] and Theodoret[54]

---

[51] Εἰ τὰ νῶτα τοῦ οὐρανοῦ πεφόρτωται ὕδασι, καθώς φησιν ἡ γραφή, ὅπερ τινὲς ἔφασαν γεγονέναι διὰ τὴν πυρώδη τῶν φωστήρων οὐσίαν, ὥστε τοῖς ἐπικειμένοις τὸν οὐρανὸν πιαινόμενον ὕδασι τῇ ὑποκειμένῃ τῶν φωστήρων φλογὶ μένειν ἀχείρωτον, πῶς οἱ ταῦτα λέγοντες ἀληθεύουσι, τῶν φωστήρων οὐκ ἐν τῷ οὐρανῷ ἀλλ' ὑπὸ τὸν οὐρανὸν κινουμένων; Εἰ δὲ τούτους ἐν τῷ οὐρανῷ λέγοιεν εἶναι, πῶς τὴν κινητικὴν ἐνέργειαν ἔχουσι, τοῦ οὐρανίου σώματος τὸ ἀκίνητον ἔχοντος; Εἰ δὲ σὺν τῷ οὐρανῷ τὰ ἄστρα λαμβάνει τὴν κίνησιν, πῶς οὐκ ἀληθεύσειεν ὁ σφαῖραν τὸν οὐρανὸν προσαγορεύων μῦθος; Εἰ δὲ τοῦτο μὲν ἀπρεπές, τὸ δὲ προλεχθὲν περὶ τῶν φωστήρων νοῆσαι ἀκόλουθον, πῶς οὐκ ἄχρηστος τῶν ἄνω ὑδάτων ἡ σύστασις; Τί δὲ καὶ αὐτὴ ἐν τῇ συντελείᾳ γενήσεται, ἄνω μὲν τῶν δικαίων, κάτω δὲ τῶν ἁμαρτωλῶν τὰς τῶν πρακτέων ἀμοιβὰς τότε μελλόντων κομίζεσθαι; A variation of this objection comes up in Augustine, *De genesi ad litteram* II. 32. 2: 'Multi enim asserunt istarum aquarum naturam super sidereum caelum esse non posse, quod sic habeant ordinatum pondus suum, ut vel super terras fluitent vel in aere terris proximo vaporaliter ferantur'.

[52] *Exp. in Ps.* 148 (ed. PG 55, col. 486; trans. Hill 1998, p. 365): Ἤκουες καὶ Μωϋσέως λέγοντος, ὅτι τῶν ὑδάτων τὰ μὲν εἴασε κάτω τὰ δὲ ὑπὲρ τῶν νώτων τῶν οὐρανίων μετεωρίζεσθαι παρεσκεύασεν, ἐν τῷ μέσῳ τῆς ἀβύσσου πήξας τὸ στερέωμα, καὶ ὑπὲρ τῶν νώτων ἀφεὶς τὰ ὕδατα μένειν. ('You hear the Moses also saying that he left some of the waters below, and caused some to float on the surfaces of the heavens, fixing the firmament in the middle of the abyss, and let the waters remain in the surfaces'). On the background to this debate see Scholten 1996, p. 271-419; Moreschini 2016.

[53] *De mundi creatione* II. 3 (ed. PG 56, col. 442): Κρυσταλλώδης ἦν ὁ οὐρανὸς ἀπὸ ὑδάτων παγείς· ἐπειδὴ ἔμελλε δέχεσθαι ἡλίου φλόγα καὶ σελήνης καὶ ἄστρων ἄπειρα πλήθη, καὶ ἦν ὅλος πυρὸς πεπληρωμένος, ἵνα μὴ ὑπὸ τῆς θερμότητος λυθῇ ἢ φλεχθῇ, ἐπέστρωσε τοῖς νώτοις τοῦ οὐρανοῦ τὰ πελάγη ἐκεῖνα τῶν ὑδάτων, ἵνα λιπαίνῃ καὶ ἐπαλείφῃ αὐτοῦ τὰ νῶτα, καὶ οὕτως ἀντέχῃ πρὸς τὴν φλόγα καὶ μὴ φρύγηται. Noted also by Voicu 2015, p. 551.

[54] Responding to Q. 11: Εἷς οὐρανὸς ἢ δύο εἰσίν; [...] διχῇ δὲ διεῖλε τῶν ὑδάτων τὴν φύσιν ὁ τῶν ὅλων Θεός, καὶ τὰ μὲν ἄνωθεν ἐπιτέθεικε στερεώματι, τὰ δὲ κάτω

held the same view, but not Gregory of Nyssa, who clearly stated that the firmament (which is called heaven) is the border of the perceptible creation, and that beyond lies spiritual (νοητός) creation which lacks form, size, place, temporal interval, colour, shape, quality and any other thing under heaven.[55] Implicit in the objection is a longer-running debate with pagans on the role of the elements. Each element had its own specific weight which determined their order in the structure of the universe. Thus to find water (a heavier element) above the air (a lighter element) in the form of supracelestial waters was impossible.[56]

In his response, Ps.-Justin concedes that, even if the luminous bodies are below the heavens, the heat from their fiery essence by its nature moves upwards. So, while accepting that the waters above the firmament cool it from the heat of the luminous bodies beneath, he adds one more reason for this configuration: the waters also weigh the firmament down so that it is not disturbed by violent winds, while sending the coolness of the winds downwards. This coolness, mixed with the heat of the sun, produces a temperate mixture of air that allows animals and plants to dwell on earth. As for the Final Judgment, Ps.-Justin states that it is not going to take place in this heaven and earth but in new ones, possibly paraphrasing Is. 65. 17: 'for heaven will be new, and the earth will be new [*not in the Septuagint text*: which I will make, and will stay for ever and ever]'; and adding further the following biblical proofs to underpin his claim: Ps. 101. 26–27: 'At the beginning it was you, O Lord, who founded the earth, and the heavens are works of your hands. They will perish but

καταλέλοιπεν ἵνα τὰ μὲν ἄνωθεν ἐπικείμενα τῇ ὑγρότητι καὶ ψυχρότητι μὴ συγχωρῇ τῷ πυρὶ τῶν φωστήρων λωβᾶσθαι τὸ στερέωμα, τὰ δὲ κάτω μεμενηκότα διατρέφῃ τοῖς ἀτμοῖς τὸν ἀέρα διαυαινόμενον καὶ ξηραινόμενον ὑπὸ τοῦ ἄνωθεν ἐπικειμένου πυρός. ('Is there one heaven or two?', Theodoret notes: 'The God of the universe made a twofold division in the nature of the waters: some He placed above the firmament, and some He left below, the purpose being that what was placed above with its moisture and coolness would not permit the firmament to be damaged by the fire of the luminous bodies, while what remained below would sustain with its mist the air parched and dried by the fire overhead'; trans. Hill in Petruccione 2007, vol. 1, p. 29–31).

[55] *Apologia in Hexaemeron* 18. See also Moreschini 2016.

[56] On the provenance of this criticism which has been attributed to Porphyry see Pépin 1964, p. 418–460 who in p. 425 refers to Ps.-Justin's Q. 104 as a parallel that echoes this debate.

you will endure and they will all become old like a garment. Like clothing you will change them, and they will be changed'; Hag. 2. 7: 'I will shake the sky and the earth'; Hebr. 12. 26.[57]

3. *Elements*

The deep resistance to Greco-Roman philosophical cosmology extended to the nature of the building blocks of the creation, the elements (στοιχεῖα). As the irreducible, basic building blocks of creation, elements had an ambivalent status in cosmological debates because they had been associated with minor deities and souls and had been worshipped as such.[58] Tatian and Aristeides had attacked the worship of the elements as idolatry. So did Theodore of Mopsuestia referring to this belief in the divinity of the elements in his commentary to Paul's letters Gal. 4. 1–3 ('de ipsis dicit sole et luna et stellis; eo quod adora-

---

[57] Κἂν ὑπὸ τὸν οὐρανόν εἰσιν οἱ φωστῆρες, ἀλλ' ἡ φορὰ τῆς τῶν πυρωδῶν οὐσιῶν ἐνεργείας κατὰ φύσιν ἐπὶ τὰ ἄνω γίνεται. διὸ εὔλογον αἰτίαν ἀποδεδώκασιν οἱ εἰρηκότες πρὸς διαμονὴν τοῦ στερεώματος πεφορτῶσθαι τοῦ οὐρανοῦ τὰ νῶτα τοῖς ὕδασιν. οὐ τοῦτο δὲ μόνον ἐστὶν αἴτιον τοῦ εἶναι τὰ ὕδατα ἐν τοῖς νώτοις τοῦ οὐρανοῦ τὸ ἀχείρωτον αὐτὸν εἶναι τῇ ὑποκειμένῃ φλογὶ τῶν φωστήρων, ἀλλὰ καὶ τὸ βαρεῖσθαι αὐτὸν ἐπὶ τὸ κάτω ὑπὸ τοῦ πλήθους τῶν ἐν νώτοις αὐτοῦ ὑδάτων καὶ μὴ δονεῖσθαι ὑπὸ τῆς βιαίας τῶν ἀνέμων φορᾶς, καὶ τὸ τὴν ἄκραν τοῦ ἡλίου θερμότητι ἀποτελεῖται τῶν ἀέρων ἡ σύγκρασις πρὸς τὴν διαμονὴν τῶν ἐπὶ τῆς γῆς ζῴων τε καὶ φυτῶν. ἐν δὲ τῇ συντελείᾳ, οὐκ ἐν τῷ νῦν οὐρανῷ καὶ ἐν τῇ νῦν γῇ κομίζονται τῶν πρακτέων τὰς ἀμοιβὰς οἱ ἄνθρωποι, ἀλλ' ἐν τῷ καινῷ οὐρανῷ καὶ ἐν τῇ καινῇ γῇ, κατὰ τὸ εἰρημένον· 'ἔσται γὰρ οὐρανὸς καινὸς καὶ ἡ γῆ καινή, ἣν ἐγὼ ποιῶ· μένει ἐνώπιον μου εἰς τοὺς αἰῶνας'. καὶ πάλιν 'κατ' ἀρχὰς σύ, κύριε, τὴν γῆν ἐθεμελίωσας καὶ ἔργα τῶν χειρῶν σου εἰσὶν οἱ οὐρανοί· αὐτοὶ ἀπολοῦνται, σὺ δὲ διαμένεις καὶ πάντες ὡς ἱμάτιον παλαιωθήσονται καὶ ὡσεὶ περιβόλαιον ἑλίξεις αὐτοὺς καὶ ἀλλαγήσονται'. καὶ πάλιν· 'ἔτι ἅπαξ ἐγὼ σείω τὸν οὐρανὸν καὶ τὴν γῆν'. τὸ δὲ σαλευόμενον δηλοῖ τὴν μετάστασιν, ἵνα μείνῃ τὰ μὴ σαλευόμενα.

[58] Lumpe 1959; Delling 1971; Pépin 1964, p. 307–313. In his handbook, Alcinous considers the elements as imbued with life / gods. *Didaskalikos* 15. 1 (ed. Whittaker 1990; trans. Dillon 1993, p. 25): Εἰσὶ δὲ καὶ ἄλλοι δαίμονες, οὓς καὶ καλοίη ἄν τις γενητοὺς θεούς, καθ' ἕκαστον τῶν στοιχείων, οἱ μὲν ὁρατοί, οἱ δὲ ἀόρατοι, ἔν τε αἰθέρι καὶ πυρὶ ἀέρι τε καὶ ὕδατι, ὡς μηδὲν κόσμου μέρος ψυχῆς ἄμοιρον εἶναι μηδὲ ζῴου κρείττονος θνητῆς φύσεως· τούτοις δὲ ὑποτέτακται τὰ ὑπὸ σελήνην πάντα καὶ τὰ ἐπίγεια. ('There are, furthermore, other divinities, the daemons, whom one could also term "created gods", present in each of the elements, some of them visible, others invisible, in ether, and fire, and air, and water, so that no part of the world should be without a share in soul or in a living being superior to mortal nature. To their administration the whole sublunar and terrestrial sphere has been assigned').

bant illa cum essent gentes ut deos, secundum legem gentium') and Col. 2. 8. The worship of the elements extended to the idea that parts of the universe and creation were also divine and worthy of worship. Athenagoras rejected this idea early on, claiming instead that 'the Demiurge and Creator of the world, God, through the medium of His word, has apportioned and ordained the angels to occupy the elements, the heavens, the world, and whatever is in the world'.[59] The premise still resonates in Q. 55 of the QRO and is also refuted in Ps.-Justin's response.[60]

Related to this constellation of beliefs about the elements is that they are sentient. Certain passages in the Bible lent themselves to this interpretation too, as Q. 60 shows.[61] Origen, in commenting on Ier. 12. 4 ('How long will the earth mourn, and the grass of every field wither because of the wickedness of its inhabitants?'), had conceded that:

Ὡσπερεὶ ἐμψύχου τῆς γῆς καὶ ἐνταῦθα διαλέγεται ὁ προφήτης λέγων τὴν γῆν πενθεῖν διὰ τὴν κακίαν τῶν ἐπιβαινόντων ἐπ' αὐτήν. Καθ' ἕκαστον οὖν ἡμῶν ἡ γῆ ἤτοι πενθεῖ ἢ εὐφραίνεται· ἢ γὰρ πενθεῖ 'ἀπὸ κακίας τῶν ἐνοικούντων ἐν αὐτῇ' ἢ εὐφραίνεται ἀπὸ ἀρετῆς 'τῶν ἐνοικούντων ἐν αὐτῇ'. Ἐφ' ἑκάστου οὖν ἡμῶν αὐτὸ τὸ στοιχεῖον ἢ εὐφραίνεται ἢ πενθεῖ· εἰ δὲ ἡ γῆ, τάχα καὶ τὰ λοιπὰ στοιχεῖα. Ὁμοίως ἐρῶ καὶ ὕδωρ καὶ ὁ ἐπὶ τοῦ ὕδατος τεταγμένος ἄγγελος, ἵνα διηγήσωμαι καὶ τὴν γῆν πενθοῦσαν ἢ μὴ πενθοῦσαν· οὐ γὰρ τοῦτο τὸ σῶμα, ἡ γῆ, 'πενθεῖ ἀπὸ τῶν κατοικούντων ἐν αὐτῇ', ἀλλὰ νόει μοι πρὸς τῇ διατάξει τοῦ παντὸς τεταγμένον τινὰ ἄγγελον ἐπὶ τῆς γῆς καὶ ἄλλον τεταγμένον ἐπὶ τῶν ὑδάτων καὶ ἄλλον ἐπὶ τοῦ ἀέρος καὶ τέταρτον ἐπὶ τοῦ πυρός. [...] Οὗτοι δὴ οἱ ἄγγελοι, μεθ' ὧν ἐσμεν ὅσον ἐσμὲν ἐπὶ γῆς, ἤτοι εὐφραίνονται, ἢ πενθοῦσιν ἐφ' ἡμῖν ὅταν ἁμαρτάνωμεν·

---

[59] *Suppl.* 10. 5 (ed. Schoedel 1972; trans. in Daniélou 1957, p. 3): [...] ὁ ποιητὴς καὶ δημιουργὸς κόσμου Θεὸς διὰ τοῦ παρ' αὐτοῦ λόγου διένειμε καὶ διέταξεν περί τε τὰ στοιχεῖα εἶναι καὶ τοὺς οὐρανοὺς καὶ τὸν κόσμον καὶ τὰ ἐν αὐτῷ καὶ τὴν τούτων εὐταξίαν. See Daniélou 1957, p. 3. For an extended discussion of this idea in Origen's work see Scott 1991, p. 127–128.

[60] Εἰ τῶν μερῶν τῆς κτίσεως οἱ δαίμονες οὐκ ἐξουσιάζουσι, διατί παρακουσθέντων τῶν χρησμῶν τοῖς Ἕλλησι τιμωρίας ἐπήγαγον καὶ θεραπευθέντων τῶν εἰδώλων ταύτας ἀνέσχον καὶ ἀγαθὰ αὐτοῖς ἀντὶ τούτων παρέσχον; Πόθεν οὖν αὐτοῖς δύναμις εἰς τὴν ἑκατέρου ἐνέργειαν;

[61] Q. 60: Εἰ τοῖς στοιχείοις οὐ πρόσεστιν αἴσθησις. Διατί Μωϋσῆς μὲν οὐρανὸν καὶ γῆν τῷ λαῷ διαμαρτύρεται [Dt. 32.1–2], Ἡσαΐας δὲ κατηγορῶν τοῦ λαοῦ τούτοις ἀκούειν ἐγκελεύεται;

The prophet here speaks as if the earth was alive when he says the earth mourned because of the wickedness of those who walked upon it. For each of us the earth either mourns or rejoices, for either it mourns 'because of the wickedness of its inhabitants' or rejoices because of the virtue 'of its inhabitants'. In each of us then this same element either rejoices or grieves, and if it is so for the earth it is also true for the other elements. Similarly, I shall say: there is water and an angel in charge of water [Apoc. 16. 5], so that I may also describe the earth which is grieving and that which is not grieving. For it is not the body earth that grieves 'because of the wickedness of its inhabitants', but understand that for the administration of the universe an angel is assigned for the earth, and another for the waters, and another for air, and a fourth for fire. Thus rise up by reason to all the order that is in animals, in plants, and in the heavenly stars. An angel is assigned to the sun, and another to the moon, and another to the stars. [...] These angels, whom we accompany as long as we are on the earth, either rejoice or grieve with us when we sin.[62]

The second-century Christian heretic Bardaisan synthesised different strands of ideas about the elements in his teachings. He subscribed to the idea that the four elements combined with each other in different balances and measures to create the various constituents of the world. He is thought to have taken from Plato's *Timaeus* 'the idea that the cosmos had been created from pre-existent matter by a demiurgical figure, who also formed the 7 planets (Mercury, Mars, Venus, Jupiter, Saturn, Earth, and the Moon). At the creation of the world, these planets were assigned their fixed paths through the heavens and each given a part in the governing of the cosmos.'[63] The same idea can be traced in numerous other works of the second century, whether Middle-Platonic, Stoic, or Christian.

Parts of this nexus of beliefs about the elements are reflected in Q. 140, and this creates the need to clarify their nature. Two views of the elements are at odds here. If deifying elements (in the form of stars or parts of the world) is an error, then surely God's pronouncement against the false gods in Jer. 10. 11

---

[62] *In Ier. hom.* 10. 6 (ed. SC 232, p. 410; trans. Scott 1991, p. 129).
[63] Denzey 2005, p. 169.

('let gods who did not make the sky and the earth perish from
the earth and from under the sky') is a pronouncement against
the elements too.[64] Invoking an oft-cited verse from Psalm 95. 5
('all the gods of the nations are demons') as an unequivocal
denunciation of foreign gods, Ps.-Justin explains how these
demons were destroyed by being stripped of their status and
honour and the names which native people had given them.[65]
Ps.-Justin then introduces the theme of the new creation, quoting Ps. 101. 27 ('they [viz. the heavens] will perish, but you
will endure, and they will all become old like a garment. Like
clothing you will change them, and they will be changed').

The role of the elements continues to be an issue in the problem of the continuity between the old creation and the new in the
divine economy. It is thus problematized in Q. 105:

> Εἰ ὡς βιβλίον τὸν οὐρανὸν ἐλίσσεσθαι καὶ τὰ ἄστρα ὡς φύλλα
> πίπτειν ἐπὶ τῆς γῆς προλέγει μὲν ὁ κύριος, καὶ ὁ προφήτης δὲ τού-
> τοις προκατήγγειλε σύμφωνα, πῶς ἡ παντελὴς τοῦ στερεώματος
> ἀπώλεια διὰ τῶν ἐκείνων λόγων οὐ δείκνυται; Τίς οὖν τῶν τοι-
> ούτων ῥημάτων διάνοια καὶ πῶς τὸ τῶν στοιχείων συνίσταται
> ἄφθαρτον;

[64] Εἰ τὰ καθόλου στοιχεῖα καὶ τὰ λοιπὰ μέρη τῆς κτίσεως κατὰ πλάνην ἐθεο-
ποίησαν εἴτουν ἐθεολόγησαν ἄνθρωποι, ποτὲ μὲν αὐτὰ καθ' αὐτὰ θαυμάσαντες, οἷον
οὐρανὸν γῆν ἥλιον σελήνην ἀστέρας πῦρ ὕδωρ ἀέρα, ποτὲ δὲ τὰ αὐτὰ ἑτέρως μυθολο-
γήσαντες, οἷον τὸν μὲν ἥλιον Ἀπόλλωνα, τὴν δὲ γῆν Δήμητραν, τὸν δὲ αἰθέρα Δία καὶ
τὰ λοιπὰ ὁμοίως, ἀπεφήνατο δὲ ὁ θεὸς κατ' αὐτῶν λέγων 'θεοί, οἳ οὐκ ἐποίησαν τὸν
οὐρανὸν καὶ τὴν γῆν, ἀπολέσθωσαν', πῶς οὐ κατὰ πάντων τῶν στοιχείων ἐξήγαγεν τὴν
τῆς ἀπωλείας ἀπόφασιν;

[65] Θεοί, ὧν τὴν ἀπώλειαν ἀπεφήνατο ἡ θεία γραφή, δαίμονές εἰσι πονηροὶ κατὰ
τὴν πλάνην τῶν ἀνθρώπων ὑπὲρ τὴν φύσιν τὴν κλῆσιν ἐσχηκότες θεοῦ κατὰ τὸ εἰρη-
μένον· 'ἔθυσαν δαιμονίοις καὶ οὐ θεῷ'. Καὶ πάλιν· 'πάντες οἱ θεοὶ τῶν ἐθνῶν δαιμόνια'.
τούτων τῶν δαιμόνων ὁ προφήτης προλέγει τὴν ἀπώλειαν. Ἀπώλεια δὲ τῶν δαιμόνων ἐστὶ τὸ πάσης μὲν τῆς ἐκ πλάνης ἀνθρώπων προγεγονυίας αὐτοῖς ἀποστερεῖσθαι
θεολογίας τε καὶ τιμῆς, ἐν τοῖς διηνεκέσι δὲ βασάνοις ζῆν ὀδυνηρῶς. τῶν δαιμόνων τε
τούτῳ τῷ τρόπῳ βασανιζομένων εἰς ἔλεγχον τοῦ μὴ ὑπάρχειν αὐτοὺς θεούς, γίνεται ἡ
ἀπώλεια τῆς ὀνομασίας αὐτῶν τε καὶ τῶν μερῶν τῆς κτίσεως, καθ' ἣν ὑπὸ τῶν πεπλανημένων ἀνθρώπων ψευδῶς ὠνομάσθησαν. Καὶ καθὼς περ ὅταν λέγῃ ἡ θεία γραφὴ
περὶ τοῦ οὐρανοῦ καὶ τῆς γῆς, ὅτι 'αὐτοὶ μὲν ἀπολοῦνται σὺ δὲ διαμένεις καὶ πάντες
ὡς ἱμάτιον παλαιωθήσονται καὶ ὡσεὶ περιβόλαιον ἑλίξεις αὐτοὺς καὶ ἀλλαγήσονται',
οὐ τὴν ἀνυπαρξίαν τῆς ὑποστάσεως αὐτῶν σημαίνει τῷ τῆς ἀπωλείας ὀνόματι, ἀλλὰ
τῆς παλαιότητος αὐτῶν, οὕτω καὶ ἐνταῦθα τῶν θεῶν λέγει τὴν ἀπώλειαν, οὐ πρὸς
σημασίαν τῆς ἀνυπαρξίας τῆς ὑποστάσεως αὐτῶν, ἀλλὰ τῆς ὀνομασίας αὐτῶν, καθ'
ἣν σὺν τοῖς μέρεσι τῆς κτίσεως θεοὶ ὑπὸ τῶν πεπλανημένων ἀνθρώπων ἐκλήθησαν.
On this apologetic argument see Wey 1957.

> If the Lord foretells that the heaven will roll up like a book scroll and the stars will fall on the earth like leaves, and the prophet foretold accordingly [Is. 34. 4], how is it that the complete loss of the firmament does not show, through their words, to be true? What is the meaning of these words and how are the elements imperishable / incorruptible?[66]

The firmly rooted belief in the incorruptibility of the elements underpins the doubts about the loss of the firmament and the apocalyptic scenario described in the Bible.[67] The same passage (Is. 34. 4), as transmitted in the *Apocalypse of Peter*,[68] was the focus of criticism by the anonymous philosopher in the *Apocriticus* of Macarius Magnes.[69] This work, by the way that the pagan objector takes exception to the apocalyptic destruction of the universe, provides a fuller rationale for understanding the ἀπορία about eschatology. That the sky would roll up like a scroll and the stars would fall on the earth like leaves was an affront to the Greek idea of an eternal, divinely ordered universe sustained by God's providence:

> [...] τὰ μὲν περὶ τὴν γῆν τετάρακται καὶ τὴν τάξιν οὐ πέφυκε σώζειν, ἀλλ' ἔστιν ἀνώμαλα, τὰ δ' ἐν τῷ οὐρανῷ τάξιν ὁμοίαν ἔχει διαπαντὸς καὶ ἀεὶ κατὰ τὰ αὐτὰ προχωρεῖ καὶ οὐδέποτε ὑπαλ-λάττεται, ἀλλ' οὐδ' ἀπαλλαγήσεταί ποτε· ποίημα γὰρ ἀκριβέστα-τον καθέστηκε τοῦ Θεοῦ· ὅθεν τὰ κρείττονος ἀξιωθέντα μοίρας λυθῆναι ἀμήχανον, ἄτε θείῳ πεπηγότα καὶ ἀκηράτῳ θεσμῷ. Τίνος δ' ἕνεκεν οὐρανὸς κριθήσεται; ἡμαρτηκὼς δὲ τί φανήσεται ποτε, ὁ τὴν ἐξ ἀρχῆς ὑπὸ Θεοῦ τάξιν δοκιμασθεῖσαν φυλάττων καὶ διαμένων ἐπὶ τῆς ταυτότητος ἀεί;

> Things in heaven have the same order forever and always move along the same [paths] and never change nor ever will change; for it was established as God's most consummate creation. Hence it is impossible that those things worthy of a superior destiny be destroyed, in so far as they have been fixed by a divine and undefiled law. And for what reason will

---

[66] On the early Christian reception of the image of the sky rolling up like a scroll see Jakab 2003.

[67] Van der Horst 1994. On the concept of 'new creation' and the exegetical debates that surrounded it see Rusell 1996; Stephens 2011.

[68] See comment in Schott & Edwards 2015, p. 211 n. 53.

[69] See also Cook 2004, p. 231–234 and Volp 2013.

heaven be judged? What fault will it ever appear to have committed, when it preserves the order approved in the beginning by God and remains always in an identical condition? [70]

This was part of a sustained attack on a number of eschatological pronouncements. Prior to this, in the same work *Apocriticus*, Paul's pronouncement in I Cor. 7. 31 ('the form of the world will pass away') had been criticised: [71]

[...] πῶς τὸ σχῆμα τοῦ κόσμου τούτου παρελθεῖν δυνατόν; Τίς δ' ὁ παράγων ἔσται καὶ τίνος χάριν; Εἰ μὲν γὰρ ὁ δημιουργὸς τοῦτο παράξειε, διαβληθήσεται, ὡς τὸ κείμενον ἀσφαλῶς κινῶν καὶ μεταφέρων. εἰ δ' ἐπὶ τὸ κρεῖττον παράξει τὸ σχῆμα, κατηγορεῖται κἂν τούτῳ πάλιν, ὡς οὐ συνιδὼν ἐν τῇ δημιουργίᾳ τὸ ἁρμόζον καὶ πρέπον σχῆμα τῷ κόσμῳ, ἀλλὰ τοῦ κρείττονος λόγου λειπόμενον ἔκτισεν αὐτὸν ὥσπερ ἀτελῆ. Πόθεν γοῦν ἰστέον ὡς εἰς τὸ καλὸν ἡ τοῦ κόσμου φύσις ὀψὲ τῶν χρόνων ἀλλαττομένη λήξει ποτέ; Τί δὲ τὸ συμφέρον τὴν τῶν φαινομένων τάξιν ἀλλαγῆναι; Εἰ μὲν γὰρ κατηφῆ καὶ λύπης αἴτια τὰ τῶν ὁρωμένων ὑπάρχει πράγματα, καταψάλλεται καὶ τούτοις ὁ δημιουργός, καταυλούμενος εὐλόγοις αἰτίαις, ὅτι λυπηρὰ καὶ ταράττοντα τὴν λογικὴν φύσιν ἐτεκτήνατο τοῦ κόσμου τὰ μέρη, καὶ μεταγνοὺς ἔκρινεν ἀλλάξαι τὸ πᾶν.

How can the form of this world pass away? Who will cause it to pass away and for what reason? For if the Creator causes this [world] to pass away, He will be slandered for setting in motion and changing that which has been firmly established, while if He alters the form for the better, for this too He would be denounced, on the grounds that, not having a clear vision of the harmonious and appropriate form for the world when He was crafting it, and lacking a better rational principle, He created it as something imperfect. At any rate, how is possible to know that the nature of the world will be changed for the better when, late in time, it comes to an end? And what is the benefit of altering the order of phaenomena? For if the things of the visible [world] are causes of grief and pain, the Creator is drummed out by the sound of these [accusations] and is piped down with good cause, because

---

[70] *Apocr.* 4. 6. 2–3 (ed. Volp 2013; trans. Schott & Edwards 2015, p. 210–211); see also Volp 2011.

[71] See Cook 2004, p. 220–222.

He devised the parts of the world as causes of pain and viola-
tions of rational nature and, later repenting, decided to alter
the whole.[72]

Ps.-Justin explains that Is. 34. 4 uses an expression, one of many
that he goes on to list: the holy scripture likened the creation
of the firmament, by means of a parable, to the stretching out of
a skin ('stretching out the sky like a skin', Ps. 103. 2)[73] and said
that 'the sky was strengthened like smoke' (Is. 51. 6). Another
time he refers to the circumference of an arch (it is said 'He has
set up heaven like a vault' [Is. 40. 22]). In sum, he states that
the Bible represents the firmament's dissolution by way of a parable, referring to it sometimes as a book-scroll, sometimes as an
element dissolved by fire, according to the apostle Peter's saying
in the second catholic epistle (II Petr. 3. 10–12), and sometimes
as an old garment (Is. 51. 6). This part of the response joins
Old Testament pronouncements about the coming Judgement
with strands of apocalyptic expectations of the end of the world,
which themselves (notably II Petr. 3. 5) were influenced by Stoic
ideas of the world's conflagration (ἐκπύρωσις)[74] which in turn
had been originally used against the 'scoffers' who believed in the
world's indestructability.[75]

The loss of the firmament and the heaven, Ps.-Justin continues, is meant to show to those who believe in the incorruptibility

---

[72] *Apocr.* 4. 3–4 (trans. Schott & Edwards 2015, p. 205–206).

[73] Elsewhere in the QRO, in Q. 77, Ps.-Justin is called upon to interpret
Ps. 18. 5 ('he set up his tent in the sun'): Εἴπομεν ἐν τοῖς ἀνωτέρω, ὅτι οὐρανοὺς
οἶδεν ἡ θεία γραφὴ καλεῖν ἢ τοὺς κατ᾽ οὐσίαν, ὡς τὸν πρῶτον οὐρανὸν καὶ τὸ στερέωμα, ἢ τοὺς κατὰ τὰ ἐν τῷ ἀέρι διαστήματα. Τὸ οὖν *ἐν τῷ ἡλίῳ ἔθετο τὸ σκήνωμα*
αὐτοῦ, ἵνα εἴπῃ τοὺς οὐρανοὺς ἔθετο σκήνωμα τοῦ ἡλίου. Ἡ γὰρ ἐκ τῆς τῶν Ἑβραίων
γλώττης εἰς τὴν τῶν Σύρων γλῶτταν μεταγωγὴ τῆς λέξεως οὕτω γεγένηται· 'ἐν αὐτοῖς
ἔθετο τοῦ ἡλίου τὸ σκήνωμα'. Δηλοῖ δὲ δι᾽ ἑτέρου ψαλμοῦ ὁ προφήτης Δαυῒδ αὐτὸ
τοῦτο, καὶ φησὶν ὁ *ἐκτείνων τὸν οὐρανὸν ὡσεὶ δέρριν·* ἡ γὰρ ἔκτασις τῶν δέρρεων τὴν
σκηνὴν ἀποτελεῖ. Τῇ ποικιλίᾳ οὖν τῶν οὐσιῶν καὶ τῇ διαφορᾷ τῶν χρειῶν δείκνυσιν
αὐτοὺς εἶναι γενητούς. Ἡ γὰρ ἀγένητος φύσις πρὸς τὴν ἀγένητον φύσιν κατὰ φύσιν
οὐκ ἔχει διαφοράν, τὸ δὲ καὶ χρείας ἕνεκεν εἶναι τοιόνδε ἢ τοιόνδε ἀλλότριόν ἐστι
τῆς ἀγενήτου φύσεως. For the considerable exegetical attention that this verses
had attracted see Gounelle 1994.

[74] Van der Horst 1994; Salles 2015.

[75] Adams 2007, p. 207 and Harrill 2010, with a review of scholarly opinion
on the contested issue of Stoic influence on II Petr. 3. 5.

of the heaven how vain their belief is.[76] Thus, the final dissolution of the firmament becomes, for Ps.-Justin, yet another opportunity for the refutation of the eternity of the world. The end of the world, however, and the defense of a new creation, continued to resonate and became the subject of the lost eighth book of Philoponus's *De aeternitate mundi contra Aristotelem*.[77]

Q. 106 probes deeper into the problem of the old versus the new creation adumbrated by biblical witnesses by enquiring about the role of the animate world and the hierarchy that God established among His creatures. If what had been created to minister to humans (i.e. animals) will perish, whereas natural elements such as the air and the sea will endure in the new creation, how will the latter not prove useless as they will not be needed (e.g. for fishing or commerce) by humans in their resurrected state?[78]

Citing Paul's declaration in I Cor. 7. 31 ('the present form of this world is passing away'), Is. 65. 17 and II Petr. 3. 17 ('a new heaven and a new earth'), Ps.-Justin insists that the natural elements will still exist in the new creation to help humans move about. This implies that the new creation will not annihilate existing natural elements, but change and use them for other purposes.[79]

---

[76] Ὥσπερ τοῦ στερεώματος τὴν ποίησιν παραβολικῶς ἡ θεία γραφὴ παρείκασε ποτὲ μὲν τῇ ἐκτάσει τῆς δέρρεως, λέγουσα 'ὁ ἐκτείνων τὸν οὐρανὸν ὡσεὶ δέρριν', ποτὲ δὲ τῷ καπνῷ στερεωμένῳ ('ὁ οὐρανός', φησίν, 'ὡσεὶ καπνὸς ἐστερεώθη'), ποτὲ δὲ τῷ περιφερεῖ τῆς καμάρας ('ὁ τανύσας' φησὶ 'τὸν οὐρανὸν ὡσεὶ καμάραν'), οὕτω καὶ τὴν ἀνάλυσιν αὐτοῦ παραβολικῶς παρείκασε ποτὲ μὲν βιβλίῳ ἑλισσομένῳ, ποτὲ δὲ στοιχείῳ λυομένῳ πυρί, καθά φησιν ὁ ἀπόστολος Πέτρος ἐν τῇ δευτέρᾳ αὐτοῦ καθολικῇ ἐπιστολῇ, ποτὲ δὲ ἱματίῳ παλαιουμένῳ· ἀνάγκη γὰρ τῇ εἰσαγωγῇ τοῦ κρείττονος οὐρανοῦ τοῦ καινῶς γινομένου ἀναιρεῖσθαι τὸ στερέωμα, ὡς ἄχρηστον ὂν πρὸς ἐκείνην τὴν κατάστασιν, ἵνα τῇ αὐτοῦ ἀπωλείᾳ κἂν τότε τὸ μάταιον τοῦ περὶ τῆς ἀγεννησίας τε καὶ ἀφθαρσίας τοῦ οὐρανοῦ φρονήματος μάθωσιν οἱ ἀΐδιόν τε καὶ ἀγένητον θεόν τε και ἔμφρονα τοῦτον εἰρηκότες.

[77] See Wildberg 1988, p. 103–104.

[78] Εἰ διὰ τὴν ἡμετέραν χρείαν κατ' ἀρχὰς ἡ παραγωγὴ τῆς κτίσεως γέγονε καὶ διὰ τὴν ἡμετέραν ὁμοίως χρείαν τὰ μὲν φθείρεται, τὰ δὲ ἀφθαρσίαν ἐν τῇ συντελείᾳ ἐνδύεται, οἷον κτήνη μὲν καὶ θηρία καὶ πετεινὰ φθείρεται, οὐρανὸς δὲ καὶ γῆ φθορᾶς ἀπαλλάσσεται. Καὶ τὰ μὲν φθείρεται, ὡς ἀνενδεοῦς ἡμῶν ἀνισταμένου τοῦ σώματος, ἐν ἀφθαρσίᾳ δὲ τὰ δηλωθέντα διαμένει στοιχεῖα, τῶν πραχθέντων ἡμῖν μελλόντων ἡμῶν ἐν αὐτοῖς κομίζεσθαι τὴν ἀντίδοσιν, ἀὴρ καὶ θάλαττα πῶς οὐκ ἄχρηστα, εἰ τότε μένει ἄφθαρτα, οὔτε εἰς ἀναπνοάς, οὔτε ἐμπορίας οὔτε ἰχθυοφαγίας ἢ ἑτέρας τινὸς βοηθείας ἐξ αὐτῶν χρηζόντων ἡμῶν διὰ τὸ ἀνενδεές, ὡς ἔφην, τοῦ σώματος;

[79] Εἰ κατὰ τὸν ἀπόστολον Παῦλον 'παράγει τὸ σχῆμα τοῦ κόσμου τούτου', δῆλον ὅτι ἐξ ἀνάγκης καὶ τὰ ἄλλα πάντα, τὰ τοῦ σχήματος ἕνεκεν τοῦ κόσμου γεγονότα,

4. *Genesis 2. 2 and God's Rest*

In Q. 148 the anonymous enquirer uses the episode of Genesis 2. 2 ('He rested on the seventh day from all the work that He had done') to pose the problem of the creation in time.[80] Gen. 2. 2 had been previously attacked by Celsus. In Origen's words:

> [...] οἰηθεὶς ταὐτὸν εἶναι τὸ 'κατέπαυσε τῇ ἡμέρᾳ τῇ ἑβδόμῃ' καὶ τὸ 'ἀνεπαύσατο τῇ ἡμέρᾳ τῇ ἑβδόμῃ' φησί· Μετὰ τοῦτο μὴν ὥσπερ τις ἀτεχνῶς πονηρὸς χειροτέχνης ἐκκαμὼν καὶ πρὸς ἀνά- παυσιν ἀργίας δεηθείς. [...] Εἶτα ὡς ἤτοι τῶν γραφῶν οὕτω λεγου- σῶν ἢ καὶ ἡμῶν αὐτῶν οὕτως διηγουμένων περὶ θεοῦ, ὅτι καμὼν ἀνεπαύσατο, φησὶν ὅτι οὐ θέμις τὸν πρῶτον θεὸν κάμνειν οὔτε χειρουργεῖν οὔτε κελεύειν.

> [Celsus] thought that to say 'He ceased on the seventh day' was the same as 'He rested on the seventh day', saying: 'After this, indeed, God exactly like a bad workman, was worn out and needed a holiday to have a rest.' [...] Then, as if it were either what the scriptures say or what we ourselves expound them to say about God, that He rested because He was tired, he [Celsus] says: 'It is not right for the first God to be tired or to work with His hands or to give orders'.[81]

In this context Origen seeks to counter Celsus's accusation of an anthropomorphic representation of God. In Q. 148 of the QRO, however, the enquiry-objection posits that this interrup- tion of God's creative will and providence meant the interrup- tion of His creative activity (ἐνεργείας). The point is illustrated by the example of fire which, once it ceases to burn, stops exist- ing (οἷον, τὸ πῦρ τοῦ καίειν καὶ φλογίζειν παυσάμενον, καὶ τοῦ εἶναι παύεται).[82]

συμπαραχθήσεται τῷ τοῦ κόσμου σχήματι, εἰσαχθήσεται δὲ 'καινὸς οὐρανὸς καὶ καινὴ γῆ', ἐν οἷς μέλλει δίδοσθαι δικαίοις τε καὶ ἀδίκοις ἡ τῶν πρακτέων ἀμοιβή. Τῷ δὲ ἀέρι, εἰ καὶ πρὸς ἀναπνοήν, τότε οὐ χρῄζομεν, ἀλλὰ πρὸς τὴν κίνησίν τε καὶ τοπικὴν μετάβασιν ἀναγκαίως αὐτῷ χρησόμεθα· 'ἁρπαγησόμεθα' γάρ, φησίν, 'ἐν νεφέλαις εἰς ἀπάντησιν τοῦ κυρίου εἰς ἀέρα'.

[80] For the difficulties presented by this verse see Alexandre 1988, p. 214–221.

[81] *Contra Celsum* 6. 61 (ed. SC 147, p. 330; trans. Chadwick 1953, p. 376). According to Cook 2004, p. 69, Celsus may have been indebted to the Hellenistic Jewish author Aristobulus 'who argued that God's resting did not imply, as some suppose, that God did nothing'.

[82] Εἰ ἡ τοῦ σαββάτου ἀργία κατά τινα τύπον τοῖς Ἰουδαίοις παραδέδοται τῆς τοῦ θεοῦ καταπαύσεως, ἤτοι ἐν τῇ κοσμοποιίᾳ, ἤτοι καὶ ἐν τῇ συντελείᾳ, κατέπαυσε

In his response, Ps.-Justin points out that this episode is a figure (τύπος), a reminder to the Jews that God was the Creator. He is very careful to distinguish between God's power and actuality (ἐνέργεια), which remained eternal and not contingent on the creation of the material world, and His will, which is separate from His being (οὐσία). God, therefore, is very much unlike fire in that the fire exists, and therefore acts (and acts, and therefore exists).[83]

As a problem of philosophical theology, this question comes close to similar προβλήματα posed by a pagan interlocutor, the iatrosophist Gesius, in the dialogue *Ammonius* by Zacharias of Mytilene:

⌜Πῶς δημιουργὸς ὁ θεός, ὦ ἑταῖρε,⌝ εἰ μὴ ἀεὶ δημιουργεῖ;
[...] οὐκοῦν οὔτε δημιουργὸς ἂν εἴη ὁ μὴ τῇ ἐνεργείᾳ δημιουργῶν καὶ τοὺς λόγους οὓς ἔχει ἐς τοὐμφανὲς προφέρων καὶ τὴν ἀνείδεον ὕλην εἰς εἶδος καὶ σχῆμα μετασκευάζων τε καὶ μεθαρμόττων.

How is God a creator, my friend, if He is not always creating? [...] He would not be a creator who does not create

---

δὲ ἢ καταπαύσει κατὰ τὸν τύπον ὁ δεσπότης τοῦ βουλήσει ἢ προνοίᾳ ἐργάζεσθαι, πῶς οὐ χρονικὴν αὐτοῦ τὴν τοῦ ἐργάζεσθαι ἐνέργειαν ὁ λόγος ὁ τοιοῦτος παρίστησι; Παυσαμένης γὰρ αὐτοῦ τῆς ἐνεργείας, δῆλον ὅτι καὶ ἡ ἐνέργεια πέπαυται. Οἷον, τὸ πῦρ τοῦ καίειν καὶ φλογίζειν παυσάμενον, καὶ τοῦ εἶναι παύεται.

[83] Ὁ μὲν δεσπότης θεὸς ἐν ταῖς ἓξ ἡμέραις πᾶσαν κτίσιν ἐκ τοῦ μὴ ὄντος εἰς τὸ εἶναι παρήγαγε καὶ τῇ ἑβδόμῃ ἡμέρᾳ κατέπαυσε τοῦ κατὰ τὰς οἰκείας ἀρχὰς ἐκ τοῦ μὴ ὄντος εἰς τὸ εἶναι παραγαγεῖν ἔτι τινά. 'καὶ κατέπαυσε' φησί 'κύριος ὁ θεὸς τῇ ἡμέρᾳ τῇ ἑβδόμῃ ἀπὸ πάντων τῶν ἔργων ὧν ἤρξατο ποιεῖν' [Gen. 2. 2]. Ἐνετείλατο δὲ τοῖς Ἰουδαίοις ἓξ ἡμέρας ἐργάζεσθαι καὶ τῇ ἑβδόμῃ ἡμέρᾳ σαββατίζειν, ἵνα, ἐργαζομένων τε αὐτῶν καὶ παυομένων τῆς ἐργασίας, τυπικῶς φυλαχθῇ ἐν αὐτοῖς ἡ μνήμη τῆς τε ἐργασίας καὶ τῆς καταπαύσεως τοῦ θεοῦ. Καὶ τὴν μὲν δύναμιν, καθ' ἣν τὴν κτίσιν πεποίηκε ὁ θεός, ἀιδίως εἶχε καὶ ἔχει. Ἐνεργεῖ δὲ κατὰ τὴν ταύτην τὴν ἀίδιον δύναμιν, ὅτε βούλεται, τῆς δυνάμεως ἐν τῇ ἰδίᾳ ἰσχύι μενούσης ἀιδίως καὶ πρὸ τῆς ἐνεργείας καὶ μετὰ τὴν ἐνέργειαν, πάσης τῆς ἐν χρόνῳ ἀποβολῆς καὶ προσλήψεως ἀπηλλαγμένης. Διὸ δύναται ποιεῖν ἀεὶ πάντα ὅσα βούλεται ποιεῖν. Οὐκ ἔτι δὲ βούλεται ποιεῖν πάντα ὅσα δύναται ποιεῖν· καὶ γὰρ πλείονας ἡλίους ἠδύνατο καὶ δύναται ποιεῖν, ἀλλ' ὅμως ἕνα μόνον ἥλιον ἐποίησεν, ὅτι ἕνα μόνον ἐβούλετο ποιεῖν· ἐπειδὴ οὖν βουλήσει καὶ οὐ τῷ εἶναι ποιεῖ ὁ θεός, διὰ τοῦτο οὐ παύεται τοῦ εἶναι [θεός], παυσαμένης τῆς ἐνεργείας αὐτοῦ· ὧν γὰρ τῇ καταπαύσει τῆς ἐνεργείας συμπαύεται καὶ τὸ εἶναι, τούτοις ἐνεργεῖν τὸ εἶναι καὶ οὐ τὸ βούλεσθαι πρόσεστιν· οἷον, τὸ πῦρ ἅμα ὑπάρχειν καὶ τὸ εἶναι καὶ τὸ ἐνεργεῖν καὶ τὸ μὴ ὑπάρχειν καὶ τὸ ἐνεργεῖν οὐχ ὑπάρχει. Διὸ καὶ ἡ κατάφασις οὐσίας τε καὶ ἐνεργείας αὐτοῦ ἀντιστρέφει· ὡσαύτως δὲ καὶ ἡ ἀπόφασις αὐτῷ· οἷον ἔστι τὸ πῦρ· ἐνεργεῖ τὸ πῦρ; ἔστι τὸ πῦρ. Οὐκ ἐνεργεῖ τὸ πῦρ; οὐκ ἔστι τὸ πῦρ. A similar line of thought appears in *Quaestiones gentilium ad Christianos* 4 (ed. CAp V, p. 340) as a response to the question of whether God creates, has created or will create, and if He does, is it with His will or without it.

---

in actuality or visibly bring forth the principles he possesses or transform and change formless matter into form and shape.[84]

To which Zacharias responds:

φαμὲν γὰρ τὸν θεὸν ἀεὶ δημιουργόν, ὡς ἔχοντα ⌜τοὺς δημιουργι-κοὺς λόγους⌝ ἐν ἑαυτῷ καὶ τούς, ⌜ὅταν ἐθέλῃ, προάγοντα.⌝ οὐ γὰρ ἀργίαν καθόλου τοῦ θεοῦ κατηγοροῦμεν, οὔτ', ἐπειδή ποτε μὴ δημιουργεῖ, δημιουργὸν εἶναι τοῦτον ἀρνούμεθα.

He is always a creator, since He has the creative principles within Himself and brings them forth when He wishes. In no way do we attribute idleness to God, nor do we deny that He is a creator, because sometimes He does not create.[85]

The emphasis that early Christian authors had been increasingly placing on the temporal beginning of the whole of creation from the fourth century on, had thrown up other more complex questions. These included: how could eternity and time conceivably overlap in the 'moment' God created? How could the timeless Creator produce a time-bound world without compromising His transcendence? These broader questions were intensely and variously debated between pagans and Christians in the fifth and early sixth centuries in Alexandria and Gaza.[86]

5. *Conclusions*

As this contribution hopes to have made clear, what seem to be isolated hesitations, concerns, and objections in fact involved (and echoed) continuing debates and competing understandings about the creation of the world. The historian of religious ideas looking for consistency or a systematic exposition and articulation of a Christian cosmological doctrine in Ps.-Justin's QRO would

[84] *Ammonius* 369, 383–385 (ed. Colonna 1973; trans. Gertz 2012, p. 112–113). For a fuller analysis of this particular debate see Gleede 2009, p. 113–119; Scholten 2000; Gleede 2011; Champion 2014, p. 150–151.

[85] *Ammonius* 387–391 (trans. Gertz 2012, p. 113). Cf. Obertello 2003; Obertello 2007; Bydén 2012.

[86] Sorabji 1983, p. 186, 196, 206, 209, 233, 249–252; Sorabji 2015; Champion 2014.

be looking for the wrong thing in the wrong place. The author of the collection, acutely aware of the possibilities that the literary format offered him, and free from any constraint to pursue a systematic exegesis of the biblical account of the world's creation, is picking up different threads of the debates that he thought relevant. The question then is, to what end?

This brings me back to my initial observations on the purpose of these collections as attested in some of the earliest examples. Having used Ps.-Justin's collection to show how they were used to investigate cosmological issues, it has been shown that these ζητήματα / προβλήματα almost certainly functioned as disputatious arguments and exercises in debate (as well as a means of instruction).[87] Other collections in the corpus attributed to Ps.-Justin, which consist only of questions, served similar aims and were most likely meant to be used in debates. In this respect, Ps.-Justin's corpus is a precursor to standard Byzantine collections of questions and answers (or only questions) compiled to be used in debates.[88] These ready-made arguments-objections enabled a participant in a debate to corner his opponent(s).[89] In his *Apocriticus*, Macarius Magnes vividly describes Christians who were on the receiving end of a barrage of intricately and elaborately constructed ἀπορίαι:

> Ταῦθ' ὁ τῆς ἑλληνικῆς δεινότητος ἔξαρχος κατὰ τῶν θείων τοῦ Χριστοῦ παιδευμάτων φθεγξάμενος, ὡς μηδενὸς ἀντιλέγοντος, ὀλίγον ἡσύχασεν. Ἡμεῖς δὲ ταὐτὸν παθόντες τῷ πολυκεφάλῳ ὕδραν τομαῖς ἐπικαίοντι, ἥτις μία δρακοντώδης τεμνομένη κεφαλὴ πολλὰς ἀντὶ μιᾶς ἐξαίφνης ἀνεδίδου, ταὐτὸν παθόντες μικροῦ συνεκάμνομεν· ἐν ὅσῃ γὰρ ⌜ἐ⌝φάπαξ τρεῖς αὐτοῦ προτά-

---

[87] A similar justification is invoked by Anastasios of Antioch to explain what he purports to be a written account of a *Streitgespräch* with a Tritheist from the middle of the sixth century AD: παρῆσαν δὲ τῇ διαλέξει τινὲς τῶν εὐλαβῶν ἀδελφῶν, οἳ καὶ γραφῆναι ταύτην ἐδοκίμασαν καλὸν εἶναι πρὸς γυμνασίαν τῶν ἴσως ἐντυγχανόντων (ed. Uthemann 1981, p. 79).

[88] For other collections, see Zacharias of Mytilene, *Adversus Manichaeos* (Ἀντίρρησις) (ed. Demetrakopulos 1886, p. 1–18); John the Grammarian's ἀπορίαι (ed. CCSG 1, p. 60–66; Déroche 1991; trans. Van der Horst 2004); Leontius of Jerusalem, *Against the Monophysites* (ed. Gray 2006; Richard 2011; Lim 1995, p. 88–89, 132, 211; Cameron 1991; Cameron 1994; Cameron 2014).

[89] For a more detailed discussion of this technique and the guidelines offered in contemporary rhetorical teatises see Papadogiannakis forthcoming.

σεις ἢ τέσσαρας ἢ πέντε πιθανῶς ἐξελύομεν, τὴν ὕδραν οὗτος τὴν
ἐν μύθοις μιμούμενος, μιᾶς λυθείσης, μυρίας ζητήσεις προὐβάλλετο
ἄπειρον ἐν τοῖς ἀπορουμένοις τὴν θεωρίαν προτείνων. Αὐτίκα δ᾽
οὖν ἐν τῷ παρόντι τοσούτων προθεὶς κεφαλαίων ζητήματα πρὸς
ἕκαστον ἡμᾶς ἔλεγεν ἀποκρίνεσθαι.

After the master of the Hellenic cleverness uttered these
things against the divine teachings of Christ, since no one
responded, he was silent for a moment. But we, experiencing
the same thing as he whose set fire to the smashed stumps
of the many-headed Hydra, which immediately grew back in
place of the one when each dragon's head had been severed,
experiencing the same thing for a moment we were similarly
hard pressed. For after we persuasively and once and for
all untangled three of his propositions, or four or five, this
fellow imitating the mythic Hydra, put forward myriad of
questions after one had been untangled, indefinitely extend-
ing [his] speculation into difficult [passages of Scripture].
For instance, presently having put forward questions on such
topics, he asked us to reply to each one.[90]

The compilations of well-honed criticisms required answers capable of countering or deflecting these criticisms, and the QRO
fits into this framework. Such collections had been compiled
by both sides in a debate.[91] It is not unusual to find collections
comprising only of the questions that attack certain views, or
just the responses. An example is the *Quaestiones Gentilium*

---

[90] *Apocr.* 3. 7 (trans. Scott & Edwards 2015, p. 114). For a discussion of more
episodes of publicly confounding an interlocutor during a public debate and on the
emotional impact of this practice see Papadogiannakis 2020. For the importance
of the *mise-en-scène* in the *Apocriticus* see Capone 2012.

[91] This is how Augustine's Manichaean opponent, Faustus, justifies the reasons for the compilation of his *Capitula* in the prologue: '[...] non ab re uisum
est, fratres carissimi, haec quoque breuia uobis et concinna responsa propter cal-
lidas et astutas conferentium nobis cum propositiones scribere, quo cum idem
uos ex more parentis sui serpentis captiosis circumuenire quaestiunculis uoluerint,
et ipsi ad respondendum uigilanter eis sitis instructi' ('it seems not unhelpful, dear
brethren, to write for you these short and polished answers on account of the
crafty and cunning statements from the conferences with us; by these, you your-
selves should be equipped to answer them vigilantly, when they should want to
surround you as well with deception by means of trifling questions, in accordance with the habit of their forefather, the serpent'; *Contra Faustum* 1. 2, CSEL
25. 1, p. 251. 22–252. 7), noted by Van den Berg 2010, p. 179. On Manichaean
κεφάλαια see Wurst 2001; Pettipiece 2009.

ad Christianos, in the same corpus, comprising lists of questions that could be used as a counterattack against the Greeks as well as responses to objections in the form of counter-questions.[92] At the same time, as well as overcoming these obstacles and deflecting criticisms, in the process of answering the questions Ps.-Justin offered his enquirers and readers rules that guided their curiosity, contained and opposed what he saw as unhealthy, misdirected and distracting patterns of speculation about the divine and the creation, and carefully defined the limits of acceptable enquiry.

Ps.-Justin's engagement with biblical creation texts highlights and reinforces the fact that theological reflection on creation emerged from an intellectual or exegetical development, prompted by the need to refute Gnostic, Marcionite, Manichaean, and Greco-Roman views on cosmogony and cosmology. This confirms the view that 'patristic interest in the natural philosophy and science of the time was customarily utilitarian and heuristic, serving apologetic, catechetical, or homiletical ends'.[93] By offering answers to a host of cosmological questions, ranging from technical and philosophical issues to exegetical ones such as the eternity (pre-existence) of matter or the ontological status of evil in the world, Ps.-Justin engaged contemporary competing views and pursued responses to cosmological theories aimed at edifying the faithful and strengthening their religious allegiance rather than cultivating an independently Christian natural philosophy to confute pagan thought.[94]

Bibliography

Primary Sources

Alcinous, *The Handbook of Platonism*, trans. J. M. Dillon, Oxford: Clarendon Press, 1993.

Alcinoos, *Enseignement des doctrines de Platon*, ed. J. Whittaker, Paris: Les Belles Lettres, 1990.

---

[92] Ed. CAp V, p. 348–367.
[93] Blowers 2012, p. 4.
[94] Blowers 2012, p. 3.

Anastasius of Sinai, *Hexaemeron*, eds C. A. Kuehn & J. D. Baggarly, Rome, 2007 (Orientalia Christiana Analecta, 278).

Aristoteles, *Physica*, ed. W. D. Ross, Oxford, 1950.

Athenagoras, *Legatio and De resurrection*, ed. W. Schoedel, Oxford, 1972.

Gregory of Nyssa, *In Hexaemeron: opera exegetica in Genesim, pars I*, ed. H. R. Drobner, Leiden, 2009.

M. W. Holmes (2007), *The Apostolic Fathers. Greek Texts and English Translations*. Grand Rapids: Baker.

John Chrysostom, *St John Chrysostom Commentary on the Psalms*, translated with an introduction by R. C. Hill, 2 vols, Brookline, Mass., 1998.

Leontius of Jerusalem, *Against the Monophysites*, ed. P. T. R. Gray, New York – Oxford, 2006.

Macarius Magnes, *Apocriticus*, translated with commentary by J. M. Schott and M. J. Edwards, Liverpool, 2015.

Macarius Magnes, *Apokritikos: kritische Ausgabe mit deutscher Übersetzung*, ed. U. Volp, Berlin, 2013 (Texte und Untersuchungen zur Geschichte der altchristlichen Literatur, 169).

Macarius Magnes. *Le monogénès*, introduction générale, édition critique, traduction française et commentaire par R. Goulet, 2 vols, Paris, 2003 (Textes et traditions, 7).

Origenes, *Contra Celsum*, trans. H. Chadwick, Cambridge: Cambridge University Press, 1953.

C. Osiek (1999), *Shepherd of Hermas: a Commentary*, Minneapolis: Fortress Press, 1999.

Pseudo-Aristotle, *On the Cosmos*, ed. J. C. Thom, Tübingen, 2014 (Sapere XXIII).

Pseudo-Justin, Θεοδωρήτου ἐπισκόπου πόλεως Κύρρου πρὸς τὰς ἐπενεχθείσας αὐτῷ ἐπερωτήσεις παρά τινος τῶν ἐξ Αἰγύπτου ἐπισκόπων ἀποκρίσεις, ed. A. Papadopoulos-Kerameus, Petersburg, 1897 (repr. Leipzig, 1975).

Pseudo-Kaisarios, *Die Erotapokriseis*, ed. R. Riedinger, Berlin, 1989.

Theodore of Mopsuestia, *In epistolas B. Pauli commentarii: the Latin Version with the Greek Fragments*, ed. H. B. Swete, Cambridge, 1880–1882.

Theodoret of Cyrrhus, *The Questions on the Octateuch*, ed. J. F. Petruccione, English translation with introduction and commentary by R. C. Hill, Washington, DC: Catholic University of America Press, 2007 (The Library of Early Christianity, 1–2).

A. von Harnack (1901), *Diodor von Tarsus. Vier pseudojustinische Schriften als Eigentum Diodors nachgewiesen*, Leipzig: Hinrichs (Texte und Untersuchungen, 21,4).

Zacharias of Mytilene, *Adversus Manichaeos* (Ἀντίρρησις), ed. A. K. Demetrakopoulos, *Bibliotheca Ecclesiastica*, Leipzig, 1886 (repr. Hildesheim, 1965), p. 1–18.

Zacharias of Mytilene, *Ammonio*, ed. M. Minniti Colonna, Naples, 1973.

Zacharias of Mytilene, *Ammonius*, translated by S. Gertz, London, 2012.

Secondary Literature

E. Adams (2007), *The Stars will Fall from Heaven: Cosmic Catastrophe in the New Testament and its World*, London: Clark (Library of New Testament Studies, 347).

M. Alexandre (1988), *Le commencement du livre Genèse I–V: la version grecque de la Septante et sa réception*, Paris: Beauchesne.

G. Bardy (1932–1933), 'La littérature patristique des "Quaestiones et responsiones" sur l'Écriture Sainte', in *Revue Biblique*, 41, p. 210–236; p. 341–369; p. 515–537; 42, p. 14–30; p. 211–229; p. 328–352.

J. D. BeDuhn (2010), *Augustine's Manichaean Dilemma: Vol. 1. Conversion and Apostasy, 373–388 C.E.*, Philadelphia: University of Pennsylvania Press.

A. Blair (1999), 'The Problemata as a Natural Philosophical Genre', in A. Grafton & N. Siraisi (eds), *Natural Particulars: Nature and Disciplines in Renaissance Europe*, Cambridge, Mass.: MIT Press, p. 171–204.

P. M. Blowers (2012), *Drama of the Divine Economy: Creator and Creation in Early Christian Theology and Piety*, Oxford: Oxford University Press.

M. D. Boeri (2009), 'Pseudo-Justin on Aristotelian Cosmology: A Byzantine Philosopher Searching for a New Picture of the World', in *Byzantion*, 79, p. 99–135.

R. Burri (2014), 'The Geography of *De Mundo*', in J. C. Thom (ed.), *Cosmic Order and Divine Power: Pseudo-Aristotle, On the cosmos*, Tübingen: Mohr Siebeck (Sapere, 23), p. 89–106.

B. Bydén (2012), 'A Case for Creationism: Christian Cosmology in the 5th and 6th Centuries', in K. Ierodiakonou & B. Bydén (eds), *The Many Faces of Byzantine Philosophy*, Athens: The Norwegian

Institute at Athens (Papers and monographs from the Norwegian Institute at Athens; Ser. 4 v. 1.), p. 79–109.

B. Bydén (2013), '"No Prince of Perfection": Byzantine Anti-Aristotelianism from the Patristic Period to Pletho', in D. Angelov & M. Saxby (eds), *Power and Subversion in Byzantium: Papers from the 43rd Spring Symposium of Byzantine Studies, Birmingham, March 2010*, Farnham, Surrey – Burlington, Vt.: Ashgate Variorum, p. 147–176.

A. Cameron (1991), 'Dispute Poems and Dialogues in the Ancient and Mediaeval Near East', in G. J. Reinink & H. L. J. Vanstiphout (eds), *Dispute Poems and Dialogues in the Ancient and Mediaeval Near East: Forms and Types of Literary Debates in Semitic and Related Literatures*, Leuven: Peeters, p. 91–108.

A. Cameron (1994), 'Texts as Weapons: Polemic in the Byzantine Dark Ages', in A. K. Bowman & G. Woolf (eds), *Literacy and Power in the Ancient World*, Cambridge: Cambridge University Press, p. 198–215.

A. Cameron (2014), *Dialoguing in Late Antiquity*, Washington, DC: Harvard University Press.

A. Cameron & R. Hoyland (eds, 2011), *Doctrine and Debate in the East Christian World, 300–1500*, Farnham: Ashgate.

A. Capone (2012), 'The Narrative Sections of Macarius Magnes' *Apocriticus*', in A. Capone (ed.), *Lessico, argomentazioni e strutture retoriche nella polemica di età Cristiana (III–V sec.)*, Turnhout: Brepols (Recherches sur les rhétoriques religieuses, 16), p. 253–270.

L. Caudano (2008), 'Un univers sphérique ou voûté? Survivance de la cosmologie antiochienne à Byzance (xiᵉ et xiiᵉ s.)', in *Byzantion*, 78, p. 66–86.

M. W. Champion (2014), *Explaining the Cosmos: Creation and Cultural Interaction in Late-Antique Gaza*, Oxford – New York: Oxford University Press.

J. G. Cook (2004), *The Interpretation of the Old Testament in Greco-Roman Paganism*, Tübingen: Mohr Siebeck (Studien und Texte zu Antike und Christentum, 23).

U. Criscuolo (2013), 'Aristotelismo a Bisanzio', in Y. Lehmann (ed.), *Aristoteles Romanus: la réception de la science aristotélicienne dans l'Empire gréco-romain*, Turnhout: Brepols (Recherches sur les rhétoriques religieuses, 17), p. 389–421.

G. Dagron (1992), 'L'ombre d'un doute: L'hagiographie en question, viᵉ–xiᵉ siècle', in *Dumbarton Oaks Papers*, 46, p. 59–68.

J. Daniélou (1957), *The Angels and Their Mission*, New York: Newman.

G. Delling (1971), 'Στοιχεῖον', in *Theological Dictionary of the New Testament*, 7, p. 670–687.

N. Denzey (2005), 'Bardaisan of Edessa', in A. Marjanen and P. Luomanen (eds), *A Companion to Second-Century Christian 'Heretics'*, Leiden: Brill (Supplements to Vigiliae Christianae, 76), p. 159–184.

E. De Ridder & K. Levrie (2015), '*Capita* Literature in Byzantium', in R. Ceulemans & P. De Leemans (eds), *On Good Authority. Tradition, Compilation and the Construction of Authority in Literature from Antiquity to the Renaissance*, Turnhout: Brepols, p. 123–137.

V. Déroche (1991), 'La polémique anti-Judaïque au VIᵉ et au VIIᵉ siècle. Un memento inédit, les *kephalaia*', *Travaux et Mémoires*, 11, p. 275–311.

W. Gass (1842), 'Die unter Justins des Märtyrers Schriften befindlichen Fragen an die Recht-gläubigen, mit Rücksicht auf andere Fragsammlungen erörtert', in *Zeitschrift für die historische Theologie*, 12, p. 35–154.

B. Gleede (2009), *Platon und Aristoteles in der Kosmologie des Proklos: ein Kommentar zu den 18 Argumenten für die Ewigkeit der Welt bei Johannes Philoponos*, Tübingen: Mohr Siebeck (Studien und Texte zu Antike und Christentum, 54).

B. Gleede (2011), 'Johannes Philoponos und die christliche Apologetik. Die Widerlegungen des Proklos und Aristoteles und die Debatte des Schöpfungsproblems in der Schule von Gaza und bei Ps-Justin', in *Jahrbuch für Antike und Christentum*, 54, p. 73–97.

B. Gleede (2012), 'Endorsing a cliché: On Liberty and Necessity in Christian and Neoplatonist Accounts of Creation', in K. Corrigan, J. D. Turner, P. Wakefield (eds), *Religion and Philosophy in the Platonic and Neoplatonic Traditions: from Antiquity to the Early Medieval Period*, Sankt Augustin: Academia, p. 277–293.

R. Gounelle (1994), '"Il a placé sa tente dans le soleil" (Ps. 18[19], 5c[6a]) chez les Pères des cinq premiers siècles', in *Le Psautier chez les Pères, Strasbourg, Centre d'Analyse et de Documentation Patristiques*, Strasbourg: Centre d'analyse et de documentation patristiques (Cahiers de Biblia Patristica, 4), p. 197–220.

J. A. Harrill (2010), 'Stoic Physics, the Universal Conflagration, and the Eschatological Destruction of the "Ignorant and Unstable" in 2 Peter', in T. Rasimus, T. Engberg-Pedersen, I. Dunderberg (eds),

Stoicism in Early Christianity, Peabody, Mass.: Baker Academic, p. 115–140.

T. Heyd (2014), 'And Yet She Moves! – The Earth Rests on Water: Thales on the Role of Water in Earth's Mobility and in Nature's Transformations', in *Apeiron*, 47, p. 485–512.

A. Hilhorst (1999), 'Biblical Scholarship in the Early Church', in J. den Boeft & M. L. van Poll-van de Lisdonk (eds), *The Impact of Scripture in Early Christianity*, Leiden: Brill, p. 1–19.

H. Inglebert (2001), *Interpretatio christiana: Les mutations des savoirs, cosmographie, géographie, ethnographie, histoire, dans l'antiquité chrétienne, 30–630 après J.-C.*, Paris: Institut d'études augustiniennes.

B. Inwood (2002), 'God and Human Knowledge in Seneca's *Natural Questions*', in D. Frede & A. Laks (eds), *Traditions of Theology: Studies in Hellenistic Theology, Its Background and Aftermath* (Philosophia antiqua, 89), Leiden – Boston: Brill, p. 119–157.

A. Jakab (2003) 'The Reception of the Apocalypse of Peter in Ancient Christianity', in J. N. Bremmer and I. Czachesz (eds), *The Apocalypse of Peter*, Leuven: Peeters, p. 174–186.

C. Jakob (2004), 'Questions sur les questions: archéologie d'une pratique intellectuelle et d'une forme discursive', in A. Volgers & C. Zamagni (eds), *Erotapokriseis: Early Christian Question and Answer Literature in Context*, Louvain: Peeters, p. 25–54.

C. Köckert (2009), *Christliche Kosmologie und kaiserzeitliche Philosophie*, Tübingen: Mohr Siebeck (Studien und Texte zu Antike und Christentum, 56).

K. Kretschmer (1889), *Die physische Erdkunde im christlichen Mittelalter*, Wien – Olmütz: E. Hölzel.

R. Krüger (2000), *Eine Welt ohne Amerika II: Das Überleben des Erdkugelmodells in der Spätantike (ca. 60 v.u.Z.-ca. 550)*, Berlin: Weidler.

S. N. C. Lieu (1992), *Manichaeism in the Later Roman Empire and Medieval China*, 2nd ed., Tübingen: Mohr Siebeck.

R. Lim (1995), *Public Disputation, Power, and Social Order in Late Antiquity*, Berkeley: Univeristy of California Press, 1995.

W. Löhr (1998), 'Der gerechte Gott und seine Verteidiger – eine altkirchliche Debatte', in J. Mehlhausen (ed.), *Recht, Macht, Gerechtigkeit*, Gütersloh: Chr. Kaiser – Gütersloher Verlagshaus, p. 387–397.

W. Löhr (2002), 'Did Marcion Distinguish Between a Just God and a Good God?', in G. May & K. Greschat (eds), *Marcion und seine kirchengeschichtliche Wirkung / Marcion and His Impact on Church History*, Berlin – New York: De Gruyter, p. 131–146.

A. Lumpe (1959), 'Elementum', in *Reallexikon für Antike und Christentum*, 4, col. 1073–1100.

J. Mansfeld (1992), '*Physikai doxai* and *Problēmata physika* from Aristotle to Aëtius (and Beyond)', in W. W. Fortenbaugh & D. Gutas (eds), *Theophrastus: his Psychological, Doxographical, and Scientific Writings*, New Brunswick – London: Transaction Publishers (Rutgers University studies in classical humanities, 5), p. 63–111.

J. P. Martín (1989), 'El Pseudo-Justino en la historia del aristotelismo', in *Patristica et mediaevalia*, 10, p. 3–19.

J. P. Martín (2000), 'Las Quaestiones de Pseudo Justino: un lector de Aristóteles en tiempos de Proclo', in *Topicos: Revista de Filosofia*, 18, p. 115–141.

G. May (1997), 'Markions Genesisauslegung und die Antithesen', in D. Wyrwa (ed.), *Die Weltlichkeit des Glaubens in der Alten Kirche: Festschrift für Ulrich Wickert zum siebzigsten Geburtstag*, Berlin: De Gruyter, p. 189–198.

R. Mayhew (ed., 2015), *The Aristotelian* Problemata Physica: *Philosophical and Scientific Investigations*, Leiden – Boston: Brill (Philosophia antiqua, 139).

M. Meeusen (2014), 'Plutarch and the Wonder of Nature. Preliminaries to Plutarch's Science of Physical Problems', in *Apeiron*, 47, p. 310–341.

M. Meeusen (2015), 'Plutarch Solving Natural Problems: For What Cause? (The Case of Quaest. Nat. 29, 919AB)', in M. Meeusen & L. Van der Stockt (eds), *Natural Spectaculars: Aspects of Plutarch's Philosophy of Nature*, Leuven: Leuven University Press (Plutarchea Hypomnemata), p. 129–142.

C. Moreschini (2016), 'Il firmamento e le acque sopracelesti di Gen 1, 6-8. Gregorio di Nissa tra oriente e occident', in B. Bakhouche (ed.), *Science et exégèse. Les interprétations antiques et médiévales du récit biblique de la création des éléments (Genèse I, 1-8)*, Turnhout: Brepols, p. 79-96.

A. A. Mosshammer (1990), 'Non-being and Evil in Gregory of Nyssa', in *Vigiliae Christianae*, 44, p. 136–167.

M. R. Niehoff (2011), *Jewish Exegesis and Homeric Scholarship in Alexandria*, Cambridge: Cambridge University Press.

L. Obertello (2003), 'Ammonius of Hermias, Zacharias Scholasticus and Boethius : Eternity of God and/or Time ?', in A. Galonnier (ed.), *Boèce ou la chaîne des savoirs : actes du Colloque international de la Fondation Singer-Polignac, présidée par Edouard Bonnefous, Paris, 8–12 juin 1999*, Louvain-la-Neuve – Louvain : Editions de l'Institut supérieur de philosophie – Peeters (Philosophes médiévaux, 44), p. 465–479.

L. Obertello (2007), 'Proclus, Ammonius of Hermias, and Zacharias Scholasticus: The Search after Eternity and the Meaning of Creations', in M. Treschow, W. Otten & W. Hannam (eds), *Divine Creation in Ancient, Medieval, and Early Modern Thought: Essays Presented to the Rev'd Dr Robert D. Crouse*, Leiden – Boston: Brill (Brill's studies in intellectual history, 151), p. 173–189.

K. Oikonomopoulou (2013), 'Ancient Question-and-Answer Literature and its Role in the Tradition of Dialogue', in S. Föllinger & G. M. Müller (eds), *Der Dialog in der Antike: Formen und Funktionen einer literarischen Gattung zwischen Philosophie, Wissensvermittlung und dramatischer Inszenierung*, Berlin: De Gruyter, p. 37–63.

Y. Papadoyannakis (2006), 'Instruction by Question and Answer in Late Antiquity: the Case of Late Antique Erotapokriseis', in S. Johnson (ed.), *Greek Literature in Late Antiquity: Dynamism, Didacticism, Classicism*, Aldershot: Ashgate, p. 91–105.

Y. Papadoyannakis (2008), 'Defining Orthodoxy in Pseudo-Justin's Quaestiones et Responsiones ad Orthodoxos', in H. Zellentin & E. Iricinski (eds), *Heresy and Identity in Late Antiquity*, Tübingen: Mohr Siebeck, p. 115–127.

Y. Papadogiannakis (2013), 'Didacticism, Exegesis and Polemics in Pseudo-Kaisarios's erotapokriseis', in M.-P. Bussières (ed.), *La littérature des questions et réponses dans l'Antiquité profane et chrétienne: de l'enseignement à l'exégèse*, Turnhout: Brepols (Instrumenta patristica et mediaevalia, 64), p. 271–289.

Y. Papadogiannakis (2014), 'Identity and the Resurrection in Some Late Antique Texts', in J. Zachhuber & A. Torrance (eds), *Individuality in Late Antiquity*, Aldershot: Ashgate, p. 129–142.

Y. Papadogiannakis (2019), 'The Use of Question-And-Answer Method and Process in Anastasius' *Hexaemeron*', in *Ephemerides Theologicae Lovanienses*, 95, p. 397–414.

Y. Papadogiannakis (2020), 'Shaming an Opponent in Debate: The Polemical Use of Emotions in Some Anti-Jewish Dialogues', in S. Morlet (ed.), *Ancient and Medieval Disputations Between Jews and Christians: Fiction and Reality*, Leuven: Peeters, p. 143–156.

Y. Papadogiannakis (forthcoming), 'Debating by Question-and-Answer: Christian *kalām* before Muslim *kalām*?', in Y. Papadogiannakis &

B. Roggema (eds), *Patterns of Argumentation and Exchange of Ideas in Late Antiquity and Early Islam*.

J. Pelikan (1993), *Christianity and Classical Culture: the Metamorphosis of Natural Theology in the Christian Encounter with Hellenism*, New Haven – London: Yale University Press.

P. Pellegrin (2009), 'The Argument for the Sphericity of the Universe in Aristotle's *De Caelo*: Astronomy and Physics', in A. C. Bowen & C. Wildberg (eds), *New Perspectives on Aristotle's* De caelo, Leiden – Boston: Brill (Philosophia antiqua, 117), p. 163–185.

J. Pépin (1964), *Théologie cosmique et théologie chrétienne (Ambroise, Exam. I 1, 1–4)*, Paris: Presses universitaires de France.

L. Perrone (1991), 'Sulla preistoria delle "quaestiones" nelle letteratura patristica. Presupposti e sviluppi del genere letterario fino al IV sec.', in *Annali di Storia dell'Esegesi*, 8, p. 485–505.

L. Perrone (1996), 'Il genere delle "Quaestiones et responsiones" nella letteratura Cristiana antica fino ad Agostino', in *De diversis quaestionibus octoginta tribus, De diversis quaestionibus ad simplicianum di Agostino D'Ippona*, Rome: Città Nuova, p. 11–44.

T. Pettipiece (2009), 'Coptic Answers to Manichaean Questions: The Erotapokritic Nature of the Kephalaia', in M.-P. Bussières (ed.), *La littérature des questions et réponses dans l'Antiquité profane et chrétienne: de l'enseignement à l'exégèse*, Turnhout: Brepols (Instrumenta patristica et mediaevalia, 64), p. 51–61.

K. Quandt (1983), 'Αἱ γὰρ τῶν ἐναντίων ἀποδείξεις ἀπορίαι περὶ τῶν ἐναντίων εἰσίν. Philosophical Program and Expository Practice in Aristotle', in *Classical Antiquity*, 2, p. 279–298.

A. Rey (2004), 'Les Erotapokriseis dans le monde byzantin: Traduction manuscrite des textes anciens et production des nouveaux textes', in A. Volgers & C. Zamagni (eds), *Erotapokriseis: early Christian question-and-answer literature in context*, Leuven: Peeters, p. 165–180.

M. Richard (2011), 'Dyophysite Florilegia of the Fifth and Sixth Centuries CE', in A. Cameron & R. Hoyland (eds), *Doctrine and Debate in the East Christian World, 300–1500*, Farnham: Ashgate, p. 321–345.

A. Rigo (ed., 2013), *Theologica Minora: the Minor Genres of Byzantine Theological Literature*, Turnhout: Brepols (Byzantios, 8).

A. M. Ritter & P. Toth (2018), 'Sechs ps.-justinische Traktate', in C. Riedweg, C. Horn & D. Wyrwa (eds), *Philosophie der Kaiserzeit und der Spätantike*, Basel: Schwabe (Grundriss der Geschichte der Philosophie, Die Philosophie der Antike), p. 2250–2263.

D. M. Russell (1996), *The 'New Heavens and New Earth': Hope for the Creation in Jewish Apocalyptic and the New Testament*, Philadelphia: Visionary Press.

R. Salles (2015), 'Two Early Stoic Theories of Cosmogony', in A. Marmodoro & B. D. Prince (eds), *Causation and Creation in Late Antiquity*, Cambridge: Cambridge University Press, p. 11–30.

I. Sandwell (2011), 'How to Teach Genesis 1.1–19: John Chrysostom and Basil of Caesarea on the Creation of the World', in *Journal of Early Christian Studies*, 19, p. 539–564.

W. Schoedel (1979), 'Enclosing not Enclosed: The Early Christian Doctrine of God', in W. R. Schoedel & R. L. Wilken (eds), *Early Christian Literature and the Classical Intellectual Tradition: in Honorem Robert M. Grant*, Paris: Beauchesne, p. 75–86.

C. Scholten (1996), *Antike Naturphilosophie und christliche Kosmologie in der Schrift* De opificio mundi *des Johannes Philoponos*, Berlin – New York: De Gruyter.

C. Scholten (2000), 'Verändert Gott, wenn er die Welt erschafft?', in *Jahrbuch für Antike und Christentum*, 43, p. 25–43.

A. Scott (1991), *Origen and the Life of the Stars: a History of an Idea*, Oxford: Clarendon Press.

D. Sedley (2007), *Creationism and its Critics in Antiquity*, Berkeley, Calif. – London: University of California Press.

R. Sorabji (1983), *Time, Creation and the Continuum: Theories in Antiquity and the Early Middle Ages*, London: Duckworth.

R. Sorabji (2015), 'Waiting for Philoponus', in A. Marmodoro & B. D. Prince (eds), *Causation and Creation in Late Antiquity*, Cambridge: Cambridge University Press, p. 71–93.

N. Spanu (2016), 'Pseudo-Kaisarios and Cosmas Indicopleustes on Genesis 1–3', in *E-Patrologos*, 2, p. 22–46.

M. B. Stephens (2011), *Annihilation or Renewal?: The Meaning and Function of New Creation in the Book of Revelation*, Tübingen: Mohr Siebeck (Wissenschaftliche Untersuchungen zum Neuen Testament, 2. Reihe, 307).

L. Taub (2015), '"Problematising" the Problems: The *Problemata* in Relation to Other Question-and-Answer Texts', in R. Mayhew (ed.), *The Aristotelian Problemata Physica: Philosophical and Scientific Investigations*, Leiden: Brill, p. 413–436.

P. Toth (2014), 'New Questions on Old Answers. Towards a Critical Edition of the Answers to the Orthodox of Pseudo-Justin', in *Journal of Theological Studies*, 65, p. 550–599.

P. Tzamalikos (2012), *The Real Cassian Revisited: Monastic Life, Greek Paideia, and Origenism in the Sixth Century*, Leiden – Boston: Brill.

K.-H. Uthemann (1981), 'Des Patriarchen Anastasius I. von Antiochien Jerusalemer Streit-gespräch mit einem Thritheiten (CPG 6958)', in *Traditio*, 37, p. 73–108.

J. A. van den Berg (2010), *Biblical Argument in Manichaean Missionary Practice: the Case of Adimantus and Augustine*, Leiden – Boston: Brill (Nag Hammadi and Manichaean studies, 70).

P. W. van der Horst (1994), '"The Elements Will be Dissolved with Fire": The Idea of Cosmic Conflagration in Hellenism, Ancient Judaism and Christianity', in P. W. van der Horst, *Hellenism, Judaism, Christianity: Essays on their Interaction*, Kampen: Kok Pharos, p. 271–292.

P. W. van der Horst (2004), 'Twenty-five Questions to Corner the Jews: a Byzantine Anti-Jewish Document from Seventh Century', in E. G. Chazon, D. Satran & R. Clements (eds), *Things Revealed: Studies in Early Jewish and Christian Literature in Honor of Michael E. Stone*, Leiden: Brill, p. 289–302

S. J. Voicu (2015), 'Due antiocheni periferici: le *Quaestiones et responsiones ad Orthodoxos* (CPG 6285) e Severiano di Gabala', in *Augustinianum*, 55, p. 543–557.

A. Volgers & C. Zamagni (2004, eds), *Erotapokriseis: Early Christian Question and Answer Literature in Context*, Louvain: Peeters.

U. Volp (2011), '"... for the Fashion of this World Passeth Away". The Apokritikos by Makarios Magnes – an Origenist's Defense of Christian Eschatology?', in H. Pietras & S. Kaczmarek (eds), *Origeniana Decima. Origen as Writer. Papers of the 10th International Origen Congress. Krakow, Poland 2009*, Peeters: Leuven (Bibliotheca Ephemeridum Theologicarum Lovaniensium, 244), p. 873–889.

U. Volp (2013), 'Der Schöpfergott und die Ambivalenzen seiner Welt. Das Bild vom Schöpfergott als ethisches Leitbild im frühen Christentum in seiner Auseinandersetzung mit der philosophischen Kritik', in H.-G. Nesselrath & F. Wilk (eds), *Gut und Böse in Mensch und Welt. Philosophische und religiöse Konzeptionen vom Alten Orient bis zum frühen Islam*, Tübingen: Mohr Siebeck (Orientalische Religionen in der Antike, 10), p. 143–159.

H. Wey (1957), *Die Funktionen der bösen Geister bei den griechischen Apologeten des zweiten Jahrhunderts nach Christus*, Winterthur: Keller.

C. Wildberg (1988), *John Philoponus' Criticism of Aristotle's Theory of Aether*, Berlin: De Gruyter (Peripatoi, 16).

G. D. Williams (2012), *The Cosmic Viewpoint: a Study of Seneca's Natural Questions*, New York: Oxford University Press.

G. Wurst (2001), 'Bemerkungen zu Struktur und genus letterarium der Capitula des Faustus von Mileve', in J. van Oort, O. Wermelinger & G. Wurst (eds), *Augustine and Manichaeism in the Latin West: Proceedings of the Fribourg-Utrecht Symposium of the International Association of Manichaean Studies*, Leiden: Brill (Nag Hammadi and Manichaean studies, 49), p. 307–324.

C. Zamagni (2004), 'Une introduction méthodologique à la littérature patristique des questions et réponses: le cas d'Eusèbe de Césarée', in A. Volgers & C. Zamagni (eds), *Erotapokriseis: Early Christian Question and Answer Literature in Context*, Louvain: Peeters, p. 1–24.

C. Zamagni (2013), 'Is the Question-and-Answer Literary Genre in Early Christian Literature a Homogenous Group?', in M. Bussières (ed.), *La litterature des questions et réponses dans l'antiquité profane et chrétienne: de l'enseignement à l'exégèse*, Turnhout: Brepols, p. 241–289.

Abstract

Collections of questions and answers (ἐρωταποκρίσεις) are a rich archive of individual and collective worries providing historians with a kaleidoscopic view of Late-Antique and Byzantine society. This contribution focuses on a rich but neglected vein of enquiries on cosmology as they are attested in Ps.-Justin's *Quaestiones et responsiones ad orthodoxos*, with a view to analysing the ways in which cosmological 'problems', objections, and enquiries are addressed as part of the process of ζήτησις ('enquiry').

BENJAMIN GLEEDE

THE PS.-JUSTINIAN CORPUS OF *EROTAPOKRISEIS* AND APOLOGETICAL TREATISES. IN SEARCH OF AN AUTHOR AND A HISTORICAL SETTING

Among the comparatively large corpus of writings ascribed to Justin the philosopher and martyr, transmitted to us mainly in the famous manuscript Parisinus gr. 450 (fourteenth century), only six remained until recently without a modern (post-nineteenth-century) critical edition.[1] Consequently, they have attracted comparatively little scholarly interest. The moral exhortations to Zena and Serenus were ascribed to the Novatian bishop Sisinnius (*c.* 400) by Batiffol in 1896 and have, as far as I can see, not undergone any closer scientific inspection since then.[2] The *Expositio fidei* is considered to be a work of Theodoret of Cyrus since Lebon[3] and is now being carefully studied and critically edited by Guinot.[4] The texts in question here are the remaining four, three of which, the *Confutatio Aristotelis* (CA), the *Quaestiones Christianorum ad gentiles* (QC), and the *Quaestiones gentilium ad Christianos* (QG),[5] clearly stand out because of their technical philosophical style and content. The fourth one, the *Quaestiones et responsiones ad orthodoxos* (QRO),[6] which also has an independent manuscript tradition attributing it to Theodoret, shares some

---

[1] On this corpus as a whole cf. Pouderon 2005.

[2] Batiffol 1896.

[3] Lebon 1930.

[4] Guinot 2001.

[5] The first two texts are quoted after CAp IV and V, the third after my own recent critical edition (Gleede 2020).

[6] Awaiting the new edition of Toth, we still have to rely on the edition of Papadopoulos-Kermaeus 1895 (repr. 1975 with a short, but interesting introduction by Hansen). On this collection, see Papadogiannakis in this volume.

Questioning the World, Greek Patristic and Byzantine Question-and-Answer Literature, ed. by Bram Demulder and Peter Van Deun, Turnhout, 2021 (*LECTIO*, 11), pp. 67-98   © BREPOLS🔊PUBLISHERS   DOI 10.1484/M.LECTIO-EB.5.121502

of their features, yet also stands apart due to its much broader variety of content.

In the course of preparing a critical edition of this text, two new collections of questions and arguments were discovered by Toth, preceding and following QRO in its most important witness, the Mosquensis GIM 394 (ninth century) originally owned by Arethas. This smaller collection of our Ps.-Justina is transmitted among the works of Theodore Abu Qurrah. The first of those new collections – called *Quaestiones contra gentiles de relatis* (QGR) by its editor [7] – is strongly reminiscent of the three aforementioned 'philosophical' Ps.-Justina in both style and content. The second, the *Capita contra Theopaschitas* (CT), advocates a 'Nestorian' Christological stance similar to the one we find in QRO 7–8 and in the preface to QGR. In the light of this new material, the examination of the old texts has to take a fresh start. The following study intends to contribute to this by examining (1) the literary shape and unity of each text one by one, (2) the corpus as a whole regarding the question of a possible unique author, (3) the possible historical context in which such an author might be situated.

1. *Literary Criticism*

Among the 'old' texts, only CA is situated by a preface dedicating the text to a certain Paul the deacon and clarifying its exact intention. Such prefaces can be found in almost the entire early Christian *erotapokriseis* literature,[8] and it was one of the more extraordinary among Toth's many accomplishments that he found a similar preface in a second witness for one of the new texts (QGR). This preface is, however, missing in the Mosquensis. It is therefore a quite plausible assumption that all the texts were originally introduced by a preface and maybe also concluded by an epilogue, both of which were, however, dropped by some redactor or copyist, probably for the sake of sustaining the pseudonymous attribution of those texts to either Justin or Theodore.

---

[7] Ed. Gleede 2020, p. 19–34.

[8] On the aspects and the development of this genre cf. Rey 2004; Papadogiannakis 2006; Zamagni 2013.

This assumption is supported by QC, where, immediately in the first refutation of the first pagan answer, a Christian person is addressed as ἡ σὴ θεοσέβεια, who obviously charged our author with the refutation of the pagan answers, but remains unidentified throughout the text.[9] A similar example can be found in the QRO, where the last question is introduced by a short transitory sentence which might be interpreted as a remnant of a dialogical frame for the questions similar to the one we find for instance in Ps.-Caesarius.[10] All of a sudden, an interlocutor rises to speak there in the first person, apologizes for taking up too much of his addressee's time and promises to ask only one last question.[11] Unfortunately, this passage is missing from the shorter and, as will be shown below,[12] more original recension but might, in my opinion, go back to the original author himself.

The clearest example of an incomplete beginning is, however, furnished by QG. There, a catalogue of questions to be resolved, looking at first sight like a simple *pinax*, is suddenly interrupted by a remark of the author concerning the selection of those *aporiai*. Due to the lack of context, this remark remains a little obscure. Instead of treating analogous *aporiai* arising from the nature of the body, our author rather wants to pick out one *aporia* concerning resurrection, which apparently was raised by certain 'stone-hearted people' (οἱ λιθοκάρδιοι) and seems – despite its 'cheap' (εὐτελής) character – much more interesting than any of the questions regarding corporeal nature.[13] After quoting the *aporia*, he challenges his opponents again in the first person and

---

[9] QC 1. 1 (CAp V, p. 250): Ἀλλ' ἐπειδὴ ἔδοξε τῇ σῇ θεοσεβείᾳ τὸ καὶ παρ' ἡμῶν ἐγγράφως ἐλεγχθῆναι τοῦ λόγου τὸ ἀσύστατον, διὰ τοῦτο ἐν συντόμῳ γράφω τὰ ὑποτεταγμένα.

[10] Cf. ed. Riedinger 1989, p. 9–10 e.a.

[11] QRO 161 (ed. Papadopoulos-Kerameus 1895, p. 146): Ἐρώτησις. Καιρὸς τοῦ λαλῆσαι καὶ καιρὸς τοῦ σιγῆσαι' φησὶν ὁ Σολομών· ἐγὼ δέ, ὁρῶν ἐμαυτὸν ἔξω καὶ τοῦ καιροῦ καὶ τῶν λόγων φερόμενον, ὅμως ἐν ἔτι τοῖς ζητήμασι προσενείρας τοῦ ἐπερωτᾶν καταπαύσω. τὸ δέ ἐστιν, εἰ [...].

[12] Cf. nn. 34-35.

[13] Otto (CAp V, p. 330) produces a rectified version of the distorted Parisinus gr. 450 text here. My critical text reads: Ταῦτα μὲν περὶ τούτων τέως ἐκ πολλῶν ὀλίγα· εἰ γὰρ ἐθέλομεν, ζητητέον καὶ τί ἐστι σῶμα καὶ ἐκ τίνων τὸ σῶμα, καὶ τὰς ἐπὶ τούτοις ἀπορίας. Ταῦτα δὲ τέως ἐάσαντες ὡς ἐν συντόμῳ μηδὲν τῶν ἀπόρων τῶν γενναιοτέρων ἐντιθέντες ἀξιοῦμεν γνῶναι τὸν περὶ τῆς ἀναστάσεως λόγον· ἐν γάρ τι τῶν εὐτελῶν ἀπόρων, τῶν παρὰ τοῖς λιθοκαρδίοις κινουμένων, ἔστι καὶ τοῦτο.

asks them to produce a properly demonstrative proof for the resurrection and reminds his readers that he would never be dealing with 'beggarly arguments' (τῶν ἀγυρτίων λόγων) like those, if there actually were proper ones.[14] This seems to be explicable only if an identification of the author, maybe the readers, and probably also the stone-hearted opponents, originally given before the catalogue of *aporiai*, was again omitted by a redactor or copyist.[15]

QG is also the most problematic one as to its literary integrity as a whole. The introductory catalogue of fourteen *aporiai* seems to be very carefully designed, ascending from the most general question (whether immaterial things exist at all), via the classification of immaterial entities (distinction between soul and God), up to two quite specific *aporiai* (concerning the beginning and end of God's creation). In the beginning of the first part of the main body of our text devoted to their refutation, they are first of all dismissed as ἐρωτήσεις ἄτεχνοι which lack the syllogistical structure demanded for a proper *aporia*.[16] The author obviously wants to distance himself from those questions, either because he just wants to stress the superiority of his own Christian position, which would not even be in need of asking questions like these, or because these questions are actually not his own, but were proposed to him for refutation from elsewhere. The latter alternative might also be suggested by what he says about the selection he makes from a larger set of *aporiai* about the resurrection, but a definitive decision is probably not possible on the basis of the incomplete text we have.

---

[14] QG pr. 15 (ed. Gleede 2020, p. 4): Καὶ ταῦτα οἷα γελῶντες οἱ λιθοκάρδιοί φασιν. Ἐγὼ δὲ παρακαλῶ ἀπορίας κατασκευαστικὸν λόγον τῆς ἀναστάσεως μαθεῖν τὸν ἐξ ἀνάγκης ἀποδεικνύντα καὶ ἀναγκ<άζοντα μ>ὴ εἶναι ἀνάστασιν διά τινων ἀποδεικτικῶν καὶ ἀληθῶν λόγων. Τῶν γὰρ ἀποδείξεων ἐρρωμένων ταῖς ἀληθείαις, οὐδένα <ἂν> τῶν ἀγυρτίων λόγον, εὖ ἴστε, ποιησοίμ<ην>. καὶ γὰρ ἄτοπον καὶ φιλόνεικον πρὸς ἐρρωμένην ἀπόδειξιν ἐθέλειν ἐρίζειν.

[15] Cf. also Riedweg 2001, p. 868–872.

[16] CAp V, p. 330–331: Οὗτοι οἱ λόγοι οὐκ εἰσὶ λογικαὶ ἀπορίαι, ἀλλ' ἐρωτήσεις ἄτεχνοι. Ὁ γὰρ λόγος, ὁ κατασκευάζων λογικὰς ἀπορίας, ἐν τοῖς ἀκολούθως πως λεγομένοις συνάγει τὸ ἄτοπον· οἷον μόνος ὁ ἄνθρωπος γελαστικόν, πᾶν γελαστικὸν ζῷον, μόνος ἄρα ὁ ἄνθρωπος ζῷον· αἵπερ εἰσὶν ἀκόλουθοι προτάσεις μέν, ἄτοπον δὲ τὸ συμπέρασμα. Ἐν δὲ τοῖς προκειμένοις λόγοις οὐδὲν ἄτοπον κατὰ ἀκολουθίαν συνήχθη· διὸ οὐκ εὐλόγως ἐκλήθησαν ἀπορίαι.

The abrupt transition following afterwards was reason enough for Otto to bridge the gap by inserting the apparently missing heading for the first *aporia* – incorrectly, as the other manuscript witnesses show. What follows here is rather some kind of introductory argument for the first *aporia*, which aims at exposing the opponents as being involved in a fundamental self-contradiction: even if they do it in an untechnical manner, they call the existence of incorporeals into question mentally, by relying on an incorporeal process, which is exactly the kind of entity they want to call into question by their *aporia*.

Similar surprises for the reader are contained in what follows. The logical sequence of the questions is apparently not maintained in their refutation, as the two questions on the existence of God and the mode of his creation precede the ones about the relationship between the diverse incorporeals. Moreover, several of the arguments adduced in the refutation do not seem to fit the respective question, but a preceding one. Thus, already Sylburg felt the need for a major change in the chronology of the text, transposing a series of six arguments from the last to the penultimate question.[17] Similarly, at least three (maybe four) out of five of the arguments following the question whether the incorporeal is more beautiful than the corporeal, actually establish nothing but the existence of incorporeals and thus seem to belong to the very first question.[18] As to this last problem, it could be argued that the problem of existence, independent existence, and superiority of incorporeals are so closely related, especially within a Platonic framework, that our author already intermingles them in the last, lengthy argument on question two, where he deals with incorporeal character of the soul and God.[19] As to the problem of inversed order, one might argue that he just anticipates the question about God's existence inspired by the aforesaid argument on the self-subsistence of incorporeals, which contains a quite detailed account of divine transcendence. In this case, however, one would expect our author to either

---

[17] Cf. Gleede 2020, p. LI.

[18] Ed. Gleede 2020, p. 7.

[19] QG 4. 2 (ed. Gleede 2020, p. 7): διὸ κάλλιον καὶ τιμιώτερόν ἐστι τοῦ σώματος, ὡς αἴτιον ὑπάρχον τοῦ καλὸν εἶναι τὸ σῶμα [...].

separate the three questions on the divine creation activity in their entirety from the one on the divine essence or to attach all of them immediately. That this topic is brutally interrupted in order to deal with the two additional questions on incorporeals, could not be explained on this line. We thus have to consider an analogous textual transposition to the one established by Sylburg in the last two questions. There, the 152 words of the very last question were probably added afterwards in an early exemplar and then integrated too early in the text by a copyist, thus interrupting the sequence of arguments on the last but one question. This leaves room for suggesting an analogous procedure concerning the 163 words of the third and fourth question. Those most probably should precede the last argument on question two in Otto's edition, which would provide a much better explanation for the introduction of the soul and God at this stage of the discussion and round off the extremely short discussion of the relationship between the soul and God in question four.

Less problematic is the fact that the text does not seem to have a proper ending, but presents the short refutation of the 'cheap *aporia*' against resurrection announced in the preface as first in line of a series of 48 *aporiai* against the pagan disbelief in bodily resurrection and divine creation in general, as we find analogous procedures also at the end of CA and QGR.

At least in the case of CA, the literary integrity of the text might, however, also be called into question on the basis of a comparison between the announcements of the preface and the actual text. At the beginning of CA, the author promised 'a selection of pagan doctrines on God and creation' (τὴν ἐκλογὴν τῶν ἑλληνικῶν περὶ θεοῦ καὶ κτίσεως δογμάτων) to be refuted,[20] but restricts himself in the main body of the extant text to a refutation of the eternalist passages of the *Physics* and the *De caelo*, thus falling short of his promise in possibly two, yet at least one respect. A reduction of the entire spectrum of pagan positions to Aristotle

---

[20] CAp IV, p. 100: [...] περὶ ὧν ἐνετείλασθέ μοι βραχεῖάν τινα ποιήσασθαι τὴν ἐκλογὴν τῶν ἑλληνικῶν περὶ θεοῦ καὶ κτίσεως δογμάτων. For a first analysis of Ps.-Justin's criticism of Aristotle cf. Boeri 2009 and Boeri's contribution to this volume. For the extraordinary character of the text compared to the rest of the Patristic discussion of Aristotle cf. Runia 1989, p. 14 and 17.

alone seems quite astonishing (especially if the text comes from the fifth century, when Neoplatonism in Athens was revitalised under Plutarch of Athens and his pupils), but conceivable. That he limits his refutation, however, entirely to Aristotle's concept of the natural world (i.e. creation) without even mentioning his theology, might indeed seem quite suspicious. As we have it, the rebuttal of Aristole's conception of the elements in *De caelo* III is immediately followed by a series of 19 *aporiai* which more or less summarize what was said in the text before and put Aristotle's so-called incoherencies forward more concisely. If those *aporiai*, however, actually marked the end of the original text, which seems highly probable to me,[21] one would expect possible missing parts of the the main body of the text (e.g. a possible refutation of *Metaphysics* XII) to come up there in one or another form. As it is also quite clear from the report of Photius that he knew CA in more or less the same shape as we do nowadays,[22] the most reasonable explanation for the tension between the promises of the preface and the actual text would probably be that our author not only sees Aristotle as the incorporation of pagan philosophy as a whole, but that he also finds his theology implied in his physics. Concluding a text by a series of *aporiai* thus seems to be one of our author's favourite means of structuring, which he employs for rounding off his texts, as those are highly technical in character and due to their very nature as *erotapokriseis* or subsequent refutations of different textual bits lack the coherence to be expected from ordinary scientific prose.

If we look at the third case of conclusion by *aporiai*, the QGR, this impression is in many respects confirmed. The preface of the text focuses on the charge of νεκρολατρία launched by the pagans against the Christian. Our author is anxious to maintain that the Christological dogma is not a new myth subjecting the transcendent God to birth and death, as the ancient pagan mythologies

---

[21] Cf. CAp IV, p. xxvi–xxvii: in the Parisinus gr. 450, the *aporiai* are repeated after QRO. However, also the Vat. gr. 1097, fol. 127ᵛ–128ʳ, a sibling of the Parisinus, proves that they originally belonged to CA.

[22] *Bibl.* 125. 94b23–28: ἔτι ἑτέρα αὐτοῦ πραγματεία κατὰ τοῦ πρώτου καὶ δευτέρου τῆς φυσικῆς ἀκροάσεως, ἤτοι κατὰ εἴδους καὶ ὕλης καὶ στερήσεως, ἐπιχειρηματικοὶ καὶ βίαιοι καὶ χρειώδεις λόγοι, καὶ κατὰ τοῦ πέμπτου σώματος ὁμοίως καὶ κατὰ τῆς ἀϊδίου κινήσεως, ἣν Ἀριστοτέλης δεινότητι λογισμῶν ἐναπέτεκεν.

did, but that – despite all the philosophical efforts to interpret this away – it is still exclusively the pagans who are blameworthy in this respect. Strangely enough, the preface does not really promise a contribution to this discussion for the following, but rather announces that, as the pagan philosophers have to admit the faulty mythological character of their theology themselves, 'we will do away with each of the remaining accusations by using the books of their accusations as advocates'.[23] Unfortunately, the text is distorted by several critical *lacunae*, which makes it impossible to tell how those 'remaining accusations' were originally presented in this preface. What follows is, at any rate, a series of 20 questions related to the Aristotelian axiom ἅμα τῇ φύσει τὰ πρός τι (*Cat.* 7. 7b15)[24] and trying to explain how this does apply to the relation between the trinitarian persons, yet does not apply to the relationship between creator and creature: if this principle is enforced to make the universe coeternal with its creator-god(s), the independence, transcendence, true divinity of those can – according to our author – not be maintained. The 16 following *aporiai* cover a much broader variety of topics: next to the indefensibleness of the pagan belief in an eternal cosmos (21. 1, 7–11, 15), they point to the victory of Christianity as historical refutation of the pagan Gods (21. 3–5) and to the inconsistencies in Plato's and Aristotle's works as definitely dismantling the trustworthiness of both philosophical authorities (21. 6, 12–14, 16). Again, a series of *aporiai* rounds off the thematically more narrow discussion of the questions and puts them into a broader argumentative context.

The main problem arising here is thus not the coherence of the QGR text itself, but its relation to QC: the five Christian questions answered there apparently by a pagan, whose answers are then refuted by the Christian, are identical with 21. 1, 7, 9, 10 and 15 of the QGR, with some alterations in the wording of

---

[23] QGR pr. (ed. Gleede 2020, p. 21): Ἐπεὶ τοίνυν ἤτε τῶν νεκρῶν θεοποιία ἤτε τῶν μύθων ἀδολεσχία καθ᾽ ἥν παρ᾽ αὐτῶν προβληθεῖσα † ...† αὐτοῖς ἄντικρυς προσοῦσα παρ᾽ αὐτῶν ἐδιδάχθη, φέρε, τῶν λοιπῶν κατηγοριῶν ἑκάστην ἀποδυσώμεθα ταῖς τῶν κατηγοριῶν βίβλοις χρώμμενος συνηγόροις.

[24] On the relevance of this axiom for the (anti-)eternalist debate of the sixth century cf. Gleede 2011, p. 84–86.

21. 7 (= QC 2 [25]) and 21. 15 (= QC 5 [26]). These could actually be identified as the systematically most important ones of the QGR series, as at least one of the remaining two concerning pagan eternalism, 21. 8, makes the – for a pagan – comparatively unproblematic point as to how the distinction between creator and creature can be upheld, if Plato calls some creatures 'Gods'.[27] Also the 11th *aporia* which argues that every generated thing has to exist in time and thus cannot be coeternal with God, as every given time span of the past has to be limited, could very simply be dismissed by a pagan as begging the question with regard to the second premise. The differences in wording and sequence make it, however, highly improbable that the pagan of QC would have produced his answers actually on the basis of his own selection from the *aporiai* of QGR. If it is actually an authentic pagan reply our author refutes there, he must have confronted his opponent with his own slightly altered selection of what were in his eyes the systematically most powerful antipagan *aporiai* in his stock.

Whether or not the answers refuted in QC actually constitute a real pagan text, is not that easy to determine. At any rate, our Christian author wants his readers to believe in the reality of his opponent, as his refutation not only sticks very closely to the details of the 'pagan text', but is also presented rather clearly as directed against a concrete individual regularly called ὁ ἀποκρινάμενος.[28]

---

[25] Ed. Gleede 2020, p. 31: Εἰ ἀδύνατον εἶναι θεὸν τὸν μηδὲν πεποιηκότα, οὐκ ἄρα ἔστιν θεός, εἰ ὁ κόσμος ἀγένητος. Cf. CAp V, p. 264: Εἰ ἀδύνατον εἶναι θεὸν τὸν μηδὲν πεποιηκότα, πῶς ἔστι θεός, εἰ ὁ κόσμος ἀγένητος, καθά τισι δοκεῖ;

[26] Ed. Gleede 2020, p. 32: Εἰ ἀγένητος ὁ οὐρανὸς καὶ ἀγένητος ὁ θεὸς καὶ οἰκεῖ ἐν τῷ οὐρανῷ ὁ θεός, πῶς οὔκ ἐστιν ὄνειδος τῷ θεῷ τὸ κατοικεῖν αὐτὸν ἐν τοῖς οὐκ αὐτοῦ; Ὃν γὰρ οὐκ ἐποίησεν οὐρανόν, οὗτος οὐκ ἔστιν αὐτοῦ. Cf. CAp V, p. 320: Εἰ ἀγένητος ὁ οὐρανὸς καὶ ἀγένητος ὁ θεὸς καὶ οἰκεῖ ἐν τῷ οὐρανῷ ὁ θεός, πῶς κατοικῶν ἐν τοῖς οὐκ αὐτοῦ ὁ θεὸς οὐχ ὑβρίζεται; Ὃν γὰρ οὐκ ἐποίησεν οὐρανόν, οὗτος οὐκ ἔστιν αὐτοῦ.

[27] Ed. Gleede 2020, p. 31: Εἰ ἀδύνατον ταὐτὸν εἶναι τῷ ποιητῇ τὰ ποιήματα, πῶς, εἰ ἀληθῆ τὸ κατὰ Πλάτωνα τὸ θεὸς θεῶν, ὧν ἐγὼ δημιουργός, οὐ ταὐτὸν τῷ δημιουργῷ τὰ δημιουργήματα, εἴ γε θεοὶ μὲν τὰ δημιουργήματα, θεὸς δὲ καὶ ὁ δημιουργῶν;

[28] Cf. QC 4. 1 (CAp V, p. 308): ᾿Ως δείξας ἀποκρινάμενος ἐν ταῖς ἄλλαις αὐτοῦ ἀποκρίσεσι τὸν κόσμον ἀγένητον, οὕτως καὶ ἐν τῇ παρούσῃ ἀποκρίσει ἐπαγγέλλεται δεῖξαι τὸν κόσμον ἀγένητον· καίτοι ἐν ταῖς ἄλλαις αὐτοῦ ἀποκρίσεσιν οὔτε ἐκ τῶν φανερῶν τε καὶ γνωρίμων τοῦ κόσμου ἐδογμάτισε τὴν ἀγενεσίαν, οὔτε διὰ τῆς ἀποδείξεως ταύτην ἔθηκεν, ἀλλὰ μόνον κατὰ τὴν οἰκείαν αὐθεντίαν τὸ δοκοῦν αὐτῷ

In his five answers, this individual presents himself as comparatively well-read in fourth- and fifth-century Neoplatonic authors using many of the arguments proposed already by Porphyry and Iamblichus against an anti-eternalist reading of the *Timaeus*.[29] The simplifications and idiosyncrasies one can find there, e.g. the complete neglect of any differentiation between intelligible causes or the labelling of both God and the cosmos as αὐτοπάρακτος (a term apparently attested only in the second pagan answer and quotations from it), can count in my opinion just as well for the authenticity of those answers as for their being forged by the Christian for the sake of easy refutation. Taking into account the considerable philosophical learning behind those answers, a Christian forger probably would not have put self-invented technical terms into the philosophers' mouths, but would rather have stuck to their standardized terminology. Another important point is the evasive character, especially of the fourth answer. The *aporia* how something generated can be coeternal with god would have been easily solvable by pointing to the difference between 'generated in time' and 'generated by cause'.[30] The pagan, however, does not give this answer straightforwardly, but rather explains why the classic accounts of world-generation must not be understood in a literal manner, i.e. the refutation of the argument is so clear to him that he immediately takes the discussion one step further. This could hardly be expected from a learned Christian forger, who would rather have tried to present the standard answer in a way which would make it easily refutable.

The only serious argument against authenticity would be the pagan's use of the phrase ἡ τῶν ὀρθοδόξων πίστις in the first answer, where he possibly alludes to Bar. 3. 38, when he says: 'and the faith of the orthodox people makes it absolutely clear, claiming God himself came down and was known by human beings'.[31] As an external perspective on the Christian faith, this

---

ἀπεφήνατο. Ἐλθὼν δὲ εἰς τὴν παροῦσαν ταύτην ἀπόκρισιν, ἐν ᾗ πειρᾶται δεῖξαι τὸν κόσμον ἀγένητον, πρῶτον μέμνηται τῶν παλαιῶν [...].

[29] Cf. Gleede 2011, p. 82–86.

[30] Cf. Dörrie & Baltes 1998, p. 130–146 (*Bausteine* 139–140).

[31] CAp V, p. 248: Ὅτι δὲ καὶ ἐνταῦθα ὄντες δύνανται οἱ ἄνθρωποι γινώσκειν τὸν θεόν, καὶ ἡ τῶν ὀρθοδόξων πίστις σαφῶς δηλοῖ, λέγουσα τὸν θεὸν αὐτὸν κατεληλυθέναι καὶ ἐγνῶσθαι τοῖς ἀνθρώποις.

in fact seems very odd. The distinction between different parties within Christianity marking themselves off in terms of ortho-doxy and heterodoxy could of course be made also by an outside observer, but normally not without qualifications like 'so-called' or 'as they call themselves'. Yet, it seems also possible that the pagan author did not want to bring in such a distinction at all, but uses ὀρθόδοξος almost as a synonym for χριστιανός, in the sense of 'mainstream-Christian'. In the period after Chalcedon, such a usage was especially prominent among the Monophysites, who did in fact represent the mainstream in most parts of the eastern half of the empire. This popular monophysitism also usually identified itself confessionally by attributing Christ's human characteristics (especially suffering and death) directly to his godhead without any qualification,[32] an example for which might be furnished by the pagan author's paraphrase of Bar. 3. 38. In this case, one would have to assume a relative ignorance of this pagan author concerning the confessional affiliation of his Christian opponent, who was probably an outspoken Nestorian. The latter, however, feels no need to correct his pagan opponent at that point, but rather cunningly turns the argument against him: once the testimony of the 'orthodox people' as recipients of divine knowledge is accepted, one also has to accept the other things they say about the beginning and end of the world.[33] All in all, our Ps.-Justin does not seem to have invested too much effort into confessional polemics, which is rare and remains rather general also in the more 'theological' texts QRO and even CT. At any rate, neither the passage just discussed nor the five pagan answers altogether seem to provide any evidence for them being a Christian forgery, which means that our author most probably did take his engagement with the remnants of paganism beyond the literary level and addressed his *aporiai* personally to a pagan

---

[32] A good example would be the Syriac novel on Julian Apostata, where the orthodox bishop Walagesh confronts the emperor Jovian twice with his simple theopaschite creed (Heidmann 1880, p. 27). For the category 'monophysisme populaire' in general cf. van Rompay 1993, p. 295–296. The only way to interpret the statement as specifically Nestorian would probably be to take it as a reflection of the 'Antiochene' reading of I Tim. 3. 16 ('God was revealed in the flesh') con-tested by the Monophysites (cf. Gleede 2010, p. 102–104), which does not seem very likely.

[33] QC 1. 3; 1. 5; 5. 2 (CAp V, p. 256; 260; 326).

intellectual, whose reply fortunately came down to us incorporated in its refutation by the Christian author of the original
aporiai of QC.

The most complicated case with respect to literary criticism is,
however, the QRO, as the three important textual witnesses
for it all testify to a different outlook of the text in its entirety.
After Papadopoulos-Kerameus had published the long recension
(LR) ascribing the text to Theodoret, which contained both 15
new questions and an in many respects better text of the ones
already known from the (Ps.-Justinian) short recension (SR),
research was convinced of having found the superior original
and to some extent even accepted its ascription to Theodoret.[34]
This conviction is, however, refuted by the Arethas codex, where
between QGR and CT (on fol. 24^v–28^r) a strange fragment
of 7 ½ questions (7, 8, 144–147, 47, 148 LR) is found, which
derives exclusively from the additional material scattered
throughout the long recension. The copyist of the codex thus
could impossibly have selected it from an original corresponding
to the long recension, the later abbreviation of which would be
the short one. Instead, the long recension has to be a later fusion
of two collections of questions, probably by the same author, one

---

[34] Riedweg 2001, p. 868–869; Toth 2014, p. 583–597. This is impossible
for several reasons, first of all the numerous exegetical divergences. Next to those
already adduced by Ehrhard 1898, one could point to the discussion of the witch
of Endor in QRO 65, which advocates the exegesis rejected by Theodoret in
Quaestiones in I Reg. 63–64, and the peculiar comparison between the visions
of Isaiah and Ezechiel from QRO 56, where the four animals are related to
Dan. 4, which is echoed nowhere in Theodoret's commentaries on the respective
passages, whereas Theodoret's recurring insistence on the invisibility of God in
commenting those visions is absent from QRO. As to the parallels to the *Expositio fidei* ascribed to Theodoret (cf. n. 4), the most important Christological
feature of QRO 8, the duality of a natural and an adopted sonship, is not only
missing from, but explicitly rejected in the *Expositio* (CAp IV, p. 36 and 48).
Yet, most importantly, the relevant manuscript tradition goes back to a title
which itself betrays its historical implausibility: 'Answers of Theodoret, the
bishop of Cyrus, one of the 630 fathers in Chalcedon, to the questions advanced
to him by a certain bishop from Egypt' (ἑνὸς τῶν ἐν Χαλκηδόνι χλ´ ἁγίων πατέρων,
πρὸς τὰς ἐπενεχθείσας αὐτῷ ἐρωτήσεις παρά τινος τῶν ἐξ Αἰγύπτου ἐπισκόπων)
obviously transfers a text which is barely concerned with Christological issues
into the Christological controversy and is therefore 'offenkundig falsch und
nur ausgedacht worden, weil man von Theodorets Fehde mit Kyrill und seinen
Anhängern wußte' (Hansen in the preface to the reprint of Papadopoulos-
Kerameus 1895 [= 1975], p. vi).

of which would be the short recension and the other the one fragmentarily preserved in the Arethas codex.

This is also confirmed by a comparison of the order of the questions in the short and in the long recension: the latter shows clear signs of a thematical regrouping of the questions. The additional material partially found in the Arethas codex is separated in three bits which are attached to thematically related questions of the short recension: the Christological questions 7 and 8 are added to the dogmatical block at the beginning (1–6 LR = 139, 144, 129, 17, 15, 16 SR), question 47 is grouped with two other ones on pure and impure food (46 and 48 LR = 35 and 99 SR). It might thus perhaps even be some kind of accident that the third block starting with a question concerning Act. 23. 3 does not follow 125 LR (115 SR), which deals with the same passage, but 126 LR (116 SR) on the relationship between Christianity and Hellenism. At any rate, the order of the QRO questions is all in all much better explicable if we suppose a partial thematic regrouping of the SR order combined with an integration of new material in LR, than if we postulate a chaotic dissolution of this partial order combined with an erratic omission of single questions in SR.[35]

The Arethas Codex thus in fact witnesses to a second, originally independent collection of *erotapokriseis*, which must have been very similar in content to the one we have extant as short recension. Due to our fragmentary information about its original character, we shall from now on call this collection QR thus distinguishing it from QRO proper, the short recension.

All this of course does not mean that the secondary long recension does not offer a better, more complete text also of the original QRO, which the scribe of the Paris manuscript obviously had to copy from a rather poor exemplar.[36] Hence, I would in fact consider the introductory clause of the last question in the long recension as original, just as the paragraph concluding the entire

---

[35] Additional clear examples of thematical regrouping would be the block on Jesus' human origin and lineage (11–15 LR = 66, 131–133, 67 SR), the pairing of 43 and 44 (33 and 122) on fixed terms in human life and the intergration of 73 (120) into the block on cosmology and eschatology (72–77 = 59–63).

[36] Cf. Toth 2014, p. 558–559.

collection,[37] which would make of the original QRO a mixed collection of *erotapokriseis* equipped with a rudimentary dialogical frame and a certain thematic focus on the relationship between Christianity and Hellenism, which is dealt with not only in the first three and the very last question, but also in several others.[38]

2. One Single Author?

Despite the relative disparity of QRO it is interesting to see that already their pre-twentieth-century editors Maranus and Otto singled them out among the Ps-Justina as belonging to the same author as CA, QC, and QG.[39] But it was not until Harnack that a formal proof of this unity of author was attempted, which – unlike his identification of this author and Diodore of Tarsus[40] – remains until now without formal refutation.[41]

Harnack obviously takes a unique author for QC and QG for granted and also rather quickly identifies him with the author of CA because of the identical philosophical interests and the identical spirit in their application.[42] That this holds true also for QGR may already seem plausible from the expositions of the

---

[37] Ed. Papadopoulos-Kermaeus 1895, p. 149–150: οὐκοῦν ἔχεις τῶν ζητημάτων τὰς λύσεις, κατὰ μὲν τὸ τῆς διανοίας ἡμῶν ἐφικτὸν ἀνελλιπεῖς, σκιὰν δὲ ὥσπερ καὶ εἰκόνα τυγχανούσας τῆς ἀληθείας· εἰ γὰρ ὁ μηδὲν ἑαυτῷ συνειδώς, ὁ τῶν ἀρρήτων μυστηρίων θεατής, Παῦλος ὁ ἀπόστολος, ἐκ μέρους γινώσκει καὶ ἐκ μέρους προφητεύει, τί θαυμαστὸν εἰ ἡμᾶς τοὺς πολὺ τῆς ἐκείνου ἀρετῆς τε καὶ πολιτείας ἀποδέοντας κατόπιν δεήσοι τῆς ἀληθείας ὀφθῆναι; διόπερ ἐνταῦθα τὸν λόγον σφραγίσαντες, μόνῃ τῇ ἀκαταλήπτῳ τριάδι πάντων ἀκριβῆ τὴν γνῶσιν κεκτῆσθαι συγχωρήσωμεν, αἰτούμενοι τῶν παρ' αὐτῆς ἡμῖν ἐπηγγελμένων αἰωνίων ἀγαθῶν ἐπιτυχεῖν χάριτι καὶ φιλανθρωπίᾳ τοῦ κυρίου ἡμῶν ᾽Ιησοῦ Χριστοῦ, ᾧ ἡ δόξα καὶ τὸ κράτος εἰς τοὺς αἰῶνας τῶν αἰώνων. ἀμήν.

[38] If one wants to include also treatment of popular pagan religious practices, one could refer to questions 10, 24, 26, 31, 42, 55, 74, 81, 89, 99 and 126.

[39] Cf. Harnack 1901, p. 46 and 52.

[40] This identification was refuted convincingly only a few years after the appearance of Harnack's book by Funk 1907, p. 323–350.

[41] On the diverse ascriptions of QRO to Theodoret and their untenability cf. n. 34.

[42] Harnack 1901, p. 53–54: 'In der That ist der Interessenkreis, der diese drei Schriften beherrscht, genau der gleiche, und ebenso ist der philosophisch-christliche Standpunkt derselbe. Wer die drei Tractate hintereinander liest, wird nirgendwo eine Veränderung wahrnehmen, sondern sich von demselben Geiste berührt und von demselben Schriftsteller angesprochen fühlen'.

previous paragraph, as this treatise not only culminates in series of *aporiai* analogous to the ones at the end of CA and QG, but also furnishes the five Christian questions of QC. The plausibility of assuming a unique author between these four 'philosophical' texts can, however, also be corroborated by a few concrete observations, partly noticed by Harnack already:

– That both QG 1 and QC 4. 3 refer to the principle of contradiction in almost the same wording,[43] was highlighted already by Otto and reflects the logical pedantry of our author in general,[44] which makes him also feel the need to explain to his opponents first of all what an *aporia* exactly is in the beginning of QG.[45]

– QG 11. 37[46] reproduces one of the core anti-Aristotelian arguments of CA,[47] namely that no natural species can be eternal, as the principle or archetype of the respective natural species has to be created in a supernatural way: neither a particular nature nor a nature as a whole can be its own principle.[48]

– Both the preface to CA and QC 5. 2 call the heavens ἄφθαρτοι, which is very unusual in a Christian context, especially considering the fact that this claim is also supported theoretically

[43] CAp V, p. 312 (ἐπὶ παντὸς γὰρ ἢ τὴν φάσιν ἀληθῆ εἶναι δεῖ ἢ τὴν ἀπόφασιν); ed. Gleede 2020, p. 5 (ἐπὶ παντὸς γὰρ ἀληθῆ τὴν κατάφασιν εἶναι δεῖ ἢ τὴν ἀπόφασιν).

[44] Similar references to the principle can be found in QC 2. 2 (CAp V, p. 270); 2. 8 (p. 280); 4. 1 (p. 308) and QGR 21. 6 (Εἰ ἀδύνατον τὴν ἀντίφασιν περὶ τοῦ αὐτοῦ ἀληθῆ εἶναι, πῶς δυνατὸν κατὰ τὴν δόξαν τοῦ γένητον εἶναι φιλόσοφον εἶναι τὸν Πλάτωνα καὶ κατὰ τὴν δόξαν τοῦ ἀγένητον εἶναι τὸν κόσμον φιλόσοφον εἶναι τὸν Ἀριστοτέλην;) and perhaps also CT 38 (Ὁ γὰρ τῆς οὐσίας λόγος οὐ δέχεται τὴν ἀντίφασιν αὐτοῦ).

[45] Cf. n. 16.

[46] Ed. Gleede 2020, p. 17: Εἰ τὸ μὴ κατὰ φύσιν γινόμενον, τούτου ἄπιστον καὶ ἀδύνατον τὴν ποίησιν χρὴ ὑπολαμβάνειν, πῶς οὐκ ἔσται καὶ τοῦ πρώτου γεγονότος ἀνθρώπου ἄπιστος καὶ ἀδύνατος ἡ ποίησις, μὴ κατὰ φύσιν γεγενημένου; Ἀδύνατον γὰρ γενέσθαι ἐξ ἀνθρώπου ἄνθρωπον κατὰ φύσιν, μὴ πρῶτον τοῦ ἀνθρώπου γινομένου ὑπὲρ φύσιν.

[47] CA 42 (CAp IV, p. 168–169): Ἄλλως γίνεται ζῷον ἐκ ζῴου, καὶ ἄλλως γέγονε ζῷον ἐκ μὴ ζῴου· καὶ τὸ μὲν ζῷον ἐκ μὴ ζῴου οὔτε κατὰ φύσιν γέγονεν οὔτε ἀεὶ γίνεται, τὸ δὲ ζῷον ἐκ ζῴου ἀεί τε καὶ κατὰ φύσιν γίνεται, ἐξ ὅτου ἔλαβεν ἀρχὴν τοῦ γίνεσθαι ἐκ ζῴου τοῦ μὴ ἐκ ζῴου. Καὶ τοῦτο ἐπὶ πάντων τῶν ἀεὶ κατὰ φύσιν γιγνομένων, οὐκ ἐπὶ τινῶν μόνον· ἀδύνατον γὰρ τὰ ἐξ ἀρχῶν γενητῶν τὴν αὐτὴν ἔχειν γένεσιν, ἣν ἐσχήκασιν αἱ ἀρχαί. Cf. CA *praef.* (p. 104); 5 (p. 120); 10 (p. 136).

[48] Cf. CA *ap.* 1 (CAp IV, p. 214): Ἡ φύσις ἡ ποιοῦσα τὰ φυσικά, ἐὰν μὴ προηγουμένως γίνηται ὑπὸ τοῦ μὴ κατὰ φύσιν ποιοῦντος, οὔτε ὑπάρχει οὔτε ποιεῖ.

by the anti-Aristotelian assertion of QG 9 that the existence of generated, yet imperishable entities is actually possible.[49]

- The philosophy of language applied in CA *ap.* 3[50] and in QG 4. 3[51] also comes into play in QGR 5[52] and (less clearly) 10: every application of human language to the divine necessarily drags it down into the corporeal world and has thus – despite its necessity for mankind – to be taken in an improper sense, in which the inapt consequences of the application of human terms and concepts to the divine can be avoided.

- The method of constructing inconsistencies in Aristotle in QGR 21. 12, 14, and 16 is quite the same as in CA, although the latter only deals with one of the *De caelo* passages adduced in QGR in a slightly different manner.[53]

Anyway, considering all the adduced observations (to which several more could undoubtedly be added) together, the common authorship of QC, QG, CA, and QGR cannot reasonably be

---

[49] I am planning to explore the background of this cosmology in a major study on the 'Antiochene', anti-Ptolemean conception of world from Diodore of Tarsus up to Cosmas Indicopleustes.

[50] CAp IV, p. 216: Εἰ τοῖς ἡμετέροις ὀνόμασι καλεῖται ὁ θεὸς πᾶν εἴ τι καλεῖται, οὐκ ἔστιν ἀνάγκη ἔπεσθαι τῷ θεῷ διὰ τὸ ὄνομα ὅσα ἔπεται τῷ ἡμετέρῳ ὀνόματι. Καλεῖται δὲ ὁ θεὸς καὶ ἀλήθεια καὶ ἀγαθός· καὶ τῇ μὲν ἀληθείᾳ ἀντίκειται τὸ ψεῦδος, τῷ δὲ ἀγαθῷ τὸ κακόν, τῷ δὲ θεῷ οὐδὲν ἀντίκειται.

[51] Ed. Gleede 2020, p. 8: Καὶ τὸν θεὸν φαμεν εἶναι ἀσώματον, οὐχ ὅτι ἔστιν ἀσώματον (ἐπέκεινα γάρ ἐστιν ὁ θεὸς τῇ αὐτοῦ οὐσίᾳ ὥσπερ τοῦ σώματος οὕτως καὶ τοῦ ἀσωμάτου, ὡς ἑκατέρου τούτων ὑπάρχων δημιουργός· οὐδὲ γὰρ ἐποίησεν ὁ θεὸς ἃ αὐτὸς ὑπάρχει), ἀλλ', ὥσπερ εἰώθαμεν ἐν τοῖς παρ' ἡμῖν τιμιωτέροις ὑλικοῖς ἀεὶ γεραίρειν τὸ θεῖον, οὕτως καὶ ἐν τοῖς ὀνόμασιν, οὐχ ὡς τοῦ θεοῦ τούτων δεομένου, ἀλλ' ἡμῶν τὴν περὶ αὐτοῦ ἔννοιαν αὐτοῖς ἐνδεικνυμένων. Τούτῳ οὖν τῷ τρόπῳ ὀνομάζομεν αὐτὸν ἀσώματον, καίτοι εἰδότες αὐτὸν ἐπέκεινα ὑπάρχοντα τοῦ ἀσωμάτου, ὡς τούτου δημιουργόν.

[52] Ed. Gleede 2020, p. 22: ἡ κτίστη φύσις [...] ἀκτίστως ἀναλαβεῖν τοῦ ἀκτίστου τὴν ἔννοιαν οὐ δύναται. Μὴ νοήσασα δὲ τὸν ἄκτιστον οὐ σῴζει ἐν ἑαυτῇ τοῦ ἀκτίστου τὴν μνήμην. ἀλλ' ἐπειδὴ τοῦτο μὲν ἀναγκαῖον ἐκεῖνο δὲ ἀδύνατον, διὰ τοῦτο τοῖς αὐτοῖς ὀνόμασι κέχρηται ἡ κτίστη φύσις πρὸς τὸ λαβεῖν τοῦ ἀκτίστου τὴν ἔννοιαν. Διὸ ἐν οἷς ἐστιν αὕτη, εἰς ταῦτα ἄγει τὸν ἄκτιστον. ἔστιν δὲ αὕτη ἐν οὐσίᾳ, ἐν τόπῳ, ἐν χρόνῳ, ἐν ἀριθμῷ, ἐν πάθει, ἄγουσα αὐτὸν εἰς οὐσίαν λέγουσα [αὐ]τὸν ἐν ὑποστάσει, ἄγουσα αὐτὸν εἰς τόπον λέγουσα εἶναι αὐτὸν πανταχοῦ, ἄγουσα αὐτὸν εἰς χρόνον λέγουσα εἶναι αὐτὸν ἀεί, ἄγουσα αὐτὸν εἰς ἀριθμὸν λέγουσα αὐτὸν ἕνα, ἄγουσα αὐτὸν εἰς πάθη λέγουσα αὐτὸν ἐλεήμονα.

[53] *De caelo* II. 3. 286a8–10 in 21. 12 and CA 52.

called into question, as it is all in all fairly obvious and self-suggesting.

That this cannot be said about relationship between those texts and QRO was also made clear by Harnack, who exactly for this reason felt the need to draw up an impressive list of 23 parallels in content and word choice and five similar stylistic features in order to substantiate his claim of a unique author.[54] If one takes a closer look at those, many of them definitely turn out to be too unspecific to prove even a common social background, let alone an identical author. Nevertheless, even after a critical examination, there are still quite a number of phrases and ideas left which are actually peculiar to this very body of texts and do not – at least according to the TLG – occur anywhere else:

– Both QRO 146[55] and QG 5[56] see God's existence and providence proved by λόγοι θείαις δυνάμεσι μεμαρτυρημένοι – a phrase attested only in those two passages and in QRO 1 (i.e. in the first and last question of this collection) in a slightly different context.

– Both QRO 77[57] and QG 1. 3[58] call the two basic epistemic faculties of the human soul καταληπτικαὶ δυνάμεις, a term which to my knowledge is used normally in the singular in a very general sense (perceptive power),[59] but never in enu-

---

[54] Harnack 1901, p. 46–54.

[55] Ed. Papadopoulos-Kermaeus 1895, p. 147: Ἔστι δὲ τῶν ὁμολογουμένων τὸ ἕνα εἶναι θεὸν δημιουργόν τε καὶ προνοητὴν τοῦ κόσμου παντός, ὃν καταγγέλλουσιν αἱ θεῖαι τῶν Χριστιανῶν γραφαὶ λόγοις θείαις δυνάμεσι μεμαρτυρημένοις· παρ' οὗ ἐστι τῶν μελλόντων ἥ τε πρόρρησις καὶ ἡ ἔκβασις.

[56] Ed. Gleede 2020, p. 8-9: Οὐ γὰρ ἂν ἦν τὰ ὄντα, μὴ τοῦ θεοῦ προϋπάρχοντος αὐτῶν, τοῦ πάντα τὰ μέρη τῆς κτίσεως χρειωδῶς πρὸς λυσιτέλειαν τῆς ὅλης κτίσεως ὑποστησαμένου, τοῦ ἡμῖν γνωσθέντος διὰ προρρήσεως καὶ διδασκαλίας προφητῶν τε καὶ τοῦ κυρίου καὶ σωτῆρος ἡμῶν Ἰησοῦ Χριστοῦ καὶ τῶν αὐτοῦ ἀποστόλων λόγοις θείαις δυνάμεσι μεμαρτυρημένος.

[57] Ed. Papadopoulos-Kermaeus 1895, p. 83: Πᾶσαι αἱ κτισταί τε καὶ λογικαὶ οὐσίαι διπλᾶς ἔχουσι καταληπτικὰς δυνάμεις, αἰσθητικήν τε καὶ νοητικήν· αἰσθητικὴν μὲν τὴν ἐννοηματικὴν λεγομένην, καθ' ἣν καταλαμβάνουσιν ἑαυτάς τε καὶ ἀλλήλας· νοητικὴν δέ, καθ' ἣν δέχονται τὴν γνῶσιν τοῦ ὑπὲρ ἐκείνας.

[58] Ed. Gleede 2020, p. 3: Δύο εἰσὶν ἐν ἡμῖν καταληπτικαὶ τῶν πραγμάτων δυνάμεις, ἥ τε αἴσθησις καὶ ἡ νόησις, ὧν αἱ ἐνέργειαι τοσούτῳ ἀλλήλων διαφέρουσιν, ὅσῳ τὰ ὑπὸ θατέρου καταλαμβανόμενα μὴ δύνανται καταλαμβάνεσθαι ὑπὸ τοῦ ἑτέρου.

[59] Cf. however Themistius, *In De anima* (CAG V/3, p. 34), where the entire perceptive part of the soul is called καταληπτικὴ δύναμις.

merations of the soul's faculties, where they are rather called κριτικαί,[60] θεωρητικαί,[61] or γνω(ρι)στικαί.[62]

- Both QRO 61[63] and QG 9. 1[64] characterize the divine imperishability as alone including ungeneratedness, as it originates in God's own essence, not in the will of someone else.

- Both QRO 114[65] and QG 11. 4[66] illustrate the divine act of creation with the same defective version of Jud 9. 5 (διενοήθης, καὶ ἐγενήθησαν ἃ ἐνενόηθης, καὶ παρέστησαν ἃ ἐβουλεύσω), which is attested nowhere else in the exact same wording.

In my opinion, those are the most striking of Harnack's observations and this would in itself already be sufficient to at least seriously consider a unique author. There can, however, be added several more:

- Both QRO 111[67] and the preface to CA[68] characterize the Christian concept of creation in relying on the opposition between νόμος φύσεως and αὐθεντία βουλῆς / βουλήσεως.

---

[60] Inspired by *De anima* III. 9. 432a15–17 e.g. in Plutarch, *De animae procreatione* 1024E or Alcinous, *Didaskalikos* 25. 7.

[61] Cf. Ammonius, *In Isag.* (CAG IV/3, p. 4); Philoponus, *In Meteor.* (CAG XIV/1, p. 1).

[62] Cf. Proclus, *In Tim.* (ed. Diehl 1903–1906, II, p. 160–161); Philoponus, *In De anim.* (CAG XV, p. 1–2 and p. 186–187).

[63] Ed. Papadopoulos-Kermaeus 1895, p. 73: Μόνος ἔχων τὴν ἀθανασίαν λέγεται ὁ θεός, ὅτι οὐκ ἐκ θελήματος ἄλλου ταύτην ἔχει, καθάπερ οἱ λοιποὶ πάντες ἀθάνατοι, ἀλλ᾽ ἐκ τῆς οἰκείας οὐσίας.

[64] Ed. Gleede 2020, p. 10: Ὣν ἡ ἀφθαρσία ἐκ τῆς ἑτέρου βουλῆς ἐξήρτηται, ταῦτα οὐ δύναται ἀγενήτως ἄφθαρτα εἶναι· διὸ μόνον τὸν θεὸν λέγομεν ἔχειν ἀθανασίαν, ὅτι ἐκ τῆς οἰκείας φύσεως καὶ οὐκ ἐκ τῆς ἑτέρου βουλῆς πρόσεστιν αὐτῷ ταῦτα.

[65] Ed. Papadopoulos-Kermaeus 1895, p. 117: οὗ δὲ ἡ δύναμις τῆς ἐνεργείας οὐ φυσικῇ ἀνάγκῃ ἀλλὰ ἰδίᾳ βουλῇ ὑφέστηκεν, οὗτος ἀνυπόβλητος τῷ τῆς ἐλαττώσεως ὀνόματι. Διενοήθης, φησί, καὶ πάντα σοι πάρεστιν.

[66] Ed. Gleede 2020, p. 12: Ἃ ποιεῖ ὁ θεός, αὐτουργικῷ ταῦτα προστάγματι ποιεῖ, σύγχρονος δὲ τῷ προστάγματι τοῦ θεοῦ ἡ ὕπαρξις τῶν ὑπ᾽ αὐτοῦ ποιουμένων. Διενοήθης, φησί, καὶ πάντα σοι παρέστη.

[67] Ed. Papadopoulos-Kermaeus 1895, p. 115: Οὐ γὰρ νόμῳ καὶ μέτρῳ φύσεως ἐργάζεται ὁ θεός, ἀλλ᾽ αὐθεντίᾳ βουλῆς τῆς ἐν μηδενὶ ἀπορουμένης πρὸς ποίησιν ὦν βούλεται ποιεῖν.

[68] CAp IV, p. 102–103: Πρὸς ἔνδειξιν δὲ τῆς θείας αὐτοῦ δυνάμεως καὶ τοῦ μὴ νόμῳ φύσεως αὐτὸν δουλεύειν, ἀλλ᾽ αὐθεντίᾳ βουλήσεως τὸ δοκοῦν ἐργάζεσθαι, τὰ μὲν ἐν ἀρχῇ τῶν ἐν γενέσει καὶ φθορᾷ φύσεως ἐκ τῆς γῆς καὶ τῶν ὑδάτων ἐποίησε [...], τὰ δὲ ἐκ τῶν γεναρχῶν γεγενημένα ἐκ τῆς καταβολῆς τοῦ σπέρματος γενέσθαι ὡρίσατο.

- Both QRO 49[69] and the preface to CA[70] use the term γεναρχής, which normally refers only to human founders or heads of families or races, in the very peculiar sense of 'principle of a natural genus' or 'prototype of a genus', which is most probably a reinterpretation of our author himself to make it fit one of his favourite arguments in CA.[71]

- Another argument peculiar to CA[72] can be found in QRO 63,[73] where from the fact that heaven and stars are useful for something else it is inferred that they have to be generated, obviously because every kind of usefulness or teleology implies a productive intellect behind the useful thing for our author.

- QGR 21. 3–5 argues historically for the superiority of Christianity in a way which is strongly reminiscent of the 'Hellenism questions' in QRO (esp. 2, 42, 74 and 146), in particular by highlighting the counterproductive effect of the persecutions[74]

---

[69] Ed. Papadopoulos-Kermaeus 1895, p. 64: Εἰ ἐν ἑκάστῳ γένει ἐστί τινα γεναρχή, καὶ τὰ μὲν γεναρχῇ ἐστιν ἔργα θεοῦ, τὰ δὲ ὑπὸ τὰ γεναρχῇ εἰσιν ἔργα φύσεως διὰ σπορᾶς [...].

[70] Cf. n. 68.

[71] Cf. n. 47.

[72] Cf. e.g. CA 53 (CAp IV, p. 194): πῶς ὑπάρχει ἐν τοῖς ἀϊδίοις τὸ εἶναι τόδε τι διὰ τὸ εἶναι ἄλλο τόδε τι, οἷον ἐπειδὴ ὁ οὐρανός ἐστιν ἀναγκαῖον εἶναι καὶ τὴν γῆν, εἰ δὲ γῆ καὶ οὐρανός ἐστι; Τοῦτο δὲ προνοίας ἐστὶν ἔργον, τῆς τόδε τὸ πᾶν ἐκ διαφόρων κατ᾽ οὐσίαν τε καὶ χρείαν μερῶν ποιησάσης. Ἢ ἄρα οὐκ ἀΐδια ὅ τε οὐρανὸς καὶ ἡ γῆ καὶ τὰ ἐν αὐτοῖς πάντα, τὰ πρὸς τὸ εἶναί τε καὶ ποιεῖν καὶ πάσχειν ἀλλήλοις συντελοῦντα, ἢ εἰ ἀΐδια, οὐκ ἀνάγκη τόδε τόδε εἶναι, ἐπειδὴ τόδε τόδε ἐστίν. Cf. also 55 (p. 202) and QG 9. 4 (τὸ γὰρ ἀγένητον χωρὶς πάσης χρειώδους αἰτίας δεῖ ὑπάρχειν ἀγένητον).

[73] Ed. Papadopoulos, p. 74: τῇ ποικιλίᾳ οὖν τῶν οὐσιῶν καὶ τῇ διαφορᾷ τῶν χρειῶν δείκνυσιν αὐτοὺς εἶναι γενητούς· ἡ γὰρ ἀγένητος φύσις πρὸς τὴν ἀγένητον φύσιν κατὰ τὴν φύσιν οὐκ ἔχει διαφοράν, τὸ δὲ καὶ χρείας ἕνεκεν εἶναι τοιόνδε ἢ τοιόνδε ἀλλότριόν ἐστι τῆς ἀγενήτου φύσεως.

[74] QGR 21. 3 (ed. Gleede 2020, p. 30: Εἰ δικαίως ἀνεῖλον οἱ ἕλληνες τοὺς χριστιανοὺς τοὺς κηρύττοντας τὴν ἀνάστασιν τῶν νεκρῶν καὶ τὸν ταύτην ποιοῦντα Χριστόν, διὰ τί μίσθον τῆς δικαιοσύνης ἀπηνέγκαντο πάσης τῆς ἑλληνικῆς δυναστείας τὴν καθαίρεσιν;); cf. QRO 74 (ἀλλ᾽ αἱ βάσανοι αὗται, αἷς πάλαι χρησάμενος ὁ ἑλληνισμὸς καὶ προσδοκήσας ἐν αὐταῖς ἄλυτον φυλάττειν ἑαυτόν, τὸν μὲν ἑλληνισμὸν ἔλυσαν, τὸν δὲ χριστιανισμὸν ἔστησαν κατὰ κράτος.); QG 11. 12 (Ποίας δὲ ἄλλης θρησκείας πολυτρόποις βασάνοις τε καὶ θανάτοις ἐβεβαιώθη τὸ δόγμα ὡς τὸ δόγμα τῆς τῶν χριστιανῶν θρησκείας περὶ τῆς τῶν νεκρῶν ἀναστάσεως;). A similar argument can be found, however, also in *Quaest. ad Antiochum ducem* 42 (Πόθεν δῆλον, ὅτι κρεῖττον πάσης τῆς ὑπ᾽ οὐρανὸν πίστεως οἱ Χριστιανοὶ πιστεύομεν;): οὐχ εὑρίσκομεν ἀπ᾽ ἀρχῆς αἰῶνος ἔθνος ὑπὸ πάντων ἐθνῶν πολεμηθὲν ἐπὶ χρόνους τοσούτους καὶ μὴ ἐξαλειφθέν,

and the crucifixion of Christ by the Jews[75] and the pagan gods' failure in foreknowledge.[76]

Fortunately, we also have one striking similarity between question 148 of the long recension, which originally belonged to QR, and QG/QC, as all three texts establish the divine will as only measure for the divine creative power by pointing to the fact that there is only one sun, whereas – considering the multitude of other stars – several other ones easily could have been created.[77]

All these parallels and similarities considered, there can in my opinion be no further reasonable doubt concerning the common authorship of CA, QC, QG, QGR, QR and QRO. The most difficult case, however, the CT, still remains to be examined. In the Arethas codex, the piece follows the QR fragment and is introduced by the not very expressive heading τοῦ αὐτοῦ πρὸς τοὺς αὐτοὺς which could in fact be counted as an ascription to the author of the preceding pieces by the manuscript tradition. Yet, this would raise the question how this entirely Christologi-

εἰ μὴ μόνον τὴν τοῦ Χριστοῦ πίστιν, ἥτις οὐκ ἂν ἔμεινεν ἀνεξάλειπτος, οὕτως ὑπὸ πάντων τῶν ἐθνῶν πολεμηθεῖσα, εἰ μὴ χεὶρ Κυρίου διεφύλαττε καὶ φυλάττει αὐτὴν ἀνεξάλειπτον (PG 28, col. 624).

[75] QGR 21. 4 (ed. Gleede 2020, p. 30: Εἰ διὰ τοῦτο ἐσταύρωσαν οἱ Ἰουδαῖοι τὸν χριστὸν ἵνα μὴ λυθῇ ὁ Ἰουδαϊσμὸς καὶ κρατήσῃ ὁ χριστιανισμός, ὡσαύτως δὲ καὶ οἱ ἕλληνες διὰ τοῦτο ἀνεῖλον τοὺς χριστιανούς, ἵνα μὴ λυθῇ ὁ ἑλληνισμὸς καὶ κρατήσῃ ὁ χριστιανισμὸς [...]); cf. QRO 108 (εἰ μὲν γὰρ ταύτῃ τῇ ἐλπίδι ἐσταύρωσαν τὸν Χριστὸν οἱ Ἰουδαῖοι, τοῦ μὴ κρατῆσαι τὴν διδασκαλίαν αὐτοῦ καὶ τοῦ μὴ λυθῆναι τὸν Ἰουδαϊσμόν [...]).

[76] QGR 21. 5 (ed. Gleede 2020, p. 30: Εἰ οὐκ ἔστι θεὸς φύσει ὁ τὸ μέλλον ἀγνοῶν, πῶς εἰσι θεοὶ οἱ τῶν ἑλλήνων θεοὶ οἱ ἐπ᾽ ἐλπίδι τῆς νίκης χριστὸν πολεμήσαντες καὶ παρ᾽ ἐλπίδα ἡττηθέντες; οὐ γὰρ ἀνεπολέμησαν χριστόν, εἰ τὴν μέλλουσαν ἀποτυχίαν τῆς νίκης προέγνων.); cf. QRO 2 (οὐδὲν ὢν προεῖπον οἱ μάντεις, ἢ κατὰ τοῦ τῆς ἀληθείας θεοῦ καὶ τῶν σεβομένων αὐτόν, ἢ ὑπὲρ τῆς συστάσεως τῶν ἑλληνικῶν πραγμάτων, τὴν ἔκβασιν ἐδέξατο) and 146 (ὧν δὲ οὐκ εἰσὶν οἱ θεοὶ θεοί, τούτων οὐδὲ οἱ μάντεις εἰσὶν ἀληθείας προφῆται, οὐδὲ ἡ δι᾽ αὐτῶν πρόρρησις ἀναπόδραστόν τε καὶ ἀψευδῆ ἔχει τὴν ἔκβασιν· εἰσὶ γὰρ ὥσπερ μακρὰν τῆς ἀληθινῆς θεότητος, οὕτως καὶ τῆς τῶν μελλόντων προγνώσεως).

[77] QR 148 (ed. Papadopoulos-Kermaeus 1895, p. 137): διὸ δύναται ποιεῖν ἀεὶ πάντα ὅσα βούλεται ποιεῖν. οὐκ ἔτι δὲ βούλεται ποιεῖν πάντα ὅσα δύναται ποιεῖν· καὶ γὰρ πλείονας ἡλίους ἠδύνατο καὶ δύναται ποιεῖν, ἀλλ᾽ ὅμως ἕνα μόνον ἥλιον ἐποίησεν, ὅτι ἕνα μόνον ἐβούλετο ποιεῖν. Cf. QG 4 (Δεῖγμα δὲ τοῦ βουλήσει τὸν θεὸν ποιεῖν τὸν κόσμον τοῦτό ἐστι, τό, δυναμένου τοῦ θεοῦ πλείονας ποιεῖν ἡλίους, οὐκ ἐποίησε πλείονας, ἀλλ᾽ ἕνα μόνον ἐποίησεν· ὁ γὰρ μὴ δυνάμενος πλείονας ποιῆσαι ἡλίους οὐδὲ ἕνα δύναται ποιεῖν, καὶ ὁ τὸν ἕνα ἥλιον δυνάμενος ποιῆσαι ἐξ ἀνάγκης καὶ πλείονας δύναται ποιεῖν.) and QC 2. 7 and 5. 2.

cal collection of arguments can be said to have the same opponent (or addressee?) as the QR fragment or even the preceding
apologetical questions, as the opponent in what follows are rather
clearly the Monophysites, who have not really come up in any
of the questions before. After all, the QR at least furnishes the
only two questions in the entire corpus which are Christological in the strict sense, i.e. which actually deal with the relationship between the two natures in Christ. Question 7 asks why
the incarnation is attributed to the second person of the trinity alone, not also to the other two, if the divine essence is one.
The answer could be understood as contradicting the CT, as
it surmises from the appropriation of the incarnation to the
Logos that we attribute τὰ τῆς οἰκονομίας to the God-Logos
κατὰ τὸν τρόπον τῆς ἀντιδείξεως,[78] whereas the CT carefully
restricts the attribution of any base attribute to Christ, the common πρόσωπον. Yet, this apparent contradiction is immediately
resolved, if we take a look at the qualification κατὰ τὸν τρόπον
τῆς ἀντιδείξεως, which should perhaps be translated as 'according to the mode of mutual indication'. How this 'mutual indication' is to be conceived, can be learned from the only other
instance of the term ἀντίδειξις in a Christological context, in the
so-called *Christian Topography* attributed by the manuscript tradition to Cosmas Indicopleustes.[79] This Nestorian text wants
to interpret Rom. 8. 32 by upholding that God's own son cannot have been given away to die and referring the phrase to the
flesh 'which is a substitute and indication for the son according
to the example of the blessed Isaak'.[80] Although the 'indication'
is not really mutual in this passage, as the flesh just 'stands for'

---

[78] Ed. Papadopoulos-Kermaeus 1895, p. 21: ἐπειδὴ οὖν ἡ ἔνσαρκος οἰκονομία
ἰδική ἐστι τοῦ θεοῦ λόγου, εἰς φανέρωσιν γὰρ αὐτοῦ τῆς σαρκὸς ἐγένετο ἡ λῆψις, διὰ
τοῦτο ἀκολούθως προσάπτωμεν τῷ θεῷ λόγῳ κατὰ τὸν τρόπον τῆς ἀντιδείξεως τὰ
τῆς οἰκονομίας.

[79] As I will try to demonstrate elsewhere, the hypothesis of Wolska (in SC
141, p. 86–93) according to which this passage derives from an anonymous
Nestorian *Treatise on the Two Conditions* is untenable.

[80] *Top. Chr.* V. 104 (SC 159, p. 157): Οὕτως καὶ ἐπὶ τοῦ Χριστοῦ τοῦ Υἱοῦ
τοῦ Θεοῦ λέλεκται· '"Ὅς γε τοῦ ἰδίου Υἱοῦ οὐκ ἐφείσατο, ἀλλ᾽ ὑπὲρ ἡμῶν πάντων
παρέδωκεν αὐτόν', κἂν ἡ σάρξ ἐστι μόνη ἡ δοθεῖσα ὑπὲρ τῆς τοῦ κόσμου ζωῆς, ἐπειδὴ
ἀδύνατον τὴν θεότητα θανεῖν· τῆς σαρκὸς διδομένης, τὸν ἴδιον Υἱὸν δίδοσθαι λέγει
ἡ Γραφή, ἀντάλλαγμα καὶ ἀντίδειξιν οὖσαν τοῦ υἱοῦ κατὰ τὸν τύπον τοῦ μακαρίου
Ἰσαάκ.

the eternal son, both texts explain 'paradoxical' Christological predication as verbal substition of one distinct entity for the other: just as the ram substituted Isaak, the human flesh of Christ substituted the divine Logos,[81] which is fundamentally in line with the position of CT. Nevertheless, considering the latter's focus on the problem of theopaschism, it is astonishing that it never touches the scriptural examples of 'theopaschite' predications (I Cor 2. 4, etc.), especially if the author has an interpretation for them on the lines of QR 7, but only deals with the wording of the *Nicaenoconstantinopolitanum* which – in his Nestorian reading[82] – offers nothing like that. Probably, the author wants to remain entirely on the conceptual level in CT without engaging into exegetical details.

This would also explain the dissimilarities between CT and QR 8, which deals with the most important anti-Nestorian charge, the alleged introduction of a duality of sons. The answer states on the one hand that a distinction of natures and sonships (natural and adopted) is necessary, as predicating both sonships of one nature would deprive the Logos of both sonships, and claims on the other hand that a duality of sons is avoided, as the form of God took the form of the servant ἐν τάξει ἑαυτῆς, i.e. confers to it the power and dignity of its own 'rank' and thus establishes with it a unity of πρόσωπον, not nature.[83] The dis-

---

[81] Cf. ed. Papadopoulos-Kermaeus 1895, p. 21: εἰς δὲ τὸν θεοῦ λόγον καὶ εἰς τὴν οἰκονομίαν οὐδαμῶς ποιεῖ τὴν τοιαύτην διαίρεσιν, ἀλλὰ κατὰ τὸν λόγον τῆς ἀντιδείξεως περὶ ἑνὸς καὶ τοῦ αὐτοῦ προσώπου ποιεῖ ἀδιαιρέτως τὴν διήγησιν *τῶν ἑκάστη φύσει διηρημένως ἁρμοττόντων.*

[82] Cf. Nestorius, *2nd Letter to Cyril* 3 (ACO I/1/1, p. 293–294): Πιστεύω τοίνυν φασί, καὶ εἰς τὸν κύριον ἡμῶν Ἰησοῦν Χριστὸν τὸν υἱὸν αὐτοῦ τὸν μονογενῆ. σκόπησον ὅπως τὸ κύριος καὶ Ἰησοῦς καὶ Χριστός καὶ μονογενής καὶ υἱός πρότερον θέντες τὰ κοινὰ τῆς θεότητος καὶ τῆς ἀνθρωπότητος ὡς θεμελίους ὀνόματα τότε τὴν τῆς ἐνανθρωπήσεως καὶ τῆς ἀναστάσεως καὶ τοῦ πάθους ἐποικοδομοῦσι παράδοσιν, ἵνα τῶν ὀνομάτων τῆς φύσεως ἑκατέρας κοινῶν τινων σημαντικῶν προκειμένων μήτε τὰ τῆς υἱότητος καὶ κυριότητος τέμνηται μήτε τὰ τῶν φύσεων ἐν τῶι τῆς υἱότητος μοναδικῶι συγχύσεως ἀφανισμῶι κινδυνεύηι.

[83] Ed. Papadopoulos-Kermaeus 1895, p. 22: τὸ δὲ ἐν τάξει τῆς μορφῆς τοῦ θεοῦ ὁρᾶσθαι τὴν τοῦ δούλου μορφὴν καὶ μὴ ἐν τῷ οἰκείῳ προσώπῳ † ...† πάσης τῆς κατὰ πρόσωπον αὐθεντίας τε καὶ τιμῆς, δυάδος υἱῶν ἐστιν ἀναιρετικόν· τὸ γὰρ ἐν τάξει ταυτόν ἐστι τῷ τάξαντι προσώπῳ καὶ οὐ φύσει. The *lacuna* is unfortunate, but a construction of the entire following phrase as apposition to τῆς μορφῆς τοῦ θεοῦ would not be possible. Cf. CT 8, where the more elaborate Nestorian doctrine of a union of two natural πρόσωπα in one πρόσωπον is presented. CT 22 (ὄνομα ἄρα δέχεται ἡ σὰρξ τοῦ θεοῦ λόγου, οὐχὶ οὐσίαν) seems, however, to restrict the

crepancies to the Christological language of CT are of course – at least partly – to be explained by the different context, as the starting point from Phil. 2 (form of God – form of a servant, natural son – adopted son [84]) is dictated by the question addressed to our author.[85] His most important conceptual tool for answering the question, the category of τάξις, might – at closer inspection – also be present in CT 34, where the flesh is claimed to receive 'the rank and the diginity of God on the basis of the union'.[86] Even more interesting is, however, the strange negative argument supporting the distinction of natures: if Christ were 'according to the same nature natural and adopted son', 'it would be necessary to conceive of the God-Logos as distinguished from both the true, proper and real and the neither true nor proper nor real son'.[87] This prima facie rather odd argument is strongly reminiscent of a point made several times in CT, i.e. that an attribution of human characteristics to the Logos would deprive him of his godhead, as the latter is absolutely incompatible with the former attributes.[88] Accordingly, our author argues in QR that, if both sonships were attributed to one nature, this would have to be an alterable nature and could not be the divinity of the Logos.

communicatio idiomatum to the mere name, and CT 31 even forbids a universal *communicatio nominum*.

[84] In CT 12 he uses the opposition son by nature – son by grace.

[85] Ed. Papadopoulos-Kermaeus 1895, p. 21–22: Οἱ λέγοντες ἡνῶσθαι τῇ τοῦ δούλου μορφῇ τὸν ἀληθῶς καὶ κυρίως καὶ ὄντως ὄντα υἱὸν τῇ ἀντιδιαστολῇ τοῦ μὴ ἀληθῶς μηδὲ κυρίως μηδὲ ὄντως ὄντος υἱοῦ, υἱοῦ δὲ ὅμως καὶ τούτου καλουμένου, πῶς δυάδι υἱῶν οὐ λατρεύουσι, κἂν ἑτεροούσια τὰ δύο τυγχάνουσι πρόσωπα.

[86] Ed. Gleede 2020, p. 43: Εἰ μένει ὁ θεὸς λόγος ὅπερ ἦν, δύναται ἡ ἑνωθεῖσα αὐτῷ σὰρξ τὴν τάξιν τε καὶ τὴν ἀξίαν ἔχειν θεοῦ ἐκ τῆς ἑνώσεως. Εἰ δὲ κατ᾽ οὐσίαν γίνεται ὁ θεὸς λόγος ἕτερος παρ᾽ ὃ ἦν, οὔτε αὐτὸς οὐσίαν ἔχει θεοῦ, οὔτε ἡ σὰρξ ἀξίαν θεοῦ.

[87] Ed. Papadopoulos-Kermaeus 1895, p. 22 (modified): εἰ γὰρ μὴ κατ᾽ ἄλλην φύσιν υἱὸς ἄθετος ὁ Χριστὸς καὶ κατ᾽ ἄλλην θετός, καθὼς ὁ τῆς ἀντιδιαστολῆς βούλεται λόγος, ἀλλὰ κατὰ τὴν αὐτὴν φύσιν ἐστὶν ἄθετος [ὁ] υἱὸς καὶ θετὸς ὁ Χριστός – ἀδύνατον γὰρ τὰς γραφικὰς φωνάς, καταγγελλούσας τὸν Χριστὸν ἄθετον καὶ θετὸν υἱόν, ἀναιρεθῆναι –, ἀνάγκη τὸν θεὸν λόγον κατὰ τὴν ἀντιδιαστολὴν τοῦ ἀληθῶς καὶ κυρίως καὶ ὄντως καὶ τοῦ μήτε ἀληθῶς μήτε κυρίως μήτε ὄντως νοεῖν υἱόν. Unlike Papadopoulos, I do not conjecture θετὸν ‹τὸν› υἱόν, but rather omit the article before, as the question always is about predicating natural and adopted sonship of Christ, not about the possibility of calling the son adopted and Christ unadopted.

[88] CT 14 cf. 5–7; 34.

The Christology of QR 7–8 is thus not only fully compatible with CT, but the latter text also shows some peculiar similarities to our corpus, of which especially the following deserve to be highlighted:

– The phrase ποιεῖσθαι τῶν φωνῶν τὴν ἔκθεσιν seems to occur only in CT 2[89] and the preface to CA.[90]

– The distinction between λόγος τῆς οὐσίας and τρόπος τῆς οἰκονομίας is apparently peculiar to CT 38[91] and QR 141.[92] The latter phrase alone is admittedly prominent especially in Cyril of Alexandria, but never contrasted with λόγος τῆς οὐσίας. The closest parallel seems to be an often quoted dictum of Basil's *Contra Eunomium* contrasting the τρόπος τῆς θεολογίας with the λόγοι τῆς οἰκονομίας.[93]

Taken all of this together, one can, in my opinion, be fairly convinced that actually all seven texts go back to one and the same Nestorian author.

3. *Historical Setting*

Any attempt to determine the historical setting of our texts has to start from Harnack again, for whom their dating at around 370 was one of the main reasons for ascribing them to Diodore. His four arguments for establishing the reign of Julian as *terminus*

---

[89] Ed. Gleede 2020, p. 37: Χρὴ πρῶτον κατὰ τὴν ἀκολουθίαν τῆς τῶν πραγμάτων φύσεως ποιεῖσθαι τῶν φωνῶν τὴν ἔκθεσιν εἶθ᾽ οὕτω κινεῖν τὰς ζητήσεις.

[90] CAp IV, p. 138: Ποιήσομαι δὲ τῶν φωνῶν τούτων τὴν ἔκθεσιν, ἐν αἷς ταῦτα ποιεῖ, ἵν᾽ ἐκ παραλλήλου γνωσθῇ τὸ ἐν αὐτῷ περιεχόμενον ψεῦδος.

[91] Ed. Gleede 2020, p. 44: Εἰ κατὰ τρόπον οἰκονομίας γίνεται ὁ θεὸς λόγος σάρξ, δύναται μένειν ὃ ἦν καὶ γενέσθαι ὃ οὐκ ἦν, τρόπος δὲ οἰκονομίας καὶ τὸ ποιῆσαι σάρκα καὶ τὸ λαβεῖν ταύτην εἰς ἐπίδειξιν ἑαυτοῦ φανερούμενος ἐν αὐτῇ. Ὁ γὰρ τῆς οὐσίας λόγος οὐ δέχεται τὴν ἀντίφασιν αὐτοῦ.

[92] Ed. Papadopoulos-Kermaeus 1895, p. 131: τὰ μὲν οὖν πρέποντα τῇ οὐσίᾳ νόει κατ᾽ οὐσίαν, καὶ τὰ πρέποντα τῇ οἰκονομίᾳ νόει κατ᾽ οἰκονομίαν, καὶ οὐδὲν ἀνακύπτει ἄτοπον· ἄλλος γὰρ ὁ λόγος τῆς θείας οὐσίας καὶ ἄλλος ὁ τρόπος τῆς θείας οἰκονομίας· ὑπὲρ ἡμᾶς γὰρ ὁ λόγος τῆς θείας οὐσίας, καθ᾽ ἡμᾶς δὲ ὁ τῆς οἰκονομίας, καθ᾽ ὃν ἡμῖν προσέρχεται ὁ θεός· ἄλλως γὰρ ἀδύνατον δέξασθαι ἡμᾶς γνῶσιν θεοῦ, μὴ τοῦ θεοῦ τούτῳ τῷ τρόπῳ εἰς γνῶσιν ἡμᾶς χειραγωγοῦντος τὴν αὐτοῦ.

[93] Basil, *Ctr. Eunom.* II. 3 (PG 29, col. 577); cf. Gregory of Nyssa, *Ctr. Eunom.* III. 3. 16. 49; Theodoret, *Eranistes*, ed. Ettlinger 1975, p. 239.

post quem are as self-evident as they are irrelevant to our discussion.[94] Of the utmost interest, however, are the three arguments for 378, the death of last 'Arian' emperor Valens, as *terminus ante quem*.[95] The third one tries to place our author's conception of the Holy Spirit before 381, without solid proof, as was shown in detail by Funk,[96] who also offers a thorough refutation of the first argument, the considerable presence of an allegedly surviving paganism in QRO.[97] Harnack clearly underestimates how long the practices of 'pagan superstition' can survive even within an in most respects consolidated *corpus Christianum*: the νεφοδιῶκται mentioned in QRO 31 are still condemned by the Concilium Quinisextum in 692,[98] and the talismans of Apollonius of Tyana referred to in QRO 24 were still extant and considered as efficient in the Byzantine Middle Ages.[99] Remains the second argument proceeding from the fact that our author considers himself to be part of a small minority of orthodox Christians oppressed by a majority of heretics. Funk's attempt to downplay those passages [100] is all in all not very convincing: in QRO 1 he wants to understand the phrase οἱ δὲ ὀρθόδοξοι μόνοι θεῷ ἀρέσκοντες Ἑλλήνων τε καὶ Ἰουδαίων καὶ πάντων αἱρετικῶν κατὰ τὸν ἀριθμὸν ὑπάρχουσιν ἥσσονες in the sense that the number of the orthodox is smaller than the one of the other groups taken all together, which would in consequence yield a relative majority for the orthodox party and thus deprive the question of its entire point. If one does not want to have the latter smaller than all the parties on their own, one could at best consider an interpretation like 'fewer in number than the pagans and the Jews taken together and

---

[94] Harnack 1901, p. 20–24.

[95] Harnack 1901, p. 24–29.

[96] Funk 1907, p. 329–332.

[97] Funk 1907, p. 332–335. On the role of paganism in QRO cf. also Rinaldi 1989, p. 116–120, who also misconceives this role relying on a too early dating of the text.

[98] Cf. Lampe 2001, s.v. The only other reference for the term apart from Matthaeus Blastares' *Collectio alphabetica* from the fourteenth century!

[99] Cf. esp. Dulière 1970 and for the early Byzantine period also Speyer 1974. About the ones in Antioch probably which our author most probably has in mind we have an extensive report from the end of the fifth century by John Malalas, *Chronographia* X. 51.

[100] Funk 1907, p. 336–338.

all the heretics taken together'. Even less convincing is his remark on QRO 22, according to which the orthodox wheat is almost suffocated by the heretical weeds (Mt. 13. 30),[101] that one would have to refer this to pagan dominance also, if one were to assign the text to the fourth century. Most important both for Harnack and for Funk is, however, QR 143, where the dominance of the Christians over the Jews because of their right faith is to be related to the dominance of the heretics over the orthodox Christians. The key problem of interpretation here are the aorists in the phrase πῶς οἱ τοιοῦτοι οὐ μόνον Ἰουδαίων, ἀλλὰ καὶ <τῶν> τὸν ἀληθῆ Χριστὸν δεσπότην τοῦ παντὸς γνωριζόντων ἐκράτησαν καὶ μυρίοις δεινοῖς περιέβαλον: whereas Harnack apparently takes especially ἐκράτησαν in an ingressive sense ('came to power and subjected them to a thousand [ongoing] repressions'), Funk prefers to refer those to events in the past, but admits that the author continues with a generalization of this past experience in the present tense.[102] Taken on its own, both readings of the question seem possible to me. Taken together with the aforesaid questions and with the other texts, especially CT, Harnack's reading undoubtedly emerges as the correct one, yet it has to be contextualized differently: the heretical emperor alluded to in this question is not an 'Arian' like Valens, but probably a Chalcedonian or Monophysite, and the text does not belong to the end of the fourth, but to the second half of the fifth or even the sixth century.

If we can grant that our author belongs to a Greek speaking Nestorian community, the establishment of a new *terminus post quem* for our texts will mostly have to rely on what we can plausibly assume concerning the development of such a community between or after the condemnations of its 'heresiarch' in Ephesus (431) and Chalcedon (451). If CT repeatedly relies on the authority of the 'two synods', would it be also imaginable that the

---

[101] Ed. Papadopoulos-Kermaeus 1895, p. 41: Εἰ τῷ σίτῳ συναυξάνεσθαι τὰ ζιζάνια ὁ κύριος καὶ δεσπότης Χριστὸς ἀπεφήνατο, πῶς τὰ μὲν ζιζάνια πεπλήθυνται, σχεδὸν δὲ ὁ σῖτος ἐξέλιπε.

[102] Ed. Papadopoulos-Kermaeus 1895, p. 132: εἰ δὲ τὸ δεσπόζειν ὀφεῖλον ὑπὸ τῆς πλάνης δεσπόζεται, πῶς τὴν δουλείαν τῶν Ἰουδαίων τῇ εἰς Χριστὸν ἀπειθείᾳ ἐπιγράφομεν, καὶ αὐτῶν σὺν τοῖς ἀληθινοῖς χριστιανοῖς τοῖς ψευδωνύμοις Χριστιανοῖς δεδουλευκότων πολλάκις;

author wrote before Chalcedon, as some Nestorians, e.g. Narsai, recognized this synod as a third one, yet of minor authority? [103] Yet, it is fairly clear that the hardliners remaining in communion with Nestorius even after the union of 433 [104] never formed a relatively fixed and self-reflecting ecclesiastical community as is presupposed in QR(O). One of those hardliners, Eutherios of Tyana, left an interesting *Protestatio*, the first chapter of which also articulates the self-conception as a minority, yet on far more dynamic and aggressive lines, i.e. not in the sense of justifying the state of a consolidated minority, but in order to bring into play again the arguments of sidelined individuals.[105] What is more, when CT referts to the authority of 'the two synods', the two creeds are meant: the original *Nicaenum* he quotes most often,[106] but also the so-called *Nicaenoconstantino-politanum*, e.g. right in CT 2, where he iuxtaposes the predicates γεννηθέντα πρὸ τῶν αἰώνων and θεὸν ἐκ θεοῦ which occur exclusively in NC and N respectively.[107] The first unequivocal reference to the text of NC are, however, the acts of 451,[108] and it was not introduced into the liturgy until after the council, by the patriarchs Peter Fullo († 488) in Antioch and Timothy († 518) in Constantinople.[109] Our texts thus definitely cannot have been produced before 451, probably even quite a while after that.

---

[103] Cf. Abramowski 1954/55.

[104] The development of the 'Antiochene network' from 433–451 is documented by Schor 2011, p. 100–130.

[105] *Prot.* 1 (SC 557, p. 86–92). Interestingly enough, Eutherios (*Prot.* 3. 70–80; SC 557, p. 104) fiercely rejects the Christological formula ἔμεινεν ὃ ἦν, ἐγένετο ὃ οὐκ ἦν happily used e.g. in CT 17 (cf. the apparatus in ed. Gleede 2020, p. 38), probably because he still knew how fond Cyril, his archenemy, was of this formula (cf. e.g. *In Lucam* V. 7 [PG 72, col. 492]; *Hom.* inc. fr. 9 [ed. Pusey 1965, III, p. 465–466]).

[106] In CT 11 and 32, for example, the concluding anathema of N, which is replaced by the extended third article in NC. For a critical edition of the two texts see Dossetti 1967.

[107] The only other instance of an allusion to a textual peculiarity of NC is CT 33 (καὶ Μαρίας τῆς παρθένου).

[108] Possible earlier traces are discussed by Ritter 1965, p. 195–208. That the most important of those, a passage in Theodore's catechetical homilies, cannot really count as a reference to NC was shown by Gerber 2000, p. 145–158.

[109] Cf. Theodor Lector, *Epitome* 428 and 501 (GCS NF 3, p. 118 and 143). According to the latter passage, the symbol used to be read before on Good Friday only.

This leaves us with the necessity of establishing a new *terminus ante quem*. This question may seem to be settled very quickly, as in QRO 71 our author clearly agrees with the world-week speculations, according to which creation is going exactly six millennia, and places himself within the sixth one. The most influential chronological conception in this vein was in fact the one by Julius Africanus, Hippolytus, Pandorus and others, who all dated the incarnation to the year 5500 of creation (i.e. creation at about 5500 BC), which would put a stop to the world exactly in the year 500.[110] If our author was following this conception at some point after 451, both the question[111] and especially the answer of our author[112] would, however, be extraordinarily sober and unexcited in tone. It is hard to belief that by 'those words were spoken in the sixth millennium, in which we are' he could actually mean 'the end of the world is in fact only a few decades away', especially as he does not show any signs of apocalyptic expectations or fears anywhere else either.[113] He thus most probably rather follows an alternative chronological conception, e.g. the one of Eusebius / Jerome, who made the world about 300 years younger.[114]

All in all, the technical philosophical character of most of the texts rather point to the sixth than to the fifth century. The only plausible argument for an earlier dating could in my opinion come from the CT. The introductory Christological alternative is here δύο φύσεις ἑτερώνυμοι ἢ μία φύσις διώνυμος and the Chalcedonian 'middle position' between those two extremes plays

---

[110] Cf. Brandes 1997, p. 25–32.

[111] Ed. Papadopoulos-Kermaeus 1895, p. 78–79: Ἐπειδή τινες περὶ τῆς τοῦ κόσμου συστάσεως ἔφασαν στοχαζόμενοι ὡς ἑξακισχίλια ἔτη μόνα συστήσεται, εἰ ἀληθὲς τοῦτο δι' ὑποδειγμάτων ἐναργῶν ἐπιδείκνυται εἴ τε ἐκ τῆς θείας γραφῆς καὶ εἰ ἄδηλον, μάθωμεν.

[112] Ed. Papadopoulos-Kermaeus 1895, p. 79: Ἔνεστι διὰ πολλῶν γραφικῶν φωνῶν τεκμήρασθαι ἀληθεύειν τοὺς λέγοντας ἑξακισχίλια ἔτη εἶναι τὸν χρόνον τῆς παρούσης τοῦ κόσμου συστάσεως, ποτὲ μὲν λέγουσα 'ἐπ' ἐσχάτων τῶν ἡμερῶν τούτων ἐλάλησεν ἡμῖν ἐν υἱῷ', ποτὲ δὲ 'εἰς οὓς τὰ τέλη τῶν αἰώνων κατήντησε', ποτὲ δὲ 'ὅτε ἦλθε τὸ πλήρωμα τοῦ χρόνου'. πᾶσαι δὲ αἱ τοιαῦται φωναὶ ἐν τῇ ἕκτῃ ἐρρέθησαν χιλιάδι, ἐν ᾗ ἐσμεν.

[113] On the apocalyptic expectations connected with the year 500 cf. Brandes 1997, esp. p. 53–62.

[114] Cf. Finegan 1964, p. 156–167.

no role in the treatise whatsoever. In CT 18 for example, it is simply stated that Christ has to have both a divine and human φύσις, ὑπόστασις and πρόσωπον without any reference to the Chalcedonian differentiation between φύσις and ὑπόστασις.[115] This actually rather clearly points to a time before the Chalcedonian restauration under Justin and Justinian, when the Monophysites were the dominating force in most of the Eastern parts of the Empire, i.e. to a time before 519, a date which is also corroborated by Voicu's obversations on the use of II Peter in QRO 94 and the baptismal practices attested in QRO 14.[116]

Bibliography

Primary Sources

Acta conciliorum oecumenicorum, ed. E. Schwartz, J. Straub & R. Schieffer, 5 vols, Berlin, 1927–1984 [ACO].

Cosmas Indicopleustes, *La Topographie chrétienne*, ed. W. Wolska, 3 vols, Paris, 1968–1973 (SC 141, 159, 197).

Cyril of Alexandria, *Alexandrini In D. Joannis evangelium*, ed. P. E. Pusey, 3 vols, Brussels, 1965.

Eutherius of Tyana, *Protestation*, ed. J. Paramelle, Paris, 2014 (SC 557).

Ps.-Caesarius of Nazianzus, *Die Erotapokriseis*, ed. R. Riedinger, Berlin, 1989 (GCS).

Ps.-Justin, *Corpus apologetarum Christianorum saeculi secundi*, ed. J. C. Otto, vol. IV and V, Jena, 1881 [CAp].

Ps.-Justin, Θεοδωρήτου ἐπισκόπου πόλεως Κύρρου πρὸς τὰς ἐπενεχθείσας αὐτῷ ἐπερωτήσεις παρά τινος τῶν ἐξ Αἰγύπτου ἐπισκόπων ἀποκρίσεις, ed. A. Papadopoulos-Kerameus, Petersburg, 1895 (repr. Leipzig, 1975).

---

[115] Ed. Gleede 2020, p. 41: Ὁ λόγος ἦν εἷς θεὸς καὶ γέγονεν εἷς ἄνθρωπος τοῦ λόγου. <Καθὸ δὲ θεός, ἦν> μία αὐτοῦ φύσις καὶ μία αὐτοῦ ὑπόστασις καὶ ἓν αὐτοῦ πρόσωπον, καὶ γέγονεν ὁ λόγος ἄνθρωπος οὐσίαν ἔχων παρὰ τὴν τοῦ λόγου | καὶ ὑπόστασιν καὶ πρόσωπον. Διὸ εἷς ὁ λόγος οὐσίᾳ καὶ ὑποστάσει καὶ προσώπῳ (εἰ δὲ οὐκ ἔστιν οὕτως, διπλοῦς ὁ λόγος), καὶ δῆλον, ὅτι οὐκ ἔστιν ὁ λόγος, ὁ γέγονεν. Εἰ ἦν ὁ λόγος θεὸς καὶ γέγονεν ἄνθρωπος καὶ ἔμεινεν ὃ ἦν, δῆλον ὅτι καὶ ὃ γέγονεν μένει, καὶ μένει πάντῃ λόγος ὁ λόγος καὶ μένει ἄνθρωπος ὁ ἄνθρωπος.

[116] Cf. Voicu 2015, 555–556.

Ps.-Justin, *Philosophische Erotapokriseis und theologische Kapitel. Quaestiones gentilium ad Christianos, Quaestiones contra gentiles de relatis. Capita contra theopaschitas*, ed. B. Gleede, Berlin – New York, 2020 (GCS NF 29).

Proclus, *In Platonis Timaeum commentaria*, ed. E. Diehl, 3 vols, Leipzig, 1903–1906 (repr. Amsterdam, 1965).

Theodor Lector, *Kirchengeschichte*, ed. G. C. Hansen, Berlin, 1995 (GCS NF 3).

Theodoret of Cyrus, *Eranistes*, ed. G. Ettlinger, Oxford, 1975.

Secondary Literature

L. Abramowski (1954/55), 'Das Konzil von Chalkedon in der Homilie des Narses über die drei nestorianischen Lehrer', in *Zeitschrift für Kirchengeschichte*, 66, p. 140–143.

P. Batiffol (1896), 'L'auteur véritable de l'Epistula ad Zenam et Serenum', in *Revue Biblique*, 5, p. 114–122.

M. D. Boeri (2009), 'Pseudo-Justin on Aristotelian cosmology. A Byzantine philosopher searching for a new picture of the world', in *Byzantion*, 79, p. 99–135.

W. Brandes (1997), 'Anastasios ὁ δίκορος: Endzeiterwartung und Kaiserkritik in Byzanz um 500 n. Chr.', in *Byzantinische Zeitschrift*, 50, p. 24–63.

H. Dörrie & M. Baltes (1998), *Der Platonismus in der Antike*, Vol. 5: *Einige grundlegende Axiome. Platonische Physik (im antiken Verständnis)*, Stuttgart: Fromann-Holzboog.

G. L. Dossetti (1967), *Il simbolo di Nicea e di Costantinopoli. Edizione critica*, Rom – Freiburg: Herder.

W. L. Dulière (1970), 'Protection permanente contre des animaux nuisibles assurée par Apollonius de Tyane dans Byzance et Antioche. Evolution de son mythe', in *Byzantinische Zeitschrift*, 63, p. 247–277.

A. Ehrhard (1898), rec. Papadopoulos-Kerameus 1895, in *Byzantinische Zeitschrift*, 7, p. 609–611

J. Finegan (1964), *Handbook of Biblical Chronology: Principles of Time Reckoning in the Ancient World and Problems of Chronology in the Bible*, Princeton: PUP.

F. X. Funk (1907), 'Pseudo-Justin und Diodor von Tarsus', in: F. X. Funk, *Kirchengeschichtliche Abhandlungen*, vol. 3, Paderborn: Schöningh.

S. Gerber (2000), *Theodor von Mopsuestia und das Nicänum: Studien zu den katechetischen Homilien*, Leiden: Brill.

B. Gleede (2010), 'Liberatus' Polemik gegen die Verurteilung der drei Kapitel und seine alexandrinische Quelle', in *Zeitschrift für antikes Christentum*, 14, p. 96–129.

B. Gleede (2011), 'Johannes Philoponos und die christliche Apologetik. Die Widerlegungen des Proklos und Aristoteles und die Debatte des Schöpfungsproblems in der Schule von Gaza und bei Ps-Justin', in *Jahrbuch für Antike und Christentum*, 54, p. 73–97.

J.-N. Guinot (2001), 'L'Expositio rectae fidei et le traité *Sur la Trinité et l'Incarnation* de Théodoret de Cyr: deux types d'argumentation pour un même propos ?', in *Recherches Augustiniennes*, 32, p. 39–74.

A. von Harnack (1901), *Diodor von Tarsus. Vier pseudojustinische Schriften als Eigentum Diodors nachgewiesen*, Leipzig: Hinrichs.

J. Heidman (1880), *Iulianos Der Abtrünnige: Syrische Erzählungen*, Leiden: Brill.

G. W. Lampe (2001), *A Patristic Greek Lexicon*, Oxford: Clarendon.

J. Lebon (1930), 'Restitutions à Théodoret de Cyr', in *Revue d'Histoire Ecclésiastique*, 26, p. 523–550.

Y. Papadogiannakis (2006), 'Instruction by Question and Answer: The Case of Late Antique and Byzantine Erotapokriseis', in S. Johnson (ed.), *Greek literature in late antiquity: dynamism, didacticism, classicism*, Aldershot: Ashgate, p. 91–106.

B. Pouderon (2005), 'Le pseudo-Justin, ou la constitution d'un corpus apologétique pseudépigraphe', in S. Crogiez-Pétrequin (ed.), *Dieu(x) et Hommes: Histoire et iconographie des sociétés païennes et chrétiennes de l'Antiquité à nos jours*, Rouen: Publications de l'Université de Rouen et du Havre, p. 49–67.

A. Rey (2004), 'Les Erotapokriseis dans le monde byzantin: Traduction manuscrite des textes anciens et production des nouveux textes', in A. Volgers (ed.), *Erotapokriseis: Early Christian Question-and-answer Literature in Context*, Leuven: Peeters, p. 165–180.

C. Riedweg (2001), 'Iustinus Martyr II (Pseudo-justinische Schriften)', in *Reallexikon für Antike und Christentum*, 19, p. 848–873.

G. Rinaldi (1989), 'Tracce di controversie tra pagani e cristiani nella letteratura patristica delle quaestiones et responsiones', in *Annali di storia dell' esegesi* 6, p. 99–124.

A. M. Ritter (1965), *Das Konzil von Konstantinopel und sein Symbol: Studien zur Geschichte und Theologie des II. Ökumenischen Konzils*, Göttingen: Vandenhoeck.

L. van Rompay (1993), 'Romanos le Mélode. Un poète syrien à Constantinople', in J. den Boeft & A. Hilhorst, *Early Christian poetry. A collection of essays*, Leiden et al.: Brill, p. 283–296.

D. Runia (1989), 'Festugière Revisited: Aristotle in the Greek Patres', in *Vigilia Christiana*, 43, p. 1–43.

A. Schor (2011), *Theodoret's people. Social Networks and Religious Conflict in Late Roman Syria*, Berkeley: UCP.

W. Speyer (1974), 'Zum Bild des Apollonios von Tyana bei Heiden und Christen', in *Jahrbuch für Antike und Christentum*, 17, p. 53–63.

P. Toth (2014), 'New questions on old answers: towards a critical edition of *Answers of the Orthodox* of Pseudo-Justin', in *Journal of Theological Studies*, 65, p. 550–599.

S. Voicu (2015), 'Due Antiocheni periferici: Le *Quaestiones et responsiones ad orthodoxos* (CPG 6285) e Severiano di Gabala', in *Augustinianum*, 55, p. 543–557.

C. Zamagni (2013), 'Is the Question-and-Answer literary genre in early Christian literature a homogenous group?', in M. Bussières (ed.), *La litterature des questions et réponses dans l'antiquité profane et chrétienne: de l'enseignement à l'exégèse*, Turnhout: Brepols, p. 241–289.

Abstract

This paper offers a historical contextualisation of the five collections of questions and answers and two polemical treatises transmitted under the name of Justin the philosopher and martyr. After a discussion of the literary form and unity of each text, the question of authorship is tackled and it is argued that all the collections under discussion can be attributed to a single, Nestorian author. Finally, the historical milieu of this author is outlined and a date between 451 and 519 is proposed.

MARCELO D. BOERI

IS THE PRIME MOVER THE SOURCE OF ALL MOVEMENT? PSEUDO-JUSTIN ON ARISTOTLE'S UNMOVED MOVER*

1. *Introduction:*
Does the Cosmos Need an Unmoved Prime Mover in Order to Maintain its Order and Regularity?

The view that there must be an Unmoved Prime Mover (UPM) of the cosmos is one of the best known and most discussed Aristotelian tenets from antiquity onwards.[1] Theophrastus, the head of the Lyceum after Aristotle's death, was the first to object to this theory. His crucial point against Aristotle concentrates on what had been one of the key problems of Platonism: to examine whether or not there is a *mutual* connection – i.e. an association or communication – between the intelligible and the natural (i.e. physical) domains (κοινωνία πρὸς ἄλληλα τοῖς τε νοητοῖς καὶ τοῖς τῆς φύσεως; Theophrastus, *Metaphysics* 4a9–11).

---

* I am grateful to the editors of this volume for their invitation to contribute a paper for this book. Special thanks go to Bram Demulder for his suggestions, objections, and careful editing work. This piece is a partial result of the Fondecyt project 1150067 (Chile).

[1] Already in antiquity this thesis was widely discussed from different philosophical and interpretative traditions. A very broad set of interpretations (followed by a critical discussion) of the ancient (Theophrastus, Alcinous, Plutarch, Alexander of Aphrodisias, Plotinus, Proclus, Themistius), medieval (Averroes, Thomas Aquinas), Renaissance (Zabarella, Fonseca), and contemporary traditions (Hegel, Bonitz, Brentano, Guthrie, Ross, Tricot, Owens, Elders, Natali) can be found in Berti 1997, p. 66–75. For thoughtful discussions of how the UPM exerts its causal action (whether as a final or a moving cause) see Broadie 1993; Berti 1997 and 2000a; Natali 1997; Laks 2000. The interpretation of Aristotle's UPM by Averroes and Alexander of Aphrodisias has been treated again by Berti 2000b, especially p. 229–241.

According to Theophrastus, it is most reasonable to think that there is a connection (συναφή) between the intelligible and the perceptible realms.[2] In fact, if a decisive assumption of Aristotelian ontology is that there are two kinds of domains (intelligible and perceptible), it would be absurd if there were no connection between them.[3] Now if there is such a connection, and if there is an 'order of beings' (some of them being prior, and others posterior), then some items must work as principles, while others should be subordinated to them (the latter items are taken to be destructible and the former indestructible).[4] Theophrastus remarks that, given that bodies moving in circles are many and that their movements of locomotion somehow are opposed and infinite, the issue regarding the 'impulsion' (or simply 'desire') of such movement[5] is simply obscure, and does not seem to be a suitable account of the cosmic changes.[6] If the mover is one, Theophrastus insists, it seems absurd that it does not move all the things with the same kind of movement. And if in each motion

---

[2] Botter has convincingly insisted on this point (cf. her 1999, p. 42; 62).

[3] One might argue that this problem goes back to Plato and is based on his view that that there are some (reasonable) ways to connect both domains through participation (μέθεξις; μετάσχεσις), presence (παρουσία), and association (κοινωνία). See Plato, *Phaedo* 100d5–6, 101c5–6; *Sophist* 250b9, 251e8–9, 256b1–2, 257a9, 259a7; *Parmenides* 132d3, 140e4, 152a2, 158d4, 160a8. In spite of the fact that, as is well-known, Aristotle is particularly critical of the notion of 'participation', I think that Plato's effort to attempt to connect what is intelligible with what is perceptible is part of the heritage Aristotle himself takes for granted when he argues that if all substances are destructible, all things are destructible (cf. Aristotle, *Metaphysics* 1071b5–6 and the next note).

[4] Theophrastus, *Metaphysics* 4a13–17. To be sure, this Theophrastean argument draws on what Aristotle himself argues when introducing his view that there must be an 'eternal unmovable substance' (*Metaphysics* 1071b4–5: ἀνάγκη εἶναι ἀίδιόν τινα οὐσίαν ἀκίνητον, this substance being the UPM): given that οὐσίαι are the first of existing things, if all the substances are destructible, all things are destructible. The basic idea is that there must be a primary and indestructible thing in order to warrant that not all the things are destructible, a view that clearly stems from Plato (*Phaedo* 65d–69d) and that Aristotle considers again and incorporates into his argument about the UPM.

[5] Towards 'the better', i.e. towards the UPM (see Theophrastus, *Metaphysics* 5a15: ἔφεσις; cf. also 11b27: τῆς εἰς τὸ βέλτιον ὁρμῆς).

[6] The use of the word ἔφεσις to signify the impulsion or tendency of something towards an end (or 'what is better') is not very common in Aristotle, but there is at least a passage where it is used by him in this sense; see *Nicomachean Ethics* 1114b5–6: ἡ δὲ τοῦ τέλους ἔφεσις οὐκ αὐθαίρετος.

there is a different mover, the principles will be multiple as well, which is also absurd, since if there are many principles, there cannot be a unique principle, i.e. there cannot be a Prime or First Mover, which is supposed to be unique, according to Aristotle.[7] Theophrastus' objection clearly attacks Aristotle's conception of the UPM as the unique, ultimate, and final cause that is responsible for the cosmic movement. And if his criticism is at all reasonable, the 'solution' Aristotle offers for explaining the connection between the UPM and the perceptible world seems seriously jeopardized. In other words, what Theophrastus is questioning is the very possibility of the existence of the UPM.

I have started this paper by pointing out one of the basic criticisms advanced by Theophrastus against the Aristotelian UPM because this kind of objection makes it clear that already in the Lyceum (maybe during Aristotle's life), there were challenges to the thesis that there must be a πρῶτον κινοῦν that guarantees and accounts for the movement of the cosmos, its order, and regularity. In addition, this brief reference to Theophrastus is helpful for my purposes here because such a criticism somehow paves the way for two objections addressed by Pseudo-Justin against Aristotle's theory of the πρῶτον κινοῦν: (i) there is no need to introduce a UPM in order to explain the whole movement of the universe insofar as there are some things (such as heaven and, more specifically, heavenly bodies) that, in being *natural* things, should have the principle of movement in themselves.[8] So, the UPM would be a superfluous cause for the movement of those things. (ii) Theophrastus, like Pseudo-Justin later, casts doubts on the distinction Aristotle makes between the rotating movement of the heavenly spheres and the rectilinear movement of the terrestrial elements, this way advancing the idea that the

---

[7] Theophrastus, *Metaphysics* 5a20–21. On the difficulties of this line see Botter, 1999, p. 46. As observed by Botter, if the desire is the best one, 'it must be one, aimed at a single object, the best in fact, for one is the best desire, the desire for the best'. In other words, there cannot be a different desire for each mover. Thus, the harmony or concordance of the rotating bodies (i.e. the heavenly bodies) moving towards the 'best desire' is not obvious at all (τὸ σύμφωνον αὐτῶν εἰς ὄρεξιν ἰόντων τὴν ἀρίστην οὐθαμῶς φανερόν).

[8] Note that this objection is based on an Aristotelian assumption: if x is a natural item, x must have the principle of movement in itself. See Aristotle, *Physics* 192b12–14 and *Metaphysics* 1025b18–21.

'laws' ruling over the heavenly things must be the same as the laws ruling over the terrestrial ones.[9]

The focus of this paper is on the critical analysis of Aristotle's UPM thesis carried out by Pseudo-Justin, a (possibly) fifth-century philosopher who devoted a whole treatise (*Confutatio dogmatum quorundam aristotelicorum*) to undermining some of the basic tenets of Aristotle's cosmology (including the doctrine of the UPM).[10] I will provide the bulk of Pseudo-Justin's criticism, and argue that at least part of his most important objections is reasonable, inasmuch as they are based on Aristotelian assump-

---

[9] Cf. Theophrastus, *Metaphysics* 5b–6a. Theophrastus' objection is mainly focused on Aristotle's UPM understood as a final cause. On this issue see Berti 2005, p. 58–67, who challenges the view that there is a *cosmic* teleology in Aristotle. See also Ross & Fobes 1929, p. 13–14. For a full discussion (both philological and philosophical) of the Theophrastus passage cited at the beginning of this note cf. Gutas 2010, p. 285–303. Of course, neither Theophrastus nor Pseudo-Justin speak in terms of 'laws' of movement in the sense we tend to understand by the word 'law'. They are rather thinking of a 'principle (or principles) of change'. As conveniently observed by Bram Demulder, both authors also seem to be interested in 'problematizing' (cf. the numerous occurrences of the verb ἀπορέω and its cognates both in Theophrastus' *Metaphysics* 5a23; 9b2; 8a21, b13 *et passim* and in Pseudo-Justin, *Confutatio* 113D6; 145B7) more than in *solving* the problems which they indicated. I am grateful to Demulder for this remark.

[10] The Greek title of Pseudo-Justin's treatise is ΑΝΑΤΡΟΠΗ ΔΟΓΜΑΤΩΝ ΤΙΝΩΝ ΑΡΙΣΤΟΤΕΛΙΚΩΝ (I shall be quoting the treatise by its Latin title *Confutatio dogmatum quorundam aristotelicorum*, abbreviated *Confutatio*). I cite Pseudo-Justin's *Confutatio* through Otto's edition of the Greek text (see Otto 1969). The issues regarding the authorship of the treatise have been discussed by von Harnack 1901, p. 240–245, and 1958, p. 99–114; famously von Harnack suggested that the author hidden behind Pseudo-Justin must be Diodorus of Tarsus (death around 390 AD). Funk 1902, on his part, has argued that the author of the *Confutatio* might be Theodoret of Cyrus, who probably died in 466 AD (a view that, as recalled by Toth 2014, p. 572, dates back to Sixtus, 1566, and Sylbung, 1593). Recently, Martín 2000, p. 137 has suggested again Theodoret of Cyrus as a possible author. In the last few years Bydén and Toth have returned to the problem of the authorship of the *Confutatio* and other treatises associated to Pseudo-Justin. Bydén, for example, interestingly observes that the *Confutatio* is the text where 'Aristotle is singled out as a prime culprit in the Christian confrontation with eternalism' (see his 2013, p. 161; Bydén thinks that our treatise should be assigned to the Alexandrian or Gazan milieux, particularly to Procopius of Gaza and Zacharias Mitylenensis, where he detects 'some tenuous, but interesting parallels', p. 161 n. 49). In his erudite 2014 paper, Toth presents and analyzes several proposals regarding the authorship (including those of Martín 2000, Riedweg 2001, and Gleede 2011, cited by Toth 2014, p. 580–581; interestingly, Gleede dates the *Quaestiones et responsiones ad orthodoxos* to the sixth century; see Toth 2014, p. 581, and Gleede in this volume).

tions and conceptual categories. While developing Pseudo-Justin's objections to Aristotle, I will be referring to some of the crucial passages in Aristotle's *Physics* VII–VIII and *Metaphysics* XII where the theory of the UPM is developed and explained. To be sure, in his *Confutatio* Pseudo-Justin only cites passages taken from Aristotle's *Physics* and *De caelo*. But in order to clarify Pseudo-Justin's arguments, I shall be quoting and commenting on some passages of Aristotle's *Metaphysics*.

My main concern in this essay is with the argumentative and conceptual framework within which the debate between Pseudo-Justin and Aristotle takes place (of course, the one who critically discusses Aristotle is Pseudo-Justin, and there is no reply in this 'debate'). What I mean is that, regardless of the many problems that the *Confutatio* involves (authorship, dating, and so on), it is a treatise where 'Byzantine philosophy' can be found. This is because there is no doubt that, in his writing, Pseudo-Justin engages *philosophically* with another philosopher. And while in the important book on Byzantine philosophy edited by Ierodiakonou in 2002, Pseudo-Justin is not mentioned even once, I hold that his treatise can be taken as an affirmative answer to the question 'Is there philosophical thinking in Byzantium?'[11] In other words, if Pseudo-Justin can be considered a 'Byzantine author' (if, as suggested by one of the alternatives considered by Ierodiakonou,[12] one assumes that Byzantine philosophy began early on in the fourth century), then I would say that his writing is a good example of 'Byzantine philosophy'.

Although I believe that the core of Pseudo-Justin's criticisms of Aristotle is sound (and for the most part they are 'internal arguments', i.e. arguments taking as their premises Aristotle's assumptions and conceptual developments[13]), Pseudo-Justin is not always charitable when citing passages from Aristotle. For example, on some occasions he omits – probably consciously – a section that would be detrimental to his critique of Aristotle. But I claim that he does so within reasonable limits and as it would be done by

---

[11] Ierodiakonou 2002, p. 1.

[12] Ierodiakonou 2002, p. 3.

[13] Such as the one pointed out above with regard to the capacity natural entities have concerning self-movement.

any philosopher interested in making a critical analysis of what another one says. Pseudo-Justin's critical examination of Aristotelian cosmology is, as usual among philosophers, designed to prove that his own standpoint is the most reasonable.

Even though his general view is not explicitly stated, it is pretty clear. (i) Time and movement are not eternal.[14] (ii) Matter – both sublunary and heavenly – has come into being. (iii) If this is so (and Pseudo-Justin believes that matter has been generated and provides some reasons which endorse his view[15]), the ether, the material component of heavenly bodies, does not exist (or it does not exist having the features Aristotle ascribes to it).[16] From this it follows (iv) that the heavenly bodies are not eternal either, and hence that (v) there cannot exist an UPM of change that is everlasting and that *continuously* sets the cosmos in motion.[17] While arguing in favor of (i), (ii), (iii), and (iv), Pseudo-Justin is explicitly denying the fundamentals of Aristotelian cosmology. Unfortunately, in so far as he does not develop a cosmology based on the rejection of these points, he does not *explicitly* propose an alternative model of the cosmos.

The upshot of Pseudo-Justin's criticism of the Aristotelian cosmology, I think, is that he anticipates a crucial tenet of Modern natural science in the seventeenth century: the laws governing the changes and movements of the terrestrial world rule the heavenly movements as well.[18] Of course, both Aristotle and Pseudo-

---

[14] Cf. Bydén 2013, p. 160–162.

[15] See *Confutatio* 116B-C, 145C and Boeri 2009, p. 105–106, 113–116.

[16] A full discussion of Aristotle's doctrine of ether (and the eternity associated to it) can be found in Wildberg 1988, p. 9–16, 37–38, 88–90.

[17] As is well-known and as I will discuss below, the eternity of heaven somehow justifies the existence of a mover (the UPM) that continuously moves: if the motion of heaven is continuous, it needs a cause of its motion that is continuous, too.

[18] Although I agree with Falcon when he states that 'while Aristotle [...] argues that the celestial world is radically different from the sublunary world, he is not envisioning two disconnected, or only loosely connected, worlds' (Falcon 2005, p. ix), and that Aristotle takes the study of the sublunary *and* the celestial world to form the single science of nature (p. 2; see also p. 8–13, 23–29), it seems to me that Pseudo-Justin's objections aim at a new consideration of the natural domain according to which there must be a sort of 'homogenization' of the principles ruling over the whole natural world. This is an important point in the consideration of the new picture of the natural domain that arises from Pseudo-Justin's

Justin reach their conclusions from a purely speculative viewpoint and in the framework of a philosophical debate. Yet this is so, one might assume, because they had no empirical science, an important point that shouldn't be overlooked when assessing the value of ancient explanations of the natural world.

2. Aristotle's View that there must be an Ultimate Principle of Change and Pseudo-Justin's Arguments against Aristotle's Unmoved Prime Mover

After dealing in detail with the issue of causality in *Physics* II.3, Aristotle analyzes again the four types of cause (in *Physics* II.7) and emphasizes the fact that the formal, final, and moving causes often coincide.[19] He also stresses that this only applies to that which moves and is moved; in other words, this procedure exclusively works in the domain of physics. Physics, according to Aristotle, is the scientific discipline that investigates beings which have in themselves the principle of both movement and rest.[20] The relations of causality existing among such entities presuppose that what is able to act upon something is also acted upon by what is caused.[21] As is well-known, Aristotle lays out three disciplines: (i) the one dealing with unmovable entities (that is,

criticism to Aristotle. Of course, I am not suggesting that this result is consciously sought out by Pseudo-Justin, but that his objections lead to those consequences.

[19] See Aristotle, *Physics* 198a24–26 where he argues that the causes understood as matter, form, mover, and that for the sake of which (τὴν ὕλην, τὸ εἶδος, τὸ κινῆσαν, τὸ οὗ ἕνεκα) often coincide (or 'come to only one thing': ἔρχεται δὲ τὰ τρία εἰς [τὸ] ἓν πολλάκις), 'for the what and that for the sake of which are one, while the primary source of motion is the same in species as these' (Revised Oxford Translation).

[20] Aristotle, *Metaphysics* 1025b18–21: ἡ φυσικὴ ἐπιστήμη [...] τὴν τοιαύτην ἐστὶν οὐσίαν ἐν ᾗ ἡ ἀρχὴ τῆς κινήσεως καὶ στάσεως ἐν αὐτῇ (see also *Physics* 192b20–22).

[21] This point is part of the conclusion of the argument developed by Aristotle in *Physics* VII.1. The first three chapters of *Physics* VII intend to show that the natural (or physical) movement entails the 'move-being moved relation', and this is so because what originates movement must be in touch with what is moved; in other words, there is no (physical) movement at distance: what physically moves is at once moved physically (see *Physics* 202a5–7, 243a32–33: Τὸ δὲ πρῶτον κινοῦν, μὴ ὡς τὸ οὗ ἕνεκεν, ἀλλ' ὅθεν ἡ ἀρχὴ τῆς κινήσεως, ἅμα τῷ κινουμένῳ ἐστί; on the meaning of ἅμα in this line see Manuwald, 1971, p. 103; 108–109 and Wardy 1990, p. 121–123).

'first philosophy'),[22] of which the object is the study of the intelligence of spheres, god, and pure forms in general; (ii) the discipline which treats the moving but indestructible entities (i.e. astronomy), of which the object of study is the heavenly bodies along with their movements, and (iii) the branch of philosophy focused on entities subject to generation and destruction, i.e. all the phenomena that take place in the sublunary sphere (physics).[23]

An important part of Aristotle's project is to show that the physicist will have to deal with *all* the forms of causality in order to explain physical phenomena (*Physics* 198a21–25). However, Aristotle claims, the principles of natural movement are of two kinds: one of them belongs to those things that move, but being moved;[24] the other one is not physical, i.e. such a principle is that which causes movement (or change) without itself moving (or changing). This must be the UPM, or, as Aristotle says in this passage, 'that which is absolutely unmovable' (what moves without being moved[25]), and 'what it is', that is, the form. According to a venerable interpretative tradition (that dates back to antiquity and that to some extent has been endorsed by contemporary scholarship), in *Physics* VII–VIII Aristotle's basic concern was to prove the necessity of the existence of the UPM, the ultimate principle that is able to explain the origin of the cosmic move-

---

[22] *Physics* 192b34–36, 194b13–15. *Metaphysics* 993a15–16, 1003b36–1004a8, and 1061b29–33, where the first philosophy is identified with 'wisdom' (σοφία). This last passage belongs to book XI of Aristotle's *Metaphysics*. Although some scholars have raised doubts about the authenticity of this book, this issue is irrelevant for my argument since Aristotle makes or suggests the same identification between first philosophy and wisdom in other passages (982a19–28, 987b27–29).

[23] Cf. Aristotle, *Metaphysics* 1026a6–32, 1073b1–8, 1077a1–9. See also *Metaphysics* 1069a30-b2, where Aristotle distinguishes two kinds of substances (or 'beings': οὐσίαι): (i) one that is perceptible (which is divided into eternal and perishable, and is 'recognized by everyone'); (ii) another one that is immovable (ἀκίνητος; Forms, mathematical objects). The substances included in (i) belong to physics (for they are accompanied by movement), but the unmovable substance belongs to 'another' science, i.e. first philosophy. In fact, Aristotle claims that 'there are as many parts of philosophy as there are kinds of substance, so that there must necessarily be among them a first philosophy' (*Metaphysics* 1004a2–3; Revised Oxford Translation). For the 'sublunar and the upper region' of Aristotle's universe see, among other passages, *Meteorologica* 340a17-b14, 342a27–33; *De caelo* 278b10–18.

[24] *Physics* 198a27: ὅσα κινούμενα κινεῖ.

[25] *Physics* 198a28–29, b1–2.

ment, and that does not depend upon another thing to impart its movement to the other things.[26] I will provide shortly some of Aristotle's main justifications of this suggestion. But before doing that, let me lay out a critical remark made by Pseudo-Justin against the Aristotelian thesis concerning the distinction between the discipline dealing with unmovable entities, and the branch of philosophy focused on the moving and destructible things just sketched above.

In *Confutatio* 128A-C, Pseudo-Justin cites and comments on *Physics* II 7, 198a35–198b3[27] (where we find the distinction of principles that are able physically to impart movement). In this context Aristotle analyzes the problem of causality again and emphasizes the (already mentioned) fact that all the forms of causality 'often can coincide'. Furthermore, Aristotle focuses on the fact that this can be applied to what is able to move *and be moved* (what in the strict sense is physical) as well as to what is able to move *without being moved*. Pseudo-Justin's criticism points to what seems to be a basic weakness (or at least a problem) in

---

[26] See Philoponus, *In Arist. Phys.* 888, 18–889, 2. Philoponus' argument runs thus. (i) If movement of parts that are subject to generation and destruction is continuous and uninterrupted (συνεχής ἐστι καὶ ἀδιάκοπος), there must be a certain eternal cause and principle, and such a principle is, for what is generated and destructible, the cause of their continuous change. (ii) If there were not an eternal and unchangeable cause (τι ἀίδιον καὶ ἀμετάβλητον αἴτιον), those things that always are partially (κατὰ μέρος) generated and destroyed would not be generated and destroyed continuously and in an uninterrupted way (συνεχῶς καὶ ἀδιακόπως), and they both would be generated and move according to their own movements. In other words, the existence of an eternal cause and principle guarantees the permanent generations and destructions of the entities belonging to the empirical world. For a similar assessment in contemporary scholarship see Verbeke 1969, p. 250, 252. Ross 1979, p. 85. Solmsen suggests that *Physics* VIII presents the Aristotelian version of the cosmological first principle, and states that that book was composed by Aristotle in order to replace book VII, where Aristotle presents a first effort to find a way to the First Mover (see Solmsen 1960, p. 222 n. 1). Natali, on his part, maintains that *Physics* VIII 'presents a discourse of *theological* content, whose purpose is to demonstrate the existence of an unmoved mover' (italics are mine; see his 1974, p. 116). If Natali is right, it still must be explained why Aristotle never uses the word 'god' in these passages. Certainly, it should be recalled that within the *Physics* the word θεός appears twice (239b15, 262a3), but it is never related to or meant to imply the UPM. Aristotle identifies his UPM with god in *Metaphysics* 1072b18–30. This is a novelty of *Metaphysics* XII.

[27] διτταὶ δὲ αἱ ἀρχαὶ αἱ κινοῦσαι φυσικῶς, ὧν ἡ ἑτέρα οὐ φυσική· οὐ γὰρ ἔχει κινήσεως ἀρχὴν ἐν αὑτῇ. τοιοῦτον δ' ἐστὶν εἴ τι κινεῖ μὴ κινούμενον, ὥσπερ τό τε παντελῶς ἀκίνητον καὶ [τὸ] πάντων πρῶτον καὶ τὸ τί ἐστιν καὶ ἡ μορφή.

Aristotle's general model of physics: the way in which the intelligible can be related to the perceptible. Aristotle's view is that there is a principle of natural (or physical) movement that is *not* physical. Pseudo-Justin's point is that it is not clear how it is possible that a non-physical principle can produce a physical movement.[28]

So Pseudo-Justin's objection is sound, it seems to me, insofar as it is reasonable to think (within a certain physicalist approach) that a non-physical factor cannot be a causal principle of what is physical (a view that surely is alien both to Aristotle and the Platonic tradition). But in Aristotle's opinion, the point is precisely this one: in order to avoid a 'movers-moved-things' *regressus ad infinitum*, it is feasible to posit an ultimate principle which is not reducible to another principle, and towards which all the movements are directed. The fact that such a principle is posited outside the perceptible domain removes the difficulty of a causal principle that, when acting upon something, also is acted upon and requires the presence of another causal factor which can explain it. In the passage quoted by Pseudo-Justin, Aristotle (according to the traditional view) seems to hold the tenet that the UPM is the final cause of every change.[29] What Pseudo-Justin's remark

---

[28] On this point see again Theophrastus' incisive remarks (*Metaphysics* 4a5–17) and Botter 1999, p. 47: 'the problem is to know how the movement is transmitted by the First Principle to the First Heaven, that is, how an unmovable mover can move'. As clearly and convincingly stated by Gutas 2010, p. 255–256, if the connection between the intelligible and perceptible realms is doubted, the universe would be episodic and disjointed.

[29] The UPM as a final cause of every change seems to be suggested by Aristotle when he talks of the UPM as 'what moves as an object of love' (*Metaphysics* 1072b3: κινεῖ δὴ ὡς ἐρώμενον; against the view that with this expression Aristotle is suggesting that the UPM is a final cause see Berti 1997, p. 64–65 and 2000a, p. 203; for the traditional view that regards this passage to indicate that the UPM is a final cause see Botter 1999, p. 47–48). The idea that the UPM is a moving cause appears to be suggested in *Metaphysics* 1071b12: κινητικὸν ἢ ποιητικόν. For discussion see Broadie 1993 and Berti 1997 and 2000a, who defend the view that the UPM is a moving, not a final cause. However, as shown by Natali 1997, p. 107, both κινοῦν and κινητικόν can mean and are used by Aristotle as signifying a final cause. In *Physics* VIII the UPM is a moving cause, although there is a brief (but significant) advance that it must be understood in terms of a final cause or, rather, as a cause that does not presuppose contact to move (cf. *Phys.* 256b20–27). Maybe the problem can be 'solved' if one follows the distinction (suggested by Aristotle in *On Generation and Corruption* 323a28–324a34, b9–17, cited by Laks 2000, p. 222 n. 40 and p. 241) between efficient causes that require a move-

appears to be challenging, reading between the lines, is that the very thesis of the causal effect of an immaterial entity on a material one (a view that will be widely debated in the Hellenistic period, and explicitly rejected by the Stoics) is doubtful.

Let us come back to Aristotle's arguments for the necessity of the existence of a UPM as the first and ultimate cause in the movers-moved series. Perhaps the demonstration of the existence of the UPM is the purpose of *Physics* VII.1, but as it has been reasonably pointed out,[30] all that Aristotle shows here is that the movement of a whole somehow depends upon the movement of its parts. When we turn to *Physics* VIII, it is clear that what Aristotle intends to show is (i) that the movement (or change: κίνησις) has always existed and will always exist (and hence time must be eternal), and (ii) that the nature of the cause on which this fact depends should be explained. While trying to account for this, Aristotle suggests (ii.i) that there is just one cause of every change, (ii.ii) that such a cause is not subject to change (i.e. it is an 'unmoved' cause), (ii.iii) that the power of such a cause is infinite, and (ii.iv) that such a cause has no magnitude and hence is an immaterial item. In *Physics* VIII.4 Aristotle is intent on proving that the first agent of any movement should be distinguished from the first (or 'proximate') agent of a particular effect, and in this way leads the discussion toward the UPM doctrine. Following the same line of reasoning, the next chapter develops the view that the mover-moved series cannot be infinite, rather it must come to an end (this view had been advanced in *Physics* VII.1).[31]

---

ment and the other efficient causes that do not require any movement, but continue to be moving causes. As observed by Salis 2005, p. 401, the first one who suggested that heaven would move for the sake of the UPM was Alexander of Aphrodisias (cf. *Quaestio* 18.62.23–24, 19.63.18–21, cited by Salis 2005, p. 401 n. 138). For discussion of the manner in which Alexander's reading is received by other interpreters in Antiquity, including Themistius and Pseudo-Alexander (probably Michael of Ephesus), see Salis 2005, p. 402–414.

[30] Wardy 1990, p. 118 n. 25.

[31] Cf. *Physics* 242b71–72: ἀνάγκη ἵστασθαι καὶ εἶναί τι πρῶτον κινοῦν καὶ κινούμενον ('[The mover-moved series] must be stopped, and there must be a first mover and a first moved'). Aristotle furnishes the following example: a stick moves the stone and is moved by the hand, which is moved by the person (who is moving the stick). So, the stick will not move unless the person moves it. This proves that the person must be a first agent of movement, that is, an agent which is not moved by something else (*Physics* 256a6–8). So, even though one can say that the stone

The first mover must be unmoved; otherwise the mover-moved series would proceed *ad infinitum*. The argument is more sophisticated, but this account suffices for my purposes.

When turning to Pseudo-Justin's objections in the *Confutatio* against Aristotle's theory of the UPM, the first thing to be noted is that there is no mention of the argument of the mover-moved series, which is so important for the Aristotelian theory to make plausible the idea that there must be a *first* mover of change, and that such a first mover must be *unmoved*.[32] It would be risky to conjecture why Pseudo-Justin omits commenting on this relevant detail in Aristotle's argument. However, I hazard the guess that he probably adopted this line of reasoning because he was mainly interested in rebutting Aristotle's cosmological picture (including, of course, the doctrine of the UPM). As I have already argued above and elsewhere,[33] what is appealing in Pseudo-Justin's argumentative strategy is that he starts discussing the Aristotelian cosmology by taking some premises and arguments accepted by Aristotle. This being so, the virtue of Pseudo-Justin's objections lies in the fact that he uses Aristotelian arguments to show that some of Aristotle's stances are wrong. On the other hand, Pseudo-Justin has his own agenda – a fundamental point of which being the view that the cosmos started to exist at a point of time and that the cause of the cosmos is God, the creator of the world. If this is so, one should assume both that Pseudo-Justin had distinct kinds of reasons for opposing the claim that both movement and time are eternal, and that his Christian agenda indeed was relevant in his whole discussion. If Aristotle is right and there is an unmoved principle of every change in the universe (a cause that is everlasting and exerts its causal powers at all times), one should accept that movement and time are eternal, which goes

---

is moved both by the last (the stick) and the first of the movers, it is more strictly moved by the first (the person who moves the stick), since the first mover moves the last, and not *vice versa*. Therefore, if there is a first agent of movement, there is no need of another agent of movement, and thereby the mover-moved series is not infinite (ἀνάγκη τι εἶναι κινοῦν ὃ οὐχ ὑπ' ἄλλου πρῶτον, εἰ δὲ τοιοῦτο τὸ πρῶτον, οὐκ ἀνάγκη θάτερον; *Physics* 256a12–17).

[32] See Aristotle, *Metaphysics* 1012b31, 1026a10, 1071b5, 1072b7, 1073a24–30; *Physics* 198b2, 201a27, 256b20, 258b4–5, 258b11–14, 259a21.

[33] Boeri 2002, p. 20–21; 2009, p. 101–102.

against the view that God created the world at a point of time which was its beginning.[34]

Indeed, Pseudo-Justin's motivations against Aristotle's cosmology can be inspired by his Christian beliefs. But this is not enough to prove that there is not an entity such as the UPM, or that there must not be an ultimate principle of change. Certainly, although one could argue that Pseudo-Justin's motivations against Aristotle are guided by his belief in a God who created the world (a God who clearly cannot be identified with Aristotle's UPM), the author of the *Confutatio* provides arguments to show that Aristotle's view on the UPM is wrong. That is the point on which I will be focused in what follows: I will explain some of Pseudo-Justin's arguments against Aristotle's UPM and in doing so I will underline the 'Aristotelian flavor' of such arguments.[35]

As I have already stressed in the previous section of this paper, in *Metaphysics* XII.6–7 Aristotle states that the UPM must be primary, eternal, and unmovable. He also tries to prove that the UPM cannot be a movement, but it must be an actuality (*Metaphysics* 1071b12–14: μὴ ἐνεργοῦν δέ τι, οὐκ ἔσται κίνησις· ἐνδέχεται γὰρ τὸ δύναμιν ἔχον μὴ ἐνεργεῖν). A crucial point in Aristotle's argument is the alleged eternity of the UPM: if movement always existed, its cause (or 'explanatory principle') should have existed

---

[34] Moreover, Aristotle states that there must always be something actual that is able to produce a change. If this were not the case, movement would go on *ad infinitum*. That which is always actual and has the power to produce change *without being changed* is the UPM; but if in fact there is an eternal cause that is *continuously* producing change, the movement should be everlasting (i.e. if there is a causal factor continuously imparting movement, the movement should be continuous; see Aristotle, *Physics* 252b10–12, 256a17–19, 28–29).

[35] The arguments are mainly contained in *Confutatio*, chapters 43–44. As I have already noted, the criticism of the ether as the material ingredient of the celestial bodies is crucial for undermining the necessity of the existence of an UPM as a causal-explicative factor of the world (I have dealt with this matter in Boeri 2009, p. 126–131). If this is so, Pseudo-Justin's criticism against the UPM also ends up destroying the fundamentals of Aristotle's theory of the celestial world. The clever strategy of Falcon is to argue in favor of the view that, even though Aristotle believes in the existence of celestial and sublunary natures, he does not believe in the *uniformity* of nature (Falcon 2005, p. 29, p. 37 n. 9, p. 87–89). This allows Falcon to show that there is a connection between both domains, although each realm has its own peculiarities.

always, and if it has existed always, it must be continuous.[36] But Pseudo-Justin addresses what I take to be a rather clever response to Aristotle; let us consider the following arguments:

A[1]:   *The argument of the superfluity of the UPM*

(*a*) If the UPM moves with a movement of locomotion (in fact, it sets the 'first heaven' in motion, i.e. the heaven of the fixed stars),[37] and (*b*) if we assume that

---

[36]   Cf. Aristotle, *Metaphysics* 1071b9–11; *Physics* 259a14–20.

[37]   The 'first heaven' or 'that which is first moved', as Aristotle calls the first heaven (i.e. the heaven of fixed stars), is everlasting and is set in motion by the Prime Mover (see Aristotle, *Physics*, 259b33–260a1; cf. *Metaphysics* 1072a23 and *De caelo*, 288a15, with Solmsen's comments 1982, p. 275–276). In *Physics* 259b32–260a19 Aristotle is at pains to show the relation of the UPM to the world through the first moved, and he insists that there must be a certain affinity between the causal and the caused factors. Thus, if the UPM is eternal, the first moved must be eternal as well. In other words, what is straightforwardly moved by the UPM is the first heaven, and what is moved by heaven (the sun), due to the fact that it at one time is at rest and at another time in motion, is not a cause of movement itself. When the sun approaches, it is a cause of this determined movement, and when it moves away it is cause of another movement. If this is so, Aristotle claims, sometimes it will produce rest and sometimes movement (cf. *Physics* 194b13; *Metaphysics* 1071a15–16; *On Generation and Corruption* 336a31–2, b17–18; see also Themistius, *In Phys. para.* 224.32–225.4). Heavenly bodies do not attain 'what is ultimate' (οὐ γὰρ ἀφικνεῖται πρὸς τὸ ἔσχατον), i.e. the Prime Mover ('the ultimate principle'), but to a certain extent they can attain the 'divine principle' (μέχρι ὅτου δύναται τυχεῖν τῆς θειοτάτης ἀρχῆς; *De caelo* 292b21–22). According to Berti 2005, p. 59–60, the 'divine principle' is not the UPM, but 'the best condition possible for each star'. It is true that, as remarked by Berti, in Aristotle 'divine' is a synonym of 'blessed and eternal, since the most divine condition, even for the stars, is a blessed and eternal life, which is warranted by the continuous movement' (p. 60). However, this does not explain why Aristotle uses the word 'principle' in the expression δύναται τυχεῖν τῆς θειοτάτης ἀρχῆς. By contrast, the first heaven attains what is ultimate 'directly through a single movement' (εὐθὺς τυγχάνει διὰ μιᾶς κινήσεως; 292b23). The bodies that are intermediate between the first heaven and the ultimate spheres attain the ultimate principle, but they do that through a multiplicity of movements. That is to say, if the Prime Mover moved things one after another, it would move them in succession, and the whole movement would not be continuous anymore, but successive. On this last point, see the appealing account by Philoponus (*In Phys.* 888, 5–16), who emphasizes the fact that if Aristotle states that movement must be eternal (ἀνάγκη ἀεὶ εἶναι κίνησιν), it should exist always. And if this is so, movement must be (ἀνάγκη) continuous and eternal (συνεχῆ εἶναι καὶ ἀίδιον). For if there is not an eternal movement, there will be an interval and hence movements will be successive (ἐφεξῆς), not continuous (συνεχεῖς). But Aristotle has proved that movement is eternal, and if this is the case, it is continuous, and if continuous it must be one. If Philoponus is right (and I think he is), Aristotle infers the uniqueness of the UPM from the continuous action it imparts.

the movement of locomotion is a property of heaven, (*c*) and that heaven is a natural body (φυσικὸν σῶμα), and (*d*) that such a body has in itself *by nature* the principle of its natural movement (φυσικῶς τῆς κατὰ φύσιν κινήσεως τὴν ἀρχήν),[38] it must follow that heaven has been moved superfluously (περιττῶς) by the UPM with a movement of locomotion.[39] In other words, if heaven is supposed to be a natural entity and thereby is able to move by itself, the UPM is not needed in order to set it in motion. As is clear, Pseudo-Justin, taking as his point of departure Aristotle's view that natural entities have in themselves the principle of movement (see *Physics* 192b13–14), shows that, if a natural body does not need anything different from itself in order to be moved, the causal power of the UPM is superfluous. And if UPM's causal power is superfluous, the UPM itself, as an explanatory entity, is superfluous as well, which is the same as saying that the UPM does not explain the movement of heaven.

Indeed, Pseudo-Justin's main purpose is to make it clear that, *according to Aristotle's own premises*, there is nothing that sets the heaven in motion. And if this is the case, there is not a UPM, or if it exists, it does not set the heaven in motion. An important ingredient of Pseudo-Justin's reasoning against Aristotle's UPM is to argue against Aristotle's assumption that heaven is composed of ether, the fifth element (actually, Pseudo-Justin simply identifies heaven with ether: διὰ τὸ εἶναι αὐτὸν [i.e. οὐρανός] πέμπτον στοιχεῖον; *Confutatio* 140C3): a basic feature of ether is that it is able to move itself, without the aid of anything else, and if this is the case, the UPM is superfluous.[40]

---

[38] In fact, inasmuch as its elemental component is ether, which is moved by itself by nature, heaven has in itself the principle of movement.

[39] Cf. *Confutatio* 140A-D; the same argument is offered in 143C.

[40] To some extent, this argument draws on what Theophrastus says when he also (indirectly) claims that the existence itself of the UPM is superfluous (see *Metaphysics* 10a22-b24). Theophrastus, like Aristotle, also regarded the connection between the intelligible and the sensible as being problematic (especially if in such a connection a principle such as the UPM is involved), but necessary: even though the principle that ultimately accounts for the change of the whole

This last remark allows me to turn to another point that Pseudo-Justin is interested in highlighting: the permanence of heaven and the heavenly bodies is a basic Aristotelian tenet which holds that, even though they are material substances, they are everlasting; and this is so because their material element, ether, is everlasting as well.[41] Further on (*Confutatio* 143C–144B), Pseudo-Justin will argue against this thesis and will try to show that there are no clear reasons to maintain that an element whose circular movement is eternal (i.e. ether) exists, or that such an element is the material component of the heavenly bodies. But before discussing Pseudo-Justin's other arguments against Aristotle, let me recall some issues that appear at the very beginning of his *Confutatio* that can be important for our understanding of his 'anti-Aristotelianism'.

The opening section of the *Confutatio* presents a distinction between (i) those 'who admitted the teaching deriving from God Himself' and (ii) 'those who distrusted the words transmitted through the prophets and are committed to the discovery of the knowledge of God through their own proper argumentations' (*Confutatio* 111A-B: οἱ μὲν παρ' αὐτοῦ τοῦ [...] θεοῦ τὴν διδασκαλίαν ἐδέξαντο [...] οἱ δέ, τοῖς διὰ τῶν προφητῶν ἀπιστήσαντες λόγοις, τοῖς οἰκείοις αὐτῶν λογισμοῖς ἐπέτρεψαν θεογνωσίας τὴν εὕρεσιν). Probably one might read here an implicit dispute between Christian and pagan thinkers, and the effort of Pseudo-Justin to show that the revealed truth is enough for the true knowledge of the empirical world as well as that of God. What is interesting is that his arguments meant to highlight the weaknesses of Aristotle's

---

universe is that which is object of desire (and because of that it is not subject to be moved), it should have an effective connection with the perceptible realm. As suggested by Aristotle himself, the UPM, in being an object of desire, sets straightforwardly in motion the first heaven (and incidentally the terrestrial things), but *without being in touch with* heaven. This is the advantage of the understanding of the UPM in terms of 'final cause' (see Aristotle, *Metaphysics* 1072b3, where the UPM is characterized 'as object of love'; cf. n. 29). Aristotle also says that good examples of what moves without being moved are what is object of desire and of thought (*Metaphysics* 1072a26–27: κινεῖ δὲ ὧδε τὸ ὀρεκτὸν καὶ τὸ νοητόν· κινεῖ οὐ κινούμενα). In *De anima* 433a15–433b1 he provides a clear account of how thinking works in terms of 'object of desire' (ὀρεκτόν; even though there he is not talking – at least not manifestly – about the UPM of the universe). By contrast, in *Physics* VIII. 5–6 the UPM never is identified with what is object of desire.

[41] See Aristotle, *De caelo* 270b20–25, 302b3–5; *Meteorologica* 339b23–27.

thesis, but following some criteria belonging to the pagan thinkers (although one can also find some presuppositions of an underlying Christian ontology, which Pseudo-Justin makes use of to try to weaken some basic Aristotelian stances: the eternity of time, of movement and hence of the world). According to Pseudo-Justin, those defending the view (i) hold the following theses: (*a*) God is one and (*b*) ungenerated; (*c*) there has been no god or gods before Him (i.e. the God Pseudo-Justin is thinking of); (*d*) there is nothing co-eternal, underlying, or opposed to God; (*e*) God possesses an incorruptible essence and has an unimpeded activity; (*f*) He is the demiurge or artisan of the world (whose principle of being and of how it persists is God's will). Almost all these views, though, had been posited and discussed by the pagan thinkers.

Thesis (*a*) dates back to the Eleatic tradition.[42] To some extent, stance (*b*) can be linked to Aristotle himself, who argues that form (εἶδος) is ungenerated (*Metaphysics* 1033a24-b9). Moreover, insofar as the Aristotelian god is an immaterial entity and somehow can be considered as a form (and thereby without matter or potentiality; cf. *Metaphysics* 1071b18–21), it is ungenerated. Besides, Aristotle describes the life of his god as an activity (ἐνέργεια; *Metaphysics* 1071b18–21), which implies that such activity should be unimpeded (cf. point (*e*)). Unlike what Pseudo-Justin seems to think, Aristotle does not believe that his god can go against the impossible: insofar as Aristotle's god is completely rational, it cannot violate the basic laws of thought. By contrast, Pseudo-Justin suggests that, given that God produces all limits, He cannot be limited, and hence He is not impeded by a necessity which imposes a limit (*Confutatio* 113E–114A). One could suspect that the implicit suggestion is that God can produce whatever He wants, including impossible things. Thesis (*d*) is like what Aristotle says about his notion of substance (οὐσία); in fact, the Aristotelian οὐσία has no opposite or something which underlies it (*Physics* 189a29; a32–33). Finally, the distinguished forerunner of view (*f*) clearly is Plato, who maintains that a demiurge

---

[42] See Xenophanes, cited by Clement of Alexandria, *Stromateis* V.109 = B23 DK; Aristotle, *Metaphysics* 986b21–25 = A30 DK; Cicero, *Academica* II.118 = A34 DK.

(i.e. a god) has produced the world out of a certain underlying disorder,[43] that is, the Platonic demiurge 'creates' the cosmos deploying its causal and rational action by imposing order in some preexisting material that is disorganized. Of course, both (c) and (f) have some genuine ingredients coming from Pseudo-Justin's cultural world: as far as I can see, there are no antecedents in Greek thought of the idea that that God's *will* is the principle of being, essence, and permanence of finite substances. Having clarified these points, we can now turn to Pseudo-Justin's second argument against Aristotle's UPM.

A²: *Argument against Aristotle's thesis of the priority of loco-motion*

In this section I shall present and discuss a set of arguments (addressed by Pseudo-Justin against the UPM) that focus on Aristotle's view that locomotion is the primary movement.[44] I divide the whole argument into five sub-arguments (A²·¹, A²·², A²·³, A²·⁴, and A²·⁵); the chief tenet that Pseudo-Justin intends to set forth is that Aristotle's view that locomotion is the primary movement is false (this is A²·¹). Once he has shown (or thinks he has proved) that locomotion cannot be the primary motion, he proceeds to discuss the manner in which the UPM imparts its movement on the first heaven and tries to argue that the manner in which eternal items (both the UPM and heaven, i.e. the heavenly bodies contained in 'heaven') are related to each other is not clear at all; this is A²·². A²·³ returns to the problem of how the UPM moves the first heaven and challenges the idea that it moves with a *continuous* movement. A²·⁴ completes the previous sub-argument by emphasizing the relation between the heavenly things and their movement, and finally A²·⁵ deals again with the finite character of locomotion.

A²·¹: In *Physics* VIII.5–6 Aristotle had pointed out the possibility of the existence of a continuous movement. Actu-

---

[43] See Plato, *Timaeus* 30a4–5: κινούμενον πλημμελῶς καὶ ἀτάκτως, εἰς τάξιν αὐτὸ ἤγαγεν ἐκ τῆς ἀταξίας.

[44] Actually, what Aristotle intends to prove is the priority of the *circular* movement in respect of place (see *Physics* VIII.9).

ally, he thinks that such a kind of movement must exist; otherwise, the causal power of the UPM, which moves continuously, could not be explained. In *Physics* VIII he states that there is a continuous movement (the demonstration of this view is carried out in *Physics* VIII.8), and that such movement is the circular movement with respect to place (*Physics* 260a26–29). This discussion (which is considered to be a 'fresh start': 260a20) follows what Aristotle had dealt with in the previous chapter, where he had suggested that the UPM acts directly upon the 'first moved' with an everlasting motion (cf. 259b32–260a1).[45] Locomotion (φορά) must be the primary movement since it is the sort of movement that must be presupposed by any other mode of change.[46]

Now in *Confutatio* 140E–142E Pseudo-Justin critically comments on *Physics* 260b15–261a7, where Aristotle tries to show that locomotion is primary. According to Aristotle, locomotion (i.e. movement in accordance with place) is prior to all the other kinds of movements (including increase and decrease, since when a thing is increased or decreased its magnitude changes with respect to place; 260b13–15). But 'prior', Aristotle claims, can be understood in several ways: from an ontological standpoint, x is prior to y when, if x does not exist (οὗ τε μὴ ὄντος; *Physics* 260b18), y will not exist, while x can exist without y.[47] In addition, x can

---

[45] As noted by Berti 1985, p. 124, interpreters (both ancient and modern) have observed that the eternity of motion that Aristotle demonstrates in *Physics* VIII is rather the eternity of successive movements, where the most representative example is the changes that occur in the sublunary world, not the absolutely continuous movement performed by the first heaven. This may have some serious implications for Aristotle's general argument when he wants to argue in favor of the UPM as a cause of the continuous movement of the sphere of the fixed stars. This is relevant since Aristotle is worried about distinguishing continuous from successive movement; in fact, even if a successive movement was an infinite chain of successive causes, it could not be a cause of the continuous change of universe.

[46] This is Themistius' (appealing) suggestion (*In Phys. para.* 225.21–25).

[47] This is the so-called 'asymmetrical existential dependence': the existence of y requires the existence of x, but the converse does not hold (see Irwin 1995, p. 81). For this meaning of 'priority' see also Aristotle, *Metaphysics* 1019a2–4. The ontological priority underlines the ontological independence of οὐσία in respect of its 'accidental' determinations, which cannot exist separated from it

also be prior in time and in substance (i.e. in the meaning of οὐσία as 'form'; τὸ τῷ χρόνῳ, καὶ τὸ κατ᾽ οὐσίαν; 260b19). Pseudo-Justin aims at proving that the Aristotelian stance of a UPM as an ultimate cause of change of the cosmic movement is false, and to do so he attempts to question the priority of the movement of locomotion. What Pseudo-Justin realizes is that, if it is possible to show an inconsistency in the alleged priority of locomotion, the way for his attack against Aristotle's UPM theory will be paved. According to Aristotle, the circular locomotion describes perfectly well the kind of movement the UPM imparts: a movement that is eternal, one, identical, regular, continuous,[48] and primary.

But Pseudo-Justin objects: if what increases (τὸ αὐξανόμενον) is generated (γενητόν), and if locomotion increases *because of a certain amount of movement* (τῷ ποσῷ τῆς κινήσεως), locomotion cannot be eternal. Pseudo-Justin attempts to take advantage of the ambiguity of the term 'increasing' (αὔξεσθαι), that can be said of what, in general, increases (such as a plant, an animal or any other entity of the sublunar domain) and, in a specific sense, of movement with respect to locomotion (in fact, one can speak of 'more or less movement with respect to place'). Thus a body that moves with respect to place has different places in which it 'produces increase of movement'; in other words, what Pseudo-Justin is warning is that locomotion increases due to the amount of movement, and given that increase is the capacity to change, one might say that locomotion 'increases' due to the amount of its movement: if quantity increases, locomotion increases, if quantity decreases, locomotion decreases. Thus, locomotion increases, but if it increases, it cannot be eternal (*Confutatio* 141C-D). Of course, Aristotle could have several responses to this argument,[49] but Pseudo-Justin's argumentative strategy is

(cf. *Metaphysics* 1028a22–24, 1028b36–37). In reality, *x* is ontologically prior to *y*, but *y* 'is' or 'exists' in the sense of something that does not exist by itself or has strictly an essence and thereby cannot be defined by itself.

[48] Not successive, since what is in succession is not continuous (*Physics* 259a16–17: καὶ γὰρ τὸ ἀεὶ συνεχές, τὸ δ᾽ ἐφεξῆς οὐ συνεχές).

[49] (i) In Aristotle's view any kind of increasing or decreasing is a kind of locomotion (think of the increase of a plant). Actually, Aristotle thinks that without locomotion there cannot be increase, since when something is increased (or decreased) its magnitude (or quantity) changes in respect of place (see *Physics*

a helpful device to show that if locomotion has its own being in coming to be and in being destroyed (actually, this is the core of Pseudo-Justin's criticism),[50] then locomotion ('whose not-being always precedes its being'; *Confutatio* 141D-E: ἧς ἀεὶ προηγεῖται τοῦ εἶναι τὸ μὴ εἶναι) is not eternal, since every change comes into being according to a change of what is not yet, but of what will be. Besides, if every locomotion is finite (because of the past), and all that is finite necessarily has a beginning (and all that is generated has a beginning), it follows that locomotion is generated (*Confutatio* 141E–142A).

If this set of objections is reasonable, locomotion cannot be prior to the body that is being moved: locomotion is locomotion of a moved body, and if locomotion cannot be prior to the moved body, then what is moved (τὸ φερόμενον) also is generated (*Confutatio* 142A1–2). So, if (i) all locomotion is finite, (ii) every finite thing has a beginning, and (iii) what has a beginning is subject to generation, it follows (iv) that locomotion must be generated. But if locomotion is generated, it cannot be considered the primary form of movement, form of movement that is imparted by the UPM.

A[2.2]: The next sub-argument (related to the alleged priority of locomotion) is specifically focused on the UPM and the manner in which it imparts its causal action upon the first heaven: if, in the domain of what is eternal, one thing (i.e. the UPM) only moves, and the other (i.e. the first heaven) only is eternally moved *with a movement of locomotion*,[51] it is impossible that what does not have a beginning (i.e. heaven) is moved with a movement having a beginning (i.e. by locomotion that, according to the previous argument, has a beginning). In other words,

---

260b14–15); (ii) Pseudo-Justin does not take into consideration the different senses of 'primary' (explicitly considered by Aristotle in the passage at stake); (iii) Aristotle does not understand 'increase' as 'an amount of movement', although it is true that, in a certain sense, it can be said that locomotion in itself 'increases' due to a bigger amount of movement developed by what is undergoing locomotion.

[50] *Confutatio* 141D5–6: ἐν τῷ γίνεσθαι καὶ ἀπογίνεσθαι τὸ εἶναι ἔχει.

[51] *Confutatio* 142A3–4: Εἰ ἐν τοῖς ἀϊδίοις τὸ μὲν μόνον κινεῖ, τὸ δὲ μόνον κινεῖται ἀϊδίως τὴν κατὰ φορὰν κίνησιν.

it is impossible that something (supposedly) eternal, such as heaven, is moved by a movement which is not eternal. Moreover, Pseudo-Justin goes on to argue, if that without which none of the other things exist (i.e. the UPM) is prior to all the other things, it is not clear how it can be said that it is ungenerated. What is absurd, he seems to suggest, is to apply a temporal category ('prior', 'posterior') to what is ungenerated. According to Pseudo-Justin, the other point that turns out to be absurd is to assume *at the same time* that there is something which is both ungenerated and prior to something which is eternal (heaven) in the realm of what is everlasting. That is to say, it does not appear reasonable to argue that *x* is prior to *y* if both *x* and *y* are eternal. If that were the case, one probably should think of 'levels of eternity', so to speak, which seems to be absurd.[52]

A[2.3]: The third sub-argument concentrates, in a more detailed way, on the manner in which the UPM moves the first heaven: (i) if it is said that the UPM moves with a *continuous* movement, and (ii) if the movement with which the UPM moves is neither according to nature (for, as it has been shown in A[1], it is superfluous insofar as heaven moves because of ether, its material natural component) nor against nature (since movement against nature is posterior to that according to nature),[53] therefore there is nothing that imparts movement with a *continuous* movement (*Confutatio* 142B8: οὐκ ἄρα κινεῖ τὴν συνεχῆ κίνησιν οὐδέν). This conclusion can be conflated with the conclusion of A[1], where Pseudo-Justin presumes to have proved that the causal power of UPM is superfluous, which aims

---

[52] Perhaps Aristotle could reply that 'prior in time' and 'prior from the ontological point of view' are not the same (see *Physics* 184a16–23; *Posterior Analytics* 71b33–72a4). But even in this case he still would have to prove the ontological priority of the UPM to heaven (something that would be easy insofar as heaven is moved by the UPM).

[53] This is almost explicitly recognized by Aristotle when arguing that disorderly movement means unnatural movement (τὸ ἀτάκτως οὐθέν ἐστιν ἕτερον ἢ τὸ παρὰ φύσιν; *De caelo* 301a4–5). See also *De caelo* 286a18–19, where he emphasizes that 'what is against nature is posterior to what is according to nature' (ὕστερον δὲ τὸ παρὰ φύσιν τοῦ κατὰ φύσιν).

at pointing out that actually there is no UPM. Thus, if there cannot be a factor which is able to move with a continuous movement, and if the UPM is supposed to be the only entity capable of moving with such a kind of movement, and it has been proven that there is nothing that moves that way, it must follow that the UPM does not exist.

A[2.4]: This argument is closely related both to A[2.2] and A[2.3] (insofar as it also makes use of the priority-posteriority category as applied to the different kinds of entities under consideration). But A[2.4], unlike the other arguments, seems to be particularly focused on the priority-posteriority relation existing between the heavenly things ('the eternal things that are subject to movement'; *Confutatio* 142B8-C1: τῶν ἀϊδίων κινουμένων) and their movement. The argumentation runs thus: (i) if, in the domain of the moved eternal things, movement is neither prior to the moved things (i.e. the celestial things) nor are they prior to movement, and (ii) if every movement exists according to a change of what is not yet, but will be,[54] it follows that all the things subject to movement have their being (or existence: τὰ κινούμενα πάντα ... τὸ εἶναι ἔχοντα) from a change that is not yet, but will be.

A[2.5]: The last argument I shall consider deals again with the finite character of locomotion; Pseudo-Justin takes as his point of departure the results of his previous argumentation: locomotion is both the primary movement of what is generated and the last of its movements (*Con-*

---

[54] This is another way to make reference to locomotion. See *Confutatio* 141C2: κατὰ μεταβολὴν τοῦ μήπω ὄντος ἀλλὰ μέλλοντος. This premise is Aristotelian in character; according to Aristotle *every* movement (or change) proceeds 'from something to something' (see *Physics* 224b1, 224b35–225a1, and 234b10–11, among many other places). But that does not mean that every movement is finite or limited: the circular or rotatory motion also proceeds 'from something to something', but Aristotle is intent on proving that it is everlasting (see *Physics* VIII.9). The case of rectilinear motion (the sort of motion Pseudo-Justin seems to be thinking of) is different, because the opposites are (or have to be) the limit of every change or movement (ἀνάγκη πάσης μεταβολῆς εἶναι πέρας τὰ ἐναντία; *Physics* 252b10–12). Aristotle develops this view in *Physics* VIII.9, where he argues that the line traversed (by a moving thing, for instance) in rectilinear movement cannot be infinite because there is no such thing as an infinite straight line (265a17–18).

futatio 142C5–6: ἡ φορὰ ὑστάτη τῶν κινήσεων). Thus if there must be another prior thing (heaven; presumably prior to its rotary movement) that moves and is moved [55] according to locomotion (i.e. φορά, but in the sense of 'rotatory locomotion'), a prior thing that, in being ungenerated, also is a cause of generation (πρότερον, ὃ καὶ τῆς γενέσεως αἴτιον ἀγένητον ὄν), then it is not clear how it is possible that the same item is the cause of generation according to nature and against nature. In other words, this other thing that is cause of generation and is ungenerated is heaven, and if locomotion is the last movement of what is subject to generation, and heaven [56] moves with a rotatory movement, it cannot be understood how the same thing can be cause of so distinct movements (movement according to nature and against nature; *Confutatio* 142C5-D1). And this is so because the UPM (what in a *primary* sense is cause of generation) cannot be generated, but 'what is moved in a primary sense [i.e. heaven] is moved so in the generation of what is primarily generated, such as later it was moved in the generation of what derives from that' (*Confutatio* 142D2–4: τὸ πρότερον κινούμενον οὕτως ἐκινεῖτο ἐπὶ τῆς γενέσεως τοῦ πρώτως γινομένου, ὡς ὕστερον ἐκινήθη ἐπὶ τῆς γενέσεως τῶν ἐξ ἐκείνου).

The general outcome of this complicated argument is the following alternative: either what is moved in an 'ungenerated manner' (ἀγενήτως; i.e. heaven) is not the cause of every generation or the UPM does not move with a continuous movement. Both alternatives will entail the destruction of Aristotle's cosmological model: no matter whether heaven is the cause of every generation (under the sphere of the moon) or whether UPM does not move with a continuous movement. The causation system of heaven as well as the UPM will be eliminated.

[55] In *Confutatio* 145C6 I take the word κινούμενον to be ambiguous (in the sense of 'heaven *moves* the heavenly things contained in it', and 'heaven *is moved* by the UPM').

[56] An ungenerated thing that is a cause of generation, according to Aristotle himself.

3. Epilogue:
How Effective are Pseudo-Justin's Arguments against Aristotle's Unmoved Prime Mover?

To conclude, I would like to stress again that, in so far as Pseudo-Justin's objections start from some of the fundamental premises of the Aristotelian cosmological model, one could say that his arguments are quite effective against Aristotle and his view of the UPM as the ultimate cause of movement of the cosmos. A point that sometimes is regarded as being negative when a philosopher attempts to reject what another philosopher states is that the one who intends to turn down the view of another one takes as his departure point premises that are alien to the author who is under scrutiny or is being criticized. But Pseudo-Justin seems to be aware of that fact and apparently tries to avoid it: if he takes as his departure point premises that are foreign to Aristotle's basic assumptions, his critique will not be reasonable or will be weak. Of course, I am not suggesting that Pseudo-Justin's objections are equally clear and cogent in all the cases: as I have pointed out above, Aristotle might respond quite well to some of the critiques contained in the *Confutatio*. I am just suggesting that Pseudo-Justin appears to have realized that, from a methodological standpoint, *ex hypothesi* he had to consider as true Aristotle's cosmological premises. Otherwise, his rejection of the Aristotelian cosmological model would be especially weak.

Finally, as I have already indicated above, both Aristotle and Pseudo-Justin develop their arguments on the cosmos and the UPM in a purely speculative manner. This can be easily explained from the fact that they had no empirical science of nature, but that does not mean that what Aristotle and Pseudo-Justin argue is not 'scientific'. From the standpoint of ancient philosophers, the procedure they follow is scientific since they provide reasons for endorsing their own theses. To be sure, Pseudo-Justin proceeds within the Aristotelian rationale, but with a peculiar concern for showing that the thesis of the existence of an eternal body (heaven) that is eternally moved by an UPM does not *necessarily* follow from Aristotle's cosmological premises.

Bibliography

E. Berti (1985), 'La suprématie du mouvement local selon Aristote: ses conséquences et ses apories', in J. Wiesner (ed.) *Aristoteles. Werk und Wirkung* (Erster Band. Aristoteles und seine Schule), Berlin – New York: Walter de Gruyter, p. 123–150.

E. Berti (1997), 'Da chi è amato il motore immobile? Su Aristotele, *Metaph.* XII 6–7', *Méthexis*, 10, p. 59–62.

E. Berti (2000a), 'Unmoved mover(s) as efficient cause(s) in *Metaphysics* Λ 6', in M. Frede & D. Charles (eds), *Aristotle's Metaphysics Lambda. Symposium Aristotelicum*, Oxford: Clarendon Press, p. 181–206.

E. Berti (2000b), 'Il movimento del cielo in Alessandro di Afrodisia', in A. Brancacci (a cura di), *La filosofia in età imperiale. Atti del Colloquio, Roma, 17–19 giugno 1999*, Napoli: Bibliopolis, p. 225–243.

E. Berti (2005), 'La finalità in Aristotele', in E. Berti, *Nuovi studi aristotelici. II Fisica, antropologia e metafisica*, Brescia: Editrice Morcelliana, p. 37–67.

M. D. Boeri (2002), *Pseudo Justino. Refutación de ciertas doctrinas aristotélicas. Traducción, Introducción y comentario*, Barranáin: EUNSA (Colección de autores medievales y renacentistas).

M. D. Boeri (2009), 'Pseudo Justin on Aristotelian Cosmology: A Byzantine philosopher searching for a new picture of the world', *Byzantion*, 79, p. 99–135.

B. Botter (1999), 'Teofrasto e i limiti della teleologia aristotelica', in C. Natali & S. Maso (eds), *Antiaristotelismo*, Amsterdam: Hakkert, p. 41–62.

S. Broadie (1993), 'Que fait le premier moteur d'Aristote ?', *Revue philosophique de la France et de l'étranger*, 118, p. 375–411.

B. Bydén, (2013), '"No Prince of perfection": Byzantine anti-Aristotelianism from the patristic period to Pletho', in D. Angelov & M. Saxby (eds), *Power and Subversion in Byzantium. Papers from the Forty-third Spring Symposium of Byzantine Studies*, Birmingham: Ashgate, p. 147–176.

A. Falcon (2005), *Aristotle and the Science of Nature. Unity without Uniformity*, Cambridge: Cambridge University Press.

F. Funk (1902), 'Le Pseudo-Justin et Diodore de Tarse', *Revue d'Histoire Ecclésiastique*, 3, p. 947–971.

B. Gleede, (2011), 'Johannes Philoponos und die christliche Apologetik: Die Widerlegungen des Proklos und Aristoteles und die Debatte des Schöpfungsproblems in der Schule von Gaza und bei Ps-Justin', *Jahrbuch für Antike und Christentum*, 54, p. 73–97.

D. Gutas (2010), *Theophrastus. On First Principles* (*known as his* Metaphysics). *Theophrastus of Eresus. Sources for His Life, Writings, Thought and Influence*, Leiden: Brill.

K. Ierodiakonou (ed., 2002), *Byzantine Philosophy and its Ancient Sources*, Oxford: Clarendon Press.

T. Irwin (1995), *Aristotle's First Principles*, New York: Oxford University Press.

A. Laks (2000), '*Metaphysics* Λ 7', in M. Frede & D. Charles (eds), *Aristotle's Metaphysics Lambda. Symposium Aristotelicum*, Oxford: Clarendon Press, p. 207–243.

B. Manuwald (1971), *Das Buch H der aristotelischen Physik: Eine Untersuchung zur Einheit und Echtheit*, Meisenheim am Glan: Verlag C. H. Beck.

J. P. Martín (2000), 'Las *Quaestiones* de Pseudo Justino: un lector cristiano de Aristóteles en tiempos de Proclo', *Tópicos*, 18, p. 139–140.

C. Natali (1974), *Cosmo e divinità. La struttura logica della teologia aristotelica*, L'Aquila: Japadre.

C. Natali (1997), 'Causa motrice e causa finale del Libro Lambda della *Metafisica* di Aristotele', *Méthexis*, 10, p. 105–123.

J. K. T. von Otto (1969), *Corpus apologetarum christianorum saeculi secundi*, IV, Wiesbaden: Saendig (= Iena, 1876), p. 100–223.

C. Riedweg, (2001), 'Iustin Martyr II (Pseudo-Justinische Schriften', in *Reallexicon für Antike und Christentum*, cols. 848–873.

W. D. Ross (1979), *Aristotle's Physics. A Revised Text with Introduction and Commentary*, Oxford: Oxford University Press.

W. D. Ross & F. H. Fobes, (1929) *Theophrastus. Metaphysics*, Oxford: Oxford University Press.

R. Salis (2005), *Il commento di pseudo-Alessandro al libro Lambda della* Metafisica *di Aristotele*, Soveria Mannelli: Rubbettino Editore.

F. Solmsen (1960), *Aristotle's System of The Physical World. A Comparison with his Predecessors*, New York: Cornell University Press.

F. Solmsen (1982), 'Plato's First Mover in the Eight Book of Aristotle's *Physics*', in F. Solmsen, *Kleine Schriften*, III, Hildesheim – Zürich – New York: Georg Olms Verlag, p. 267–278.

P. Toth (2014), 'New Questions on Old Answers: Towards a critical edition of the Answers to the Orthodox of Pseudo-Justin', *Journal of Theological Studies*, 65, 2, p. 550–599.

G. Verbeke (1969), 'L'argument du livre VII de la *Physique*. Une impasse philosophique', in I. Düring (ed.), *Naturphilosophie bei Aristoteles und Theophrast*, Heidelberg: Lothar Stiehm Verlag, p. 250–267.

A. von Harnack (1901), *Diodor von Tarsus. Vier pseudojustinische Schriften*, Leipzig: Hinrichs Verlag.

A. von Harnack (1958), *Geschichte der altchristlichen Literatur bis Eusebius*, I, Leipzig: Hinrichs Verlag.

R. Wardy (1990), *The Chain of Change. A Study of Aristotle's Physics VII*, Cambridge: Cambridge University Press.

C. Wildberg (1988), *John Philoponus' Criticism of Aristotle's Theory of Aether*, Berlin – New York: Walter De Gruyter.

Abstract

The view that there must be an Unmoved Prime Mover (UPM) is at the core of Aristotle's cosmology. Theophrastus was the first to object to this theory. He paved the way for the objections addressed by Pseudo-Justin, who devoted a whole treatise to undermining some of the basic tenets of Aristotle's cosmology (*Confutatio dogmatum quorundam aristotelicorum*). The focus of this paper is on Pseudo-Justin's critical analysis of Aristotle's UPM thesis. After providing the bulk of Pseudo-Justin's criticism, I argue that at least part of his most important objections is reasonable, inasmuch as they are based on Aristotelian assumptions. My main concern is with the argumentative and conceptual framework within which the Pseudo-Justin's discussion of Aristotle takes place: I hold that Pseudo-Justin engages philosophically with Aristotle. On the other hand, Pseudo-Justin is not always charitable when citing passages from Aristotle. I claim, though, that he does so within reasonable limits and as it would be done by any philosopher interested in making a critical analysis of what another one says.

SÉBASTIEN MORLET

UNE POLÉMIQUE CONTRE PHILON D'ALEXANDRIE DANS LA QUESTION 69 *AD ORTHODOXOS* ATTRIBUÉE À JUSTIN ?*

La *Patrologie grecque* de Migne contient trois séries de questions-réponses attribuées à Justin : 1) les *Quaestiones et responsiones ad orthodoxos*[1] ; 2) les *Quaestiones Christianorum ad Graecos*[2] ; 3) les *Quaestiones Graecorum* (ou *gentilium*) *ad Christianos*, récemment rééditées par B. Gleede[3]. Les *Quaestiones et responsiones ad orthodoxos* font elles aussi l'objet d'un travail de réédition, mené par P. Toth dans le cadre de l'équipe réunie autour de Y. Papadogiannakis[4]. Ce travail modifiera en profondeur notre approche de ces textes. Nous bénéficierons sous peu d'une nouvelle édition, qui permettra de jeter un regard neuf sur la question débattue de l'auteur ou des auteurs de ce texte, et donc sur son milieu de production[5]. Les *Quaestiones ad orthodoxos* ont, la plupart du temps, été attribuées à un auteur antiochien : Diodore de Tarse[6], Théodoret[7], ou un antiochien inconnu du vᵉ siècle[8].

---

* Nous remercions Agnès Lorrain, Ioannis Papadogiannakis et Peter Toth pour les remarques précieuses dont ils nous ont fait part à propos de cet article.

[1] PG 6², col. 1249–1400.

[2] PG 6², col. 1401–1464.

[3] Voir Gleede 2020. L'ancienne édition se trouve en PG 6², col. 1464–1490.

[4] Toth 2014.

[5] Toth rappelle que les *Quaestiones* présentent une unité de style et d'intention qui indique *a priori* qu'elles ont un seul auteur (Toth 2014, p. 552).

[6] Hypothèse proposée pour la première fois en 1721 par Maturin La Croze (voir Toth 2014, p. 573). Elle fut reprise par Harnack 1901.

[7] L'hypothèse fut proposée dès le xvIᵉ siècle, pour des raisons essentiellement stylistiques, par Sixte de Sienne (voir Toth 2014, p. 571).

[8] C'est l'hypothèse que proposa en 1742 Prudent Maran dans son édition du texte (voir Toth 2014, p. 574).

Questioning the World, Greek Patristic and Byzantine Question-and-Answer Literature, ed. by Bram Demulder and Peter Van Deun,
Turnhout, 2021 (*LECTIO*, 11), pp. 127-144   ©BREPOLS✳PUBLISHERS   DOI 10.1484/M.LECTIO-EB.5.121504

Dans une partie de la tradition manuscrite, elles sont attribuées, de fait, non à Justin, mais à Théodoret. D'autres attributions ont pu être proposées, plus tardives que Théodoret[9]. Aujourd'hui, cependant, c'est l'attribution à Théodoret, ou à un antiochien du vᵉ siècle, qui est majoritaire[10].

Notre intention n'est pas ici de revenir directement sur ce problème, mais de proposer quelques réflexions sur une question abordant la thématique cosmologique. La Question 69, dans le volume de Migne, est consacrée au nombre 7 et à sa place dans la nature. Nous en donnons une traduction, sur la base du texte reproduit par Migne et correspondant à l'édition de Prudent Maran (1742) :

Ἐρώτησις ξθ′.

Διὰ τί ὁ ἑπτὰ ἀριθμὸς ἐναλλαγὴν δέχεται ; Καὶ γὰρ ἐν σαββάτῳ ὡς τὰ πολλὰ ὁ ἀὴρ μεταβάλλεται, καὶ ἡ τοῦ ἀνθρώπου κατὰ τὴν ἡλικίαν προκοπὴ ἐν τούτῳ τῷ ἀριθμῷ λαμβάνει ἐπίδοσιν, ὀδόντων μὲν φυομένων τῷ ἑβδόμῳ μηνί, τῷ δ' αὐτῷ ἔτει ἀλλασσομένων τούτων, διπλασιασθέντων δὲ πάλιν σπερματικὴν προσκτωμένων δύναμιν, καί, ἵνα συντόμως εἴπω, ὁ ἀριθμὸς τῶν ἑπτὰ τὴν αὔξησιν καὶ λῆξιν τῶν ἀνθρώπων ἐργάζεται, καὶ τῶν νοσημάτων ποιεῖται διάκρισιν, καὶ ἐν νόμῳ τῶν λοιπῶν ἀριθμῶν τὸ αἰδέσιμον κέκτηται.

Ἀπόκρισις.

Πρὸς τὴν δύναμιν τῆς φύσεως τῶν ἔργων τῆς φύσεως ἡ ἐκπλήρωσις γίνεται, καὶ οὐ πρὸς τὴν χρονικὴν παράστασιν ἑβδομάδι μηνῶν ἢ ἐνιαυτῶν ὡρισμένην. Διὸ τὰ ὀνομασθέντα ἔργα τῆς φύσεως ἐν τῇ ἐρωτήσει πολλάκις θᾶττον ἢ βραδύτερον τῶν ἑπτὰ ἀριθμῶν ἐπὶ τὴν οἰκείαν ἄγει ἡ φύσις τελειότητα· ἅπερ οὐκ ἂν ἐγίνετο, εἰ ἡ φύσις τῇ ἑβδομάδι καὶ μὴ ἡ ἑβδομὰς τῇ φύσει ἠκολούθει. Οὐχ ἡ ἑβδομὰς οὖν ἐστιν αἰτία τῆς ἐκπληρώσεως τῶν ἔργων τῆς

---

[9] Voir par exemple celle de Gleede, qui attribue les *Quaestiones* à un auteur de l'entourage de Jean Philopon (Gleede 2011) ou encore Tzamalikos, qui veut attribuer le texte à un auteur du vɪᵉ siècle, Cassien le Sabaïte (Tzamalikos 2012, p. xɪ–xɪɪ).

[10] Elle est défendue par Toth 2014. Mais Toth, dans une correspondance récente, nous a fait part de ses réserves. Actuellement, il pencherait plutôt pour un auteur anonyme plus tardif que Théodoret (fin vᵉ – début vɪᵉ siècle). Papadogiannakis nous a fait remarquer également que, à son jugement, les similitudes qui ont été relevées par la critique entre Ps.-Justin et Théodoret sont contrebalancées par de vraies différences, notamment dans l'exégèse des mêmes passages bibliques (cf. Gass 1842). Selon lui, le Ps.-Justin ne peut pas être Théodoret. Voir aussi la contribution de Gleede dans ce volume.

φύσεως, ἀλλὰ ἡ δύναμις τῆς φύσεως αἰτία τῆς ἑβδομάδος, καθ' ἣν οὖν λαμβάνει τῇ φύσει τὰ οἰκεῖα ἔργα ἐκτελέσαι. Ὡσαύτως δὲ καὶ περὶ τῶν ἄλλων ἀριθμῶν μηνῶν τε καὶ ἐνιαυτῶν, δι' ὧν ἐκπληροῦται τὸ ἔργον τῆς φύσεως ἐν τοῖς λοιποῖς ζῴοις τε καὶ φυτοῖς, ἡ δύναμις τῆς φύσεώς ἐστιν αἰτία τοῦ ἴσου χρόνου, καὶ τοῦ πλείονος καὶ τοῦ ἐλάττονος. Αἰδεσιμώτερος δὲ ἐν τῇ θείᾳ γραφῇ ὁ ἑπτὰ ἀριθμὸς παρὰ τοὺς λοιποὺς ἀριθμούς, ὅτι ἐν αὐτῷ ὁ πᾶς χρόνος τῆς τε τοῦ κόσμου ποιήσεως καὶ τῆς τοῦ πεποιηκότος αὐτὸν καταπαύσεως· ἑξὰς μὲν τῆς ποιήσεως, μονὰς δὲ τῆς καταπαύσεως. Ἵνα οὖν φυλαχθῇ ἡ μνήμη τῆς τοῦ κόσμου ποιήσεως ἐν τοῖς ἀνθρώποις, διὰ τοῦτο τιμιώτερον τῶν ἄλλων εὑρίσκειν ἔταξε τὸν ἑπτὰ ἀριθμὸν ἐν τῇ θείᾳ γραφῇ. (PG 6², col. 1309C–1312A)

Question 69.

Pourquoi le nombre sept implique-t-il un changement ? De fait, le jour du sabbat, l'air se modifie la plupart du temps. Et la progression de l'âge de l'homme augmente avec ce nombre : les dents poussent le septième mois, et elles tombent au bout du même nombre d'années. Sept ans plus tard, les hommes acquièrent la puissance de procréer. Et, pour dire les choses en un mot, le nombre sept opère augmentation et cessation chez les hommes ; des maladies, il fait le moment critique ; et, dans la Loi, il possède un caractère vénérable par rapport aux autres nombres.

Réponse.

L'accomplissement des œuvres de la nature advient du fait de la puissance de la nature et non de l'intervalle temporel délimité par une hebdomade de mois ou d'années. C'est pourquoi les œuvres de la nature mentionnées dans la question, la nature, la plupart du temps, les amène à la perfection qui leur est propre, plus ou moins vite que les sept premiers nombres. Ce qui, précisément, n'arriverait pas, si c'était la nature qui suivait l'hebdomade, et non l'hebdomade qui suivait la nature. Ce n'est donc pas l'hebdomade qui est cause de l'accomplissement des œuvres de la nature, mais la puissance de la nature qui est cause de l'hebdomade, selon laquelle chaque œuvre reçoit sa perfection de la nature. Il en va de même des autres nombres de mois et d'années, par lesquels l'œuvre de la nature s'accomplit dans les autres êtres vivants et les autres plantes : c'est la puissance de la nature qui est cause du temps égal, ou plus ou moins grand. Mais le nombre sept est plus vénérable que les autres nombres, dans l'Écriture divine, parce que c'est en lui que s'est accompli tout le temps de la création du monde et du repos de celui qui l'a créé : une hexade, pour la création, une monade, pour le repos. C'est donc pour que soit conservée la mémoire de la création du monde chez les hommes qu'il a ordonné que, dans l'Écriture divine, on trouve le nombre sept plus honorable que les autres.

Le caractère polémique de cette question est tout à fait évident. En apparence, la question posée revient à s'interroger sur la puissance du nombre 7. On attend, à la suite de cette question, un développement de type arithmologique tel qu'on en trouve, tout au long de l'Antiquité, dans les textes grecs, juifs ou chrétiens. Le cadre de ces développements est celui de l'arithmétique scolaire et philosophique, très populaire sous l'Empire romain, et très influencée par le pythagorisme : il suppose que les nombres ont des vertus ou une puissance et qu'ils peuvent, en tant que tels, être appréhendés comme des principes de la nature[11].

Or la réponse donnée dans le texte, loin de s'inscrire dans cette tradition, constitue au contraire une prise de position contre ce type de développement arithmologique. L'auteur ne répond pas vraiment à la question posée. Il préfère au contraire remettre en cause sa légitimité : ce n'est pas la nature qui suivrait le nombre 7, mais le nombre 7 qui suivrait la nature, et la meilleure preuve de ce fait serait que la plupart des événements que l'on associe au nombre 7 adviennent dans un temps qui est plus ou moins grand que l'hebdomade, mais n'y correspond pas tout à fait. C'est une remise en question fondamentale du socle pythagoricien sur lequel est fondé tout l'enseignement de l'arithmétique à l'époque impériale[12].

L'auteur est pourtant confronté à une difficulté : la Loi fait du nombre 7 le nombre le plus vénérable (allusion probable à Gen. 2. 3, où Dieu bénit le septième jour, mais peut-être aussi, plus généralement, à tous les usages du nombre 7 dans la Loi). Il répond que, si le nombre 7 est le plus vénérable, ce n'est pas pour célébrer l'hebdomade en elle-même, mais simplement pour que l'homme se souvienne des sept jours de la Création.

[11] Voir à ce propos Marrou 1948, p. 267–270 ; Kalvesmaki 2013 ; Morlet 2016, p. 123–126.

[12] Voir par exemple, sur la puissance des nombres dans le monde, le fragment B 11 de Philolaos dans la collection Diels-Kranz.

L'hostilité très marquée de l'auteur à l'égard de l'arithmologie n'est pas seulement une prise de position très forte à l'égard du monde païen. Elle constitue également une rupture par rapport à la tradition patristique. Chez Clément d'Alexandrie[13], chez Origène[14], chez Basile de Césarée[15], l'arithmologie grecque est régulièrement utilisée comme une voie d'accès aux mystères de la nature et au sens du texte biblique. Cependant, l'arithmétique grecque est alors en voie de christianisation : les auteurs connaissent les significations attribuées aux nombres par les Grecs, mais vont peu à peu les modifier, en assignant aux nombres des significations nouvelles, en rapport avec l'histoire du salut, et en fondant leurs spéculations sur des exemples pris à l'Écriture plutôt que sur des raisonnements proprement arithmologiques. Ce mouvement de christianisation de l'arithmétique est très visible de Clément à Origène[16]. Les deux textes rassemblés sous le titre *Sur l'origine de l'homme* et attribués à Basile de Césarée supposent encore un pas de plus dans cette direction : son auteur, à propos du septième jour de la Création, commence par évoquer les significations attribuées par les spécialistes au nombre 7[17], mais préfère se fonder sur les usages du nombre 7 dans l'Écriture pour associer le jour du repos de Dieu à celui de la délivrance des péchés[18]. Ainsi, écrit l'auteur, 'nous nous approprions l'hebdomade' (οἰκειούμεθα ἡμεῖς τὴν ἑβδομάδα)[19].

Le texte du Ps.-Justin s'inscrit dans le même mouvement d'appropriation de l'arithmétique, mais l'auteur va beaucoup plus loin que Basile. Ce dernier exprime déjà ses doutes sur l'utilité de l'arithmologie pour l'exégèse du texte, mais il transmet tout de même quelques théories arithmétiques, et affirme que

---

[13] Voir *Stromates* VI, 80–85.

[14] Voir par exemple *Homélies sur la Genèse* 2, 5 ; *Homélies sur l'Exode* 9, 3.

[15] Voir *Sur l'origine de l'homme* 2, 8–11. Les deux homélies qui constituent ce texte sont parfois attribuées à Grégoire de Nysse. Nous conservons sous toute réserve l'attribution à Basile, défendue dans le volume des SC 160 mais sans préjuger de sa valeur.

[16] Voir Morlet 2016, p. 135–139 : Origène commente les dimensions de l'arche de Noé d'une façon analogue à Clément, mais cherche davantage que son prédécesseur les significations des nombres dans l'Écriture.

[17] *Sur l'origine de l'homme* 2, 8.

[18] *Sur l'origine de l'homme* 2, 9–11.

[19] *Sur l'origine de l'homme* 2, 9.

'l'arithmétique est quelque chose de grand' (μέγα ἀριθμητική), dont l'Écriture contiendrait les germes.

Notre auteur, quant à lui, conteste d'une façon beaucoup plus radicale la légitimité de l'arithmologie pour la compréhension du texte biblique et de la nature. Il plaide pour une inversion de la perspective traditionnelle : ce n'est pas l'arithmétique qui expliquerait la nature, mais la nature qui expliquerait l'arithmétique ; ce n'est donc pas l'arithmétique qui peut expliquer pourquoi le nombre 7 est utilisé dans l'Écriture, mais au contraire l'exégèse du texte qui permet d'expliquer pourquoi le nombre 7 y est utilisé. L'usage du nombre 7 dans le récit de la Création n'est pas justifié par notre auteur par la mise en évidence des vertus de l'hebdomade, mais au contraire par l'intention du texte biblique, marquée par ἵνα. Il y a là un type d'explication psychologique que l'on envisage souvent comme une caractéristique des exégètes antiochiens[20]. On trouve 268 occurrences de ἵνα dans les *Questions* de Théodoret, tant sur l'Octateuque que sur les livres historiques. La plupart du temps, il s'agit d'expliquer l'intention de l'Écriture. L'idée exprimée à la fin de la Question 69 – le 7 est honoré dans l'Écriture pour que les hommes se souviennent du Créateur – trouve d'ailleurs des parallèles chez l'évêque de Cyr[21].

Une étude plus poussée doit être menée sur ce texte et sur ses sources. Une première approche permet cependant de détecter quelques échos dans la littérature patristique, mais pas de source réelle[22]. Dans l'éventail des textes que nous avons pu consulter, c'est chez Philon d'Alexandrie que l'on trouve les parallèles les plus frappants : dans le *De decalogo* (96–105), le *Legum allegoriae* (I, 8–18), et surtout le *De opificio mundi* (89–128)[23].

---

[20] Sur l'exégèse psychologique chez Théodoret, voir Guinot 1995, p. 435–438.

[21] Voir par exemple *Questions sur les Nombres* 51 (éd. Fernández Marcos & Sáenz-Badillos 1979) : Ἵνα ἀκέραιον διαφυλαχθῇ τοῦ Ἰούδα τὸ σπέρμα ; *Questions sur II Règnes* 21 (éd. Fernández Marcos & Busto Saiz 1984) : Ταῦτα δὲ εἰς τὴν τῆς εὐσεβείας καὶ εὐνομίας βεβαίωσιν εἴρηκεν, ἵνα τῶν εὐεργεσιῶν μεμνημένος θεραπεύῃ τὸν εὐεργέτην ; *Questions sur IV Règnes* 35 : ἵνα φυλαχθῇ τοῦ βασιλικοῦ σπέρματος ὁ σπινθήρ.

[22] Voir par exemple les références données par Alexandre 1988, p. 221.

[23] Sur l'usage des nombres dans l'exégèse de Philon, voir Robbins 1921 ; Staehle 1931 ; Moehring 1995. Avant Philon, Aristobule avait lui aussi disserté sur le nombre 7 à partir du repos de Dieu le septième jour (cité par Eusèbe, *Prépa-*

Les échos à Philon sont tellement précis qu'on échappe difficilement à l'impression que l'auteur juif constitue la cible directe de la Question 69. Les traités d'arithmologie conservés n'offrent pas de parallèles aussi précis[24].

---

ration évangélique, XIII, 12, 9–16). Selon Walter, il aurait puisé dans un florilège de textes poétiques relatifs aux nombres de la décade (Walter 1964, p. 166–171). L'étude de Moehring donne d'autres textes moins importants chez Philon sur le nombre 7. Voir surtout *Abr.* 28–30 ; *Her.* 221–225 ; *Spec.* I, 177 ; II, 56–59 ; *Mos.* II, 102–103 ; 209–211 ; *QEx* II, 68 ; 78. Les commentaires que Philon consacre au repos de Dieu le septième jour sont étudiés par Calabi 2011.

[24] Le traité d'Anatolius *Sur la décade* contient un développement sur le nombre 7, qui n'offre pas de parallèles aussi clairs (p. 11–14 Heiberg). Il existe des points communs plus précis entre la Question 69 et les Θεολογούμενα ἀριθμητικά de Nicomaque de Gérasa, perdus, mais largement cités dans les Θεολογούμενα τῆς ἀριθμητικῆς attribués à Jamblique, éd. Romano 1995 (voir notamment l'idée que les dents tombent au bout de sept ans : ch. 65 ; ou encore, qu'il existe dix âges de la vie comportant chacun sept ans : ch. 66 ; ou que, pour les médecins, le 7 est un nombre critique : ch. 67). Mais les points communs sont beaucoup plus nombreux chez Philon et certaines idées, évoquées dans la Question 69, manquent chez Nicomaque alors qu'elles sont présentes chez Philon (par exemple l'idée qu'il y a une influence de la lune sur l'air – cf. *infra* –, là où Nicomaque n'évoque que l'influence de la lune sur l'océan : ch. 60). Il paraît évident que Philon et Nicomaque ont une source commune (Nicomaque cite par exemple le traité de Proros le Pythagoricien, Περὶ τῆς ἑβδομάδος : ch. 57). On ne peut exclure que l'auteur de la Question 69 polémique contre cette source plutôt que contre Philon, mais c'est une hypothèse peu économique. Le seul indice qui pourrait à la rigueur l'étayer réside dans le fait qu'il évoque une théorie (la poussée des dents au bout de 7 mois) qui ne se trouve que chez Nicomaque, et non chez Philon (voir *infra*). Selon Roscher, elle remonterait au péripatéticien Straton et à Dioclès de Carystos, explicitement cités au début du développement de Nicomaque consacré au nombre 7 dans la vie humaine, tout comme dans le développement parallèle de Macrobe (*Commentaire sur le Songe de Scipion* I, 6 ; cf. Roscher 1913, p. 92–98). Ces deux développements évoquent également la division de la vie humaine en dix âges de sept ans. Roscher pense que Nicomaque et Macrobe dépendent du commentaire de Posidonios sur le *Timée* (p. 92). L'étude de Roscher contient un nombre important de textes parallèles sur les théories médicales de l'hebdomade. Voir également Roscher 1906. L'autre ouvrage mathématique de Nicomaque, conservé, lui (l'*Introduction arithmétique*), ne contient pas de développement théologique sur le nombre 7 (éd. Hoche 1866). Le développement de Philon trouve aussi des parallèles dans le traité hippocratique *Des semaines*. Mais comme Philon cite ce traité, tout comme Anatolius (voir la note suivante), il semble plus probable que l'un et l'autre dépendent, non directement d'Hippocrate, mais d'un intermédiaire. D'ailleurs le développement de Philon comporte de nombreux développements qui ne se trouvent pas dans le texte hippocratique. On trouve d'autres parallèles à Philon dans le traité hippocratique *Des chairs* 19 (les maladies s'évaluent suivant les semaines ou les fractions de semaines, les enfants changent de dents à sept ans). La fin du passage annonce un autre ouvrage consacré plus spécialement au nombre 7, qui n'est peut-être pas le traité *Des semaines*.

On pense en priorité au passage du *De opificio mundi*, qui constitue un commentaire de Gen. 2. 2–3, sur le repos de Dieu le septième jour, évoqué à la fin de la réponse du Ps.-Justin. Philon y applique le type d'exégèse que conteste l'auteur des *Quaestiones* : il cherche à expliquer la mention du septième jour en décrivant 'la nature de l'hebdomade' (τὴν ἑβδομάδος φύσιν, 90). Le commentaire de Philon comporte d'abord un long développement purement arithmétique, visant à illustrer la perfection du nombre 7 dans ses rapports avec les autres nombres (90–98). Il évoque notamment le fait que, seul de tous les nombres de la décade, le 7 n'engendre ni n'est engendré (99). Pour cette raison, note-t-il, certains philosophes l'identifient à Athéna, vierge sans mère, tandis que les pythagoriciens l'assimilent au recteur de l'univers (100). Philon essaye ensuite de retrouver la présence du 7 dans le monde :

- D'abord, dans les révolutions de la lune : il lui faut sept jours, note Philon, pour atteindre son premier quartier ; sept autres jours pour arriver en son plein, puis deux fois sept jours pour retrouver sa forme initiale (101).

- Ensuite, dans tout corps organisé, qui comporte trois dimensions et quatre limites – le point, la ligne, la surface et le volume (102).

Ces deux exemples permettent à Philon de soutenir que, dans le domaine du sensible, le nombre 7 est un nombre 'maturateur' (τελεσφόρος, 102) et qu'il fait que toutes les réalités terrestres 's'améliorent' (βελτιοῦσθαι, 101).

Philon prend ensuite un troisième exemple dans les âges de la vie humaine, qui seraient tous, selon lui, séparés par une période de sept ans : les dents poussent pendant les sept premières années ; pendant le second septénaire se constitue la semence ; pendant le troisième apparaît la barbe ; le quatrième correspond à 'l'accroissement des forces' (πρὸς ἰσχὺν ἐπίδοσις) ; le cinquième, au moment des noces ; le sixième, à l'apogée du jugement ; le septième, à 'l'amélioration et l'amplification à la fois de l'intellect

Ces remarques doivent compléter le jugement de Moehring, qui faisait l'hypothèse, chez Philon, de 'some Neopythagorean work either on arithmology in general, or on the number seven' (Moehring 1995, p. 159).

et de la parole' (βελτίωσις ἀμφοῖν καὶ συναύξησις νοῦ καὶ λόγου) ; le huitième, à la perfection dans les deux domaines ; le neuvième, à la modération et au calme ; le dixième correspond enfin au terme désirable de la vie (103). Philon s'appuie ensuite, pour illustrer ce point, sur l'autorité de Solon (dix âges de sept ans : 104) puis d'Hippocrate (sept âges de sept ans, et chute des premières dents à sept ans : 105)[25].

Après avoir montré le caractère maturateur du 7, Philon décrit son caractère harmonique (107–110). Il revient ensuite sur l'omniprésence du 7 dans la nature : 'Se trouve-t-il parmi les êtres de ce monde une partie qui n'aime pas l'hebdomade ?' (τί γὰρ οὐ φιλέβδομον τῶν ἐν τῷ κόσμῳ μέρος, 111). Philon évoque surtout le cas des sept planètes, qui agiraient sur l'air en le changeant (τρέπουσι) en saisons et qui le modifieraient (μεταβάλλουσι) selon diverses transformations dues au calme des vents, à la sérénité du ciel, à l'agglomération des nuages ou à la violence des ouragans (113). Philon donne ensuite d'autres exemples destinés à montrer l'influence des sept planètes sur la croissance des êtres vivants et des plantes (ζῷά τε αὖ καὶ φυτά, 113).

Puis il évoque le cas de la grande ourse, composée de sept étoiles, comme les Pléiades (114–115). Quand ces dernières se couchent, dit-il, on creuse les sillons pour semer. Une fois levées, elles donnent le signal de la moisson (115). Chaque équinoxe du soleil, ajoute Philon, tombe le sept du mois. La Loi commande d'organiser de grandes fêtes à chacun de ces jours, car c'est alors que tout ce que porte la terre arrive à maturité (116).

Vient ensuite un développement sur la présence du 7 dans l'homme – dans l'âme, mais aussi dans le corps (117–125). Ce développement se termine par une allusion à diverses doctrines que Philon prête à Hippocrate, et notamment l'idée que les maladies graves atteignent leur point critique le septième jour (ἑβδόμῃ μάλιστά πως ἡμέρᾳ διακρίνονται, 125). L'ensemble se termine par une illustration du nombre sept au sein des disciplines de la culture (126–127).

---

[25] Citation du traité *Des semaines* 5. Le même témoignage d'Hippocrate est évoqué à cet égard par Anatolius à propos du nombre 7 (*Sur la décade* p. 13. 23 Heiberg ; texte cité dans les Θεολογούμενα τῆς ἀριθμητικῆς attribués à Jamblique, 55–56). L'édition de Littré donne la citation de Philon seule comme témoin du texte grec du traité *Des semaines* (Littré 1853, p. 636).

Conclusion : le nombre sept 'a reçu dans la nature les honneurs les plus hauts' (τιμὰς μὲν ἔλαχεν ἐν τῇ φύσει τὰς ἀνωτάτω, 128), il est le nombre le plus honoré chez les Grecs comme chez les barbares, et Moïse l'a honoré spécialement dans la Loi, en ordonnant l'abstention des travaux le septième jour (128).

Le premier livre des *Legum allegoriae* développe des idées similaires : 'la nature se réjouit de l'hebdomade' (χαίρει δὲ ἡ φύσις ἑβδομάδι, 8). Il y a sept planètes. Les phases de la lune se font en sept jours. Elle produit des changements dans l'air (μεταβολὰς ἐργάζεται), surtout par ses formes hebdomadaires. Les âges de l'homme correspondent à des périodes de sept ans (10). Il y a sept parties dans l'âme (11). Le corps présente sept mouvements, sept viscères et sept membres (12). 'Dans les maladies, le septième jour est le plus critique' (ἔν γε μὴν ταῖς νόσοις κριτικωτάτη ἑβδομάς, 13). Le 7 se retrouve dans les arts (14). De tous les nombres, il est le plus parfait (15). Ce développement, beaucoup moins long que celui du *De opificio*, en reprend la matière et la logique générale, mais sous une forme nettement résumée.

Le *De decalogo* donne un exposé encore plus succinct, insistant avant tout sur l'excellence du nombre 7 et l'existence des sept planètes (102–105).

Ces différents textes de Philon, notamment celui de *De opificio*, contiennent des parallèles précis avec la Question 69 du Ps.-Justin. La question proprement dite présente, avec ce texte, les points communs suivants :

– L'idée selon laquelle le nombre 7 indiquerait le changement (= *De opificio*, 101–102).
– L'exemple des âges de la vie (= *De opificio*, 103).
– L'allusion aux modifications que le nombre 7 provoquerait chez les hommes (= *De opificio*, 115–116).
– L'idée selon laquelle le septième jour est le jour critique dans le cas des maladies (= *De opificio*, 125).
– L'idée enfin, selon laquelle la Loi aurait honoré le 7 d'une façon particulière (= *De opificio*, 128).

On le voit, ces idées sont évoquées dans la question initiale dans l'ordre où elles apparaissent dans le texte de Philon, ce qui constitue un indice supplémentaire, et fort, en faveur d'une dépendance littéraire de la Question 69 à l'égard de Philon ou d'un texte très semblable aux réflexions de Philon[26]. Par ailleurs, l'expression 'pour le dire en un mot' témoigne probablement du fait que l'auteur de la Question résume un propos plus long[27]. Le texte présente de fait tous les traits d'un résumé : des dix âges de la vie, il n'évoque que les deux premiers, et, là où Philon parle du septième jour comme du jour critique pour les maladies *graves*, l'auteur de la Question parle simplement des 'maladies', sans plus de précision.

La réponse consiste par ailleurs à réfuter la thèse qui est au fondement des commentaires de Philon : celle selon laquelle, d'après les *Legum allegoriae*, 'la nature se réjouit de l'hebdomade'. Mais la phrase de conclusion de la réponse n'est pas très éloignée du point de vue proposé par Philon à la fin de son propre développement, dans le *De decalogo* : si le nombre 7 a été honoré d'une façon particulière, dit-il, c'est parce que, à travers lui, mieux que tout autre nombre, on contemple le Créateur agissant, créant le monde et gouvernant l'univers (105). Cette idée fait allusion aux différents effets du nombre 7 que Philon reconnaît dans l'univers – la croissance des êtres et leur harmonie – mais l'allusion à Dieu comme Créateur renvoie aussi au nombre 7 tel qu'il est présenté en Gen. 2. 3, c'est-à-dire comme indiquant la fin de la Création. L'auteur de la Question 69 développe finalement une thèse proche lorsqu'il affirme que le nombre 7 est honoré pour que les hommes gardent à l'esprit la Création[28].

Il y a donc des raisons sérieuses de penser que Philon est à la fois la source et la cible essentielles, sinon exclusives, de la Question 69[29]. Il y a cependant deux éléments, dans la question initiale, qui ne semblent pas se trouver chez Philon :

---

[26] Clément d'Alexandrie, par exemple, s'inspire de Philon dans un développement sur les vertus du nombre 7 (*Stromates* VII, 143–145), qui pourrait aussi compter parmi les sources de la Question 69.

[27] Toth rappelle que l'expression ne se trouve qu'ici dans les *Quaestiones*, et affirme en avoir trouvé huit parallèles chez Théodoret (Toth 2014, p. 595 n. 207).

[28] On retrouve une autre explication proche de celle de Théodoret chez Procope de Gaza, qui explique que l'institution du Sabbat (le repos le septième jour) avait pour fonction de rappeler aux hommes le souvenir de Dieu (PG 87.1, col. 141C). Voir désormais Metzler 2015, p. 89.

[29] On ajoutera que la manière dont l'auteur de la Question distingue l'hexade de la Création du septième jour rappelle Philon, *Spec.* II, 58.

– L'idée selon laquelle, le jour du sabbat, l'air change la plupart du temps ;

– L'idée selon laquelle les dents poussent en sept mois, puis tombent au bout de la septième année.

La première idée ne paraît pas formulée de cette manière chez Philon. Le texte du *Legum allegoriae* attribue cependant à la lune une influence sur l'air (I, 8). Et le *De opificio* rappelle que chaque phase de la lune correspond à une période de sept jours (101). Il est donc possible que l'auteur de la Question 69 ait eu connaissance par ailleurs du fait que le sabbat correspondait, chez les juifs, au septième jour marquant le terme de chaque cycle lunaire. Le fait qu'il formule une idée qui ne se trouve pas telle quelle chez Philon mais qui pouvait se *déduire* de Philon pourrait s'expliquer par le fait qu'il résume fortement sa source, peut-être à travers un souvenir de lecture. Ce fait n'indique pas nécessairement que Philon ne puisse être sa source.

La seconde idée en revanche, ne correspond pas à ce que dit Philon, qui évoque bien la poussée des dents, mais au cours des sept premières années, et non des sept premiers mois. Cette idée n'est pourtant pas une vue de l'esprit : on la trouve dans les Θεολογούμενα ἀριθμητικά de Nicomaque de Gérase. Ce texte, après vérification, ne peut cependant pas expliquer le reste de la Question 69. Il est donc possible que, sur ce point précis, l'auteur ait disposé d'une autre source, ou, plus probablement, ait connaissance d'une autre théorie, à partir de Nicomaque ou d'un autre auteur, et qu'elle se soit retrouvée, dans son souvenir, mêlée aux idées de Philon, qui évoque bien par ailleurs la poussée des dents lors d'un premier septénaire – d'années, et non de mois.

Nous faisons donc l'hypothèse, sous toute réserve, que l'auteur a travaillé à partir de souvenirs de lecture de Philon et de connaissances arithmétiques qu'il a pu acquérir suite à d'autres lectures ou simplement au cours d'arithmétique. La mention de la Loi dans la question initiale est un indice fort en faveur de l'hypothèse d'une source juive ou chrétienne plutôt que païenne.

Il resterait théoriquement possible que la vraie cible de la Question 69 soit un commentaire chrétien inspiré par Philon. On a perdu par exemple tout commentaire d'Origène sur Gen.

2. 2–3[30], comme la section correspondante du commentaire de Didyme sur la Genèse[31]. Les chaînes ne permettent pas de combler significativement cette lacune[32]. On ne peut donc pas exclure par principe qu'un commentaire, surtout un commentaire alexandrin, ait pu s'inspirer fortement de Philon. Mais il faudrait imaginer une reprise très proche. Il arrive à Origène d'expliquer le texte biblique grâce à l'arithmétique[33]. Il devait sûrement le faire à propos de Gen. 2. 2–3, mais on ne trouve pas, chez lui, la confiance et l'enthousiasme à l'égard de l'arithmologie que l'on trouve chez Philon[34].

La Question 69 nous paraît donc témoigner d'une polémique à la fois particulière et générale : particulière, en ce qu'elle semble dirigée contre un auteur, Philon d'Alexandrie[35] ; plus générale, parce qu'elle visait sans doute, dans l'esprit de l'auteur, à dénoncer une certaine manière (la manière alexandrine ?) d'user de l'arithmétique dans le commentaire de l'Écriture, et, plus largement encore, la confiance placée par les Grecs comme par certains juifs et certains chrétiens dans l'arithmétique comme voie d'accès aux secrets de la nature. Dans le monde grec, cette confiance s'était imposée à la suite des réflexions de Platon, qui présente l'arithmétique, dans la *République*, comme un chemin conduisant aux intelligibles[36]. Si la ou l'une des cibles de notre auteur est Philon, ou, à travers Philon, les exégètes alexandrins, on disposerait sans doute, à travers la Question 69, d'un nouvel élément en faveur

---

[30] Voir les témoignages rassemblés par Metzler 2010.

[31] Cf. *Commentaire sur la Genèse* 80–81. Le texte conservé donne un commencement d'explication sur le repos de Dieu le septième jour, mais la suite manque.

[32] Voir la note 37.

[33] Voir notre note 14.

[34] Toth nous signale un autre parallèle entre la Question 69 et David, *Prolegomena philosophiae* p. 53. 16–21 Busse (VIe siècle). Le texte de David reprend l'exemple des âges de la vie, mais là s'arrêtent les points communs. Il ne peut être selon nous la cible de la Question 69, mais témoigne plutôt, avec d'autres textes (voir la note 24) de l'importance de l'arithmologie dans la culture scolaire et philosophique de la fin de l'Antiquité.

[35] Philon ne paraît pas explicitement nommé dans les *Quaestiones*. Dans les Questions 82 et 86, l'auteur évoque une *Interprétation des noms hébreux* qui peut correspondre à l'ouvrage qu'Eusèbe attribue à Philon (*Histoire ecclésiastique* II, 18, 7).

[36] *République* VII, 525c.

de l'attribution des *Quaestiones* à un auteur antiochien, Théodoret ou un autre[37].

Dans les *Questions sur la Genèse*, Théodoret ne commente pas le passage biblique sur les dimensions de l'arche de Noé, comme le faisaient Origène et Clément pour y trouver les fondements d'une explication spirituelle[38]. Dans les *Questions sur l'Exode*, il commente bien les dimensions de la Tente (Ex. 28), mais sans les spéculations arithmologiques de ses prédécesseurs[39]. En revanche, son œuvre ne paraît pas témoigner de prise de position explicite contre l'arithmétique. La *Thérapeutique* l'évoque, avec la géométrie, parmi les sciences acceptables[40], et, dans l'*Histoire ecclésiastique*, Théodoret cite l'arithmétique, de même, parmi les disciplines de la culture grecque dans lesquelles Didyme d'Alexandrie aurait été formé[41]. Mais dans le *Compendium des fables hérétiques*, il mentionne Monoïme, qui aurait constitué son hérésie à partir de l'arithmétique[42]. Dans les *Discours sur la Providence*, il range l'arithmétique parmi 'les curiosités qui dépassent la mesure' (τὰς πέρα τοῦ μέτρου πολυπραγμοσύνας)[43]. Théodoret avait donc un point de vue nuancé sur l'arithmétique, comme la plupart de ses prédécesseurs chrétiens. Il l'évoque tantôt comme une discipline utile, tantôt comme une science vaine

---

[37] Il faudrait vérifier également si la Question 69 ne dérive pas d'un intermédiaire qui aurait déjà développé cet argument contre l'exégèse philonienne. Nous n'avons pas trouvé de texte qui puisse correspondre à un tel intermédiaire. Mais notre recherche n'a pas pu être exhaustive, et cet intermédiaire, s'il existe, est peut-être perdu. Les *Homélies sur la Genèse* de Chrysostome ne commentent pas le repos de Dieu au septième jour, pas plus que les *Homélies sur la Création* de Sévérien de Gabala ou les *Glaphyres sur la Genèse* de Cyrille d'Alexandrie. Nous n'avons rien trouvé non plus dans les fragments caténaires rassemblés par Devreesse 1959, ou par Petit 1977. Le *Commentaire sur la Genèse* d'Eusèbe d'Émèse commente le repos de Dieu le septième jour, mais, semble-t-il, sans préoccupation arithmologique (voir ter Haar Romeny 1997, p. 212). Il existe chez Éphrem un commentaire sur le repos du septième jour, mais qui ne peut pas être la source de la Question 69 (cf. Tonneau 1965, p. 19).

[38] Voir *Questions sur la Genèse* 50.

[39] *Questions sur l'Exode* 60.

[40] VI, 52. Même point de vue dans les *Discours sur la Providence*, PG 83, col. 605B.

[41] IV, 30.

[42] PG 83, col. 369A.

[43] PG 83, col. 624C.

voire pernicieuse. Ce point de vue est assez banal et n'est pas très utile pour identifier l'auteur de la Question 69.

En revanche, il existe, dans les *Questions sur la Genèse* de Théodoret, une question parallèle à la Question 69, formulée de la façon suivante : 'Pourquoi donc Dieu a-t-il béni le septième jour d'une façon particulière ?' (Τί δή ποτε διαφερόντως τὴν ἑβδόμην ἡμέραν εὐλόγησεν ὁ Θεός ;)[44]. Théodoret répond que chaque jour précédent avait impliqué (ἐδέξατο) une création particulière. Si Dieu a béni le septième jour, c'était pour que celui-ci ne restât pas sans récompense (ἀγέραστος). Il y a deux différences majeures entre cette question et la Question 69 :

– La question posée est celle de savoir pourquoi Dieu a béni le septième *jour*, alors que la question initiale, dans la Question 69, consiste à demander pourquoi le *nombre* 7 implique un changement dans la nature.

– La réponse de Théodoret est beaucoup moins polémique que celle de la Question 69. Elle ne consiste pas à remettre en cause l'exégèse arithmologique.

Cependant, cette absence de la polémique n'est pas en elle-même pertinente : elle peut s'expliquer, justement, parce que c'est moins la question de la vertu du nombre 7 qui est en jeu que celle du septième jour.

Il reste des points communs évidents entre Théodoret et la Question 69 :

– L'allusion au repos de Dieu le septième jour, même si elle paraît secondaire dans la Question 69.

– L'absence de tout raisonnement arithmologique chez Théodoret, qui ne s'explique peut-être pas seulement par la question initialement posée, mais aussi par un refus, plus délibéré, de ne pas expliquer l'honneur fait au nombre 7 en invoquant ses vertus.

– Le même usage du verbe δέχεσθαι pour évoquer ce qui est *impliqué* par le septième jour – même emploi, dans la Question 69, à propos du nombre 7.

---

[44] *Questions sur la Genèse* 21.

Ce dernier constat s'ajouterait aux remarques stylistiques faites plus haut, qui orienteraient assez bien en direction de Théodoret[45]. L'opposition à l'égard de Philon, et peut-être, plus largement, à une façon alexandrine, ou ressentie comme telle, d'utiliser l'arithmétique pour commenter l'Écriture, oriente en tout cas, *a priori*, en direction d'un auteur antiochien.

Bibliographie

M. Alexandre (1988), *Le commencement du Livre. Genèse I–V. La version grecque de la Septante et sa réception*, Paris : Éditions Beauchesne.

F. Calabi (2011), 'Le repos de Dieu chez Philon d'Alexandrie', dans S. Inowlocki & B. Decharneux (éd.), *Philon d'Alexandrie. Un penseur à l'intersection des cultures gréco-romaine, orientale, juive et chrétienne*, Turnhout : Brepols, p. 185–204.

R. Devreesse (1959), *Les anciens commentateurs grecs de l'Octateuque et des Rois (fragments tirés des chaînes)*, Città del Vaticano : Biblioteca apostolica vaticana.

N. Fernández Marcos & J. R. Busto Saiz (éd., 1984), *Theodoreti Cyrensis Quaestiones in Reges et Paralipomena*, Madrid : Consejo Superior de Investigaciones Científicas.

N. Fernández Marcos & A. Sáenz-Badillos (éd., 1979), *Theodoreti Cyrensis Quaestiones in Octateuchum*, Madrid : Consejo Superior de Investigaciones Científicas.

W. Gass (1842), 'Die unter Justins des Märtyrers Schriften befindlichen Fragen an die Rechtgläubigen, mit Rücksicht auf andere Fragsammlungen erörtert', dans *Zeitschrift für die historische Theologie*, 12, p. 35–154.

B. Gleede (2011), 'Johannes Philoponos und die christliche Apologetik : Die Widerlegungen des Proklos und Aristoteles und die Debatte des Schöpfungsproblems in der Schule von Gaza und bei Ps-Justin', dans *Jahrbuch für Antike und Christentum*, 54, p. 73–97.

B. Gleede (2020), *Philosophische Erotapokriseis und theologische Kapitel. Quaestiones gentilium ad Christianos. Quaestiones contra Gentiles de relatis. Capita contra Theopaschitas*, Berlin – New York: De Gruyter.

J.-N. Guinot (1995), *L'exégèse de Théodoret de Cyr*, Paris : Beauchesne.

---

[45] Voir la note 21.

R. B. ter Haar Romeny (1997), *A Syrian in Greek Dress. The Use of Greek, Hebrew, and Syriac Biblical Texts in Eusebius of Emesa's Commentary on Genesis*, Louvain : Peeters.

A. Harnack (1901), *Diodor von Tarsus : Vier pseudojustinische Schriften als Eigentum Diodors nachgewiesen*, Leipzig : J. C. Hinrichs.

R. Hoche (éd., 1866), *Nicomachi Geraseni Pythagorei introductionis arithmeticae libri II*, Leipzig : B. G. Teubner.

J. Kalvesmaki (2013), *The Theology of Arithmetic : Number Symbolism in Platonism and Early Christianity*, Washington, DC : Center for Hellenic Studies.

É. Littré (1853), *Œuvres complètes d'Hippocrate*, VIII, Paris : J.-B. Baillère.

H.-I. Marrou (1948), *Histoire de l'éducation dans l'Antiquité. I : Le monde grec*, Paris : Éditions du Seuil.

K. Metzler (2010), *Origenes. Die Kommentierung des Buches Genesis*, Berlin – New York : W. de Gruyter.

K. Metzler (éd., 2015), *Prokop von Gaza. Eclogarum in libros historicos Veteris Testamenti epitome*. Teil 1 : *Der Genesiskommentar*, Berlin : De Gruyter (GCS, N.F. 22).

H. R. Moehring (1995), 'Arithmology as an Exegetical Tool in the Writings of Philo of Alexandria', dans J. P. Kenney (éd.), *The School of Moses. Studies in Philo and Hellenistic Religion*, Atlanta : Scholars Press, p. 141–176.

S. Morlet (2016), *Les chrétiens et la culture. Conversion d'un concept (Ier–VIe s.)*, Paris : Les Belles Lettres.

F. Petit (1977), *Catenae Graecae in Genesim et in Exodum*, Turnhout – Leuven : Brepols (CCG, 2).

F. E. Robbins (1921), 'Arithmetic in Philo Judaeus', dans *Classical Philology*, 16, p. 345–361.

F. Romano (éd., 1995), *Giamblico. Il numero e il divino*, Milano : Rusconi.

W. H. Roscher (1906), *Hebdomadenlehren der griechischen Philosophen und Ärtze*, Leipzig : B. G. Teubner.

W. H. Roscher (1913), *Die hippokratische Schrift von der Siebenzahl in ihrer vierfachen Überlieferung*, Paderborn : F. Schöningh.

K. Staehle (1931), *Die Zahlenmystik bei Philon von Alexandreia*, Leipzig – Berlin : B. G. Teubner.

R. M. Tonneau (éd., 1965), *Sancti Ephraem Syri in Genesim et in Exodum commentarii*, Louvain : Peeters (CSCO, 153).

P. Toth (2014), 'New Questions on Old Answers. Towards a Critical Edition of the Answers to the Orthodox of Pseudo-Justin', dans *Journal of Theological Studies*, 65, p. 550–599.

P. Tzamalikos (2012), *The Real Cassian Revisited : Monastic Life, Greek Paideia, and Origenism in the Sixth Century*, Leiden – Boston : Brill.

N. Walter (1964), *Der Thoraausleger Aristobulus*, Berlin : Akademie-Verlag.

Abstract

The *Quaestio ad orthodoxos* 69 attributed to Justin contains a harsh criticism against arithmological speculations on the number 7. This essay demonstrates that the text is probably a response to Philo of Alexandria, notably his *De opificio mundi*. This suggestion would support the widely held hypothesis that the author of the *Quaestiones* was an Antiochian writer. A few details recall the style of Theodoret, whom critics most often name as the likely author of the *Quaestiones*, although this attribution remains uncertain.

PART 2
MAXIMUS THE CONFESSOR

VLADIMIR CVETKOVIĆ

RE-INTERPRETING TRADITION: MAXIMUS THE CONFESSOR ON CREATION IN *AMBIGUA AD IOANNEM**

Maximus the Confessor's *Ambigua ad Ioannem* represents a composition of 66 elucidations on ambiguous passages from the works of Gregory Nazianzen. The collection was written between 628 and 630 and dedicated to a certain John, whose identity is still under scholarly scrutiny.[1] Although *Ambigua*, as a collection of various *scholia*, is mainly an exegetical work it may be to some extent subsumed under the popular Byzantine literary genre of *erotapokriseis* or question-and-answer literature, since the recipient of the work had selected different passages from Gregory and asked Maximus to ponder over their meaning. One of Maximus' intentions in writing this work is the dismissal of Gregory's alleged Origenistic or heterodox leaning (as in *Ambiguum* 7)[2] and the justification of Gregory's virtual infallibility and of his designation the 'Theologian' (as in *Ambiguum* 21).[3] Moreover, Maximus displays his immense capacity to synthesize divergent theological traditions and to present them as parts of one coherent theological system.

The aim of this paper is to show how by utilizing different Christian and philosophical doctrines Maximus developed his original teaching on creation. In doing this, I will first look at the historical importance of the question of creation for Christians

* This article was realised with the support of the Ministry of Education, Science and Technological Development of the Republic of Serbia, according to the Agreement on the realisation and financing of scientific research.

[1] Jankowiak & Booth 2015, p. 25–26, 28–29.
[2] Cvetković 2016, p. 750.
[3] Louth 1996, p. 22.

Questioning the World, Greek Patristic and Byzantine Question-and-Answer Literature, ed. by Bram Demulder and Peter Van Deun, Turnhout, 2021 (*LECTIO*, 11), pp. 147-179   ©BREPOLS✠PUBLISHERS   DOI 10.1484/M.LECTIO-EB.5.121505

and on the main philosophical arguments for the creation of the world that circulated in the sixth century. Next, I will show how, in *Ambiguum* 7, Maximus does not only refute the Origenistic view on creation associated with this passage, but also refutes certain anti-Origenistic stances that compromised the ortho-dox position by idealizing the historical condition of human beings. The following sections will explore the way in which Maximus developed his most representative doctrines, such as the doctrines of moving and rest and of λόγοι (*Ambiguum* 7), of cosmological processions, ontological expansions and provi-dence (*Ambiguum* 10), and of five divisions within creation (*Ambiguum* 41), by reinterpreting previous Christian traditions of Origen, Gregory Nazianzen, Gregory of Nyssa, Nemesius of Emesa and Dionysius the Areopagite in a new key.

1. *Introduction*

The Christian view on the creation of the world out of nothing (*ex nihilo*) has been the subject of philosophical debates between Christians and representatives of the pagan philosophical schools from the second century onward.[4] However, before the second century the question of the creation of the world occupied pri-marily the attention of Jewish thinkers who intended to harmo-nize the Old Testament view on the genesis of the world with the teachings of Greek philosophical schools. The most famous representative of Jewish thought and at the same time a heir of Aristotelian, Platonic, and Stoic traditions,[5] Philo of Alexandria, attempted to philosophically justify Moses' stances from the book of Genesis with the help of Plato's doctrine on the creation of the world by the Demiurge and of Stoic teaching on the periodical beginnings of time cycles.[6] The problem of the creation of the world had a subtle elaboration later on in the works of Christian authors such as Irenaeus of Lyon, Origen, Athanasius the Great,

---

[4] May 2004, p. 1–5.

[5] Wolfson 1948, p. 319–320.

[6] *De opificio mundi* 26. 4 (ed. Cohn 1896): ἐπεὶ γὰρ διάστημα τῆς τοῦ κόσμου κινήσεώς ἐστιν ὁ χρόνος; *De aeternitate mundi* 4. 8–9 and 52. 5–7 (ed. Cohn & Wendland 1915): ὥστ' εὐθυβόλως ἀποδεδόσθαι πρὸς τῶν εἰωθότων τὰ πράγματα ὁρίζεσθαι χρόνον διάστημα τῆς τοῦ κόσμου κινήσεως.

and the Cappadocian Fathers. However, the common character-istic of all these positions is that they remained within the realm of Christian apologetics, attempting to substantiate their reli-gious position with convincing philosophical argumentation in order to refute pagan cosmology.

A comprehensive philosophical justification of the Christian position on the creation of the world came from Christian rep-resentatives of the Alexandrian Academy, which existed until the beginning of the seventh century. One of the greatest philo-sophical minds of the sixth century, who countered first Proclus and then Aristotle on the question of the world's eternity from a purely Christian perspective, was John Philoponus (490–570). With him Christianity acquired a completely different position in relation to the Greek philosophical heritage, distinct from the defensive attitude that it had adopted for centuries.

In his comments on Aristotle's *Physics* from 517, Philoponus claimed, contrary to Aristotle and in conformity with Christian tradition, that the world has a beginning. Philoponus exposed some of his main arguments first in his work *Against Proclus on the Eternity of the World* (*De aeternitate mundi contra Proclum*). Subsequently he developed these arguments and added a number of new ones in his most significant work, *Against Aristotle on the Eternity of the World* (*De aeternitate mundi contra Aristotelem*), composed of eight books. The main arguments brought by Philo-ponus in favor of the view on the world's beginning are focused on motion. First, for Philoponus, motion is a result of impetus, regardless of whether a body is set in motion by the soul or this impetus comes from outside, like in the case of inanimate nature. In both cases, the instigator of motion is God.[7] Second, Philo-ponus prioritizes the linear motion over other types of motions, because, unlike the circular motion considered perfect by Aristo-tle, it is not doomed to repetition but reaches its goal.[8] Third, by

---

[7] Philoponus, *De aeternitate mundi contra Aristotelem* 7. 78. 28–79. 2 (ed. Heiberg 1894). His argumentation set forth in the second book of *Against Aristotle on the Eternity of the World* and especially his theory of impetus, Philoponus developed further in the discourse about the creation of the world that is inspired by the book of *Genesis*. Cf. *De Opificio Mundi* 28. 20–29. 9 (ed. Reichardt 1897). See also Mueller-Jourdan's contribution to this volume.

[8] Wildberg 1987, p. 52.

commencing from Aristotle's definition of motion as a motion towards a goal, Philoponus considers that the goal or the rest of every movement is in God. On the basis of these arguments, Philoponus develops a theory of the limited capacity (δύναμις) of physical bodies to move, arguing that, if the moving capacity of physical bodies is infinite, then they would be coeternal with God and they would not be moved towards him as a goal.[9] Thus, for Philoponus, God as creator is the instigator of every movement of creatures. He is also the one who directs the movement towards himself and the goal of every movement in which creatures can experience their rest.

One can find all three aspects of Philoponus' critique of the eternity of the world in Maximus the Confessor (580–662). A possible link between Maximus and Philoponus might be Stephanus of Alexandria, the last headmaster of the Alexandrian Academy,[10] who came to the imperial court of Heraclius to teach philosophy at the time when, according to the (Greek) Vita, Maximus the Confessor was already appointed the chief of the imperial office (πρωτοασηκρῆτις).[11] Since at the beginning of the seventh century there was no need for Christian rebuttal of the pagan position on the world's eternity, because pagan philosophical opposition was lacking by then, Maximus used the theme of the creation of the world to re-evaluate the previous Christian tradition. He demonstrated that the aforementioned three arguments present in Philoponus, as well as some new reasoning for the creation of the world by God had been already extant in the Christian tradition of the Cappadocians, Nemesius, and Dionysius. However, although there exists resemblance between Philoponus' and Maximus' views on creation, one should not interpret it as a matter of influence, but rather as a common indebtedness to the same Christian predecessors.

---

[9] Philoponus, De aeternitate mundi contra Proclum 1. 2. 2. 10–14 (ed. Rabe 1899). For Philoponus' arguments on generability and perishability see Judson 1987.

[10] Both Louth and Tollefsen believe that one should start the exploration of Maximus' philosophical sources from those who have had a direct impact on his life, and this is above all Stephanus of Alexandria, through whom the young imperial officer could obtain insight into the work of Christian commentators of Aristotle. See Tollefsen 2008, p. 15–16 and Louth 1998, p. 67–84.

[11] Maximus claims himself that he was in the imperial service (Ep. 12. 505B). Cf. Lackner 1971, p. 63–65.

2. *Maximus' View on the Creation of the World between Origenism and Anti-Origenism*

Anyone who is even remotely familiar with the work of Maximus the Confessor knows his famous triad γένεσις ('creation') – κίνησις ('movement') – στάσις ('rest').[12] Although it recalls Philoponus' arguments about God who not only provides impetus for creaturely movement by creating the world, but also directs and is the final goal of every movement, this triad, according to Sherwood's view, actually represents Maximus' rearrangement of Origen's triad μονή – κίνησις – γένεσις and as such is the backbone of his refutation of Origenism.[13] Maximus' rearrangement of Origen's triad aims especially to refute the Origenist myth which claims that the original fall of creatures was a result of their satiety (κόρος) in contemplating God.[14] There are some differences in contemporary scholarship with regard to Origen's point of view. Thus, unlike Sherwood, Louth mentions another triad represented by Origen, which is γένεσις – στάσις – κίνησις.[15] The reason for this apparent discrepancy lies in the fact that one may think of two creations in Origen. The first creation is from eternity, in which God eternally creates beings that contemplate his essence, while the second creation represents the divine response to the movement of creatures and their attachment to angelic, human, or demonic bodies, and it is the divine punishment for their violation of the original unity. Origen's triad can have a twofold interpretation. If one takes into account the eternal creation, it would be in the form of γένεσις – στάσις – κίνησις, while in the case of the second creation, in which the human being is imprisoned in a material body, the creation should be seen as a consequence of the movement, and the triad would be in the form of στάσις – κίνησις – γένεσις.

On the one hand, it would be wrong to conclude that Maximus' triad was developed in the course of refuting Origenism and that there is no foundation in his work except in *Ambiguum* 7, where Maximus largely contested the Origenist stance. On the

---

[12] *Amb.* 7, 1069B–1073B (ed. Constas 2004, I, p. 76–77).

[13] Sherwood 1955a, p. 92.

[14] Origenes, *De principiis* II. 1. 1 (ed. Görgemanns & Karpp 1976).

[15] Louth 1996, p. 67.

other hand, it would be equally erroneous to admit that this triad represents the backbone of Maximus' ontology while continuing to restrict its application only to the Confessor's rebuttal of Origenism: this would create the impression that the whole of Maximus' work is focused on refuting this sixth-century heresy. In order to avoid possible pitfalls in the understanding of Maximus' thought, it would be appropriate to consider this aspect from the perspective of contemporary scholarly developments. In the first edition of his *Cosmic Liturgy* (1941), Balthasar interpreted Maximus' work in the light of Origenistic influence.[16] Balthasar claimed that *The Centuries on Theology and Economy of the Incarnate Son of God* (CPG 7694) prove a certain Origenistic crisis in Maximus' monastic life. Sherwood contested Balthasar's claim first in *An Annotated Date-list of the Works of Maximus the Confessor*.[17] Later, in *The Earlier Ambigua of St Maximus the Confessor*, he showed that Maximus took quite the opposite side in relation to the Origenistic position.[18] Although Balthasar conceded Sherwood's arguments and revised his approach in the second edition of his *Cosmic Liturgy*, Maximus' works continued to be perceived within the dialectical pair Origenism – anti-Origenism. In later Maximian scholarship, Balthasar's approach, linked to the first edition of *The Cosmic Liturgy*, was combined with Sherwood's discovery, leading some scholars to draw a division in Maximus' life between two distinct, if not divergent, periods, one Origenist and another anti-Origenist.[19] Tunberg opposed such claim, pointing to the fact that Maximus' (*Greek*) *Vita* does not mention any changes in his views; on the contrary, it argues that his thought remained unchanged throughout the course of his life.[20] If one takes a closer look at Maximus' work, one may conclude on the basis of both his *Vitae* and the works allegedly composed under Origenist influence, such as *The Gnostic Centuries*, that Maximus held a coherent and consistent position toward Origenism, and that

[16] Balthasar 1941, p. 27–35.
[17] Sherwood 1952, p. 3.
[18] Sherwood 1955a.
[19] Garrigues 1976, p. 35–75.
[20] Thunberg 1995, p. 11.

there is no question of a possible Origenist influence. I do not intend to follow Sherwood's line of research further in order to demonstrate that Maximus held his anti-Origenist position throughout his works, but rather to move the focus away from his anti-Origenism, because I think that it would be counterproductive to stress Origenistic issues in Maximus work or to look on the entire Maximus' opus as one massive critique of Origenism. Maximus lived nearly a hundred years after the climax of the Origenist crisis, at a time when its consequences had largely been overcome. His terminology from *Ambiguum* 7, which Maximus used as a weapon against those who have expressed their position in those terms, should not be viewed as Origenistic. As recent research of Benevich[21] and Lévy[22] shows, the aim of Maximus' reconsideration of the Origenistic problem is not a restoration of the discussions with Origenists, but a precise definition of the orthodox attitude in relation to extreme anti-Origenism, which questioned the form of salvation and the future of deification of human body. Therefore, the second part of *Ambiguum* 7 is exclusively dedicated to the questions of the metaphysical structure of human being, his concrete, historical condition, and his finality and it aims to refute anti-Origenistic claims that in the future life human beings would continue breathing air and preserve veins coursing with blood, arguing instead that human beings will be fully infused with the fullness of God.[23]

In regard to both Origenist and anti-Origenist vocabulary one may conclude that Maximus' terminology is deeply rooted in the orthodox tradition and does not constitute an *ad hoc* invention, since the basic contours of Maximus' triad γένεσις – κίνησις – στάσις can already be found in the work of Gregory of Nyssa.[24] Therefore, Maximus repeats the orthodox arguments of previous Church Fathers creatively applying them to the seventh-century situation.

---

[21] Benevich 2009, p. 5–15; Benevich, Biriukov & Shufrin 2007.

[22] Lévy 2006, p. 131.

[23] *Amb.* 7, 1088C (ed. Constas 2014, I, p. 112–113). Cf. Cvetkovic 2016, 756–757.

[24] Blowers 1992a, p. 151–171.

3. *The Five Divisions of Beings*

Already in the opening lines of his *Ambiguum* 41, Maximus exposes his doctrine of five divisions of being, pointing to its consistency with the previous tradition in the following words:

> Οἱ τὰ πολλὰ τῶν θείων μυστηρίων ἐκ τῶν ὁπαδῶν *καὶ ὑπηρετῶν γενομένων* τοῦ *Λόγου, καὶ αὐτόθεν ἀμέσως τὴν* τῶν ὄντων μυηθέντων γνῶσιν, κατὰ διαδοχὴν διὰ τῶν πρὸ αὐτῶν εἰς αὐτοὺς διαδοθέντα παραλαβόντες ἅγιοί φασιν πέντε διαιρέσεσι διειλῆφθαι τὴν πάντων τῶν γεγονότων ὑπόστασιν·

> Having received the greater part of the divine mysteries handed down to them in succession from those who before them were the followers and ministers of the Word and being directly initiated into the knowledge of beings through these mysteries, the saints say that the existence of all things that have come into being is marked by five divisions.[25]

According to Maximus, then, one of the doctrines passed down by tradition is that everything existing may be perceived through five divisions. The first division is that of uncreated and created nature, which has received its being through creation.[26] Already with this first division it becomes obvious that Maximus stands in the tradition of Gregory of Nyssa.[27] Regarding this first division Maximus explains, again referring to the tradition, that in his goodness God created the orderly arrangements but that it was not immediately clear to the saints what God is and how He exists in these orderly arrangements. Therefore they called the ignorance that distinguishes the creation from God 'division'.[28] This epistemological gap is caused by the ontological division, because the realities, which do not possess one and the same λόγος and therefore cannot be united in the single essence, are naturally divided among themselves.

---

[25] *Amb.* 41, 1304D (ed. and trans. Constas 2014, II, p. 102–103).

[26] *Amb.* 41, 1304D (ed. Constas 2014, II, p. 102–103): ὧν πρώτην μέν φασιν εἶναι τὴν διαιροῦσαν τῆς ἀκτίστου φύσεως τὴν κτιστὴν καθόλου φύσιν καί διὰ γενέσεως τὸ εἶναι λαβοῦσαν.

[27] Gregorius Nyssenus, *Contra Eunomium* I (ed. GNO I, p. 270–272).

[28] *Amb.* 41, 1305A (ed. Constas 2014, II, p. 102–103): Φασὶ γὰρ τὸν Θεὸν ἀγαθότητι πεποιηκότα τῶν ὄντων ἀπάντων λαμπρὰν διακόσμησιν, μὴ αὐτόθεν αὐτῇ καταφανῆ γενέσθαι τίνα καὶ ὁποῖον εἶναι, τὴν περὶ τοῦτο τὴν κτίσιν τοῦ Θεοῦ διακρίνουσαν ἄγνοιαν 'διαίρεσιν' λέγοντες.

Although Maximus' doctrine of λόγοι of essences or natures, which represent divine wills about creation, has been considered a 'lonely meteorite' in the night sky of Byzantine thought, Louth admits a possible influence of Dionysius the Areopagite on Maximus on this issue.[29] Maximus himself points to Dionysius' teaching on predestination as the source for his doctrine of λόγοι.[30] It should be added that Maximus' doctrine of λόγοι can also be found in its underdeveloped form in Gregory of Nyssa, who thinks of λόγοι as spiritual manners of looking on things,[31] which corresponds to Maximus' usage of this term in the aforementioned passage of *Ambiguum* 7.

Maximus points next to the division between intelligible and sensible nature, and then to the division of sensible nature into heaven and earth. The fourth division is the division of the earth between paradise and οἰκουμένη or the inhabited world, and the fifth division is within human nature separating male from female.[32]

The creation of the world that took place through these five divisions can be referred to by means of the Neoplatonic notion of 'procession' often used by Maximus. Thus, Maximus describes the philosophical problem of one and the many, manifested in relation to the one Λόγος of God with many λόγοι of creation, by using the Neoplatonic dialectical pair 'procession' (πρόοδος) – 'return' (ἐπιστροφή):

> κατὰ μὲν τὴν ἀγαθοπρεπῆ εἰς τὰ ὄντα τοῦ ἑνὸς ποιητικήν τε καὶ συνεκτικὴν πρόοδον πολλοὶ ὁ εἷς, κατὰ δὲ τὴν εἰς τὸν ἕνα τῶν πολλῶν ἐπιστρεπτικήν τε καὶ χειραγωγικὴν ἀναφοράν τε καὶ πρόνοιαν, ὥσπερ εἰς ἀρχὴν παντοκρατορικὴν ἢ κέντρον τῶν ἐξ αὐτοῦ εὐθειῶν τὰς ἀρχὰς προειληφός, καὶ ὡς πάντων συναγωγός, εἷς οἱ πολλοί.

> According to the creative and sustaining procession of the One to individual beings, which is befitting of divine goodness, the One is many. According to the revertive, inductive,

---

[29] Louth 2009, p. 593.

[30] *Amb.* 7, 1085A (ed. Constas 2014, I, p. 106–107).

[31] Gregorius Nyssenus, *De opificio hominis* 24 (ed. PG 44, col. 212–213).

[32] *Amb.* 41, 1305A-B (ed. Constas 2014, II, p. 102–105). Gregory of Nyssa devotes the whole chapter 16 of his *De opificio hominis*, to the topic of division between male and female.

and providential return of the many to the One – as if to an all-powerful point of origin, or to the center of a circle precontaining the beginnings of the radii originating from it – insofar as the One gathers everything together, the many are One.[33]

The divine act of creating of the world is a process of procession, which includes the establishment of five divisions within creation. The opposite process of return (ἀναφορά) is undertaken by human beings, who, by uniting divided poles, gradually ascend to God.[34] The movement parallel to the movement of procession is the movement of expansion (διαστολή) and it pertains to the ontological structure of creation or to the relationship between universals and individuals. Maximus describes this process in his *Ambigua* 10 as a downward movement from the most generic λόγος of being and nature, through the λόγοι of generic genera (γενικώτερα γένη), specific species (εἴδη) and most specific species (εἰδικώτατα εἴδη), to the λόγοι of individuals (ἄτομα).[35]

The act of creation consists of two parallel processes: a process of procession, by which Maximus portrays the relationship between one and the many, and another process of expansion, which aims to determine the relationship between universals and particulars. For Tollefsen, the process of expansion refers to the ontological arrangement of the world, while he understands the process of procession as a 'metaphysical structure establishing the limits of creation and consummation within which the historical process takes place'.[36]

4. The Creation of Time and Age

In his *Ambiguum* 10, Maximus claims that the whole existing nature can be divided into intelligible and sensible.[37] The question as to which division is primary, the division into created

---

[33] *Amb.* 7, 1081C (ed. and trans. Constas 2014, I, p. 100–103).

[34] *Amb.* 41, 1305C (ed. Constas 2014, II, p. 104–107).

[35] *Amb.* 10, 1177C (ed. Constas 2014, I, p. 288–289). Cf. also *Amb.* 41, 1312D (ed. Constas 2014, II, p. 116–101).

[36] Tollefsen 2008, p. 78.

[37] *Amb.* 10, 1153A (ed. Constas 2014, I, p. 240–241).

and uncreated nature or the division into intelligible and sensible nature, may be resolved by the terminological analysis of the notions employed. There is no doubt that for Maximus division between created and uncreated nature is primary, because, when referring to the existing nature (τῶν ὄντων φύσις), Maximus thinks of created nature. It is a matter of linguistic finesse, as Daniélou has shown in his analysis of Gregory of Nyssa, who applies the term τὰ ὄντα only to created nature, while referring to God as τὸ ὄντως ὄν.[38]

Maximus claims that the intelligible nature may be described as eternal due to its creation in age or αἰών, and sensible nature as temporal due to its creation in time.[39] Maximus draws a clear division within the created nature, not only on the basis of the dichotomy mind-senses, but also on the basis of the dichotomy eternal-temporal. Thus, the intelligible or spiritual nature exists within age (αἰών), while the sensible or physical nature exists within time. However, this division does not say anything about the nature of eternity, nor time. In *The Centuries on Theology and Economy*, Maximus reflects on the nature of time:

> Ἡ ἀρχὴ καὶ ἡ μεσότης καὶ τὸ τέλος, τῶν χρόνῳ διαιρετῶν εἰσι γνωρίσματα· εἴποι δ᾽ ἄν τις ἀληθεύων, καὶ τῶν ἐν αἰῶνι συνορωμένων. Ὁ μὲν γὰρ χρόνος, μετρουμένην ἔχων τὴν κίνησιν, ἀριθμῷ περιγράφεται· ὁ αἰὼν δὲ συνεπινοουμένην ἔχων τῇ ὑπάρξει τὴν πότε κατηγορίαν, πάσχει διάστασιν, ὡς ἀρχὴν τοῦ εἶναι λαβών. Εἰ δὲ χρόνος καὶ αἰὼν οὐκ ἄναρχα, πολλῷ μᾶλλον τὰ ἐν τούτοις περιεχόμενα.

> Beginning, middle, and end are characteristics of beings distinguished by time and it can be truly stated that they are also characteristics of beings comprehended in age. Indeed time, which has measured movement, is circumscribed by number, and age, which includes in its existence the category of

---

[38] Daniélou 1970, p. 7.

[39] *Amb.* 10, 1153A (ed. Constas 2004, I, p. 240–241): [...] καὶ τὰ μὲν λέγεται καὶ ἔστιν αἰώνια, ὡς ἐν αἰῶνι τοῦ εἶναι λαβόντων ἀρχήν, τὰ δὲ χρονικά, ὡς ἐν χρόνῳ πεποιημένα, καὶ τὰ μὲν ὑποπίπτει νοήσει, τὰ δὲ αἰσθήσει [...]. Although Louth 1995, p. 124 and Ponsoye 1994, p. 211 translate the term αἰών with 'eternity' and 'un principle éternel' respectively, it should be noted that these terms do not render the Greek term properly. Thus, αἰών as created category that has a beginning but not an end should not be mistaken for the divine eternity. Berthold translation of αἰών with 'history' is inappropriate (Berthold 1985, p. 128–130).

'when', admits of a separation in so far as it began to be. And if time and age are not without beginning, so much less are those things which are contained in them.[40]

In this passage Maximus provides several important initial premises. First, that everything exists, either in time or in age. Time actually determines the scope of beings that exist within it, and each being has a beginning, middle, and end within time. On the other hand, the distinction between the beginning, middle, and end only expresses the way in which beings are defined by temporal categories, without excluding them from the existence in age. This calls into question the previous assumption that everything exists either in time or in αἰών, and that by this division one may clearly draw a line between sensible and intelligible, and in fact it indicates that a disjunction is not applicable to the existing reality, which simultaneously exists both in age and time.[41] What is then the difference between age and time? For Maximus, time is measured by movement and circumscribed by number. On the other hand, age includes the category of 'when' and, at the same time, it indicates a certain distance (διάστασις) since it has a beginning.[42] The common characteristic of time and age is that they are not without beginning. Time and age have their beginnings because God is the creator of 'every essence, power, and act, as well as every beginning, middle, and end' (πάσης οὐσίας καὶ δυνάμεως καὶ ἐνεργείας, ἀρχῆς τε καὶ μεσότητος καὶ τέλους ποιητική).[43] Thus, both time and age were created and have their beginning in creation. In addition, both time and age include some distance between their inception and the present moment.

---

[40] Cap. Theol. I. 5 (ed. PG 90, col. 1085A; trans. Berthold 1985, p. 129–130; Berthold's translation is slightly modified).

[41] The most common conclusion of scholars in the interpretation of this passage is that time is attributed to the physical nature, while the spiritual or angelic nature belongs to the realm of age (Balthasar 2003, p. 137–138 and Plass 1980, p. 261–262). Even those scholars who have argued that there is no essential difference between age and time, returned at the end to the position of clear separation of age from time (Völker 1963, p. 33).

[42] One may notice here that Maximus prefers the term διάστασις to the term διάστημα, which entered his terminology by being borrowed from Gregory of Nyssa. For more about the use of these terms in Maximus see Thunberg 1995, p. 57–60.

[43] Cap. Theol. I. 5 (ed. PG 90, col. 1084D; trans. Berthold 1985, p. 129–130).

The difference consists primarily in the fact that time can be measured by movement and expressed by number, while age cannot. Maximus offers a definition of time and age in *Ambiguum* 10. 31, claiming that time, when it is deprived of movement, is age, and that age, when it is measured by movement, is time.[44] Time is relative to movement and change and as such it can be measured or expressed by number. In contrast to time, age represents a distance in which there is no movement, and thus no possibility to be measured, because measurement and quantification are only viable in relation to a change. If one expresses change within beings that exist in age by means of temporal categories, then one may speak about beginning, middle, and end. It is a matter of debate whether all temporal categories may be applied to age, since Maximus refers here only to the beginning as a common feature of time and age, as well as all beings that exist within them. Maximus actually defends a principal Christian belief that God is the Creator out of nothing and that everything that exists was created by him, and therefore must have a beginning in time, or in age:

> Καὶ ὑπὸ τὸ 'πότε,' ὡς ἐν χρόνῳ πάντως ὄντα, συναποδειχθήσεται, ἐπειδὴ μὴ ἁπλῶς, ἀλλὰ πῶς τὸ εἶναι ἔχουσι, πάντα ὅσα μετὰ Θεὸν τὸ εἶναι ἔχει. Καὶ διὰ τοῦτο οὐκ ἄναρχα.

> This will also demonstrate that beings are subject to the category of 'when', as completely existing in time, since no being after God exists simply, but in a certain way, and for this reason beings are not without a beginning.[45]

At this point, by refuting the pagan cosmology which presupposes the eternity of the world, Maximus offers at least two reasons for the non-eternal nature of the creation. The first reason is that everything that exists is under the category of 'when' (πότε), which is applicable to both time and age. The second reason is that the existence of everything created cannot be labeled as simple, since it will always be put under the category of 'how' (πῶς). Maximus additionally explains the aforementioned reason by arguing that the category of 'how' describes how something is,

---

[44] *Amb*. 10, 1164B-C (ed. Constas 2014, I, p. 262–263).
[45] *Amb*. 10, 1180C-D (ed. and trans. Constas 2014, I, p. 292–293).

but not that it is, or that always was (ἦν).[46] While creatures are known on the basis of their mode or 'how' of existence, of God is known only that 'he is' and that 'he was' simply, boundlessly and absolutely. Maximus goes further than this, arguing that being derives from God, but He is not being, being above being.[47] In addition to a temporal reference, all creatures have a spatial reference, because one is inseparably related to the other. Space, according to Maximus, cannot be conceived apart from time, because they are by nature thought together.[48] In addition, Maxim claims that:

> Μήποτε οὖν, ἔργα μὲν Θεοῦ χρονικῶς ἠργμένα τοῦ εἶναί ἐστι, πάντα τὰ ὄντα μετέχοντα· οἷον αἱ διάφοροι τῶν ὄντων οὐσίαι. Τὸ γὰρ μὴ ὄν, ἔχουσι αὐτῶν τοῦ εἶναι πρεσβύτερον. Ἦν γάρ ποτε, ὅτε τὰ ὄντα μετέχοντα οὐκ ἦν. Θεοῦ δὲ ἔργα τυχὸν οὐκ ἠργμένα τοῦ εἶναι χρονικῶς, τὰ ὄντα μεθεκτά, ὧν κατὰ χάριν μετέχουσι τὰ ὄντα μετέχοντα· οἷον, ἡ ἀγαθότης, καὶ πᾶν εἴ τι ἀγαθότητος ἐμπεριέχεται λόγῳ. Καὶ ἁπλῶς πᾶσα ζωή, καὶ ἀθανασία καὶ ἁπλότης καὶ ἀτρεψία καὶ ἀπειρία, καὶ ὅσα περὶ αὐτὸν οὐσιωδῶς θεωρεῖται· ἅτινα καὶ ἔργα Θεοῦ εἰσι, καὶ οὐκ ἠργμένα χρονικῶς.

> God's works which began in time are all beings which share, for example, the different essences of beings, for they have nonbeing before being. For God was when participated beings were not. The works of God which did not happen to begin to be in time are participated beings, in which participated beings share according to grace, for example, goodness and all that the term goodness implies, that is, all life, immortality, simplicity, immutability, and infinity and such things which are essentially contemplated in regard to him; they are also God's works, and yet they did not begin in time.[49]

For Maximus, God is the creator of all that exists, which came to being from non-being. However, although the creation came from non-being into being by the will and goodness of God,

---

[46] By the imperfect of the verb 'to be' in the third person singular (ἦν), Maximus refers to eternal existence. The usage of the verb 'to be' in this form in the Christian tradition to refer to the eternal existence has its origins in the Prologue of St John's Gospel. Cf. Louth 1996, p. 209.

[47] *Amb.* 10, 1180D (ed. Constas 2014, I, p. 294–295).

[48] *Amb.* 10, 1180B-C (ed. Constas 2014, I, p. 292–293).

[49] *Cap. Theol.* I. 48 (ed. PG 90, col. 1100C-D; trans. Berthold 1985, p. 136).

it does not possess being in itself, but it exists in a certain way. The way in which creatures possess being is determined by the natural position of each being, as well as by the limit imposed by its particular λόγος.[50] All created nature, states Maximus, has a duality within its being. The duality of sensible nature consists of physical properties and form, and the duality of the intelligible nature consists of the common essence and its individual properties.[51] In addition, age and time fall under the category of relationship (πρός τι), and everything created that is within which is relative.[52] For Maximus, the entire cosmos is limited by its own λόγοι and it is determined by place and duration of those beings that are within it. This limit is also the limit of space and time, because the limit of space is at the same time the limit of the universe, and the limit of time is the limit of movement.[53] Therefore, in his *Mystagogy*, Maximus claims that God, who brought everything into being, contains, gathers, and limits all beings, which are separated by space and time, but undivided from God and among themselves due to divine providence.[54] For Maximus, God, who is the cause and beginning, as well as the goal of everything created, holds all things separated by nature one from another, making them to converge one to another by the singular force of their relationship to him as origin.[55]

In addition to this static definition of the creatures determined by place and duration, by which the creator separated beings one from another, for Maximus the creation has also a dynamic dimension that derives from the relationship of creation with God as the origin of all things. However, apart from beings related to God as their origin, the created beings are also related to him as provider, who maintains everything in existence, as well as the goal towards which everything naturally

---

[50] *Amb.* 10, 1180D–1181A (ed. Constas 2014, I, p. 294–295): [...] ὑπὸ τοῦ ποῦ εἶναι διὰ τὴν θέσιν καὶ τὸ πέρας τῶν ἐπ᾽ αὐτοῖς κατὰ φύσιν λόγων [...].

[51] *Amb.* 67, 1400C (ed. Constas 2014, II, p. 294).

[52] *Cap. Theol.* I. 68.

[53] *Thal.* 65, 532–534 (ed. CCSG 22): Οὐκοῦν ὁ μὲν κόσμος τόπος ἐστὶ πεπερασμένος καὶ στάσις περιγεγραμμένη, ὁ δὲ χρόνος περιγραφομένη καθέστηκε κίνησις.

[54] *Myst.* I. 132–138 (ed. CCSG 61, p. 11–12).

[55] *Myst.* I. 135–138 (ed. CCSG 61, p. 12).

inclines. Therefore, Maximus claims that God is beginning, middle, and end:

> Ἀρχὴ γάρ ἐστιν ὡς δημιουργός· καὶ μεσότης, ὡς προνοητής· καὶ τέλος, ὡς περιγραφή. Ἐξ αὐτοῦ γάρ, φησί, καὶ δι᾿ αὐτοῦ, καὶ εἰς αὐτὸν τὰ πάντα.

> For he is beginning as creator, middle as provider, and end as goal, for it is said, 'From him and through him and for him are all beings' (Rom. 11. 36).[56]

The dynamic dimension is the participation of creatures in divine attributes, which was not made in time, such as life, immortality, simplicity, immutability, and infinity.[57] Therefore, Maximus claims that one who is rendered worthy of divine grace is above any age, time and place.[58] One may notice that Maximus allows creatures the possibility to transcend their natural limits by striving for their creator, who is at the same time the final goal of their aspirations. This means, in final instance, that, on the basis of their relationship with God, the created beings potentially extend beyond age and time.

5. The Existence of the World from Eternity

In order to portray the relation of creatures to God in all its fullness, one should expand the scope of the investigation from the categories of time and age to the notion of eternity. The main reason of expanding the scope is Maximus' claim that the created beings preexisted from eternity in God's foreknowledge. Maximus argues that:

> Τὴν ἐξ ἰδίου ἐν ἑαυτῷ ὁ Δημιουργὸς τῶν ὄντων προϋπάρχουσαν γνῶσιν, ὅτε ἐβουλήθη, οὐσίωσε καὶ προυβάλετο.

> The Creator when He willed gave substance to and sent forth His eternally pre-existent knowledge of beings.[59]

---

[56] *Cap. Theol.* I. 10 (ed. PG 90, col. 1088A; trans. Berthold 1985, p. 130).
[57] *Cap. Theol.* I. 48.
[58] *Cap. Theol.* I. 68.
[59] *De Carit.* IV. 4 (ed. PG 90, col. 1048D; trans. Sherwood 1955b, p. 192–193). Although Maximus uses the adverbial clause of time ὅτε, this in no case

However, for Maximus, not only the essences of the existing creatures, but also the individual beings existed in the divine foreknowledge from eternity. In the dispute which took place at Bizya with Theodosius, the bishop of Caesarea, Maximus claimed that God preordained from eternity the individual life of each created being in his providence.[60] This does not mean that God, by doing this, limited the freedom of intelligible beings, because Maximus differentiates between that which belongs to essences of created intelligible beings and that which belongs to their free will. In the act of creation, God granted being and eternity or eternal being (εἶναι καὶ ἀεὶ εἶναι; τὸ ὄν καὶ τὸ ἀεὶ ὄν) to the essences of intelligible beings, while at the same time goodness or well-being and wisdom (εὖ εἶναι καὶ σοφία) are bestowed to their free will.[61] Therefore, when pointing to predestination (προορισμός) of creatures, Maximus refers to those properties of beings, which are not dependent on them. On the one hand, these properties are attributed to the essences of creatures, and in general they belong to the realms of being and eternal being, which are fully dependent on the divine will. On the other hand, God has foreknowledge (πρόγνωσις) of our thoughts, words and deeds, which as expressions of our free will fully depend on us.[62]

Arguing about the way in which God knows himself and other beings, Maximus claims:

> Ὁ μὲν Θεὸς ἑαυτὸν γινώσκει ἐκ τῆς μακαρίας οὐσίας αὐτοῦ· τὰ δὲ ὑπ᾽ αὐτοῦ γεγονότα ἐκ τῆς σοφίας αὐτοῦ, δι᾽ἧς καὶ ἐν ᾗ τὰ πάντα ἐποίησεν.

> God knows Himself from His own blessed essence, and the things He has made from His Wisdom through which and in which He made all things.[63]

---

entails that there was a moment in eternity when God began to create. For Maximus, the beginning of divine creative act is covered by a veil of mystery and, therefore, it is unattainable to the human mind (*De Carit.* IV. 5).

[60] *Disp. Biz.* 3 (ed. Allen & Neil 2002, p. 78): Ἡ πρόγνωσις τῶν ἐφ᾽ ἡμῖν ἐννοιῶν καὶ λόγων καὶ ἔργων ἐστίν· ὁ προορισμὸς δὲ τῶν οὐκ ἐφ᾽ ἡμῖν συμβαινόντων ἐστί.

[61] *De Carit.* III. 24–25.

[62] *Disp. Biz.* 3.

[63] *De Carit.* III. 22 (ed. PG 90, col. 1024A; trans. Sherwood 1955b, p. 176).

In regard to God's knowledge of himself, it also implies that God's essence, on the basis of which he knows himself, remains forever hidden to creatures, because of the gulf of ignorance that divides the uncreated from the created nature, and that the only way for created beings to know God is by their participation in his uncreated properties or energies.[64] When referring to the way God knows his creatures, Maximus evokes passages from the Psalms and the Book of Wisdom stating that wisdom existed from eternity in God and by wisdom God created all wonderful things. Here Maximus identifies wisdom with the Λόγος of God, from whom, by whom and for whom everything is created. Moreover, in his *Ambiguum 7*, Maximus claims that one who knows the divine reason (λόγος) and wisdom by which everything is created, on the basis of mutual indivisibility and unconfused specificity of λόγοι in accordance to which everything is created, can also recognize the Λόγος of God in the multitude of created beings.[65] Thus, Maximus points that the λόγοι of created beings are contained in one God from the eternity due to the possible differentiated apprehension of the Λόγος of God in every particular λόγος.[66]

6. *The Creation of Human Beings*

God created human beings according to his image and likeness (κατ'εἰκόνα καὶ ὁμοίωσιν Θεοῦ), whereby the divine image points to being by resembling the being of the One who is, and to eternal being by resembling the eternal being of the One who always was, while the likeness points to the goodness, fashioned according to the goodness of the Good One, and to wisdom, fashioned according to the wisdom of the Wise One.[67] Maximus draws on Dionysus the Areopagite's doctrine of processions (πρόοδοι) here, but he adapts it to serve his purpose.[68]

---

[64] *Cap. Theol.* I. 48.

[65] *Amb.* 7, 1077C (ed. Constas 2014, I, p. 94).

[66] Blowers 1992b, p. 574. On the relationship between one Λόγος and many λόγοι see Dalmais 1952, p. 244–249; Thunberg 1995, p. 75–77; Tollefsen 2008, p. 64–127.

[67] *De Carit.* III. 25.

[68] Cf. Cvetkovic 2011, p. 140–141.

Firstly, Maximus adopts Dionysius' assertion that goodness, being, life, and wisdom are divine processions.[69] However, by replacing the term 'goodness' (ἀγαθότης) with the term 'well-being' (εὖ εἶναι), and the term 'life' (ζωή), which in Dionysius means everlasting life, with the term 'eternal being' (ἀεὶ εἶναι) he utilizes them exclusively in an anthropological context. Therefore, according to Maximus, God creates the human being according to his image and likeness, endowing being and eternal being to human essence in order to reflect God's image in human being, and goodness and wisdom to the realm of human will in order to reflect divine likeness.

In addition to goodness (or well-being) and wisdom (ἀγαθότητος καὶ σοφίας), by which the creator has endowed human free will, human beings have the capacity to direct their free will toward the opposites, such as evil and ignorance (κακίαν καὶ ἀγνωσίαν).[70] However, according to Maximus, these last two categories have no ontological foundation, but they represent a lack of goodness and wisdom. Since human beings were created in the image and likeness of God, human inclination toward evil and ignorance represent a privation of God's attributes. There is no contradiction in God, but only the fullness of all the attributes in which the intelligible created nature participates. A human inclination toward evil and ignorance has direct consequences on human will, but this inclination cannot have any consequence on matters that are within the realm of divine will, like existence or non-existence of creation:

> Ὥσπερ τὸ κακὸν στέρησίς ἐστιν ἀγαθοῦ καὶ ἡ ἀγνωσία στέρησις γνώσεως, οὕτω καὶ τὸ μὴ ὂν στέρησίς ἐστι τοῦ ὄντος, οὐ τοῦ κυρίως δὲ ὄντος· οὐκ ἔχει γὰρ ἐναντίον· ἀλλὰ τοῦ κατὰ μέθεξιν τοῦ κυρίως ὄντος. Καὶ αἱ μὲν τῶν προτέρων στερήσεις τῇ γνώμῃ τῶν γεγονότων ἕπονται· ἡ δὲ τοῦ δευτέρου ἐν τῇ βουλήσει τοῦ πεποιηκότος ὑπάρχεται, τοῦ ἀεὶ δι' ἀγαθότητα βουλομένου εἶναι τὰ ὄντα καὶ ἀεὶ ὑπ' αὐτοῦ εὐεργετεῖσθαι.

As evil is the privation of the good, and ignorance of knowledge; so not-being is privation of being, not of true Being (for it has no contrary), but of participated true Being. The

---

[69] *De divinis nominibus* 5. 2 (ed. Suchla 1991, p. 181).
[70] *De Carit.* III. 27 (ed. PG 90, col. 1025A).

former privations follow the will and judgment of crea-
tures; the latter rests with the will of the Maker. And He of
His goodness ever wills beings to be and always to receive
His benefits.[71]

Maximus argues here that the rational beings may choose privation of goodness and wisdom, but even refusing their participation in the true being, they do not have the capacity to return
to non-being, because this decision depends on divine will.
Since God always wills for creation 'to be' and 'to be forever',
he would not make such a decision to return created beings into
non-being even this is their will. This raises the question about
the divine prospects of the beings, which voluntarily dwell in
deprivation of divine attributes. God does not know a mode
of existence which is contrary to the natural λόγος of every created being. By dwelling in deprivation of divine goods and by
failing to reflect divine likeness, created beings oppose their natural λόγοι of being and eternal or ever-being. On the one hand,
created beings do not have the capacity to return to non-being
from which they derive, and subsist on the basis of being as divine
gift. On the other hand, by representing the fullness of all his
attributes in which the creatures participate, God does not contain within himself the opposites or privation of those attributes, including relative non-being (μὴ ὄν). Therefore, by opting
for evil, ignorance, and non-being, the created beings are torn
between their inclinations toward the privation of divine goods
and immense divine life reflected through the divine good.
Maximus describes this state of being by the technical term τὸ φεῦ
εἶναι ('evil-being' or 'ill-being'), which is diametrically opposed
to the state of τὸ εὖ εἶναι ('well-being').[72] The God of Christians,
for Maximus, is not a cruel tyrant who punishes rational created beings for moral transgressions, because the choice of created beings to be deprived of divine goods is already a judgment
and punishment for them. If the created beings persist in opposing their natural λόγοι and continue to dwell in deprivation

[71] *De Carit.* III. 29 (ed. PG 90, col. 1025C; trans. Sherwood 1955b, p. 178).
[72] *Amb.* 42, 1329A (ed. Constas 2014, II, p. 148–149).

of divine goods, their state of ill-being extends into eternity as ever ill-being (ἀεὶ φεῦ εἶναι).[73]

7. God's Design of Universals and Particulars and λόγος-τρόπος Distinction

For Maximus, the principal λόγος of everything created is the λόγος of being, which is bestowed on all created nature, regardless of whether it is spiritual or material, rational or sensible. Maximus claims that in a way known only to Him, God completed once and for all the primary λόγοι and universal essences of created beings.[74] However, according to Maximus, God did not just create general essences of being, which he preserves now through his providential role, but he formed the individual parts that potentially exist in general essence, constantly caring for their development and survival. Maximus argues that by his providence God conforms particulars to universals until creaturely inclinations are voluntarily united with the general λόγος of rational beings, through the movement of the individual creatures toward well-being. Moreover, God makes them compliant and self-moving both in relation to each other and in relation to the overall creation.[75] A view that God exercises his divine providence not only over universals, but also over particulars has been already developed by Nemesius of Emesa, in his refutation of Aristotelianism, and Maximus closely followed the bishop of Emesa on this point.[76]

Maximus makes a distinction between natural λόγος of beings (λόγος τοῦ εἶναι τῶν ὄντων), which is embodied in their nature, and individual modes of existence (τρόπος ὑπάρξεως) of these beings. While these λόγοι of beings depend on God, the modes of their existence are given to the free will of rational creatures. The λόγοι of beings are reflected in the essences of beings as their

---

[73] *Amb.* 65, 1392C (ed. Constas 2014, II, p. 278–279).

[74] *Thal.* 2 (ed. CCSG 7, p. 51): Τοὺς μὲν πρώτους τῶν γεγονότων λόγους ὁ Θεὸς καὶ τὰς καθόλου τῶν ὄντων οὐσίας ἅπαξ, ὡς οἶδεν αὐτός, συμπληρώσας [...].

[75] *Thal.* 2 (ed. CCSG 7, p. 51).

[76] *De natura hominis* 42 (ed. Morani 1987, p. 124).

ultimate scope (ὅρος).[77] Maximus links the mode of being to individual or personal existence and in practice this mode is reflected in creatures' employment of their free will. Therefore, Maximus claims that by the variation of a person's actions one may know his mode of being, while by the immutability of human natural energies one may know his λόγος of being.[78] Maximus uses an Aristotelian conceptual framework in describing the relationships between the λόγος of beings and the mode of existence of these beings in terms of πρᾶξις and ἐνέργεια. However, Tollefsen notes that in contrast to Aristotle, who claims that a being actualizes itself in action (πρᾶξις) on the basis of its potentiality (ἐνέργεια), and that the action includes the end (τέλος) in itself, Maximus maintains that the τέλος cannot be reached within the framework of natural actualization.[79] In *The Centuries on Theology and Economy*, Maximus reflects on the triad ἀρχή – μεσότης – τέλος in the context of the Aristotelian triad οὐσία – δύναμις – ἐνέργεια. He argues that each τέλος, naturally limited by its own λόγος, is a fulfillment of potentiality, which derives from the essence and which conceptually precedes the τέλος.[80] This seemingly contradicts Tollefsen's claim that Maximus does not conceive the τέλος outside the natural framework of beings. However, in *Ambiguum* 7 he clarifies that everything that comes into being does not have τέλος in itself, since it is not self-caused.[81] This apparent contradiction can be explained by the natural limit of λόγος, which does not represent the end of being, but only the end of its natural λόγος, reflected in its essence and realized in its natural energies. Maximus explains this as follows:

> Ὅσα μὲν ἐν χρόνῳ κατὰ χρόνον δημιουργεῖται, τελειωθέντα ἵσταται, λήγοντα τῆς κατὰ φύσιν αὐξήσεως. Ὅσα δὲ κατ᾿ ἀρετὴν ἐπιστήμη Θεοῦ κατεργάζεται, τελειωθέντα πάλιν κινεῖται πρὸς αὔξησιν. Τὰ γὰρ τέλη αὐτῶν, ἑτέρων ἀρχαὶ καθεστήκασιν.

---

[77] *Cap. Theol.* I. 3.

[78] *Opus.* 10 (ed. PG 91, col. 137A): Ὅθεν ἐν μὲν τῷ τρόπῳ τὸ παρηλλαγμένον τῶν προσώπων κατὰ τὴν πρᾶξιν γνωρίζεται· ἐν δὲ τῷ λόγῳ, τὸ τῆς φυσικῆς ἀπαράλλακτον ἐνεργείας.

[79] Tollefsen 2008, p. 115.

[80] *Cap. Theol.* I. 3.

[81] *Amb.* 7, 1072B (ed. Constas 2014, I, p. 82–83).

> All things created in time according to time become perfect when they cease their natural growth. But everything that the knowledge of God effects according to virtue, when it reaches perfection, moves to further growth. For the end of the latter becomes the beginning of the former.[82]

The end of natural growth represents reaching the natural limit of λόγος, but it does not represent the end of the rational beings, whose τέλος coincides with the cause of their existence, i.e. God. Thus, one may conclude that the natural growth occurs in time and is restricted by time. Maximus identifies the realm of natural λόγοι with the law, which regulates temporal matters exposed to generation and corruption.[83] Therefore, human beings grow in their natural λόγος through the cycles of generation and corruption. According to Maximus, although rational soul is confined to this biological time, she collects and recognizes the virtuous and spiritual λόγοι of everything that exists.[84] However, by existing in time and by recognizing the λόγοι of beings, the human being is led to transcend both time and the λόγοι of beings. Maximus mentions the experiences of the saints, who by discerning the permanence, the order, and the position of created beings, as well as their mode of existence, according to which everything is unconfused and without disorder, concluded that the world is ruled by divine providence.[85] Maximus argues that the way in which the cosmic time passes in regular intervals of the Earth's rotation and revolution, which causes the alternating change of day and night and the seasons, led saints to come to their conclusion about the divine creative and providential role.

8. *The λόγοι of Well-being and Eternal Well-being*

For Maximus the soul does not only contemplate the natural λόγοι of beings but also the spiritual λόγοι of virtues. The spiritual λόγοι of virtues direct the soul to transcend the closed cycle of

---

[82] *Cap. Theol.* I. 35 (ed. PG 90, col. 1096C; trans. Berthold 1985, p. 134–135).

[83] *Cap. Theol.* I. 35.

[84] *Cap. Theol.* I. 42.

[85] *Amb.* 10, 1176C (ed. Constas 2014, I, p. 284–285).

generation and corruption, and through loving ecstasy to move towards God as the centre of all λόγοι.[86] Maximus argues that one who through his virtuous activity stopped the establishment of corruption will experience in himself the realization of divine principles.[87] This means that by knowing the virtue and by acting in accordance to it, one may be carried out from the closed cycle of corruption and, thus, be elevated in his knowledge from the creation to the creator. The virtuous life is a mode of existence for rational beings, and it corresponds to the human realization and multiplication of gifts of goodness and wisdom, which are granted to the human being in the act of creation. However, these gifts are not something fixed by the will of God in the creation and dependent on the same divine will, like it is the case of the λόγοι of beings, but they are left to the free will of the rational creation. Therefore, whether the rational being will opt for goodness and wisdom, and thus gain the likeness of God, or will opt for their opposites or deprivations, depends upon the creaturely mode of existence. The τρόπος of being can be in conformity with nature (κατὰ φύσιν) if the rational being follows his purpose or his λόγος of being according to which he is created, or against nature (παρὰ φύσιν) if deviating from its natural λόγος. It should be noted here that this λόγος of being is not a most general λόγος, or the λόγος relating to a particular substance, but the λόγος of individual being. The τρόπος of each rational being may be in conformity with his λόγος (κατὰ λόγον) or in opposition to his λόγος (παρὰ λόγον). Maximus claims that if the τρόπος of the rational being is in conformity with the appropriate λόγος, then it is given an opportunity for spiritual growth or transition to a higher state of being, which he refers to as well-being (εὖ εἶναι). As the λόγος of being is linked to divine being, so the λόγος of well-being is linked to God's goodness and wisdom. Therefore, well-being represents participation in the divine goodness and wisdom as the uncreated energies of God. At the level of the λόγος of well-being the general plan is combined with the personal one. The created rational being will only be able to take part in

---

[86] *Cap. Theol.* I. 39; II. 4; *Amb.* 7, 1081C (ed. Constas 2014, I, p. 100–104); *Myst.* 1, 189–193 (ed. CCSG 61, p. 13).

[87] *Cap. Theol.* I. 35.

the λόγος of well-being, if he acts in accordance with his own particular λόγος. By attaining the λόγος of well-being, one does not reach the end of his spiritual growth, because there is another level ahead. The last stage, which is endless for Maximus, is to achieve eternal being (ἀεὶ εἶναι). Maximus applies various analogies on the triad εἶναι – εὖ εἶναι – ἀεὶ εἶναι. Thus, in *The Centuries on Theology and Economy* he symbolically compares it with the sixth, seventh and eighth day of creation:

> Ἡ ἕκτη ἡμέρα, τὸν τοῦ εἶναι τῶν ὄντων λόγον ὑποδηλοῖ· ἡ δὲ ἑβδόμη, τὸν τοῦ εὖ εἶναι τῶν ὄντων τρόπον ὑποσημαίνει· ἡ δὲ ὀγδόη, τὸ τοῦ ἀεί εὖ εἶναι τῶν ὄντων ἄρρητον μυστήριον ὑπαγορεύει.

> The sixth day reveals the principle of being of things, the seventh indicates the manner of the well-being of things, the eighth communicates the ineffable mystery of the eternal well-being of things.[88]

Maximus employs here a metaphor of creation in order to explain his metaphysical principles. Thus, Saturday is the end of the six-day creation in which everything was created and in which God laid the foundations of being; therefore, it points to the λόγος of being. As a symbol of God's rest, the seventh day represents the entire history of the human drama of elevating toward God through virtuous life, or the λόγος of well-being. Being out of the circle of creation as never-ending day, the eighth day points to eternity for which all things were made and to the λόγος of eternal beings as the participation in the eternal life of God. Moreover, by explaining Gregory the Theologian's views on the three births from his oration *On the Theophany*, Maximus, in his *Ambiguum* 42, offers again a symbolic representation of the aforementioned triad.[89] Thus, the first birth as a physical birth, which results in the union between soul and body, is gaining of being. The second birth is the result of baptism through which human beings obtain well-being in abundance. The third birth is the fruit of resurrection, by which God through his grace (διὰ χάριτος) receives the human beings into the eternal well-

---

[88] *Cap. Theol.* I. 56 (ed. PG 90, col. 1104C; trans. Berthold 1985, p. 138).
[89] Gregorius Nazianzenus, *Or.* 38, 11 (*In theophania*) (ed. SC 358).

being.[90] Although the eternal life or eternal being is bestowed on the rational beings by nature, the divine grace of eternal well-being is not automatically spilled out on created beings, being dependent on their mode of existence or on their participation in the λόγος of well-being. As mentioned above, the λόγοι of being and of eternal being represent the image of God, according to which the human being was created, and they are stored in human essence. As every creature that has been translated from non-being into being acquires its being due to participation in the λόγος of being, he also acquires his eternal being by participating in God as eternity. The former is something that is already realized in human nature, while the latter, although it is attributed in potentiality to human essence, is something whose mode each individual being receives according to the grace (κατὰ χάριν) of God. The well-being is reflected in human free choice (κατὰ πρόθεσιν) of the mode of existence, and as such it does not depend on the will of God. Therefore, if a human being opts for the life in accordance with his λόγος of well-being, then he receives the divine gift of eternal well-being. Maximus refers often to eternal being as the eternal well-being, because by his choice of well-being, human beings establish themselves in the eternal well-being by divine grace. However, if by inclining toward evil and ignorance, as privations of goodness and wisdom, the human free will is utilized contrary to the λόγος of being, then human being acquires the life in ill-being (τὸ φεῦ εἶναι).[91] By choosing the ill-being, human beings establish themselves in eternal ill-being (τὸ ἀεὶ φεῦ εἶναι), because they are eternal by nature.[92]

9. The Purpose of Creation – The Eternity of Creation

Maximus' symbolic comparison of the λόγοι of being, well-being, and eternal being with the sixth, the seventh, and the eighth day of creation has its elaboration within the categories of time and eternity as well:

---

[90] *Amb.* 42, 1316AC (ed. Constas 2014, II, p. 122–125).
[91] *Amb.* 42, 1329A (ed. Constas 2014, II, p. 148–149).
[92] *Amb.* 65, 1392D (ed. Constas 2014, II, p. 280–281).

Ἡ ἕκτη κατὰ τὴν Γραφὴν ἡμέρα, τὴν τῶν ὑπὸ φύσιν ὄντων εἰσηγεῖται συμπλήρωσιν· ἡ δὲ ἑβδόμη, τῆς χρονικῆς ἰδιότητος περιγράφει τὴν κίνησιν· ἡ δὲ ὀγδόη, τῆς ὑπὲρ φύσιν καὶ χρόνον ὑποδηλοῖ καταστάσεως τὸν τρόπον.

According to Scripture, the sixth day brings in the completion of beings subject to nature. The seventh limits the movement of temporal distinctiveness. The eighth indicates the manner of existence above nature and time.[93]

In relation to this passage one may discern the distinction between temporal and eternal realm. For Maximus, the sixth day refers to the cosmological or biological time and it represents the fullness of creation, in which are placed the λόγοι of beings. The sixth day is under the category of nature and time, and it symbolically points to the creation of all beings according to the preexisting λόγοι of God.[94] Maximus does not refer only to the essences that have come into being, but also to the individual beings that had their λόγοι from eternity in God.[95] Therefore, Maximus perceives the relationship between the individual created beings and their λόγοι in terms of time or opportune moment:

[...] κἂν εἰ αὐτὰ τὰ πάντα, τά τε ὄντα καὶ τὰ ἐσόμενα, οὐχ ἅμα τοῖς ἑαυτῶν λόγοις, ἢ τῷ γνωσθῆναι ὑπὸ Θεοῦ, εἰς τὸ εἶναι παρήχθησαν, ἀλλ᾽ ἕκαστα τῷ ἐπιτηδείῳ καιρῷ κατὰ τὴν τοῦ Δημιουργοῦ σοφίαν πρεπόντως κατὰ τοὺς ἑαυτῶν λόγους δημιουργούμενα καὶ καθ᾽ ἑαυτὰ εἶναι τῇ ἐνεργείᾳ λαμβάνῃ.

[...] even though all things – things present and things to come – were not called into existence simultaneously with their *logoi* or with their being known by God. Instead, in the wisdom of the Creator, individual things were created at the appropriate moment in time, in a manner consistent with their *logoi*, and thus they received in themselves actual existence as beings.[96]

Maximus employs the term καιρός in order to point to a certain moment or period in time within which the divine providence

---

[93] *Cap. Theol.* I. 51 (ed. PG 90, col. 1102C; trans. Berthold 1985, p. 137).
[94] *Amb.* 7, 1081A (ed. Constas 2014, I, p. 98–101).
[95] *Amb.* 10, 1188D–1192B (ed. Constas 2014, I, p. 308–313).
[96] *Amb.* 7, 1081A (ed. and trans. Constas 2014, I, p. 98–101).

is realized. Time is perceived neither as consequence of Adam's fall, nor as the continuous circulation of planets and an endless circle of generation and corruption, but as medium, whose λόγοι of time (οἱ λόγοι τοῦ χρόνου) eternally preexisted in God.[97] The divine purpose of time is to be a medium in which the created beings may grow up in both λόγοι of nature and λόγοι of virtues. Therefore, time is a medium in which created beings realize their own natural λόγοι, and every creature has an opportune moment (καιρός) for the growth in his own λόγοι in the course of time. The end of time is not the end of creatures, but rather a transition of well-being into the eternal well-being. Time plays an important role in the divine plan of creation and it was created by God, like everything else, to be good. However, depending on the manner in which beings use their spiritual and physical abilities, time receives its context, which features creaturely movement towards good or in the opposite direction. Time exists only along this movement of beings, because it does not accompany them in the divine life of the age to come. The created beings then abide in Christ, who is the successor of both time and age.[98] Therefore, as the realization of the λόγοι of beings belongs to the sixth day or time, the λόγοι of eternal beings, no matter whether eternal well-being or eternal ill-being, find their realization in the eighth day, which is outside nature and time.

10. *Conclusion*

Maximus the Confessor's *Ambigua ad Ioannem* represents an important moment in the emergence of patristic tradition as a source of authority. Maximus not only firmly established the theological authority of Gregory Nazianzen, whose writings were under direct scrutiny, but he also dealt harmoniously with different patristic voices. Maximus the Confessor's view on creation exposed in *Ambigua ad Ioannem* is a good example of both his theological originality and synthetic capabilities. He does not see himself as an inventor of novel teachings, but rather as a close follower of the previously exposed doctrines by the saints and

---

[97] *Amb.* 10, 1164B (ed. Constas 2014, I, p. 262–263).
[98] *Amb.* 10, 1164B (ed. Constas 2014, I, p. 262–263).

the Fathers of the Church. By references to the Church Fathers, especially Gregory Nazianzen and Dionysius the Areopagite, but also Gregory of Nyssa and Nemesius of Emesa, Maximus attempts to prove that he is just a humble interpreter of the previous teachings on the subject of the creation of the world. In the cases where the Christian perspective of the doctrine of creation is jeopardized by heterodox views, like in the case of Origen's teaching of double creation, one from eternity and another as divine punishment of the creatures' movement away from God, Maximus exposes a fierce refutation of such teachings. However, his refutation of Origenist myth is again grounded in previous orthodox tradition. Therefore, in arguing against Origenistic views in his *Ambiguum* 7, Maximus employs Gregory of Nyssa's teaching on movement toward God and rest in him, as the most distinctive feature of everything created. When combating the extreme anti-Origenism of the seventh century, Maximus again made use of Church Fathers such as Dionysius to show that human body is created to undergo transformation from physical to spiritual.

In *Ambiguum* 41 Maximus draws on Gregory of Nyssa's stance on the division within the being, commencing from the first division between male and female until the last division between uncreated and created nature. He skillfully combines these aspects of Nyssen's doctrine with the doctrine on λόγοι as preexisting divine wills about creation, which he borrowed in sketch from Dionysius the Areopagite and further developed. Maximus develops a view on the creation of human being by interpreting the biblical verse of the creation of human being in the divine image and likeness, in the light of Dionysius' doctrine of four divine processions (being, life, wisdom and goodness). Maximus borrows from Nemesius of Emesa a critique of the Aristotelian stance that God is the creator and provider not only of universals, but of particulars too. Thus, in his *Ambiguum* 10, by pairing Nemesius' doctrine of divine providence with his doctrine of λόγοι, Maximus develops a view on pre-existence of λόγοι of individual human and angelic beings in God from eternity and on divine care about them. In addition, Maximus exposes all these ideas in philosophical language based on Neoplatonic, Stoic, and Aristotelian notions. This may suggest his direct or indirect acquaintance either with the teachings of Alexandrian Neoplatonic thinkers such as John Philoponus and Stephanus of Alexandria or the teachings of earlier Neoplatonic schools, such as the Athenian Academy. Nevertheless, although his teachings are camouflaged in the philosophical language of late Neoplatonism they perfectly accomplish the purpose of Christian metaphysics. By gathering previous teachings on creation in an inclusive synthesis, Maximus the Confessor offers a most comprehensive account of the Christian philosophy of creation.

Bibliography

Primary Sources

Dionysius Areopagiticus, *Corpus Dionysiacum.* I: *De Divinis Nominibus* (= *DN*), ed. B. R. Suchla, Berlin: de Gruyter, 1990, p. 107–231.

Gregorius Nazianzenus, *Orationes* 38–41, ed. C. Moreschini, Paris 1990 (Sources Chrétiennes 358).

Gregorius Nyssenus, *De opificio hominis*, PG 44.

Gregorius Nyssenus, *Contra Eunomium*, vol. 1.1 & 2.2, ed. W. Jaeger, Leiden: Brill, 1960 (Gregorii Nysseni Opera = GNO 1).

Ioannes Philoponus, *De aeternitate mundi contra Aristotelem*, ed. J. L. Heiberg, Berlin, 1894.

Ioannes Philoponus, *De opificio mundi*, ed. G. Reichardt, Lipsiae: Teubner, 1897.

Ioannes Philoponus, *De aeternitate mundi contra Proclum*, ed. H. Rabe, Lipsiae: Teubner, 1899.

Maximus Confessor, *Ambiguorum liber, Ambig. Ioan.* (= *Amb.*) 6–7, PG 91, col. 1061–1417.

Maximus Confessor, *On the Difficulties in Church Fathers. The Ambigua*, ed. and trans. M. Constas, 2. vols. Cambridge, Mass.: Harvard University Press, 2014.

Maximus Confessor, *Capitum theologicorum et oeconomicorum duae centuriae* (= *Cap. Theol.*), PG 90, col. 1084–1173.

Maximus Confessor, *Capita de caritate, quattuor centuriae* (= *De Carit.*), PG 90, col. 960–1073.

Maximus Confessor, *Epistulae* (1–45) (= *Ep.*), PG 91, col. 361–650.

Maximus Confessor, *Mystagogia* (= *Myst.*), ed. C. Boudignon, Turnhout: Brepols 2011 (CCSG 69).

Maximus Confessor, *Opuscula theologica et polemica* (= *Opusc.*) 1–27, PG 91, col. 9–285.

Maximus Confessor, *Disputatio Bizyae cum Theodosio* (= *Disp. Biz.*), ed. P. Allen & B. Neil, Turnhout: Brepols, 1990, p. 73–151 (CCSG 39).

Maximus Confessor, *Quaestiones ad Thalassium* (= *Thal.*) 1–55, ed. C. Laga & C. Steel, Turnhout: Brepols, 1980 (CCSG 7).

Maximus Confessor, *Quaestiones ad Thalassium* (= *Thal.*) 56–65, ed. C. Laga & C. Steel, Turnhout: Brepols, 1990 (CCSG 22).

Nemesius Emesenus, *De natura hominis*, ed. M. Morani, Leipzig: Teubner, 1987.

Origenes, *De principiis*, ed. H. Görgemanns & H. Karpp, Darmstadt: Wissenschaftliche Buchgesellschaft, 1976.

Philo Alexandrinus, *Opera quae supersunt*, ed. L. Cohn et al., Berlin: Reimer, 1896-, I: *De opificio mundi*, ed. L. Cohn (1896).

Philo Alexandrinus, *Opera quae supersunt*, ed. L. Cohn et al., Berlin: Reimer, 1896-, VI: *De aeternitate mundi*, ed. L. Cohn & P. Wendland (1915).

Simplicius, *In Aristotelis quattuor libros de caelo commentaria*, ed. J. L. Heiberg, Berlin: Reimer, 1984.

Translations and Secondary Literature

P. Allen & B. Neil (2002), *Maximus the Confessor. Documents from Exile*, Oxford: Oxford University Press.

P. Allen & B. Neil (2015), *The Oxford Handbook of Maximus the Confessor*, Oxford: Oxford University Press.

H. U. von Balthasar (1941), *Kosmische Liturgie, Maximus der Bekenner: Höhe und Krise des griechischen Weltbilds*, Freiburg: Weltbilds.

H. U. von Balthasar (2003), *Cosmic liturgy: the universe according to Maximus the Confessor*, San Francisco: Ignatius Press.

G. Benevich (2009), 'Maximus the Confessor's polemics against anti-Origenism: Epistulae 6 and 7 as a context for the Ambigua ad Iohannem', in *Revue d'histoire ecclésiastique*, 104, p. 5–15.

G. I. Benevich, D. S. Biriukov & A. M. Shufrin (2007), *Prp. Maksim Ispovednik: Polemika s Origenizmom i Mononergizmom*, Sankt-Peterburg: SPbGU – RkhGA.

G. S. Berthold (1985), *Maximus Confessor. Selected Writings*, New York: Paulist Press.

P. M. Blowers (1992a), 'Maximus the Confessor, Gregory of Nyssa, and the Concept of "Perpetual Progress"', in *Vigiliae Christianae*, 46, p. 151–171.

P. M. Blowers (1992b), 'The Logology of Maximus the Confessor and His Criticism of Origenism', in R. J. Daly (ed.), *Origeniana Quinta: Historica, Text and Method, Biblica, Philosophica, Theologica, Origenism and Later Developments*, Leuven: Leuven University Press – Peeters, p. 570–575.

V. Cvetković (2011), 'Predeterminations and Providence in Dionysius and Maximus the Confessor', in F. Ivanović (ed.), *Dionysius the Areopagite between Orthodoxy and Heresy*, Newcastle: Cambridge Scholars Publishing, p. 135–156.

V. Cvetković (2016), 'Maximus the Confessor's Reading of Origen between Origenism and Anti-Origenism', in A.-C. Jacobsen (ed.), *Origeniana Undecima: Origen and Origenism in the History of Western Tradition*, Leuven: Peeters, p. 747–758.

I.-H. Dalmais (1952), 'La théorie des "logoi" des créatures chez S. Maxime le Confesseur', in *Revue des sciences philosophiques et théologiques*, 36, p. 244–249.

J. Daniélou (1970), *L'être et le temps chez Grégoire de Nyssa*, Leiden: Brill.

J.-M. Garrigues (1976), *Maxime Le Confeseur: Le Charité, avenir divin de l'homme*, Paris: Beauchesne.

M. Jankowiak & P. Booth (2015), 'A New Date-List of the Works of Maximus the Confessor', in P. Allen & B. Neil (eds), *The Oxford Handbook of Maximus the Confessor*, Oxford: Oxford University Press, p. 19–83.

L. Judson (1987), 'God or Nature? Philoponus on Generability and Perishability', in R. Sorabji (ed.), *Philoponus and the Rejection of Aristotelian Science*, London: Duckworth, p. 179–196.

W. Lackner (1971), 'Der Amtstitel Maximos des Bekenners', in *Jahrbuch der österreichischen Byzantinistik*, 20, p. 63–65.

A. Lévy (2006), *Le créé et le incréé. Maxime le Confesseur et Thomas d'Aquin: Aux sources de la querelle palamienne*, Paris: Vrin.

A. Louth (1996), *Maximus the Confessor*, London: Routledge.

A. Louth (1998), 'Recent research on St Maximus the Confessor: A survey', in *St Vladimir's Theological Quarterly*, 42, p. 67–84.

A. Louth (2009), 'The Reception of Dionysius in the Byzantine World: Maximus to Palamas', in *Modern Theology*, 24, p. 585–599.

G. May (2004), *Creatio ex Nihilo. The Doctrine of 'Creation out of Nothing' in Early Christian Thought*, London & New York: T&T Clark International.

P. Plass (1980), 'Transcendent time in Maximus the Confessor', in *The Thomist*, 44, p. 259–277.

E. Ponsoye (1994), *Saint Maxime le Confesseur. Ambigua*, Paris: Suresnes.

P. Sherwood (1952), *An Annotated Date-list of the Works of Maximus the Confessor*, Romae: Studia Anselmiana.

P. Sherwood, (1955a), *The Earlier Ambigua of Saint Maximus the Confessor and his Refutation of Origenism*, Romae: Studia Anselmiana.

P. Sherwood (1955b), *St Maximus the Confessor. The Ascetic Life and the Four Centuries on Love*, London: Longman, Greens and Co.

L. Thunberg (1995), *Microcosm and Mediator: The Theological Anthropology of Maximus the Confessor*, 2nd ed., Chicago and La Salle: Open Court.

T. Tollefsen (2008), *The Christocentric Cosmology of St Maximus the Confessor*, Oxford: Oxford University Press.

P. Van Deun & P. Mueller-Jourdan (2015). 'Maxime Le Confesseur', in C. G. Conticello (ed.), *La théologie byzantine et sa tradition*, vol. I/1, Turnhout: Brepols, p. 387–510.

W. Völker (1963), *Maximus Confessor als Meister des Geistlichen Lebens*, Weisbaden: Franz Steiner Verlag.

C. Wildberg (1987), *Philoponus. Against Aristotle, on the Eternity of the World*, London: Duckworth.

H. A. Wolfson (1948), *Philo, Foundations of Religious Philosophy in Judaism, Christianity and Islam*, Cambridge, Mass.: Harvard University Press.

Abstract

The paper aims to analyze Maximus the Confessor's views on creation focusing on his *Ambigua ad Ioannem*. Particular attention will be given to Maximus' doctrines of the *logoi* of the creation (*Ambiguum* 7), of the logical structure of the creation (*Ambiguum* 10) and of the five divisions of the creation (*Ambiguum* 41). The paper also attempts to discern the possible sources of Maximus' teachings, exploring his indebtedness to Origen, Gregory of Nyssa, Dionysius the Areopagite, Nemesius of Emesa, as well as to Aristotle's Neoplatonic commentators. Finally, the paper intends to connect the ontological, logical and cosmological aspects of Maximus' view on creation in one comprehensive synthesis, showing his originality in interpreting previous views on creation.

TORSTEIN THEODOR TOLLEFSEN

ST MAXIMUS THE CONFESSOR ON THE MYSTERY OF CHRIST

Armstrong says, commenting on Plotinus: 'There is no deliberate action on the part of the One, and no willing or planning or
choice or care for what is produced.'[1] If this is correct, which it
probably is, then there is a marked difference between the Neoplatonic doctrine of the creation and preservation of the cosmos
as we find it in Plotinus and Proclus and the doctrine of the Late-
Antique Christian philosopher St Maximus the Confessor. This
difference is probably not only between these thinkers, but rather
between pagan Neoplatonist cosmological doctrines in general
and the cosmology of Christian thinkers who were preoccupied
with these topics, like St Basil and St Augustine. One might ask
a few questions. Is the act of creation due to a divine act of will?
Does God care for creatures? Are they made for a definite purpose? These three questions correspond to St Paul's 'metaphysics
of prepositions' as we find it in Romans 11. 36: 'For of Him and
through Him to Him are all things, to whom be glory forever.
Amen.' (ὅτι ἐξ αὐτοῦ καὶ δι' αὐτοῦ καὶ εἰς αὐτὸν τὰ πάντα· αὐτῷ ἡ
δόξα εἰς τοὺς αἰῶνας· ἀμήν.) Things are made by God (ἐξ αὐτοῦ),
are preserved by God (δι' αὐτοῦ), and have their goal in God
(εἰς αὐτόν). In this article I shall try to show that pagan Neoplatonism (as we find it in Plotinus and Proclus) answers these questions in a different way than Maximus. In the last part of this
article I shall show that, according to Maximus, the cosmos is
made for a particular purpose. This purpose is the transformation of all beings into the condition of deification. In short,

---

[1] Armstrong 1980, p. 240.

Questioning the World, Greek Patristic and Byzantine Question-and-Answer Literature, ed. by Bram Demulder and Peter Van Deun,
Turnhout, 2021 (*LECTIO*, 11), pp. 181-200   © BREPOLS✠PUBLISHERS   DOI 10.1484/M.LECTIO-EB.5.121506

God does not only care for the general framework of the world, but for each creature within the system of the whole. In connection with this we shall turn to a couple of texts in what may be called a question-and-answer commentary, viz. the *Quaestiones ad Thalassium* 22 and 60. I shall argue that Maximus claims the purpose of creation is to achieve the economy of the Incarnation in order to establish the conditions for the deification of all beings. That is to say that the Incarnation is not a divine rescue operation when something went wrong among historically existing humans, but is rather God's eternal purpose: God made the world because He eternally sought to communicate His gift of deification.

Why is there a cosmos at all? Neoplatonists and Christians would agree to the following answer: because of divine goodness. For pagan Neoplatonism this would be the classic answer, taken from Plato's *Timaeus*.[2] However, since the understanding of divine activity differs between Neoplatonism and Christian thought, the similarity stops at this point. We may ask our first question: is the act of creation due to a divine act of will? There are two terms here that make a difference, viz. act of creation and act of will. Plotinus, Proclus, and Maximus would agree that an act of creation is behind the cosmos even if they would disagree as to the nature of this act. When it comes to the act of will they would definitely disagree. Since there is a cosmos, there must be a divine act of creation behind it, but the nature of that act depends upon how the divine act of will is executed.

The One of Plotinus has a basic feature, viz. it is 'abiding' or 'remaining'. All entities in the Plotinian cosmos, as long as they *remain* in being (ἕως μένει), produce something out of their own essences.[3] The One produces as well. Metaphorically speaking the One is like the sun radiating light.[4] The productive activity of the One may also be compared with perfume diffusing scent. Neither

---

[2] Cf. *Timaeus* 29d–30c. However, one should keep in mind that Proclus' Demiurge *participates* in Goodness by receiving it from the One. The Demiurge belongs to the intellective gods in Proclus' intricate hierarchy of being, while the Good as such transcends everything. Cf. Proclus, *In Timaeum* I.360, 364 on the Demiurge, with trans. Runia & Share 2008, p. 22–24.

[3] *Ennead* 5.1.6.

[4] *Ennead* 5.1.6.

the sun nor perfume send forth their activities of light and scent as a result of any conscious process. However, we cannot immediately turn Plotinian metaphors into philosophical doctrine and draw the conclusion that the One unconsciously produces as if it just 'overflowed' with energy. First we shall have to find out more about what remaining means.

In *Ennead* 5.4.2 we learn that every entity possesses an activity that belongs to its essence (i.e. an internal activity) and an activity that goes out of its essence (i.e. an external activity). In *Ennead* 6.8.13 Plotinus writes on the will of the One and creates the impression that the internal activity of the One is its essence as actively willing.[5] Willing what? One might picture for oneself the situation of one thing willing another, but that cannot be the case here. There is no duality. There is no distinction between willing and its accomplishment. It is a reasonable interpretation that the One is essentially a *willing to be itself*, and, one might suppose, this is what the remaining consists in: willing to be itself. It is probably also reasonable to draw the conclusion that this willing to be itself is a willing to be itself as good. The One is not as it is because it cannot be otherwise, but because being what it is is the best. There is no necessity involved.[6] If the willing of the One is the willing of itself as the Good, then one may guess that the One wills itself as that which becomes the principle of an external activity of making.[7]

Of course, we should remember that all this talk about the One is the talk of something that cannot be talked about adequately, since the One is beyond all intellectual grasp. However, even if Plotinus often stresses this fact, he also talks about the One in order to accommodate a slight philosophical grasp of what goes on in the generation of the cosmos. The idea that the One wills itself as the Good might be a convenient starting point for considering the One as Creator. We should expect of a Creator that

[5] It is important to note that, according to Plotinus, the enquiry into the topic of will is for the sake of persuasion, or, as Rist 1980, p. 79, says, 'we must begin to use language of the One which is not strictly appropriate' in order to accommodate understanding.

[6] *Ennead* 6.8.9.

[7] Rist 1980, chapter 6, has an interesting discussion of 'Emanation and Necessity' that is relevant for the present topic.

it is conscious of itself and of what it is going to make. However, this is not the case with Plotinus' One. The One is not self-thinking thought, does not think or contemplate at all, and is not even conscious of itself.[8] Plotinus explicitly denies that God foresees and calculates how this cosmos should come into being.[9] The cosmos has no beginning but is, as we now can expect, everlasting.

If the One still, despite its lack of conscious activity, is to be the source of all subsequent levels of being, then it is tempting to draw the conclusion that the beings after the One results from eternal necessity: 'All things which exist, as long as they remain in being, necessarily produce from their own essences, in dependence on their present power, a surrounding reality directed to what is outside them [...]' (καὶ πάντα τὰ ὄντα, ἕως μένει, ἐκ τῆς αὐτῶν οὐσίας ἀναγκαίαν τὴν περὶ αὐτὰ πρὸς τὸ ἔξω αὐτῶν ἐκ τῆς παρούσης δυνάμεως δίδωσιν αὐτῶν ἐξηρτημένην ὑπόστασιν [...]).[10] The One, which is always perfect in its remaining, produces everlastingly (ἀΐδιον). Since the divine act of will has the character we have seen above, the act of creation has to be conceived of not as an act of an instantaneous divine initiative to make, but rather as an activity that eternally conditions the being of lower levels of reality. Rist remarks on this challenge: 'If emanation follows from the One's nature and the One's nature is caused by the One's will, the emanation will be an act of a kind of free will and Plotinus will be freed from the shackles of a deterministic universe.'[11] Rist concludes his treatment of necessity with saying that '[c]reation is as free, no more and no less, than the One itself'.[12]

It is, of course, difficult to understand or even imagine such a concept of free will: there is no choice between different options; the One cannot want not to be itself since the will is directed towards what is good and that only. On the other hand, to speak in a non-accurate way, since goodness is the basic reality, to want

[8] *Ennead* 3.9.9.
[9] *Ennead* 3.2.1.
[10] *Ennead* 5.1.6; ed. and trans. Armstrong 1978–1988.
[11] Rist 1980, p. 76.
[12] Rist 1980, p. 83.

what is good or to want oneself as good may intuitively be conceived of as the highest bliss of freedom. Still, from the creaturely point of view, it only means that the One is directed monadically towards itself.

How, then, shall we understand the act of creation? When Plotinus surprisingly says that making is *accidental*, this might seem strange.[13] Should we not expect by now that when the One freely wants to be itself, external activity *necessarily* follows? However, it does not have to be understood this way. The creative source did not have the production in view. In short, the internal activity of the One is executed *for its own sake* and not for the sake of the lower levels of being. In this regard the production is incidental to the preoccupation of the cause. However, given the internal activity, the external effect necessarily results.[14] The freedom of the One, the accidental coming to be of what is other than the One, and the necessary dependence of other things on the One should, for the sake of understanding, even if interconnected in the Plotinian system, be distinguished from one another.

The cosmos experienced by human beings consists in diversity and plurality. The One desires none of this. The first level after the One is the Intellect that somehow is the more proximate maker of sensible things, but it is actually the Soul that produces the material world. In *Ennead* 5.2.1 Plotinus shows us how the whole of reality is interconnected: while the principle above (i.e. the One) remains in calmness, it produces the next hypostasis (i.e. the Intellect) and the activity mediated through the primary hypostases reaches all the way down to the Soul's creation of the sensible world. The Soul directs its attention to its source and 'is filled' (πληροῦται).[15] Its source is the Intellect. This probably means that the Forms contemplated in the Intellect become, in the gaze of the Soul, the paradigm of the lower and material world. However, even if the Soul plays such an important role in the constitution of the lower world, the creative energy comes hierarchically from the two hypostases above (the One and the

---

[13] *Ennead* 6.1.22.
[14] See the quotation from *Ennead* 5.1.6 above.
[15] *Ennead* 5.2.1.

Intellect) that execute 'no willing or planning or choice or care for what is produced', to quote Armstrong's words once more.

We get a similar picture in Proclus even if his system is more difficult to analyze because of its complexity. He says that if the cosmos is an entity that has come into being, and everything that has come into being has a cause, the cosmos must necessarily have a cause.[16] One of the basic causes is the Demiurge, and the Demiurge should be distinguished from the first God that transcends everything and is unparticipable.[17] The Demiurge participates in goodness.[18] He looks to the paradigmatic causes, that is the paradigm on a higher level of reality, and makes all things according to the Forms he contemplates.[19] It is obvious that the Maker, being eternal and receiving goodness eternally, eternally makes the cosmos.[20] However, the cosmos as such does not belong to eternal things.[21] It is not an entity that simply 'is' or 'is imperishable', rather it 'becomes' imperishable. It does not exist eternally, but extends (or becomes) everlastingly to all time.[22]

Chlup holds that Proclus follows Plotinus and 'denies that the creativity of the One would be a result of its conscious decision or intent of any kind'.[23] The description of the demiurgic activity in Proclus' *In Timaeum* brings forward that the Demiurge lacks envy and *wants* for that reason to make all things like himself.[24] Proclus advances a detailed argument for creation from eternity, with the cosmos as a temporally everlasting result.[25]

[16] *In Timaeum* I.296.

[17] *In Timaeum* I.359 and 364.

[18] On the mechanism of participation, see Chlup 2012, p. 99–111. An important set of distinctions in Proclus is between unparticipated, participated, and participating. Chlup's book is an admirably clear introduction to Proclus' philosophy, something of a pedagogical miracle.

[19] *In Timaeum* I.366.

[20] *In Timaeum* I.367–368.

[21] *In Timaeum* I.366.

[22] *In Timaeum* I.367–368. Cf. Runia & Share 2008, 228 n. 92 on the difference between αἰώνιος and ἀΐδιος / ἀεί in Proclean usage.

[23] Chlup 2012, p. 62.

[24] *In Timaeum* I.365–368.

[25] The argument is similar to Proclus' first two arguments summarized by Philoponus in *De aeternitate mundi contra Proclum*. The first argument is lost in its original Greek, but is translated from Arabic in Share 2004. The first argument states that the Demiurge, being what he is (i.e. good and powerful), creates

The reference to divine will is not as detailed as in Plotinus. The pages from the *In Timaeum* referred to above give the impression that the divine will is conceived of as quite generalized: the Demiurge is good and it is natural that he acts according to his nature, but without any conscious decision or any particular care for the entities of the cosmos. Of course, providence may extend to the whole of particulars in this general way, since what is created is set in eternal harmony, proportion and order.[26] God is not, however, interested in particular beings as such.

In some sense creation is due to a divine act of will in these Neoplatonist thinkers. This act of will, however, is conceived of in such a way that the act of creation is eternal and results in an everlasting cosmos. Proclus makes this quite clear in his *In Timaeum*: it is contrary to argument to suppose that the cosmos came into being after not having existed before.[27] If the Demiurge once was inactive, was that because he did *not want* to create or because he was *not able* to create? Neither of these options is considered possible. Further, created beings are cared for by the divinities even if only by being within the general divine scheme of things. But is there even such a divine purpose for particular beings? There is probably no purpose beyond being at a particular place at a particular time and fulfilling one's nature within the general scheme of the whole. In short, there is no particular divine care or purpose for the particular being. The care for the particulars is so to say 'general'.

What then with St Maximus the Confessor? First we should remember that in Maximus' Christian system there is no room for a hierarchy of divinities or hypostases 'between' God and the created cosmos. The God of Maximus is conceived of as

---

eternally. The second states that, since the paradigm used by the Demiurge is eternal (and since the Demiurge is good and powerful), creation should be eternal too.

[26] Cf. Proclus' reference to Porphyry at *In Timaeum* I.366. Cf. Proclus' *Decem quaestiones circa providentiam* 2.7 (ed. Boese 1960; trans. Opsomer & Steel 2012): καὶ ὅλως πάντα κατὰ τὴν ἑαυτῆς ὕπαρξιν καὶ οὐ τὴν τῶν γινωσκομένων ('and, in general, it will know all things in accordance with its own existence, not in accordance with the existence of the objects known'). Proclus argues that providence stretches to particular beings even within the sensible world, but the knowledge and care of the higher principles for what is below is in accordance with the ontological constitution of the higher things.

[27] *In Timaeum* I.366–367.

a purely transcendent reality, rather to be compared with the One of Plotinus and Proclus than with their Demiurge. On the other hand, Maximus' God *is* the Demiurge or Creator of the world, and therefore all the conditions for creating have to be sought in Him. What are these conditions? We find an important section on this in Maximus' *Capita de caritate* (4.1–9).[28] The text puts forward the following elements: that God exists eternally as Creator (4.3), that there is an eternally pre-existing divine knowledge of beings (4.4), that creatures are brought into existence from nothing (4.1), that this happened 'when He willed it' (ὅτε ἐβουλήθη, 4.4; cf. 4.3), that God created the world recently (προσφάτως, 4.5), that God's wisdom is inscrutable (4.1 and 4.3), that we may seek the reason (ἡ αἰτία) for God's creation (4.5), but that we may not search for 'how and why' (πῶς καὶ διὰ τί) He created recently since that is beyond our grasp (4.5).

How does Maximus conceive of God as eternal Creator? In this section of *Capita de caritate* there are indications that Maximus wants to profile his doctrine of creation over against the rival views of the Platonic schools. He is conscious of the fact that 'some say' (τινές φασι) created beings exist eternally with God, something he holds to be impossible (4.6): 'For how can what is limited in every way eternally coexist with what is wholly infinite? Or how are they really creatures if they are coeternal with the Creator?' (Πῶς γὰρ τῷ πάντη ἀπείρῳ, τὰ κατὰ πάντα πεπερασμένα, συνυπάρχειν δύναται ἐξ ἀϊδίου; ἢ πῶς κυρίως δημιουργήματα, εἰ συναΐδια τῷ Δημιουργῷ;) This argument sounds like a slightly more elaborate section from *Ambigua ad Iohannem* 7:

Ἐπειδὴ ὁ μὲν ἀεὶ κατ' ἐνέργειάν ἐστι Δημιουργός, τὰ δὲ δυνάμει μέν ἐστιν, ἐνεργείᾳ δὲ οὐκ ἔτι· ὅτι μηδὲ οἷόν τε τῶν ἅμα εἶναι τὸ ἄπειρον καὶ τὰ πεπερασμένα, οὐδέ τις δεῖξαι λόγος ἀναφανήσεται τῶν ἅμα εἶναι δύνασθαι τὴν οὐσίαν καὶ τὸ ὑπερούσιον καὶ εἰς ταὐτὸν ἀγαγεῖν τῷ ἐν μέτρῳ τὸ ἄμετρον καὶ τῷ ἐν σχέσει τὸ ἄσχετον καὶ τὸ μηδὲν ἔχον ἐπ' αὐτοῦ κατηγορίας εἶδος καταφασκόμενον τῷ διὰ πάντων τούτων συνισταμένῳ.

---

[28] *Capita de caritate*, PG 90, col. 1048b–1049b.

> For the Creator is always in actuality, but they are potential and only later in actuality, since it is not possible for the infinite and the finite to exist simultaneously on the same level of being. Indeed no argument will ever be able to demonstrate the simultaneous existence of being and what transcends being, or to bring into the same that which transcends measure with what is measured, or that which transcends relation with what is related, or that something of which no category can be predicated can be placed in the same species as what is constituted by all categories.[29]

It is well known that *Amb.Io.* 7 is directed against Origenist theology.[30] Even the paragraph just quoted may be understood in that light. However, the paragraph is even so constructed in a general way that grows beyond that limited scope. Like the statements from *Capita de caritate* this is an implied correction of Platonic metaphysics and cosmology. For a start we should remember that Maximus' concept of the demiurgic creator is different from the Neoplatonist concept. The Proclean Demiurge is not the all-powerful, simple, uniform, and unqualified divinity of Maximus.[31] However, we shall not enter into a detailed discussion of the soundness of the present Maximian claim about the impossibility of simultaneous existence. It is worth noticing, though, that in *Car.* he argues against 'Greeks' who admit God as Creator not of the substance of cosmic being, but only of the properties.[32] This seems to be directed more against Plato's *Timaeus* and its more conservative interpreters than against a Proclean interpretation of the same.[33] On the other hand, the two questions put forward above, about how the limited can coexist with the infinite and how beings can be creatures if they coexist with the Creator, could be intended as directed against Plotinian and Proclean versions of Platonism.

---

[29] *Amb.Io.* 7, PG 91, col. 1081a-b. I have modified Constas' translation. I should like to add that I usually find his translation quite satisfactory.

[30] See also Cvetković in this volume. I use the abbreviations for Maximus' writings from Allen & Neil 2015, p. xix–xx.

[31] *Car.* 4.9, PG 90, col. 1049b.

[32] *Car.* 4.6, PG 90, col. 1049a.

[33] Proclus would probably not have admitted that any 'substance' came 'before' (temporally or even ontologically) the properties.

There is one problem that naturally pops up in this connection, viz. whether Dionysius the Areopagite, one of the main sources of inspiration behind Maximus' philosophy, is more 'Greek' than Christian in his doctrine of creation. I have argued elsewhere that Dionysius' doctrine of creation does not seem to be orthodox by the standards of mainstream Late-Antique and early Byzantine theology.[34] There can be no doubt that Dionysius, even if utilizing the legacy of Proclus, abolishes the whole Neoplatonic hierarchy of divine hypostases between the One and sensible beings.[35] There is one God, the Holy Trinity, that is the Maker and Provider of the cosmos. However, did the cosmos have a temporal beginning recently (προσφάτως), in the sense claimed by for instance St Basil the Great, and later by Maximus?[36] In the *De divinis nominibus* (7.2) Dionysius says: 'The Divine Wisdom then, by knowing itself, will know all things [...].' (Ἑαυτὴν οὖν ἡ θεία σοφία γινώσκουσα γνώσεται πάντα [...].)[37] This probably means that God by knowing Himself, knows Himself as the source of all beings. In this knowledge God knows within Himself the paradigms of all creatures.[38] However, there does not seem to be any clear notion of divine will in Dionysius. There is definitely not any clearly conceived notion of a will that accommodates itself from eternal contemplation to the making of temporal things. It doesn't help much, I should think, that the paradigms of the cosmos are called 'divine and good acts of will' (θεῖα καὶ ἀγαθὰ θελήματα).[39] The analogy with the sun put forward in *De divinis nominibus* 4.1 is therefore quite telling:

> Καὶ γὰρ ὥσπερ ὁ καθ᾽ ἡμᾶς ἥλιος οὐ λογιζόμενος ἢ προαιρούμενος, ἀλλ᾽ αὐτῷ τῷ εἶναι φωτίζει πάντα τὰ μετέχειν τοῦ φωτὸς αὐτοῦ κατὰ τὸν οἰκεῖον δυνάμενα λόγον, οὕτω δὴ καὶ τἀγαθὸν ὑπὲρ ἥλιον ὡς ὑπὲρ ἀμυδρὰν εἰκόνα τὸ ἐξηρημένως ἀρχέτυπον

---

[34] Cf. Tollefsen 2008b and 2012, p. 101–118. I have no prestige in this claim and should very much appreciate to be proven wrong.

[35] Cf. *De divinis nominibus* 5.2, p. 181 ed. Suchla 1990.

[36] For Basil, cf. *In hexaemeron* 1.6, PG 29, col. 16b.

[37] *De divinis nominibus* 7.2, p. 197 ed. Suchla 1990.

[38] *De divinis nominibus* 7.3, p. 197–198 ed. Suchla 1990; cf. 5. 8, p. 188 ed. Suchla 1990.

[39] *De divinis nominibus* 5.8, p. 188 ed. Suchla 1990.

αὐτῇ τῇ ὑπάρξει πᾶσι τοῖς οὖσιν ἀναλόγως ἐφίησι τὰς τῆς ὅλης
ἀγαθότητος ἀκτῖνας.

> For, even as our sun, not as calculating or choosing, but by its
> very being, enlightens all things able to partake of its light in
> their own degree, so too the Good, which is superior to the
> sun in the way the archetype *par excellence* is superior to an
> obscure image, by Its very existence sends to all things that be,
> the rays of Its whole goodness, according to their capacity.[40]

Somehow this makes the impression that God manifested the
cosmos eternally from Himself, without any definite act of will.
If this is the case, one should like to know if there is a divine
providence for particular beings or if such beings are just cared
for within the more general scheme of universal providence.
If my interpretation is reasonable, this is probably the most distinctive Neoplatonic feature of Dionysius' thought. However,
every author does not have to cover every piece of orthodox teaching in everything he writes. One should not necessarily expect
Dionysius to be quite clear on all matters. Maximus considered
Dionysius orthodox and has to my knowledge nowhere uttered
any critique of his cosmology. That, of course, is in itself not
decisive. On the other hand, maybe Maximus did not expect
the great theologian to state his mind in detail on every issue, and
therefore felt no need to correct Dionysius in this regard. However that may be, the picture Dionysius makes leaves something to
be desired in regard to the doctrine of creation.

Whatever we think about Dionysius, we have to answer the
question of what Maximus has in mind when he claims that
God is eternally a Creator, which is the same as the fact that the
Creator exists always in actuality. If this is the case, would it not
naturally lead to the corollary that the cosmos is eternally manifested as an everlasting system from God as cause? Would this not
be to endorse claims put forward by Proclus? Maximus obviously
denies such a thing. He does not seem to put forward any arguments though.[41] On the other hand, Maximus makes an impor-

---

[40] *De divinis nominibus* 4.1, p. 144 ed. Suchla 1990.

[41] If Maximus had known Philoponus' books against Proclus on the eternity
of the world, he could have interpreted his 'in actuality' in accordance with Philo-

tant distinction that might highlight his notion of God as eternal Creator in actuality.

This distinction is found in *Amb.Io.* 7 and sheds light on a couple of subjects in the text from *Car.* 4.[42] Maximus says that the *logoi* of all things are fixed in God and that God knows all things in these *logoi* before they came into being. (Let us just say that these *logoi* are the divine Ideas for the essences of creatures.[43]) However, things present and things that are to come were not brought into being simultaneously (οὐχ ἅμα) with their being known by God: 'Instead, in the wisdom of the Creator, individual things were created at the appropriate moment in time, in a manner consistent with their *logoi*, and thus received in themselves actual existence as beings' (ἀλλ' ἕκαστα τῷ ἐπιτηδείῳ καιρῷ κατὰ τὴν τοῦ Δημιουργοῦ σοφίαν πρεπόντως κατὰ τοὺς ἑαυτῶν λόγους δημιουργούμενα καὶ καθ' ἑαυτὰ τὸ εἶναι τῇ ἐνεργείᾳ λαμβάνη).[44] The distinction applied here is between *logoi* as *principles of knowledge* and as *principles of making*.[45] God may eternally know all beings that He might want to create, but actual creation takes place at the appropriate time for each creature. For this reason God may be considered to exist eternally as Creator (cf. *Car.* 4.3), since He contains eternally the knowledge of creatures (cf. *Car.* 4.4). On the other hand, creation occurred 'when He willed it' (*Car.* 4.3 and 4).

We are not going to dive into the intricacies involved in the accommodation of eternal knowledge by the creative act into temporal existence, even if tempting. We should note, however, that in the text from *Car.* we are told to abstain from inquiry

---

ponus' (Aristotelian) distinction between first and second actuality, cf. *De aeternitate mundi contra Proclum*, the third argument against Proclus. But Maximus does not talk about first and second actuality here. If Maximus was acquainted with Alexandrian Neoplatonism, it strikes me as rather strange that he does not apply Philoponus' important work in regard to the doctrine of creation.

[42] *Amb.Io.* 7, PG 91, col. 1081a.

[43] For the doctrine of the *logoi*, see Tollefsen 2008a and 2015.

[44] *Amb.Io.* 7, PG 91, col. 1081a, Constas' translation.

[45] The distinction is argued by Philoponus in *De aeternitate mundi contra Proclum*, argument 2–3. Did Maximus know this book? He might have found the distinction in Philoponus, but he might also have worked it out by himself. Thomas Aquinas later applies the same distinction in his doctrine of creation, cf. *Summa theologiae* 1, question 15, article 3.

into 'how and why' (πῶς καὶ διὰ τί) God created recently since that is beyond human capacity. God's wisdom, Maximus tells us, is inscrutable. These words are probably a warning against philosophical speculations since the immature person may go astray like the 'Greeks'. On the other hand, we may seek the reason (ἡ αἰτία) why God created, 'for this is knowledge' (ἔστι γὰρ γνῶσις).[46] Where does this direct us? We may probably find Maximus' ideas about the reason for God's creation in *Quaestiones ad Thalassium* 60.

The text opens with a question put to Maximus by Thalassius. The question is based on I Petr. 1. 20: προεγνωσμένου μὲν πρὸ καταβολῆς κόσμου φανερωθέντος δὲ ἐπ' ἐσχάτου τῶν χρόνων δι' ὑμᾶς [...]. ('He indeed was foreknown before the foundation of the world, but was manifest in these last times for you [...].') The question is *by whom* Christ was foreknown. Maximus answers that Christ was foreknown by the Trinity not as God, but as human being, i.e. in His incarnate condition.[47] Foreknowledge of Christ as incarnate is the same as the foreknowledge of 'the mystery of Christ' (τὸ τοῦ Χριστοῦ μυστήριον).[48] This mystery is exactly the *hypostatic union* between divinity and humanity in the hypostasis of the Logos, the Son of God.

This is the reason why God made the world, viz. to become incarnate. Maximus says: 'Because of Christ, or rather, the mystery of Christ, all the ages and those beings that are in the ages have received the beginning and end of their being in Christ.' (Διὰ γὰρ τὸν Χριστὸν, ἤγουν τὸ κατὰ Χριστὸν μυστήριον, πάντες οἱ αἰῶνες καὶ τὰ ἐν αὐτοῖς τοῖς αἰῶσιν ἐν Χριστῷ τὴν ἀρχὴν τοῦ εἶναι καὶ τὸ τέλος εἰλήφασιν.)[49] It is interesting to see here that Maximus does not present the human Fall as the condition of the Incarnation, but rather that the cosmos is created for the sake of the Logos becoming man. Maximus simply says that the hypostatic union is the divine mystery conceived before the ages and this is the goal for which everything exists.[50] One might, of course,

[46] *Car.* 4.5, PG 90, col. 1048d.
[47] *Q. Thal.* 60, CCSG 22, p. 79–81.
[48] *Q. Thal.* 60, CCSG 22, p. 73.
[49] *Q. Thal.* 60, CCSG 22, p. 75.
[50] *Q. Thal.* 60, CCSG 22, p. 75.

suggest that God foresaw the Fall and eternally made His plans for that reason. Philosophically speaking I think God must have foreseen the Fall, but there is not a single word in *Quaestiones ad Thalassium* 60 or 22 that suggests the Fall as a divine motive for the Incarnation. On the other hand, there is a saying in *Amb.Io.* 41 that might suggest that the Fall is the motivation for God to become incarnate. Maximus says that God became a human being 'in order to save lost humanity' (ἵνα σώσῃ τὸν ἀπολόμενον ἄνθρωπον).[51] The whole sequence can as a matter of fact be interpreted that way.[52] However, I don't think this has to change the picture found in *Quaestiones ad Thalassium*. As pointed out above, God wanted eternally to become incarnate and, we may add, knew simultaneously that there would be a Fall and wanted to remedy it.

However, what has just been said widens the scope of Maximus' understanding of the Incarnation. The cosmos is not just created because of a divine desire to become incarnate. The divine objective includes a further concern. So why does God eternally desire to become incarnate? This question is definitely answered in *Quaestiones ad Thalassium* 60:

> Ἔδει γὰρ ὡς ἀληθῶς τὸν κατὰ φύσιν τῆς τῶν ὄντων οὐσίας δημι-
> ουργὸν καὶ τῆς κατὰ χάριν αὐτουργὸν γενέσθαι τῶν γεγονότων
> θεώσεως, ἵνα ὁ τοῦ εἶναι[53] δοτὴρ φανῇ καὶ τοῦ ἀεὶ εὖ εἶναι χαρι-
> στικός.

> For truly He who by nature is the Creator of the essence of beings had also to become the Author of the deification of creatures by grace, in order that the Giver of being might also appear as the gracious Giver of eternal well-being.[54]

God wants to become incarnate *for the sake of His creatures*. The quote might suggest that Maximus thinks God *qua* Creator is *bound* to become the Saviour of His creatures. But I should

---

[51] *Amb.Io.* 41, PG 91, col. 1308d.

[52] Cf. *Amb.Io.* 41, PG 91, col. 1308c-d.

[53] The text in CCSG 22, p. 79 has εὖ εἶναι here. According to the critical apparatus some manuscripts omit the εὖ. I cannot judge the soundness of the choice of εὖ εἶναι, but I am convinced that the logic of the sequence demands that the εὖ is omitted.

[54] *Q. Thal.* 60, CCSG 22, p. 79.

think there is nothing substantial in Maximus' writings to the effect that he conceives of God as constrained by anything.[55] We saw above how he understood the act of creation, and everything seems to indicate that he thinks of God as a completely free agent – however that freedom should be understood. I suppose what Maximus has in mind is something like this: He who eternally willed to be the cause of the cosmos willed simultaneously to become the Saviour of what He made, therefore he had to become the Author of deification. It is almost as if the divinity made a promise to Himself for the sake of creatures.

The same motif, that God desires to become incarnate for the sake of created beings, is found in the *Quaestiones ad Thalassium* 22. Maximus answers a question about how two sayings by St Paul in respectively Eph. 2. 7 and I Cor. 10. 11 shall be related to one another. The first says that 'in the ages to come He [i.e. God] might show the exceeding riches' (ἵνα ἐνδείξηται ἐν τοῖς αἰῶσιν τοῖς ἐπερχομένοις τὸ ὑπερβάλλον πλοῦτος) and the second uses the formula 'upon whom the ends of the ages have come' (εἰς οὓς τὰ τέλη τῶν αἰώνων κατήντηκεν). How should we accommodate the 'end of the ages' to 'ages to come'? Maximus answers that God divided the ages between those intended for God to become human (and those ages have come to an end) and those intended for human beings to become God (which are the ages to come).[56] The rest of the text has the ages to come as a main topic, viz. how the Incarnation of Christ is the divine means by which humanity may achieve deification through grace.

In *Quaestions ad Thalassium* 60 Maximus says that the divine economy is the great and hidden mystery for which all things are made, but that this preconceived purpose itself 'exists on account of nothing' (αὐτὸ δὲ οὐδενὸς ἕνεκα).[57] What could this mean? It probably means that there is nothing outside of God that motivates the making and saving work of God. This could,

---

[55] So how should we understand the ἔδει? Does it mean that the Creator *had* to become the Saviour, that He was bound to it, that it was inevitable for Him to become so, or that it was proper that He became so? I suppose that this should be taken in the sense that God eternally took it upon Himself and stood by this eternal intention.

[56] *Q. Thal.* 22, CCSG 7, p. 137.

[57] *Q. Thal.* 60, CCSG 22, p. 75.

of course, be taken to indicate that even the Christian God of Maximus does not care essentially for His creatures, but I really doubt this is a reasonable interpretation of the saying. I suppose this rather directs us to a very distinctive feature that Maximus perceives in the Christian God, viz. God's love for His creatures, especially His love for human beings.[58] The motif of divine love and divine philanthropy is central to Maximus thought. If it is correct to interpret the 'on account of nothing' in this direction, we might say that divine love needs no motif outside of God Himself but springs freely and abundantly from God as beginning and end of creaturely movement.

It is always taken for granted that when we speak of the Christian God as the Maker and Saviour of the world, divine care is directed to human individuals (or personal beings) and not to generalities such as the whole cosmos or to the human species. However, the texts we have considered so far paint a picture with a rather broad brush and if we look beyond modern Christian preconceptions Maximus' vision is *cosmic* rather than directed to the human particular. This is the world-view of the Christian philosopher. It may be compared with the philosophy of the Platonic schools. There are, on the other hand, some aspects of Maximus' philosophy that would immediately be felt as scandalous by the pagan Neoplatonist philosopher, for instance that the highest God *contemplated* the making of the world and *willed* the world to exist with a temporal beginning, i.e. recently (προσφάτως). The greatest scandal would, of course, be that the eternal Godhead should want to become a human being and that God became so out of love for creatures. Love for what is 'below' in the scale of being (and becoming) would from a Neoplatonist perspective be seen as a Fall. It would definitely not be worthy of the divinity and therefore unthinkable.

What then about human individuals, does God care for them? Does God care for particular creatures at all? Maximus definitely thinks so. There is not just a love for humanity. There is love for

---

[58] This motif may be found in almost every text Maximus wrote. Here I just point to *Amb.Io.* 41, PG 91, col. 1308b-c.

each human being. However, the love for particulars cannot be isolated from divine care for the whole.

In *Amb.Io.* 7 we learn that God eternally contained within Himself the pre-existing *logoi* of created things.[59] As already said, these *logoi* are divine Ideas or plans for creaturely being. By the *logoi* He created and creates all things,[60] *universals as well as particulars* (τὰ καθόλου τε καὶ τὰ καθ' ἕκαστον). I think it is important to note that it is not just particular beings that are created. Universals are created as well. God does not only *create* universals and particulars, His *providence* comprises both.[61] However, universals subsist in the particulars and do not have their *logos* of being and subsistence in themselves. This probably means that they do not exist as independent hypostases. On the other hand, even if wholes (i.e. universals) subsist in the parts (i.e. particulars), parts also subsist in the wholes.[62] This interconnectedness of all beings – parts in their wholes, wholes in still more inclusive wholes – still does not have to be interpreted as if God cares in a special sense for particulars. It might just mean that particulars are within God's providence in the general way we found above in Neoplatonism.

However, things become much clearer in *Amb.Io.* 7.[63] Maximus writes about the *logoi* and calls them, pointing to Dionysius the Areopagite, 'predeterminations' and 'divine wills' (προορισμοί and θεῖα θελήματα). God of course knows His own will and He knows beings, i.e. His creatures, 'as His own wills' (ὡς ἴδια θελήματα ὁ θεὸς τὰ ὄντα γινώσκει). In other words, the divine *logoi* belong here to the divinity itself and not to any divine Intellect lower in the scale of being. The one and supreme God determines the content of these *logoi* for each being in such a way that He knows creatures in His own will to make them.

---

[59] *Amb.Io.* 7, PG 91, col. 1080a.

[60] I should just like to remark on this 'all things' that there is in my opinion no reason to hold that the doctrine of divine *logoi* is restricted: each natural entity has a *logos* in God, and I also claim that 'natural entities' includes particulars as well as universals.

[61] *Amb.Io.* 10, PG 91, col. 1189c.

[62] *Amb.Io.* 10, PG 91, col. 1189c-d. I have called this mutual relationship between whole and part in Maximus 'holomerism' (Tollefsen 2015, p. 316–319).

[63] *Amb.Io.* 7, PG 91, col. 1085a-c.

We saw above that the Plotinian One does not think and is not even conscious of itself. We also saw that the Proclean first God is beyond any particular interest in what is 'below'. Even Proclus' hypostatic Providence does not know contingent things the way they are, but knows them only in the mode of necessity in accordance with its own nature.[64] Beings are, therefore, known from their causes in the divine world and not as they are in themselves. Somehow this is similar to what Maximus says about God's knowledge, but one major difference is, as just said, that Maximus' God is the one and only highest divinity and not any lower entity in the scale of being. On the other hand, we might ask about the manner of divine knowledge: in what *way* does God know particulars? Does He know them as contingent beings or does He know them in the mode of necessity?

This of course drags with it a whole lot of problems concerning necessity, contingency, and human freedom that cannot be dealt with here. From what is shown above I think we may conclude that Maximus' God knows particular beings and cares for each of them. Armstrong's words at the beginning of this paper may be adapted: there is deliberate action on the part of the One, and willing and planning and choice and care for what is produced. We may also address the three questions formulated initially. Is the act of creation due to a divine act of will? Does God care for creatures? Are they made for a definite purpose? From Maximus' Christian point of view all three definitely have a positive answer. The conclusion should, however, be made even more explicit: God cares for the particulars and each particular is made for a purpose. The purpose of creation is in a lot of places in Maximus' writings shown to be the final deification of all beings.[65]

---

[64] Proclus, *Decem quaestiones circa providentiam* 2. 8; trans. Opsomer & Steel 2012, p. 76.

[65] Cf. for instance *Q. Thal.* 60, CCSG 22, p. 75–79 and *Amb.Io.* 41, PG 91, col. 1308b.

Bibliography

Primary Sources

Maximus the Confessor, *On Difficulties in the Church Fathers, The Ambigua*, 2 vols, ed. and trans. N. Constas, Cambridge, MA: Harvard University Press, 2014.

Dionysius the Areopagite, *De divinis nominibus*, ed. B. R. Suchla, Berlin: De Gruyter, 1990 (Patristische Texte und Studien 33).

Philoponus, *Against Proclus On the Eternity of the World 1–5*, trans. M. Share, London: Duckworth, 2004.

Plotinus, *The Enneads*, 7 vols, trans. A. H. Armstrong, Cambridge, MA: Harvard University Press, 1978–1988.

Proclus, *Commentary on Plato's Timaeus. Book 2: Proclus on the Causes of the Cosmos and its Creation*, trans. D. T. Runia & M. Share, Cambridge: Cambridge University Press, 2008.

Proclus, *Ten Problems Concerning Providence*, trans. J. Opsomer & C. Steel, London: Bristol Classical Press, 2012.

Proclus, *Ten Problems Concerning Providence*, in *Procli Diadochi tria opuscula*, ed. H. Boese, Berlin: De Gruyter, 1960, p. 5–108.

Secondary Literature

P. Allen & B. Neil (2015), *The Oxford Handbook of Maximus the Confessor*, Oxford: Oxford University Press.

A. H. Armstrong (ed., 1980 [= 1967]), *The Cambridge History of Later Greek and Early Medieval Thought*, Cambridge: Cambridge University Press.

R. Chlup (2012), *Proclus, An Introduction*, Cambridge: Cambridge University Press.

J. M. Rist (1980 [= 1967]), *Plotinus. The Road to Reality*, Cambridge: Cambridge University Press.

T. T. Tollefsen (2008a), *The Christocentric Cosmology of St Maximus the Confessor*, Oxford: Oxford University Press.

T. T. Tollefsen (2008b), 'The Doctrine of Creation according to Dionysius the Areopagite', in *Papers and Monographs of the Finnish Institute at Athens*, 14, p. 75–89.

T. T. Tollefsen (2012), *Activity and Participation in Late Antique and Early Christian Thought*, Oxford: Oxford University Press.

T. T. Tollefsen (2015), 'Chrisocentric Cosmology', in P. Allen & B. Neil (eds), *The Oxford Handbook of Maximus the Confessor*, Oxford: Oxford University Press, p. 307–321.

Abstract

In this paper the author investigates likenesses and differences between pagan (*i.c.* Neoplatonist) and Christian (*i.c.* Maximus the Confessor's) doctrines of creation. The primary object is to describe Maximus' teaching against the background of Plotinian and Proclean cosmology. The basic principle of creation is divine goodness, but both Plotinus and Maximus bring divine will into the picture. In Plotinus this is primarily the will of the One to be itself, from which act the eternal generation of the intelligible world has its source. In Maximus, on the other hand, it is the will that directs God's being in love both to make and save His creatures within the horizon of a temporality with a definite, recent beginning. The mystery of Christ is, therefore, the mystery of divine love as this is manifested cosmologically as well as soteriologically.

CHRISTIAN BOUDIGNON

JAMBLIQUE ET MAXIME LE CONFESSEUR, COSMOLOGIE ET THÉURGIE

à Pascal Mueller-Jourdan

Le principal texte antique de cosmologie et de théurgie est écrit sous forme de questions et réponses. Il s'agit des *Mystères d'Égypte* de Jamblique, ou plutôt, pour lui rendre son vrai titre, de la *Réponse d'Abamon, son professeur, à la Lettre de Porphyre à Anébon*. Le titre lui-même nous signifie qu'on est bien dans le jeu des questions et réponses. En effet, la *Lettre à Anébon* de Porphyre[1] est reprise par extraits qui constituent autant de questions, auxquels répond Jamblique. Ainsi, en 1.3, la concession de Porphyre sur l'existence des dieux devient un 'dit' (λέγομενον) traité par Jamblique comme une question mal posée qui appelle à une rectification, comme c'est couramment le cas dans la tradition des questions et réponses. Plus encore, en 1.4, on a affaire au questionnement de Porphyre : 'Et ce que tu recherches : quelles sont les propriétés de chacun des genres supérieurs, propriétés qui les séparent les uns des autres ?' (ἃ δ' ἐπιζητεῖς ἰδιώματα τίνα ἐστὶν ἑκάστῳ τῶν κρειττόνων γενῶν, οἷς κεχώρισται ἀπ' ἀλλήλων [...])[2]. Car c'est une véritable question si l'on comprend bien le sens du verbe ἐπιζητεῖς ('rechercher') qui correspond à une interrogation de l'ordre de la recherche. Le troisième questionnement sur l'activité ou la passivité débouche, de l'aveu de Jamblique, sur une question double. Jamblique reproche alors à Porphyre la confusion qui règne 'sur la fin de la question' (ἐπὶ τῷ τέλει τῆς ἐρωτήσεως, 1.4)[3]. Il n'y a plus de doute que les citations de Porphyre

---

[1] Saffrey & Segonds 2012.
[2] Saffrey & Segonds 2013, p. 7, l. 21–24.
[3] Saffrey & Segonds 2013, p. 9, l. 24.

Questioning the World, Greek Patristic and Byzantine Question-and-Answer Literature, ed. by Bram Demulder and Peter Van Deun, Turnhout, 2021 (*LECTIO*, 11), pp. 201-227   © BREPOLS⬦PUBLISHERS   DOI 10.1484/M.I.LECTIO-EB.5.121507

sont traités comme des ἐρωτήσεις. On pourrait donner encore une foule d'autres exemples. La *Réponse d'Abamon* relève donc de la littérature érotapocritique.

Quelle a été la réception de ce texte et de son hypo-texte, la *Lettre à Anébon*, en milieu chrétien ? La *Lettre à Anébon* de Porphyre, pour nous perdue, est citée dans le monde chrétien par Eusèbe de Césarée dans sa *Préparation évangélique*, dans la *Cité de Dieu* d'Augustin, et dans l'*Hypomnèsticon* de Joseph de Tibériade. Serait-il surprenant que la *Réponse d'Abamon* ait été connue des chrétiens[4] ? Oui, pour Saffrey et Segonds, les derniers éditeurs de la *Réponse d'Abamon*[5], qui écrivent que 'le texte de Jamblique est demeuré entièrement inconnu des chrétiens, aussi bien en Orient qu'en Occident, chez les Grecs comme chez les Latins'[6]. Mais Van Liefferinge est beaucoup moins catégorique et suggère qu'Augustin dans la *Cité de Dieu* fait bien allusion aux démons pervers de la *Réponse d'Abamon*.

Je ferai l'hypothèse que la définition et la défense de la théurgie que propose Jamblique dans la *Réponse d'Abamon* (que Saffrey et Segonds datent entre 301 et 305[7]) ont considérablement influencé l'esprit de la *Mystagogie* de Maxime le Confesseur (CPG 7704). Ce commentaire de la messe pourrait dater peut-être du début des années 630[8]. Je ne suppose pas que Maxime ait pris connaissance directement de l'ouvrage de Jamblique, – encore qu'une telle possibilité ne puisse être exclue. Mais puisque Jamblique est le véritable fondateur de la théologie platonicienne jusqu'à Proclus et Damascius, il est fort possible que Maxime ait connu un livre néoplatonicien de théurgie. Il aurait eu ainsi indirectement accès à l'ouvrage érotapocritique de Jamblique qu'est la *Réponse d'Abamon*[9].

---

[4] Van Liefferinge 1999, p. 86–87.

[5] Je choisis ce titre en résumé qui correspond aux premiers mots du titre original plutôt que celui que donnent Saffrey & Segonds 2013 : *Réponse à Porphyre*, qui est artificiel. Ils choisissent d'ailleurs en grec d'abréger en Ἀβάμωνος ἀπόκρισις.

[6] Saffrey & Segonds 2012, p. XLVI.

[7] Saffrey & Segonds 2013, p. XXXII.

[8] Jankowiak & Booth 2015, p. 30. Cette datation demeure cependant discutable, cf. Van Deun 2015, p. 407.

[9] Il n'était pas de toute façon moralement pensable pour le moine qu'est Maxime de revendiquer une telle influence jamblichéenne. Au contraire, son attitude serait plutôt de feinte défiance, comme au chapitre 23 de la *Mystagogie*

Ajoutons que ce n'est pas seulement par le biais des écrits du Pseudo-Denys l'Aréopagite (qu'on date du tout début du VIᵉ siècle) que Maxime a eu part à cette philosophie. Car la logique même de la *Mystagogie* de Maxime repose sur l'idée que l'église est l'image et la figure de Dieu et du monde, idée absente chez le Pseudo-Denys. Au contraire, les *Hiérarchies ecclésiastiques* du Pseudo-Denys reposent sur l'idée que l'efficacité du culte chrétien vient d'un contact entre les ordres célestes, notamment les anges, et les ordres ecclésiastiques, notamment l'évêque. Ce sont deux logiques très différentes, même si Maxime emprunte çà ou là tel ou tel élément au Pseudo-Denys.

Dans son étude sur *La Mystagogie de Maxime le Confesseur dans la culture philosophique de l'Antiquité tardive*, Mueller-Jourdan[10] montre que Maxime a repris de la *Réponse d'Abamon* éventuellement certains mots-clés comme ἐπιβολή ('intuition')[11] ou ἀναγωγή ('montée' vers les causes explicatives des choses)[12]. Il rapproche également la *Mystagogie* des autres œuvres de Jamblique[13] et d'autres textes, il met 'en doute l'idée d'une tradition philosophique *commune* au christianisme et au néoplatonisme'[14], et refuse[15] l'idée que la *Mystagogie* soit un 'véritable traité philosophique sur les symboles'[16].

Je montrerai pourtant que l'on peut établir des rapprochements solides entre les deux ouvrages, à défaut de citation directe de la *Réponse d'Abamon* par Maxime. Mais, et c'est là la thèse que je défendrai, la structure même de la *Mystagogie* repose sur les conceptions théurgiques de Jamblique.

Il convient donc de démontrer les parallélismes entre les deux œuvres. Pour cela, je me concentrerai sur six points :

1. qu'est-ce qu'une image et qu'une figure ?
2. pourquoi l'église est-elle image de Dieu et du monde ?

(Boudignon 2011, p. 50, l. 790–791), où il attaque τοὺς ἀσόφους τῶν παρ᾽ Ἕλλησι λεγομένων σοφῶν ('les *non-sages* de ceux que chez les païens on appelle sages').

[10] Mueller-Jourdan 2005, p. 16–17, n. 25–26.
[11] Saffrey & Segonds 2013, p. 85, l. 14–15.
[12] Saffrey & Segonds 2013, p. 86, l. 6.
[13] Voir l'index de Mueller-Jourdan 2005, p. 202, à l'entrée Jamblique.
[14] Mueller-Jourdan 2005, p. 13.
[15] Mueller-Jourdan 2005, p. 12.
[16] Boudignon, 2000, p. 38.

3. pourquoi l'entrée du grand-prêtre est-elle l'image de la venue de Dieu au monde ?

4. en quoi l'église peut-elle recevoir le divin ?

5. en quoi la liturgie n'est pas magie ?

6. quelle élévation de l'âme pour les ignorants ?

1. *Qu'est-ce qu'une image et qu'une figure ?*

S'il n'est pas l'inventeur de la théurgie qui remonte aux *Oracles chaldaïques*, Jamblique en est le véritable promoteur. Van Liefferinge l'a montré parfaitement :

> [P]our résoudre les deux grands problèmes de l'inefficacité des rites et de la contrainte exercée sur les dieux lors des rites, c'est à la théurgie que Jamblique fait appel. Il lui donne la définition suivante : 'C'est l'accomplissement des actions ineffables accomplies divinement au-delà de toute intellection, ainsi que le pouvoir des symboles [inexprimables] pensés seulement par les dieux qui opèrent l'union théurgique' [ἡ τῶν ἔργων τῶν ἀρρήτων καὶ ὑπὲρ πᾶσαν νόησιν θεοπρεπῶς ἐνεργουμένων τελεσιουργία ἥ τε τῶν νοουμένων τοῖς θεοῖς μόνον συμβόλων ἀφθέγκτων δύναμις ἐντίθησι τὴν θεουργικὴν ἕνωσιν[17]][18].

Elle ajoute : 'Deux mots clés dans cet extrait : actions (ἔργα) et symboles (σύμβολα).'

Or si l'on se reporte à la *Mystagogie* de Maxime, la première partie (ch. 1–7) traite plus particulièrement de l'église comme symbole, tandis que la seconde traite plus proprement des actions liturgiques dans l'église (ch. 8–24). Il s'agit d'une reprise des deux éléments constitutifs de la théurgie jamblichéenne : ἡ τῶν ἔργων τελεσιουργία (la célébration des actes) et ἡ τῶν συμβόλων δύναμις (le pouvoir des symboles). Mais les deux termes ne sont pas sans relation l'un avec l'autre. Nous le verrons plus loin[19].

---

[17] Saffrey & Segonds 2013, p. 73, l. 5–8.

[18] Van Liefferinge 1994, p. 209. À part cette traduction (légèrement retouchée), toutes les autres sont les miennes.

[19] Voir la troisième partie.

Tout lecteur attentif de la *Mystagogie* aura remarqué le leitmotiv qui revient sans cesse de l'image-figure, aux chapitres 1, 2 et 8 :

Τὴν τοίνυν ἁγίαν ἐκκλησίαν κατὰ πρώτην θεωρίας ἐπιβολὴν τύπον καὶ εἰκόνα θεοῦ φέρειν ἔλεγεν ὁ μακάριος γέρων ἐκεῖνος, ὡς τὴν αὐτὴν αὐτῷ κατὰ μίμησιν καὶ τύπον ἐνέργειαν ἔχουσαν[20].

La sainte église donc, selon une première intuition contemplative, ce bienheureux Ancien disait qu'elle portait la *figure* et l'*image* de Dieu, dans la mesure où elle avait la même activité que lui par imitation et figure.

Κατὰ δευτέραν δὲ θεωρίας ἐπιβολήν, τοῦ σύμπαντος κόσμου, τοῦ ἐξ ὁρατῶν καὶ ἀοράτων οὐσιῶν ὑφεστῶτος, εἶναι τύπον καὶ εἰκόνα τὴν ἁγίαν τοῦ θεοῦ ἐκκλησίαν ἔφασκεν, ὡς τὴν αὐτὴν αὐτῷ καὶ ἕνωσιν καὶ διάκρισιν ἐπιδεχομένην[21].

Mais selon une deuxième intuition contemplative, il disait que la sainte église de Dieu était la *figure* et l'*image* du monde entier, constitué de substances visibles et invisibles, dans la mesure où elle recevait à la fois la même union et la même division que lui.

Τὴν μὲν οὖν πρώτην εἰς τὴν ἁγίαν ἐκκλησίαν τοῦ ἀρχιερέως κατὰ τὴν ἱερὰν σύναξιν εἴσοδον, τῆς πρώτης τοῦ Υἱοῦ τοῦ θεοῦ καὶ σωτῆρος ἡμῶν Χριστοῦ διὰ σαρκὸς εἰς τὸν κόσμον τοῦτον παρουσίας τύπον καὶ εἰκόνα φέρειν ἐδίδασκεν [...][22].

La première entrée donc dans la sainte église du grand prêtre lors de la messe sacrée, il enseignait qu'elle portait la *figure* et l'*image* de la première venue par la chair en ce monde du Fils de Dieu, notre sauveur le Christ [...].

Ces trois textes me serviront de fil d'Ariane. Or cette association de l'image et de la figure se retrouve au début de la *Réponse d'Abamon* :

τὰ δ' εἰκόνα τινὰ ἄλλην ἀποσώζει, καθάπερ δὴ καὶ ἡ γενεσιουργὸς φύσις τῶν ἀφανῶν λόγων ἐμφανεῖς τινας μορφὰς ἀπετυπώσατο·[23]

[Certaines actions cultuelles] conservent une certaine autre *image*, comme précisément la nature génératrice, elle aussi, a *figuré* des raisons invisibles en certaines formes manifestes.

---

[20] Boudignon 2011, p. 10, l. 129–131. Pour la question du 'bienheureux Ancien', voir Boudignon 2002 et 2015.

[21] Boudignon 2011, p. 14–15, l. 207–209.

[22] Boudignon 2011, p. 37, l. 604–607.

[23] Saffrey & Segonds 2013, p. 28, l. 15–18.

Les images-figures ou images-types gardent une forme d'empreinte de leurs λόγοι ou raisons d'être. L'idée fondamentale de Jamblique (suivi ici par Maxime) est que le démiurge a déposé dans le monde des éléments, des συνθήματα, qu'on pourrait traduire par 'signaux' ou 'symboles'. Ces *symboles* envoyés dans le monde sont l'*empreinte*, la *trace* d'une action du démiurge dans la création, pour ainsi dire la *marque* qu'il a laissée. Ils renvoient à la cause unique créatrice. *Empreinte, trace, marque*, tout cela correspond concrètement en grec au mot τύπος que l'on traduit traditionnellement par 'figure'. Comme l'empreinte d'un pas sur le sable, la *figure* est aussi une *image* (εἰκών), qui reçoit du fait de son inscription dans l'espace une mesure. La forme de l'image est le produit de l'impression d'une raison créatrice, invisible. Il y a donc un lien de ressemblance visuelle entre l'image et son modèle et un lien de cause entre la figure et son auteur[24].

On a tout à gagner à situer l'image et la figure dans une perspective jamblichéenne, car c'est sur cet arrière-fond que se comprend ce que dit Maxime de l'église 'image' et 'figure' de Dieu et du monde. Pour Jamblique, le culte (ἁγιστεία), le rite (θεραπεία) imite l'ordre des dieux et celui des astres :

> οὐχ αὕτη μὲν κατὰ θεσμοὺς θεῶν νοερῶς τε κατ᾽ ἀρχὰς ἐνομοθετήθη, μιμεῖται δὲ τὴν τῶν θεῶν τάξιν, τήν τε νοητὴν καὶ τὴν ἐν οὐρανῷ;[25]

> N'a-t-il pas été réglé intellectivement et à l'origine par les décrets des dieux, et n'imite-t-il pas l'ordre des dieux qu'il soit intelligible ou que ce soit celui du ciel ?

L'imitation de l'ordre céleste des dieux conduit Maxime à poser que l'église, en tant que principe du rituel, est

1. image et figure de Dieu
2. et aussi image et figure du monde.

---

[24] Certes, on peut comme Mueller-Jourdan 2005, p. 125, interpréter en termes de figure géométrique le lien de l'image à son modèle et de la figure à la cause qui l'engendre, notamment à travers la figure géométrique de l'angle qui est chez Maxime aussi une définition de l'église dans la 53ᵉ *Question à Thalassios*. Mais ce n'est là qu'un cas particulier de la relation de l'image au modèle et de la figure à la cause.

[25] Saffrey & Segonds 2013, p. 49, l. 3–6.

Ces deux premiers points chez Maxime ont clairement un parallèle dans la figuration jamblichéenne, par les images, de Dieu et des êtres intelligibles. Ce rapprochement permet de comprendre le sens de l'imitation du premier chapitre de la *Mystagogie* : l'église est image et figure de Dieu en tant qu'elle imite son ordre créateur. Cette idée est, à mon avis, unique dans la pensée chrétienne. Elle trouve au contraire ici un parallèle net dans la pensée de Jamblique, pour qui

1. le culte imite l'ordre des dieux, c'est-à-dire celui des êtres intelligibles invisibles
2. et il imite celui des êtres visibles dans le ciel, à savoir les astres.

2. *Pourquoi l'église est-elle image de Dieu et du monde ?*

Allons plus loin. La religion grecque telle qu'elle est défendue par Jamblique dans la *Réponse d'Abamon* se compose principalement de trois parties : les apparitions divines[26], les oracles[27] et les sacrifices[28]. Une lecture de la partie sur les apparitions montre qu'en fait derrière la notion d' ἐπιφάνεια ('apparition' ou 'épiphanie')[29] se cache celle de παρουσία ('parousie', 'visite', 'venue' ou 'présence')[30] des êtres divins, et plus particulièrement la question du culte associé à la 'statue' (ἄγαλμα) du dieu installée dans un temple. Jamblique veut défendre le culte traditionnel rendu aux statues en le refondant sur la philosophie platonicienne. Il propose ainsi une nouvelle interprétation de la 'statue cultuelle' (ἄγαλμα). Le mot ἄγαλμα désigne traditionnellement une 'statue de culte', comme dans la *Lettre d'Abamon*, où les 'statues consacrées' (ἱερὰ ἀγάλματα) sont associées aux 'temples' (τεμένη)[31]. Or les astres et le ciel en général sont image et figure

---

[26] Saffrey & Segonds 2013, p. 52, l. 20 – p. 73, l. 27.

[27] Saffrey & Segonds 2013, p. 75, l. 6 – p. 135, l. 2.

[28] Saffrey & Segonds 2013, p. 149, l. 5 – p. 179, l. 7.

[29] Saffrey & Segonds 2013, p. 52, l. 20.

[30] Saffrey & Segonds 2013, p. 52, l. 22.

[31] Saffrey & Segonds 2013, p. 23, l. 15. On regrettera leur traduction quasi systématique du mot ἄγαλμα par 'image', alors justement qu'ici, ils traduisent bien par 'statue'. La dimension traditionnelle, cultuelle, est masquée par ce changement de vocable dans la traduction française.

des dieux intelligibles, incorporels et invisibles. À ce titre, en tant qu'imitation des dieux, le ciel et le monde sont définis comme τὸ τῶν θεῶν ἐμφανὲς ἄγαλμα ('statue manifeste des dieux')[32]. C'est ce qu'explique Jamblique : ὅπερ δὴ καὶ ὁ σύμπας μιμούμενος οὐρανὸς καὶ κόσμος τὴν ἐγκύκλιον περιφορὰν περιπολεῖ [...] ('c'est cela [la présence de la lumière divine dans les êtres] qu'imite le ciel et le monde tout entiers quand ils font leur course circulaire [...]')[33]. Si l'on met en rapport ces passages de la *Lettre d'Abamon*, on comprend le lien qui unit les deux genres de statue cultuelle, celles que sont les astres, et celles qui sont fabriquées par les hommes et installées à l'intérieur des temples. Les astres parce qu'ils resplendissent de lumière imitent le divin, tout comme les statues que le rituel théurgique fait volontiers resplendir lors de cérémonies où les dieux sont censés apparaître.

En employant ce mot d'ἄγαλμα à propos des astres célestes, et notamment du soleil qui resplendit, Jamblique reprend la tradition du dialogue pseudo-platonicien de l'*Epinomis* (983e) qui fait des astres θεῶν εἰκόνας ὡς ἀγάλματα ('des images des dieux, en tant que statues') fabriquées par les dieux eux-mêmes. Selon ce principe, les images fabriquées par les hommes sont dans un troisième degré d'éloignement par rapport aux dieux. Il y a les dieux, les images des dieux que sont les astres, puis en troisième lieu les images des dieux que sont les statues. On comprend bien le défaut de légitimité de ces dernières images, surtout quand l'adversaire de Jamblique, Porphyre, insiste sur l'incorporalité des dieux : θεοὺς εἶναι νόας καθαρούς ('les dieux sont de purs intellects')[34], et donc indirectement sur l'impossibilité de les représenter, puisque ce n'est alors qu'εἰδωλοποιία ('fabrication de simulacre') pour Porphyre[35]. Il faut donc justifier ces statues autrement que par une ressemblance. C'est ce que fait Jamblique en reprenant la phraséologie des *Oracles chaldaïques*, quand il écrit : τὰ μὲν τῶν θεῶν ἀγάλματα φωτὸς πλέον ἀστράπτει ('les statues cultuelles des dieux ont plus de fulgurance que la lumière')[36]. En resplendissant grâce

---

[32] Saffrey & Segonds 2013, p. 24, l. 19.

[33] Saffrey & Segonds 2013, p. 24, l. 9–11.

[34] Saffrey & Segonds 2012, p. 12, fragment 16.

[35] Saffrey & Segonds 2012, p. 18, fragment 29b.

[36] Saffrey & Segonds 2013, p. 58, l. 10–11.

à des jeux de lumière, les statues cultuelles deviennent en quelque sorte des astres, images vivantes des dieux. Mieux, elles sont censées briller plus que les astres !

On peut trouver un parallélisme à ces affirmations dans ce qu'écrit Maxime à propos de l'univers qui est pour ainsi dire, dans son existence, une église céleste, ou plutôt une église non faite de main d'hommes. L'église terrestre, le bâtiment ecclésial, ou plutôt l'église faite de main d'homme en est le reflet, pour qui sait regarder les choses avec sagesse (ch. 2) :

> ἄλλη πως ὑπάρχων ἀχειροποίητος ἐκκλησία διὰ ταύτης τῆς χειροποιήτου σοφῶς ὑποφαίνεται [...] [37].

> [Le monde entier] qui a l'existence d'une certaine façon d'une église non faite de mains d'hommes, transparaît dans la sagesse à travers cette église-ci faite de mains d'hommes.

Par ce biais, Maxime souligne que l'on a une forme de tripartition : Dieu, le monde issu de Dieu et l'église. En fait, et c'est un point qu'avait souligné Mueller-Jourdan, le monde a une réelle activité en tant que lieu qui contient les êtres[38]. Mais c'est l'église terrestre qui révèle cette activité existentielle du monde. En effet, dans le premier chapitre, Maxime a expliqué que l'église est image de Dieu en tant qu'il rassemble les êtres. Dans le deuxième chapitre, il dit que l'église est image du monde en tant qu'il unit dans la distinction les êtres. On conviendra que la nuance est fine entre l'activité providentielle de Dieu qui unit les êtres entre eux et à lui-même et celle du monde qui unit les êtres entre eux, tout en préservant leur distinction. La principale différence est que le monde est second par rapport à Dieu, premier, puisque l'univers est ἐκ θεοῦ κατὰ γένεσιν παρηγμένος ('produit par Dieu par naissance', autrement dit 'engendré par Dieu')[39], selon une formulation plus néoplatonicienne que chrétienne : il semble

---

[37] Boudignon 2011, p. 16, l. 229–231.

[38] Mueller-Jourdan 2015, p. 110 écrit : 'Chaque chose est ainsi gardée de la confusion par une cause qui, dans le néoplatonisme, peut être rapportée respectivement au lieu et au temps comme "puissance de l'un". C'est ce qu'on peut déduire des propos de Simplicius lorsqu'il tente de comprendre au terme du *Corollarium de loco* la nature de la cause qui retient les êtres de la dispersion à l'infini ou de la confusion'.

[39] Boudignon 2011, p. 16, l. 225.

exercer un vicariat providentiel sur les êtres qui sont en lui. Mais c'est plus finalement l'église terrestre qui montre cette activité de rassemblement, notamment lors de la messe qui est dite en grec précisément σύναξις ('rassemblement'). Le monde, lui, échappe aux regards : seule la sagesse permet de discerner cette activité du monde par la médiation de l'église terrestre. En ce sens, le monde est une église céleste. On retrouve là une pensée qui n'est pas sans affinité avec ce que disait Jamblique : le monde et le ciel sont certes τὸ τῶν θεῶν ἐμφανὲς ἄγαλμα ('la statue manifeste des dieux')[40] mais τὰ μὲν τῶν θεῶν ἀγάλματα φωτὸς πλέον ἀστράπτει ('les statues cultuelles des dieux ont plus de fulgurance que la lumière')[41].

3. *Pourquoi l'entrée du grand-prêtre est-elle l'image de la venue de Dieu au monde ?*

Le rituel de la théurgie est même plus précisément évoqué par Jamblique pour réfuter l'accusation d'inefficacité des statues de cultes : Porphyre accuse les statues de dieu de ne pas avoir de pouvoir divin. Porphyre parle à ce propos de τὸ ἀπατηλόν, τὸ τῆς περιαυτολογίας ('l'effet trompeur, celui de la forfanterie')[42]. Cette forfanterie est associée par Porphyre (dans une autre citation faite par Jamblique qu'il faut évidemment rattacher à la précédente) à ces images désormais réduites au rang de vains simulacres des dieux :

> κοινόν ἐστι <τὸ> τῆς εἰδωλοποιίας καὶ τῆς περιαυτολογίας θεῶν καὶ δαιμόνων καὶ τῶν ἄλλων [...][43].
>
> [L'effet trompeur] de la fabrication d'idoles et de la forfanterie est commun aux dieux, démons et autres [...].

La 'fabrication de statues cultuelles' est associée au charlatanisme et ravalée au rang d' εἰδωλοποιία ('fabrique de simulacres', littéralement 'd'idoles')[44] par Porphyre. Jamblique, lui, reprend le mot

---

[40] Saffrey & Segonds 2013, p. 24, l. 19.
[41] Saffrey & Segonds 2013, p. 58, l. 10–11.
[42] Saffrey & Segonds 2012, p. 18, fragment 29a.
[43] Saffrey & Segonds 2012, p. 18, fragment 29b.
[44] Le mot d'εἴδωλον ('simulacre'), est employé par Jamblique pour qualifier une fausse apparition d'Apollon, qui est en fait celle d'un défunt gladiateur,

traditionnel d'ἄγαλμα que l'on rapproche étymologiquement dès l'Antiquité du verbe ἀγάλλομαι ('exulter, ressentir une joyeuse fierté de')[45]. Ce mot qui signifie littéralement 'joyau' ou 'parure' chez Homère, se spécialise chez Hérodote et dans la langue attique au sens de 'statue offerte à un dieu, qui le représente généralement et est adorée'[46]. Le choix par Jamblique d'un tel mot associé à la joie, pour corriger Porphyre, n'est donc pas innocent[47]. C'est une première réponse, formelle, à Porphyre.

Mais sur le fond, Jamblique répond en évoquant une erreur possible dans le rituel théurgique pour justifier une inefficacité éventuelle :

> Πότε οὖν συμβαίνει τὸ λεγόμενον ὑπὸ σοῦ ἀπατηλόν, τὸ τῆς περιαυτολογίας; ἡνίκα ἂν ἁμάρτημά τι συμβαίνῃ περὶ τὴν θεουργικὴν τέχνην, καὶ μὴ οἷα δεῖ τὰ αὐτοπτικὰ ἀγάλματα ἀλλ' ἕτερα ἀνθ' ἑτέρων ἀπαντήσῃ.[48]

> Quand donc se produit 'cet effet trompeur' dont tu parles, 'celui de la forfanterie' ? Quand une certaine faute se produit touchant l'art théurgique et si ce ne sont pas les bonnes statues cultuelles objet de vision directe mais d'autres à leur place qui se présentent.

Je soulignerai trois choses. *Primo*, pour Jamblique les statues sont 'autoptiques' dans la mesure où elles permettent la 'vision directe' des dieux. Ce qui justifie les statues cultuelles est pour Jamblique le mystère, en fait la perception du mystère qu'on nomme en grec ἐποπτεία, c'est-à-dire 'survision', 'vision au-delà de la réalité', une vision de la présence divine dans le monde. Cette ἐποπτεία

---

comme en témoigne Eunape dans sa *Vie des sophistes*. Cf. Giangrande 1956, p. 40, l. 9–15.

[45] Le lexique d'Hésychius définit ainsi l'ἄγαλμα· πᾶν ἐφ'ᾧ τις ἀγάλλεται. Cf. Chantraine, 1999, p. 6.

[46] Chantraine, 1999, p. 7.

[47] Je remercie Bram Demulder qui me fait remarquer que Platon, *Timée* 37c, employait déjà ἄγαλμα avec εἰκών pour décrire le *cosmos* créé par le démiurge comme τῶν ἀιδίων θεῶν γεγονὸς ἄγαλμα 'représentation des dieux éternels'. En général, il est clair que Jamblique se réfère ici au *Timée*, comme aussi par exemple pour la question de la *genèse* des figures matérielles qui 'reçoivent des empreintes qui proviennent de ces réalités éternelles' (τυπωθέντα ἀπ' αὐτῶν [sc. τῶν ὄντων ἀεὶ], *Tim.* 50c).

[48] Saffrey & Segonds 2013, p. 68, l. 25 – p. 69, l. 2.

devient chez Jamblique une αὐτοψία, c'est-à-dire 'vision directe', une perception des dieux. Par la statue cultuelle resplendissante, ce sont les dieux que l'on voit directement dans les statues, comme à travers le soleil on voit l'image du Bien.

Secundo, quand il est question d'apparition ou plutôt de fausse apparition, Jamblique réplique en parlant de théurgie, et plus précisément de faute dans l'usage rituel des statues. Cela prouve bien que toute la partie concernant les apparitions traite en fait principalement, même si c'est indirectement, de la question des statues, ou plutôt du rituel autour des statues.

Tertio, on est en droit de se demander si le rituel en question n'est pas ici la télestique, ou l'art d'animer les statues[49]. Car, l'erreur ne viendrait pas du sculpteur mais du prêtre qui consacre les statues et doit les rendre vivantes et animées. En cas de réussite du rituel, le dieu vient les habiter, elles deviennent autoptiques. En plus, les statues sont alors elles-mêmes en mouvement, elles viennent à la rencontre (ἀπαντήσῃ) des fidèles – si du moins le rituel se passe comme il faut ! On retrouve là l'idée traditionnelle de ces statues animées ou 'statues de Dédale' (τοῖς Δαιδάλου ἀγάλμασι) qu'évoque Platon dans le *Ménon* (97a) et 'qui s'échappent en secret et s'enfuient si on ne les attache pas' (ταῦτα, ἐὰν μὲν μὴ δεδεμένα ᾖ, ἀποδιδράσκει καὶ δραπετεύει). Mais si le prêtre se trompe dans les symboles, il fait alors venir des démons dans les statues des dieux, qui sont alors trompeuses. L'inefficacité d'une statue qui la relègue au rang d'idole ou de simulacre relève donc non pas de la question de la nature de la statue, mais des actions du prêtre. C'est donc là que se noue le lien entre statue et prêtre...

Cela me conduit à cette question fondamentale : comment expliquer une influence de ce culte païen sur la description du culte chrétien ? De fait, Jamblique répondait indirectement aux

---

[49] Van Liefferinge 1999, p. 96–97, pense que la télestique serait plutôt à trouver chez Proclus que chez Jamblique. Cependant, contrairement à ce qu'elle conclut, le rapprochement entre le traité appelé l'*Asclepius*, qui parle de la force qui se trouve dans les dieux terrestres (en fait les statues creuses), due à la présence en eux d'herbes, pierres et aromates et la *Réponse d'Abamon* (Saffrey & Segonds 2013, p. 174, l. 2–3) est tout à fait légitime. Il s'agit bien chez Jamblique de la 'fabrication d'un réceptacle parfait où le dieu peut résider' comme le comprennent Saffrey & Segonds 2013, p. 316, n. 1, et donc de télestique.

attaques du christianisme contre ce que les chrétiens appellent idolâtrie. De plus, il n'y a pas de statue sacrée dans le christianisme antique. Néanmoins, le mot d'ἄγαλμα apparaît métaphorique-ment, et cet usage rhétorique va nous conduire insensiblement à l'adaptation de la théorie jamblichéenne au christianisme.

On lit ainsi chez le Pseudo-Denys l'Aréopagite :

> Δεῖ δὴ οὖν ἡμᾶς – ἐντὸς γὰρ εἶναι τῶν πανιέρων οἴομαι – τὸ νοη-τὸν τοῦ πρώτου τῶν ἀγαλμάτων ἀπογυμνώσαντας εἰς τὸ θεοειδὲς αὐτοῦ κάλλος ἐνατενίσαι καὶ τὸν ἱεράρχην ἐνθέως ἰδεῖν ἀπὸ τοῦ θείου θυσιαστηρίου μέχρι τῶν ἐσχάτων τοῦ ἱεροῦ μετ'εὐοσμίας ἰόντα καὶ πάλιν ἐπ'αὐτῷ τελειωτικῶς ἀποκαθιστάμενον[50].

> Il nous faut donc à la vérité – car je pense que nous sommes à l'intérieur d'un temple tout sacré –, dénudant la beauté intelligible de la première des *statues* fixer du regard sa beauté déiforme et voir divinement le grand-prêtre venir, au milieu des douces fragrances, du divin autel jusqu'aux extrémités du temple et ensuite se réinstaller auprès de l'autel à la façon de quelqu'un qui accomplit un rite mystique.

Le rite dionysien de la descente du grand-prêtre dans la nef et sur-tout de son retour auprès de l'autel est métaphoriquement inter-prété sur le modèle de la contemplation des statues cultuelles. Contempler la beauté de la statue, c'est voir venir le grand-prêtre...

Maxime de son côté, quand il décrit l'entrée du grand-prêtre dans l'église de l'extérieur (d'une façon différente de Denys, qui lui considère que le grand-prêtre est déjà dans l'église quand commence la messe), emploie le terme d'*image* et de *figure*. Voici le texte de Maxime que nous avons déjà cité (ch. 8) :

> Τὴν μὲν οὖν πρώτην εἰς τὴν ἁγίαν ἐκκλησίαν τοῦ ἀρχιερέως κατὰ τὴν ἱερὰν σύναξιν εἴσοδον, τῆς πρώτης τοῦ Υἱοῦ τοῦ θεοῦ καὶ σωτῆρος ἡμῶν Χριστοῦ διὰ σαρκὸς εἰς τὸν κόσμον τοῦτον παρουσίας τύπον καὶ εἰκόνα φέρειν ἐδίδασκεν [...][51].

> La première entrée donc dans la sainte église du grand-prêtre lors de la messe sacrée, il enseignait qu'elle portait la *figure* et l'*image* de la première venue par la chair en ce monde du Fils de Dieu, notre sauveur le Christ [...].

---

[50] *Les hiérarchies ecclésiastiques*, III, 3, éd. Heil & Ritter 1991, p. 82, l. 13–17.
[51] Boudignon 2011, p. 37, l. 604–607.

Les différences entre le culte chrétien et le culte hellène sautent aux yeux : là où Jamblique décrivait une théurgie liée aux statues auto-révélatrice, Maxime décrit l'entrée du grand-prêtre dans l'église. Il suit la métaphore du Pseudo-Denys. Cependant, en termes maximiens, le grand-prêtre représente la venue, la première parousie du Christ. Or ce mot était employé par Porphyre pour interroger Jamblique sur le culte grec et les apparitions divines que, lui, Porphyre qualifiait de parousies :

> τί τὸ γνώρισμα θεοῦ παρουσίας ἢ ἀγγέλου ἢ ἀρχαγγέλου ἢ δαίμονος ἢ τινος ἄρχοντος ἢ ψυχῆς[52];
>
> Quelle est la marque de la *venue* d'un dieu, d'un ange, d'un archange, d'un démon, d'un certain archonte ou d'une âme ?

Ce n'est pas seulement le mot de παρουσία, mais le concept même de la *venue* d'un dieu dans le monde qui est centrale dans le cas de la *Mystagogie* et dans le cas de la théurgie. Car, chose que conteste Porphyre mais que défend Jamblique, la théurgie n'est rien d'autre qu'une technique pour faire venir le dieu, – dont les moyens sont en fait le rituel autour des statues ou télestique, la divination et les sacrifices.

Or le Christ devient présent dans la suite du texte de la *Mystagogie*, ce qui suppose en effet, que l'image et la figure que représente l'entrée du grand-prêtre dans l'église ont été efficaces. C'est désormais le Christ qui est le grand-prêtre ; en effet, le fidèle qui se convertit du vice à la vertu (ch. 9) :

> κυρίως τὲ καὶ ἀληθῶς Χριστῷ τῷ θεῷ καὶ ἀρχιερεῖ νοείσθω τὲ καὶ λεγέσθω συνεισιέναι εἰς τὴν ἀρετήν, ἐκκλησίαν τροπικῶς νοουμένην[53].
>
> Qu'il soit dit et pensé que proprement et véritablement il entre en compagnie du Christ dieu et grand-prêtre dans la vertu, c'est-à-dire l'église conçue métaphoriquement.

On est passé d'une métaphore (τροπικῶς) à la réalité proprement dite (κυρίως τε καὶ ἀληθῶς). Le Christ est réellement présent dans l'entrée du grand-prêtre.

---

[52] Saffrey & Segonds 2012, p. 16–17, fragment 28a.
[53] Boudignon 2011, p. 39, l. 638–640.

4. *En quoi l'église peut-elle recevoir le divin ?*

Ce passage est capital puisqu'il établit le lien entre la première et la seconde partie du traité. Ce qui était dit théoriquement de l'église comme image et figure du démiurge et du monde prend une résonance pratique : l'entrée dans l'église du grand-prêtre, c'est-à-dire de l'évêque, devient l'image et la figure de l'entrée dans notre monde matériel du Verbe démiurge. Or le but de la théurgie, nous l'avons vu, consiste précisément à faire venir le divin. Mais comment ?

Un passage de la *Réponse d'Abamon* peut être mis en rapport. Il concerne en fait les sacrifices matériels, dont Porphyre contestait la légitimité. Or Jamblique établit l'existence d'une matière qu'il qualifie de καθαρὰ καὶ θεία[54] ('pure et divine') et de θεῶν ὑποδοχή[55] ('réceptacle des dieux'). Cette matière est qualifiée de καταβολὴ πρώτη[56] ('fondation première') divine, comme si non seulement la victime du sacrifice, mais aussi la statue de culte et le temple étaient faits de cette matière divine. On notera soigneusement ce lien matériel qui fonde temple, statue et sacrifice. D'une façon explicite, il écrit :

> Οὐ γὰρ δὴ δεῖ δυσχεραίνειν πᾶσαν ὕλην, ἀλλὰ μόνην τὴν ἀλλο-τρίαν τῶν θεῶν, τὴν δὲ οἰκείαν πρὸς αὐτοὺς ἐκλέγεσθαι, ὡς συμφωνεῖν δυναμένην εἴς τε θεῶν οἰκοδομήσεις καὶ καθιδρύσεις ἀγαλμάτων καὶ δὴ καὶ εἰς τὰς τῶν θυσιῶν ἱερουργίας. Οὐδὲ γὰρ ἂν ἄλλως τοῖς ἐπὶ γῆς τόποις ἢ τοῖς δεῦρο κατοικοῦσιν ἀνθρώποις μετουσία ἂν γένοιτο τῆς τῶν κρειττόνων λήψεως, εἰ μή τις τοιαύτη καταβολὴ πρώτη προενιδρυθείη[57].

> Car il ne faut pas rechigner devant toute matière, mais seule-ment devant celle qui est étrangère aux dieux, et choisir celle qui leur est apparentée, dans la mesure où elle peut convenir à la construction de demeures pour les dieux, à l'installa-tion de leurs statues, et en particulier à la cérémonie sacrée des sacrifices. En effet, il n'y a pas d'autre manière pour les lieux de la terre ou pour les hommes qui habitent ici-bas d'avoir part à la réception des êtres supérieurs, que de fonder à l'avance une première fondation de cette sorte.

[54] Saffrey & Segonds 2013, p. 173, l. 12–13.
[55] Saffrey & Segonds 2013, p. 173, l. 15–16.
[56] Saffrey & Segonds 2013, p. 174, l. 13.
[57] Saffrey & Segonds 2013, p. 174, l. 5–14.

Jamblique avance un argument pragmatique : si l'on refuse le culte matériel, si la matière n'a aucun rapport avec le divin, alors on sombre dans un intellectualisme ravageur comme Porphyre, et il n'y a quasiment plus aucun moyen pour le simple mortel d'entrer en contact avec le divin. Pour éviter cette extrémité, Jamblique recourt à l'idée de 'matière divine', et ce non seulement pour les victimes de sacrifices : pierres, plantes, animaux et parfums... mais aussi pour les statues et les temples. Le lecteur que je suis ne peut s'empêcher d'avoir en tête les bétyles[58], ces pierres noires tombées du ciel. Jamblique de Chalcis appartenait à la grande famille sacerdotale des Sampsigéramides qui régnaient sur le territoire de la cité syrienne d'Emèse[59] et le bétyle du dieu Elagabal trônait dans le temple d'Emèse[60]. Jamblique emploie cependant un mot particulièrement révélateur qui est celui de καταβολή, qui renvoie à la 'fondation' d'un temple, comme si la première pierre d'un temple était divine. On y voit volontiers une allusion au temple d'Emèse, mais cela est valable pour tous les temples, car il faut que les hommes aient des lieux sur terre pour entrer en contact avec le divin :

> Ἐπεὶ γὰρ ἔδει καὶ τὰ ἐν γῇ μηδαμῶς εἶναι ἄμοιρα τῆς θείας κοινωνίας, ἐδέξατό τινα ἀπ' αὐτῆς θείαν μοῖραν καὶ ἡ γῆ, ἱκανὴν οὖσαν χωρῆσαι τοὺς θεούς[61].

> En effet, puisqu'il fallait que les choses terrestres ne fussent pas sans communion avec le divin, la terre, elle aussi, a reçu de cette [communion] une certaine portion divine, capable de contenir les dieux.

Cette partie divine que la terre a reçue des dieux, c'est au moins l'espace sacré où se trouvent le temple des dieux, la statue de culte et l'autel des sacrifices. Mais la façon de dire de Jamblique repose sur la théorie de la sympathie universelle, des relations nécessaires

---

[58] Jospeh de Tibériade, dans son *Hypomnèsticon*, parle ainsi comme moyens de divination de τὰ ἐν τοῖς ναοῖς βαιτύλια ('les bétyles conservés dans les temples'), cf. Saffrey & Segonds 2012, p. 28, l. 12.

[59] Saffrey & Segonds 2013, p. XVI qui citent la *Vie d'Isidore* de Damascius (Zintzen 1967, p. 317).

[60] On se rapportera à la pittoresque anecdote sur le bétyle d'Emèse dans la *Vie d'Isidore* de Damascius (Zintzen 1967, p. 274–278).

[61] Saffrey & Segonds 2013, p. 173, l. 21–24.

qui existent entre le monde terrestre des hommes et le monde céleste des dieux[62].

Maxime établit de la même façon la correspondance entre le monde sensible, c'est-à-dire matériel, et le monde intelligible (ch. 2) :

> Δεῖ γὰρ τὰ ἀλλήλων ὄντα δηλωτικὰ πάντως ἀληθεῖς καὶ ἀριδήλους τὰς ἀλλήλων ἔχειν ἐμφάσεις καὶ τὴν ἐπ' αὐταῖς σχέσιν ἀλώβητον[63].

> Car il faut que les choses qui se montrent mutuellement aient en tout cas un reflet clair et distinct les uns des autres et une relation indéfectible à ces reflets.

C'est par cette relation qui existe entre la matériel et le spirituel, le sensible et l'intelligible, le visible et l'invisible, que le matériel peut accueillir le spirituel, ou comme le dit Jamblique : χωρῆσαι τοὺς θεούς[64] ('faire place aux dieux').

Cette relation repose sur une fondation, qui chez Maxime est celle de l'incarnation du Verbe[65]. On ne sera pas surpris que le référent soit plutôt la parousie du Verbe démiurge que la création. En effet, comme le dit Maxime juste après la mention de l'entrée du grand-prêtre image et figure de cette venue, le Verbe a restauré la création dans son état premier par sa parousie (ch. 8) :

> [...] δι' ἧς τὴν δουλωθεῖσαν τῇ φθορᾷ καὶ παθοῦσαν ὑφ' ἑαυτῆς τῷ θανάτῳ διὰ τῆς ἁμαρτίας καὶ βασιλευομένην τυραννικῶς ὑπὸ τοῦ διαβόλου τῶν ἀνθρώπων φύσιν ἐλευθερώσας τε καὶ λυτρωσά-μενος, καὶ πᾶσαν τὴν ὑπὲρ αὐτῆς ὀφειλὴν ὡς ὑπεύθυνος ἀποδοὺς ὁ ἀνεύθυνος καὶ ἀναμάρτητος, πάλιν πρὸς τὴν ἐξ ἀρχῆς ἐπανή-γαγε τῆς βασιλείας χάριν[66].

---

[62] On se rapportera aussi aux premiers mots du traité attribué à Proclus, *De sacrificio et magia* ou Περὶ τῆς καθ' Ἕλληνας ἱερατικῆς τέχνης (Bidez 1948, p. 148) dont le chapitre 2 de la *Mystagogie* se démarque.

[63] Boudignon 2011, p. 17, l. 255–257.

[64] Saffrey & Segonds 2013, p. 173, l. 24. Je remercie encore Bram Demulder qui me signale que ce verbe χωρῆσαι semble faire écho à la description dans le *Timée* 52 du 'lieu' (χώρα) qui, avec l'être et le devenir, existait avant la naissance du ciel et reçoit la forme qui entre dans la matière, forme à la ressemblance de la forme intelligible en soi.

[65] Pour Maxime, la création est ordonnée à l'incarnation. Dans le 33ᵉ *Passage difficile, à Jean*, Maxime parle de trois incarnations, ou plutôt 'incorporations' du Christ : dans le monde, dans les Écritures, et dans la chair. Cf. Tollefsen 2015, p. 308.

[66] Boudignon 2011, p. 37, l. 607–613.

> [...] à travers laquelle il a libéré contre rançon la nature humaine asservie à la corruption, punie par elle-même de mort à travers le péché et soumise à la tyrannie du diable, il en a versé le prix comme quelqu'un qui avait des comptes à rendre alors qu'il n'avait de compte à rendre à personne et qu'il était sans péché, et il l'a de nouveau restaurée dans la grâce du royaume qu'elle avait à l'origine.

À travers ces mots, c'est en fait le Verbe, en tant qu'il n'est pas soumis au sensible, qui a restauré la nature humaine dans sa dignité intellective, elle qui par le péché s'était soumise au sensible en s'y dévoyant, comme Maxime l'a expliqué dans l'introduction des *Questions à Thalassios*[67]. L'entrée dans le monde du démiurge est donc bien le rétablissement de la juste relation entre le sensible et l'intelligible, la matière et l'esprit, la création et son créateur.

En ce sens, l'église est figure et image du démiurge qui tient ensemble les deux mondes, le sensible et l'intelligible et sauvegarde par son rituel l'interpénétration des deux.

Car Maxime fonde toute sa *Mystagogie*,

1. sur une construction symbolique, architecturale, et statique du bâtiment qui en tant que contenant, signifie à la fois la capacité du démiurge de tenir ensemble le monde et l'unité du monde dont les éléments s'interpénètrent,

2. et sur l'animation de cette structure dans la description symbolique d'entrées et sorties de personnages, notamment celle du grand prêtre qui marque la restauration du monde sensible dans sa dignité première et son lien avec le démiurge.

Dans la mesure où l'entrée de personnages qualifie l'espace, on peut rapprocher cela de la télestique qui par le rituel qualifie les statues divines, en les rendant vivantes, ou plutôt habitées. En ce sens, il y a bien une continuité entre les deux premières figures et images statiques et la troisième figure et image dynamique en ce qu'elles se supposent mutuellement. Sans l'entrée du grand-prêtre, l'église resterait un bâtiment vide et vain ; sans la structuration symbolique de l'espace, l'entrée du grand-prêtre ne ferait pas d'effet.

---

[67] Laga-Steel 1980, p. 35, l. 303 – p. 37, l. 326.

5. *En quoi la liturgie n'est pas magie ?*

Toute cette construction pourrait faire penser à la magie. De fait, elle en reprend les structures. Mais le souci de Jamblique est justement de distinguer magie et théurgie pour répondre à Porphyre, dans la mesure où la magie cherche à contraindre le divin, tandis que la théurgie, comme l'a clairement établi Van Liefferinge[68], élève 'le théurge jusqu'aux être supérieurs sur lesquels il n'exerce donc aucune contrainte'. En fait, la théurgie conduit au bonheur de l'union avec les dieux, comme le dit Jamblique à la fin de son traité :

> δύναμιν δ' ἔχει πρώτην μὲν ἀγνείαν τῆς ψυχῆς πολὺ τελειοτέραν τῆς τοῦ σώματος ἀγνείας, ἔπειτα κατάρτυσιν τῆς διανοίας εἰς μετουσίαν καὶ θέαν τοῦ ἀγαθοῦ καὶ τῶν ἐναντίων πάντων ἀπαλλαγήν, μετὰ δὲ ταῦτα πρὸς τοὺς τῶν ἀγαθῶν δοτῆρας θεοὺς ἕνωσιν[69].

> [La théurgie] a comme premier effet une pureté de l'âme bien plus parfaite que la pureté du corps, ensuite une préparation de la pensée à la participation au Bien et à la vision du Bien et un abandon des réalités contraires, et après cela, une union avec les dieux dispensateurs des biens.

L'église n'est pas, elle non plus, un dispositif magique pour attirer le divin, même si tout ce qui a été dit jusqu'à présent le supposait. C'est en fait un dispositif contemplatif pour faire monter l'âme vers Dieu par le spectacle des actions liturgiques, comme l'explique Maxime au ch. 23 :

> Ἄθρει τοιγαροῦν, ὅστις τῆς μακαρίας τοῦ Χριστοῦ σοφίας γνήσιος καθέστηκας ἐραστής, νοὸς ὀφθαλμοῖς κατὰ τὴν πρώτην εἴσοδον τῆς ἁγίας συνάξεως ἀπὸ τῆς ἔξωθεν τῶν ὑλικῶν πλάνης καὶ ταραχῆς, [...] ἐρχομένην τε τὴν ψυχὴν καὶ προτοπάδην φεύγουσαν καὶ ὥσπερ εἰς ἐκκλησίαν καὶ ἄσυλον εἰρήνης ἀνάκτορον τὴν ἐν Πνεύματι φυσικὴν θεωρίαν τὴν ἄμαχον καὶ πάσης ἐλευθέραν ταραχῆς μετὰ Λόγου τὲ καὶ ὑπὸ τοῦ Λόγου τοῦ μεγάλου καὶ ἀληθοῦς ἡμῶν θεοῦ καὶ ἀρχιερέως εἰσερχομένην[70].

---

[68] Van Liefferinge 1999, p. 57.
[69] Saffrey & Segonds 2013, p. 216, l. 3–8.
[70] Boudignon 2011, p. 49–50, l. 784–787 & 798–803.

Voilà pourquoi, regarde donc, toi qui es désormais l'amant légitime de la sagesse bienheureuse du Christ, avec les yeux de l'intellect, dans la première entrée de la sainte messe, l'âme qui vient, se précipite en fuyant hors de l'égarement et du trouble extérieurs des réalités matérielles [...] et entre avec le Verbe et sous la houlette du Verbe, notre grand et vrai Dieu et grand-prêtre, comme dans une église et dans un palais inviolable de paix, dans la contemplation de la nature dans l'Esprit, contemplation invincible et libre de tout trouble.

Il s'agit bien ici, à travers le symbole que représente la première entrée, du début d'un processus intellectuel d'élévation, qui commence par une libération du trouble matériel à travers une πρᾶξις ('pratique morale'). Cela correspond bien à la purification dont parle Jamblique. La pratique morale est associée simultanément à la φυσικὴ θεωρία ('contemplation de la nature'), pour repérer dans la nature les marques de la présence du Verbe démiurge.

La deuxième étape se produit à l'occasion à la seconde entrée de la liturgie grecque (ch. 23) :

κἀντεῦθεν πάλιν ἔξω γενομένην τῶν αἰσθητῶν, ὡς ἡ τῶν θυρῶν τῆς ἁγίας τοῦ θεοῦ ἐκκλησίας νοεῖν ὑποτίθεται κλεῖσις, ἐπὶ τὴν δηλουμένην διὰ τῆς εἰσόδου τῶν ἀρρήτων μυστηρίων ἄϋλον καὶ ἁπλῆν καὶ ἀναλλοίωτον καὶ θεοειδῆ καὶ παντὸς ἐλευθέραν εἴδους καὶ σχήματος ἐπιστήμην τῶν νοητῶν ἄγοντα·[71]

Et de là, de nouveau, [regarde le Verbe] conduire [l'âme] qui sort du sensible – comme on peut comprendre intellectuellement la fermeture des portes de la sainte église de Dieu –, vers la science des réalités intelligibles qui est signifiée à travers l'entrée des mystères ineffables, science immatérielle, simple, immuable, déiforme, et libre de toute forme et configuration.

Après la φυσικὴ θεωρία vient l'ἐπιστήμη τῶν νοητῶν ('science des réalités intelligibles'), c'est-à-dire la θεολογία ('théologie'), qui se fait par un dépassement de la contemplations des choses sensibles. Cette 'théologie' correspond à bien à l'expression : τῶν ἐναντίων πάντων ἀπαλλαγή ('l'abandon de tout ce qui est contraire' au Bien), qu'employait Jamblique plus haut[72].

---

[71] Boudignon 2011, p. 51–52, l. 824–828.
[72] Saffrey & Segonds 2013, p. 216, l. 3–8. La différence entre Jamblique et Maxime sur ce point est que Maxime associe la 'contemplation de la nature'

La dernière étape correspond à l'union de l'âme avec le divin (ch. 23) :

> κατ' εὐχὰς τὸν θεὸν Πατέρα μυστικόν τε χάριτι καὶ μόνον ἔχουσα πρὸς τὸ ἓν τῆς αὐτοῦ κρυφιότητος κατ' ἔκστασιν πάντων συναχθήσεται, καὶ τοσοῦτον πείσεται μᾶλλον ἢ γνώσεται τὰ θεῖα[73].

> Conformément à ses vœux, [l'âme] aura Dieu pour seul père par grâce dans le mystère, elle s'unira à lui, l'Un de l'occultation divine, dans une *extase* [qui la conduit hors] de tout, et elle éprouvera le divin plus qu'elle ne le connaîtra.

Maxime décrit ici littéralement une 'extase', une 'sortie' hors de tout qui permet à l'âme l'union avec Dieu de façon que la connaissance soit abolie dans une passivité réceptive.

Le programme jamblichéen est donc manifestement repris, même si, différence notoire, il est transféré du théurge au chrétien gnostique, à la ψυχὴ γνωστική[74] ('âme connaissante') c'est-à-dire à l'âme du fidèle qui a développé une certaine connaissance de la théologie. Le gnostique est le plus haut degré d'une échelle qui va du simple fidèle au gnostique en passant par le pratique, c'est-à-dire le chrétien qui développe une pratique morale. En ce sens, Maxime se distingue du Pseudo-Denys qui rapportait ses explications au grand-prêtre, c'est-à-dire à l'évêque en tant qu'acteur conscient de la liturgie et véritable théurge chrétien.

6. *Quelle élévation de l'âme pour les ignorants ?*

Mais, quelle efficacité la théurgie chrétienne peut-elle avoir sur le simple fidèle ? Maxime écrit que (ch. 24) :

> κἂν αὐτὸς μὴ αἰσθάνηται, εἴπερ τῶν ἔτι κατὰ Χριστὸν νηπίων ἐστὶ καὶ εἰς τὸ βάθος τῶν γινομένων ὁρᾶν ἀδυνατεῖ[75]

> même s'il ne sent rien lui-même, puisqu'il est encore un enfant en Christ et qu'il ne peut voir la profondeur de ce qui survient

---

à la première étape, alors que pour Jamblique la 'préparation de la pensée à la participation et à la vision du Bien' appartient à la deuxième étape – si, du moins, on peut rapprocher φυσικὴ θεωρία et κατάρτυσις τῆς διανοίας εἰς μετουσίαν καὶ θέαν τοῦ ἀγαθοῦ.

[73] Boudignon 2011, p. 54, l. 868–871.
[74] Boudignon 2011, p. 49, l. 777.
[75] Boudignon 2011, p. 56, l. 894–895.

la liturgie le transforme μεταπλάττουσα ἐπὶ τὸ θειότερον ἀναλόγως ἑαυτῷ ('en le modelant sur un modèle plus divin en proportion de ce qu'il peut recevoir')[76]. C'est exactement la position de Jamblique quand il définit la théurgie, comme Van Liefferinge[77] le rappelait au début de cette étude :

> ἡ τῶν ἔργων τῶν ἀρρήτων καὶ ὑπὲρ πᾶσαν νόησιν θεοπρεπῶς ἐνεργουμένων τελεσιουργία ἥ τε τῶν νοουμένων τοῖς θεοῖς μόνον συμβόλων ἀφθέγκτων δύναμις ἐντίθησι τὴν θεουργικὴν ἕνωσιν[78].

> Mais c'est la célébration des actes indicibles accomplis religieusement *au-delà de toute intellection*, et aussi le pouvoir des symboles inexprimables, *compris seulement des dieux*, qui procurent l'union théurgique.

Bien sûr, Jamblique combat en fait ici l'intellectualisme plotinien défendu par Porphyre comme seule voie d'accès au divin. Mais dans cette défense, seuls les dieux comprennent intellectuellement les actions et les symboles, et c'est d'ailleurs la raison pour laquelle ils se rendent présents lors des actes religieux et dans les symboles qu'ils ont eux-mêmes institués. Jamblique établit ailleurs une tripartition, lui aussi, parmi les fidèles, entre ceux qui sont soumis aux puissance naturelles, ceux qui s'en sont affranchis pour se soumettre à l'intellect et ceux qui sont entre les deux. Il n'en reste pas moins que la théurgie n'est pas d'ordre intellectuel, mais au-delà de l'intellect. A ce titre, même les hommes soumis aux puissances naturelles peuvent avoir une religion matérielle, c'est-à-dire que τὴν θρησκείαν ἐπιτηδεύουσι τῇ φύσει πρόσφορον καὶ τοῖς κινουμένοις ὑπὸ τῆς φύσεως σώμασι ('ils pratiquent le culte adapté à la nature et aux corps qui sont mis en mouvement par la nature')[79]. Mais, et c'est là que le bât blesse, il est plus difficile alors de supposer que le culte ne soit pas une captation magique du divin mais au contraire une élévation des âmes jusqu'à l'union avec le divin. Maxime s'en sort par le principe d'analogie : les simples fidèles sont divinisés *un peu*,

---

[76] Boudignon 2011, p. 55, l. 892-p. 56, l. 894.
[77] Van Liefferinge 1994, p. 209.
[78] Saffrey & Segonds 2013, p. 73, l. 5–8.
[79] Saffrey & Segonds 2013, p. 167, l. 11–13.

ἀναλόγως ἑαυτῷ ('à proportion de ce qu'ils peuvent recevoir')[80]. Jamblique lui se tire d'affaire par la variété des rites, qui les uns purifient, les autres perfectionnent, πάντα δὲ προσήγορα τοῖς ὅλοις κρείττοσιν ἡμῶν ἀπεργάζεται ('mais tous nous mettent en rapport avec les êtres supérieurs à nous')[81] : les fidèles matérialistes reçoivent donc, eux, surtout une purification, – dont ils ont bien besoin !

7. *Conclusion*

Au terme de cette étude, j'espère avoir démontré la dépendance intellectuelle, directe ou indirecte, de la *Mystagogie* vis-à-vis de la *Réponse d'Abamon*, dont la structure érato-apocritique a sans doute contribué à une utilisation plus facile par les lecteurs postérieurs.

On peut établir un parallèle entre l'idée, centrale dans la *Mystagogie*, d'image et de figure, et ce que dit Jamblique. Pour lui, les symboles ont un lien de causalité avec le divin qui les a fondés (cela correspond à la figure maximienne), et les images reproduisent une forme, celle que leur impose leur raison d'être, et donc la nature génératrice.

J'ai tenté de montrer que ce que dit Jamblique des statues de culte suppose une tripartition du monde entre les dieux intelligibles, les dieux corporels ou astres et enfin les statues des dieux. Les astres sont les statues vivantes des dieux intelligibles tandis que les statues des dieux sont pour ainsi dire des astres vivants qui reflètent le divin. Cette division explique que Maxime définisse lui aussi une tripartition entre Dieu, le monde et l'église terrestre, puisque Dieu, le monde et l'église tiennent les êtres unis. Le monde est en quelque sorte une église céleste, dont l'église terrestre est le reflet.

Ce que dit Jamblique des apparitions divines suppose un art de consacrer les statues, une véritable télestique, qui fait que l'efficacité des statues repose en partie sur l'art des prêtres de les faire habiter par un dieu. On peut mettre cela en rapport avec ce que

---

[80] Boudignon 2011, p. 56, l. 893.
[81] Saffrey & Segonds 2013, p. 172, l. 27 – p. 173, l. 1.

dit Maxime de l'entrée du grand-prêtre dans l'église : il s'agit bien de faire venir dans l'église-monde le Verbe démiurge, qui par sa venue au monde, a refondé le monde. L'imitation déclenche donc apparemment une parousie, au moins symbolique, du Christ dans l'église. Car le matériel est attaché au spirituel par des liens de causalité et de ressemblance pour Maxime, ce qui est une autre formulation du principe de sympathie universelle défendu par Jamblique.

Cependant, ce principe risque de transformer la théurgie ou la liturgie en magie. C'est la raison pour laquelle, inversant le regard magique, ce n'est pas le divin qui descend – même s'il y en a toutes les apparences –, mais au contraire le fidèle qui doit élever son âme jusqu'à l'union avec le divin. Maxime reprend à sa façon le triple principe de purification, de contemplation divine et d'union avec le divin qu'établissait Jamblique. Il répond lui aussi à la difficulté que cette théorie suppose quand il s'agit de fidèles ignorants.

Il faut donc conclure que l'architecture de la *Mystagogie* repose sur un armature néoplatonicienne que la *Réponse d'Abamon* de Jamblique, parmi d'autres textes, exprime parfaitement. Et chose unique dans le christianisme, c'est l'activité démiurgique de Dieu sur le monde qui est imitée par l'église : une certaine cosmologie néoplatonicienne sous-tend donc ce commentaire liturgique, d'une façon irréductible à l'influence du Pseudo-Denys. On peut donc bien parler en ce sens, avec bien sûr toutes les réserves nécessaires, 'd'une certaine tradition philosophique *commune* au néoplatonisme et au christianisme'.

Bibliographie

Sources antiques

Corpus Dionysiacum II. Pseudo-Dionysius Areopagita. De Coelesti Hierarchia. De Ecclesiastica Hierarchia. De Mystica Theologia. Epistulae, éd. G. Heil & A. M. Ritter, Berlin : De Gruyter, 1991 (Patristische Texte und Studien 36).

Damascius, *Vitae Isidori reliquiae*, éd. C. Zintzen, Hildesheim: Olms, 1967 (Bibliotheca Latina et Graeca Suppletoria 1).

Eunapius, *Vita Sophistarum*, éd. G. Giangrande, Rome, 1956 (Scriptores Graeci et Latini consilio Academiae Lynceorum editi).

Jamblique, *Réponse à Porphyre (De Mysteriis)*, éd. H. D. Saffrey & A.-Ph. Segonds, Paris : Les Belles Lettres, 2013.

Maximus Confessor, *Mystagogia, una cum latina interpretatione Anastasii Bibliothecarii*, éd. C. Boudignon, Turnhout : Brepols, 2011 (Corpus Christianorum Series Graeca 69).

Maximus Confessor, *Questiones ad Thalassium, I, quaestiones I–LV una cum latina interpretatione Ioannis Scotti Eriugenae iuxta posita*, éd. C. Laga & C. Steel, Turnhout : Brepols, 1980 (Corpus Christianorum Series Graeca 7).

Porphyre, *Lettre à Anébon l'Egyptien*, éd. H. D. Saffrey & A.-Ph. Segonds, Paris : Les Belles Lettres, 2012.

Platon, *Opera*, éd. J. Burnet, Oxford : Oxford University Press, 1900–1907.

Proclus, *In Platonis Timaeum commentaria*, éd. E. Diehl, vol. II, Leipzig: Teubner, 1904.

Proclus, *De sacrificio et magia*, éd. J. Bidez, *Catalogue des manuscrits alchimiques grecs*, Bruxelles: Lamertin, 1928, vol. 6, p. 148–151.

Littérature secondaire

P. Annala (2015), 'From the Exterior to the Interior, and Beyond : Spiritual Topography in St Maximus' *Mystagogia*', dans A. Lévy, P. Annala & O. Hallama (éd.), *The architecture of the Cosmos, St Maximus the Confessor New Perspectives*, Helsinki : Luther-Agricola Society, p. 279–297.

C. Boudignon (2000), 'La *Mystagogie*, ou *traité sur les symboles de la liturgie* de Maxime le Confesseur (580–662)' (thèse de doctorat non publiée, Université d'Aix-Marseille).

C. Boudignon (2002), 'Maxime le Confesseur et ses maîtres', dans G. Filoramo (éd.), *Maestro e Discepolo, Temi e problemi della direzione spirituale tra VI secolo a. C. e VII secolo d. C.*, Brescia : Morcelliana, p. 317–330.

C. Boudignon (2015), 'Pseudo-Macarius as source of the *Mystagogy* of Maximus the Confessor', dans A. Lévy, P. Annala, O. Hallama & T. Lankila (éd.), *The Architecture of the Cosmos, St Maximus the Confessor, New Perspectives*, Helsinki : Luther-Agricola Society, p. 39–50.

P. Chantraine (1992), *Dictionnaire étymologique de la langue grecque. Histoire des mots*. Nouvelle édition avec un supplément, Paris : Klincksieck.

M.-L. Charpin-Ploix (2005), *Maxime le Confesseur. La Mystagogie*, Paris : Migne (Les Pères dans la foi 92).

M. Jankowiak & P. Booth (2015), 'A new date-list of the works of Maximus the Confessor', dans P. Allen & B. Neil (éd.), *The Oxford Handbook of Maximus the Confessor*, Oxford : Oxford University Press, p. 19–83.

W. Lackner (1962), *Studien zur philosophischen Schultradition und zu den Nemesioszitaten bei Maximos dem Bekenner*, Graz (dissertation dactylographiée).

P. Mueller-Jourdan (2005), *Typologie spatio-temporelle de l'*Ecclesia *byzantine. La* Mystagogie *de Maxime le Confesseur dans la culture philosophique de l'Antiquité tardive*, Leyde : Brill (Supplements to *Vigiliae Christianae*).

P. Van Deun & P. Mueller-Jourdan (2015), 'Maxime le Confesseur', dans G. C. Conticello (éd.), *La théologie byzantine et sa tradition*, I/1, Turnhout : Brepols, p. 374–514.

C. Van Liefferinge (1994), 'La théurgie, outil de restructuration dans le *De Mysteriis* de Jamblique', dans *Kernos*, 7, p. 207–217.

C. Van Liefferinge (1999), *Le théurgie, Des Oracles chaldaïques à Proclus*, Liège : Centre international d'étude de la religion grecque antique (*Kernos*, supplément 9).

H.-U. von Balthasar (1947), *Liturgie cosmique, Maxime le Confesseur*, Paris : Aubier (Théologie 11).

T. T. Tollefsen (2008), *The Christocentric Cosmology of St. Maximus the Confessor*, Oxford : Oxford University Press (Oxford Early Christian Studies).

T. T. Tollefsen (2015), 'Christocentric cosmology', dans P. Allen & B. Neil (éd.), *The Oxford Handbook of Maximus the Confessor*, Oxford : Oxford University Press, p. 307–321.

Abstract

The purpose of this paper is to study the possible links between Maximus the Confessor's *Mystagogia* and Iamblichus' *Letter of Abamon*, better known as *De mysteriis Aegyptiorum*. The Maximian notions of image and figure reflect the Iamblichean idea of symbols, the causes and models of which are the gods. In the first part of the *Mystagogia*, the church is described as image and figure of God and of the world. This is to be read in connection with Iamblichus' division of the universe into three elements: cult statues, divine stars, and invisible gods, along with the idea that the statues are reflections of the gods. In the second part of the *Mystagogia*, the entrance of the high priest into the church could recall the telestic art, the ritual which aims to summon the divine in the statues. Its effectiveness is based upon the correspondences between the intelligible and the sensible which the 'universal sympathy' supposes. But neither liturgy nor theurgy are pure magic, because they are deemed to raise the soul of the faithful or of the theurgic priest up to the divine union, through purification and contemplation. One problem remains: how to understand the effect of the theurgy or liturgy on the faithful who are ignorant or materialist?

BRAM ROOSEN

WHAT THEODOSIUS OF GANGRA WANTED TO KNOW FROM MAXIMUS THE CONFESSOR

The genre known as ἐρωταποκρίσεις or question-and-answer literature is not the easiest genre to study. This has nothing to do with the subjects it deals with – virtually anything –, nor with the language – often of a delightful clarity. It is our struggle to reconstruct the 'original text' that causes problems. As a primarily educational genre these ἐρωταποκρίσεις were excerpted, rewritten, adapted, ..., all of them procedures that obscure the path to the original text and drive even the hardiest editor to despair. As such, it should come as no surprise that some of the most influential collections still await a critical edition or that editors are forced to select only a part of the frequently abundant manuscript tradition. For other texts, however, fate had another destiny in mind: they were more or less forgotten, survive only fragmentarily and are, therefore, all too often overlooked by editors in search of more glamorous texts to devote their attention to.

In the following pages we will deal with an example of the latter kind: a collection of ἐρωταποκρίσεις of which, according to the title, Maximus the Confessor and Theodosius of Gangra were the protagonists.[1] Unfortunately, only two ἀποκρίσεις with-

---

[1] In this contribution, which is an adapted version of some pages from my doctoral dissertation (Roosen 2001) the following abbreviations will be used for the writings of or associated with Maximus the Confessor: *Add.* = *Additamenta e variis codicibus* [*CPG* 7707]; *D.B.* = *Disputatio Bizyae* [*CPG* 7735]; *Ep.* = *Epistulae XLV* [*CPG* 7699]; *Op.* = *Opuscula theologica et polemica* [*CPG* 7697]; *Q.D.* = *Quaestiones et dubia* [*CPG* 7689]; *R.M.* = *Relatio motionis inter Maximum et principes* [*CPG* 7736]. The number following *Add.* and *Op.* refers to the subdivision one can find in *CPG*. The most up-to-date version of the *CPG* can now be consulted in Open Access in the *Clavis Clavium* (https://clavis.brepols.net/clacla/).

Questioning the World, Greek Patristic and Byzantine Question-and-Answer Literature, ed. by Bram Demulder and Peter Van Deun,
Turnhout, 2021 (*LECTIO*, 11), pp. 229-267   © BREPOLS✠PUBLISHERS   DOI 10.1484/M.LECTIO-EB.5.121508

out their respective questions have survived, but for each of these answers two different versions are extant. Together with the relatively rich manuscript tradition this makes for a rather complex dossier that is certainly worth our attention. We start with the as yet unpublished fragment.

1. 'What is the Difference between Foreknowledge (πρόγνωσις) and Predestination (προορισμός)?'

The question of the difference between πρόγνωσις and προορισμός is famously addressed by Maximus at the start of the *Disputatio Bizyae*, a debate between Maximus and the bishop of Bithynian Caesarea, Theodosius, that took place in Maximus' place of exile, Bizya, in August 656. When Theodosius asked Maximus how he was doing, Maximus' answer sparked a short discussion on the aforementioned difference – I quote the relevant part of the text as it is found in the critical edition, slightly correcting the punctuation in the last paragraph [2] –:

> Θεοδόσιος· Τί ἐστιν αὐτὸ τοῦτο τὸ προέγνω καὶ προώρισε;
>
> Μάξιμος· Ἡ πρόγνωσις τῶν ἐφ' ἡμῖν ἐννοιῶν καὶ λόγων καὶ ἔργων ἐστίν· ὁ δὲ προορισμὸς τῶν οὐκ ἐφ' ἡμῖν συμβαινόντων ἐστί.
>
> Θεοδόσιος· Ποῖα εἰσὶ τὰ ἐφ' ἡμῖν, καὶ ποῖα τὰ οὐκ ἐφ' ἡμῖν;
>
> [...]
>
> Μάξιμος· Ἐφ' ἡμῖν ἐστι τὰ ἑκούσια πάντα, ἤγουν ἀρεταὶ καὶ κακίαι· οὐκ ἐφ' ἡμῖν δὲ αἱ ἐπιφοραὶ τῶν συμβαινόντων ἡμῖν κολαστικῶν τρόπων, ἢ τῶν ἐναντίων. Οὔτε γὰρ ἐφ' ἡμῖν ἐστιν ἡ κολάζουσα νόσος, οὔτε ἡ εὐφραίνουσα ὑγεία· κἂν αἱ ποιητικαὶ τούτων αἰτίαι. Οἷον· αἰτία νόσου ἀταξία, ὥσπερ καὶ ὑγείας εὐταξία· καὶ βασιλείας οὐρανῶν αἰτία ἡ τῶν ἐντολῶν φυλακή, ὥσπερ καὶ πυρὸς αἰωνίου ἡ τούτων παράβασις.
>
> Θεοδόσιος· Τί οὖν; Διατοῦτο θλίβῃ ἐν τῇ ἐξορίᾳ ταύτῃ, ἐπειδὴ ἄξια τινὰ ἐποίησας ταύτης τῆς θλίψεως;
>
> Μάξιμος· Παρακαλῶ ἵνα ὁ Θεὸς ταύτῃ τῇ θλίψει περιορίσῃ τὰς ἐκτίσεις ὧν ἥμαρτον αὐτῷ ἐν τῇ παραβάσει τῶν αὐτοῦ δικαιωτικῶν ἐντολῶν.

---

[2] See *D.B.* 31–73 (ed. Allen & Neil 1999, p. 75–81). On this punctuation, see Roosen 2001a, p. 120–121.

Θεοδόσιος· Οὐκ ἔστι καὶ δοκιμῆς ἕνεκεν ἐπαγομένη πολλοῖς θλίψις;

Μάξιμος· Ἡ δοκιμὴ τῶν ἁγίων ἐστίν, ἵνα φανερωθῶσι διὰ τῆς θλίψεως τῷ βίῳ τῶν ἀνθρώπων, αἱ περὶ τὸ φύσει καλὸν διαθέσεις αὐτῶν, ἑαυταῖς συνεκφαίνουσαι τὰς ἠγνοημένας πᾶσιν αὐτῶν ἀρετάς, ὡς ἐπὶ τοῦ Ἰὼβ καὶ Ἰωσήφ. Ὁ μὲν γὰρ ἐπὶ φανερώσει τῆς ἐγκεκρυμμένης ἀνδρείας ἐπειράζετο· ὁ δὲ ἐπ᾽ ἐκφάνσει τῆς ἁγιαστικῆς σωφροσύνης ἐδοκιμάζετο· καὶ πᾶς τῶν ἁγίων ἀκουσίως ἐν τῷ αἰῶνι τούτῳ θλιβεὶς ἐπί τισι τοιαύταις οἰκονομίαις ἐθλίβετο, ἵνα διὰ τῆς ἀσθενείας τῆς συγχωρουμένης αὐτοῖς ἐπαχθῆναι, τὸν ὑπερήφανον καὶ ἀποστάτην πατήσωσι δράκοντα, τουτέστι τὸν διάβολον. Ἡ γὰρ ὑπομονή, δοκιμῆς ἔργον ἐστὶν ἐφ᾽ ἑκάστου τῶν ἁγίων.

Θεοδόσιος· Μὰ τὴν ἀλήθειαν τοῦ Θεοῦ, καλῶς εἶπας· καὶ ὁμολογῶ τὴν ὠφέλειαν, καὶ ἐζήτουν ἐν τοῖς τοιούτοις ἀεὶ συνδιαλέγεσθαι ὑμῖν. Ἀλλ᾽ ἐπειδὴ ἐπ᾽ ἄλλῳ κεφαλαίῳ κἀγὼ καὶ οἱ δεσπόται μου οἱ μελλοπατρίκιοι πρὸς σὲ γεγόναμεν, καὶ τοσαῦτα διαστήματα ἤλθομεν, παρακαλοῦμέν σε τὰ παρ᾽ ἡμῶν προτεινόμενα δέξασθαι καὶ χαροποιῆσαι πᾶσαν τὴν οἰκουμένην.

This discussion has no real importance for the rest of the debate and with Ἀλλ᾽ ἐπειδὴ ἐπ᾽ ἄλλῳ κεφαλαίῳ ... πρὸς σὲ γεγόναμεν Theodosius even breaks it off in order to turn to the real purpose of his visit to Maximus.

Interestingly, the passage seems to offer us a glimpse of how the *D.B.* was made. For, although the text presents itself as a faithful account of an actual discussion, there is little chance that it is. Of course the gist may, and probably does, go back to what was said, but the text as we have it is clearly the result of a thorough redaction process.[3] Besides polishing and 'dramatizing' the text, this process also seems to have involved the search for and the use of Maximian texts. For the *D.B.* there is evidence for at least two such passages. One is the close and hardly coincidental similarity between l. 479–489 of the *D.B.* and some lines of *Op.* 24 (*PG* 91, col. 269 A7 – B9).[4] The other is the aforementioned discussion on the meaning of πρόγνωσις and προορισμός. The source of these lines, discovered quite recently by Dr Basile Markesinis,[5] is catalogued as *CPG* 7707.38.

---

[3] See recently Ohme 2016, p. 306–346.
[4] See Roosen 2001a, p. 114–115.
[5] Dr Markesinis kindly gave us the permission to study and edit the text.

Add. 38 is preserved in two different versions in only three manuscripts. Since we have already dealt with these manuscripts and with the way they are related in an earlier article,[6] we can limit ourselves to the following facts.

The longest version of *Add.* 38 is found on one of the last folios of the little accessible MS *Ohrid, Naroden Muzej, fonds principal 86 (Mošin 84)*, henceforth *Aa*.[7] The manuscript, dating from the late thirteenth – early fourteenth century, is famous for the extraordinarily rich *Florilegium Achridense* that occupies the second part of the manuscript (p. 133–212). *Add.* 38 (p. 203, l. 8–23) is the 33rd of the 35 fragments in the 24th chapter, i.e. the one that is entitled Περὶ θείας προγνώσεως καὶ προορισμοῦ, προνοίας τὲ καὶ κρίσεως· οὐδὲν γὰρ ἀόριστον παρὰ θεῷ, ἀλλ'ἡ ἁμαρτία καὶ μόνον.[8] It is followed by the lines from the *D.B.* quoted above, viz. l. 24–73 (p. 203, l. 24–204, l. 24).[9]

Neither chronologically nor textually *Aa* can be considered the ancestor of the other two manuscripts, *Me* and *Od*. Their *sigla* refer to:

- MS *München, Bayerische Staatsbibliothek, gr. 270*[10], to which Dr Markesinis quite convincingly assigns an Italian origin between the middle of the eleventh century and the achievement of its direct copy *Od*. Between 1551 and 1557 the manuscript was acquired by Hieronymus Wolf for Johann Jakob Fugger's library, of which he was the librarian. In 1571

---

[6] See Roosen 2001a, p. 117–121.

[7] We have dealt with this quite badly preserved and, therefore, at times difficult to read manuscript on earlier occasions: see my doctoral dissertation Roosen 2001, p. 131–132 (and p. 759–762, p. 765–766, p. 792–794 and p. 800–801 for the edition of several fragments from the *Florilegium Achridense*); Roosen 2001a, p. 113–131 (see especially p. 117 n. 10 for some codicological details and a list of the older literature); Roosen 2015, p. 236.

[8] For a detailed description of the 24th chapter, see Appendix I of Roosen 2001a, p. 122–130.

[9] For a discussion of this fragment in relation to the edition of the *D.B.* by Allen and Neil, see Roosen 2001a, p. 118–121.

[10] Parchment; 203 × 130 mm.; 1 col.; 26–28 l.; presently III.168 fol., but the manuscript lost an undeterminable number of folios at the end. For summary descriptions of this manuscript, see Hardt 1806–1812, III, p. 124–128 and Fedwick 1993–2000, III, p. 114. B. Markesinis kindly made his thorough, yet unfortunately still unpublished description available to us.

Fugger's books were incorporated in the *Hofbibliothek* of Albrecht V.[11]

- and its direct copy, MS *Oxford, Bodleian Library, Cromwell 7*,[12] which was copied by a certain Gerasimus,[13] probably on Sicily[14] before the year 1181/1182.[15] At least from 1371, but probably already from 1354, onwards until 1473 the manuscript was found in the then Venice ruled city of Methoni on the Peloponnesus.[16] In the late sixteenth or early seventeenth century *Od* was acquired by Giacomo Barocci. Via William Herbert and Oliver Cromwell it finally ended up in the Bodleian library in 1654.[17]

In both these manuscripts *Add.* 38 ends with the word ἔπαινον (l. 8), after which comes an appendix in the form of a scholium not found in *Aa*. There is little doubt that this is a secondary

---

[11] Cf. Hartig 1917, p. 242 and n. 936 in the table on p. 368.

[12] Parchment; 190 × 135 mm.; 1 col.; 24–26 l.; presently II.654 p., but the manuscript lost two folios before the present p. 1, the first folio of the second quire and the complete 21st quire, i.e. between the present p. 314 and 315. Finally, p. 651–654, i.e. the last two folios of the manuscript, do not form part of the quires anymore. More details, also on the disturbance of the order of the first 12 pages, will be found in Markesinis' description. But as long as that description has not been published, one can benefit from Coxe 1853, col. 425–427; Allen & Neil 1999, p. 55–56; Bibikov 1996, p. 151–153.

[13] See the note in the upper margin of p. 424 (μνήσθητι ἀδελφὲ τοῦ γράψαντος γερασίμου ἁμαρτωλοῦ). On Gerasimus, see in the first place Gamillscheg & Harlfinger & Hunger 1981–1989, I n. 50 and II n. 65 (with bibliography). The assertion found there that Catania is situated in Asia Minor is a mistake.

[14] Gerasimus is thought to have been the brother of Martinianus, the higoumenos of a monastery near or in the Sicilian city of Catania, and he may have worked as a scribe for him. See the subscription in MS *Berlin, Staatsbibliothek zu Berlin (Preussischer Kulturbesitz), Phillipps 1491 (87)* and the word ἀδελφὲ in the note on p. 424 of our manuscript. Cf. Vogel & Gardthausen 1909, p. 67.

[15] According to the subscriptions of MSS *Jerusalem, Patriarchikê bibliothêkê, Panaghiou Taphou 57 (a.* 1181/1182) and *Genova, Biblioteca Franzoniana, fonds principal Urbani 30 (s.* XII), Gerasimus became higoumenos and archimandrite of the Νέα Μονή on the isle of Chios before 1181/1182. Since in our manuscript he does not yet call himself higoumenos and archimandrite, it may be concluded that our manuscript predates his appointment. For these subscriptions, see Euangelatou-Notara 1982, p. 214 (number 456) and p. 221 (number 492) respectively, but for the latter manuscript, see rather Cataldi Palau 1996, p. 77–81 (for the text of the note, see p. 79).

[16] We refer to the description by Markesinis for the evidence.

[17] Cf. Madan & Craster 1922, p. 11–12.

evolution and that the author of the scholium had a longer text in front of him than the one presently found in *Me* and *Od*.[18] *Add.* 38 is again followed by almost the same passage from the *D.B.* as in *Aa*, as can be seen in the following table:

	Me	*Od*
Q.D. I, 68; II, 18; 40 and 189	fol. 161ᵛ–163ᵛ	p. 608–617
Add. 38 (short version + scholium)	fol. 165ᵛ	p. 623–624
D.B., l. 24–70 of *D.B.*	fol. 165ᵛ–166ᵛ	p. 624–626
Q.D. 19 and 16	fol. 166ᵛ–167	p. 627–629
Capita V spiritualia [*CPG* 7707.39[19]]	fol. 167ʳ⁻ᵛ	p. 629–631
Op. 5	fol. 167ᵛ–168ᵛ	p. 631–635

The data adduced above only confirm the stemma we drew in 2001:[20]

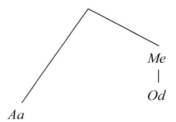

2. 'How do the Philosophers and the Fathers Define φύσις, οὐσία, ἄτομον and ὑπόστασις?'

Also of the second fragment two versions exist.

The shorter version, *Op.* 26a, presents for the terms φύσις, οὐσία, ἄτομον and ὑπόστασις each time two definitions: one in

---

[18] Indeed, the words εἴ τι τούτοις συνεπινοεῖται of the scholium are too resemblant of the words οὔ τι τῶν τούτοις συνεπινοουμένων in the text not to consider the latter as the source of the former.

[19] These chapters are actually chapters 36–38, 49 and 56 from John of Karpathos' *Capita theologica et gnostica* [*CPG* 7856]. Therefore, number 7707.39 should be deleted from the *Clavis Patrum Graecorum*.

[20] See Roosen 2001a, p. 120.

accordance with the philosophers (κατὰ φιλοσόφους) and one in accordance with the fathers (κατὰ τοὺς πατέρας). Five manuscripts come into play:

Ac   *Athêna, Ethnikê Bibliothêkê tês Hellados (EBE), Fonds principal 225 (s. XIV), fol. 185*

Mb   *Milano, Biblioteca Ambrosiana, fonds principal Q 74 sup. (Martini-Bassi 681) (s. X), fol. 150ʳ⁻ᵛ*

Ug   *Vaticano, Biblioteca Apostolica Vaticana, Vat. gr. 504 (a. 1105), fol. 147*

Uh   *Vaticano, Biblioteca Apostolica Vaticana, Vat. gr. 507 (a. 1344), fol. 131ʳ⁻ᵛ*

Ui   *Vaticano, Biblioteca Apostolica Vaticana, Vat. gr. 508 (s. XII–XIII), fol. 206ᵛ–207*

We have discussed all of these manuscripts and the relevant parts of their contents in two earlier articles and there is no need to do this exercise again.[21] Suffice it to repeat the stemma of *Ac Ug Uh Ui* and devote some attention to the position of *Mb*.

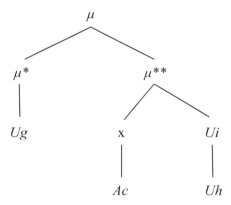

While *Mb* is clearly the oldest manuscript of this group, its text is distinctive enough to exclude the possibility of an identification with μ. But whether *Mb* goes back to μ or shares an ancestor with μ is impossible to establish.

---

[21] For *Ac, Ug, Uh* and *Ui* I refer to Roosen 2014, p. 254–260 and to Roosen 2015, p. 209–210. A description of *Mb* can be found in Roosen 2015, p. 210–212.

As for most of Maximus' texts, the *editio princeps* of *Op.* 26a is due to Fr. Combefis and dates from 1675.[22] In his *Elenchus operum sancti Maximi*,[23] written 15 years earlier, Combefis had written 'Testimonia SS. Patrum de duabus Voluntatibus & Operationibus in una persona Christi, ex Clemente Alexandrino, Irenaeo, Justino, & c. Cod. Vatic. DVIII.' The list of authors and the reference to wills and energies indicate that Combefis certainly refers to *Op.* 26b and *Op.* 27. However, he probably also refers to *Op.* 26a, since the way in which *Op.* 26b follows *Op.* 26a in his edition suggests that according to Combefis *Op.* 26a and *Op.* 26b were one and the same text. So, despite the lack of textual evidence to back this up, it is quite safe to assume that Combefis and therefore also the reprint of this edition as volumes 90 and 91 of the *Patrologia Graeca* are based on our manuscript *Ui.* As usual, Combefis' edition is not free of faults: on l. 14 he added δὲ after Ὑπόστασις and on l. 15–17 he completely remodelled the definition by adding ὁ before καθ'ἕκαστον, writing ἄνθρωπος for ἄνθρωπον and changing ἀφοριζόμενον into ἀφοριζόμενος.

The longer version, *Add.* 20, consists of the full text of *Op.* 26a plus five additional definitions of ὑπόστασις, all but one taken from Maximus' *Ep.* 13 and *Ep.* 15. The manuscript tradition of *Add.* 20 is richer than that of *Op.* 26a, but most manuscripts miss the start of the text due to a fault in the textual transmission.[24] Moreover, in two manuscripts, i.e. MS *Vaticano, Biblioteca Apostolica Vaticana, Ottob. gr. 43 (Uott)* and its copy, MS *Vaticano, Biblioteca Apostolica Vaticana, Vat. gr. 197 (Uz)*, the text is missing due to the loss of some folios.[25]

---

[22] Cf. Combefis 1675, p. 151.

[23] For an edition of the *Elenchus*, see de Montfaucon 1715, p. 309.

[24] We have dealt with most of these manuscripts already in Roosen & Van Deun 2006, p. 66–69.

[25] The correct order of folios in *Uott* is fol. 66–73ᵛ, 94–107ᵛ after which some folios were lost, fol. 86–93ᵛ, 74ʳ⁻ᵛ, fol. 75, of which the upper half was cut off, fol. 75bis–85ᵛ, after which again some folios were lost. (The manuscript can be consulted at https://digi.vatlib.it/view/MSS_Ott.gr.43.) In *Uz*, the second part of which was copied from *Uott* by Vivianus Brunorus, the order of the folios was partly corrected and the texts relevant to this contribution are found on fol. 122–138ᵛ and fol. 146–153. Since *Op.* 26a – *Add.* 22 is not found in these manuscripts anymore, we will not go into further detail as concerns their characteristics and history.

We begin with the manuscripts that miss the start of *Add.* 20:

Pd   or MS *Paris, Bibliothèque nationale de France (BnF), gr. 11*[26] was made of three different parts: the first (p. 1–265a) was copied in the year 1186 by Leo Gabalas, Bishop of Nymphaion (modern Nif in Turkey);[27] the second part, the one relevant to us (p. 265b–328), is possibly a little younger and was copied by Manuel, the notary of a certain Cometas of Sozopolis; we have no further information on the third part (p. 329–456). In 1730 *Pd* was sent from Constantinople to France.

Ff   or MS *Firenze, Biblioteca Medicea Laurenziana, Plut. 09. 08*[28] was written by an eleventh-century, possibly Cypriot hand. In 1510, at the latest, it became part of the Medicean library.

Pv   or MS *Patmos, Monê tou Hagiou Iôannou tou Theologou, fonds principal 205*[29] can be dated to the twelfth century, but, unfortunately, does not provide us with information about its place of origin, scribe, further history, …

Uy   or MS *Vaticano, Biblioteca Apostolica Vaticana, Vat. gr. 2224*,[30] finally, was written in the early fourteenth century and donated to the Athonite monastery of the Laura shortly after. Via the collections of Johannes de Salviatis in the sixteenth century and the Colonna family in the eighteenth century the manuscript entered the *Vaticana* in 1821.

---

[26] Membranaceus; 255 × 185 mm; 1 col.; 460 p. (+ the blank pages 265a and 265b), preceded by three unnumbered folios and two folios numbered A and B. Cf. Omont 1886–1888, I, p. 2–3. (The manuscript can be consulted at https://gallica.bnf.fr/ark:/12148/btv1b55006074f.).

[27] Cf. Gamillscheg & Harlfinger & Hunger 1981–1989, II n. 329.

[28] Membranaceus; 320 × 205 mm.; 1 col.; 35 l.; now I.354 fol., but after fol. 350 eight folios are missing, which are now found as fol. 9–16 in codex *Lipsiensis, Bibliothecae Universitatis graecus 46*. Cf. Bandini 1764–1770, I, p. 395–403; Beneševič 1972², p. 137–140; Kotter 1959, p. 25 (number 195A); Burgmann & Troianos 1979, p. 35; Uthemann 1981, p. xli–xlii and ccxxvi–ccxxviii; Burgmann et al. 1995, p. 80–82.

[29] Membranaceus, except fol. 1–30 and fol. 415; 2 col.; 33 l.; at present 418 fol. Cf. Sakkelion 1890, p. 114; Konidaris 1982, p. 27–31; Van der Wal & Stolte 1994, p. xlix; Burgmann et al. 1995, p. 241–242.

[30] Chartaceus; 222 × 154 mm.; 1 col.; 27–32 l.; I.294 fol. See in the first place Lilla 1985, p. 272–291.

Ay or MS *Hagion Oros, Monê Ibêrôn, fonds principal 190 (Lam-bros 4310)* [31] is undeniably of South-Italian origin: it was copied in the year 1297/1298 by Kalos of Saint Peter of Galatina in the theme of Otranto.[32] Before 1841 the manuscript was conveyed to Mount Athos.

These manuscripts present some remarkable similarities as far as (part of) their contents is concerned:

I.   A series of texts built around the second chapter of Anasta-sius Sinaita's *Viae dux*: [33]

1. Anastasius Sinaita, *Viae dux* II, 1, 1–7, 86.[34]

   (*Pd*, p. 266–284; *Ff*, fol. 289ᵛ–298; *Uott*, fol. 66–73ᵛ + 94–99; *Uz*, fol. 122–132; *Pv*, fol. 185ʳa–196ʳa; *Uy*, fol. 262–274; *Ay*, fol. 118[162]–121[165])

2. A definition of κατάχρησις not found in the *Viae Dux*.[35]

   (*Pd*, p. 284; *Ff*, fol. 298; not in *Uott*; not in *Uz*; not in *Pv*; not in *Uy*; *Ay*, fol. 121 [165])

3. A neochalcedonian treatise edited by S. Helmer on the basis of *Pd*.[36]

   (*Pd*, p. 284–286; *Ff*, fol. 298–299ᵛ; *Uott*, fol. 99–100ᵛ; *Uz*, fol. 132–133ᵛ; *Pv*, fol. 196ʳb–197ᵛb; *Uy*, fol. 274–276; *Ay*, fol. 121[165]ʳ⁻ᵛ)

---

[31] Early chartaceus without watermarks; 215 × 135 mm.; 1 col., except in the case of poems; originally 191 fol., now only 143. Cf. Lampros 1895–1900, II, p. 53–54; Hoffmann 1985–1986, p. 251–261; Van Deun 1991, p. CLII; Uthemann 1993, p. 252. It is, however, impossible to describe this manuscript without referring to MS *Paris, Bibliothèque nationale de France (BnF), suppl. gr. 681*, which contains some folios of *Ay*, that in 1841 were stolen by Minoïdes Mynas. On this Parisian manuscript, see Omont 1886–1888, III, p. 297; Hoffmann 1987, p. 115–127; Ph. Hoffmann in Astruc et al. 1989, p. 79–81 and plates 83–86. On Minoïdes Mynas, see Gourevitch & Roselli 2006, p. 481–503.

[32] Cf. Gamillscheg & Harlfinger & Hunger 1981–1989, II n. 298.

[33] The fact that the first florilegium of *Pf* was also made on the basis of chapter II of Anastasius Sinaita's *Viae dux* seems to be a coincidence, as there are considerable differences between both florilegia.

[34] For more details on the text in our manuscript, see Uthemann 1981, p. CCXXVI.

[35] For the text of this definition, see Uthemann 1981, p. CCXXVI n. 21.

[36] Cf. Helmer 1962, p. 275–278.

4. Anastasius Sinaita, *Viae dux* II, 8, 101–137.

(*Pd*, p. 286–287; *Ff*, fol. 299ᵛ–300; *Uott*, fol. 100ᵛ–101ᵛ; *Uz*, fol. 133ᵛ–134; *Pv*, fol. 197ᵛb–198ʳb; *Uy*, fol. 276ʳ⁻ᵛ; *Ay*, fol. 121[165]ᵛ ³⁷)

5. Anastasius Sinaita, *Viae dux* II, 8, 1–7, 18–26, 46, 87–100.

(*Pd*, p. 287–288; *Ff*, fol. 300; *Uott*, fol. 101ᵛ–102; *Uz*, fol. 134ʳ⁻ᵛ; *Pv*, fol. 198ʳb–198ᵛb; *Uy*, fol. 285ʳ⁻ᵛ; *Ay*, fol. 121[165]ᵛ–122[166]ᵛ ³⁸)

6. ἕτεροι ὅροι. Τί ὁμώνυμον, συνώνυμον, παρώνυμον, ἑτερώνυμον, πολυώνυμον.

= a collection of definitions of the words mentioned in the title, followed by definitions of the words πρότερον, ἅμα, ἄτομον, κατάφασις, ἀπόφασις and ἀντίφασις.³⁹

(*Pd*, p. 288–290; *Ff*, fol. 300–301; *Uott*, fol. 102–103; *Uz*, fol. 134ᵛ–135; *Pv*, fol. 198ᵛb–200ʳa; *Uy*, fol. 276ᵛ–277ᵛ; *Ay*, fol. 122[166]ᵛ–123[167])

II. A collection of texts with close parallels in the 3ʳᵈ florilegium of *Pf* (the titles given below are those of *Uott*, qualitatively the best manuscript; for the texts not found there anymore, we copied *Pd*):

1. Ὅροι σύντομοι ἁγίων πατέρων, περὶ οὐσίας καὶ φύσεως, ὑποστάσεως τὲ καὶ προσώπου. Τοῦ ὁσίου Μαξίμου μοναχοῦ καὶ ὁμολογητοῦ, Πρὸς Κοσμᾶν διάκονον Ἀλεξανδρείας ἐπιστολὴ περὶ κοινοῦ καὶ ἰδίου, ἤγουν οὐσίας καὶ ὑποστάσεως, φύσεώς τε καὶ προσώπου.

= Maximus Confessor, the first part of *Ep.* 15, ending with the words καθέστηκε λόγος (= *PG* 91, col. 553 C5).

---

³⁷ While in the other manuscripts of this branch the text covers lines II, 8, 101–137 (p. 72–73 in the edition by Uthemann 1981), in *Ay* the text ends on l. 119, the scholium on l. 120–137 being transposed after the following text (I. 5).

³⁸ Here we have the most significant difference with the rest of the manuscripts in this group: *Ay* does not have the short version of the *Etymologicum* like the other manuscripts, but the full text, except for II, 8, 69–72.

³⁹ See the edition by Roosen – Van Deun 2006, p. 53–76.

(*Pd*, p. 290–298; *Ff*, fol. 301–304; *Uott*, fol. 103–107ᵛ;[40] *Uz*, fol. 135ᵛ–138ᵛ;[41] *Pv*, fol. 200ʳa–204ᵛa; *Uy*, fol. 277ᵛ–281ᵛ; *Ay*, fol. 123[167]–125[169])

2. Τοῦ μακαρίου Κλήμεντος πρεσβυτέρου Ἀλεξανδρείας ἐκ τοῦ Περὶ προνοίας[42] λόγου.

   = Ps.-Clemens Alexandrinus, fr. 37.[43]

   (*Pd*, p. 298; *Ff*, fol. 304; *Uott*, †; *Uz*, †; *Pv*, fol. 204ᵛa; *Uy*, fol. 282; *Ay*, fol. 126[170]ᵛ)

3. Τοῦ ὁσίου Ἀναστασίου πατριάρχου Ἀντιοχείας.

   = A collection of definitions which is closely paralleled by the one in *Pf*, fol. 130ᵛ, l. 7–27.[44] In *Ff* the title was omitted, making the collection seem part of the forego-ing text.[45]

   (*Pd*, p. 298–300; *Ff*, fol. 304–305; *Uott*, †; *Uz*, †; *Pv*, fol. 204ᵛa–205ᵛa; *Uy*, fol. 282ʳ⁻ᵛ; *Ay*, fol. 126[170ᵛ]–127[171])

4. Τοῦ ἁγίου Σωφρονίου πατριάρχου Ἱεροσολύμων, ἐκ τῶν πρὸς Ὀνώριον πάπα Ῥώμης.

   In the same way as in *Ug*, also in *Pd Ff Pv Uy* and *Ay* the definition Φύσις οὐσία καὶ μορφὴ ταυτόν ἐστιν· ἄτομον ὑπόστασις καὶ πρόσωπον ταυτόν ἐστιν is attributed to Sophronius. We refer to the description of *Pf* below (no. 6) for more details.

   (*Pd*, p. 300; *Ff*, fol. 305; *Uott*, †; *Uz*, †; *Pv*, fol. 205ᵛa; *Uy*, fol. 282ᵛ–283; *Ay*, fol. 127[171])

---

[40] Due to the loss of some folios, the text breaks off with the words πρὸς τοὺς, i.e. *PG* 91, col. 553 B3, where, however, πρὸς ἄλλους is written.

[41] Like in *Uott* the text of Maximus' *Ep.* 15 in *Uz* ends with the words πρὸς τοὺς. In the margin Vivianus Brunorus himself wrote πολὺ λείπει.

[42] *Pd* reads ἀνοίας.

[43] Stählin 1909, p. 219. Stählin's edition was updated in 1970 (cf. Stählin & Früchtel & Treu 1970²).

[44] See our description of *Pf* below.

[45] For this collection in *Ff*, see Uthemann 1980, p. 333–334. The situation in *Ff* caused Uthemann to write that the collection 'sich als Exzerpt aus des Klemens' von Alexandrien Schrift *De Providentia* ausgibt' (p. 333).

5. Without a title or any other sign of transition, the definition attributed to Sophronius is followed by *Add.* 20, but only from Ἄτομον (l. 9) onwards.

(*Pd*, p. 300–301; *Ff*, fol. 305; *Uott*, f. †; *Uz*, f. †; *Pv*, fol. 205ᵛa–206ʳa; *Uy*, fol. 283; *Ay*, fol. 127[171]ʳ⁻ᵛ)

6. Περὶ οὐσίας καὶ φύσεως καὶ ὑποστάσεως.
= *Op.* 23c
(*Pd*, p. 301; *Ff*, fol. 305ʳ⁻ᵛ; *Uott*, fol. 86 [l. 9–16 only]; *Uz*, fol. 146 [l. 9–16 only];[46] not in *Pv*; not in *Uy*; *Ay*, fol. 127 [171]ᵛ)

7. Τοῦ μακαρίου Μαξίμου, Περὶ τῶν β' φύσεων, τοῦ Κυρίου καὶ Θεοῦ καὶ Σωτῆρος ἡμῶν Ἰησοῦ Χριστοῦ, Κεφάλαια ι'.
= *Op.* 13[47]
(*Pd*, p. 302–304; *Ff*, fol. 305ᵛ–306ᵛ; *Uott*, fol. 86–87ᵛ; *Uz*, fol. 146–147; *Pv*, –; *Uy*, fol. 283–285; *Ay*, fol. 125[169]ʳ⁻ᵛ)

8. Ὅροι σαφηνίζοντες τί οὐσία καὶ φύσις, πρόσωπόν τε καὶ ὑπόστασις, ὡσαύτως, τί ἐνούσιον καὶ ὁμοούσιον, ἐνυπόστατόν τε καὶ ὁμοϋπόστατον καὶ τὰ ἰδίως τούτοις θεωρούμενα. Τοῦ μακαρίου Μαξίμου.

= *Add.* 21
(*Pd*, p. 304–308; *Ff*, fol. 306ᵛ–308; *Uott*, fol. 87ᵛ–90; *Uz*, fol. 147–149; *Pv*, fol. 206ʳa–208ʳa; *Uy*, –; *Ay*, fol. 125[169]ᵛ–126[170])

9. Τοῦ μακαρίου Μαξίμου, Περὶ τῶν δύο θελημάτων Χριστοῦ τοῦ Θεοῦ ἡμῶν.

= *Op.* 24
(*Pd*, p. 308–311; *Ff*, fol. 308–309; *Uott*, fol. 90–91ᵛ; *Uz*, fol. 149–150; not *Pv*; not in *Uy*; not in *Ay*)

[46] These line numbers refer to the edition of *Op.* 23c in my doctoral dissertation, Roosen 2001, p. 719. They correspond to *PG* 91, col. 265 D6–268 A4.
[47] Ed. Levrie 2017.

10. Τοῦ αὐτοῦ Περὶ οὐσίας καὶ φύσεως, ὑποστάσεως τὲ καὶ προσώπων.

= *Op.* 23a

(*Pd*, p. 311–312; *Ff*, fol. 309–310; *Uott*, fol. 91ᵛ–92ᵛ; *Uz*, fol. 150–151; not in *Pv*; not in *Uy*; *Ay*, fol. 126[170]ʳ⁻ᵛ)

11. Ἰωάννου μοναχοῦ, Περὶ τῆς καθ᾽ὑπόστασιν ἑνώσεως.

= Iohannes Damascenus, *Dialectica* brev. 50/fus. 67; brev. 28/fus. 45; brev. 29/fus. 46; brev. 32/fus. 49.[48]

(*Pd*, p. 312–316; *Ff*, fol. 310–311ᵛ; *Uott*, fol. 92ᵛ–93ᵛ + 74ʳ⁻ᵛ; *Uz*, fol. 151–153; not in *Pv*; not in *Uy*; *Ay*, fol. 127[171]ᵛ–129[173]])

These manuscripts have to be related: the list of works described above is just too characteristic to believe otherwise and they, indeed, have a number of readings in common, the most remarkable of which certainly is the omission of the title and the first 8 lines, but there are also the readings ἀφοριζόμενος for ἀφοριζόμενον (coincidentally also *Mb*) (l. 17) and τῶν ὄντων for τῶν ἐν τῷ (l. 31). Moreover, for historical, codicological and textual reasons there is no doubt that *Uz* is a direct copy of *Uott* and there are some remarkable textual similarities between *Pv* and *Uy*.[49] But that is about it: neither our collations of the present text nor our collations of texts I, 6 and II, 2, 6, 9 and 10 above allowed us to further reduce the number of manuscripts in the critical apparatus. With all due caution because of the shortness of the text(s) involved, we, therefore, draw the following stemma:

---

[48] This combination of four *capita* from Iohannes Damascenus' *Dialectica* was given a number of its own in *CPG*, viz. *CPG* 6915. The mistake was caused by Helmer 1962, who failed to identify the text and, therefore, edited it on p. 266–270.

[49] In any case, all faults and variants of *Pv* are also found in *Uy* (except for some orthographica) and the readings proper to *Uy* are by no means convincing: ἄτομον μὲν for Ἄτομόν ἐστι and om. of μὲν (l. 9); ἄλλῳ for ἄλλου (l. 10); and addition of τοῖς before ἰδίοις (l. 12). As such, we have decided to leave *Uy* out of the critical apparatus. At this moment, the only counterargument against the dependency of *Uy* on *Pv* are some differences in the build-up of the set of texts described above, but to answer that problem more research is needed.

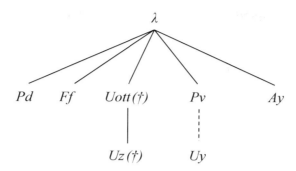

Two manuscripts remain, both having also a title and the opening lines of *Add.* 20. The first one is the complex thirteenth-century miscellany *Pf* or MS *Paris, Bibliothèque nationale de France (BnF), gr. 854,*[50] notorious for the alternative versions of Maximian *opuscula* it contains on fol. 121–136ᵛ. It is noteworthy that these two quaternions are contemporary to the rest of the manuscript, but no original part of it.[51] The second one is *Ob* or MS *Oxford, Bodleian Library, Auct. T.1.1 [Misc. 179]*, which was the personal notebook of the famous Jesuit editor of patristic texts, Fronto Ducaeus, between 1580 and 1624.[52] In it he copied a number of texts from a variety of manuscripts, one of which was *Pf.*[53]

---

[50] Because of the miscellaneous nature of the manuscript, it has been dealt with on a considerable number of occasions. See, of course, the catalogue description by Omont 1886–1888 I, p. 159–160 and III, p. 394, but e.g. also Westerink 1948, p. 7; Munitiz 1974, p. 160; Sotiroudis 1989, p. 23–25. For an interesting find on the history of the manuscript, see Markesinis 2000, p. 302–306 (with pl. 54). The manuscript can be consulted at https://gallica.bnf.fr/ark:/12148/btv1b10722105h.

[51] The codicological characteristics of these two quaternions are the following: bombycinus; 260 × 150 mm.; 1 col.; 35 l.; quire numbers α on fol. 128ᵛ and β on fol. 129 and 136ᵛ in the middle of the lower margin. Other scholars having dealt specifically with these folios are Uthemann 1981, p. LIX–LX, CCXXXIV and n. 1; Uthemann 1980, p. 334–335; and Declerck 2002, p. CCCVI–CCCXIII.

[52] Chartaceus; 355 × 230 mm.; 1 col.; 46–60 l.; I+524 p. (+ p. 53a, 54a, 65a, 66a, 73a, 74a, 145a, 146a, 415a, 416a, 459a, 460a, but p. 262–282 and p. 467–488 are lost). For more details on this manuscript, see Coxe 1853, col. 724–733; Aubineau 1968, p. 161; Van De Vorst & Delehaye 1913, p. 366–367; Van Dieten 1970, p. 26; Uthemann 1981, p. XXXIII and Van Deun 1991, p. XXXII–XXXIII.

[53] This relationship becomes clear already from a comparison of the relevant parts of the contents of both manuscripts. Moreover, *Ob* has all the readings proper to *Pf* and some extra of its own. As far as *Add.* 20 is concerned, *Ob* has

The text on fol. 121–136ᵛ of *Pf* consists of five thematic florilegia, each headed by a general title:

I. (fol. 121–125ᵛ) Σὺν θεῷ ὅροι διάφοροι, κατὰ τὴν παράδοσιν καὶ πίστιν τῆς ἁγίας καθολικῆς καὶ ἀποστολικῆς ἐκκλησίας, συλλεγέντες ἀπό τε τοῦ μεγάλου Κλήμεντος τοῦ Στρωματέως, καὶ ἑτέρων ὁσίων καὶ μακαρίων πατέρων, ...⁵⁴

II. (fol. 125ᵛ–130) Σὺν θεῷ ὅροι δογματικοὶ τῶν ἁγίων καὶ διαφόρων μυσταγωγῶν καὶ πανσόφων πατέρων καὶ διδασκάλων τῆς ἁγίας καθολικῆς καὶ ἀποστολικῆς ἐκκλησίας.⁵⁵

III. (fol. 130–134) For a description of the third florilegium, see below.

IV. (fol. 134–136) Σὺν θεῷ ὅροι σύντομοι τῶν ἁγίων καὶ θεοφόρων μυσταγωγῶν καὶ πανσόφων διδασκάλων τῆς ἁγίας καθολικῆς ἐκκλησίας σαφῶς δηλοῦντες τί ἐστι θέλημα.

V. (fol. 136ʳ⁻ᵛ) Σὺν θεῷ ὅροι διάφοροι τῶν ἁγίων, καὶ θεοφόρων μυσταγωγῶν καὶ πανσόφων πατέρων καὶ διδασκάλων, περὶ ἐνεργείας.⁵⁶

Relevant to this contribution is only the third florilegium. A detailed description will clearly reveal the similarities with the other manuscripts of *Op.* 26a / *Add.* 20:

1. (fol. 130, l. 27–29) The general title of this third florilegium is: Σὺν θεῷ ὅροι σύντομοι τῶν ἁγίων καὶ θεοφόρων μυσταγωγῶν, καὶ πανσόφων διδασκάλων τῆς ἁγίας καθολικῆς ἐκκλησίας, περὶ οὐσίας καὶ φύσεως, ὑποστάσεώς τε καὶ προσώπου

two readings of its own: the omission of ἀριθμῷ (l. 3) and the omission of Ὑπόστασις – δηλωτική (l. 20/22).

⁵⁴ This is an adaptation of the collection of definitions in Anastasius of Sinai's *Viae dux*. See Uthemann 1981, p. LIX–LX n. 114 and p. CCXXXIV.

⁵⁵ For the edition of the fragment Τοῦ ἁγίου καὶ μακαρίου καὶ μεγάλου φωστῆρος καὶ διδασκάλου Αὐγουστίνου ἐπισκόπου Ἱππονιρισίου, ἐκ τοῦ δογματικοῦ διαλόγου πρὸς Φιλικιανόν on fol. 128ᵛ, see J. Noret in Thomson 1994, p. 325–327.

⁵⁶ Chapter IV and V are known as the Pseudo-Maximian *Add.* 24 and 25 respectively. They were edited for the first time by Epifanovič 1917, p. 72, l. 25–75, l. 25 and p. 76, l. 1–77, l. 8. For a critical re-edition together with *Op.* 26b and *Op.* 27, of which they are alternative versions, see Roosen 2001, p. 781–786 and p. 819–823.

2. (fol. 130, l. 30–130ᵛ, l. 1) Τοῦ ἁγιωτάτου καὶ μακαριωτάτου Κλήμεντος πρεσβυτέρου Ἀλεξανδρείας ἐκ τοῦ περὶ προνοίας λόγου

= Ps.-Clemens Alexandrinus, fr. 37.[57]

3. (fol. 130ᵛ, l. 1–6) Without a title or any other sign of a transition, the text continues with what has become known as fr. 38 of Ps. Clemens' *De providentia*. Actually, this is nothing but the last part, viz. l. 11–16 (*PG* 91, col. 265 D9–268 A4), of *Op.* 23c. This partial transmission of *Op.* 23c in *Pf* seems to be the result of a fault in the textual tradition, not of a decision made by a scribe. Indeed, in the previous text, the last words καὶ τὸ πῶς εἶναι seems to have been substituted by θεωρούμενον. The result, however, is senseless: 'the divine providence gives to the things that come into being τὸ εἶναι θεωρούμενον'. An addition in the text of *Op.* 23c as found in *Pd Ff Uott Uz* and *Ay* suggests a tempting explanation. Between l. 9 and l. 10 (*PG* 91, col. 265 D6–7 and D8) these manuscripts repeat the second definition of *Op.* 23c (l. 4/5 [*PG* 91, col. 265 C11–12]). The last word of that definition is ἐνθεωρούμενον, of which θεωρούμενον is only one syllable short. Thus, θεωρούμενον is probably not to be considered as the last word of III. 2, but as the first word of III. 3. The fact that in *Pd Ff Uott Uz* and in *Ay* there is still one more definition, viz. that on l. 10 (*PG* 91, col. 265 D8) between the additional definition and the definition Φύσις – πεφυκέναι (l. 11 [*PG* 91, col. 265 D9]), before which θεωρούμενον is found in *Pf*, is no serious counterargument. Either it was dropped at an earlier stage due to an *Augensprung*, which is easy enough in a series of three Φύσις-definitions, or in the *Pf* branch the additional definition and the definition on l. 10 (*PG* 91, col. 265 D8) were found in reverse order.

---

[57] Stählin, *Clemens Alexandrinus*, III, p. 219. See also text II. 2 in our description of *Pd* and its related manuscripts above.

4. (fol. 130ʳ, l. 7–27) Τοῦ ὁσίου πατρὸς ἡμῶν Ἀναστασίου πατριάρχου Ἀντιοχείας, ἐκ τῆς βίβλου ἧς ἡ ἐπιγραφή· Περὶ τῶν καθ'ἡμᾶς τῆς ἀληθείας δογμάτων.

= a collection of definitions attributed to and indeed for the most part taken from Anastasius I Antiochenus' *Definitiones* or *Capita philosophica* [*CPG* 6945].[58]

5. (fol. 130ʳ, l. 28–131, l. 2) Τοῦ μακαρίου Λεοντίου μοναχοῦ τοῦ Βυζαντίου, ἐρημίτου ὀρθοδόξου, καὶ μεγάλου φιλοσόφου, ἐκ τοῦ περὶ οὐσίας, καὶ ὑποστάσεως λόγου, κεφάλαιον α΄.

= an excerpt from Leontius of Byzantium's *Libri tres contra Nestorianos et Eutychianos* [*CPG* 6813], more exactly *PG* 86, col. 1280 A5–15 (ἡ μὲν γὰρ φύσις – ἐν ἀλλήλοις κεκτημένα).

6. (fol. 131, l. 2–8) Τοῦ ἐν ἁγίοις πατρὸς ἡμῶν Σωφρονίου πατριάρχου Ἱεροσολύμων, ἐκ τῶν πρὸς Ὀνώριον πάπαν Ῥώμης, γραφέντων.

The title heads three definitions.

The first one, viz. Φύσις, καὶ οὐσία, καὶ μορφή, ταυτόν ἐστιν· ἄτομον, ὑπόστασις καὶ πρόσωπον, ταυτόν ἐστιν, is also found in *Ug*[59] and in *Pd Ff Pv Uy* and *Ay*.[60] While in *Ug* the title hardly gives any details (Τοῦ ἁγίου Σωφρονίου), in *Pf* and *Pd Ff Pv Uy* and *Ay* it explicitly states that Sophronius is the seventh-century Patriarch of Jerusalem and that the text is addressed to Pope Honorius.[61] But

---

[58] For this collection in our manuscript, see Uthemann 1980, p. 334–335.

[59] See Roosen 2014, p. 255 and n. 52.

[60] See number II. 4 in the description of these manuscripts higher in this contribution.

[61] It seems obvious to think of Sophronius' *Epistula synodica ad Sergium Constantinopolitanum* [*CPG* 7635], of which we know that it was also sent to Honorius: Photius' codex 231, for example, contained a synodical letter of Sophronius to Pope Honorius, of which the contents seem to have been the same as the contents of the letter to Sergius (cf. Henry 1967, p. 64, l. 13–65, l. 35) and two of the *testimonia* Patriarch Nicephorus I of Constantinople appended to his *Antirrhetici* are entitled Τοῦ ἁγίου Σωφρονίου ἀρχιεπισκόπου Ἱεροσολύμων, ἐκ τῆς πρὸς Ὀνώριον (τὸν) πάπαν Ῥώμης ἐπιστολῆς and are indeed also found in Sophronius' *Epistula synodica* to Sergius (cf. Pitra 1852, p. 350 and p. 486–487). However, as far as the definition in our manuscripts is concerned, one searches the letter in vain. There is another quite tempting possibility, viz that the definition was part of the 600 testimonies from the fathers, Sophronius asked Stephen

despite these details, we have not been able to identify the definition.

The two other definitions in *Pf*, however, are found neither in *Ug* nor in *Pd Ff Pv Uy Ay*[62] and are, therefore, very likely secondary additions.[63]

7. (fol. 131, l. 8–33) Τοῦ ἐν ἁγίοις Μαξίμου τοῦ μεγάλου, καὶ θεόφρονος διδασκάλου, ἐκ τῶν ἐρωτηθέντων αὐτῷ παρὰ Θεοδοσίου μοναχοῦ.

= *Add.* 20, the text we are editing in this contribution. The text is characterised by the omission of the patristic definition of ὑπόστασις up to and including the first five words of the part proper to *Add.* 20 (κατὰ – ἰδιωμάτων, l. 15/18), an omission not encountered in the other manuscripts of *Add.* 20 and very likely the result of an *Augensprung*.

8. (fol. 131, l. 33–132ᵛ, l. 13) Τοῦ αὐτοῦ θεόφρονος Μαξίμου τοῦ ὁμολογητοῦ, καὶ μεγάλου διδασκάλου, ὅτι οὐσία καὶ φύσις ταυτόν ἐστιν.

= *Add.* 21

9. (fol. 132ᵛ, l. 14–133ᵛ, l. 17) Τοῦ αὐτοῦ μακαρίου θεοσόφου καὶ θεόφρονος Μαξίμου τοῦ μεγάλου φιλοσόφου καὶ ὁμολογητοῦ, Κεφάλαια περὶ οὐσίας, καὶ ὑποστάσεως.

= *Add.* 22, i.e. *Op.* 23a lengthened with some extra lines in the beginning and at the end.

---

of Dora to bring to Honorius in Rome. See the testimony of Stephen of Dora in his *Libellus Stephani episcopi Dorensis* [*CPG* 9399.1], which was inserted into the acts of the Lateran Synod of 649 (ed. Riedinger 1984, p. 38, l. 11 – p. 46, l. 36, especially p. 40, l. 20–21).

[62] It is possible that in *Pd Ff Pv Uy* and *Ay* the following two definitions were dropped together with the first part of the following text, viz. *Add.* 20, but the situation in *Ug* makes this assumption if not impossible, then at least less probable.

[63] The second definition, viz. Οὐσία ἐστὶν πρώτως τὲ καὶ κυρίως, πᾶν ὅτιπερ αὐθυπόστατον ὑπάρχει, καὶ μὴ ἐν ἑτέρῳ ἔχει τὸ εἶναι, is clearly related to Theodorus Rhaïthu's *Praeparatio* [*CPG* 7600], p. 201, l. 13–15 (ed. Diekamp 1938); the third definition, viz. Οὐσία ἐστὶ τὸ δι'ὅλου ὑφεστός, is the same as the third definition in the fragment from the Ps. Clementine *De providentia* as found in *PG* 91, col. 264B and in the edition by Stählin & Früchtel & Treu 1970², 219.

10. (fol. 133ᵛ, l. 18–134, l. 12) Τοῦ αὐτοῦ, τί ὑπόστασις, καὶ τί ἐνυπόστατον, ἐκ τῆς πρὸς Κοσμᾶν διάκονον Ἀλεξανδρείας δογματικῆς ἐπιστολῆς.

= *Add.* 23, which is an addition to Maximus the Confessor's *Ep.* 15.

The fact that *Pf* does have the title and the opening lines of *Add.* 20 is a clear indication that the manuscript cannot go back to λ: its ancestor, which will be called ι, must be situated higher in the stemma. Now, the question is whether *Add.* 20 is a lengthened version of *Op.* 26a? Or is it the other way around and is *Op.* 26a a shortened version of *Add.* 20? A positive answer to the former question suggests the stemma to the left, a positive answer to the latter question the stemma to the right:

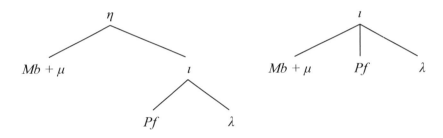

Unfortunately, there are no faults and variants that can help us decide. However, the contrast between the lines *Op.* 26a and *Add.* 20 have in common and the lines proper to *Add.* 20 can hardly be greater. On the one hand, there is a very strict structure with the four terms that are at the centre of the post-chalcedonian christological debates (φύσις, οὐσία, ἄτομον and ὑπόστασις) each defined in two different ways. On the other hand, there is the seemingly haphazard accumulation of ὑπόστασις definitions in the lines proper to *Add.* 20, an accumulation probably provoked by the fact that *Op.* 26a ends with a ὑπόστασις definition. Moreover, if one accepts Maximus' authorship of *Add.* 38 and of the lines *Op.* 26a and *Add.* 20 have in common – in the following section of this contribution we will try to adduce some arguments in favour of Maximus' authorship –, this almost necessarily leads to the conclusion that the ὑπόστασις definitions are later additions:

it seems, indeed, quite unlikely that Maximus would have quoted so extensively from his own writings.

Add. 20 was edited for the first and only time in 1917 by S. L. Epifanovič.[64] As he indicates himself,[65] he used *Pf* for his edition, a lucky coincidence, as it is the only independent manuscript presenting the title and the first lines of *Add.* 20. The edition, which only presents those lines not found in the edition of *Op.* 26a in the *Patrologia graeca*, is quite faithful and proposes two emendations.[66]

3. *Where do these Fragments Come from?*

One important question remains, that of the origin of these two short texts and, thus, their author. We start with the title.

In the two independent manuscripts of *Add.* 38 this title is virtually identical and reads:

Ἐκ τῶν ἐρωτηθέντων παρὰ <u>Θεοδοσίου μοναχοῦ</u>, <u>πρεσβυτέρου Γαγγρῶν</u> <u>ὀρθοδόξου</u> (*Me*)

or:

Ἐκ τῶν ἐρωτηθέντων παρὰ <u>Θεοδοσίου</u> ταπεινοῦ καὶ ἁμαρτώλου μοναχοῦ, <u>ὀρθοδόξου</u> <u>πρεσβυτέρου</u> <u>Γαγγρῶν</u> (*Aa*)

The title in *Op.* 26a – *Add.* 20 is less detailed with regard to the identity of Theodosius, but still very similar to that of *Add.* 38. However, the situation was involuntarily obscured by Combefis, who edited *Op.* 26a under the title:

Ἐκ τῶν ἐρωτηθέντων αὐτῷ παρὰ <u>Θεοδώρου</u> μοναχοῦ

It is this reading which made it to the *Clavis Patrum Graecorum*, as *E quaestionibus a Theodoro monacho illi propositis.*[67] Surpris-

---

[64] Cf. Epifanovič 1917, p. 67, l. 25 – p. 68, l. 8.

[65] Cf. Epifanovič 1917, p. 67 n. 1.

[66] On l. 24 ἤ was rightly corrected into ἢ and on l. 25 ἀτόμων was rightly corrected into ἀτόμῳ.

[67] Cf. *CPG* 7697. 26.

ingly, *Add.* 20 is mentioned in *CPG* with the exact same Latin title, although Epifanovič faithfully followed *Pf* in writing:

Ἐκ τῶν ἐρωτηθέντων αὐτῷ παρὰ Θεοδοσίου μοναχοῦ

Upon examination of the manuscript evidence, however, it becomes clear that Combefis misinterpreted the abbreviation of the name in *Ui*. The different versions in the independent manuscripts of *Op.* 26a are – we try to reproduce the extant manuscripts as photographically as possible –:

θεοδ)° in *Ug*

θε in *Ac Ui*

Thus, Combefis, who used *Ui* for his edition, only had the letters θε as a basis to decide on the name. Apparently, he thought of Theodore of Rhaithu when he decided to write Θεοδώρου.[68] Already Diekamp considered Combefis' identification as highly unlikely, but his arguments hardly convince.[69] Diekamp's scepticism is confirmed not only by *Pf,* but more importantly also by *Ug.* Because of the final o and the absence of an accent, the abbreviation in that last manuscript is indeed much more fitting for Θεοδοσίου than for Θεοδώρου. Even if one assumes that this is one of the rare cases where the scribe of *Ug* made an orthographical mistake and wrote an omikron for an omega, one still would expect to find an accent.[70] In other words, we are convinced that the title in the one family that transmits *Op.* 26a is identical to the title in *Pf* and reads:

Ἐκ τῶν ἐρωτηθέντων αὐτῷ παρὰ Θεοδοσίου μοναχοῦ

The conclusion that *Add.* 38, *Op.* 26a and *Add.* 20 are headed by almost exactly the same title adds credibility to the informa-

---

[68] See *PG* 91, col. 276 n. 39: 'Videtur hic ipse presbyter Rhaithu, ad quem Περὶ οὐσίας καὶ φύσεως, nec forte alius ad quem Περὶ τῶν δύο θελημάτων.' As a matter of fact, the interpretation of the abbreviation in *Ui* as being short for Θεοδώρου was also made by Demetrius Cabasilas Canisces, the scribe of *Uh*. Instead of just θε like in *Ui* he wrote something that resembles θ)ε̄δρ'.

[69] Cf. Diekamp 1938, p. 174: 'Dagegen spricht aber, dass Theodor von Raïthu, der über die Häresien seiner Zeit handelt, mit keinem Worte den Monotheletismus oder Monoenergismus erwähnt'.

[70] One would expect Θεοδώρου to be shortened to θεοδω' or, with an orthographical mistake, to θεοδ°'.

tion this title provides. In the case of *Op.* 26a and *Add.* 20, which are closely related, such an identical title is of course exactly what one would expect. However, between *Op.* 26a – *Add.* 20 on the one hand and *Add.* 38 on the other there is, as far as we can see, no such relationship, so that, to explain for the presence of this almost identical, clearly non-generic title in two different, mutually independent fragments, we must assume that this title goes back to the source text.

Now, if we look at the information in the title, this source text appears to have been a set of questions and answers (cf. Ἐκ τῶν ἐρωτηθέντων). Unfortunately, both in the case of *Add.* 38 and in the case of *Op.* 26a – *Add.* 20 there is, as already said, no trace of the question anymore, at least if one disregards the situation in *Me.* This manuscript seems to consider the words Ἡ πρόγνωσις τὰ ἐφ'ἡμῖν περιέχει πάντα, τίμιά τε καὶ ἄτιμα (l. 1/2) as a question by putting the word ἐρώτησις in the left margin and writing the sign frequently used for the end of a paragraph, i.e. a colon followed by a short horizontal line, at the end of this sentence. At level with the following words, viz. ὁ προορισμὸς, the manuscript has ἀπόκρισις in the left margin. However, since it is difficult to see how this first sentence can be understood as a question, the rest as the answer and since, moreover, this situation is not seen in *Aa*, it has to be assumed that the situation in *Me* was caused by the words Ἐκ τῶν ἐρωτηθέντων from the title.

The person asking the questions is identified in the following part of the title, but while the manuscripts of *Op.* 26a – *Add.* 20 only have παρὰ Θεοδοσίου μοναχοῦ, the manuscripts of *Add.* 38 add πρεσβυτέρου Γαγγρῶν ὀρθοδόξου. Even if it is quite likely that there has been more than one orthodox priestmonk in Gangra named Theodosius, in combination with the unanimous attribution of *Add.* 38 and *Op.* 26a – *Add.* 20 to Maximus the Confessor, it is almost certain that we are dealing with the brother of Theodore Spoudaeus, the recipient of a letter by Anastasius Apocrisiarius [*CPG* 7733], the possible author of the *Hypomnesticum* [*CPG* 7968] and one of the followers of Maximus Confessor.[71]

---

[71] On Theodosius of Gangra, see Winkelmann 2001, p. 509 (nº 7816), where however the article by Simonetti 1987, p. 113–146 is not mentioned.

But what to think of this unanimous attribution of the two fragments to Maximus the Confessor? In other words, is it possible that Maximus provided the answers to Theodosius' questions? If so, it would evidence the dynamics at work in the relationship between Theodosius and Maximus, i.e. those between a teacher and a student, who, if we judge by the rather basic level of the fragments, still had a lot to learn.

Needless to say, Maximus was acquainted with the genre of the ἐρωταποκρίσεις: his *L.A.*, e.g., is a beautiful example, as are his *Q.D.* But this is like saying that a present-day writer knows what a novel is. It hardly is an argument.

A much stronger argument in favour of the attribution is the aforementioned similarity between *Add.* 38 and the opening lines of the *D.B.* Since this similarity is, as already said, clear enough to suggest that the former is the source of the latter – not the other way around, since it would make it very hard to explain the relationship between *Add.* 38 and *Op.* 26a – *Add.* 20 –, it allows us to pinpoint the origin of *Add.* 38 (and, thus, indirectly also *Op.* 26a – *Add.* 20) not later than the first half of the seventh century and at least in the proximity of Maximus the Confessor.

For *Op.* 26a – *Add.* 20 there is no such direct link with Maximus the Confessor. Still, attention should be drawn to the fact that the intellectual traditions in which the definitions are situated fit Maximus and his time very well. Although the original part, i.e. l. 1–17, makes a strict distinction between the definitions of the philosophers and those of the fathers, reality is, as usual, much less black and white. Indeed, most definitions appear in philosophical as well as in theological texts. Major influences are, as can be seen in the *apparatus fontium et locorum parallelorum*, the neoplatonic school of Alexandria with authors like Elias and David, and the sixth-century Chalcedonian party, with authors like Leontius of Byzantium and Anastasius of Antioch. Moreover, there are a number of parallels between the eight definitions which constitute *Op.* 26a – *Add.* 20, l. 1–17 and texts for which Maximus' authorship is undisputed. In fact, these parallels also call into question Thunberg's opinion that Maximus 'refers almost with disdain' to the definitions κατὰ τοὺς φιλοσόφους.[72]

---

[72] See Thunberg 1995², p. 86 n. 237. Thunberg's opinion is also rejected by

In other words, Maximus Confessor was certainly able to write a text like *Op.* 26a – *Add.* 20, l. 1–17.

Finally, there is an indirect tradition of *Op.* 26a – *Add.* 20 that still needs to be discussed and which seems to provide an argument in favour of Maximus' authorship. This indirect tradition consists of three quite similar collections of mostly alphabetically ordered definitions:

DOtt   Definitions in MS *Vaticano, Biblioteca Apostolica Vaticana, Ottob. gr. 43* (*s.* XI–XII), fol. 1–49

DPatm Definitions in MS *Patmos, Monê tou Hagiou Iôannou tou Theologou, fonds principal 263* (*s.* X), fol. 120–191

DVat   Definitions in MS *Vaticano, Biblioteca Apostolica Vaticana, Vat. gr. 1778* (*s.* XVI), fol. 25–84

Our investigations of these collections of definitions have shown that the first two are quite closely related, but that one is not dependent on the other. *DVat* then has added at least one more collection, possibly one close to the considerably shorter collection of definitions found in MS *Vaticano, Biblioteca Apostolica Vaticana, Vat. gr. 447* (*s.* XII), fol. 315–329.

Now, if we take a closer look, it is remarkable that, just like *Mb*, none of these collections of definitions has the opening lines devoted to φύσις and that a marginal M̄ for Maximus the Confessor accompanies two definitions also found in our text, i.e. the double definition of ἄτομον on l. 9–13 and the definition of ὑπόστασις σύνθετος on l. 29–36. In the case of the latter, the correctness of this attribution can easily be checked since the source text, Maximus' *Ep.* 13, is still extant. In the case of the former, it is additional evidence for the attribution of *Op.* 26a – *Add.* 20, l. 1–17 to Maximus.[73]

Karayiannis 1993, p. 36 n. 7. Karayiannis refers to Prestige 1952, p. 279 as sharing Thunberg's opinion, but this reference is based upon a misinterpretation of Thunberg's footnote.

[73] That is, of course, unless one assumes that the definition entered the collections of alphabetically ordered definitions not via the original set of ἐρωταποκρίσεις between Maximus and Theodosius, but via the excerpt as we have it. In that case, the marginal attribution has no value whatsoever.

4. *Ratio edendi and Edition*

The critical edition of the texts in this contribution is made with as much respect for the manuscripts as can be justified on the basis of present-day scholarly standards. This has the following consequences:

- *punctuation*: the manuscripts have been double-checked for the position of the punctuation marks. As a result, every punctuation mark in our edition corresponds to a punctuation mark in the majority of the manuscripts, although not all punctuation marks have been preserved;

- *accentuation*: special attention has been payed to the accentuation in the manuscripts, which as is well-known, differs from the rules in school grammars, especially in the case of enclitics. As such, the reader will find orthotone τις, even though it is used as an indefinite pronoun, or an oxytone word followed by an oxytone εἰσι. Moreover, since the use of a gravis before 'weak punctuations' like a comma is quite common in manuscripts (and, as a matter of fact, quite justified), we decided to preserve also this feature; [74]

- *apostrophe*: except in fairly late manuscripts, scribes rarely end a line with an apostrophe, and would rather write καθ᾽ἕ|καστον than καθ᾽|ἕκαστον, thus revealing the close connection they felt between the apostrophized word and the next word. Therefore, as in French or Italian, we never added a space (or punctuation mark) after an apostrophe. Moreover, we followed the manuscripts in adding an apostrophe after οὐχ.

---

[74] See Panteghini 2011, p. 142: 'Anzi, parebbe in molti casi che la scelta dell'accento discenda da una percezione del grado d'indipendenza di un κῶλον all'interno della superiore gerarchia sintattica: se dipende da un verbo finito che si trova altrove – o nell'enunciato principale o nel κῶλον successivo –, o se è in relazione stretta con elementi che con circondano, la μέση non determina quel grado di indipendenza che le consente di impedire la baritonesi'.

Add. 38   Ἐκ τῶν ἐρωτηθέντων παρὰ Θεοδοσίου μοναχοῦ,   Ineditum
πρεσβυτέρου Γαγγρῶν ὀρθοδόξου

Ἡ πρόγνωσις τὰ ἐφ' ἡμῖν περιέχει πάντα, τίμιά τε καὶ
ἄτιμα, ὁ προορισμὸς τὰς τῶν οὐκ ἐφ' ἡμῖν τιμὰς ἢ
ἀτιμίας, καὶ συντόμως εἰπεῖν, τὰ προορισθέντα πάντα,
ἢ κολαστικὰ εἰσὶ τῶν ἐφ' ἡμῖν πονηρῶν, ἢ ἐπαινετικὰ
5   τῶν ἐφ' ἡμῖν ἀγαθῶν. Καὶ οὐδὲν διαφεύγει τῆς θείας
προγνώσεως, καὶ τοῦ θείου προορισμοῦ τὸν λόγον, οὐκ
αἰὼν, οὐ χρόνος, οὐ μέρος χρόνου, οὐ τόπος, οὐχ' ὕλη
πρὸς ἔπαινον (1) ἢ ὕβριν, οὐ πρόφασις, οὔ τι τῶν
τούτοις συνεπινοουμένων, ἀλλὰ πάντα περιέχεται τῷ
10   λόγῳ τῆς θείας προνοίας καὶ κρίσεως, ἐν τῇ ἀπορρήτῳ
σοφίᾳ τοῦ καλῶς καὶ ἀπείρως ἀγαθότητι πάντα τὰ
ὁπωσοῦν ὄντα οἰακίζοντος. Ὄντα δὲ λέγω [τὰ τῷ λόγῳ
τῆς δημ περιεχόμενα, καὶ] τὰ τῷ λόγῳ τῆς δημιουργίας
περιεχόμενα ὑπέρ{± 5 litt.}, καὶ τὰ τῷ λόγῳ γινόμενα τῆς
15   καθ' ἡμᾶς φυσικῆς αὐτεξουσιότητος ἀγαθά· τὰ γὰρ
ἁμαρτήματα κἂν ἐφ' ἡμῖν τυγχάνωσιν, ἀλλ' οὐ τῷ
λόγῳ τῆς δημιουργίας ἢ τῆς φύσεως περιέχεται. Ἔστιν
οὖν ὡς ἐν συντόμῳ φᾶναι, ἡ μὲν πρόγνωσις, τῶν
ἑκουσίων καὶ ἐφ' ἡμῖν ἀποδεικτική· ὁ δὲ προορισμὸς,
20   τῶν ἀκουσίων καὶ οὐκ ἐφ' ἡμῖν ἐπακτικός. Ἔτι
συντομώτερον περὶ τούτων εἰπεῖν, τῶν ἀκουσίων καὶ
προωρισμένων τὰ ἑκούσια καὶ προεγνωσμένα, αἴτια
τυγχάνει, ὡς εἶναι τὰ ἀκούσια διὰ τὰ ἑκούσια, ἤγουν τὰ
οὐκ ἐφ' ἡμῖν διὰ τὰ ἐφ' ἡμῖν.

Scholium   (1) Ἰδοὺ φανερῶς οὗτος ὁ μέγας πατὴρ τὰ τέσσαρα, ἤγουν τὸν
χρόνον, καὶ τὸν τόπον, τόν τε τρόπον καὶ τὴν ὕλην, καὶ πᾶν εἴ τι
τούτοις συνεπινοεῖται προωρίσθαι παρὰ θεοῦ φησίν.

— Apparatus fontium et locorum parallelorum

1/24 cf. Max. Conf. in (Max. Conf.), D.B., l. 31–49 (p. 75–77)

— Sigla

Aa^(sine scholio)   *Me*^(usque ad ἔπαινον [l. 8] et cum scholio)

— Apparatus criticus

Indicatio auctoris   τοῦ ἁγίου μαξίμου *Aa*; τοῦ ὁσίου πατρὸς ἡμῶν μαξίμου μοναχοῦ
καὶ μάρτυρος *Me*

Tit. 1 μοναχοῦ] ταπεινοῦ καὶ ἁμαρτώλου *praem. Aa*   **2** ὀρθοδόξου] *a.* πρεσβυτέρου
trps. Aa

Txt. 1 Ἡ] ἐρώ(τησις) *in margine praem. Me*   **2** ὁ] ἀπό(κρισις) *in margine praem. Me*   **4** ἢ¹] *om. Me*   ἢ ἐπαινετικὰ] ἡ ἐπαινετὴ καὶ *Me*

5 διαφεύγει] διαφεύγη *Me*   **7** οὐχ᾿ὕλη] οὐ χειλη *Aa*   **8/24** ἢ ὕβριν – διὰ τὰ ἐφ᾿ἡμῖν]
om. Me   **12/13** τὰ – καὶ] *(sic) Aa, seclusi*   **14** ὑπέρ{...}] *non liquet Aa*

Scholium 3 συνεπινοεῖται] *correxi*; συνέπινοῆται *(sic) Me*   προωρίσθαι] *correxi*;
προόρισθαι *Me*   φησίν] *correxi*; φασίν *Me*

<table>
<tr><td>Op. 26a
+ Add. 20</td><td style="text-align:center">Ἐκ τῶν ἐρωτηθέντων αὐτῷ
παρὰ Θεοδοσίου μοναχοῦ</td><td>PG 276A
Epifan. 67</td></tr>
</table>

¹ **Φύσις ἐστὶ, κατὰ μὲν φιλοσόφους, ἀρχὴ κινήσεως καὶ
ἠρεμίας, κατὰ δὲ τοὺς πατέρας, εἶδος κατὰ πολλῶν
καὶ διαφερόντων τῷ ἀριθμῷ, ἐν τῷ ὁποῖον τί ἐστι
κατηγορούμενον.**

5 ² **Οὐσία ἐστὶ, κατὰ μὲν φιλοσόφους, αὐθυπόστατον
πρᾶγμα, μὴ δεόμενον ἑτέρου πρὸς σύστασιν, κατὰ δὲ
τοὺς πατέρας, ἡ κατὰ πολλῶν καὶ διαφερόντων ταῖς
ὑποστάσεσιν ὀντότης φυσική.**

³ **Ἄτομόν ἐστι, κατὰ μὲν φιλοσόφους, ἰδιωμάτων
10 συναγωγὴ, ὧν τὸ ἄθροισμα ἐπ᾿ ἄλλου θεωρεῖσθαι οὐ
δύναται, κατὰ δὲ τοὺς πατέρας, οἷον Πέτρος ἢ Παῦλος
ἢ τίς ἕτερος τῶν καθ᾿ αὑτὰ ἰδίοις προσωπικοῖς ἰδιώμασι
τῶν ἄλλων ἀνθρώπων ἀφοριζόμενος.**

⁴ **Ὑπόστασίς ἐστι, κατὰ μὲν φιλοσόφους, οὐσία μετὰ
15 ἰδιωμάτων, κατὰ δὲ τοὺς πατέρας, καθ᾿ ἕκαστον
ἄνθρωπον προσωπικῶς τῶν ἄλλων ἀνθρώπων
ἀφοριζόμενον.**

Add. 20   ⁵ Ὑπόστασίς ἐστιν, οὐσία μετὰ ἰδιωμάτων ἀριθμῷ
τῶν ὁμογενῶν διαφέρουσα, **οἷον ὁ δεῖνα.** |
20   ⁶ Ὑπόστασίς ἐστι, τὸ καθ᾿ αὑτὸ διωρισμένος **τῶν**   Epifan. 68
ὁμογενῶν τε καὶ **ὁμοειδῶν** ὑφεστώς.
⁷ **Ὑπόστασίς ἐστι, προσώπου δηλωτική·** ⁸ **Ὅρος
ὑποστάσεως ἁπλῶς λεγομένης** – Ὑπόστασίς
ἐστιν, οὐσία τίς μετὰ ἰδιωμάτων, ἢ οὐσία τίς τῶν
25   καθ᾿ ἕκαστα περιληπτική, τῶν ἐν τῷ οἰκείῳ ἀτόμῳ
πάντων ἰδιωμάτων. Τὴν προσδιωρισμένως
ἀλλ᾿ οὐχ᾿ ἁπλῶς λεγομένην ὁρίζοντες ὑπόστασιν
λέγομεν, – ⁹ **Ὅρος ὑποστάσεως συνθέτου** –
Ὑπόστασις σύνθετός ἐστι, οὐσία τίς σύνθετος
30   μετὰ ἰδιωμάτων, ἢ οὐσία τίς σύνθετος τῶν
καθ᾿ ἕκαστα περιληπτική, τῶν ἐν τῷ οἰκείῳ ἀτόμῳ
πάντων ἰδιωμάτων· τὰ γὰρ κοινῶς ἐν τοῖς ὑπὸ τὸ
αὐτὸ εἶδος ἀτόμοις θεωρούμενα, τὸ τῆς οὐσίας
ἤτοι φύσεως χαρακτηρίζει προηγουμένως ἐν τοῖς
35   ὑπ᾿ αὐτὴν ἀτόμοις γενικόν. Πάντων δὲ κοινὸν τῶν
ὑπὸ τὸ σύνθετον εἶδος ἀτόμων<, τὸ σύνθετον>.

— Apparatus fontium et locorum parallelorum

1/2 ¹ (Φύσις – ἠρεμίας) Arist., Phys. VIII, 3 (253b7–9). Cf. ibid. II, 1 (192b13–14.21–22); id., Met. VI (1025b19–21). Saepe laudatur ab Aristotelis commentatoribus: e.g. Ioh. Philop., In Arist. Phys. (p. 298, l. 23–24), David, In Porph. Isag. (p. 192, l. 27–28). Vide et Ps. Plut., Plac. Phil. I, 1 (875 B1–2 [p. 70], B10 – C1, C3 [p. 71]). Saepe laudatur etiam in scriptis christianis: e.g. Ioh. Scyth., Scholia (PG 4, 296 B14–15; 324 B9–10 et C1–2); Pamph., Qu. II, 192–193 (p. 143); Theodor. Raith., Praep. (p. 202, l. 10–11); Ps. Max. Conf., Op. 23c (l. 9; PG 91, col. 265 D6–7); Anast. Sin., Viae dux, VIII, 5, 117–118 (p. 133); Ioh. Dam., Dial., fus. 41 (brev. 24), 2 et 4–7 (p. 107). Vide et collectiones definitionum anonymas: e.g. Oxon., 11, l. 27 (fol. 11; p. 164); DOtt, fol. 46; DPatm, fol. 184ᵛ; DVat, fol. 78ᵛ; DRom, fol. 328 (bis)

2/4 (κατὰ – κατηγορούμενον) Leont. Schol., De sectis (PG 86, 1193 A7–10) – ad definitionem vocabuli εἶδος ut κατὰ πλειόνων καὶ διαφερόντων ἀριθμῷ ἐν τῷ τί ἐστι κατηγορούμενον, vide apud philosophos, e.g. Porph., Isag. (p. 4, l. 11–12); Alex. Aphr., In Arist. Topica (p. 47, l. 10–12); Dexipp., In Arist. Cat. (p. 30, l. 20–21); Ammon., In Porph. Isag. (p. 70, l. 3–4); Ioh. Philop., In Arist. Cat. (p. 67, l. 27–28); Elias, In Porph. Isag. (p. 61, l. 26–27); David, In Porph. Isag. (p. 144, l. 18–19); Ps. Elias / David, In Porph. Isag. 32, 10 (p. 80); DPatr 33 (p. 258, l. 21–23) – ad εἶδος ut ...ἐν τῷ ὁποῖον τί ἐστι κατηγορούμενον, vide quae dicit Ammon., In Arist. Cat. (p. 124, l. 18–125, l. 8)

5/6 ² (Οὐσία – σύστασιν) Ad originem huius definitionis, cf. Arist., Cat. 5 (2a11–13), sed vide praesertim Aristotelis commentatores, e.g. Ammon., In Arist. Cat. (p. 33, l. 11–13); Ioh. Philop., In Arist. Anal. post. (p. 31, l. 1–2); id., In Arist. Cat. (p. 49, l. 19–20); Olymp. phil., In Arist. Cat. (p. 43, l. 14–15); Asclep. Trall., In Arist. Metaphys. (p. 208, l. 30–31); et theologos, e.g. Pamph., Qu. II, 24–26 (p. 134–135); Anast. Ant., Cap. philos. 46 (p. 349); Ps. Anast. Ant., Expl. fid. orth. (PG 89, 1401 A3–5; vide et duas alias recensiones huius operis editas a LILLA, Un opusculo, p. 52, l. 10–11 et p. 54, l. 10–11); Theodor. Raith., Praep. (p. 201, l. 13–16; vide et p. 202, l. 3–5); Max. Conf., Ep. 15 (PG 91, 564 B10–12); DPatr 6, XVI (p. 40, l. 25–26)

6/8 (κατὰ – φυσική) cf. Max. Conf., Ep. 12 (PG 91, 488 B2–4)

9/11 ³ (Ἄτομόν – δύναται) Vide e.g. Porph., Isag. (p. 7, l. 21–23); Elias, In Porph. Isag. (p. 76, l. 3–4); David, In Porph. Isag. (p. 167, l. 22–24); Ps. Elias / David, In Porph. Isag. 38, 11 (p. 99); DPatr 33 (p. 252, l. 13–14) – ut definitio vocabuli ὑπόστασις: cf. e.g. Leont. Byz., Epil. (PG 86, 1945 B12 – C2); Theodor. Raith., Praep. (p. 205, l. 15–17) – ad definitionem vocabuli ὑπόστασις modo ut συνδρομὴ ἰδιωμάτων vel ἰδιοτήτων, et cetera similia, vide e.g. Bas. Caes., Adv. Eun. II, 4, 20–21 (p. 20); Ps. Bas. Caes., Ep. 38 (revera Greg. Nyss., Ad Petrum fratrem), 6, l. 4–6 (p. 89; = Pamph., Qu. XI, 8–10 [p. 201]; = Anast. Ant., Cap. philos. 60 [p. 352]; = DPatr 33 [p. 265, l. 8]); Anast. Ant., Cap. philos. 59 (p. 351)

11/13 (κατὰ – ἀφοριζόμενος) Vide e.g. Ps. Eulog. Alex., Defensiones (revera Ioh. Gramm., Apol.), l. 67–69 (p. 51); Leont. Byz., C. Nest. et Eutych. I (PG 86, 1277 D3–4); id., Epil. (PG 86, 1928 C6–9); Pamph., Qu. I, 83–84 (p. 131); ibid. VII, 18–20 (p. 173–174); Max. Conf., Ep. 15 (PG 91, 552 B13–15 et C14 – D5)

14/15 ⁴ (Ὑπόστασις – ἰδιωμάτων) Apud philosophos hanc definitionem non invenimus. Ut definitio patrum (κατὰ τοὺς θεοφόρους πατέρας) laudatur in DPatr 11, XV (p. 72, l. 1–2). Vide et e.g. Heracl. Chalc., Ad Soterichum (p. 42, l. 21–24); Leont. Hierosol., C. Nest. (PG 86, 1485 B5); id., Contra Monophys. 61 (PG 86, 1804 B6–8); Pamph., Qu. I, 7 (p. 128); Max. Conf., Ep. 13 et Ep. 15, cf. infra ad

l. 14–15 et 18–21 – similia inveniuntur e.g. apud Bas. Caes., Ep. 214, 4, l. 9–11 (p. 205); Iust. imp., Contra monophys. 22 (p. 11, l. 41); Ps. Eulog. Alex., Defensiones (revera Ioh. Gramm., Apol.), l. 204–205 (p. 55); cf. Ps. Max. Conf., Op. 23c (l. 8; PG 91, col. 265 D4–5)

15/17 (κατὰ – ἀφοριζόμενον) eadem fere definitio est ac definitio κατὰ τοὺς πατέρας vocabuli ἄτομον (cf. supra l. 11–13)

18/19 ⁵Max. Conf., Ep. 15 (PG 91, 557 D13–15); Ps. Anast. Ant., Expl. fid. orth. (PG 89, 1401 B1–2; vide et duas alias recensiones huius operis editas a LILLA, *Un opusculo*, p. 53, l. 16–17 et p. 54, l. 19–20)

20/21 ⁶Max. Conf., Ep. 15 (PG 91, 557 D12–13)

23/28 ⁸Max. Conf., Ep. 13 (PG 91, 528 A10–14)

29/36 ⁹Max. Conf., Ep. 13 (PG 91, 528 A14 – B7)

— *Sigla*

Op. 26a (l. 1–13): *Ug Ac Ui Mb*⁽ⁱⁿᵈᵉ ᵃᵇ ᵒὐˢⁱᵃ ⁽ˡ· ⁵⁾⁾ – **Add. 20 (l. 1–28):** *Pf Pd*⁽ⁱⁿᵈᵉ ᵃᵇ Ἄᵗᵒμόⁿ ⁽ˡ· ⁹⁾⁾ *Ff*⁽ⁱⁿᵈᵉ ᵃᵇ Ἄᵗᵒμόⁿ ⁽ˡ· ⁹⁾⁾ *Pv*⁽ⁱⁿᵈᵉ ᵃᵇ Ἄᵗᵒμόⁿ ⁽ˡ· ⁹⁾⁾ *Ay*⁽ⁱⁿᵈᵉ ᵃᵇ Ἄᵗᵒμόⁿ ⁽ˡ· ⁹⁾⁾ – ²*DOtt*, fol. 32 *DPatm*, fol. 163ᵛ *DVat*, fol. 58 ³*DOtt*, fol. 5ᵛ *DPatm*, fol. 127ᵛ (cum attrib. "M̅") ⁴*DOtt*, fol. 43ᵛ *DPatm*, fol. 180ᵛ *DVat*, fol. 75ᵛ ⁵⁻⁶*DOtt*, fol. 43 *DPatm*, fol. 180ᵛ *DVat*, fol. 75 ⁸⁻⁹*DOtt*, fol. 43ᵛ (⁹ cum attrib. "M̅") *DPatm*, fol. 180ᵛ– 181 (⁹ cum attrib. "M") *DVat*, fol. 75ᵛ

— *Apparatus criticus*

Indicatio auctoris τοῦ ἁγίου μαξίμου *Ug Ac Ui*; μαξίμου *Mb*; τοῦ ἐν ἁγίοις μαξίμου τοῦ μεγάλου. καὶ θεόφρονος διδασκάλου *Pf*

Tit. 1/2 Ἐκ – μοναχοῦ] *om. Mb*

Txt. 5/6 αὐθυπόστατον πρᾶγμα] αὐθύπαρκτον πρᾶγμα *Mb*; ἰδιωμάτων συναγωγὴ *DOtt DPatm DVat* **6** δεόμενον] δεομένου *DOtt*; δεομένη *DPatm*; δεομένων *DVat* **7** διαφερόντων] τῷ ἀριθμῷ κατηγορούμενα. καὶ μήποτε καθότι οὖν ἐπὶ προσώπω περιοριζόμενα *add. DPatm*ᵃ· ᶜᵒʳʳ· *(pars est definitionis sequentis)* **7/8** ταῖς ὑποστάσεσιν] ὑποστάσεων *Mb* **8** ὀντότης φυσική] ταυτότης φυσική *Mb*; οντον τῇ φυσικῇ *(sic) DOtt*; ὄντων τῆς φυσικῆς *DPatm DVat* **9** Ἄτομόν ἐστι] οὐσία ἐστιν τὸ διόλου ὑφεστός *praem. Mb* **10** ἄλλου] ἄλλους *Ug DPatm* **11** πατέρας] ἁγίους *praem. DOtt DPatm* **12** ἢ τίς ἕτερος] ἢ τις ἕτερος *Ug Pf*; ἢ ἕτερός τις *Mb* τῶν] τὰ *Pv* καθ᾽αὐτὰ] καθ᾽ἑαυτὰ *Ff* προσωπικοῖς] προσώποις *Pf*ᵃ· ᶜᵒʳʳ· ᵘᵗ ᵛⁱᵈᵉᵗᵘʳ ἰδιώμασιν *Pv*ᶠ ᶜᵒʳʳ· **14** Ὑπόστασίς ἐστι] τὸ καθεαυτὸν ὑφεστώς. ὑπόστασίς ἐστιν *add. Mb* οὐσία μετὰ ἰδιωμάτων] ἰδιωμάτων συναγωγὴ *DOtt DPatm DVat* **15/18** κατὰ – ἰδιωμάτων] *om. Pf* **15/16** καθ᾽ἕκαστον ἄνθρωπον] ὁ καθ᾽ἕκαστον ἄνθρωπος *Mb*; καθ᾽ἕκαστον ἀνθρώπων *Ff* **17** ἀφοριζόμενον] ἀφοριζόμενος *Mb Pd Ff Pv Ay DOtt DPatm DVat* **19/21** διαφέρουσα – ὁμογενῶν] *om. DOtt* **20** τὸ καθ᾽αὐτὸ] τὸ καθ᾽αὐτὸ *Pd Ff*; τῷ καθ᾽ἑαυτῷ *DPatm*; τὸ καθ᾽ἑαυτὸ *DVat* διωρισμένος] διωρισμένη *Pd* **21** ὑφεστώς] ὑφεστός *Pf Ay DVat* **22** Ὑπόστασίς – δηλωτικὴ] *om. Pf Pv* ἢ] ἡ *Ay* **22/23** Ὅρος ὑποστάσεως ἁπλῶς λεγομένης] *om. Pd Ff Pv Ay* ἡ *Pf*, ἡ *Pv* **23** ἀτόμῳ] ἀτόμων *Pf Pd Ff Pv Ay* **26** Τὴν] ἡ οὐσία σύνθετ *(sic) praem. Ay*ᵗ· ᶜᵒʳʳ· προσδιωρισμένως] προσδιωρισμένην *Pd*, πρὸσδιόρισμένος *(sic) Pv* **27** λεγομένην] λεγομένης *Pd* **28** Ὅρος ὑποστάσεως συνθέτου] *om. Ay DOtt DPatm DVat* **29** Ὑπόστασις σύνθετός ἐστιν] ὑπόστασίς ἐστι σύνθετος *Pv* **30** τίς] *om. Ay* σύνθετος] αὔθετος *(sic) Pv* **31** καθ᾽ἕκαστα] καθέκαστον *(sic) Pd* περιληπτικὴ] παραληπτικὴ *Ay* τῶν ἐν τῷ οἰκείῳ ἀτόμῳ] τῶν ὄντων οἰκείῳ ἀτόμω *Pd Ay*; τῶν ὄντων οἰκείων ἀτόμων *Ff Pv* **32** ἰδιωμάτων] τῶν *praem. Pd Ay* τὰ] τὸ *Pf Pd Ff Ay DOtt DPatm DVat* **33** θεωρούμενα] θεωρούμενον *Ay DOtt DPatm*

DVat; θεωρούμεν (sic) Pd 34 χαρακτηρίζει] χαρακτηρίζειν DVat προηγουμένως]
ουμένως fenestrae causa Ay 35 αὐτήν] αὐτὸν Pd γενικόν. Πάντων δὲ γενικῶν,
πάντων δὲ Ff Πάντων] πᾶν DOtt DPatm DVat κοινόν] κοινῶν Pd Pv τῶν] τὸ
DPatm DVat 36 τὸ σύνθετον²] addidi coll. Max. Conf.; om. codd.

Bibliography

Primary Sources [75]

Alex. Aphr., In Arist. Topica – Alexander Aphrodisiensis, *In Aristotelis Topicorum libros octo commentaria*, ed. M. Wallies, Berolini, 1891 (Commentaria in Aristotelem Graeca, II, 2).

Ammon., In Arist. Cat. – Ammonius, *In Aristotelis Categorias commentarius*, ed. A. Busse, Berolini, 1895 (Commentaria in Aristotelem Graeca, IV, 4), p. 15–106.

Ammon., In Porph. Isag. – Ammonius, *Commentarium in Porphyrii Isagogen sive quinque voces*, ed. A. Busse, Berolini, 1891 (Commentaria in Aristotelem Graeca, IV, 3), p. 16–128.

Anast. Ant., Cap. philos. – Anastasius I Antiochenus, *Definitiones (Capita philosophica)* [CPG 6945], ed. Uthemann 1980; two other recensions of this text were edited by S. Lilla (1973), 'Un opusculo sulla teologia trinitaria in quattro codici Vaticani', in *Vetera Christianorum*, 10, p. 51–58.

Ps. Anast. Ant., Expl. fid. orth. – Ps. Anastasius I Antiochenus, *Explicatio fidei orthodoxa* [CPG 6969], ed. PG 89, col. 1400–1404.

Anast. Sin., Viae dux – Anastasius Sinaita, *Viae dux (Hodegos)* [CPG 7745], ed. K.-H. Uthemann, Turnhout – Leuven, 1981 (Corpus Christianorum. Series Graeca, 8).

Arist., Cat. – Aristoteles, *Categoriae*, ed. L. Minio-Paluello, Oxonii, 1949 (Scriptorum Classicorum Bibliotheca Oxoniensis), p. 3–45.

Arist., Met. – Aristoteles, *Metaphysica*, ed. W. Jaeger, Oxonii, 1957 (Scriptorum Classicorum Bibliotheca Oxoniensis).

Arist., Phys. – Aristoteles, *Physica*, ed. W. D. Ross, Oxonii, 1950 (Scriptorum Classicorum Bibliotheca Oxoniensis).

Asclep. Trall., In Arist. Metaphys. – Asclepius Trallianus, *In Aristotelis Metaphyicorum libros A-Z commentaria*, ed. M. Hayduck, Berolini, 1888 (Commentaria in Aristotelem Graeca, VI, 2).

---

[75] This list of primary sources contains the texts mentioned in the *Apparatus fontium et locorum parallelorum* of the editions.

Bas. Caes., Adv. Eun. – Basilius Caesariensis, *Adversus Eunomium libri I–III* [*CPG* 2837], ed. B. Sesboüé & G.-M. de Durand & L. Doutreleau, 2 vols, Paris, 1982–1983 (Sources Chrétiennes, 299 & 305).

Bas. Caes., Ep. – Basilius Caesariensis, *Epistulae* [*CPG* 2900], ed. Y. Courtonne, 3 vols, Paris, 1957 / 1961/1966.

Dexipp., In Arist. Cat. – Dexippus, *In Aristotelis Categorias commentarium*, ed. A. Busse, Berolini, 1888 (Commentaria in Aristotelem Graeca, IV, 2).

David, In Porph. Isag. – David, *In Porphyrii Isagogen commentarium*, ed. A. Busse, Berolini, 1904 (Commentaria in Aristotelem Graeca, XVIII, 2), p. 80–219.

DPatr – *Doctrina Patrum de incarnatione Verbi* [*CPG* 7781], ed. Diekamp, Phanourgakis & Chrysos 1981[2].

Elias, In Porph. Isag. – Elias, *In Porphyrii Isagogen commentarium*, ed. A. Busse, Berolini, 1900 (Commentaria in Aristotelem Graeca, XVIII, 1), p. 35–104.

Ps. Elias / David, In Porph. Isag. – Ps. Elias / David, *In Porphyrii Isagogen commentarium*, ed. L. G. Westerink, Amsterdam, 1967, p. 49–136.

Ps. Eulog. Alex., Defensiones – Ps. Eulogius Alexandrinus, *Defensiones* [*CPG* 6972], vide apud Ioh. Gramm., Apol.

Greg. Nyss., Ad Petrum fratrem – Gregorius Nyssenus, *Ad Petrum fratrem de differentia essentiae et hypostaseos* [*CPG* 3196], vide apud Bas. Caes., Ep. 38.

Heracl. Chalc., Ad Soterichum – Heraclianus Chalcedonensis, *Ad Soterichum* [*CPG* 6800], fragmenta in DPatr 6, XVIII; 21, VII; 29, XI–XII; 30, I, ed. Diekamp, Phanourgakis & Chrysos 1981[2], p. 42, l. 18 – p. 43, l. 15; p. 134, l. 11–14; p. 207, l. 19 – p. 208, l. 27; p. 216, l. 18 – p. 217, l. 15.

Ioh. Dam., Dial. – Iohannes Damascenus, *Dialectica* [*CPG* 8041], ed. Kotter 1969, p. 47–146.

Ioh. Gramm., Apol. – Iohannes Caesariensis grammaticus, *Apologia concilii Chalcedonensis*, fragmenta graeca [*CPG* 6855], ed. M. Richard, Turnhout – Leuven, 1977 (Corpus Christianorum. Series Graeca, 1), p. 49–58.

Ioh. Philop., In Arist. Anal. post. – Iohannes Philoponus, *In Aristotelis Analytica posteriora commentaria*, ed. M. Wallies, Berolini, 1909 (Commentaria in Aristotelem Graeca, XIII, 3), p. 1–440.

Ioh. Philop., In Arist. Cat. – Iohannes Philoponus, *In Aristotelis Cate-*

gorias commentarium, ed. A. Busse, Berolini, 1898 (Commentaria in Aristotelem Graeca, XIII, 1).

Ioh. Philop., In Arist. Phys. – Iohannes Philoponus, *In Aristotelis Physicorum libros commentaria*, ed. H. Vitelli, Berolini, 1887–1888 (Commentaria in Aristotelem Graeca, XVI–XVII).

Ioh. Scyth., Scholia – Iohannes Scythopolitanus, *Scholia in corpus Areopagiticum* [*CPG* 6852], ed. *PG* 4, col. 15–423, col. 527–576.

Iust. imp., Contra monophys. – Iustinianus imperator, *Contra monophysitas* [*CPG* 6885], ed. E. Schwartz (1939), *Drei dogmatische Schriften Justinians*, München (repr. Milano, 1973²) (Abhandlungen der Bayerischen Akademie der Wissenschaften, Philosophisch-historische Klasse, N.F. 18), p. 7–43.

Leont. Byz., C. Nest. et Eutych. – Leontius Byzantinus, *Libri tres contra Nestorianos et Eutychianos* [*CPG* 6813], ed. *PG* 86, col. 1268–1396.

Leont. Byz., Epil. – Leontius Byzantinus, *Epilysis* vel *Solutio argumentorum Severi* [*CPG* 6815], ed. *PG* 86, col. 1916–1945.

Leont. Hierosol., Contra Monophys. – Leontius Hierosolymitanus, *Contra Monophysitas* [*CPG* 6917], ed. *PG* 86, col. 1769–1901.

Leont. Hierosol., C. Nest. – Leontius Hierosolymitanus, *Contra Nestorianos* [*CPG* 6918], ed. *PG* 86, col. 1400–1768.

Leont. Schol., De sectis – Leontius Scholasticus, *Liber de sectis* [*CPG* 6823], ed. *PG* 86, col. 1193–1268.

Max. Conf., Ep. – Maximus Confessor, *Epistulae* [*CPG* 7699], ed. *PG* 91, col. 364–649.

Max. Conf. in (Max. Conf.), D. B. – Maximus Confessor prout loquitur in (Ps.?) Maximi Confessoris *Disputatione Bizyae* vel *Actis in primo exsilio seu dialogo Maximi cum Theodosio episcopo Caesareae in Bithynia* [*CPG* 7735], ed. Allen – Neil 1999, p. 73–151.

Ps. Max. Conf., Op. 23c – Ps. Maximus Confessor, *De substantia seu essentia et natura et hypostasi* [*CPG* 7697.23c], ed. Roosen 2001, p. 719 and *PG* 91, col. 265–268.

Olymp. phil., In Arist. Cat. – Olympiodorus philosophus, *In Aristotelis Categorias commentarium*, ed. A. Busse, Berolini, 1902 (Commentaria in Aristotelem Graeca, XII, 1), p. 26–148.

Oxon. – Fragmenta philosophica e cod. *Oxoniensi, Bibliothecae Bodleianae, Auctarii T.1.6 [Miscellaneo 184]* (s. XII), fol. 1–32ᵛ [*CPG* 8042], ed. Kotter 1969, p. 151–173.

Pamph., Qu. – Pamphilus theologus, *Capitulorum diversorum seu dubitationum solutio* [*CPG* 6920], ed. J. H. Declerck in J. H.

Declerck & P. Allen (1989), *Diversorum postchalcedonensium auctorum collectanea* I, Turnhout – Leuven (Corpus Christianorum. Series Graeca, 19), p. 127–261.

Ps. Plut., Plac. Phil. – Ps. Plutarchus, *De placentibus philosophis*, ed. G. Lachenaud (1993), *Plutarque. Œuvres morales*, XII². *Opinions des philosophes*, Paris.

Porph., Isag. – Porphyrius, *Isagoge sive quinque voces*, ed. A. Busse, Berolini, 1887 (Commentaria in Aristotelem Graeca, IV, 1), p. 1–22.

Theodor. Raith., Praep. – Theodorus Raithenus (Pharanita), *Praeparatio* [*CPG* 7600], ed. Diekamp 1938, p. 173–227.

Secondary Literature

P. Allen & B. Neil (1999), *Scripta saeculi VII vitam Maximi Confessoris illustrantia una cum latina interpretatione Anastasii Bibliothecarii iuxta posita*, Turnhout – Leuven (Corpus Christianorum. Series Graeca, 39).

Ch. Astruc et al. (1989), *Les manuscrits grecs datés des XIIIᵉ et XIVᵉ siècles conservés dans les bibliothèques publiques de France*, I. *XIIIᵉ siècle*, Paris.

M. Aubineau (1968), *Codices Chrysostomici Graeci*, I. *Codices Britanniae et Hiberniae*, Paris (Documents, Études et Répertoires publiés par l'Institut de Recherche et d'Histoire des Textes, XIII).

A. M. Bandini (1764–1770), *Catalogus codicum manuscriptorum Bibliothecae Mediceae Laurentianae, varia continens opera graecorum patrum*, 3 vols, Florentiae.

G. Bausenhart (1992), *'In allem uns gleich außer der Sünde'. Studien zum Beitrag Maximos' des Bekenners zur altkirchlichen Christologie mit einer kommentierten Übersetzung der 'Disputatio cum Pyrrho'*, Mainz (Tübinger Studien zur Theologie und Philosophie, 5).

V. Beneševič (1972²), *Синагога въ 50 титуловъ и другіе юридическіе сборники Іоанна Схоластика*, Leipzig (Subsidia Byzantina, I).

M. V. Bibikov (1996), *Византийский Прототип Древнейшей Славянской Книги (Изборник Святослава 1073г.)*, Moscow.

L. Burgmann & Sp. Troianos (1979), 'Appendix Eclogae', in D. Simon (ed.), *Fontes Minores*, III, Frankfurt am Main (Forschungen zur byzantinischen Rechtsgeschichte, 4), p. 24–125.

L. Burgmann et al. (1995), *Repertorium der Handschriften des byzantinischen Rechts*, I. *Die Handschriften des weltlichen Rechts (Nr. 1–327)*, Frankfurt am Main (Forschungen zur byzantinischen Rechtsgeschichte, 20).

A. Cataldi Palau (1996), *Catalogo dei manoscritti greci della Biblioteca Franzoniana (Genova), (Urbani 21–40)*, Roma (Bollettino dei classici. Supplemento, 17).

F. Combefis (1675), *S. Maximi Confessoris, Graecorum Theologi eximiique Philosophi, Operum Tomus primus (secundus). Ex probatissimis quaeque mss. Codicibus, Regiis, Card. Mazarini, Seguierianis, Vaticanis, Barberinis, Magni Ducis Florentinis, Venetis, etc., eruta, nova Versione subacta, Notisque illustrata*, Parisiis.

H. O. Coxe (1853), *Catalogi codicum manuscriptorum Bibliothecae Bodleianae*, t. I, *recensionem Codicum Graecorum continens*, Oxford.

J. H. Declerck (2002), *Eustathii Antiocheni, patris Nicaeni, Opera quae supersunt omnia*, Turnhout – Leuven (Corpus Christianorum. Series Graeca, 51).

B. de Montfaucon (1715), *Bibliotheca Coisliniana, olim Segueriana; sive manuscriptorum omnium Graecorum, quae in ea continentur, accurata descriptio, ubi operum singulorum notitia datur, aetas cuiusque Manuscripti indicatur, vetustiorum specimina exhibentur, aliaque multa annotantur, quae ad Palaeographiam Graecam pertinent*, Parisiis.

F. Diekamp (1938), *Analecta patristica. Texte und Abhandlungen zur griechischen Patristik*, Roma (Orientalia Christiana Analecta, 117).

F. Diekamp, B. Phanourgakis & E. Chrysos (1981[2]), *Doctrina Patrum de incarnatione Verbi. Ein griechisches Florilegium aus der Wende des 7. und 8. Jahrhunderts*, Münster.

S. L. Epifanovič (1917), *Матеріалы къ изученію жизни и твореній преп. Максима Исповѣдника*, Kiev.

F. Euangelatou-Notara (1982), «*Σημειώματα*» *ἑλληνικῶν κωδίκων ὡς πηγὴ διὰ τὴν ἔρευναν τοῦ οἰκονομικοῦ καὶ κοινωνικοῦ βίου τοῦ Βυζαντίου ἀπὸ τοῦ 9ου αἰῶνος μέχρι τοῦ ἔτους 1204*, Athens (Ἐθνικὸν καὶ Καποδιστριακὸν Πανεπιστήμιον Ἀθηνῶν, Φιλοσοφικὴ Σχολή. Βιβλιοθήκη Σοφίας Ν. Σαριπόλου, 47).

P. J. Fedwick (1993–2000), *Bibliotheca Basiliana Universalis. A Study of the Manuscript Tradition of the Works of Basil of Caesarea*, Turnhout (Corpus Christianorum).

E. Gamillscheg, D. Harlfinger & H. Hunger (1981–1989), *Repertorium der griechischen Kopisten 800–1600*, 2 vols, Wien (Österreichische Akademie der Wissenschaften. Veröffentlichungen der Kommission für Byzantinistik, III, 1–2).

D. Gourevitch & A. Roselli (2006), 'Mynoïde Mynas, un "drôle de pistolet": érudition, escroquerie et histoire politique autour de l'indépendance de la Grèce, à propos de la "Gymnastique" de

Philostrate', in *Ecdotica e ricezioni dei testi medici greci. Atti del V Convegno Internazionale, Napoli 1–2 ottobre 2004*, Napoli (Collectanea, 24).

I. Hardt (1806–1812), *Catalogus codicum manuscriptorum Bibliothecae Regiae Bavaricae*, Monachii.

O. Hartig (1917), *Die Gründung der münchener Hofbibliothek durch Albrecht V und Johann Jakob Fugger*, München (Abhandlungen der königlichen Bayerischen Akademie der Wissenschaften. Philosophische-philologische und historische Klasse, 28, 3).

S. Helmer (1962), 'Der Neuchalkedonismus. Geschichte, Berechtigung und Bedeutung eines dogmengeschichtlichen Begriffes' (Inaugural-dissertation), Bonn.

R. Henry (1967), *Photius. Bibliothèque*, Tome V. «Codices» 230–241, Paris (Collection Byzantine).

Ph. Hoffmann (1985–1986), 'Une lettre de Drosos d'Aradeo sur la Fraction du Pain (Athous Iviron 190, a.D. 1297/1298)', in *Rivista di Studi Bizantini e Neoellenici*, n.s. 22–23, p. 245–284.

Ph. Hoffmann (1987), 'Un recueil de fragments provenant de Minoïde Mynas: le Parisinus suppl. gr. 681', in *Scriptorium*, 41, p. 115–127.

V. Karayiannis (1993), *Maxime le Confesseur. Essence et énergies de Dieu*, Paris (Théologie Historique, 93).

J. Konidaris (1982), 'Die Epitome einer justinianischen Novelle aus dem Patmiacus 205', in D. Simon (ed.), *Fontes Minores*, V, Frankfurt am Main (Forschungen zur byzantinischen Rechtsgeschichte, 8), p. 27–31.

B. Kotter (1959), *Die Überlieferung der Pege Gnoseos des Hl. Johannes von Damaskos*, Ettal (Studia Patristica et Byzantina, 5).

B. Kotter (1969), *Die Schriften des Johannes von Damaskos*, I. *Institutio elementaris. Capita philosophica (Dialectica). Als Anhang die philosophischen Stücke aus cod. Oxon. Bodl. Auc. T.1.6*, Berlin (Patristische Texte und Studien, 7).

W. Lackner (1962), 'Studien zur philosophischen Schultradition und zu den Nemesioszitaten bei Maximos dem Bekenner' (Inaugural-dissertation), Graz.

S. P. Lampros (1895–1900), *Κατάλογος τῶν ἐν ταῖς βιβλιοθήκαις τοῦ Ἁγίου Ὄρους ἑλληνικῶν κωδίκων*, 2 vols, Cambridge.

K. Levrie (2017), *(Pseudo-)Maximus Confessor, Capita de duabus Christi naturis necnon Capita gnostica*, Turnhout – Leuven (Corpus Christianorum. Series Graeca, 89).

S. Lilla (1985), *Codices Vaticani graeci. Codices 2162–2254 (Codices*

Columnenses), In Bibliotheca Vaticana (Bibliotecae Apostolicae Vaticanae Codices manu scripti recensiti).

F. Madan & H. H. E. Craster (1922), *A Summary Catalogue of Western Manuscripts in the Bodleian Library at Oxford which have not hitherto been catalogued in the Quarto Series, with References to the Oriental and other Manuscripts*, II, 1. *(Collections received before 1660 and miscellaneous MSS, acquired during the first half of the 17ᵗʰ Century) Nos. 1–3490*, Oxford.

B. Markesinis (2000), 'Janos Laskaris, la bibliothèque d'Avramis à Corfou et le Paris. gr. 854', in *Scriptorium*, 54, p. 302–306 (with pl. 54).

J. A. Munitiz (1974), 'Synoptic Greek Accounts of the Seventh Council', in *Revue des Études Byzantines*, 32, p. 147–186.

H. Ohme (2016), 'Maximos Homologetes († 662) : Martyrium, Märtyrerbewusstsein, „Martyriumssucht"?', in *Zeitschrift für Antikes Christentum*, 20, p. 306-346.

H. Omont (1886–1888), *Inventaire sommaire des manuscrits grecs de la Bibliothèque nationale et des autres bibliothèques de Paris et des départements*, 3 vols, Paris.

P. Piret (1983), *Le Christ et la Trinité selon Maxime le Confesseur*, Paris (Théologie Historique, 69).

J. B. Pitra (1852), *Spicilegium Solesmense complectens Sanctorum Patrum Scriptorumque ecclesiasticorum anecdota hactenus opera*, I, Parisiis.

G. L. Prestige (1952), *God in Patristic Thought*, London.

R. Riedinger (1984), *Acta Conciliorum Oecumenicorum*, Series II, Volumen 1. *Concilium Lateranense a. 649 celebratum*, Berlin.

B. Roosen (2001), 'Epifanovitch Revisited. (Pseudo-)Maximi Confessoris Opuscula varia: a critical edition with extensive notes on manuscript tradition and authenticity' (unpublished doctoral thesis, KULeuven).

B. Roosen (2001a), 'On the Recent Edition of the Disputatio Bizyae. With an Analysis of Chapter XXIV De providentia of the Florilegium Achridense and an Index manuscriptorum in Appendix', in *Jahrbuch der Österreichischen Byzantinistik*, 51, p. 113–131.

B. Roosen (2014), 'Precepts for a Tranquil Life. A new edition of the Ad neophytos de patientia [CPG 7707.32]', in *Jahrbuch der Österreichischen Byzantinistik*, 64, p. 247–283.

B. Roosen (2015), 'Eulogii Alexandrini quae supersunt. Old and new fragments from Eulogius of Alexandria's oeuvre (CPG 6971–6979)', in *Medioevo Greco*, 15, p. 201–240.

B. Roosen & P. Van Deun (2006), 'Les collections de définitions philosophico-théologiques appartenant à la tradition de Maxime le Confesseur: le recueil centré sur ὁμώνυμον, συνώνυμον, παρώνυμον, ἑτερώνυμον...', in M. Cacouros & M.-H. Congourdeau (ed.), *Philosophie et Sciences à Byzance de 1204 à 1453*, Leuven – Paris – Dudley, MA (Orientalia Lovaniensia Analecta, 146), p. 53–76.

I. Sakkelion (1890), *Πατμιακὴ βιβλιοθήκη ἤτοι ἀναγραφὴ τῶν ἐν τῇ βιβλιοθήκῃ τῆς κατὰ τὴν νῆσον Πάτμον γεραρᾶς καὶ βασιλικῆς μονῆς τοῦ Ἁγίου Ἀποστόλου καὶ Εὐαγγελιστοῦ Ἰωάννου τοῦ Θεολόγου τεθησαυρισμένων χειρογράφων τευχῶν*, Athens.

M. Simonetti (1987), 'Un falso Ippolito nella polemica monotelita', in *Vigiliae Christianae*, 24, p. 113–146.

A. Sotiroudis (1989), *Die handschriftliche Überlieferung des «Georgius Continuatus» (Redaktion A)*, Thessaloniki (Ἀριστοτέλειο Πανεπιστήμιο Θεσσαλονίκης. Ἐπιστημονικὴ Ἐπετηρίδα τῆς Φιλοσοφικῆς Σχολῆς. Παράρτημα, 68).

O. Stählin (1909), *Clemens Alexandrinus*, III. *Stromata Buch VII und VIII. Excerpta ex Theodoto – Eclogae propheticae – Quis dives salvetur – Fragmente*, Leipzig (Die Griechischen Christlichen Schrifsteller der ersten [drei] Jahrhunderte, 17).

O. Stählin, L. Früchtel & U. Treu (1970²), *Clemens Alexandrinus*, III. *Stromata Buch VII und VIII. Excerpta ex Theodoto – Eclogae propheticae – Quis dives salvetur – Fragmente*, Leipzig (Die Griechischen Christlichen Schrifsteller der ersten [drei] Jahrhunderte, 17).

F. J. Thomson (1994), 'L'évolution de la manière de traduire chez les slaves au Moyen Âge. Comparaison et édition de deux traductions slavonnes (Xᵉ-XIVᵉ siècles) de passages d'Irénée et d'un pseudo-Augustin', in *Revue d'Histoire des Textes*, 24, p. 313–336.

L. Thunberg (1995²), *Microcosm and Mediator. The Theological Anthropology of Maximus the Confessor*, Chicago – La Salle, Illinois.

K.-H. Uthemann (1980), 'Die "Philosophischen Kapitel" des Anastasius I. von Antiochien (559–598)', in *Orientalia Lovaniensia Periodica*, 46, p. 306–366. Reprinted with additions in id. (2017), *Studien zu Anastasios Sinaites mit einem Anhang zu Anastasios I. von Antiochien*, Berlin – Boston, p. 384–436 + 530–538 (Texte und Untersuchungen zur Geschichte der altchristlichen Literatur, 174).

K.-H. Uthemann (1981), *Anastasii Sinaitae Viae dux*, Turnhout – Leuven (Corpus Christianorum. Series Graeca, 8).

K.-H. Uthemann (1993), '"Die Ἄπορα des Gregorius von Nyssa"? Ein Beitrag zur Geistmetaphysik in Byzanz mit einer Edition von CPG 1781', in *Byzantion*, 63, p. 237–327. Reprinted with additions in id. (2017), *Studien zu Anastasios Sinaites mit einem Anhang zu Anastasios I. von Antiochien*, Berlin – Boston, p. 207–275 + 518–520 (Texte und Untersuchungen zur Geschichte der altchristlichen Literatur, 174).

N. Van der Wal & B. H. Stolte (1994), *Collectio tripartita. Justinian on Religious and Ecclesiastical Affairs*, Groningen.

P. Van Deun (1991), *Maximi Confessoris Opuscula exegetica duo*, Turnhout – Leuven (Corpus Christianorum. Series Graeca, 23).

C. Van De Vorst & H. Delehaye (1913), *Catalogus Codicum Hagiographicorum Graecorum Germaniae Belgii Angliae*, Bruxelles (Subsidia hagiographica, 13).

J.-L. Van Dieten (1970), *Zur Überlieferung und Veröffentlichung der Panoplia dogmatike des Niketas Choniates*, Amsterdam (Zetemata Byzantina, 3).

M. Vogel & V. Gardthausen (1909), *Die griechischen Schreiber des Mittelalters und der Renaissance*, Leipzig (repr. Hildesheim, 1966) (Zentralblatt für Bibliothekswesen, Beiheft 33).

L. G. Westerink (1948), *Michael Psellus De Omnifaria doctrina. Critical Text and Introduction*, Nijmegen.

F. Winkelmann et al. (2001), *Prosopographie der mittelbyzantinischen Zeit*, Erster Abteilung (641–867), 4. Band, Platon [# 6266] – Theophylaktos [# 8345], Berlin – New York.

Abstract

The contribution presents the critical edition of *CPG* 7707.38 and *CPG* 7697.26a + 7707.20. This is what remains of a collection of ἐρωταποκρίσεις of which Maximus the Confessor and Theodosius of Gangra were the protagonists. The edition of these fragments is preceded by a study of their manuscript tradition and the attribution to Maximus the Confessor.

PART 3
COSMOLOGIES
IN SIXTH-CENTURY BYZANTIUM

PASCAL MUELLER-JOURDAN

LES CONDITIONS DE L'AVÈNEMENT DE LA LUMIÈRE DANS LE *DE OPIFICIO MUNDI* DE JEAN PHILOPON. DIFFICULTÉS ET SOLUTIONS

La présente contribution entend interroger les conditions d'avènement et le statut de la lumière primitive dans le *De opificio mundi* de Jean Philopon. Ce choix en délimite naturellement le cadre. Nous proposons ici un travail exploratoire qui n'a d'autres prétentions que de trier et de sérier les principales difficultés qui ressortent de cette question. S'il y parvient, il aura atteint son but. Le sujet est délicat, car la question de la lumière soulève d'inextricables difficultés philosophiques à commencer par l'examen de son statut ontologique, en particulier le problème de sa corporéité ou, au contraire, de son incorporéité. Ce fut là un point de désaccord entre Platon, pour qui la lumière est une sorte de feu, et Aristote, pour qui la lumière est incorporelle[1]. Ce désaccord fut source d'embarras pour les commentateurs tardo-antiques, et de Platon et d'Aristote, soucieux de faire ressortir l'accord foncier de leurs doctrines. Mais il faut compter avec une difficulté supplémentaire qui provient, pour l'essentiel, du texte biblique qui affirme la création de la lumière avant même que ne soient produits, et le firmament, et les corps qui, en lui, constitueront le substrat nécessaire à la lumière, à savoir les luminaires. Enfin une dernière difficulté, et non des moindres, car il s'agit d'une difficulté de méthode : Nous prétendons, en effet, déterminer une certaine théorie de la lumière dans un commentaire biblique qui n'a pas pour visée spécifique de nous fournir, de façon construite, les données que nous cherchons à récolter. En raison de l'absence

---

[1] Cf. Sorabji (2005), p. 274–289.

Questioning the World, Greek Patristic and Byzantine Question-and-Answer Literature, ed. by Bram Demulder and Peter Van Deun, Turnhout, 2021 (*LECTIO*, 11), pp. 271-309   © BREPOLS✠PUBLISHERS   DOI 10.1484/M.LECTIO-EB.5.121509

de systématicité dans l'exposé de la question de la lumière, nous ne pouvons échapper au risque d'un travail de reconstruction qui n'aura sans doute pas su éviter de valoriser exagérément tel ou tel point mineur, et de minorer, voire d'omettre, tel ou tel aspect pourtant indispensable[2].

Pour saisir la question de la lumière au cœur même du *De opificio mundi*, dans ce qui s'impose comme une exégèse philosophique de la cosmogonie mosaïque, il conviendra donc de clarifier le contexte de son apparition. Pour ce faire, nous nous arrêterons aux raisons qui ont poussé Philopon à commenter le récit de la Genèse. Nous y découvrirons les présupposés teintés de concordisme qui président à l'exégèse opérée. Nous décrirons d'abord la nature et le contenu de la première geste divine qui fait advenir successivement : ciel/terre, lumière puis firmament[3], et ce avant la création des luminaires, dans l'ordre d'importance : soleil, lune, étoile de l'aurore puis astres en général. Nous nous focaliserons sur la nature de cette lumière primitive, antérieure aux luminaires donc, et aux multiples problèmes qu'elle soulève.

1. *Le* De opificio mundi : *Contexte et visée générale*

La biographie et la bibliographie de Philopon, sur lesquelles nous ne nous attarderons que très peu, s'éclairent mutuellement. Elles ont fait ces dernières années l'objet de nombreuses recherches[4]. On s'accorde en général à reconnaître plusieurs pé-

---

[2] Un certain nombre de points de la présente contribution ont été discutés dans le cadre d'un séminaire de recherche que nous conduisons avec Bertrand Ham, Maître de Conférences à l'Université catholique de l'Ouest à Angers, et ce depuis plusieurs années. Les discussions que nous y avons eues ont largement contribué à réduire les insuffisances dont pourrait encore témoigner ce travail. Celles qui restent nous reviennent. Nous voudrions spécialement remercier Bertrand Ham pour sa compétence de philologue et d'historien généreusement mise à notre disposition mais aussi les étudiants qui nous ont fait l'honneur de suivre nos travaux cette année : Sr Claire Cachia osb, Anne Greffard, Romain Cohergne et Antoine Leclercq.

[3] Cf. Philopon, *De opificio mundi* [*De opif.*] 161.19–21.

[4] Depuis les travaux de Verrycken 1990, les recherches chronologiques sur le développement de la pensée de Philopon ont considérablement progressé. L'article de Wildberg 2018 du *Stanford Encyclopedia of Philosophy* fait un bon état des lieux de ces questions. Il va cependant de soi que cet article n'a pas prétention à embrasser toutes les difficultés qui proviennent de la carrière de Philopon, mais

riodes dans la vie de Philopon au regard de la datation de ses productions qui manifestent des préoccupations qui évoluent lentement.

En une simple esquisse ici, nous pouvons dire qu'il avait, dans une première phase de sa carrière, assuré l'édition de certains séminaires d'Ammonius d'Hermeias, maître de l'Ecole platonicienne d'Alexandrie, en y ajoutant, comme les titres l'attestent, certaines observations personnelles[5]. Il avait également proposé quelques commentaires de son propre cru. Dans une seconde période de son activité, il devait longuement réfuter l'idée même d'éternité du monde qui s'enracinait autant dans l'exégèse, tenue pour orthodoxe, du *Timée* de Platon, celle de Proclus en particulier, que dans la théorie de la *quinta essentia* d'Aristote à qui il reproche d'avoir introduit dans la pensée grecque la conception de l'éternité du monde[6]. Il s'était risqué sur le tard à la théologie

il constitue un premier guide sûr pour s'engager en particulier dans les recherches qui ont trait à la physique, et notamment à la lumière. Pour une recherche documentaire fouillée, voir : Giardina 2012.

[5] (1) De Jean grammairien d'Alexandrie, *Notes scolaires sur le premier livre des 'Premiers Analytiques' à partir des séminaires d'Ammonius d'Hermeias* (CAG 13.2) ; (2) Jean d'Alexandrie, *Notes scolaires à partir des séminaires d'Ammonius d'Hermeias, avec quelques observations personnelles, sur le premier livre des 'Analytiques Postérieurs' d'Aristote* (CAG 13.3) ; (3) De Jean grammairien d'Alexandrie, *Notes scolaires à partir des séminaires d'Ammonius d'Hermeias, avec quelques observations personnelles, sur le premier des livres 'De la génération et de la corruption' d'Aristote* (CAG 14.2) ; (4) De Jean d'Alexandrie, *Sur le traité 'De l'âme' d'Aristote, notes scolaires à partir des séminaires d'Ammonius d'Hermeias, avec quelques observations personnelles* (CAG 15). Au stade de nos propres recherches qui doivent encore faire l'objet d'importants approfondissements, nous ne parvenons pas à la conviction définitive de savoir si ces notes résultent d'une commande officielle de l'école ou si elles sont de l'initiative de Philopon.

[6] Comme il le rappelle dans *De opif.* (82.3–12) : Ἀρχὴν οὖν τοῦ εἶναι τοῦ κόσμου λαβόντος μόνος γέγονε Μωϋσῆς ἀξιόχρεως ὑποφήτης θεοῦ, τὸν κόσμον ὡς γέγονε τὴν ἀρχὴν σαφῶς διηγήσασθαι καὶ ἕτερος μετ' αὐτὸν οὐδείς. [...] Ἀριστοτέλης δὲ καινὴν ἐξεῦρεν ὁδόν, πρῶτος τῶν φυσικῶν ἄναρχον εἶναι τὸν κόσμον καὶ ἀγένητον ὑποθέμενος. ('Sur le commencement de l'univers, seul Moïse a été un interprète conséquent de Dieu ; il a expliqué clairement comment fut créé l'univers au commencement, et nul autre après lui ne l'a fait [...]. Mais Aristote a ouvert une *voie nouvelle*, en émettant, *le premier des physiciens*, l'hypothèse que le monde était sans commencement et inengendré.') On peut noter également que pour Philopon, Platon n'a pas soutenu la thèse de l'éternité, ou du caractère inengendré du monde contrairement à ce que Proclus, contre le médioplatonicien Atticus, devait admettre. Philopon affirme (*De opif.* 80.10–12) : πάντων τῶν πάλαι φυσικῶν φιλοσόφων μέχρις αὐτοῦ Πλάτωνος ἀρχὴν τοῦ εἶναι τῷ κόσμῳ δεδωκότων ('tous les philosophes naturalistes jusqu'à Platon lui-même, ont donné au monde un

stricto sensu. Ses productions sur la Trinité et sur la Résurrection (i. e. sur les corps ressuscités) contribuèrent à l'inscrire durablement sur la longue liste de ceux qui sont identifiés pour avoir tenu des opinions erronées en matière de théologie dogmatique[7]. Mais le *De opificio mundi*, qui se situe à la charnière de la deuxième et de la troisième période des productions philoponiennes, et que les travaux d'érudition récents[8] datent des années qui ont précédé le deuxième Concile de Constantinople (553), n'a sans doute pas reçu toute l'attention qu'il méritait dans le domaine des recherches sur la cosmologie byzantine.

Le préambule du *De opificio mundi* informe sur l'une des raisons principales du travail entrepris. Philopon affirme en effet :

Πολὺς μὲν ἐμοὶ περὶ τῆς τοῦ κόσμου γενέσεως ἐν πολλαῖς πραγματείαις διήνυσται λόγος, τούς τε ποικίλους τῶν συλλογισμῶν καὶ δυσδιεξόδους ἀνελίσσοντι λαβυρίνθους, δι᾽ ὧν οἱ ἐκ τῆς σεμνῆς φιλοσοφίας μὴ γεγονέναι τουτονὶ τὸν κόσμον δεικνύειν ἔδοξαν, ὡς κινδυνεύειν ἐντεῦθεν μηδ᾽ ὅλως αὐτοῦ δημιουργὸν εἶναι πιστεύειν θεόν, εἰ μὴ τοῦτον οὐκ ὄντα παρήγαγε· δέδειχα δὲ καὶ ὡς ἀρχὴν ἔχει τοῦ εἶναι, πλείοσιν ἐπιβολαῖς τοῦτο συλλογισάμενος. πολλοὶ δὲ διὰ ταῦτα συνεχῶς ἡμῖν ἠνώχλουν ἠρέμα πως καὶ ὑπωνείδιζον, ὡς τῶν ἐξωτερικῶν μὲν λόγων πρὸς ἔλεγχον διηγώνισταί μοι τάχα που καὶ πέρα δυνάμεως, τῶν δὲ τοῦ μεγάλου Μωϋσέως περὶ τῆς τοῦ κόσμου παραγωγῆς θεόθεν ἡκόντων ἀμελήσαιμι ῥημάτων, περιελκομένων οὐκ ἀνεκτῶς ὑπὸ τῶν ἐπεσκέφθαι τοῦ παντὸς φρυαττομένων τὴν διακόσμησιν, ὡς οὐ τοῖς φαινομένοις Μωϋσῆς πεφυσιολόγηκε σύμφωνα. (*De opif.* 1.6–2.4)

J'ai déjà mené une longue étude sur l'origine du monde dans plusieurs textes ; j'y ai parcouru les labyrinthes variés et inextricables des syllogismes par lesquels les tenants de la philosophie savante crurent démontrer que ce monde n'est

commencement dans l'être', ou pour être plus littéral, ont donné au monde un principe d'être). Philopon joue contre Proclus sur la polysémie d'*ἀρχή* (principe, commencement *temporel*, origine, etc.) car Proclus ne récuse pas au monde le fait d'avoir un principe d'être, autrement dit, il ne lui récuse pas le fait d'être issu du principe de toute réalité, l'*un* ; mais il s'agit là d'un tout autre présupposé métaphysique avec lequel Philopon a rompu si tant est qu'il y ait une seule fois réellement adhéré. On peut par ailleurs signaler que Philopon fait de Platon un héritier de Moïse qu'il aurait imité en de nombreux points (*De opif.* 4.17–15.16).

[7] Cf. Jean Damascène, *De Haeresibus* 83 (éd. Kotter 1984). Voir également : Hainthaler 1996 ; Lang 2001.

[8] Cf. Schamp 2000.

pas engendré ; à tel point qu'ils risquent d'en déduire que Dieu n'en est absolutément pas le démiurge, s'il n'a pas mené à l'être ce qui n'existait pas[9]. Mais j'ai démontré aussi que ce monde a commencé à être, en multipliant pour cela les argumentations. Mais beaucoup de gens, à cause de cela, ont commencé peu à peu à me troubler et à me faire des reproches : j'aurais prétendument combattu, presque jusqu'au-delà de mes forces, pour réfuter les discours étrangers à notre foi, mais que j'aurais négligé les paroles inspirées du grand Moïse sur la production du monde, paroles qui, chez ceux qui s'enorgueillissent d'avoir examiné l'ordonnance de l'univers, ont été abusivement détournées, au point de nous laisser croire que Moïse n'a pas donné une explication de la nature qui soit conforme aux phénomènes[10].

Le préambule rappelle brièvement le motif du *De opificio mundi*. A ses dires, il lui fut reproché de s'être, par le passé, longuement attardé à discuter la question de l'origine du monde contre la thèse notamment de l'éternité prétendue de celui-ci, et ce en négligeant les propos de Moïse sur la production du monde, en laissant le champ libre à ceux qui, dit-il, les auraient abusivement détournés. La suite du *De opificio mundi* atteste clairement que Philopon désigne, sans le nommer ici, Théodore d'Antioche, évêque de Mopsueste qui se trouve être la principale autorité exégétique à y être réfutée en raison notamment des attaques que Théodore avait menées contre *l'Hexaéméron* de Basile de Césarée dans la tradition duquel Philopon prétendait s'inscrire (cf. *De opif.* 2.16–25). Outre Théodore, il faut compter avec ceux qui, au siècle de Philopon, se positionnaient dans la tradition du théologien antiochien, et dont Cosmas Indicopleustès, auteur d'un véritable traité de cosmographie biblique raisonnée, était alors l'un des principaux représentants. Cette école d'exégèse littérale du récit biblique refusait systématiquement les recherches physiques et

[9] Il ne saurait s'agir de la tradition platonicienne et donc de Proclus car, à la différence de la tradition péripatéticienne, les platoniciens de l'Antiquité tardive ne font pas abstraction d'une cause agente démiurgique dans leurs conceptions cosmologiques. Cf. les dix-huit arguments de Proclus pourtant réfutés par Philopon dans le *Contra Proclum*.

[10] De façon générale, nous suivrons les traductions de Rosset & Congourdeau 2004 en y apportant des précisions et corrections en particulier pour ce qui concerne le vocabulaire philosophique. Sur cette traduction, voir : Laramée 2008.

astronomiques grecques qui ne corroboraient pas les descriptions cosmographiques de la Bible pour laquelle, croyait-on alors, la terre est plate, en forme d'édifice oblong, et est surmontée d'une voûte arrondie et allongée : le ciel[11]. On découvre à la lecture du propos de Philopon que ceux qui s'enorgueillissent d'avoir commenté Moïse, Théodore et selon toute vraisemblance Cosmas, qu'il ne nomme jamais bien qu'il le connaisse, en avaient détourné les propos au profit d'une cosmologie qui ne s'appuie pas sur le caractère contraignant des faits ou phénomènes physiques. Le reproche que Philopon leur adresse porte clairement sur l'absurdité de leurs théories cosmologiques en ce que, par leur manque de rigueur scientifique, ils vont jusqu'à exposer inutilement le dogme chrétien aux critiques et au mépris[12].

C'est dans le souci de réhabiliter l'autorité du texte mosaïque sur toutes les explications scientifiques de la génération et de l'organisation du monde que Philopon s'engage dans un commentaire qui a pour but principal :

> αὐτὸ γὰρ δὴ τοῦτο δεῖξαι πρὸς δύναμιν [...], ὡς οὐδὲν ἐν τῇ τοῦ προφήτου κοσμογονίᾳ τῇ διατάξει τοῦ παντός ἐστιν ἀσύμφωνον, τοὐναντίον δὲ πολλὰ τῶν ὕστερον αἰτιολογηθέντων ὑπὸ τῶν φυσικῶν ἐκ τῶν Μωϋσεῖ γραφέντων εἴληφε τὴν ἀρχήν. (*De opif.* 6.19–24)
>
> [...] de montrer, autant que possible, que rien dans la cosmogonie du prophète n'est en désaccord avec l'organisation de l'univers, mais qu'au contraire, les explications causales données ultérieurement par les physiciens trouvent en de nombreux points, leur origine dans les écrits de Moïse.

Il ressort d'ailleurs de façon continue du commentaire de Philopon le souci de montrer que non seulement les propos de Moïse sont en accord constant avec l'agencement ordonné des réalités, mais aussi que c'est à lui que physiciens, astronomes et philosophes ont emprunté ce qu'ils ont, d'une certaine manière à sa suite, porté à la connaissance de tous[13].

---

[11] Cf. Cosmas Indicopleustès, *Top. chrét.* II.17.1–18.8.

[12] Cf. Philopon, *De opif.* 126.14–24.

[13] Par exemple, sur la découverte de la sphère sans astres, extérieure à tout, qu'Hipparque et Ptolémée auraient empruntée à Moïse, voir : Philopon, *De opif.* 15.17–16.14. Il est fort probable que cette théorie de l'emprunt soit pour Philopon plus rhétorique que tenue pour historiquement fondée. Car si la doctrine

2. *Les fondements de la cosmographie biblique selon Philopon*

Pour Philopon, le récit biblique relève à la fois, de la cosmogonie qui décrit les phases de développement du monde, et de la cosmographie qui en décrit l'organisation et l'ordre. Philopon se défend pourtant de faire de Moïse un physicien au sens où on pouvait l'entendre en son siècle[14]. La visée du Législateur biblique, en effet, est différente de celle des théoriciens de la nature en ce que ces derniers s'adonnent à l'explication positive des rapports de causalité qui traversent tous les phénomènes naturels, alors que Moïse, par ses paroles inspirées, a pour but de conduire les âmes, même dépourvues de l'intelligence des phénomènes physiques, à la connaissance du Dieu invisible, et ce à partir d'une certaine contemplation de la nature et de son ordre[15].

Rappelons, pour mieux situer la question de la lumière, que les choses qui la concernent directement se déroulent en quatre jours et se présentent successivement dans l'ordre suivant :

1. Création du ciel et de la terre, appel de la lumière, séparation de la lumière et de la ténèbre, appellation de la lumière ('jour') et de la ténèbre ('nuit') : Jour Un.

2. Etablissement du firmament pour séparer les eaux d'en haut et les eaux d'en bas : deuxième jour.

3. Apparition de la terre sèche par amoncellement des eaux qui sont sous le ciel (= firmament) en une seule masse, apparition du végétal portant sa propre semence : troisième jour.

4. Apparition des luminaires au firmament du ciel pour séparer le jour et la nuit, pour éclairer la terre : quatrième jour.

---

cosmologique des 'Grecs', méprisée par la tradition antiochienne, a pour origine Moïse lui-même et est de ce fait dans un accord foncier avec les écrits du Rédacteur biblique, Théodore et Cosmas qui luttent contre la cosmographie sphérique hellénique luttent en fait contre Moïse lui-même qui en assume en un sens la paternité. Pour Cosmas, voir : Cosmas Indicopleustès, *Top. chrét.* I.1.1–32.12.

[14] Refuser de faire de Moïse un *physicien*, quand bien même on le tient pour la source des recherches physiques grecques, retire toute légitimité à la tradition antiochienne qui cherche à fonder sa cosmographie et sa physique sur les prétendues données *physiques* du texte biblique, et ce précisément contre la cosmologie grecque.

[15] Cf. Philopon, *De opif.* 2.16–14.14. On peut se demander si une partie de la démiurgie exprimée dans le *Timée* de Platon, notamment la partie narrative, ne se donne pas pour fin une visée assez proche de celle-là.

Avant de traiter de l'appel à l'existence de la lumière, il est utile d'avoir assez précisément à l'esprit l'interprétation et l'extension théorique que Philopon donne au premier verset de la Genèse. Ciel et terre sont produits ἐν ἀρχῇ. Pour Philopon, qui suit en de nombreux points Basile dans son inventaire des significations du mot ἀρχή [16], l'auteur du texte biblique veut signifier que, alors qu'ils n'étaient pas, le ciel et la terre sont apparus ἐν ἀρχῇ, autrement dit dans le premier maintenant inétendu, principe de toute réalité et du temps.

Ciel et terre désignent d'abord les limites ultimes d'un espacement sphérique, vers la périphérie, ou vers le haut pour le ciel, vers le centre, ou vers le bas pour la terre. Mais Philopon précise et ajoute que dans le même instant, dans cette ἀρχή qu'il affirme être 'infiniment petite et sans dimension' (ἀκαριαίαν καὶ ἀδιάστατον) [17], se trouve constituée avec le ciel et la terre, autrement dit en même temps (ἅμα) qu'eux, la nature des quatre éléments, le feu, l'air, l'eau et la terre, à partir desquels adviendront les corps composés [18]. Philopon précise ailleurs que Moïse 'fut le seul à transmettre avec exactitude la position naturelle des éléments et leur rang, en disant que l'eau est située au-dessus de la terre, et l'air non illuminé au-dessus de l'eau' (τὴν φυσικὴν δὲ τῶν στοιχείων θέσιν τε καὶ τάξιν μόνος ἀπέδωκεν ἀκριβῶς, γῇ μὲν εἰπὼν τὸ ὕδωρ ἐπεῖναι, ὕδατι δὲ τὸν ἀφώτιστον ἀέρα) [19]. Philopon veut donc voir, ἐν ἀρχῇ, dans l'instant inétendu et principe du temps, l'apparition immédiate d'une étendue spatiale sphérique tridimensionnée, le ciel et la terre comme limites ultimes du cosmos et des éléments distribués dans des lieux – sphériques eux aussi – qui sont conformes à leur nature [20].

---

[16] Cf. Philopon, *De opif.* 7.8–11.3. Voir également : Basile de Césarée, *In hexaem.* 1. 5–6.

[17] Pour une brève discussion du sens de l'ἀδιάστατον dans le *De opificio mundi*, voir : Laramée 2008, p. 542–543.

[18] Cf. Philopon, *De opif.* 15.5–6 : Ὥστε ἅμα τῷ οὐρανῷ καὶ ἡ τῶν τεσσάρων στοιχείων συνυπέστη φύσις, ἐξ ὧν τὰ σύνθετα γέγονεν.

[19] Philopon, *De opif.* 164.1–4. On notera que curieusement, il n'est fait nulle mention du feu, à moins qu'on ne considère implicitement que la mention primitive du ciel en tient lieu. Sur la place des éléments chez les physiciens, voir : Aristote, *Meteor.* 354b23–26 : τοῦ γὰρ ὕδατος περὶ τὴν γῆν περιτεταμένου, καθάπερ περὶ τοῦτο ἡ τοῦ ἀέρος σφαῖρα καὶ περὶ ταύτην ἡ λεγομένη πυρός. τοῦτο γάρ ἐστι πάντων ἔσχατον, εἴθ᾽ ὡς οἱ πλεῖστοι λέγουσιν εἴθ᾽ ὡς ἡμεῖς.

[20] Cette répartition originelle des éléments primitifs ne contrevient pas au fait

Mais Philopon donne une étendue plus vaste encore à la sobriété du donné biblique, car, dès cet instant unique et premier qui voit se produire l'acte de création par excellence, il affirme que Dieu a déposé, dans les éléments primitifs, les raisons spermatiques des réalités à venir[21]. Mais si une telle affirmation, dans l'intention de Philopon, explique d'abord la raison pour laquelle la génération première des êtres vivants procède d'une injonction donnée au milieu naturel des êtres à produire[22], elle permet surtout de comprendre, qu'au sens strict, seuls sont créés *ex nihilo,* et ce dans le même instant inétendu, le ciel, la terre, les quatre éléments et toutes les raisons spermatiques des réalités à venir.

Mais ce point établi, d'autres opérations lui succèdent dans ce qui sera appelé, non pas premier jour, mais Jour Un auquel Philopon attribue la puissance générative des jours suivants[23] :

qu'ils feront l'objet d'une réorganisation économique spécifique dans le but d'accueillir les êtres animés ou non d'ailleurs. On voit par exemple que dans la disposition originale des éléments, toute l'eau entoure toute la terre qui de ce fait est invisible. Il faudra une injonction divine à l'eau qui est au-dessous du ciel pour que, rassemblée en un rassemblement unique, elle laisse apparaître la terre sèche qui recevra à son tour l'injonction divine pour qu'elle fasse pousser une pâture d'herbe (Gen. 1. 11). Voir par exemple : Philopon, *De opif.* 161.22–162.21.

[21] Cf. Philopon, *De opif.* 216.24–25 : τοὺς σπερματικοὺς ἄρα τῶν ἐσομένων λόγους ἐν τοῖς στοιχείοις ὁ θεὸς ἐξ ἀρχῆς ἐναπέθετο.

[22] Par exemple *De opif.* 162.9–11 : 'βλαστησάτω ἡ γῆ βοτάνην χόρτου' καὶ τὰ ἑξῆς· ἅμα γὰρ τῷ θείῳ λόγῳ τὸ δυνάμει αὐτῆς εἰς ἐνέργειαν προσελήλυθεν ('"que la terre fasse germer une pâture d'herbe" et la suite [Gen. 1. 11] ; au moment où Dieu dit cela, ce qu'elle était en puissance, elle le devint en acte') ; voir également : *De opif.* 167.11–16 ; 176.19–20 ; 177.26–178.2 ; 182.17–24 ; 189.14–15. Cet exemple indique que la parole divine convoque les raisons spermatiques précontenues dans les éléments en les faisant passer de la puissance à l'acte. Comparer à propos de la terre : Basile de Césarée, *In hexaem.* 2.3.38–42 (éd. SC 26 bis) : ὠδίνουσα μὲν τὴν πάντων γένεσιν διὰ τὴν ἐναποτεθεῖσαν αὐτῇ παρὰ τοῦ δημιουργοῦ δύναμιν, ἀναμένουσα δὲ τοὺς καθήκοντας χρόνους, ἵνα τῷ θείῳ κελεύσματι προαγάγῃ ἑαυτῆς εἰς φανερὸν τὰ κυήματα. ('[La terre] portait en son sein le germe de toutes choses, en vertu de la puissance déposée en elle par le Créateur, mais elle attendait le temps où elle devrait, selon l'ordre divin, produire ses fruits à la lumière').

[23] Comme Philopon l'affirme en effet (*De opif.* 108.13–22) : εἰκότως ἄρα μίαν αὐτὴν καὶ οὐ πρώτην ὠνόμασε Μωϋσῆς, ἅτε δὴ τῶν ἑξῆς ἁπασῶν οὖσαν γεννητικήν, ὡς καὶ ἡ μονὰς μία ἐστὶ τῇ ἰδίᾳ ἀνακυκλήσει τοὺς ἑξῆς ἀριθμοὺς γεννῶσα. Εὔλογον οὖν τὸ αἴτιον μὴ ποιεῖν τοῖς αἰτιατοῖς σύστοιχον, ἀλλ' ἐκεῖνα μὲν ἐκ τῆς πρὸς αὐτὸ σχέσεως ἔχειν τὸ δεύτερα εἶναι καὶ τρίτα, τοῦτο δὲ ὡς ἐκείνων ἐξῃρημένον τῇ δυνάμει ἄσχετον πρὸς αὐτὰ τὴν προσηγορίαν ἔχειν, ἓν λεγόμενον καὶ μία καὶ εἷς, οὐχὶ δὲ πρῶτος καὶ πρώτη καὶ πρῶτον. ('Vraisemblablement Moïse l'a appelé "un" et non pas "premier", puisqu'il est vraiment puissance d'engendrement toute la suite des autres, comme la monade "un" génère par sa propre révolution tous les nombres qui suivent.

L'appel de la lumière, la séparation de la lumière et de la ténèbre et la nomination de la lumière ('jour') et de la ténèbre ('nuit').

Une précision s'impose ici, car Philopon soutient l'idée d'une cosmogénèse marquée par des séquences temporelles qui voit des choses advenir successivement, certaines antérieurement, d'autres postérieurement, jusqu'à ce que le cosmos parvienne à sa stature définitive. Cette remarque est importante dans la mesure où ce programme, temporellement séquencé, se démarque des rapports causaux explicatifs de ce cosmos-ci apportés par le platonisme athénien, dont Proclus est, sans conteste, l'un des plus éminents représentants. Ces rapports causaux explicatifs, même séquencés par la nécessité de la narration du mythe vraisemblable qu'est le discours du *Timée*, ne s'inscrivent pas dans l'extension temporelle et sont de fait concomitants les uns aux autres. En effet, les explications du platonisme tardo-antique ne font pas entrer la cosmogénèse dans cette forme d'actuation progressive qui ressort des propos de Philopon[24], mais elles la conçoivent comme une actuation permanente[25].

Il est donc juste de ne pas confondre la cause avec les causés, mais les causés tiennent de leur relation à la cause le fait d'être deuxième et troisième, tandis que la cause, séparée d'eux autant que possible, a une dénomination non liée à la leur, on l'appelle "un", "une" ou "un", et non "premier", "première" ou "premier"').

[24] Voir par exemple *De opif.* 304.9–17 : Διὰ τί ἐν ἓξ ἡμέραις τὸν κόσμον ἐποίησεν ὁ θεός, οὐ δίκαιον μὲν ἴσως περιεργάζεσθαι· – τί γάρ, εἰ καὶ ἐν πλείοσιν ἢ καὶ ἐλάττοσιν ἐγεγόνει, λέγειν εἴχομεν ἢ καὶ ἀθρόον καὶ ἅμα πᾶς ; – ἤρκει δὲ καὶ ἡ μέχρι νῦν τοῦ παντὸς διάταξις καὶ ἡ ὑπὸ πάντων ἀνθρώπων ἑβδοματικὴ τῶν ἡμερῶν ἀπαρίθμησις ἀπόδειξιν ἱκανὴν ἔχουσα τοῦ ἐν τοσαύταις ἡμέραις τὸν πάντα κόσμον δημιουργῆσαι τὸν θεόν, τῆς ἑβδόμης ὥσπερ ἑορτῆς ἐπὶ συμπληρώσει τῆς γενέσεως τοῦ παντὸς ὑπαρχούσης· ('Pourquoi Dieu a fait le monde en six jours, il n'est peut-être pas juste de s'y arrêter. Pourquoi en effet devrions-nous dire s'il l'a fait en plus ou moins de jours, ou même en un instant et tout à la fois ? Mais l'ordre de l'univers jusqu'à nos jours, et le dénombrement hebdomadaire des jours par les hommes, sont une démonstration suffisante du fait que Dieu a créé le monde entier en autant de jours, puisque l'hebdomade est comme une célébration de l'achèvement de la création de l'univers').

[25] Cette question est particulièrement difficile et elle provient, bien antérieurement au commentaire scripturaire proposé ici par Philopon, des présupposés exégétiques qui ont commandé plusieurs écoles d'interprétation du *Timée* de Platon qui, du moins en son objet, le cosmos, et en sa forme narrative, présente quelque parenté avec le récit de la Genèse. Le dilemme est le suivant. (1) Soit on les interprète littéralement et on considère que la forme narrative décrit les étapes réelles d'une cosmogénèse temporelle, et on court alors le risque d'imputer au démiurge lui-même la contrainte de la temporalité en raison des opérations qu'il ne peut engager que l'une après l'autre comme n'importe quel artisan. Cette posi-

Mais avant d'en venir à la lumière au sens strict, il faut brièvement clarifier le statut de la ténèbre qui la précède et son sens.

3. *La ténèbre primitive*

De façon générale, Philopon distingue la ténèbre totale antérieure à la production de la lumière 'qui ne subsiste pas, une fois la lumière produite' (μηδ᾽ ὅλως γενομένου φωτὸς παρυπέστη, *De opif.* 92.8–9), de la ténèbre nocturne dont l'existence accidentelle provient de l'interception de la lumière solaire par des corps qui s'interposent à sa diffusion, comme c'est le cas la nuit lorsque le soleil passe sous la terre[26], mais aussi dans le cas de l'ombre. On devrait peut-être ajouter, comme nous le verrons ci-après, qu'il y a une phase intermédiaire entre ces deux-là dans l'agencement progressif du cosmos et de ses lois par l'acte démiurgique. Nous voulons parler du positionnement provisoire de la ténèbre sitôt la lumière créée. A cet instant, en effet, Dieu sépara, d'un côté la lumière, d'un côté la ténèbre et ce en l'absence d'un agent illuminant précisément localisé. Cet état intermédiaire qui n'existe plus sous cette forme à l'avènement des luminaires est fondateur de la loi physique d'alternance du jour et de la nuit, de la lumière et de la ténèbre.

---

tion fut pour le *Timée*, celle de Plutarque de Chéronée et d'Atticus que Proclus réfute longuement mais aussi celle de Philopon qui réfute Proclus réfutant les deux médio-platoniciens (cf. *Contra Proclum*). (2) Soit on considère que Platon n'a fait usage de la forme narrative temporalisée qu'à des fins didactiques. C'est la position de Proclus et avant lui celle de son maître Syrianus (cf. *In Metaph.* 181.29–32). Le démiurge dans ce cas est toujours démiurge en acte et ainsi opérant toujours, le résultat de son opération, le cosmos, est toujours également en acte sans qu'on puisse distinguer temporellement un moment où le cosmos n'aurait pas encore été cosmos, un moment où le cosmos n'aurait été encore que cosmos en puissance. Dans l'état actuel de nos propres recherches, il nous est difficile de savoir si la cosmogénèse biblique qui est temporelle pour Philopon impacte temporellement l'action divine induisant dans le Dieu Créateur de la Bible de la puissance, non encore actualisée, de faire d'abord ceci, puis cela, enfin cela encore. Il faudrait pour clarifier ce point revoir le détail de l'argumentation du *Contra Proclum* de Philopon que les limites de cette contribution n'autorisent pas.

[26] Cf. *De opif.* 85.6–8 ; 92.6–10. Mais aussi *De opif.* 130.10–12 : ἡ δὲ νὺξ οὐδὲν ἄλλο ἐστὶν ἢ σκίασμα γῆς [...] ὑπ᾽ αὐτὴν τοῦ ἡλίου γενομένου· ('La nuit n'est rien d'autre que l'ombre de la terre [...] quand le soleil est sous elle').

Enfin et surtout, ce que l'Ecriture nomme, avant la création de la lumière, la ténèbre (τὸ σκότος) n'est logiquement que la condition de privation dans laquelle se trouvent ἐν ἀρχῇ, dans l'instant inétendu premier, les corps diaphanes (τὰ διαφανῆ σώματα), l'air et l'eau[27], qui ne sont pas encore illuminés (μήπω πεφωτίσθαι)[28]. Et, lorsque le texte biblique affirme : 'la ténèbre était au-dessus de l'abîme' (Gen. 1. 2), par abîme, l'auteur biblique désigne – pour Philopon – l'eau et par ténèbre l'air non illuminé (ὁ ἀὴρ ἀφώτιστος)[29]. Philopon retient donc par priorité l'usage des anciens physiciens et celui de l'Ecriture pour lesquels le nom 'ténèbre' désigne l'air non éclairé[30] qui tient lieu de substrat[31] à la présence ou à l'absence de lumière conçue comme qualité incorporelle. Le rapport qui lie dialectiquement ténèbre et lumière n'est pas un rapport de contrariété, mais un rapport d'opposition sur le mode de la privation (στέρησις), ou de la possession (ἕξις) d'une qualité appelée 'lumière' qui affecte d'abord le support air en lui conférant, ou plus exactement en actualisant

---

[27] Les deux autres éléments, la terre et le feu, privés de caractère diaphane, sont des corps qui s'interposent (ἀντιφρακτικὰ γάρ ἐστι γῆ καὶ πῦρ διαφανείας ἐστερημένα, De opif. 119.9–10).

[28] Cf. De opif. 72.5–8 ; 73.4–8, 10–11, 19–21.

[29] Il faut toutefois noter que le texte biblique n'est pas dépourvu d'ambiguïté lorsqu'il fait usage des noms 'air' et 'eau' et ce en raison de leur très grande parenté (συγγένεια) et de leur facile transmutation réciproque (ἡ εἰς ἄλληλα ῥᾳδίαν αὐτῶν μετάπτωσις, dans De opif. 152.19–21). En effet, l'Ecriture a coutume de nommer l'eau de multiples façons comme le rappelle Philopon en un dossier qui n'entend sacrifier ni les phénomènes physiques, ni l'usage scripturaire allégorique de ces termes (voir : De opif. 142.25–156.23).

[30] Ainsi que l'affirme Philopon (De opif. 12.18–25) : Καὶ γὰρ καὶ ἡ τῶν παλαιῶν χρῆσις καὶ ἡ συνήθεια πάντων καὶ ἡ θεία γραφὴ τὸ νυκτερινὸν τοῦ ἀέρος κατάστημα καὶ μάλιστα τὸ ζοφῶδες καὶ παντελῶς ἀφεγγὲς ἐκ τῆς ἑπομένης τῷ ἀέρι τοῦ φωτὸς στερήσεως, ἐν ᾧ καὶ τὸ παρ' ἡμῖν ὑφίσταται φῶς, τὸν ὅλον ἀφώτιστον ἀέρα συνηρημένως ὀνομάζουσι σκότος. κυρίως γὰρ σκότος ἐστὶν ἡ τοῦ φωτὸς ἀπουσία καὶ στέρησις. ('L'usage des anciens, l'habitude générale et l'Ecriture divine soulignent le caractère nocturne de l'air et surtout son opacité, son absolue ténèbre du fait de la privation de la lumière pour l'air qui pour nous [i. e. dans l'expérience que nous en avons présentement] est le support de la lumière ; si bien qu'ils dénomment en général "ténèbre" l'air entièrement dépourvu de lumière. La ténèbre est au sens propre l'absence et la privation de lumière.') Voir également : De opif. 62.8–14 ; 63.8 ; 69.8–10 ; 70.21–22 ; 72.5–8 ; 91.13–15.

[31] Cf. De opif. 69.8–10 : ἄλλο δέ ἐστι τῷ ἀέρι <τὸ> εἶναι καὶ ἄλλο τὸ πεφωτίσθαι ἢ ἀφωτίστῳ εἶναι, ὅπερ σκότος ὠνόμασται. ('C'est une chose pour l'air d'exister et une autre d'être illuminé ou non illuminé, ce que nous appelons "ténèbre"').

en lui transparence (i. e. diaphanie) et luminosité. Car la ténèbre n'est elle-même ni une qualité, ni *a fortiori* une substance, mais elle est simplement privation ou absence (ἀπουσία) de cette qualité-là pour l'air[32].

4. *L'avènement de la lumière : Position du problème*

Pour Philopon qui vise ici à respecter scrupuleusement la littéralité du propos biblique, 'la lumière n'a pas commencé à exister avec le ciel' (τὸ μὴ συνυποστῆναι τῷ οὐρανῷ τὸ φῶς, *De opif.* 91.15–16), autrement dit en même temps que lui. Mais, sur la parole divine, elle est générée sans rupture, sans intervalle (διάλειμμα), directement (εὐθέως) *après* la production simultanée (ἄμα) du ciel, de la terre et des éléments primitifs. La lumière advient donc *après* et il y a eu un instant non mesurable, car sans dimension (= sans durée), où la lumière n'était *pas encore*[33]. Une telle affirmation soulève d'importantes questions que nous pourrions sérier comme suit :

- D'où vient cette réalité, cette qualité incorporelle, appelée 'lumière' ?

- Est-elle produite *ex nihilo* l'instant qui succède sans intervalle la création initiale ?

- Est-elle déjà présente en puissance dans la première geste, sous forme de raison spermatique comme nous le mentionnions précédemment ?

- Pourquoi est-elle créée avant les luminaires qui seront, dans l'économie cosmique, les agents de sa diffusion ?

- Philopon ne se trouve-t-il pas emporté dans d'inextricables difficultés à vouloir tenir simultanément : (a) la contrainte qu'imposent les règles de la physique qui obligent une qua-

---

[32] Cette question est longuement discutée par Philopon, dans *De opif.* 69.6–73.24.

[33] Philopon ne le dit pas explicitement mais il faut, nous semble-t-il, admettre qu'avec l'avènement de la lumière se manifeste pour la première fois et au sens strict le temps, qui suppose nécessairement, selon sa propre définition, un premier rapport d'antériorité et de postériorité. Ce rapport advient pour la première fois avec la génération de la lumière.

lité à ne pas exister sans le corps, et (b) la littéralité du texte biblique qui contrevient à cette règle, en faisant apparemment exister la qualité lumière indépendamment d'un corps ?

Mais il y a un autre problème que Philopon semble ne pas vouloir prendre en compte ici. Il s'agit du rapport de la lumière primitive et du feu primitif, lequel est pourtant, au même titre que les autres éléments, concomitant à la production ἐν ἀρχῇ du ciel et de la terre. À ce stade de nos recherches, il nous est encore impossible de nous expliquer la raison de la non-prise en compte de ce rapport. Ceci est d'autant plus troublant que Philopon affirme clairement, quelques chapitres plus tard, que 'la capacité d'éclairer et la capacité de brûler n'appartiennent qu'au feu' (μόνῳ τῷ πυρὶ τὸ φωτιστικὸν ἅμα καὶ καυστικὸν ὑπάρχει, *De opif.* 185.23–24). Et il admet ensuite que 'les luminaires dans le ciel tiennent du feu le pouvoir d'éclairer' (οἱ κατ᾽ οὐρανὸν φωστῆρες τὸ φωτιστικὸν ἔχουσι τοῦ πυρός, *De opif.* 186.1–2). Il se réfère enfin à Platon qui a dit que 'le pouvoir éclairant du soleil, de la lune et des autres astres [...] participent principalement de l'élément feu[34] – le pouvoir éclairant n'appartient <donc> à aucun élément simple en dehors du feu' (τὸ φωτιστικὸν ἡλίου τε καὶ σελήνης καὶ τῶν λοιπῶν ἀστέρων πλείστου πυρὸς μετέχειν [...] – οὐδενὶ γὰρ ὑπάρχει τῶν ἁπλῶν πλὴν πυρὶ τὸ φωτιστικόν, *De opif.* 118.13–16)[35].

---

[34] Répété quelques lignes plus bas : *De opif.* 120.8–9.

[35] La tradition byzantine postérieure semble avoir admis de façon très précise cette association. Pour Jean Damascène (*c.* 676–749) en effet, le feu et la lumière qui en provient sont simultanés (ἅμα) et il n'y a pas d'abord le feu et après la lumière. La lumière, qui est toujours engendrée du feu, est toujours en lui n'étant jamais séparée de lui. La lumière qui est toujours inséparablement engendrée du feu, et demeurant toujours en lui, n'a pas sa propre hypostase à côté du feu car elle est la qualité naturelle du feu. Voir : Jean Damascène, *Expositio fidei* (éd. Kotter 1984) 8.99–107, 154–165. On peut noter que la position de Damascène s'approche étonnamment de celle de Proclus que Philopon combat dans son *Contra Proclum*. Proclus ne dit pas autre chose que cela, à savoir que la lumière émise n'a pas sa propre hypostase et qu'elle est toujours inséparablement engendrée du feu. Ce que Philopon récuse. Il tentera de démontrer qu'il faut traiter différemment la lumière comme forme du luminaire et le rayon lumineux et soutiendra que l'un et l'autre n'ont pas la même raison formelle. Pour le détail de cet argument : Philopon, *Contra Proclum* 14.24–23.23. Enfin on peut ajouter que, contrairement à ce qu'on trouve chez Philopon, Damascène semble considérer que la création de l'élément *feu* est assimilée à la création de la lumière. Voir *Expositio fidei* 21.3–7 : 'Καὶ εἶπεν ὁ θεός. Γενηθήτω φῶς, καὶ ἐγένετο φῶς.' Οὐχ ἕτερον γάρ ἐστι τὸ πῦρ εἰ μὴ τὸ φῶς, ὥς τινές φασιν.

Or si l'élément feu auquel seul on impute le pouvoir d'illuminer est bien simultané au ciel, à la terre et aux autres éléments, comme nous pensons que Philopon le croit aussi, comment expliquer qu'il soit, antérieurement à l'appel de la lumière, privé du pouvoir illuminateur qui lui est propre et qu'on lui concède ensuite à plusieurs reprises ? Il est étonnant que Philopon n'apporte aucune solution réelle à ce problème dans le commentaire du premier jour. Le moins qu'on puisse dire est que le rapport de la lumière et du feu y est mal élucidé.

5. *De la nature de la lumière primitive*

Sur ces apories scripturaires que sont la nature et le mode d'existence de la lumière primitive, Philopon constituera un dossier dont voici les pièces principales.

Il commence par pointer la difficulté que nous avons déjà signalée, qui découle de la loi physique universelle qui veut qu'aucune qualité n'existe par elle-même sans un corps[36], comme c'est le cas, par exemple, pour le chaud, le froid, le blanc, le doux, le mou et le dur. Ces qualités jamais ne sont trouvées en soi en dehors d'un corps qui leur donne lieu d'être, et qu'en retour elles qualifient. Il affirme donc :

> Ἐπειδὴ [...] τὸ φῶς δὲ ποιότης ἐστὶν ἐν σώμασιν ὑφεστῶσα, σελήνῃ τε καὶ ἡλίῳ καὶ ἄστροις καὶ πυρί, ζητεῖται εἰκότως, μήπω τῶν φωστήρων γενομένων τί ἦν ἐκεῖνο τὸ πρωτόγονον φῶς, καὶ πῶς ἀνὰ μέρος ὑποχωρούντων ἀλλήλοις φωτός τε καὶ σκότους ἡμέρα καὶ νὺξ ἐγίνετο. οὐδὲ γὰρ ἀντιπαραχωρεῖν ἀλλήλοις τοὺς τόπους σωμάτων χωρὶς οὐδὲ εἶναι ὅλως ἠδύναντο. (*De opif.* 74.10–16)

> Puisque la lumière est une qualité qui réside dans les corps (dans la lune et le soleil, les astres, le feu)[37], on a raison de chercher alors que les luminaires[38] n'avaient pas encore été créés, qu'est-ce qu'était cette lumière primitive[39], et com-

---

[36] Cf. Philopon, *De opif.* 74.8–9 : ποιότης οὐδεμία καθ' αὑτὴν σώματος ὑπάρχει χωρίς.

[37] Le feu dont il est ici question peut être soit le corps simple élémentaire, le feu dans son état premier, soit le feu dont nous faisons ici-bas l'expérience.

[38] Qu'en est-il alors du feu pourtant mentionné ?

[39] Cf. *De opif.* 74.13 ; 78.9 ; 186.27.

ment, la lumière et la ténèbre se retirant l'une devant l'autre tour à tour, il y eût le jour et la nuit. Elles ne pouvaient en effet sans corps, ni se céder la place tour à tour, ni tout simplement être.

Ce paragraphe pose clairement comme présupposé que la lumière est une qualité. Cela signifie, nous l'avons déjà dit, qu'elle n'est pas un corps mais qu'elle réside nécessairement dans un corps.

Le propos comporte deux objets de recherche. (1) Le premier porte sur la nature de la lumière primitive préexistant aux luminaires. (2) Le deuxième porte sur la modalité du rapport de la lumière et de la ténèbre qui jamais n'occupent la même portion d'air, air qui leur tient lieu de substrat corporel.

Nous pouvons déjà observer que Philopon appréhende la lumière de deux manières différentes.

(1) Dans le premier cas, destinée à résider dans la lune, le soleil, les astres et le feu, la lumière est une qualité essentielle déterminant la nature de chacune des entités qu'elle informe. En effet, elle entre dans la définition des luminaires qui tirent d'elle leur nom, et ce faisant, elle se trouve du côté de l'essence, de la forme constitutive de chacun d'eux. Retirer la lumière, dans cette acception-là, reviendrait à réduire à néant l'agent illuminant.

(2) Dans le deuxième cas, il n'est plus question de la qualité essentielle des luminaires préexistant aux corps destinés à illuminer mais de la lumière qui cède la place à sa privation, à savoir la ténèbre. Cette alternance ne peut se produire que dans un substrat corporel dont l'existence ne dépend pas de la qualité reçue ou de sa privation. Il ne peut donc s'agir que du corps diaphane, ici de l'air. Comme l'affirme ailleurs Philopon : 'C'est une chose pour l'air d'exister et une autre d'être illuminé ou non illuminé, ce que nous appelons "ténèbre"' (ἄλλο δέ ἐστι τῷ ἀέρι <τὸ> εἶναι καὶ ἄλλο τὸ πεφωτίσθαι ἢ ἀφωτίστῳ εἶναι, ὅπερ σκότος ὠνόμασται, *De opif.* 69.8–10).

La conception philoponienne de la lumière repose foncièrement sur la distinction nécessaire qu'il convient de faire entre ces deux cas. À ce propos, Philopon avait affirmé dans le *Contra Proclum* :

ἐπειδὴ τὸ φῶς διττόν ἐστιν, τὸ μὲν ἐν αὐτῇ συνυποστὰν τῇ τοῦ
ἡλίου σφαίρᾳ οὐσιωμένον φῶς εἰδοποιόν τέ ἐστιν καὶ συμπλη-
ρωτικὸν τῆς τοῦ ἡλίου φύσεως, <ὡς> παντί τῳ δῆλον· (*Contra
Proclum* 16.25–28)

Puisque la lumière est double, d'un côté, comme il est clair
pour n'importe qui, la lumière substantielle, qui vient dans
la sphère du soleil coexister avec elle, est ce qui donne la forme
et l'achèvement à la nature du soleil.

Τὸ δὲ ἐν ἀέρι χεόμενον φῶς οὐκ ἀεὶ τὸ αὐτὸ ὑπάρχει· φθαρτὸν
γὰρ εἶναι ὡμολόγηται· διαδέχεται γὰρ αὐτὸ σκότος· (*Contra
Proclum* 17.15–17)

Mais d'un autre côté la lumière qui se diffuse dans l'air
n'est pas toujours la même. Il est en effet admis qu'elle est
corruptible, car la ténèbre lui succède.

Philopon affirmera d'ailleurs, à propos de cette seconde acception de la lumière qui diffère de la nature de la première, cause
formelle du luminaire : 'la limite de la lumière est commencement
de la ténèbre et la limite de la ténèbre est commencement de la
lumière' (τὸ πέρας τοῦ φωτὸς ἀρχή ἐστι τοῦ σκότους καὶ τοὐμπαλιν
τὸ πέρας τοῦ σκότους ἀρχή ἐστι τοῦ φωτός, *De opif.* 83.10–12).
Il est certain que cette lumière-là est celle qui, diffuse, a l'air pour
substrat et qu'elle est, du moins Philopon le défend-t-il, corruptible car elle peut être ou n'être pas, c'est le propre de l'accident,
ce qui n'est pas possible pour la première acception : la lumière
forme, ou qualité essentielle, des agents illuminant[40].

L'objectif de sa recherche est alors d'interroger la nature
de la lumière primitive qu'il conçoit d'abord comme la forme
préexistante de l'agent illuminant. Il recense pour cela les positions en présence et les solutions envisagées par ses prédécesseurs. Il faut constater que les opinions évaluées ont toutes pour
visée de résoudre l'aporie révélée par le texte biblique, même si
tel ou tel aspect est emprunté plus directement à la philosophie.

---

[40] Nous pourrions ajouter en nous référant une fois encore au *Contra Proclum* (18.4–6) que la nature de la lumière dans l'air n'a pas toujours fait consensus ainsi que Philopon le rappelle : πολλὴ γὰρ ἡ περὶ τῆς ὑπάρξεως αὐτοῦ ζήτησις,
εἴτε ἐνέργεια τοῦ φωτίζοντος εἴτε εἶδος εἴτε πάθος τοῦ ἀέρος. ('Il y a, dit-il, de nombreuses discussions sur son mode d'existence : si elle est acte de l'agent illuminant, ou forme, ou affection qualitative de l'air.').

La tradition philosophique en tant que telle n'est pas directement concernée par le problème de la préexistence temporelle de la lumière sur les luminaires qu'elle informera. Pour Philopon :

> Τινὲς μὲν οὖν τῶν ἐξηγησαμένων οὐδ᾽ αὐτό γε τοῦτο τοῖς εἰρημένοις ἐπέστησαν, ἀλλὰ βασάνου χωρὶς τὸν τόπον παρεληλύθασιν· ἕτεροι δὲ τὴν τοῦ πυρὸς οὐσίαν τοῦτο τὸ φῶς ἔφασαν ὑπάρχειν. συμμεμιγμένων γὰρ ἀλλήλοις, φασί, κατ᾽ ἀρχὴν τῶν στοιχείων – οἷόν τι καὶ ὁ Ἐμπεδοκλῆς ἔλεγεν – καὶ μήπω καθαρῶς διακεκριμένων, τὸ πῦρ ἅτε δὴ λεπτομερέστατον ὑπάρχον καὶ ὀξυκινητότατον ἁπάντων προεξήλατο τῶν ἄλλων στοιχείων κελεύσαντος θεοῦ· ʽγενηθήτω φῶςʼ καὶ τὴν ἄνω χώραν κατείληφεν. (*De opif.* 74.17–26)

> [*Thèse 1*] Certains des commentateurs donc n'ont même pas traité ce point dans leur propos mais ils ont sauté le passage sans l'examiner ;

> [*Thèse 2*] d'autres ont soutenu que cette lumière était la substance du feu. Les éléments, disent-ils, étaient au commencement mélangés les uns aux autres – Empédocle par exemple a dit quelque chose de semblable[41] – et ne pouvaient pas encore être distingués de façon pure, si bien que le feu parce qu'il était le plus subtil et le plus vif de tous, s'élança avant les autres éléments quand Dieu ordonna : 'Qu'advienne lumière', et s'empara de toute la région d'en-haut.

Le premier groupe ne présente que peu d'intérêt car il esquive simplement la question[42].

Le second groupe est difficile à identifier. En affirmant que la lumière est la substance du feu (ἡ τοῦ πυρὸς οὐσία), il fait de la lumière la forme constitutive du corps feu qu'elle informe. L'ensemble de la thèse présente d'importantes similarités avec le platonisme pour qui la lumière est une sorte de feu[43]. Pour Proclus, que Philopon a ailleurs longuement combattu, il existe au ciel du feu, la lumière qui est une forme du feu (τὸ φῶς, εἶδος ὂν

---

[41] Cf. Eusèbe de Césarée, *Praep. evang.* I.8.10.

[42] L'examen des commentaires patristiques montre qu'ils ne font, de façon générale, pas cas des problèmes physiques soulevés par la création de la lumière. On se livre plutôt à la lecture allégorique et aux discours exhortatifs qu'à la recherche scientifique jugée peu utile pour l'édification de l'Eglise. Cf. Basile de Césarée, *In hexaem.* 1.8.2–9.

[43] Cf. Platon, *Tim.* 58c5–d1 : πυρός [...] γένη.

πυρός, *In Tim.* II.47.10) le montre. Les tenants de cette seconde thèse posent avant la création de la lumière qui est en un sens, pour eux, avènement du feu en sa pureté, la théorie du mélange primitif. Nous pouvons le rapprocher d'un état d'indistinction comparable à celui que Platon pensait trouver dans la première phase de la cosmogénèse dans laquelle les éléments, non encore régulés par la proportion, agitaient la matrice-réceptacle originelle de mouvements chaotiques. Le démiurge, voulant que toutes choses fussent bonnes, conduit ensuite cette masse agitée du désordre à l'ordre, de l'indistinction chaotique des éléments à leur distinction ordonnée[44].

Enfin, pour renforcer l'accent platonicien de cette position, il faudrait signaler la mention du caractère le plus subtil (λεπτομερέστατον), le plus vif (ὀξυκινητότατον), imputé à la corporéité du feu, ainsi que la très grande rapidité à se mouvoir. Ces trois puissances font penser à une section du commentaire de Proclus au *Timée*. Le Lycien rapporte alors la théorie des trois puissances fondamentales de chacun des quatre éléments qu'il attribue à Timée de Locres, le Pythagoricien qui serait à l'origine de la cosmologie de Platon[45].

Mais dans tous les cas, bien que la source soit selon toute vraisemblance platonicienne, il s'agit de l'usage qu'en aurait fait un auteur chrétien dans le but d'expliquer, d'un point de vue physique, le propos de Moïse sur la création de la lumière et sa préexistence sur les luminaires[46]. L'avènement de la lumière aurait, pour cette thèse, résulté d'une parole efficace restituant au feu

---

[44] Cf. Platon, *Tim.* 30a2–7 ; 53a7–b5.

[45] Cf. Proclus, *In Tim.* II.39.19–21 : μόνος δὴ οὖν ὁ Τίμαιος καὶ εἴ τις τούτῳ κατηκολούθησεν ὀρθῶς οὔτε μίαν οὔτε δύο τοῖς στοιχείοις ἀπονέμει δυνάμεις, ἀλλὰ τρισσάς, τῷ μὲν πυρὶ λεπτομέρειαν, ὀξύτητα, εὐκινησίαν.

[46] La thèse liant la lumière et le feu trouve un écho assez inattendu chez Cosmas Indicopleustès (*Top. Chr.* X.22.6–7), l'un des adversaires chrétiens de la physique et de la cosmologie philoponiennes, dans un très court propos du premier livre de l'*Hexaéméron* de Sévérien de Gabala qu'il rapporte : Εἶπεν ὁ Θεός· 'Γενηθήτω φῶς', καὶ ἐγένετο τοῦ πυρὸς ἡ φύσις. ('Dieu a dit : "Qu'advienne Lumière". Et advint la nature du feu.') Mais cette affirmation consonne assez mal avec la thèse deux présentée par Philopon car cette dernière ne fait pas advenir le feu à l'appel de la lumière, mais affirme qu'il lui préexiste, bien que ce soit de façon confuse. L'avènement de la lumière révèle plutôt le feu dans sa pureté et indique les lieux que dorénavant il occupera : toute la région d'en-haut.

sa place, sa pureté et son pouvoir naturel d'éclairer. Dans ce cas, la lumière cosmique, assimilée au feu, est corporelle. Cette thèse s'expose à la critique du Stagirite[47]. Philopon la réfutera brièvement après l'exposé de la thèse suivante.

Il rapporte donc une troisième position au problème de l'antériorité de la lumière sur les luminaires :

> ἕτερος δέ φησι τὸν ἀέρα τῇ κινήσει τοῦ αἰθερίου σώματος θερμαινόμενον ἄλλας ἐν ἄλλοις αὐτοῦ μέρεσι ἐκλάμψεις ποιεῖν, οἷά ἐστι τὰ καλούμενα σέλα, πῇ μὲν μικράς, πῇ δὲ μείζονας, ἃς ὕστερον ἐξαφθείσας τελείως ἥλιον καὶ σελήνην καὶ τῶν ἀστέρων ποιῆσαι τὸ πλῆθος. (*De opif.* 75.14–19)

> [*Thèse 3*] Un autre dit que l'air échauffé par le mouvement du corps éthéré produit différentes étincelles dans différentes parties de lui-même, telles celles que nous appelons lueurs, ici petites, là plus importantes ; par la suite, une fois qu'elles sont parfaitement enflammées, sont créés le soleil, la lune et la multitude des astres.

L'objection de Philopon reprend l'une après l'autre ces deux positions en les écartant comme suit :

> ἀλλ᾽ ἤδη τῶν στοιχείων γεγονότων, πῶς τὸ ἤδη ὂν πῦρ αὖθις γενέσθαι προσέταξεν ὁ θεός; οὐ γὰρ εἶπεν· 'ἐξαγαγέτω ἡ γῆ φῶς' ἀλλὰ 'γενηθήτω φῶς' τὸ μήπω ὂν ὑποστῆναι κελεύσας· καὶ ὅτι τὸ φλογῶδες τοῦτο πῦρ ἐν μόνοις τοῖς ὑπὸ σελήνην τόποις ὑφίσταται ὑπερβολῇ πυρὸς ὂν καὶ οὐ διαρκοῦν εἰς ἀεί, ὡς διαρκοῦσιν οἱ φωστῆρες, καὶ ὅτι ἐν τῷ στερεώματι, ὅπερ ἐκάλεσεν οὐρανόν, τοὺς φωστῆρας ἔθηκεν ὁ θεός, οὐκ ἐν τῷ πρὸς ἡμᾶς ἀέρι. (*De opif.* 75.19–27)

---

[47] Aristote en effet en une page célèbre du *De anima* (418b14–17), très vraisemblablement supposée ici, rappelle à propos de ce qu'est la lumière : οὔτε πῦρ οὔθ᾽ ὅλως σῶμα οὐδ᾽ ἀπορροὴ σώματος οὐδενός (εἴη γὰρ ἂν σῶμά τι καὶ οὕτως), ἀλλὰ πυρὸς ἢ τοιούτου τινὸς παρουσία ἐν τῷ διαφανεῖ· οὔτε γὰρ δύο σώματα ἅμα δυνατὸν ἐν τῷ αὐτῷ εἶναι [...]. ('Il ne s'agit, ni de feu, ni, en général, d'un corps, ni même de l'effluve d'un corps quelconque, car il s'agirait également d'une sorte de corps dans ces conditions, mais de la présence du feu ou d'un élément analogue au sein de la transparence. Et de fait, deux corps ne peuvent se trouver ensemble au même endroit.') Il semble en effet que Philopon ait cette règle à l'esprit qu'il avait autrefois commentée (*In De anima* 343.6–29 et 343.30–344.10) lorsqu'il considère la lumière comme une qualité incorporelle dont l'être n'a pas lieu d'être sans un corps. À cela, il faut préciser que pour Bodéüs 1993, p. 169 n. 1 : 'Le mot "présence" doit [...] s'entendre, non comme celle du corps agent lui-même [*i. e.* du feu], mais comme celle de son acte qu'il transmet'.

[*Objection thèse* 2] Mais les éléments ayant déjà été produits, comment Dieu a-t-il à nouveau donné l'ordre que soit le feu, puisqu'il existait déjà ? Il n'a pas dit : 'Que la terre produise la lumière', mais 'Qu'advienne lumière' ordonnant ainsi que vienne à l'existence quelque chose qui n'était pas encore.

[*Objection thèse* 3] Ce feu ardent n'existe que dans les lieux sublunaires, étant une surabondance de feu et ne devant pas durer toujours comme les luminaires célestes qui doivent durer, et Dieu a établi les luminaires dans le firmament que nous appelons 'ciel', et non pas dans l'air de chez nous.

Nous proposons, avant d'en venir à la réfutation de la deuxième thèse, d'interroger la troisième et sa mise à l'écart par Philopon.

Cette nouvelle opinion convoquée est assez énigmatique. Il est difficile de savoir si elle fut tenue par quelque exégète du récit mosaïque cherchant à expliquer la naissance de la lumière primitive car, à la différence de la thèse deux, aucune référence au texte biblique n'y est faite. Ce seul exégète, car il n'est question que d'un autre au singulier, fait provenir les luminaires d'un enchaînement de causes mécaniques. Le mouvement du corps éthéré produit un échauffement de l'air qui produit des étincelles appelées lueurs. C'est au moment où ces étincelles atteignent un certain seuil critique, en s'enflammant parfaitement, que sont créés les luminaires, le soleil, la lune et les astres. La préexistence de la lumière se réduit à la préexistence d'étincelles appelées lueurs. Là encore, loin d'être une qualité incorporelle, les étincelles, assimilées à la lumière, sont des corpuscules enflammés du conglomérat desquels résulteront les luminaires.

Nous ne sommes pas parvenus à trouver dans la tradition patristique l'écho d'une telle interprétation qui se réfère manifestement aux *Météorologiques* d'Aristote traitant des processus de production de réalités enflammées[48]. Mais cet emprunt est pour

---

[48] Cf. Aristote, *Meteor.* 340b10–14 : φερομένου δὲ τοῦ πρώτου στοιχείου κύκλῳ καὶ τῶν ἐν αὐτῷ σωμάτων, τὸ προσεχὲς ἀεὶ τοῦ κάτω κόσμου καὶ σώματος τῇ κινήσει διακρινόμενον ἐκπυροῦται καὶ ποιεῖ τὴν θερμότητα. ('Comme le premier élément [*i. e.* l'éther], avec les corps qu'il renferme, est animé d'un mouvement circulaire, ce qui, du monde inférieur et du corps qui le compose, se trouve en permanence en contact du premier élément, dissous par le mouvement s'enflamme et produit la chaleur.') Et Aristote de préciser plus bas que le feu qui est une forme d'incandescence résulte d'un excès de chaleur (cf. *Meteor.* 340b23). Le feu pour Aristote n'est qu'une réalité sublunaire dont la permanence semble ici assurée par la permanence du mouvement du ciel.

le moins curieux en ce que, pour Aristote, les astres, ne sont ni produits, ni faits de feu. Ils sont de la même nature éthérée que toute la sphère céleste. De plus, le feu et la chaleur produits par frottement le sont dans les lieux sublunaires (cf. ἐν τῷ πρὸς ἡμᾶς ἀέρι) présidés par les lois de la génération et de la corruption comme Aristote l'entendait. Il ne saurait donc constituer la matière des luminaires qui eux, dira Philopon, doivent durer[49]. Cette exégèse confond simplement les deux domaines en induisant à partir des phénomènes météorologiques de la région sublunaire, le mode d'avènement et d'existence des réalités supralunaires, autrement dit pour le Philopon interprète des Ecritures : le mode d'avènement et d'existence du firmament et des astres qui l'occupent. Ces derniers, à défaut d'être éternels, doivent, pour Philopon, se maintenir semblables à eux-mêmes pendant toute la durée du monde qui n'est pas, pour lui, éternel.

Nous avons omis la discussion de la thèse deux insérée entre la thèse trois et sa réfutation. Il nous faut brièvement y revenir.

Nous apprenons que, pour Philopon, la nature de la lumière primitive qui advient alors qu'elle n'était pas encore est à dissocier de la production ἐν ἀρχῇ du feu qui la précède. Ce que ne font pas les tenants de cette thèse que nous qualifiions de platonicienne. À quoi, il faut rappeler que pour eux, la lumière, essentiellement liée au feu puisqu'elle en est la substance, est, à ce qu'il semble, assimilée au corps qu'elle informe ou du moins solidaire de celui-ci. Ce que Philopon ne saurait à la suite d'Aristote admettre. Dans le commentaire de Philopon, l'antécédence du feu sur la lumière ne fait aucun doute, mais le *black-out* qu'il fait ici sur la nature du feu primitif, pourtant naturellement doté, du moins dans l'économie cosmique actuelle, de la puissance d'illuminer, est propice à générer bien de l'embarras. L'affirmation que la lumière advint alors qu'elle n'était pas encore (τό μήπω ὄν), sans l'élucidation de son rapport au feu, n'est pas vraiment de nature à le dissiper.

---

[49] En rigueur de termes, pour Philopon, le ciel lui-même comme la totalité du cosmos est engendré au commencement et connaîtra donc ultimement une corruption même si, du point de vue de notre propre champ de perception, il paraît durer toujours. C'est d'ailleurs ce paraître durer toujours du ciel qui devait induire l'hypothèse de sa pérennité, de son éternité et ce faisant celle de l'éternité du monde.

Mais il faut suspendre cette question en ce que Philopon ne laisse transparaître aucun indice à sa solution. Le sujet traité, en effet, porte d'abord sur l'existence d'une qualité qui sera dans l'ordre cosmique définitif, tant la 'forme des luminaires' (τὸ τῶν φωστήρων εἶδος, *De opif.* 76.21), du soleil, de la lune et des astres, que le rayonnement lumineux diffus qui en résultera[50]. C'est le mode antérieur et paradoxal d'existence de cette qualité simple et incorporelle, appelée lumière, qui est ici interrogé.

Vient enfin la position de Basile de Césarée[51] que Philopon convoque et dans la lignée duquel, il prétend s'inscrire contre Théodore de Mopsueste :

> Ὁ δὲ μέγας Βασίλειος τὸ ἡλιακὸν φῶς αὐτὸ προϋποστῆναί φησι τοῦ ἡλιακοῦ σώματος, δυνάμει θείᾳ τούτου γενομένου, ὅπερ φυσικῶς γενέσθαι ἀδύνατον· ὑπόδειγμα δὲ τοῦ λόγου ποιεῖται τὸ ἐπὶ τοῦ βάτου φανὲν τῷ Μωϋσεῖ πῦρ. διττῆς γὰρ οὔσης τῆς τοῦ πυρὸς δυνάμεως, φωτιστικῆς τε καὶ καυστικῆς, καὶ χωρίσαι ταῦτα μὴ δυναμένης τῆς φύσεως, ἐπὶ τοῦ βάτου τὸ μὲν φωτιστικὸν τοῦ πυρὸς ἐνήργει, τὸ δὲ καυστικὸν ἄπρακτον ἔμεινεν, τοῦ αὐτοῦ καὶ ἐπὶ τῶν ἐν τῇ καμίνῳ παίδων γενομένου τῇ ἐν Βαβυλῶνι· εἰς αὐτοὺς γὰρ τὸ καυστικὸν ἀνενέργητον ἔμεινεν. οὐκ ἀδύνατον ἄρα θεῷ καὶ χωρὶς σώματος ὑποστῆσαι τὸ φῶς. (*De opif.* 76.3–15)

> Basile le Grand dit que la lumière solaire a existé avant le corps solaire ; elle existait par la puissance divine avant qu'il lui fût possible d'exister dans la nature ; il donne pour exemple à son raisonnement le feu apparu à Moïse dans le buisson [cf. Ex. 3. 2]. Double en effet est la puissance du feu, capacité d'illuminer et capacité de brûler, et la nature ne peut s'écarter de ces deux caractéristiques ; pour le buisson, la faculté illuminative du feu était active, sa capacité à brûler demeurait inopérante ; on retrouve le même phénomène dans la fournaise des enfants à Babylone [cf. Dan. 3][52] : sur

---

[50] Cf. Philopon, *De opif.* 184.2–7. Nous pourrions interroger le fait que ce ne sont pas les seuls luminaires célestes qui sont luminescents. En effet, les comètes, la foudre, le feu là-haut ou ici-bas, certains corps ici-bas le sont aussi. Mais Philopon ne s'intéresse dans ces lignes qu'au rapport que la lumière primitive entretient avec les corps célestes qui demeurent et demeureront toute la durée du cosmos et ce à la différence des réalités luminescentes de la région sublunaire.

[51] Cf. Basile de Césarée, *In hexaem.* 6.3.1–18. Philopon, bien qu'il respecte globalement les idées avancées par Basile, le glose et le commente.

[52] Cet exemple n'est pas mentionné par Basile qui en convoque un autre. Il mentionne le témoignage du psalmiste qui affirme : 'La voix du Seigneur qui

eux aussi, la capacité de brûler demeurait inactive. Il n'était donc pas impossible à Dieu d'établir la lumière sans un corps[53].

Basile associe explicitement la lumière primitive et la lumière solaire préexistante au corps solaire. Mais il y a une relative imprécision dans la position de l'Évêque de Césarée, car il est difficile de savoir ce qu'il entend par lumière solaire. S'agit-il, c'est probablement le cas, de la forme essentielle du soleil, ou des rayons que celui-ci émet et qui ont dès lors pour substrat l'air auquel se trouvent conférées transparence et luminosité ? Les deux hypothèses doivent être envisagées.

Pour Basile, qui ne paraît pas avoir anticipé la distinction que Philopon fera, la préexistence de la lumière solaire relève de l'exception providentielle, car c'est la puissance divine qui donne à la lumière solaire d'exister avant l'astre duquel ultérieurement elle proviendra. De Basile, Philopon paraît retenir principalement le fait qu'il n'est pas impossible à Dieu d'établir la lumière, qu'il tient pour incorporelle, sans un substrat corporel.

---

du feu sépare la flamme' (Ps. 28. 7). Basile (*In hexaem.* 6.3.19–23 ; éd. SC 26 bis) le commente ainsi : Ὅθεν καὶ ἐν ταῖς τῶν βεβιωμένων ἡμῖν ἀνταποδόσεσι λόγος τις ἡμᾶς ἐν ἀπορρήτῳ παιδεύει, διαιρεθήσεσθαι τοῦ πυρὸς τὴν φύσιν, καὶ τὸ μὲν φῶς, εἰς ἀπόλαυσιν τοῖς δικαίοις, τὸ δὲ τῆς καύσεως ὀδυνηρὸν, τοῖς κολαζομένοις ἀποταχθήσεσθαι. ('De là vient aussi que, dans la rétribution due aux actes de notre vie, une sentence mystérieuse nous avertit que doivent être divisées les propriétés naturelles du feu : la lumière s'en détachera pour la jouissance des justes, la brûlure douloureuse pour ceux qui ont mérité un châtiment').

[53] Ce qui est démontré, c'est le pouvoir que possède Dieu, indépendamment des lois de la physique, de faire exister une substance sans l'une de ses puissances naturelles (le feu et sa puissance illuminative naturelle). Mais l'appel à Basile est étonnant car ce qu'il faut démontrer pour la lumière primitive, c'est le contraire. Ce n'est pas que Dieu soit en mesure de priver une substance de sa puissance naturelle, mais c'est qu'il puisse faire exister la puissance naturelle incorporelle d'une réalité sans sa substance, autrement dit la puissance illuminative sans le corps feu, ici la lumière solaire avant le soleil. La conclusion qu'en tire Philopon lorsqu'il affirme οὐκ ἀδύνατον ἄρα θεῷ καὶ χωρὶς σώματος ὑποστῆσαι τὸ φῶς (*De opif.* 76.13–15) n'est fondé que sur l'affirmation, non vérifiable, du pouvoir divin libre des lois physiques qu'il a par ailleurs établies. La principale idée que Philopon retient du propos de Basile est finalement celle que ce qui est impossible à la nature n'est pas impossible à Dieu. Nous pourrions en déduire que l'acte démiurgique qui instaure pas à pas les lois physiques n'y est lui-même pas soumis.

Philopon envisage donc, tour à tour, chacune des distinctions concernant la lumière : celle de la forme essentielle du luminaire et celle qui résulte de l'effet produit dans l'air lorsqu'il est présent.

> Καὶ ἐρεῖ τις τούτῳ συνηγορῶν, ὅτι καθάπερ τῶν μελλόντων ὑπὸ σελήνην γίνεσθαι προϋπέστησε τὰς ὑλικὰς αἰτίας ὁ θεός, ὡς εἰπόντες ἔφθημεν, οὕτως ἐπὶ τῶν φωστήρων τὸ ἐναντίον γέγονε· πρὸ τῆς σωματικῆς αὐτῶν οὐσίας καὶ ὑλικῆς τὸ φῶς ὑπέστησεν ὁ θεός, ὅπερ ἐστὶ τὸ τῶν φωστήρων εἶδος, εἶτα ἐκ τῆς προϋποκειμένης ὕλης διαπλάττει τὰ σώματα. ἀδύνατον δὲ θεῷ λέγειν, ὅπερ καὶ τῇ φύσει, θέμις ἐστὶν οὐδέν. ταῦτα δὲ συνάψας ἄμφω τοὺς ἐξ αὐτῶν φωστῆρας ἀνέδειξεν. (*De opif.* 76.16–25)

> [*Distinction 1 : la lumière, cause formelle des luminaires*]
> On dira à l'appui de cette thèse que, alors que, pour les choses qui devaient se trouver sous la lune, Dieu créa leurs causes matérielles avant elles, comme nous l'avons dit auparavant, au contraire, pour les luminaires, c'est l'inverse qui se produit : avant la substance corporelle et matérielle, Dieu a donné réalité à la lumière qui est justement la forme des luminaires, et ensuite, à partir de la matière préexistante il façonne les corps. Il n'est pas permis de dire que ce qui est impossible à la nature est impossible à Dieu. Ayant uni les deux, il montra les luminaires formés à partir d'elles[54].

Cherchant semble-t-il à appuyer la position de Basile en la clarifiant, Philopon commence par envisager la lumière solaire, non comme les rayons solaires ayant pour substrat l'air, mais comme la cause formelle du luminaire. L'exception providentielle est surtout un privilège démiurgique dissociant la causalité formelle et la causalité matérielle du luminaire. Philopon reprendra d'ailleurs cette idée lorsque, commentant la création des luminaires au quatrième jour, il affirmera :

> Πρότερον μὲν οὖν τὸ εἶδος ἁπλῶς τοῦ φωτὸς ὑπέστησεν ὁ θεός, ἁπλοῦν τὴν φύσιν καὶ διαφορὰν οὐδεμίαν ἔχον· νυνὶ δὲ τὰ ὑποκείμενα τούτῳ ποιήσας καὶ ἄμφω συνθεὶς τοὺς φωστῆρας εἰργάσατο. (*De opif.* 184.16–19)

---

[54] Le caractère composite du luminaire et la préexistence de sa forme seront à nouveau convoqués dans le commentaire du quatrième jour.

D'abord donc, Dieu créa la forme de la lumière sur le mode simple[55], <forme> qui a une nature simple non différenciée ; une fois qu'il a fait les objets qui lui servent de substrat, et assemblé les deux, il fabrique les luminaires.

L'appel de la lumière se classe donc, ainsi qu'il l'admet lui-même, dans le cas des choses qui sont impossibles à la nature, confirmant le *hiatus* métaphysique d'une telle position d'autant plus que, si on comprend exclusivement la lumière primitive comme la forme essentielle des luminaires, elle est trouvée sans la matière qui constituera avec elle la réalité physique concrète de l'agent illuminant.

Sans précision supplémentaire ici, Philopon délaisse provisoirement le postulat de la lumière primitive comme forme des luminaires pour l'envisager comme la lumière diffuse dans l'air. C'est la deuxième distinction :

Ἔστι δὲ κἀκεῖνο εἰπεῖν, ὡς οὐδ' αὐτὸ τὸ φῶς σώματος ὑπέστη χωρίς· ἀλλ' ὥσπερ καὶ τὸ ἐξ ἡλίου νῦν ἐν τοῖς διαφανέσι χωρὶς τοῦ ἡλιακοῦ γίνεται σώματος, ὑποκείμενον ἔχον αὐτὰ τὰ διαφανῆ σώματα, οὕτως εἰπόντος τοῦ θεοῦ· 'γενηθήτω φῶς' ὅπερ ποιεῖ τοῖς διαφανέσιν ὁ ἥλιος, φωτίζων αὐτά, τοῦτο τὸ θεῖον ἐποίησε πρόσταγμα ἐν αὐτοῖς κελεῦσαν ὡς ἐν ὑποκειμένοις ἐκλάμψαι τὸ φῶς. (*De opif.* 77.3–10)

[*Distinction 2 : la lumière dans le corps diaphane*] Il est possible *aussi* de dire que la lumière n'a pas existé en elle-même sans un corps ; mais de même que maintenant, ce qui vient du soleil se trouve dans les corps diaphanes sans le corps solaire, étant donné qu'il a comme substrat les corps diaphanes eux-mêmes, ainsi quand Dieu dit : 'Qu'advienne lumière', cet ordre divin fit dans les corps diaphanes ce que le soleil fait en eux quand il les illumine, en ordonnant que la lumière brille en eux comme dans leurs substrats.

Outre le fait que Philopon parvient à montrer ainsi que la lumière n'est jamais trouvée sans corps, il désigne clairement la lumière primitive comme le résultat de l'action d'un agent illuminant réalisant luminosité et transparence dans les corps diaphanes,

[55] Il dira peut avant (*De opif.* 184.4–7) qu'elle est une simple qualité (τὸ μὲν τὴν ἁπλῆν ποιότητα) et que le luminaire est le composé d'un substrat corporel et d'une qualité (τὸ δὲ τὸ ἐκ τοῦ ὑποκειμένου σώματος καὶ τῆς ποιότητος σύνθετον).

en l'absence duquel, ils ne sont que ténèbre. Mais ce propos n'est pas sans difficulté car, dans le cas du soleil, la lumière diffuse qui se propage instantanément dans l'air, bien que dissociée du luminaire quant à son mode d'être propre, est tributaire de sa source en l'absence de laquelle elle s'estompe. Que dire alors de l'agent de cette lumière primitive diffuse en l'absence de luminaires ? De qui, de quoi, résulte-t-elle ? Pour Philopon, il semble que ce soit l'ordre divin qui assume le rôle d'agent, ordre divin qui fait dans les corps diaphanes, l'air et dans une moindre mesure l'eau, ce que fera en eux le soleil, quand Dieu l'aura façonné. Pour le dire autrement, l'ordre divin actualiserait transparence et luminosité dans les corps qui en sont – au premier instant du monde – privés. Et ce, avant que le soleil, la lune et les astres ne deviennent définitivement les agents cosmiques de la propagation lumineuse[56].

La suite de son commentaire voit Philopon laisser de côté la question de la nature de la lumière primitive. Il ne la conçoit provisoirement plus comme la forme essentielle anticipée des luminaires et plus précisément du soleil, mais comme de la lumière propagée dans l'air, autrement dit, même s'il évite les termes philosophiques ici, comme l'acte du diaphane rendu possible par la présence de l'agent illuminant. Il devait, en effet, concevoir la lumière primitive autrement que comme la seule forme du luminaire pour expliquer la séparation de la lumière et de la ténèbre qui ne concerne évidemment pas la cause formelle, mais la lumière diffuse et sa privation dans le corps diaphane.

6. *La séparation de la lumière et de la ténèbre*

Il aborde maintenant la deuxième partie du problème, celui des modalités physiques du rapport que la lumière entretient sitôt créée avec sa propre privation : la ténèbre. Ce sont des modalités principielles dans la mesure où elles commandent et président ce que seront dorénavant ces rapports, en particulier l'alternance du jour et de la nuit. Il demande donc

---

[56] Une fois encore, nous sommes contraints de constater que demeure non élucidé, dans ce commentaire, le rapport que la lumière primitive aurait pu entretenir avec l'élément feu.

[...] πῶς ἀνὰ μέρος ὑποχωρούντων ἀλλήλοις φωτός τε καὶ σκότους ἡμέρα καὶ νὺξ ἐγίνετο. οὐδὲ γὰρ ἀντιπαραχωρεῖν ἀλλήλοις τοὺς τόπους σωμάτων χωρὶς οὐδὲ εἶναι ὅλως ἠδύναντο. (*De opif.* 74.13–16)

[...] comment, la lumière et la ténèbre se retirant l'une devant l'autre tour à tour, il y eût le jour et la nuit. Elles ne pouvaient en effet sans corps, ni se céder la place tour à tour, ni tout simplement être.

Pour élucider les conditions de ce retrait, Philopon commente le verset de la Genèse qui affirme, sitôt la lumière venue à l'existence sur appel de Dieu, la séparation de celle-ci d'avec la ténèbre. Il s'agit en fait, si l'on veut être exact, de la venue ou du retrait de la lumière, autrement dit de sa génération et de sa corruption, car il est entendu qu'au sens strict la ténèbre n'est pas quelque chose mais la privation de quelque chose. Ceci étant précisé, le fait de se céder tour à tour la place vient confirmer, selon lui, le fait que la lumière, bien que qualité incorporelle, n'est dès l'origine, pas sans corps qui lui tienne lieu de substrat, lui donne lieu d'être et permette physiquement le passage d'un état lumineux de quelque corps à son état contraire. C'est en raison du fait qu'elle trouve dans le corps diaphane un substrat que l'on peut, selon Philopon, comprendre le 'se retirer' ou le 'céder sa place' de la lumière autant que sa séparation physique d'avec la ténèbre.

Τὸ δέ· 'καὶ διεχώρισεν ὁ θεὸς ἀνὰ μέσον τοῦ φωτὸς καὶ ἀνὰ μέσον τοῦ σκότους' ὑπόνοιαν ἡμῖν ἐντίθησιν, ὡς οὐκ ἀθρόον ὅλον ἅμα τὸ διαφανὲς διειλήφει τὸ φῶς. οὕτω γὰρ ἂν πανταχόθεν ὅλον ἠφανίζετο σκότος, ὡς μηδὲ εἶναι λοιπὸν σκότος μηδαμοῦ· ὅλου γὰρ τοῦ πέριξ πεφωτισμένου σκίασμα λοιπὸν οὐκ ἦν οὐδαμοῦ. πῶς οὖν εἶπεν· 'καὶ διεχώρισεν ὁ θεὸς ἀνὰ μέσον τοῦ φωτὸς καὶ ἀνὰ μέσον τοῦ σκότους· καὶ τὸ μὲν φῶς ἡμέραν, τὸ δὲ σκότος ἐκάλεσεν νύκτα'; ὡς ἑκατέρου μὲν ὑπάρχοντος, διακεχωρισμένων δὲ τοῖς τόποις ἀλλήλων· ἅμα γὰρ ἄμφω ἐν ἑνὶ τόπῳ εἶναι ἀδύνατον ἦν· οὔτε γὰρ τὰ ἐναντία, οὔτε στέρησιν καὶ ἕξιν ἅμα συνυπάρχειν ἐνδέχεται. εἰ οὖν χωρὶς μὲν ἦν τὸ σκότος, χωρὶς δὲ τὸ φῶς, οὐχ ὅλον ἅμα τὸν κόσμον κατειλήφει τὸ φῶς. (*De opif.* 77.13–78.3)

La parole : 'Et Dieu sépara d'un côté la lumière, d'un côté la ténèbre' nous fait conjecturer que la lumière n'a pas embrassé tout ensemble d'un seul coup le <corps> diaphane.

En effet, la ténèbre aurait alors été éclairée de tous côtés de sorte qu'il ne resterait plus aucune ténèbre ; tout l'alentour étant éclairé, il ne resterait plus d'ombre où que ce soit. Et pourquoi alors aurait-il dit : 'Et Dieu sépara la lumière d'avec la ténèbre. Il appela la lumière "jour" et la ténèbre "nuit"', comme si chacune d'elles existait et qu'elles avaient été séparées l'une de l'autre par les lieux qu'elles occupaient ? Car il était impossible que les deux se trouvent en même temps en un même lieu. Il n'est loisible ni pour les contraires, ni pour une privation et un état d'exister ensemble en un même lieu[57]. Si donc, il y avait séparément, et la ténèbre, et la lumière, c'est que la lumière ne s'était pas emparée en même temps de l'univers tout entier.

L'acte divin qui suit l'appel de la lumière est une séparation. Or, pour comprendre la conjecture explicative de Philopon, à savoir que 'la lumière n'a pas embrassé tout ensemble d'un seul coup le <corps> diaphane', et la conclusion du propos 'que la lumière ne s'était pas emparée en même temps de l'univers tout entier', il peut être utile de recourir à une clarification que Philopon n'apporte que quelques pages plus bas[58]. Dans l'analyse détaillée d'un point de syntaxe du grec de la *Septante* que les traductions peinent parfois à restituer[59], Philopon fait remarquer que le texte biblique dit en un parallèle évident : 'Dieu sépara, d'un côté (ἀνὰ μέσον) la lumière, d'un côté (ἀνὰ μέσον) la ténèbre'[60]. Pour Philopon, l'expression ἀνὰ μέσον, que nous traduisons ici par 'd'un côté', d'abord utilisée pour la lumière, puis utilisée pour la ténèbre, atteste de la répartition de l'une et de l'autre en deux domaines clairement distincts[61]. Cette séparation radicale (car, pour Philopon, Dieu a rendu leur nature, pure de

---

[57] Ils peuvent cependant exister ensemble mais dans des lieux différents comme dans la configuration cosmique définitive.

[58] Pour la totalité du développement : Philopon, *De opif.* 82.13–83.26.

[59] Nous sommes parfaitement conscients que notre traduction 'et Dieu sépara d'un côté la lumière, d'un côté la ténèbre' sans doute trop littérale infléchie le texte dans le sens où le comprend Philopon.

[60] Philopon signalait d'ailleurs le choix interprétatif de la *Septante*, qu'il retient ici, par contraste d'avec les versions d'Aquila et de Symmaque qui proposent respectivement : καὶ διεχώρισεν ὁ θεὸς μεταξὺ τοῦ φωτὸς καὶ μεταξὺ τοῦ σκότους. ὁ δὲ Σύμμαχος ἀντὶ τοῦ διεχώρισεν 'διέστειλεν' ἔφη (*De opif.* 82.16–19).

[61] Cf. Philopon, *De opif.* 82.22–83.4.

tout mélange et de toute communion)[62] peut s'entendre de trois manières qui ne sont d'ailleurs pas exclusives[63].

(1) La claire discrimination entre lumière et ténèbre s'opère d'abord sur le *plan logique et métaphysique* car la disposition (ἕξις) est inconciliable avec la privation (στέρησις). Ainsi que le précise Philopon : 'La limite de la lumière est le commencement de la ténèbre et, inversement, la limite de la ténèbre est le commencement de la lumière' (τὸ πέρας τοῦ φωτὸς ἀρχή ἐστι τοῦ σκότους καὶ τοὔμπαλιν τὸ πέρας τοῦ σκότους ἀρχή ἐστι τοῦ φωτός, *De opif.* 83.10–12).

(2) Elle s'opère ensuite au regard de la *catégorie de lieu.* Lumière et ténèbre ne peuvent en effet occuper le même lieu. Nous allons revenir sur cette modalité.

(3) La discrimination s'opère enfin au regard de la *catégorie de temps,* selon une alternance qui semble réguler dès l'origine le jour et la nuit. Dès que la lumière paraît, instantanément, d'un coup, la ténèbre disparaît. Certes, il y a des degrés d'intensité de la lumière mais dans les faits, pour Philopon, ou il y a lumière à l'instant, ou il n'y a plus lumière à l'instant.

Mais pour Philopon, le propos de la Genèse qui affirme : 'Et Dieu sépara d'un côté la lumière, d'un côté la ténèbre' vise avant tout la séparation locale. Parfaitement observable dans l'économie cosmique une fois les luminaires créés, cette séparation spatiale, qui vise à démontrer que 'la lumière n'a pas embrassé tout ensemble d'un seul coup le <corps> diaphane' (*De opif.* 77.14–16), est problématique, si l'on considère son statut primitif avant que l'Univers ne soit achevé et configuré. En effet, dans la configuration cosmique définitive, il est facile de se représenter une séparation locale de la lumière et de la ténèbre, laquelle ténèbre résulte de la présence d'un corps s'interposant à l'étendue de l'action d'un agent illuminant précisément localisé[64]. Comment expli-

---

[62] Cf. Philopon, *De opif.* 83.5–6 : ἄμικτόν τε καὶ ἀκοινώνητον αὐτῶν τὴν φύσιν ποιήσας.

[63] Pour ce développement, voir : Philopon, *De opif.* 83.5–26.

[64] Ainsi que l'affirme Philopon (*De opif.* 83.14–17) qui n'offre comme exemple à la séparation locale que le cas du cosmos achevé : ὅτε γὰρ ὑπὲρ γῆν ἐστιν ὁ ἥλιος φωτίζων τὰ πρὸς ἡμᾶς, ὑπὸ γῆν ἐστιν ὁ σκότος· καὶ ἔμπαλιν, ὅτε ὑπὸ γῆν ἐκεῖνος, ὁ σκότος τὸν ὑπὲρ γῆν ἀέρα κατέχει. ('Quand le soleil est au-dessus de

quer, en effet, que résident côte à côte lumière et ténèbre alors que Philopon vient de conjecturer que 'la lumière n'a pas embrassé tout ensemble d'un seul coup le <corps> diaphane' ? Quelle est donc la cause qui retient la lumière dans des bornes aussi sévères, alors qu'aucun corps n'est dit s'interposer à sa diffusion ? Cette cause limitant la lumière, est-elle corporelle, incorporelle, physique ou métaphysique ?

Philopon est conscient que c'est là une position difficilement tenable d'un point de vue strictement physique. C'est sans doute pourquoi il poursuit ainsi :

> Γνωρίμῳ δέ τινι ὑποδείγματι χρήσομαι, ὅπερ ἐπὶ τῶν κομητῶν ὁρῶμεν γιγνόμενον ἐν μέρει τινὶ τοῦ περιέχοντος ἀέρος λαμβανόντων ὑπόστασιν καὶ συμπεριπολούντων τῷ παντί, συνανατελλόντων τε καὶ συνδυομένων τῷ μέρει, καθ᾽ ὃ ἂν συστῶσιν· οὕτω καὶ τὸ πρωτόγονον ἐκεῖνο φῶς μέρος ἐπέχον τοῦ διαφανοῦς, οἷον φέρε τῶν ἡμισφαιρίων ἕν, ὥσπερ νῦν τῇ ἀνατολῇ μὲν τοῦ ἡλίου γίνεται ἡμέρα, τῇ δύσει δὲ νύξ, οὕτω καὶ τοῦ φωτὸς ἐκείνου συμπεριπολοῦντος τῷ παντί, δυομένου μὲν νύξ, συνανατέλλοντος δὲ ἡμέρα ἐγίνετο. (*De opif.* 78.4–14)

> J'utiliserai un exemple connu : c'est ce que nous voyons se passer pour les comètes qui prennent consistance dans une partie de l'air ambiant, qui font leur révolution avec l'univers qui s'élèvent et qui plongent avec lui du côté où elles se sont formées. Il en va ainsi pour cette lumière primitive qui occupe *une partie* de ce qui est transparent, comme par exemple l'un des hémisphères ; de même que maintenant avec le lever du soleil a lieu le jour, avec son coucher la nuit, ainsi cette lumière <primitive> tournant avec l'univers quand elle se couchait c'était la nuit, quand elle se levait avec l'univers, c'était le jour.

La lumière primitive occupe donc bien, pour lui, une portion de ce qui est transparent concomitamment à la ténèbre qui en occupe une autre. Il reste cependant imprécis sur la portion occu-

---

la terre et éclaire notre monde, la ténèbre est sous la terre ; et à rebours, quand le soleil est sous la terre, la ténèbre domine l'air qui est sur terre.') Cf. *De opif.* 85.7–8 : αὐτὸ τὸ μόνῃ τῇ ἀντιφράξει τοῦ φωτὸς παρυφιστάμενον ('[la ténèbre] n'existe que par l'interception de la lumière') ; puis encore *De opif.* 130.10–12 : ἡ δὲ νὺξ οὐδὲν ἄλλο ἐστὶν ἢ σκίασμα γῆς [...] ὑπ᾽ αὐτὴν τοῦ ἡλίου γενομένου ('la nuit n'est rien d'autre que l'ombre de la terre [...] quand le soleil est sous elle').

pée car la tournure de Philopon : 'comme par exemple l'un des
hémisphères', n'est pas une affirmation claire qui permette de
fonder le fait que lumière et ténèbre se partagent effectivement
alors l'espace cosmique en deux zones égales. Le cas de la comète
convoqué pour illustrer la non-impossibilité de poser l'existence
d'une réalité luminescente entourée de ténèbre n'est pas très clair
non plus. Au mieux dit-il que la lumière primitive semble atta-
chée au mouvement de l'univers qu'elle suit dans sa rotation.
Ce serait donc qu'il y a une forme d'alternance primitive suivant la rotation de l'univers où, tour à tour, les deux hémisphères
seraient illuminés, puis privés de lumière, et ce au moins jusqu'au
quatrième jour, au moment où sont formés les luminaires auxquels la lumière est destinée. Une fois encore, cet état primitif
n'étant qu'un moment de la cosmogénèse, on se meut dans d'in-
vérifiables conjectures sur les étapes préparatoires qui verront la
lumière, forme, qualité incorporelle, informer les luminaires qui,
dans l'économie d'un monde enfin achevé, assureront l'alternance du jour et de la nuit telle que depuis nous les connaissons.

Ainsi Philopon pourra conclure :

> Μήποτε δὲ καὶ ἐνσώματος ἦν οὐσία τὸ φῶς ἐκεῖνο, οὐχ οὕτω
> διεσχηματισμένον, ὡς νῦν οἱ ἀστέρες καὶ οἱ δύο φωστῆρες ὑπάρ-
> χουσιν, ὕστερον δὲ εἰς τὴν νῦν αὐτὸ τάξιν ἤγαγεν ὁ θεός, εἰς ἥλιον
> καὶ σελήνην καὶ τοὺς λοιποὺς ἀστέρας τὸ φῶς ἐκεῖνο καταμε-
> ρίσας· καὶ οὕτω μὲν οὐδὲν ἀδύνατον ἐφάνη συμβαῖνον· τάχα
> δὲ πάλιν ἐντεῦθεν ὁ Πλάτων εἰληφώς· 'βουληθεὶς ὁ θεός' φησίν
> 'ἀγαθὰ μὲν πάντα, φλαῦρον δὲ μηδὲν εἶναι κατὰ δύναμιν, οὕτω
> δὴ πᾶν, ὅσον ἦν ὁρατὸν παραλαβὼν οὐχ ἡσυχίαν ἄγον, ἀλλὰ
> κινούμενον πλημμελῶς καὶ ἀτάκτως εἰς τάξιν αὐτὸ ἤγαγεν ἐκ τῆς
> ἀταξίας· ἡγησάμενος ἐκείνου τοῦτο πάντως ἄμεινον'. ὁρατὸν δὲ
> ἄνευ φωτὸς οὐδέν. (*De opif.* 78.15–27)

Cette lumière n'était pas encore une substance incorporée,
elle qui n'avait pas encore cette forme achevée qu'ont maintenant les astres et les deux luminaires, mais c'est par la suite
que Dieu la mena à l'ordre, le même que maintenant : il répar-
tit cette lumière entre le soleil, la lune et les astres restants ;
et il semble bien possible que ce fut ainsi[65]. Platon s'en inspire
peut-être bien quand il dit : 'Dieu, voulant que toutes choses

---

[65] On notera cette réserve qui semble admettre le caractère délicat d'une telle
conjecture qui se comprend surtout comme une étape préparatoire explicative
du cosmos que nous ne connaissons que dans sa forme achevée.

fussent bonnes et que rien ne fut mauvais dans la mesure
du possible, a pris tout ce qui était visible, dépourvu de tout
repos et qui se mouvait sans mesure et sans ordre, et il l'a
amené du désordre à l'ordre, car il estimait que l'ordre vaut
infiniment mieux que le désordre' [Platon, *Timaeus* 30a].
Mais sans lumière rien n'est visible [cf. Aristote, *De Anima*
418a31–b3].

Il revient dans cette conclusion à la conception de la lumière
comme forme des luminaires. Il rappelle qu'elle n'est pas encore
substance incorporée bien qu'elle ne soit pas trouvée sans un
substrat corporel, à savoir l'air dont elle n'est simplement pas la
forme constitutive.

Force est d'admettre finalement que, postuler l'existence tant
de la cause formelle des luminaires avant leur cause matérielle,
que l'existence de la lumière dans l'air en l'absence d'agent physique illuminant, est assez délicat à tenir. Cela constitue peut-
être moins une entorse aux lois de la physique qui s'établissent
progressivement, qu'un privilège du Démiurge qui précisément
fonde, étape par étape, les lois physiques qui, au terme de la
création, apparaîtront comme les règles constitutives du cosmos
et de tous les phénomènes qui s'y peuvent observer. En effet,
le 'mener la lumière à l'ordre, le même que maintenant' comme
l'affirme Philopon, renforcé par la citation du *Timée* qui rapporte
le passage à l'ordre de tout le visible par l'action démiurgique,
l'un et l'autre de ces points viennent indiquer que nous sommes
bien dans un moment déterminé de la cosmogénèse, moment
qui, en tant que tel, n'a pas à répondre aux lois physiques contrai-
gnantes une fois l'ordre cosmique définitif établi.

Philopon semble conscient de la difficulté que soulèvent ces
étapes préparatoires et fondatrices du monde, étapes finalisées
certes, mais qui restent pour une part conjecturales, car il esquive
par deux fois de s'en expliquer en renvoyant de potentiels contra-
dicteurs à leurs propres difficultés à rendre compte des anomalies et irrégularités d'un ciel qu'ils tiennent pourtant pour divin,
en raison de sa régularité et de la permanence de son mouvement.
C'est ce qui lui fait affirmer :

Εἰ δέ τις ἡμᾶς ἀπαιτοίη τὴν αἰτίαν τοῦ ταῦτα οὕτω κατ' ἀρχὴν
διαταξάμενον ποιῆσαι τὸν θεόν, πρῶτον μὲν τὸ οὐκ ἀδύνατον
τοῦ πράγματος ποικίλως ἐδείχθη· ὅταν δὲ τῆς φαινομένης ἐν

τοῖς ἄστροις ἀνωμαλίας κατά τε μεγέθη καὶ θέσιν καὶ τάξιν καὶ χρώματα καὶ πρὸς ἄλληλα σχέσιν, καὶ τῆς ἐν διαφόροις χρόνοις τῶν πλανωμένων ἀποκαταστάσεως τὰς αἰτίας εἴποι, καὶ ἄλλων μυρίων τῶν ἐν τῷ κόσμῳ διατεταγμένων, δι᾽ οὓς λόγους ταῦθ᾽ οὕτως ἔχειν πεποίηκεν ὁ θεός, τότε καὶ ἡμᾶς τῶν ὑπὸ Μωϋσέως κατὰ θείαν ἐπίπνοιαν περὶ τῆς κατ᾽ ἀρχὴν κοσμογονίας ἑκάστου λόγον αἰτείτω. (*De opif.* 79.5–16)

Si quelqu'un demandait la raison pour laquelle Dieu a créé en procédant ainsi à l'origine, tout d'abord on a démontré qu'il ne lui était pas impossible de réaliser cela de diverses façons. Quand on nous dira les causes des anomalies qui apparaissent dans les astres pour la grandeur, la position, le rang, les couleurs ou leurs relations mutuelles et les raisons du retour des planètes à leur point de départ à différents moments, et pour quelles raisons Dieu a fait les milliers d'autres phénomènes qui sont réglés dans le monde, qu'on nous réclame alors la raison de chacune des choses énoncées par Moïse sous l'inspiration divine à propos de l'origine de la cosmogonie[66].

Le Jour Un étant achevé, ce n'est plus *ex nihilo* qu'adviennent les réalités qui lui succèdent dans des phases successives dont il est le principe. L'action est alors démiurgique, artisanale, dans la mesure où rien de nouveau n'est introduit dans le monde qui n'y soit déjà sous la forme de la matière préexistante et des raisons spermatiques contenues dans les éléments.

Si les éléments feu et terre semblent occuper une place prépondérante dans la toute première phase de la création, comme on peut par ailleurs le constater dans le commentaire tardo-antique du *Timée* de Platon[67], ce sont les corps diaphanes, l'air et l'eau, qui sont sollicités au deuxième jour au moment de la création du firmament dans lequel, au quatrième jour, viendront prendre place les luminaires, en particulier le soleil et la lune, qui présideront dans l'économie cosmique à l'alternance du jour et de la nuit, à la présence de la lumière et à sa privation autrement appelée 'ténèbre', 'nuit', 'ombre', etc.

---

[66] Il reproduira une seconde fois un propos similaire : Philopon, *De opif.* 117.15–23.

[67] Cf. Proclus, *In Tim*. II.5.31–13.14.

7. *Conclusion*

Nous nous proposions, dans ce travail exploratoire, de discuter les conditions d'avènement de la lumière primitive ainsi que sa nature. Nous avons vu que le texte biblique soulève d'importantes difficultés quand nous tentons, dans un effort ouvertement concordiste, de faire converger la cosmogénèse qu'il expose, avec ce qui peut s'observer des processus physiques d'avènement de la réalité. Philopon s'est engagé dans cette forme de justification du texte mosaïque. Il intervient contre l'École d'Antioche d'abord qui, par sa lecture littérale et naïve du récit de la Genèse et son hostilité déclarée aux données qu'imposent les faits d'observation, ne peut que provoquer du mépris pour la conception judéo-chrétienne de l'Univers. Il intervient dans un souci apologétique ensuite pour montrer que rien, dans le propos du Prophète, n'est en désaccord avec les phénomènes mais qu'en un sens Moïse a précédé les recherches des physiciens qui lui emboîteront le pas. Outre ce souci de concordisme qui constitue le présupposé de son exégèse, Philopon entendait élucider les difficultés qui découlaient de l'appel de la lumière au Jour Un dans l'instant qui suit sans intervalle la création *ex nihilo* proprement dite. Nous avons vu que la création ἐν ἀρχῇ voit apparaître simultanément le ciel et la terre, la nature des quatre éléments et les raisons spermatiques de tous les êtres à venir. Nous avons vu également que, dans ce premier instant inétendu et principe du temps, la lumière n'était pas encore, laissant non élucidé le rapport de cette dernière avec l'élément feu qui la précède, lequel élément feu est pourtant naturellement doté de la puissance d'illuminer comme Philopon l'admet lui aussi.

Nous avons vu que Philopon imposait de considérer la lumière diversement, selon qu'on la tient pour la forme des luminaires, ou qu'on la tient pour l'état du corps diaphane résultant de la présence d'un agent illuminant paradoxalement absent au premier jour. Mais Philopon, conscient de ces difficultés, semble avoir admis le fait que ce qui est impossible à la nature n'est pas impossible à Dieu et semble s'être accommodé de ce fait qu'il ne prend pas la peine d'argumenter face à de possibles détracteurs, les renvoyant à leurs propres difficultés à expliquer leur théorie concernant le ciel.

De ce travail exploratoire, on peut cependant relever la mobilisation d'un certain nombre de données sur la lumière ressortant du *De opificio mundi* qu'il faut lire avec, en arrière-plan, les recherches que Philopon avait déjà conduites par le passé, dans le commentaire d'Aristote et dans le *Contra Proclum*. Nous avons ainsi pu noter que la lumière est double, selon qu'on la considère comme la forme constitutive de l'agent illuminant (soleil, lune, astres et feu), ou selon qu'on l'envisage comme la lumière qui naît dans l'air à l'approche d'un tel agent. Dans le premier cas, elle est une forme incorporelle, de nature simple. Elle est incorruptible. Dans le *Contra Proclum*, Philopon précise qu'elle est acte du soleil (ἐνέργεια). En tant que cause formelle du soleil, elle est cause efficiente de la diaphanie, de la transparence et de la luminosité dans l'air (cf. *De opif.* 70.6–8). Quant à la lumière dans l'air, elle est, selon Philopon, une affection qualitative de l'air (πάθος τοῦ ἀέρος, *Contra Proclum* 18.6) et non l'acte de l'agent illuminant (ἐνέργεια τοῦ φωτίζοντος, *Contra Proclum* 18.5) puisqu'elle est corruptible. Ce n'est en effet pas toujours la même lumière qui, dans l'économie cosmique, se trouve dans une région de l'air, mais toujours une lumière autre à un moment autre, en un lieu autre. Ces distinctions, peu développées dans le *De opificio mundi*, et ce à la différence du *Contra Proclum*, n'en sont pas moins centrales et omniprésentes dans ce commentaire scripturaire[68]. Mais dans le cas de la lumière primitive, nous sommes dans une phase antérieure à celle-là, car il n'y a pas d'agent illuminant. La lumière primitive, tantôt envisagée comme la cause formelle du luminaire anticipant l'apparition de ce dernier, tantôt envisagée comme la lumière diffuse dans l'air n'embrassant pas totalement le corps diaphane, devait surtout indiquer une étape préparatoire aux lois et règles cosmiques qui, une fois les luminaires créés, sont irrévocables. Cette 'photographie' du Jour Un est surtout indicative d'une Intelligence à l'œuvre dans un ensemble d'opérations qui amènent progressivement le monde à sa stature définitive et à son ordre.

Il reste que, comme tel, Philopon n'a pas élucidé dans ce commentaire le rapport de la lumière primitive et du feu primitif. C'est ainsi que ce parcours exploratoire, dans l'un des commentaires tardo-antiques de la Genèse qui compte parmi les plus fouillés, s'achève sur une aporie.

---

[68] Philopon y renvoie explicitement. Voir : Philopon, *De opif.* 88.12–27.

Bibliographie

Sources primaires

Jean Damascène, *De Haeresibus 83 addit.*, dans *Die Schriften des Johannes von Damaskos, Vol. 4. Liber de haeresibus. Opera Polemica*, éd. B. Kotter, Berlin : De Gruyter, 1981, p. 50–55.

Jean Philopon, *De Aeternitate Mundi contra Proclum*, éd. H. Rabe, Leipzig : Teubner, 1899.

Jean Philopon, *De opificio mundi*, éd. G. Reichhardt, Leipzig : Teubner, 1897.

Jean Philopon, *La création du monde*, trad. M.-C. Rosset & M.-H. Congourdeau, Paris : Migne, 2004 (Les Pères dans la foi).

Jean Philopon, *De Aeternitate Mundi contra Proclum*, 3 vol., éd. C. Scholten, Freiburg i. Br. – Basel : Herder, 2009–2011 (Fontes Christiani).

Jean Philopon, *Against Aristotle. On the Eternity of the World*, trad. C. Wildberg, London : Duckworth, 1987.

Proclus, *In Platonis Timaeum commentaria*, 3 vol., éd. E. Diehl, Leipzig : Teubner, 1903–1906.

Proclus, *Commentaire sur le Timée*, 5 vol., trad. A.-J. Festugière, Paris : Vrin – CNRS, 1966–1968.

Proclus, *On the Eternity of the World*, trad. H. S. Lang & A. D. Macro, Berkeley – Los Angeles : University of California Press, 2001.

Simplicius, *Against Philoponus on the Eternity of the World*, trad. C. Wildberg, London : Duckworth, 1991.

Littérature secondaire

R. Bodéüs (1993), *Aristote. De l'âme*, Paris : Flammarion.

L. Fladerer (1999), *Johannes Philoponos. De opificio mundi. Spätantikes Sprachdenken und christliche Exegese*, Stuttgart – Leipzig : Teubner.

G. R. Giardina et al. (2012), 'Philopon (Jean-)', dans R. Goulet (éd.), *Dictionnaire des philosophes antiques*, vol. Va, Paris : CNRS, p. 455–502.

P. Golitsis (2008), *Les Commentaires de Simplicius et de Jean Philopon à la Physique d'Aristote*, Berlin – New York : Walter de Gruyter (Commentaria in Aristotelem Graeca et Byzantina 3).

J. C. De Groot (1983), 'Philoponus on *De Anima* II.5, *Physics* III.3, and the Propagation of Light', dans *Phronesis*, 28, p. 177–196.

J. De Groot (1991), *Aristotle and Philoponus on Light*, New York – London: Garland.

T. Hainthaler (1996), 'Jean Philopon, philosophe et théologien à Alexandrie', dans A. Grillmeier (éd.), *Le Christ dans la tradition chrétienne, II.4 : L'Église d'Alexandrie, la Nubie et l'Éthiopie après 451*, Paris : Cerf, p. 165–215.

P. Hoffmann (1987), 'Sur quelques aspects de la polémique de Simplicius contre Jean Philopon : De l'invective à la réaffirmation de la transcendance du ciel', dans I. Hadot (éd.), *Simplicius, sa vie, son œuvre, sa survie*, Berlin – New York : Walter De Gruyter, p. 183–221.

U. M. Lang (2001), *John Philoponus and the Controversies over Chalcedon in the Sixth Century. A Study and Translation of the 'Arbiter'*, Leuven : Peeters.

S. Laramée (2008), 'À propos de *La Création du monde* de Jean Philopon', dans *Laval théologique et philosophique*, 64, p. 541–548.

P. Mueller-Jourdan (sous presse), 'De l'acte du diaphane à l'énergie opérative. Notes sur la nature de la lumière dans le commentaire de Jean Philopon au *De Anima* d'Aristote', dans P. Hoffmann e.a. (éd.), *Essence, puissance, activité dans l'Antiquité classique et tardive*, Paris : Classiques Garnier.

C. Osborne (1989), 'Philoponus on the Origins of the Universe and other Issues', dans *Studies in History and Philosophy of Science*, 20, p. 389–395.

S. Sambursky (1958), 'Philoponus' Interpretation of Aristotle's Theory of Light', dans *Osiris*, 13, p. 114–126.

S. Sambursky (1987), *The Physical World of Late Antiquity*, London : Routledge and Kegan Paul.

J. Schamp (2000), 'Photios et Jean Philopon : sur la date du *De opificio mundi*', dans *Byzantion*, 70, p. 135–154.

C. Scholten (1996), *Antike Naturphilosophie und christliche Kosmologie in der Schrift 'De opificio mundi' des Johannes Philoponos*, Berlin – New York : Walter de Gruyter.

L. Siorvanes (1996), *Proclus : Neo-Platonic Philosophy and Science*, New Haven – London : Yale University Press.

R. Sorabji (éd., 1990), *Aristotle Transformed. The Ancient Commentators and Their Influence*, London : Duckworth.

R. Sorabji (2005), *The Philosophy of the Commentators, 200–600 AD. A Sourcebook*, vol. 2., Ithaca – New York : Cornell University Press.

A. Vasiliu (1997), *Du diaphane*, Paris : Vrin (Études de philosophie médiévale).

G. Verbeke (1988), 'La physique d'Aristote et l'interprétation de

Jean Philopon', dans M. A. Sinaceur (éd.), *Aristote aujourd'hui*, Paris : Érès, p. 300–314.

K. Verrycken (1990), 'The development of Philoponus' thought and its chronology', dans R. Sorabji (éd.), *Aristotle Transformed. The Ancient Commentators and Their Influence*, London : Duckworth, p. 233–274.

K. Verrycken (1997), 'Philoponus' Interpretation of Plato's Cosmogony', dans *Documenti e Studi sulla tradizione filosofica medievale*, 8, p. 269–318.

K. Verrycken (1998), 'Johannes Philoponos', dans *Reallexikon für Antike und Christentum*, 18, p. 534–553.

C. Wildberg (1988), *John Philoponus' Criticism of Aristotle's Theory of Aether*, Berlin – New York : Walter de Gruyter.

C. Wildberg (2018), 'John Philoponus', dans E. N. Zalta (éd.), *The Stanford Encyclopedia of Philosophy*, https://plato.stanford.edu/archives/win2018/entries/philoponus/.

W. Wolska (1962), *La Topographie chrétienne de Cosmas Indicopleustès. Théologie et science au VIᵉ siècle*, Paris : P.U.F.

Abstract

The commentary of John Philoponus on the narration of the Creation of the world is characterised by an obvious concordance and the will to make the Scriptures and the nature of physical phenomenons observed by both Aristotle and Plato converge. It presents several difficulties including that of the status that must be granted to the primitive light when on the first day, upon the divine calling, the incorporeal quality "light" happens alone without the luminescent body of which however it will constitute the formal reason on the fourth day of the creation. What must be thought of this hiatus? How to understand it? To put it simply, what is the nature of the primitive light in these conditions? The present contribution especially seeks to organise the questions that emerged from this aporia yet without completely answering them.

ISTVÁN PERCZEL

PRE-EXISTENCE AND THE CREATION OF THE WORLD IN PSEUDO-CAESARIUS

1. *Introduction*

In three previous studies – 'Finding a Place for the *Erotapokriseis* of Pseudo-Caesarius: A New Document of Sixth-century Palestinian Origenism', 'Clandestine Heresy and Politics in Sixth-century Constantinople: Theodore of Caesarea at the Court of Justinian' and 'Universal Salvation as an Antidote to Apocalyptic Expectations: Origenism in the Service of Justinian's Religious Politics'[1] – I investigated the milieu of provenance, the doctrinal background, and the authorship of the *Questions and Answers* (QA) attributed to Caesarius, the brother of Gregory of Nazianzus. I have come to the conclusion that, the work's seemingly anti-Origenist stance notwithstanding, it was written by a member of the sixth-century movement deemed 'Origenist'. In an attempt to identify the author of the work, I suggested that, once the elements we had about the author are combined with these recognitions, we obtain a clear phantom image of him, which perfectly coincides with the figure of Theodore, Archbishop of Caesarea in Cappadocia, nicknamed 'the Wine-sack' (Ἀσκιδᾶς). This Theodore was the main advisor of Justinian in religious affairs during the period between 536 and 553; also, according to Cyril of Scythopolis, he was one of the leaders of the 'Isochrist Origenist' party. The Isochrists constituted one faction of the 'Origenists' so-called, which was accused by its opponents – that is, both the anti-Origenist Sabaite monks and their fellow-'Origenist' Protok-

---

[1] Perczel 2006–2007; Perczel 2017a; Perczel 2017b.

Questioning the World, Greek Patristic and Byzantine Question-and-Answer Literature, ed. by Bram Demulder and Peter Van Deun, Turnhout, 2021 (*LECTIO*, 11), pp. 311-360   ©BREPOLS❦PUBLISHERS   DOI 10.1484/M.LECTIO-EB.5.121510

tist monks of Firminus' Lavra – of professing the doctrine that, in the final Restoration to the original bliss of all the rational beings, there will be no difference between Christ and the divinised saints: all of them will be equal to Christ.[2] Thus, in 'Clandestine Heresy and Politics', I outlined the historical context for Theodore's activity, his 'Origenism' and also his denial of Origen when he signed, in an act of concealment, the Alexandrian master's condemnation by the Permanent Synod in Constantinople in 542/43,[3] as well as his move to counteract the intrigues of the anti-Origenist party, led by the Deacon Pelagius, the legate of Pope Vigilius and his personal enemy, by promulgating the condemnation of the Three Chapters.

The thesis that Pseudo-Caesarius, his apparent anti-Origenism notwithstanding, must have belonged to the Origenist movement, which I first outlined in 'Finding a Place', has had a rather uneven reception history. The first to accept and endorse it, although in a perplexing way, was Tzamalikos in his voluminous twin monograph about Cassian the Sabaite.[4] He widely approved of my thesis of the Origenism of Pseudo-Dionysius, as well as my attribution of the Pseudo-Didymian De trinitate and of the Pseudo-Caesarian Erotapokriseis to sixth-century Origenism. Yet, he nowhere references my work, while introducing some important changes. So, while I had adduced several arguments to prove that the author of the De trinitate is identical with that of the Pseudo-Dionysian Corpus,[5] and attributed the Erotapokriseis to the Origenist leader Theodore of Caesarea,[6] Tzamalikos attributes both the De trinitate and the Erotapokriseis, while maintaining their Origenism, to Cassian the Sabaite, one of the leaders of the anti-Origenist movement of Palestine, about whom Tzamalikos is writing interesting but undemonstrated stories, such as Cassian's meeting with Pseudo-Dionysius in the monastery of the

---

[2] On this issue, see Perczel 2017a, ch. 4.

[3] The accepted date for the condemnation is 543. However, the only point of repair for the dating is that the edict was promulgated in Palestine in February 543. The Constantinopolitan condemnation could well have happened in late 542, or in January 543.

[4] See Tzamalikos 2012a and 2012b.

[5] See Perczel 1999, p. 690–701, and Perczel 2013.

[6] See Perczel 2006–2007.

Akoimetai in Constantinople and about Damascius converting to Christianity at the end of his life and settling in the monastery of the *Akoimetai* after his return from Persia.[7] Tzamalikos' claim of a Greek monk authoring the kernel of the work later created under the name of John Cassian of Marseille has been duly examined and refuted by Stewart, who has shown that the Greek Cassian is simply an abbreviated version of the Latin Corpus, which has well attested external witnesses to its existence before the time of activity of Cassian the Sabaite, so it cannot be attributed to him.[8] In 'Clandestine Heresy and Politics' I re-examined all the existing testimonies to Cassian the Sabaite, showing that he was reputed to be one of the leaders of the anti-Origenist strife in Palestine and that the attribution to him of an extended pseudonymous corpus of Origenist tendency has no foundation.[9]

At the opposite end of Tzamalikos, Papadogiannakis has expressed his doubts on the attribution of the *Erotapokriseis* to an Origenist author because of the latter's explicit attacks on Origen and on his doctrine of a spiritual paradise and the leather garments of Gen. 3. 21, meaning the human bodies received after the Fall.[10] Yet, Papadogiannakis seems to ignore the general political context of the condemnation of Origen in 542/3 and its aftermath, when the prominent leaders of the Origenist movement, Theodore of Caesarea and Domitian of Ancyra, were forced to sign the anti-Origenist edict. This was a move that led to a psychological crisis in the case of Domitian and to a sustained double speak in the case of Theodore, who remained outspoken in his condemnation of Origen until the fifth oecumenical council in 553, while remaining faithful to his Origenist convictions.[11] To Papadogiannakis' doubts, a more detailed answer will be given in the present study, whose philological analyses will show

---

[7] On the identification of Cassian and Pseudo-Caesarius see Tzamalikos 2012a, p. 373–440. On the attribution of the *De trinitate* to Cassian the Sabaite, see his p. 441–619. On the meeting of Cassian and Pseudo-Dionysius, see p. 8, 15, 481. On Damascius' conversion to Christianity, see p. 474.

[8] Stewart 2015.

[9] See Perczel 2017a, p. 160–168.

[10] Papadogiannakis 2013, p. 274 and note 12. Cf. also Macé 2015, p. 6, note 30.

[11] See my treatment of this context and of the divergent reactions of the Origenist leaders, testified to by contemporary documents in Perczel 2006–2007, p. 73–74 and, in more detail, in Perczel 2017a, p. 147–156.

how the seemingly anti-Origenist passages of the *Erotapokriseis* should be understood.

Also, there are passages of manifest Origenian and Evagrian inspiration, which Papadogiannakis does not recognise. Thus, when he presents Ps.-Caesarius' interpretation of Ps. 118 (119). 73 'your hands have made me and fashioned me' (αἱ χεῖρές σου ἐποίησάν με καὶ ἔπλασάν με) in QA 137 and 138, according to which the 'making' (ποίησις: see Gen. 12. 7) refers to the creation of the soul, and the 'fashioning' (πλάσις: see Gen 2. 7) to that of the body, while the hands of God are the Son and the Holy Spirit, he does not recognise that Ps.-Caesarius reproduces here Evagrius' exegesis, based on Origen's double creation theory.[12] Also, when Papadogiannakis presents Ps.-Caesarius' explaining away, in QA 217, of Paul's teaching on the final salvation of the entire Israel (Rom. 1. 25–27), saying that Israel does not mean here the Jews but 'the mind seeing God' (νοῦς ὁρῶν θεόν) and that those Jews who will not convert will be punished in hell, he does not recognise that this etymology comes from Origen rather than from Philo and that, precisely in his commentary on the same verses of the Epistle to the Romans, Origen gives the same etymology and the same interpretation of the damnation of the unrepented Jews, adding however, that hell is a purifying fire that would come to an end.[13]

I should also cite Spanu, who has mentioned my identification of Ps.-Caesarius with Theodore of Caesarea along with the views of Papadogiannakis and Tzamalikos without, however, taking sides.[14] Finally, in a study treating Justinian's Novella 146, De Lange mentions the same identification and my conclusion that Theodore of Caesarea might be the mind behind Justinian's legislation in a similarly neutral manner.[15]

[12] Papadogianakis 2013, p. 273. See (Ps.-)Origen, *Fragmenta in Psalmos* 118. 73 (in Pitra 1883, p. 278–279). Below, when treating Ps.-Caesarius apparent anti-Origenism, I will study this passage in detail.

[13] Papadogianakis 2013, p. 277. See Origen, *In Rom.* VIII. 12 (ed. PG 14, col. 1195–1198). Yet, I must admit that, while treating this passage in the QA and demonstrating its Origenian and Evagrian inspiration, I also failed to note this obvious parallelism in the interpretation of the same Pauline verses. See Perczel 2006–2007, p. 69–71 and, more extensively, Perczel 2017b, p. 132–140. Thus, my conclusions in those publications need to be modified based on this Origenian parallel.

[14] Spanu 2016, p. 25. See also Spanu 2014, p. 2.

[15] De Lange 2016, p. 221 and 225.

After this survey of the reactions to my initial publication on this issue, I can only express my hope that the detailed analyses of the last three studies, including the present one, would trigger more interest and perhaps a more sympathetic reception than the first study alone was able to secure.

If the hypothesis that Theodore of Caesarea is the real author of the Ps.-Caesarian *Questions and Answers* is correct, this means that, in principle, this piece of writing should contain the 'Isochrist Origenist' doctrine, a doctrine about which we know hardly anything more than the – necessarily biased – accusations of the condemnatory documents. Given the historical context, even if this doctrine is expressed somewhere, it could only be found in a hidden manner, so that it would not be manifest for a superficial reader but would be clearly indicated, even exposed, for those initiated. In other words, it would be *encoded* in seemingly innocent, or even striking but at face value incomprehensible, passages. Now, if there is an *encoding*, there should also be a *decoding*, revealing the original intention and thought of the author. However, a decoding endeavour is always risky: one might risk at the end not to find what there is in reality but what one wishes to see. In order to avoid such an illusion, I formulated, at the end of 'Clandestine Heresy', six general methodological principles that should guide, at least in the form of a methodological working hypothesis, the decoding endeavour. These I called the *principles of intentionality, of individual coherence, of respect, of the existence of encoded languages, of symmetry,* and *of efficiency*.[16] In 'Universal Salvation'[17] I tried to apply these principles to samples of the eschatological material contained in the *Questions and Answers*. This has led to the elaboration of a decoding methodology for understanding the complicated allegorical scriptural exegesis used by the Ps.-Caesarius, which has some peculiarities, of which I was able to discover the following:

1. Ps.-Caesarius, his vociferous condemnation of Origen and of some 'Origenist' tenets notwithstanding, is largely relying on the particular allegorical exegeses given by Origen and Evagrius of Pontus, often alluding to some of their texts – controversial

---

[16] See Perczel 2017a, p. 168–171.
[17] See Perczel 2017b.

in the sixth century – *verbatim*. This contradiction – condemning Origen overtly while following Origen's and Evagrius' tradition secretly – corresponds to the historically known attitude of Theodore of Caesarea, whose secret 'Origenism' was finally revealed only in 553, and who used the precedent of the *post mortem* condemnation of Origen as a pretext for promoting the *post mortem* condemnation of Theodore of Mopsuestia.[18] The method of hiding controversial texts under a paraphrase I called *the method of the background texts*. According to the *principle of symmetry*, which states that the decoding methods should correspond to the encoding methods, the recognition of the background texts, if the intertextual relationship is analysed carefully and cautiously, and if it is combined with other methods, should lead to the understanding of the texts' hidden meaning.

2. There is also another method, which was presented in 'Finding a Place' but did not get much emphasis in 'Universal Salvation', namely using the technique of paraphrasing standard theological texts from the great tradition but giving them a twist so that their meaning changes, often to the opposite. This method I would call *the method of the twisted authorities*.

3. For encoding his message, the author generally uses duplicates and, in the case of very important passages even triplicates. That is, he is using terms whose meaning is not clear in the given passage, while the key for understanding this hidden meaning can be found in a parallel passage or passages where, on the other hand, terms whose usage was clear in the first passage remain unclear. Thus, the author established a structure, which resembles systems of equations with multiple variables. Therefore, the decoding following the recognition of this encoding method is similar to the solution of such equation systems. One has to use the methods of elimination or substitution for a given variable until the values of all the variables are found. This method I dubbed *the method of the duplicates*.

---

[18] See ACO IV/1, p. 18. 24–25; 24. 19; 27. 9 and 24; 104. 30–115; 143. 14; 185. 12.

4. In some cases I found correspondences according to the meaning and even verbal coincidences between the expressions used by Ps.-Caesarius and the texts of the anti-Origenist condemnations of the fifth ecumenical council of 553.[19] As the condemnatory texts are later than, or at least independent of, the text of the *Questions and Answers*, the recognition of these parallels is methodologically different from the recognition of the Origenian and Evagrian background texts. They reveal that the condemnatory texts were composed in the knowledge and on the basis of testimonies coming from the 'Origenist' monks of Palestine, pointing toward either written or oral sources. Although this is not an encoding method used for decoding, using such recognitions greatly help us understanding the text. Thus, I would call this *the method of the condemnatory parallels*.

In what follows, I will, once again, use these methodological observations. First I will treat the general structure of the *Questions and Answers*, after which I will examine how the author's vociferous condemnations of the 'most unholy Origen's' doctrines should be understood, before exploring another element of Ps.-Caesarius's systematic thought expressed through his subtle writing technique, namely his teaching on the pre-existence of the rational beings and of their subsequent fall leading to the creation of the material universe.

2. *The General Structure of the Questions and Answers and Ps.-Caesarius's Apparent Anti-Origenism*

The work intends to be a universal compendium of the Christian faith, exposed in the form of questions and answers. After a rhetorical introduction in QA 1, which treats very important epistemological questions in a rather allusive manner, it enters the

---

[19] In Perczel 2006–2007, p. 55 and Perczel 2017a, p. 154–155, I explained why Diekamp's widely accepted hypothesis (Diekamp 1899, p. 97–98), according to which 'Origenism' was condemned at a pre-session of the fifth ecumenical council by the Permanent Synod and why the consequent claim that there have never been any ecumenical condemnation of Origenism, is untenable. According to my reconstruction, the condemnation of 'Origenism' was the subject of a second session of the ecumenical council.

field of theology. For all these theological questions Ps.-Caesarius chooses the *Ancoratus* of Epiphanius as basic background text, moulding his message in a paraphrase of this old anti-heretical – and anti-Origenist – compendium.[20]

The questions and answers comprise, first, the Trinitarian doctrine (QA 2–17), after which there begin long musings about the Son, pertaining to a mixture of what the Cappadocian Fathers have called *theologia*, i.e. the intra-Trinitarian relations, and *oikonomia*, i.e. the Incarnation (QA 18–41); two questions (QA 42–43) are related to the Holy Spirit, after which Ps.-Caesarius treats the angels (QA 44–49), the penultimate question (QA 48) being about the Devil, who had earlier been an angel. With QA 50 begin the chapters about the creation of the material universe, a literal-historical exegesis based on the commentaries on Genesis of Severian of Gabala and, to a lesser extent, of Basil of Caesarea, through which, at the most unpredictable places, transpires an allegorical exegesis suggesting the most daring tenets. In QA 50–117, the author comments upon the first five days of the creation and – accordingly – upon all the elements of the material creation with the exception of man, created on the sixth day.

Here one would expect that the exposition should continue with the creation of man but, instead, there comes a series of odd questions and answers, pertaining to a number of miscellaneous subjects (QA 118–134). Their placement here is entirely illogical from the point of view of the plan of the work, so Ps.-Caesarius justifies this interruption of the original plan by an inappropriate question of his interlocutors, whom he scolds for this.[21] The questions have apparently nothing to do with each other: first, the interlocutor asks about the meaning of a parable of Christ (QA 118), secondly about the question why and how God gave Job over to the Devil (QA 119–120), thirdly there comes a series of questions about the fall of Adam and Eve and the role of the Devil and his previous fall (QA 121–124), fourthly a series of Christological questions concerning the incarnate Christ (QA 125–134), including the question on what would

---

[20] See Riedinger 1964.
[21] QA 118. 6–9.

happen to the Kingdom of Christ, whether it will take an end or remain forever (QA 126; 128).

There follows a long sequence of questions and answers on the creation of man, apparently the central problem of the whole work (QA 135–188). The structure of this set of questions is the following. As an introduction, there are three general questions about the creation of man, two about the question why David disparages, and Solomon magnifies man (QA 135–136) and one about the difference between the ποίησις ('creation') and the πλάσις ('moulding') of man (QA 137). Here Ps.-Caesarius distinguishes between the creation of man in Gen. 1. 26, which he understands as the creation of the soul, and the moulding of man from earth in Gen. 2. 7, which he understands as the fashioning of the body.[22] Then, Ps.-Caesarius avoids a question concerning the anthropomorphite understanding of God, which proposes that the fact that the human being is created 'according to the image and likeness' of God should mean that God is also similar to us. Postponing the answer until later, Ps.-Caesarius rather indulges in the physiological details of the conception of the human being (QA 139). Within this framework he refutes traducianism (which he calls 'co-existence', συνύπαρξις, of soul and body) but also the idea that the body would be anterior to the soul (which he calls 'posterior existence', μεθύπαρξις) as well as the 'pre-existence' of the souls to the body (προΰπαρξις), affirming that only the composite can be called 'man'. By this, he establishes a paradox or, rather, a riddle: the soul is neither coeval, nor pre-existent, nor posterior to the body.

Having made these distinctions, Ps.-Caesarius proceeds to the treatment of the corporeal 'fashioning' of man (QA 140–158), followed by questions concerning the Paradise of Eden (QA 159–167), where the emphasis is on the earthly nature of Paradise as over against the allegorical interpretation, here explicitly attributed to 'the most unholy Origen' (Ὠριγένην τὸν ἀνοσιώτατον, QA 166. 24). In all this, Ps.-Caesarius's unavowed source is Epiphanius' *Ancoratus*, whose anti-Origenist arguments it uses. The next section refutes the interpretation, presented again as 'Origen's poisonous and destructive doctrine' (τὰ Ὠριγένους

---

[22] See above, page 314 and note 12.

[...] δηλητήρια καὶ φθοροποιὰ δόγματα, QA 168), of the 'leather garments' (Gen 3. 21) being the bodies received by the fallen souls who had to leave the celestial Paradise and the idea, upheld by 'those who are babbling Origen's doctrines' (τοὺς Ὠριγένους φληνάφους, QA 170), that embodiment is a punishment of pre-cosmic sin (QA 168–173). In QA 173 he returns to the distinction between 'creation' and 'fashioning', which he still distinguishes as two distinct acts inseparable in time, to refute the idea of pre-existence. It is to be noted that Ps.-Caesarius's criticisms of the Origenian tenets, which have earned for him the reputation of being a dedicated anti-Origenist,[23] are all concentrated in this section and, thus, belong to his refutation of the idea of the pre-existence of the souls to their bodies.

QA 174–188 contain a detailed exegesis of the meaning of the human being's being created 'according to the image and resemblance' of God (Gen 1. 27). Ps.-Caesarius finds that this is not in any one of the constituents of the human being, neither in the body, nor in the soul but 'in the immortality of the soul, and in the human being's rule over the whole creation' (ἐν τῷ ἀθανάτῳ τῆς ψυχῆς καὶ ἐν τῷ πάντων ἄρχειν αὐτόν, QA 174. 4–5). So it is in neither one of the two constituents (QA 175), nor in the mind (QA 176–178), the human being being entirely dissimilar from God, but, as advanced in QA 174 but reformulated in QA 179 in an ambivalent manner, 'in the immortality and the ruling nature' or rather 'in the immortal and principal element of the soul' (ἐν τῷ ἀθνήτῳ καὶ ἀρχικῷ τῆς ψυχῆς, QA 179. 5–6) (QA 179–187). The ambiguity is grammatical: this can either mean the fact that the soul is immortal and ruling, or that there is an immortal and ruling, i.e. divine, element in the soul. The continuation shows that Ps.-Caesarius adheres to the second interpretation. The rest of the treatment exploits this ambiguity and it is here that Ps.-Caesarius enters poetic heights describing the absolute ruling power of the divinised saints who remain in this immortal, ruling principle. Finally, it is in QA 188 that Ps.-Caesarius returns to the question asked in QA 139 about the anthropomorphite interpretation of God's nature. Having established the total dissimilarity of the human constitution to God, he interprets its

---

[23] See Grillmeier 1989, p. 421 and Papadogiannakis 2013, p. 273.

creation according to the image and likeness as a prophecy about the Incarnation of the Word thus making the human being the divine image.

Mentioning the Incarnation gives opportunity to Ps.-Caesarius for placing a blow on the Jews (QA 189), after which come speculations on virtue (QA 190–192). Clearly, here begins the part on eschatology, virtue being the means for divinisation. There follows a number of explanations of obscure scriptural passages and parables (QA 193–215). These explanations are characterised by bold allegorisation, which permits Ps.-Caesarius to expound several aspects of his doctrine, among others, in QA 214, an allegory on God's infinite mercifulness in a system of pardoning not only seven times but seventy times seven times (Mt. 18. 21–22) meaning that not only 'the one who had once killed' (τὸν ἅπαξ φονεύσαντα, QA 214. 90; i.e. Cain), but also 'the one who had once reneged on God' (τὸν ἅπαξ που ἀρνησάμενον τὸν θεόν, QA 214. 91–92; the subject is unspecified, but the hint seems to be at Satan) will be pardoned. The last three questions, occupying roughly one seventh of the entire work, deal with the end of human history and the fate of the Jews (QA 216–218). This amounts to an entire semi-independent anti-Jewish treatise using *the method of the twisted authorities*. In fact, it uses and paraphrases much of John Chrysostom's anti-Jewish homilies[24] but its aim is to refute Chrysostom's teaching about the eschatological conversion and final historical salvation of the Jewish people as a people, which constituted the theological basis for the survival of the Jewish community in the Byzantine polity.[25] The whole treatise is completed by a call on the Emperor to punish the perfidious Jews for all their sins.[26] Apparently, the political aim of this great theological compendium was to give a new theological interpretation to the role of the Jews, denying their salvation as a people, in order to prepare Justinian's anti-Jewish legislation. I see even much in common between the language

---

[24] John Chrysostom, *Against the Jews*, homilies IV–VI (ed. PG 48, col. 876–904), see Riedinger's *apparatus criticus*.

[25] See John Chrysostom, *Commentary on the Epistle to the Romans*, XIX, 2–3 (ed. PG 60, col. 585–587).

[26] QA 218. 899–900. I have treated this part in its connection to Ps.-Caesarius' Origenist eschatology in Perczel 2017b, p. 129–132.

of the *Questions and Answers* and Novella 146 of Justinian *On the Hebrews*,[27] a problem that will be treated in a forthcoming publication. Thus, I would set as a *terminus ante quem* for the composition of the work the 8 February 553, that is, the date of publication of the Novella.[28]

3. Ps.-Caesarius's Anti-Origenian Polemic: A Sincere Stance, Hypocrisy, or Reservatio Mentalis?

As mentioned above, Ps.-Caesarius's anti-Origenian polemic is concentrated in the part of the *Questions and Answers* dealing with the soul-body relationship and especially with the doctrine, attributed to Origen, of the pre-existence of the souls to the bodies. If the identification that I am proposing of the author with Theodore of Caesarea, reputedly the leader of the Isochrist Origenists of the New Lavra in Palestine, holds, an examination of this polemic promises much: the comprehension of his internal thoughts when signing Justinian's anti-Origenist edict of 542/43, a condemnation that he maintained during all his life and which served as a pretext for him for promoting the posthumous condemnation of Theodore of Mopsuestia and of the Three Chapters. So, was he sincerely condemning Origen, or was he simply a hypocrite as Cyril of Scythopolis claims,[29] or is there a subtler relationship between his doctrines and those condemned by the edict?

In fact, if one examines this text carefully, one finds out that Ps.-Caesarius's criticism of Origen is a typical example of encoding, using *the method of the twisted authorities*. He uses, besides the standard text of Epiphanius, that of Justinian's *Letter to Menas* written in 542/43,[30] which he cites almost verbally and which he subtly criticises.

---

[27] Ed. Schöll & Kroll 1912, p. 714–716. On the Novella, see Veltri 1994; De Lange 1999 and 2016; Rutgers 2003.

[28] This is confirming Riedinger's conclusions who had established as approximate date for the composition the early 550s. See Riedinger 1969, p. 235–459.

[29] Cyril of Scythopolis, *Life of Saint Sabas*, in Schwartz 1939, p. 191. 32–192. 11, cited and treated in detail in Perczel 2017a, p. 147–149.

[30] *Iustinianus contra Origenem* in ACO III, p. 189–214.

Here are a few examples:

Justinian, *Edict against Origen*	Ps.-Caesarius, *Questions and Answers*
1. ACO III, p. 191. 24–35.	1. QA 168. 12–18.
Εἰ δὲ <u>κατὰ τὴν</u> Ὠριγένους <u>βλασφη-μίαν</u> προϋπῆρχον αἱ ψυχαὶ καὶ διὰ τὸ ἁμαρτῆσαι αὐτὰς τιμωρίας χάριν εἰς τὰ σώματα κατεπέμφθησαν, ἵνα παι-δευθεῖσαι σωφρονήσωσιν, <u>ἐχρῆν</u> <u>αὐτὰς</u> <u>μηκέτι ἁμαρτάνειν</u>. εἰ γὰρ πρὸς κόλασιν τῆι ψυχῆι διὰ τὴν ἁμαρτίαν ἐδόθη τὸ σῶμα, ὥστε αὐτὴν ὀδυνομένην παιδευθῆ-ναι πρὸς τὸ τιμᾶν τὸν θεόν, πῶς συνεργεῖ καὶ συναγωνίζεται αὐτῆι τὸ σῶμα πρὸς τὸ ἁμαρτάνειν; <u>δεσμοὶ γὰρ καὶ φυλακαὶ</u> <u>καὶ πέδαι καὶ συντόμως εἰπεῖν τὰ τοιαῦτα</u> <u>ἐφεκτικὰ τοῦ ἀδικεῖν καὶ τοῦ ἁμαρτάνειν</u> <u>τοῖς κολαζομένοις γίνονται</u>. οὐ γὰρ ὅπως ὁ ἁμαρτήσας πλέον ἁμαρτήσηι, συνεργὸς αὐτῶι πρὸς τὴν ἁμαρτίαν ὁ δεσμὸς δίδο-ται, ἀλλ᾽ ὅπως παύσηται τοῦ ἁμαρτάνειν διὰ τῶν δεσμῶν βασανιζόμενος. πρόδηλον τοίνυν ὅτι οὐ διὰ σωφρονισμὸν προλαβου-σῶν ἁμαρτιῶν τοῖς σώμασιν ἐνεβλήθησαν αἱ ψυχαὶ κατὰ τοὺς ἐκείνου λήρους, ἀλλὰ κατὰ ταυτὸν ὁ θεὸς τό τε σῶμα τήν τε ψυχήν, τουτέστι τέλειον τὸν ἄνθρωπον ἐδημιούργησεν.[31]	Ἤδη ἀνωτέρω αἰσθόμενος ἔφην ὑμᾶς <u>τὰ</u> <u>Ὠριγένους</u> φρονεῖν <u>δηλητήρια καὶ φθορο-ποιὰ</u> δόγματα, τοὺς ἁπλουστέρους σκελί-ζοντα. οὐ γὰρ κατ᾽ οὐρανὸν ἁμαρτοῦσαι ψυχαὶ ἐν σώμασιν κατεκρίθησαν τιμω-ρεῖσθαι, μηκέτι δυνάμεναι συνπεριπο-λεῖν τῇ ὑπερκοσμίῳ τελετῇ. εἰ γὰρ πρὸς διόρθωσιν καὶ νῆψιν τοῖς σώμασιν τού-τοις κατεκλείσθησαν, <u>πῶς ἐν τούτῳ βα-ρυτέρως ἁμαρτάνουσιν</u>; ὁ δὲ ἐν φρουρίῳ τιμωρούμενος δηλονότι καὶ βουλόμενος ἁμαρτεῖν οὐχ οἷός τε ὑπάρχει.[32]
	2. QA 137. 1–7.
	Πεῦσις Τί δηλοῖ ὁ Δαυὶδ λέγων τῷ θεῷ· *αἱ χεῖρές σου ἐποίησάν με καὶ ἔπλασάν με*; ἆρα ἕτερόν τι σημαίνει τὴν πλάσιν καὶ ἄλλο τὴν ποίησιν; ἐκ δὲ τούτου διφυεῖς ἑαυτοὺς νοῦμεν; ποίας δὲ ἄρα χεῖρας χρὴ λέγειν ἐπὶ θεοῦ;
	Ἀπόκρισις <u>Τὴν</u> <u>ποίησιν ἐπὶ τῆς ψυχῆς</u> <u>μοι δοκεῖ νοεῖσθαι, τὴν δὲ πλάσιν ἐπὶ τῆς</u> <u>σωματικῆς πηλοπλασίας·</u> χεῖρας δὲ τοῦ θεοῦ καὶ πατρὸς τὸν υἱὸν καὶ τὸ πνεῦμά

(cont.)

[31] 'If, according to Origen's <u>blasphemy</u>, *the souls pre-existed and were sent down to the bodies in order to be punished, so that, having been disciplined, they become sober*, <u>they</u> <u>should</u> <u>have</u> <u>stopped</u> sinning. If the body was given to the soul as a punishment because of sin, so that, afflicted, she would be disciplined to venerate God, how does the body contribute and strive together with her to sinning? <u>For the chains, the jails, the shackles and, to make it brief, all the suchlike</u> <u>are given to those punished in order to prevent them from committing injustice</u> <u>and from sinning</u>. For chains are not given as a collaborator to the one who has sinned, in order that he might continue sinning, but in order that he may stop sinning, being tortured by the chains. Thus, it is manifest that the souls were not thrown into bodies in order to be corrected from previous sins according to their stupidities, but that God created together the body and the soul, that is, the complete human being'.

[32] 'Even before, when I heard this, I told that you [the interrogators] are professing Origen's <u>poisonous</u> <u>and</u> <u>destructive</u> <u>doctrines</u>, which are thwarting the

Justinian, *Edict against Origen*	Ps.-Caesarius, *Questions and Answers*
2. ACO III, p. 192. 27–30. Ὁ θεὸς γὰρ εἰπὼν *ποιήσωμεν ἄνθρωπον κατ' εἰκόνα ἡμετέραν καὶ ὁμοίωσιν* ἀμφότερα κατὰ ταυτὸν ἐδημιούργησε, τουτέστι σῶμά τε πλάσας καὶ ψυχὴν νοεράν τε καὶ λογικὴν δημιουργήσας. ἅμα γὰρ σῶμα ἔπλασεν ὁ θεὸς καὶ τὴν ψυχὴν ἐδημιούργησε τέλειον τὸν ἄνθρωπον ἀποτελέσας.[33] 3. ACO III, p. 192. 31. Οὐδὲ γὰρ σῶμα χωρὶς ψυχῆς οὐδὲ ψυχὴ χωρὶς σώματος ἄνθρωπος.[34] 4. ACO III, p. 194. 26–30. Εἰ δὲ προϋπῆρχον αἱ ψυχαὶ ἐν ἑτέραι τάξει ὑπάρχουσαι κατὰ τοὺς Ὠριγένους	φημι, πρὸς οὓς καί φησιν· *ποιήσομεν ἄνθρωπον κατ' εἰκόνα καὶ ὁμοίωσιν ἡμετέραν.*[35] 3. QA 139. 59–61. Οὔτε οὖν ἡ ψυχὴ καθ'ἑαυτὴν οὔτε τὸ σῶμα ὑπάρχει ἄνθρωπος· ἑκατέρων γὰρ τὴν συνάφειαν καὶ ἕνωσιν ἀπηρτῆσθαι βροτὸν ὁ τῶν θείων συγγραφεὺς Μωσῆς ἀπεφήνατο.[36] 4. QA 168. 18–20. Διά τι δὲ ἄρα καὶ τοὺς δαίμονας ἅμα τῷ διαβόλῳ νόας ὑπάρχοντας καὶ ἀσωμάτους ἁμαρτήσαντας καὶ τῶν οὐρανῶν καταρραγέντας μὴ ἐν σώμασιν καθ' ὑμᾶς

simple-minded. *For it is not true that the souls committing sin in the heavens were condemned to be punished in bodies*, not being able to go around together with the supracosmic initiation [cf. Plato, *Phaedrus* 246b]. *For if they had been enclosed in these bodies for correction and sobering down*, how comes that in the body they are sinning even more seriously? It is clear that the one who is punished by detention in jail, even if he wants to sin is not capable to do so'.

[33] 'For God, when he said, "*Let us make man according to our image and likeness*" [Gen. 1. 26], created both by the same act, that is, by moulding the body and by creating the intellectual and rational soul. For it was together that God moulded the body and created the soul, completing the perfect man'.

[34] 'For neither the body without the soul, nor the soul without the body is man'.

[35] 'Q. What does David indicate when he says to God: "Your hands made me and fashioned me" [Ps. 118. 73]? Does he indicate that the moulding and the making are two different things? Should we understand from this that we are double-natured? Also, what kind of hands should we understand concerning God? A. You should understand that the making refers to the soul, while the moulding to the corporeal fashioning of the clay, while I call hands of God the Father, the Son and the Spirit, to whom he says: "*Let us make man according to our image and likeness*" [Gen. 1. 26]'.

[36] 'Therefore, neither the soul by itself, nor the body by itself is man. For the author on things divine Moses declared that the conjunction and union of the two composes the mortal'.

Justinian, *Edict against Origen*	Ps.-Caesarius, *Questions and Answers*
μύθους, διὰ τί μόνον τὸν Ἀδὰμ ἔπλασεν ὁ θεός; ἆρα μόνον ἡ ψυχὴ τοῦ Ἀδὰμ τότε ἦν ἁμαρτήσασα καὶ διὰ τοῦτο ἓν σῶμα ἔπλασεν ὁ θεός; εἰ γὰρ ἦσαν πρὸ τούτου καὶ ἄλλαι ψυχαί, ἔδει καὶ ἄλλα σώματα ἅμα πλασθῆναι ὑποδεχόμενα τὰς ψυχάς.[37]	αὐτοὺς πρὸς νῆψιν καὶ διόρθωσιν κατησφαλίσατο;[38]

I think these parallels show the subtle way in which Ps.-Caesarius engages with the text of the anti-Origenist condemnations in a complex intertextual debate, formally accepting them but subtly criticising their arguments. This is so much so that I would claim that it is only in the light of Justinian's edict that Ps.-Caesarius's speculations on the creation of man and his ambiguous rejection of the theory of pre-existence become comprehensible.

In parallel 1, he takes over the edict's argument that, if the souls had pre-existed and their embodiment had been the result of punishment, the punishment should serve to prevent further sinning. Since the body participates in sinning, it cannot be considered an efficient corrective to the previous sin.

Parallel 2 shows a complicated intertextual relationship: Justinian's criticism targets Origen's doctrine, according to which the creation of man in Gen. 1. 26 refers to the creation of the soul, while the moulding of man from earth in Gen. 2. 7 refers to the body:

> Hunc sane hominem, quem dicit *ad imaginem Dei factum*, non intelligimus corporalem. Non enim corporis figmentum Dei imaginem continet, neque *factus* esse corporalis homo dicitur, sed *plasmatus*, sicut in consequentibus scriptum est.

---

[37] 'If the souls pre-existed existing in a different order according to Origen's myths, why did God fashion only Adam? *Had only Adam's soul sinned alone, so that for this reason God fashioned only one body? For if there were also other souls before that, he should have fashioned also other bodies together with that one, to receive the souls*'.

[38] 'Also, given that the demons together with the Devil are also minds, *when they sinned in the incorporeal state and were thrown down from heaven, why did God not secure them human bodies for sobering down and correction?*'

Ait enim: *Et plasmavit Deus hominem*, id est finxit, *de terrae limo*. Is autem qui *ad imaginem Dei factus est*, interior homo noster est, invisibilis et incorporalis et incorruptus atque immortalis.[39]

We do not understand, however, this man indeed whom Scripture says was made *according to the image of God* [Gen. 1. 26] to be corporeal. For the form of the body does not contain the image of God, nor is the corporeal man said to be *made* but *fashioned*, as is written in the words that follow. For the text says: *And God fashioned man*, that is, *moulded, from the mud of the earth* [Gen. 2. 7].[40]

Apparently, it is this theory that Justinian rejects by affirming that the creation and fashioning are one and the same act. Ps.-Caesarius, on his turn, using *the method of the twisted authorities*, engages with this view. He maintains the difference of the two acts but accepts their simultaneity as, according to parallel 3, in which Ps.-Caesarius literally echoes Justinian, neither constituent can be called man, but only the composition out of the two. Yet, in parallel 2, Ps.-Caesarius returns from Justinian to Origen and Evagrius via a complex Origenian/Origenist exegetical tradition interpreting Ps. 118. 73 and transmitted through the glosses of the Palestinian Catena on the Psalms. Modern research has identified one of these glosses as written by Evagrius of Pontus:

Πεποίηται μὲν ἡ ψυχή, πέπλασται δὲ τὸ σῶμα· ποιήσωμεν γὰρ, φησὶ, ἄνθρωπον κατ' εἰκόνα ἡμετέραν. καὶ πάλιν· λαβὼν χοῦν ἀπὸ τῆς γῆς ἔπλασεν.[41]

---

[39] Origen, *Homiliae in Genesin* 1. 13. 56; ed. Doutreleau 1985.

[40] Translation slightly modified from Heine 1982, p. 63.

[41] See (Ps.-)Origen, *Fragmenta in Psalmos* 118:73 (in Pitra 1883, p. 278–279). Pitra's text consists of a string of glosses on the verse, the first of which Marie-Joseph Rondeau identified, based on the witness of MS Vat. graec. 754, as written by Evagrius (Rondeau 1960, p. 345). On fol. 300ᵛ of Vat. graec. 754, this gloss is transmitted anonymously and bears the number 32. In other manuscripts it is attributed to Origen. I owe all the clarification on this gloss and the following ones to Paul Géhin, who not only generously shared with me the critical text of this gloss prepared for his forthcoming edition of the *Scholia in Psalmos* of Evagrius, but also gave extensive explanations on the other glosses interpreting this verse and on the secondary literature (e-mail communication by Paul Géhin dated 25.10.2018). I thank him warmly for all this!

The soul is *made*, while the body is *fashioned*. For Scripture says: *let us make man according to our image* [Gen. 1. 26]; and again: *taking dust from the earth He fashioned* [Gen. 2. 7].

That this was a controversial theory is clear not only from Justinian's condemnatory text but also from a note in the Palestian Catena, which attributes this distinction between making and fashioning to Origen and his followers, and rejects it.[42] Another gloss, which Vat. graec. 754 attributes to Jerome but Vat. graec. 2057 transmits under the fivefold lemma 'of Origen, Cyril, Athanasius, Didymus, Evagrius', says the following:

> ὠριγένους· κυρίλλου· ἀθανασίου· διδύμου· εὐαγρίου: τὸ ἀνυστικὸν τῆς ἐνεργείας αὐτοῦ σημαίνει καὶ δημιουργικὴν ἐνέργειαν · χεῖρες δὲ θεοῦ. ὁ υἱὸς καὶ τὸ πνεῦμα τὸ ἅγιον, δι' ὧν τὰ πάντα · μάλιστα δὲ τὸν ἄνθρωπον ἐδημιούργησεν · καὶ τὸ μὲν ἐποίησε νοήσεις. καὶ ἐπὶ τῆς ψυχῆς καὶ τοῦ σώματος: ποίημα γὰρ θεοῦ τὰ ἀμφότερα · τὸ δὲ ἔπλασαν. ἐπὶ τοῦ σώματος νοητέον:- [43]

This means the efficiency of his activity and his creative activity. *The hands of God are the Son and the holy Spirit*, through whom he created all things and especially man. And you should understand 'he made' to refer both to the soul and to the body, as both are the make of God, while 'they have moulded' should be understood to refer to the body.

Regardless of the complicated transmission history of these glosses, it is clear that this entire exegetical tradition goes back

---

[42] See Marguerite Harl 1972, vol. I, p. 301. 1. 10–12, on the history of this distinction in the Origenist movement, see Harl 1972, vol. II, p. 648–650.

[43] Vat. graec. 2057, fol. 254ᵛ. The text of Vat. graec. 754, fol. 300ᵛ, is different and more complicated: ἱερονύμου: τὸ ἀνυστικὸν τῆς ἐνεργείας αὐτοῦ σημαίνει. καὶ δημιουργικὴν ἐνέργειαν · ὅλοις μὲν ὁ θεὸς χεὶρ ἔστιν. ὡς τὰ πάντα διερευνῶν · χεῖρες δὲ θεοῦ. ὁ υἱὸς καὶ τὸ πνεῦμα τὸ ἅγιον, δι' ὧν τὰ πάντα μάλιστα δὲ τὸν ἄνθρωπον ἐδημιούργησε · καὶ τὸ μὲν ἐποίησε γε νοήσεις. καὶ ἐπὶ τῆς ψυχῆς καὶ τοῦ σώματος: ποίημα γὰρ θεοῦ ἀμφότερα · τὸ δὲ ἔπλασεν. τὰ γὰρ ἄλλα πάντα λόγῳ δημιούργησας: ἐπὶ τοῦ ἀνθρώπου φήσας. ἐπὶ τοῦ σώματος νοητέον: – In the same manuscript, this gloss is followed by another one, belonging to the same exegetical tradition: Ποιήσωμεν ἄνθρωπον λέγων ἐπὶ τῷ μονογενεῖ καὶ πνεύματι ἁγίῳ. οὓς νῦν ἐκάλεσε χεῖρας · κεῖται δὲ τῷ κυρίῳ παριτὸν τὸ ῥητόν: λέγει δὲ · τὸ μὲν ἐποίησαν ἐπὶ τῆς ψυχῆς · τὸ δὲ ἔπλασαν ἐπὶ τοῦ σώματος: – For a detailed discussion of the textual transmission and the variants of these glosses, see Dorival 1974, p. 727–728.

to Origen and Evagrius and is the heritage of the Palestinian Origenian/Origenist tradition. It is in this tradition in which Ps.-Caesarius inserts himself and which he uses in his subtle reply to and correction of Justinian's anti-Origenist edict. All this shows how Ps.-Caesarius applies here the encoding *method of the twisted authorities*, combining it with the *method of the background texts*.

In parallel 4, where Ps.-Caesarius's text is the direct continuation of the text cited in parallel 1, he turns Justinian's argument in and out and gives the solution to the riddle, which he earlier established, according to which the soul is neither coeval, nor pre-existent, nor posterior to the body. He seemingly takes over Justinian's argument according to which, had more souls than that of Adam pre-existed, more bodies should have been fashioned by God and not only one. Yet, he subtly shifts the argument from the alleged pre-existence of the souls to the pre-existence of the incorporeal minds, which become souls only in their contact with the body at the creation of the composite human being, or composite demonic beings. Thus, he acknowledges that the demonic beings are originally also pure minds, just like the human beings, and applies their previous existence and subsequent fall to the idea of the bodies as a means of punishment, which he apparently does not accept and which, in fact, had never been Origen's true doctrine either. So, he argues that, if the bodies were means of punishment, then the demons, thrown down from heaven after their sin, should also have been enclosed in human bodies for correction. Yet, this is not the case. Note also Ps.-Caesarius' subtle way of smuggling into the rewriting of Justinian's condemnatory texts the idea of the original creation of the rational beings – including the demons – as pure, incorporeal minds, a doctrine later to be condemned by Anathema 2 of the anti-Origenist council of 553.[44]

---

[44] *Canones XV contra Origenem sive Origenistas*, ACO IV/1, p. 248, 5–13: Εἴ τις λέγει πάντων τῶν λογικῶν τὴν παραγωγὴν νόας ἀσωμάτους καὶ ἀΰλους γεγονέναι δίχα παντὸς ἀριθμοῦ καὶ ὀνόματος... ἀνάθεμα ἔστω. ('If someone says that the creation of all the rational beings has brought about incorporeal and immaterial minds without any number or name, ... let him be anathema!').

Also, Justinian's refutation – citing John Chrysostom as authority – is based on a literal interpretation of Gen 2. 7, according to which the body was first fashioned, before God breathed the soul into it:

> Ὥσπερ γὰρ ὁ οὐρανὸς καὶ ἡ γῆ καὶ ἥλιος καὶ σελήνη καὶ τὰ ἄλλα πάντα ἐδημιουργήθη καὶ μετὰ ταῦτα πάντα ὁ ἄνθρωπος ὁ τούτων πάντων τὴν ἀρχὴν μέλλων ἐγχειρίζεσθαι, τὸν αὐτὸν δὴ τρόπον καὶ ἐν αὐτῆι τῆι διαπλάσει τοῦ ἀνθρώπου πρότερον τὸ σῶμα πλάττεται καὶ τότε ἡ ψυχὴ ἡ τιμιωτέρα. ὃν γὰρ τρόπον τὰ ἄλογα τὰ πρὸς ὑπηρεσίαν μέλλοντα εἶναι χρήσιμα πρὸ τοῦ ἀνθρώπου δημιουργεῖται, ἵνα ἑτοίμην ἔχηι τὴν ὑπηρεσίαν ὁ μέλλων τῆς τούτων χρείας ἀπολαύειν, οὕτω καὶ τὸ σῶμα πρὸ τῆς ψυχῆς δημιουργεῖται, ἵνα ἐπειδὰν κατὰ τὴν ἀπόρρητον αὐτοῦ σοφίαν ἡ ψυχὴ παραχθῆι, ἔχηι τὰς οἰκείας ἐνεργείας ἐπιδείκνυσθαι διὰ τῆς τοῦ σώματος κινήσεως.[45]

> For just as the heaven and the earth, the sun and the moon and all the other things had been created and only later the man, who was going to be entrusted with the rule over all these, in the same way, in the very fashioning of man, first the body is fashioned and only later the more precious soul. In fact, just as the irrational animals that were to become useful for service, had been created before man, so that the latter, who was going to need and enjoy them, may receive their service immediately, in the same way the body is created before the soul, so that, when due to God's ineffable wisdom the soul was to come to being, it might display its proper activities through the movement of the body.

Now, once again according to the encoding *method of the twisted authorities*, this is refuted by Ps.-Caesarius as 'the stupid doctrine of posterior existence' (ἡ ληρουμένη μεθύπαρξις, QA 139. 53–61) making man 'older and younger than himself' (πρεσβύτερος καὶ νεώτερος αὐτὸς ἑαυτοῦ, QA 170. 38–39). Thus, when Ps.-Caesarius is criticising the theory of the 'posterior existence', he is not only criticising Justinian, whose edict he knows because he cites it *in extenso*, but also John Chrysostom, about whom he knows that he is the authority cited by Justinian.

---

[45] *Iustinianus contra Origenem*, ACO III, p. 194. 7–17, where Justinian cites as authority John Chrysostom (*Hom. in Gen.* 13 [ed. PG 53, col. 107]).

The parallels could be followed further, but the material presented here should be enough for showing that Ps.-Caesarius, while seemingly following the text and the ideas of Justinian's anti-Origenist edict, creatively engaged with it, replied to, corrected and criticised most of its arguments. If the *Questions and Answers* were indeed written by Theodore of Caesarea, this analysis shows how he was able to sign the anti-Origenian edict in relatively good conscience, practicing some *reservatio mentalis*: in fact, the condemned doctrines did not represent his own views, nor were they faithful representations of those of the Alexandrian master. Thus, the critical engagement with Justinian's edict gave Theodore the opportunity to expose his own, much subtler theory of the pre-existence of the common substance of the rational beings, out of which a gradual individuation constituted the pre-cosmic Fall, whose final result is the birth of the composite individual, the soul becoming soul only in the moment of the conception of the human being. It is now to the positive elaboration of this doctrine that we must turn our attention.

4. *Pre-existence and the Hierarchical Gradation of the Universe after the Original Fall*

The third question of Ps.-Caesarius' *Questions and Answers* concerns the dogma of the consubstantiality of the Son with the Father. His presentation of this doctrine, although full of baroque expressions, is traditional, based on the teachings and vocabulary of the Cappadocian Fathers:

> Ἀγέννητος οὖν ὁ πατήρ, γεννητὸς ὁ υἱός, ἐκπορευτὸν τὸ πνεῦμα· τρία ἐν ἀλλήλοις φῶτα, ὡς ἐν τρισὶν ἡλίοις τοῖς προσώποις ἐχόμενοι ἀλλήλων μήτε διιστάμενοι μήτε συναλειφόμενοι, ὁμόφωτοι, ἀείφωτοι, ἀδιαιρέτως χωριζόμενοι ταῖς ὑποστάσεσιν ἤγουν προσώποις καὶ ἀσυναλείπτως ἑνούμενοι τῇ ὑπερουσίῳ οὐσίᾳ καὶ ὑπὲρ νοῦν συναφείᾳ καὶ διαστάσει ἀδιαστάτῳ. καὶ οὔτε αἱ τρεῖς ὑποστάσεις εἰς τοσαύτας φύσεις τέμνουσιν τὴν μίαν τῆς θεότητος οὐσίαν οὔτε ἡ μία οὐσία εἰς ἓν πρόσωπον καὶ μίαν ὑπόστασιν συναλείφει καὶ συναιρεῖται τὴν τρίστομον καὶ τρισαένναον κρήνην τῆς θεότητος.[46]

---

[46] QA 3, 23–29.

So the Father is unborn, the Son is born, the Spirit is proceeding: three lights in each other, as if in three suns connected to each other by their faces, neither separated, nor coalescing, of the same brightness, eternally bright, separated without division by their hypostases, that is, persons, and united without coalescing by the super-substantial substance and the supra-mental conjunction and the undistinguished distinction, so that neither do the three hypostases cut into so many natures the one substance of the godhead, nor does the one substance blend and fold into one person and one hypostasis the three-sourced and thrice-inexhaustible fountainhead of the divinity.

This is indeed traditional doctrine, and also traditional vocabulary influenced by, besides the Cappadocian Fathers, Ps.-Dionysius. It is this influence that betrays the only dissonant element: the Dionysian-sounding vocabulary notwithstanding, this doctrine is formulated as a reply and a denial of the Ps.-Dionysian Trinitarian doctrine. While, for Ps.-Dionysius quoting Origen, 'the only source of the super-substantial divinity is the Father' (μόνη δὲ πηγὴ τῆς ὑπερουσίου θεότητος ὁ πατήρ[47]), Ps.-Caesarius stresses that the three hypostases together constitute the unique fountainhead of the divinity. Thus, here we can sense a subtle polemics with a Ps.-Dionysian tenet, in which Ps.-Dionysius proves to be a faithful follower of Origen.

The rest of the Trinitarian passage continues this thought:

Φῶς τοίνυν ὁ πατήρ, φῶς ὁ υἱός, φῶς τὸ θεῖον πνεῦμα, ἀλλ' οἱ τρεῖς ἓν ὑπάρχουσι φῶς ὑπέρχρονον, προαιώνιον, ἄναρχον, τρι-πρόσωπον, τρισυπόστατον, τριδέσποτον, τρίθρονον, τριλαμπές, τριαυγές, ἰσολαμπές, ἀειλαμπές, ἀναλλοίωτον, ἀμείωτον, ἀνύκτε-ρον, ἀχείρωτον, ἀλώβητον· μία οὐσία, μία συνσθενία, μία εὔκλεια, μία βασιλεία, μία θεότης, ἓν θέλημα, δρᾶμα καὶ πρόσταγμα· πᾶσα ἑνότης καὶ ἰσότης καὶ ταυτότης ἐν τριάδι πλὴν ἀγεννησίας καὶ γεννήσεως καὶ ἐκπορεύσεως, ἑκάστης ὑποστάσεως ἰδιαζόντως

---

[47] Ps.-Dionysius, *DN* II. 5. 641D; ed. Suchla 1990, p. 128. 11–12, quoting Origen, *De princ.* I. 3. 7; ed. GCS p. 60. 2–4: '[C]um *unus deitatis fons* verbo ac ratione sua teneat universa, spiritu vero oris sui quae digna sunt sanctificatione sanctificet […].' I have treated this Dionysian doctrine in Perczel 1999 and Perczel 2001.

οὔσης καὶ ἐσομένης, οὐκ ἀρξαμένης, οὐ παυσαμένης, ἀλλ᾽ ἀεὶ ὡσαύτως ἐχούσης καὶ ἀμεταβλήτου μενούσης.[48]

Therefore, light is the Father, light is the Son, and light is the divine Spirit but the three are one light, above time, before eternity, without beginning, in three persons, in three hypostases, in three lordships, three thrones, three radiations, three brightnesses, of equal brightness, eternal brightness, without change, without decrease, without night, untouchably, undamageably – one substance, one common power, one glory, one kingdom, one divinity, one will, activity and command. Everything is oneness, equality and identity in the Trinity, with the exception of the unbegottenness, the begottenness and the procession, so that every hypostasis exists and will exist individually, without beginning, without end, remaining eternally in the same condition without any change.

This is, as will be shortly seen, an exordium to a lengthy but rather loose paraphrase of a passage, based on the famous sun metaphor in Plato's *Republic*, from *Oratio* 40 of St Gregory of Nazianzus, *On the Holy Baptism*, that is, from one of the best known but also one of the most daring texts of Late-Antique theological discourse,[49] which I will quote here *in extenso*, because it will be important for the analysis of Ps.-Caesarius' text:

Θεὸς μέν ἐστι φῶς τὸ ἀκρότατον, καὶ ἀπρόσιτον, καὶ ἄρρητον, οὔτε νῷ καταληπτὸν, οὔτε λόγῳ ῥητόν, πάσης φωτιστικὸν λογικῆς φύσεως. Τοῦτο ἐν νοητοῖς, ὅπερ ἐν αἰσθητοῖς ἥλιος· [...] αὐτὸ ἑαυτοῦ θεωρητικόν τε καὶ καταληπτικόν, ὀλίγα τοῖς ἔξω χεόμενον. Φῶς δὲ λέγω, τὸ ἐν Πατρὶ, καὶ Υἱῷ, καὶ ἁγίῳ Πνεύματι θεωρούμενον· ὧν πλοῦτός ἐστιν ἡ συμφυΐα, καὶ τὸ ἓν ἔξαλμα τῆς λαμπρότητος. Δεύτερον δὲ φῶς ἄγγελος, τοῦ πρώτου φωτὸς ἀπορροή τις, ἢ μετουσία, τῇ πρὸς αὐτὸ νεύσει καὶ ὑπουργίᾳ τὸν φωτισμὸν ἔχουσα· οὐκ οἶδα, εἴτε τῇ τάξει τῆς στάσεως μεριζομένη τὸν φωτισμὸν, εἴτε τοῖς μέτροις τοῦ φωτισμοῦ τὴν τάξιν λαμβάνουσα. Τρίτον φῶς ἄνθρωπος, ὃ καὶ τοῖς ἔξω δῆλόν ἐστι.

---

[48] QA 3. 30–37.

[49] To what extent this text of Gregory the Theologian was important for Ps.-Caesarius and, per consequent, to what extent he used it, has escaped the attention of his modern students. However, Kertsch 1983 discovered one fragment of Gregory's *Homily on Baptism* in QA 61.

Φῶς γὰρ τὸν ἄνθρωπον ὀνομάζουσι, διὰ τὴν τοῦ ἐν ἡμῖν λόγου δύναμιν· καὶ ἡμῶν αὐτῶν πάλιν οἱ θεοειδέστεροι, καὶ μᾶλλον Θεῷ πλησιάζοντες. Οἶδα καὶ ἄλλο φῶς, ᾧ τὸ ἀρχέγονον ἠλάθη σκότος, ἢ διεκόπη, πρῶτον ὑποστὰν τῆς ὁρατῆς κτίσεως, τήν τε κυκλικὴν τῶν ἀστέρων περίοδον, καὶ τὴν ἄνωθεν φρυκτωρίαν, κόσμον ὅλον αὐγάζουσαν.[50]

God is the highest, inapproachable and ineffable Light, neither comprehensible to the mind, nor utterable to the word, illuminating the whole rational nature. It is among the intelligible beings what the sun is among the perceptible beings[51] [...] It contemplates and comprehends Itself, [from which knowledge] It pours out just a little bit to those outside. By Light I mean that which we contemplate in the Father, the Son and the Holy Spirit, whose wealth is the community of nature and the one outburst of brightness. A second light is the angel, an emanation from or participation in the first Light, which receives its illumination due to its inclination toward the first Light and from its service rendered to It. I do not know whether its illumination is proportioned to the rank of its state, or whether it receives its state according to its illumination. The third light is man – which fact is clear even to those outside [that is, to the heathen Greeks]: they call man 'light'[52] because of the virtue of the reason in us – but even among us rather those who are more similar to God and approach God more. I also know another light, by which the original darkness was expelled, or rather divided, the first visible creature to come to existence, and also the circular motion of the stars and the beacon from on high, which irradiates the entire world.

After his Trinitarian hymn, based on Gregory the Theologian, Ps.-Caesarius presents the relationship between God and the creature, thus continuing his paraphrase of Gregory:

ἀεὶ γὰρ ὑπῆρχεν ὁ θεὸς καὶ πατὴρ ἀεὶ ὢν πατὴρ παιδὸς μονογενοῦς, αὐδῆς ἐνυποστάτου πάντα δρώσης, ἀεὶ ξυνόντος αὐτοῖς

[50] Gregory of Nazianzus, *Oratio* 40, *On the Holy Baptism* 5 (ed. PG 36, col. 364. 14–36).

[51] See Plato, *Republic* VI. 508C–509D.

[52] This is a wordplay: in Greek 'light' is φῶς and 'man' is φώς, only the accent being different in writing, but – by the fourth century AD when Gregory wrote – the pronunciation of the two being indistinguishable.

τοῦ θείου πνεύματος καὶ συνπροσκυνουμένου παρὰ πάσης νοερᾶς
τε καὶ λογικῆς φύσεως· οὐ πρόγονός τις ἐξ αὐτῶν οὐδ' ἐπίγονος,
οὐκ αὔξων, οὐ λήγων κατὰ τὸ αἰσθητὸν φῶς ἢ τὰς ὑπερκοσμίους
δυνάμεις· αἱ ταὐτὸν μὲν τῇ οὐσίᾳ πᾶσαι ὑπάρχουσαι, ὁμοίως καὶ
αἱ λογικαὶ βροτῶν ψυχαὶ ταὐτὸν ὑπάρχουσαι τῇ οὐσίᾳ πᾶσαι, αἱ
μὲν τυγχάνουσιν τάξει, αἱ δὲ στάσει, ἕτεραι δὲ παραστάσει καὶ
λειτουργίᾳ, ἐπιβολαῖς καὶ μεταβολαῖς καὶ μετατροπαῖς αὐθαιρέτως πρὸς τὸ χεῖρον ἢ κρεῖττον ῥέπουσαι, οὐκ ἀνάγκη δὲ φυσικῇ
ἐκπίπτουσαι κατὰ τὸ μεῖζον καὶ ἧττον, ἐν τούτοις τὸ διάφορον
ἔχουσαι τῆς ὑπεροχῆς.[53]

For God the Father eternally existed, eternally being the
Father of the only begotten Son, of the all-acting enhypostasised Sound, while together with them was eternally the
divine Spirit who is worshipped, together with them, by the
entire intellectual and rational nature. Neither one of them
is first-born, nor last-born, nor are they increasing or ceasing to be, unlike the perceptible light or the supra-mundane
virtues, which are all of identical substance, just as all the
rational souls of the mortals are also of the same substance,
but some of them are according to their rank, others according to their state, again others according to their position and
service, their attention, changes and subsequent alterations,
out of their own free choice, inclining toward the worse or
the better, and falling out, some more and some less, without any natural necessity – in these conditions acquiring the
differences of superiority <or inferiority>.

The sophisticated composition of this text is entirely calqued
upon the passage of Gregory of Nazianzus cited above. From
this paraphrase a clear metaphysical doctrine unfolds: the Trinity
is one unchangeable Light of identical substance, worshipped by
the 'entire intellectual and rational nature' (παρὰ πάσης νοερᾶς τε
καὶ λογικῆς φύσεως),[54] apparently also conceived as being of one
substance, but with the important difference that the individual
members of this common intellectual and rational nature, *a posteriori*, after a certain 'falling out' (ἐκπίπτουσαι), have acquired different ranks and conditions, according to their inclination toward

[53] QA 3. 37–45.
[54] Corresponding to 'illuminating the whole rational nature' (πάσης φωτιστικὸν λογικῆς φύσεως) in Gregory's text.

the worse or the better (πρὸς τὸ χεῖρον ἢ κρεῖττον ῥέπουσαι), being a motion entirely depending on the free will (αὐθαιρέτως).

It is remarkable to see how Ps.-Caesarius transforms and moulds Gregory's thought, which he uses as the basic tissue of his discourse. In fact, here we can observe a masterly application of the *method of the twisted authorities*. Gregory indeed says something very daring: he says that the 'second light', the angel, is either 'a kind of emanation from' (ἀπόρροή τις) or a 'participation in' (μετουσία) the first Light, that is, God; that its 'inclination toward the first Light' and its 'service' rendered to God are the immediate cause of its enlightenment by the first Light. By saying this, Gregory poses the alternative of an emanationist model, represented by 'a kind of emanation from', and of a creationist one, represented by 'participation in', without clearly deciding between the two. Gregory also remains wavering between two theories about the way the angelic hierarchies were formed: as he says, he does not know whether the enlightenment of every angelic rank is simply proportioned to its state (a creationist model), or whether it is the state which is proportioned to the enlightenment, the latter, as we have seen, depending on the angels' 'inclination' toward God and their 'service' rendered to him (an emanationist model, where individual virtue assigns its rank to each angelic being). Apparently, Gregory is keen not to go too far and not to decide between the two theoretical alternatives. However, when Ps.-Caesarius paraphrases Gregory's text, he makes it as unequivocal as possible: he could not be more emphatic in stating that it is the heavenly powers' independent and voluntary motions, their individual measure of 'falling out' (ἐκπίπτουσαι) from their original state and their post-lapsarian inclinations, which determine their rank, acquired *a posteriori* in the angelic hierarchy. Moreover, this 'falling out' closely corresponds, as we shall shortly see, to the emanationist model presented by Gregory as one of the possible explanatory alternatives. Ps.-Caesarius does not even mention the other, creationist alternative, still maintained by Gregory as an equally viable theoretical possibility.

In fact, what Ps.-Caesarius presents here in his paraphrasis of Gregory, is a standard doctrine from Origen to the sixth-century condemnations, of the Christian intellectual trend nicknamed

'Origenism': that of a pre-existing unique intellectual substance, called a ἑνάς ('unity'), disturbed by an original motion causing a 'falling out from the henad' (ἀπόπτωσις τῆς ἑνάδος), in which the rational beings followed their individual motions determined by their free will, motions that finally resulted in the creation of the material world. This was already the teaching of Origen in his great work *On the Principles*, fragments of which were condemned by Justinian's anti-Origenist edict in 542/3, even though the edict gave these fragments a twisted interpretation:

Περὶ τῆς προϋπάρξεως τῶν ψυχῶν, ἐκ τοῦ πρώτου λόγου τοῦ Περὶ ἀρχῶν βιβλίου. Ἐξ ἰδίας αἰτίας τῶν μὴ προσεχόντων ἑαυτοῖς ἀγρύπνως γίνονται τάχιον ἢ βράδιον μεταπτώσεις, καὶ ἐπὶ πλεῖον ἢ ἐπ' ἔλαττον, ὡς ἀπὸ ταύτης τῆς αἰτίας κρίσει θείαι συμπαραμετρούσηι τοῖς ἑκάστου βελτίοσιν ἢ χείροσι κινήμασι καὶ τὸ κατ' ἀξίαν ὁ μέν τις ἕξει ἐν τῆι ἐσομένηι διακοσμήσει τάξιν ἀγγελικὴν ἢ δύναμιν ἀρχικὴν ἢ ἐξουσίαν τὴν ἐπί τινων ἢ θρόνον τὸν ἐπὶ βασιλευομένων ἢ κυρείαν τὴν κατὰ δούλων, οἱ δὲ οὐ πάνυ τι ἐκπεσόντες τὴν ὑπὸ τοῖς εἰρημένοις οἰκονομίαν καὶ βοήθειαν ἕξουσι. καὶ οὕτως κατὰ μὲν τὸ πλεῖστον ἀπὸ τῶν ὑπὸ τὰς ἀρχὰς καὶ τὰς ἐξουσίας καὶ τοὺς θρόνους καὶ τὰς κυριότητας, τάχα δὲ ἔσθ' ὅτε καὶ ἀπ' αὐτῶν συστήσεται τὸ τῶν ἀνθρώπων γένος ἐν τῶι καθ' ἕνα κόσμωι.[55]

On the pre-existence of the souls from the first book *On the Principles*: 'From the same reason [as that of the original fall], there occur renewed falls, at a faster or slower speed, to a greater or smaller degree, of those who do not beware of themselves. As of this cause the divine judgment measures according to each one's better or worse motion the rank that it deserves in the arrangement to come, that is, an angelic rank, or the power of principality, or authority over other beings, or that of being a throne over those ruled, or lordship over the servants. Those who have not entirely fallen out will be provided for and helped by the aforementioned [angelic orders]. In this way, for the most part the human kind in an individual world will consist mostly of those who are subject to the principalities, the authorities, the thrones and the lordships, but in some cases also of these beings themselves.'

---

[55] *Iustinianus contra Origenem*, ACO III, p. 210. 28–211. 7. This corresponds to *De principiis* I. 6. 2 (ed. Görgemanns & Karpp 1976, p. 220). The Greek text here follows the edition of Görgemanns & Karpp.

Similar is also another fragment of *On the Principles* condemned by the same edict:

> Περὶ τῆς τῶν ἄνωθεν εἰς σῶμα καταγωγῆς. Οὕτω δὴ ποικιλω-
> τάτου κόσμου τυγχάνοντος καὶ τοσαῦτα διάφορα λογικὰ περιέ-
> χοντος τί ἄλλο χρὴ λέγειν αἴτιον γεγονέναι τοῦ ὑποστῆναι αὐτὸν
> ἢ τὸ ποικίλον τῆς ἀποπτώσεως τῶν οὐχ ὁμοίως τῆς ἑνάδος ἀπορ-
> ρεόντων; [56]

> On the descent from on high into the bodies: 'Given that
> there is such a variegated world containing so many different
> rational creatures, what else should we name as the cause of
> its creation, than the differences of the falling out of those
> who in a non-identical way emanated from the unity?'

It is worthwhile noting the coincidence between Origen's expression in the second fragment, 'emanated from the unity' (τῆς ἑνάδος ἀπορρεόντων) and Gregory's first alternative, 'a kind of emanation from the first Light' (τοῦ πρώτου φωτὸς ἀπορροή τις). One may also note that in Origen 'falling out' (ἀπόπτωσις) and 'emanation from the unity' (τῆς ἑνάδος ἀπορρεόντων) are just two facets of the same doctrine. Clearly, when Gregory presents his first, emanationist alternative explanation of the angelic state, he presents Origen's doctrine as a possibly acceptable one, as over against the creationist solution, without deciding between the two. Thus, when Ps.-Caesarius, in his paraphrase of Gregory, echoes Origen's words about the Fall ('falling out [ἐκπίπτουσαι], some more and some less, without any natural necessity'), entirely omitting the creationist alternative still considered viable by Gregory, he also decides for the emanationist interpretation of the universe. This he does precisely in the wake of Origen's condemnation in 543, which had endorsed the creationist model, rejecting and branding as 'Origenism' the emanationist explanation of the world's diversity. This shows what precisely Ps.-Caesarius thought about Justinian's anti-Origenist edict, which, as we have seen in the previous section, he knew only too well and which, if he is indeed identical to Theodore of Caesarea, he had signed with his own hand.

---

[56] *Iustinianus contra Origenem*, ACO III, p. 211. 13–16. This corresponds to *De principiis* II. 1. 12 (ed. Görgemanns & Karpp 1976, p. 284–285).

Moreover, while some sceptical reader might judge the terminological similarities between Ps.-Caesarius' text and the afore-cited excerpts from *On the Principles* of Origen as being of an arguable character, it would be very difficult to contest that the train of thought is very similar in the two cases. According to both authors, the conscious movement of the individual beings that have separated themselves from the original common substance of the 'entire intellectual and rational nature' (in Ps.-Caesarius' terms), or the original henad (in Origen's terms), determines their position in the 'arrangement' following the fall and the subsequent creation of a world (in Origen's terms: ἐν τῇ ἐσομένῃ διακοσμήσει). Origen is more explicit than Ps.-Caesarius; he says that the angelic ranks and the birth of some beings in the human condition are due to these renewed motions, fallings and re-fallings, to which the divine judgment measures the distribution of ranks, that is to say, the divine judgment assigns a place to each being in the universe that, from the original equality in the unity, has become hierarchical as a result of the fall. On the other hand, Ps.-Caesarius is elusive: he does not name the individual angelic ranks resulting from the diverse motions but, still, he is clear enough: he speaks of the hierarchical arrangement of the universe as resulting from the free motions, and of the ranks and services acquired as a result of these. Ps.-Caesarius is also alluding to the doctrine of subsequent downward motions after the original fall, when he speaks about 'changes and subsequent alterations' (μεταβολαῖς καὶ μετατροπαῖς) echoing the 'subsequent falls' (μεταπτώσεις) in Origen. Moreover, although Ps.-Caesarius uses grammatical structures permitting some slight ambiguity, he also makes it quite explicit that the angelic orders and the souls of men are issued from the same original substance, which he calls 'the entire intellectual and rational nature'.

Finally, one sees the common Aristotelian background of the two teachings. This doctrine is based, both in Origen and in Ps.-Caesarius, on the Aristotelian principle that substance is not receptive of any 'more or less' [57] and that 'being the same and one

---

[57] Aristotle, *Cat.* 3b33–36: Δοκεῖ δὲ ἡ οὐσία οὐκ ἐπιδέχεσθαι τὸ μᾶλλον καὶ τὸ ἧττον [...].

in number' it can receive opposite qualities.[58] Thus, the created substance of the rational beings, being the same and one in number, is receptive of opposite qualities. In both our authors these opposites are created by the diverse post-lapsarian movements of the rational creatures, which doctrine in Origen's fragment is expressed in the following way: 'at a faster or slower speed, to a greater or smaller degree' (τάχιον ἢ βράδιον [...] ἐπὶ πλεῖον ἢ ἐπ' ἔλαττον), while in Ps.-Caesarius by these expressions: 'toward the worse or the better [...], some more and some less' (πρὸς τὸ χεῖρον ἢ κρεῖττον [...] κατὰ τὸ μεῖζον καὶ ἧττον). According to the emanationist doctrine, apparently professed both by Origen and by Ps.-Caesarius, this reception, after the Fall, of the opposites into the original unique substance, serving as the substrate (ὑποκείμενον) of the movement generating the opposites, is the mediate, or catalysing, or instrumental cause of the creation of our diversified material universe.

Thus, one may see that the metaphysical doctrines conveyed by Origen's fragment from *On the Principles* and by Ps.-Caesarius' paraphrase of Gregory of Nazianzus, as well as their philosophical roots and their theological connotations, are very similar. There is a slight difference in the context and a great difference in clarity. The difference in clarity can be easily explained by the fact that Ps.-Caesarius wrote his text after repeated condemnations of the doctrine of pre-existence, which is at stake here, and especially after the Justinianian edict condemning this doctrine in 542/43. If he wanted to maintain and transmit an 'Origenist' teaching, necessarily he had to hide it. However, the difference in the context has another reason. In fact, while Ps.-Caesarius definitely echoes some of Origen's thoughts and expressions, the framework and the context of his fragment at hand is much closer to another text, which is perhaps contemporary to the *Questions and Answers* of Ps.-Caesarius, or even antedates it, but must have been composed independently of it. This text comes from another type of anti-Origenist documents, written to prepare the Council of Constantinople in 553. So here is a parallel text of Ps.-Caesarius' QA 3 and Anathema 2 of 553:

---

[58] Aristotle, *Cat.* 4a10–11: Μάλιστα δὲ ἴδιον τῆς οὐσίας δοκεῖ εἶναι τὸ ταὐτὸν καὶ ἓν ἀριθμῷ ὂν τῶν ἐναντίων εἶναι δεκτικόν· [...].

Ps.-Caesarius, *Questions and Answers,* QA 3. 37–45.	Fifteen Canons against the Origenists, Anathema 2, ACO IV/1, p. 248. 5–13.
ἀεὶ γὰρ ὑπῆρχεν ὁ θεὸς καὶ πατὴρ ἀεὶ ὢν πατὴρ παιδὸς μονογενοῦς, αὐδῆς ἐνυ-ποστάτου πάντα δρώσης, ἀεὶ ξυνόντος αὐτοῖς τοῦ θείου πνεύματος καὶ συν-προσκυνουμένου παρὰ πάσης νοερᾶς τε καὶ λογικῆς φύσεως· οὐ πρόγονός τις ἐξ αὐτῶν οὐδ᾽ ἐπίγονος, οὐκ αὔξων, οὐ λήγων κατὰ τὸ αἰσθητὸν φῶς ἢ τὰς ὑπερκοσμί-ους δυνάμεις· αἱ ταὐτὸν μὲν τῇ οὐσίᾳ πᾶσαι ὑπάρχουσιν, ὁμοίως καὶ αἱ λογι-καὶ βροτῶν ψυχαὶ ταὐτὸν ὑπάρχουσαι τῇ οὐσίᾳ πᾶσαι, αἱ μὲν τυγχάνουσιν τάξει, αἱ δὲ στάσει, ἕτεραι δὲ παραστάσει καὶ λειτουργίᾳ, ἐπιβολαῖς καὶ μεταβολαῖς καὶ μετατροπαῖς <u>αὐθαιρέτως πρὸς τὸ χεῖρον ἢ κρεῖττον</u> ῥέπουσαι, οὐκ ἀνάγκη δὲ φυσικῇ ἐκπίπτουσαι κατὰ τὸ μεῖζον καὶ ἧττον, <u>ἐν τούτοις τὸ διάφορον ἔχουσαι τῆς ὑπερο-χῆς.</u>[59]	Εἴ τις λέγει πάντων τῶν λογικῶν τὴν πα-ραγωγὴν *νόας ἀσωμάτους καὶ ἀΰλους* γε-γονέναι δίχα παντὸς ἀριθμοῦ καὶ ὀνόμα-τος, *ὡς ἑνάδα πάντων τούτων γενέσθαι τῇ ταυτότητι τῆς οὐσίας καὶ δυνάμεως καὶ ἐνεργείας* καὶ τῇ πρὸς τὸν θεὸν Λόγον ἑνώσει τε καὶ γνώσει, κόρον δὲ αὐτοὺς λαβεῖν τῆς θείας θεωρίας <u>καὶ πρὸς τὸ χεῖ-ρον τραπῆναι κατὰ τὴν ἑκάστου ἀναλο-γίαν τῆς ἐπὶ τοῦτο ῥοπῆς· καὶ εἰληφέναι σώματα λεπτομερέστερα ἢ παχύτερα, καὶ ὄνομα κληρώσασθαι διὰ τὸ ὡς ὀνο-μάτων οὕτω καὶ σωμάτων διαφορὰς εἶναι τῶν ἄνω δυνάμεων·</u> καὶ ἐντεῦθεν τοὺς μὲν χερουβὶμ τοὺς δὲ σεραφὶμ τοὺς δὲ ἀρχὰς καὶ ἐξουσίας ἢ κυριότητας ἢ θρό-νους καὶ ἀγγέλους καὶ ὅσα ἐστὶν οὐράνια τάγματα γεγονέναι τε καὶ ὀνομασθῆναι, ἀνάθεμα ἔστω.[60]

[59] 'For God the Father eternally existed, eternally being the Father of the only begotten Son, of the all-acting enhypostasised Sound, while together with them was eternally the divine Spirit, who is worshipped, together with them, by *the entire intellectual and rational nature.* Neither one of them is first-born, nor last-born, nor are they increasing or ceasing to be, unlike the perceptible light or *the supramundane virtues, which all are of identical substance, just as all the rational souls of the mortals are also of the same substance,* but some of them are according to their rank, others according to their state, again others according to their position and service, their attention, changes and subsequent altera-tions, <u>out of their own free choice, inclining toward the worse or the better,</u> and falling out, some more and some less, without any natural necessity – <u>*in these conditions acquiring the differences of superiority <or inferiority>.*</u>' See also above, p. 333–334.

[60] 'If anyone says that the creation of all the rational beings meant *that incor-poreal and immaterial minds* came to existence without any number and name, so that *there came to existence a unity (henad) of all these by the identity of the substance, the power and the activity,* as well as by the union to and knowledge of God the Word; but because they became satiated of the divine contempla-tion, <u>they turned toward what is worse according to the proportion of each one's inclination toward this,</u> *so that they received lighter or coarser bodies and each was assigned a name, because just as there are different names of the virtues on high, so also they have different bodies* and, therefore, some of them became cherubs, others seraphs, others principalities and authorities, lordships or thrones and

Once again, the vocabulary of the two texts differs, but here the doctrine is virtually identical. According to the condemned doctrine, at the beginning an unique incorporeal universal substance, containing pure minds, was created, which the text of the anathema calls a 'henad', or 'unity' and Ps.-Caesarius calls 'the entire intellectual and rational nature'. Thus, from the origin, all rational creatures are of one only substance. However, there occured a mysterious 'satiation' (Anathema: κόρος) of the divine contemplation, so that they turned away from God and 'inclined' (ῥοπή: an emphatic word in both the Anathema and Ps.-Caesarius) toward something else, but individually in different measures and proportions. This 'inclination' and 'falling out' (Origen: ἀπόπτωσις, Ps.-Caesarius: ἐκπίπτουσαι[61]) determined the place and the function of the fallen minds in the new cosmic structure. The condemned doctrine also adds an important element, which seems to be absent from Ps.-Caesarius but is, in fact, implicit in it: once the measure of this inclination determines the hierarchical place of a rational being in the newly developed universe, the fallen being receives a body that corresponds to its function: this may be an angelic, a human, or a demonic body, in which it will act according to its condition. The body is not freely chosen but assigned by divine judgment, while the inclination, that is, the diversion from the original contemplation, had indeed been an act of free will (Ps.-Caesarius: αὐθαιρέτως) without any compelling necessity flowing from the being's intrinsic nature (Ps.-Caesarius: οὐκ ἀνάγκη δὲ φυσικῇ). Here the meaning of Ps.-Caesarius's text is clarified by our application of the *method of the condemnatory parallels*.

5. *The First-Created Light and the Lower Beings*

Interesting is also the continuation of Ps.-Caesarius' text:

φὼς δὲ καὶ ὁ βροτὸς προσαγορεύεται, φῶς καὶ ὁ ἥλιος καὶ ἡ σελήνη καλεῖται, φῶς καὶ ἡ ποικίλη τῶν ἄστρων χορεία κατω-

---

angels, and all the other heavenly orders and they also got names accordingly – let such a person be anathema!'

[61] The expression is found only in the second Origenian fragment quoted above and in Ps.-Caesarius.

νόμασται· ἀλλὰ τῶν εἰρημένων πλείστων ὑλικῶν καὶ διαφόρων
φώτων πολυμερῶς καὶ πολυτρόπως ποιητὴς καὶ δημιουργὸς
ὑπάρχει τὸ ἀληθινὸν καὶ ἄϋλον φῶς, ὁ ἐπὶ πάντων θεὸς καὶ πατὴρ
σὺν τῷ μονογενεῖ αὐτοῦ παιδὶ καὶ τῷ θείῳ πνεύματι [...].[62]

The mortal is also called light, the sun and the moon are also
called light, and the variegated dance of the stars is also called
light, but of all these so many, material and different lights,
'in many ways and in diverse manners' [Hebr. 1. 1] Maker
and Creator is the true and immaterial Light, 'God above all'
[Rom. 9. 5] and Father, together with his only begotten Child
and with the divine Spirit.

Obviously, here Ps.-Caesarius continues his paraphrasis of Gregory
the Theologian by mentioning the third and the fourth 'lights'
that Gregory lists in his inventory of the lights. The third light
is man and the fourth the celestial luminaries, while, according
to Ps.-Caesarius, the distinguishing character of all these lights
mentioned – that is, of the second, third, and fourth lights according to Gregory's classification – is that they are material, that is,
incorporated in a body, while God is entirely immaterial.

Now, we know that Anathema 2 of the anti-Origenist council of 553 was followed by two anathemas condemning specific
Origenist doctrines about the creation of the sun, the moon, and
the stars, as well as of men and demons.

Εἴ τις λέγει τὸν ἥλιον καὶ τὴν σελήνην καὶ τοὺς ἀστέρας, καὶ αὐτὰ
τῆς αὐτῆς τῶν λογικῶν ἑνάδος ὄντα, ἐκ παρατροπῆς τῆς ἐπὶ τὸ
χεῖρον γεγονέναι τοῦτο ὅπερ εἰσίν, ἀνάθεμα ἔστω.[63]

If anyone says that the sun, the moon and the stars themselves
belong to the same unity (henad) of the rational beings and by
turning away toward the worse became what they are, let such
a man be anathema!

And:

Εἴ τις λέγει τὰ λογικὰ τὰ τῆς θείας ἀγάπης ἀποψυγέντα σώμασι
παχυτέροις τοῖς καθ᾽ ἡμᾶς ἐνδεθῆναι καὶ ἀνθρώπους ὀνομασθῆναι,
τὰ δὲ ἐπὶ τὸ ἄκρον τῆς κακίας ἐληλακότα ψυχροῖς καὶ ζοφεροῖς

---

[62] QA 3. 45–49.
[63] *Anti-Origenist Canons*, Anathema 3, ACO IV/1, p. 248. 14–16.

ἐνδεθῆναι σώμασι καὶ δαίμονας ἢ πνευματικὰ τῆς πονηρίας εἶναί τε καὶ καλεῖσθαι, ἀνάθεμα ἔστω.[64]

If anyone says that those rational beings that have cooled down from the divine love were bound into the coarser bodies of our kind and were called human beings, while those which ran until the extremity of vice were bound into cold and dark bodies, so that they are demons and spirits of evilness, let such a man be anathema!

Comparing Ps.-Caesarius' text to these anathemas, we may see that, after a rather close doctrinal correspondence between the previous Ps.-Caesarian fragment and Anathema 2, there is a structural correspondence between the text of Ps.-Caesarius and the two subsequent anathemas. Is this a fortuitous coincidence, let alone an optical illusion, or does it indicate a real relationship? In fact, the actual formulation of the Ps.-Caesarian text sounds so innocent that one would be led to doubt such a connection, the close connection of the formerly analysed Ps.-Caesarian fragment with Anathema 2 notwithstanding. However, Gregory of Nazianzus' text, serving as a basis for Ps.-Caesarius, seems to offer a clue: it says that man is called 'light' because of the capacity of reason in it (διὰ τὴν τοῦ ἐν ἡμῖν λόγου δύναμιν), that is, that 'light' is, in a sense, a metaphor for reason. So if we were to substitute 'reason' to light, we would get the doctrine condemned by Anathemas 3 and 4: man is and is called a rational being (light), the sun and the moon are also called rational beings (light), and the stars are also called rational beings (light). Would this deciphering and hermeneutics be too daring? Do we have the right to read such hindsights behind Ps.-Caesarius' words?

After the discovery of so many clever techniques used to convey hidden meaning in Ps.-Caesarius, we definitely have the right to attempt such a reading. Still, the above suggestion would certainly be a rather daring hermeneutics, had Ps.-Caesarius not explained himself in the same sense, applying his usual *method of the duplicates*, by taking over the same subject in another part of his work, where he himself clearly makes the identification light (and fire) = reason. This he does when he speaks about the

[64] *Anti-Origenist Canons*, Anathema 4, ACO IV/1, p. 248. 17–20.

creation of the original light on the first day of the creation, in QA 57–59. This section of the *Questions and Answers* is thus a very useful and enlightening complement to the text of QA 3.

In QA 55–57 the interlocutors of Ps.-Caesarius ask him the question where one finds the creation of fire in the Scriptures. After all, we do not read about God saying 'Let there be fire!' To which question Ps.-Caesarius answers:

> Μωσῆς γράφει· καὶ εἶπεν ὁ θεός· γενηθήτω φῶς, καὶ ἐγένετο φῶς, ἡ τοῦ πυρὸς δηλονότι φύσις· οὐ γὰρ μόνον τὸ παρ' ἡμῖν πῦρ ὑπάρχει, ἀλλὰ καὶ αἱ ἄνω δυνάμεις πῦρ εἶναί μοι δοκοῦσιν συγγενὲς τοῦ παρ' ἡμῖν.[65]

> Moses writes: 'And God said: let there be light! And there became light' (Gen. 1. 3), that is, the nature of the fire. For there is not only the fire of here-below, but it seems to me that the virtues on high are also fire, akin to this fire.

Here, once again, Ps.-Caesarius employs the *method of the twisted authorities*. He simply repeats the words of Severian of Gabala about the creation of fire in his first homily on the creation of the world:

> Λοιπὸν λείπεται δεῖξαι, ποῦ τὸ πῦρ ἐγένετο. Εἶπεν ὁ Θεός · Γενηθήτω φῶς, καὶ ἐγένετο ἡ τοῦ πυρὸς φύσις · οὐ γὰρ μόνον τοῦτο τὸ πῦρ ἐστιν, ἀλλὰ καὶ αἱ ἄνω δυνάμεις πῦρ εἰσι, καὶ συγγενές ἐστι τὸ ἄνω πῦρ τούτου τοῦ παρ' ἡμῖν.[66]

> There remains to show where [in Scripture] the fire came to existence. 'God said: let there be light!' And there came to existence the nature of the fire. For there is not only this fire, but the virtues on high are also fire and the fire on high is akin to this fire.

So, in the cited sentences of QA 57, Ps.-Caesarius barely does anything else than repeat the words of Severian of Gabala, a scriptural commentator famous for his exegesis of the literal sense of the Scriptures, a great foe of any allegorical explanation. How will we find in this mere repetition the allegory that we sup-

---

[65] Ps.-Caesarius, *Questions and Answers*, QA 57. 4–6.

[66] Severian of Gabala, *On the Creation of the World* I. 4 (ed. PG 56, col. 434. 23–27). The reference is indicated by Riedinger's *apparatus criticus* (ed. GCS).

pose Ps.-Caesarius has hidden in it? *Si duo dicunt idem, non est idem* and by the mere repetition of Severian's words, Caesarius has already given them a significant twist. This twist consists in the fact that the 'virtues on high' (αἱ ἄνω δυνάμεις) mean different things for Severian and for Ps.-Caesarius. As the context shows, Severian meant by this expression the celestial bodies, that is, the sun, the moon and the stars, while for Ps.-Caesarius it means the angels in general and a certain rank of angels in particular.[67]

In the next, 58th, question Ps.-Caesarius' interlocutors continue asking him about this issue. Their question concerns the 'kinship', mentioned in the answer to the previous question, between the 'fire on high' and 'our fire':

> Καὶ πῶς τὸ ἄνω τοῦ παρ' ἡμῖν ἔσται συγγενές, τοῦ μὲν ἀσβέστου ὄντος, τοῦ δὲ σβεννυμένου; [68]

> And how will the fire on high be akin to our fire, given that it is unquenchable, while ours goes out?

Once again, this is just a repetition of the words of Severian of Gabala:

> Ζητεῖται δὲ, ὅτι τὸ μὲν σβέννυται, τὸ δὲ οὐ σβέννυται.[69]

> The problem is to know why this one goes out, while the other does not go out.

So, until now, what we have here is nothing else than a repetition of Severian's words, with the important twist of a change of meaning for the expression 'virtues on high'. The real transformation of the meaning of Severian's exegesis comes in Ps.-Caesarius'

---

[67] See QA 3. 40–42: [...] τὰς ὑπερκοσμίους δυνάμεις· αἱ ταὐτὸν μὲν τῇ οὐσίᾳ πᾶσαι ὑπάρχουσαι, ὁμοίως καὶ αἱ λογικαὶ βροτῶν ψυχαὶ ταὐτὸν ὑπάρχουσαι τῇ οὐσίᾳ πᾶσαι [...] (cited above, p. 334); QA 44. 9–12: ἑπτὰ δὲ τυγχάνουσιν τάγματα, καθὼς Ἰούδας ἔγραψεν καὶ ὁ ὑψηλὸς ἐξαριθμεῖται ἀπόστολος, ᾧ καὶ ἑπόμενοι οἱ τῆς θείας τελετῆς ἱερεῖς ἀναφωνοῦσιν θεῷ· 'σὲ ὑμνοῦσιν ἄγγελοι ἀρχάγγελοι θρόνοι κυριότητες ἀρχαὶ ἐξουσίαι δυνάμεις' – a most interesting doctrine, plainly contradicting the Dionysian hierarchisation of the angels in nine orders.

[68] QA 58. 1–2.

[69] Severian of Gabala, *On the Creation of the World* I. 4 (ed. PG 56, col. 434. 28–29; with the correction of an error through iotacism in the PG text, which printed Ζητεῖτε).

answer to the above question. For this transformation Ps.-Caesarius uses precisely the aforecited text of Gregory the Theologian; through this allusion he transforms Severian's words into a text expressing the sixth-century Origenist doctrine on the pre-existence. To show the subtle writing technique of Ps.-Caesarius, here I give his text in parallel with that of Severian, with an indication of the Nazianzenian element utilised for the transformation.

Ps.-Caesarius, *Questions and Answers*, QA 58. 1–14.	Severian of Gabala, *On the Creation of the World* I. 4 (ed. PG 56, col. 434. 27–41).
Πεῦσις Καὶ πῶς τὸ ἄνω τοῦ παρ' ἡμῖν ἔσται συγγενές, τοῦ μὲν ἀσβέστου ὄντος, τοῦ δὲ σβεννυμένου; **Ἀπόκρισις** Παραπλησίως ἀγγέλων καὶ τῶν ἡμετέρων ψυχῶν τὸ ὅμοιον ἔχειν φημί· ἀμφότερα γὰρ πνεύματα ὑπάρχει παρὰ θεοῦ τὴν γένεσιν ἔχοντα, τὰ μὲν ἐν τοῖς σώμασιν ἡμῶν λαμπάδων δίκην φαίνοντα καὶ οἱονεὶ σβεννύμενα τῇ διαζεύξει τῆς ἐνεργείας παυόμενα. φῶς γὰρ βροτοὶ παρὰ τοῖς πάλαι σοφοῖς προσαγορεύονται διὰ τὴν τοῦ λόγου δύναμιν. ὁμοίως δὲ καὶ πῦρ προσαγορεύονται, ὡς μικρὸν ὕστερον ἀποδείξω τοῦ λόγου προϊόντος ἐπὶ τὴν ἡμετέραν γένεσιν. τοὺς δ' ἀγγέλους φημὶ πνεύματα ἄσβεστα, μὴ ἔχοντα σωματικὴν συνάφειαν καὶ διάστασιν· τὴν δὲ ψυχῶν καὶ ἀγγέλων ὁμοιότητα καὶ οἱ τρεῖς ἅγιοι παρέστησαν παῖδες, εὐλογεῖτε φάσκοντες	Ζητεῖται δὲ, ὅτι τὸ μὲν σβέννυται, τὸ δὲ οὐ σβέννυται. Ἐπεὶ καὶ τοὺς ἀγγέλους ἐποίησεν ὁ Θεὸς πνεύματα, καὶ τὰς ψυχὰς ἡμῶν πνεύματα, ἀλλὰ τὰς μὲν ψυχὰς ἡμῶν ἐν σώμασι, τοὺς δὲ ἀγγέλους ἐκτὸς σωμάτων. ὥσπερ οὖν ἐπὶ τῶν ψυχῶν καὶ τῶν ἀγγέλων, οὕτω καὶ ἐπὶ τοῦ πυρός ἐστιν ἰδεῖν. Τὸ πῦρ τὸ ἄνω ἄνευ ὕλης, τὸ πῦρ τὸ κάτω μετὰ ὕλης· τὸ γὰρ ἄνω πῦρ συγγενὲς τούτων ἐστί, ὥσπερ καὶ ἡ ψυχὴ ἡμῶν συγγενὲς ἀγγέλων· καθὸ κἀκεῖνοι πνεύματα, καὶ αὗται πνεύματα, ὡς καὶ οἱ τρεῖς παῖδες λέγουσι· *Εὐλογεῖτε, πνεύματα καὶ ψυχαὶ δικαίων·* καὶ πάλιν· *Ὁ ποιῶν τοὺς ἀγγέλους αὐτοῦ πνεύματα.* Οὔτε οὖν ψυχὴ ἄνευ σώματος φαίνεται, οὔτε πῦρ ἄνευ στυππείου, ἢ κληματίδος, ἢ ἑτέρας ὕλης ἔστιν ἰδεῖν.[70]

[70] 'The problem is to know why this one goes out, while the other does not go out. God created both the angels as spirits and our souls as spirits, but our souls he created in bodies, while the angels without bodies. So the relationship between the two fires is analogous to the one between the souls and the angels. The fire on high is without fuel [or matter] the fire here-below is with fuel [or matter]. For the fire on high is akin to these fires, just as our soul is akin to the angels. Just as they are spirits, in a like manner the souls are also spirits, as the three young men say: "Bless, o spirits and souls of the just [the Lord]!" [Dan. 3. 86] and again: "who makes his angels spirits" [Ps. 103. 4]. So neither does the soul appear without a body, nor can we see a fire without some oakum, or vine-branch, or other fuel [or matter]'.

Ps.-Caesarius, *Questions and Answers*, QA 58. 1–14.	Gregory of Nazianzus, *Oratio* 40, *On the Holy Baptism* 5 (ed. PG 36, col. 364. 29–32).
πνεύματα καὶ ψυχαὶ δικαίων τὸν κύριον· καὶ πάλιν ἐν μελῳδίαις ὁ Δαυίδ φησιν· ὁ ποιῶν τοὺς ἀγγέλους αὐτοῦ πνεύματα, τὸ δ' ὅμοιον αὐτῶν πρὸς τὰς ἡμῶν ψυχὰς παριστῶν φησιν· ταχὺ εἰσάκουσόν μου κύριε, ἐξέλιπεν τὸ πνεῦμά μου.[71]	Τρίτον φῶς ἄνθρωπος, ὁ καὶ τοῖς ἔξω δῆλόν ἐστι. Φῶς γὰρ τὸν ἄνθρωπον ὀνομάζουσι, διὰ τὴν τοῦ ἐν ἡμῖν λόγου δύναμιν· καὶ ἡμῶν αὐτῶν πάλιν οἱ θεοειδέστεροι, καὶ μᾶλλον Θεῷ πλησιάζοντες.[72]

In the previous QA Ps.-Caesarius operated a twist, transferring Severian's words about the 'fire on high' from the celestial luminaries to the angelic beings. Here, through the hidden quote from Gregory of Nazianzus, he completes the transfer in the most daring way. In fact, Severian established a kind of proportion: the relation between the unquenchable fire on high and the quenchable fire here-below is just as the relation between the angelic spirits and our souls; the fire on high is without a fuel and the earthly fire with a fuel, just like the angels are bodiless and the souls in a body. However, the same becomes an identification for Ps.-Caesarius: the unquenchable fires on high are the angels and the quenchable earthly fires are the souls of the mortals, both being portions of the same 'light' or 'fire' created on the first day of creation, meaning as clearly as possible the originally created intellectual substance, which, according to the anti-Origenist

---

[71] 'Q. And how will the the fire on high be akin to our fire, given that it is unquenchable, while ours goes out?

A. I say that they are similar just as the angels and our souls. For they are both spirits who owe their existence to God; the latter are just as lamps shining in our bodies and are so to say going out because by the fact of the separation they cease of their operation. For the ancient sages call the mortals "light" because of the power of reason. They are also called fire, as I will demonstrate a little later, when we will treat our creation. I would say that the angels are unquenchable spirits, who have no bodily conjunction and extension. The holy three young men have also shown the likeness of souls and angels, when they said: "Bless, o spirits and souls of the just, the Lord!" [Dan. 3. 86] and again, David who in his songs says: "who makes his angels spirits" [Ps. 103. 4] shows their likeness to our souls saying: "Quickly, listen to me my Lord, because my spirit has failed" [Ps. 142. 7]'.

[72] 'The third light is man – which fact is clear even to those outside: they call man "light" because of the virtue of the reason in us – but even among us rather those who are more similar to God and approach God more'.

anathemas of 553 AD, the Origenists called a unity or henad.
Ps.-Caesarius also interprets death in the classical Platonist sense
as a mere separation of the unquenchable fire, the immortal
soul, from its fuel, the body. This identification with the angelic
spirits of the 'fires on high', which originally meant for Severian
of Gabala the celestial luminaries, is all the more logical, given
that for Ps.-Caesarius the sun and the moon are also from the
same original light-substance, created on the first day, from where
the angelic spirits and the souls originate.[73]

After these clarifications it is worth going back to the text of
QA 3, which follows the almost overtly Origenist account of the
Fall:

> φὼς δὲ καὶ ὁ βροτὸς προσαγορεύεται, φῶς καὶ ὁ ἥλιος καὶ ἡ σελήνη
> καλεῖται, φῶς καὶ ἡ ποικίλη τῶν ἄστρων χορεία κατωνόμασται·
> ἀλλὰ τῶν εἰρημένων πλείστων ὑλικῶν καὶ διαφόρων φώτων πολυ-
> μερῶς καὶ πολυτρόπως ποιητὴς καὶ δημιουργὸς ὑπάρχει τὸ ἀληθι-
> νὸν καὶ ἄϋλον φῶς, ὁ ἐπὶ πάντων θεὸς καὶ πατὴρ σὺν τῷ μονογενεῖ
> αὐτοῦ παιδὶ καὶ τῷ θείῳ πνεύματι [...].[74]

If now we reread this text in the light of the clarifications received
from the analysis of QA 57 and 58, it does not sound exaggerated
anymore to connect it to the doctrines condemned by Anathemas 3 and 4 of the anti-Origenist council of 553. Our text says
in a hidden but logically decodable manner that the mortal man,
the sun and the moon are equally particles of the original light
created on the first day, the light meaning a universal and immortal – although created – unique rational substance, from where
all the rational, that is, light-natured, beings, such as the angels,
the celestial luminaries, the human beings, and the demons originate. Their separate existence is precisely due to the original Fall,
described in QA 3, immediately preceding the text analysed
above, in a manner which could not be much clearer than it is.

6. The Devil and the Fall of Adam and Eve

Thus, in Ps.-Caesarius we have discovered the doctrine, condemned in 553, of the creation of the angels, human beings, and

---

[73] QA 92, 1–16.
[74] QA 3. 45–49, translated above.

celestial luminaries out of a unique light-natured rational substance, subsequent to a mysterious original Fall. However, what should we think about the demons? According to the doctrine condemned in 553 AD, the demons are equally from the original henad, but they are those who, after the original 'turning away towards the worse' (ἐκ παρατροπῆς τῆς ἐπὶ τὸ χεῖρον), 'ran until the extremity of vice' (ἐπὶ τὸ ἄκρον τῆς κακίας ἐληλακότα), so that they 'were bound into cold and dark bodies' (ψυχροῖς καὶ ζοφεροῖς ἐνδεθῆναι σώμασι).[75] Does Ps.-Caesarius say something about these issues as well?

In QA 121–122 Ps.-Caesarius sets out to explain the meaning of St Paul's words: 'For I was alive without the law once: but when the commandment came, sin revived, and I died' (Rom. 7. 9). First, he explains that St Paul says this in the person of Adam. He lived in Paradise for forty days – forty being here a symbolic number, representing an indefinite period of time – before he ate from the fruit of the forbidden tree.[76] The question remains, as formulated by Ps.-Caesarius's interlocutors, the following:

> Ἁμαρτία ἡ παρακοὴ καὶ πᾶσα κακία ὀνομάζεται, πρὸ δὲ τοῦ Ἀδὰμ οὐδεὶς ἀνθρώπων ἥμαρτεν· οὔτε γὰρ ἦν. ὑπὸ τίνος οὖν πραχθεῖσα προϋπῆρχεν νεκρὰ καὶ ἀνέζησεν ἐλθούσης τῆς ἐντολῆς; τῶν δύο γὰρ τὸ ἕτερον, ἢ φύσιν ὑποτίθει ἁμαρτίας ὑπάρχειν ἢ πραχθεῖσαν αὐτὴν ὑπό τινος πρὸ τοῦ Ἀδάμ.[77]

> Disobedience and all other vice are called sin. Before Adam no man sinned, given that no man existed; then, by whom was sin committed, so that after that it preexisted being dead and revived when the commandment came? For one of the two must be true: either you suppose that there exists a nature of the sin, or somebody else committed it before Adam.

To which question the following remarkable answer is given:

> Ἄπαγε φύσιν λέγειν τῶν κακῶν· ἁμαρτία δ' ἐμοὶ δοκεῖ πᾶσα τοῦ κρείττονος ἀντίστασις καὶ ἀντιπαράταξις. ταύτην δέ φημι ὑπάρχειν τὸν διάβολον οὐ φύσει, ἀλλὰ προαιρέσει ἐπὶ τὸ χεῖρον τραπέντα. ἐκ γὰρ τοῦ διαβάλλειν θεῷ τὰς τῶν ἀγγέλων χορείας

---

[75] *Anti-Origenist Canons* 3 and 4, ACO IV/1, p. 248. 15 and 19–20.

[76] QA 121. 39–50.

[77] QA 122. 1–4.

φερωνύμως ἐκλήθη διάβολος, ὑπάρχων ἀρχάγγελος. τῶν δὲ ὑπερ-
κοσμίων καταρραγεὶς ὑπῆρχεν τῇ πράξει ἐχθρὸς μήπω γενομένου τοῦ ὁρατοῦ τούτου κόσμου μηδὲ ὑπάρχοντος τοῦ παρ' αὐτοῦ
ὑπαχθέντος ἀνθρώπου· γενομένου δὲ αὖθις διαβάλλει τὸν θεὸν τῷ
Ἀδὰμ βασκανίας αὐτῷ καταληρῶν [...] γυμνώσας τοίνυν αὐτοὺς
καὶ ὧν εἴχοσαν ἀθανασίας καὶ ἀφθαρσίας καὶ μακαριότητος, ἀνέ-
ζησεν τῇ πράξει ὁ μισόθεος καὶ ἀνθρωποκτόνος καὶ αὖθις διαβάλλει θεῷ τὸν ἄνθρωπον παραβάντα.[78]

God forbid to speak about a nature of evil! It seems to me that
sin is all the resistance and fight against what is good. And
I say that this is the Devil, who had turned toward what
is worse, not by nature, but by free choice. He was called Devil
[i.e. 'Accuser'] from the fact that he accused to God the angelic
hosts, himself being an archangel. Having been thrown down
from the supramundane region he was an enemy by his deeds
before the coming to existence of this visible world, when
man, whom he had cheated [or: dragged down], did not yet
exist. When he [that is, man] came to being, the Devil accused
God to Adam, speaking to him bewitchingly [... here follows
an account on the temptation of Eve and Adam in Paradise
...] Having deprived them even of that immortality, inde-
structibility, and blessedness that they had had, then the god-
hating and man-murdering one revived in deed and, on his
turn, accused to God man as transgressor.

The above text is in close correspondence both with Ps.-Caesarius'
QA 3, analysed above, and with the anathemas of 553 AD. Moreover, it conveys a very interesting doctrine on the first Fall from
the immaterial henad and on the second Fall from Paradise.
Let us first see the literal correspondences. They are indicated in
the following table.

Anti-Origenist Canons, ACO IV/1, p. 248. 8–11; 17–20.	Ps.-Caesarius, *Questions and Answers*, QA 3. 40–45.	Ps.-Caesarius, *Questions and Answers*, QA 122. 6–11.
Anathema 2: [...] κόρον δὲ αὐτοὺς λαβεῖν τῆς θείας θεωρίας καὶ **πρὸς τὸ χεῖρον**	[...] αἱ μὲν τυγχάνουσιν τάξει, αἱ δὲ στάσει, ἔτεραι δὲ παραστάσει καὶ	Ἄπαγε φύσιν λέγειν τῶν κακῶν· ἁμαρτία δ' ἐμοὶ δοκεῖ πᾶσα τοῦ κρείττονος

[78] QA 122. 6–25.

Anti-Origenist Canons, ACO IV/1, p. 248. 8–11; 17–20.	Ps.-Caesarius, *Questions and Answers*, QA 3. 40–45.	Ps.-Caesarius, *Questions and Answers*, QA 122. 6–11.
τραπῆναι κατὰ τὴν ἑκάστου ἀναλογίαν τῆς ἐπὶ τοῦτο ῥοπῆς· καὶ εἰληφέναι σώματα λεπτομερέστερα ἢ παχύτερα, καὶ ὄνομα κληρώσασθαι διὰ τὸ ὡς ὀνομάτων οὕτω καὶ σωμάτων διαφορὰς εἶναι τῶν ἄνω δυνάμεων· Anathema 4: Εἴ τις λέγει τὰ λογικὰ τὰ τῆς θείας ἀγάπης ἀποψυγέντα σώμασι παχυτέροις τοῖς καθ' ἡμᾶς ἐνδεθῆναι καὶ ἀνθρώπους ὀνομασθῆναι, <u>τὰ δὲ ἐπὶ τὸ ἄκρον τῆς κακίας ἐληλακότα</u> ψυχροῖς καὶ ζοφεροῖς ἐνδεθῆναι σώμασι καὶ <u>δαίμονας ἢ πνευματικὰ τῆς πονηρίας</u> εἶναί τε καὶ καλεῖσθαι, ἀνάθεμα ἔστω.	λειτουργία, ἐπιβολαῖς καὶ μεταβολαῖς καὶ μετατροπαῖς αὐθαιρέτως πρὸς τὸ χεῖρον ἢ κρεῖττον ῥέπουσαι, οὐκ ἀνάγκῃ δὲ φυσικῇ ἐκπίπτουσαι κατὰ τὸ μεῖζον καὶ ἧττον, ἐν τούτοις τὸ διάφορον ἔχουσαι τῆς ὑπεροχῆς.	<u>ἀντίστασις καὶ ἀντιπαράταξις.</u> ταύτην δὲ φημι ὑπάρχειν τὸν διάβολον οὐ φύσει, ἀλλὰ προαιρέσει ἐπὶ τὸ χεῖρον τραπέντα. ἐκ γὰρ τοῦ διαβάλλειν θεῷ τὰς τῶν ἀγγέλων χορείας φερωνύμως ἐκλήθη διάβολος, ὑπάρχων ἀρχάγγελος. τῶν δὲ ὑπερκοσμίων καταρραγεὶς ὑπῆρχεν τῇ πράξει ἐχθρὸς μήπω γενομένου τοῦ ὁρατοῦ τούτου κόσμου [...].

A comparison of the three texts suggests the following relationships between them. The first part of our first text, that is Anathema 2, formulates a general principle: the cause of the creation of the variegated universe out of the original created unity (henad) was a 'satiation of the divine contemplation' and a subsequent 'turning away' from God, resulting in a series of disorderly motions, which brought the moving beings to diverse locations in the new universe, created by their very motions. It was according to these entirely free motions (in proportion to their direction and speed) that they were assigned diverse bodies and, corresponding to these, diverse denominations. The second part of our first text, that is, Anathema 4, applies the principle, according to which every denomination in the newly created universe corresponds to the previous actions of the rational beings, to two sub-categories: those of them in whom the 'divine love' simply cooled down were bound into coarser bodies than the fiery bodies of the angels

– they became the human beings; but those rational beings whom their impetus and free motion brought 'as far as the extremity of vice' (ἐπὶ τὸ ἄκρον τῆς κακίας), were bound into cold and dark bodies and were called demons.

Our second text, that of QA 3 in Ps.-Caesarius, only partly cited here, repeats the principle stated in Anathema 2, according to which the hierarchical arrangement of the universe is due to prenatal actions. It further emphasises the freedom of the motion, which brings each being to a corresponding birth: no natural necessity is at play, it is all due to their free choice (αὐθαιρέτως) and to the degree (κατὰ τὸ μεῖζον καὶ ἧττον) to which they have 'fallen out' (ἐκπίπτουσαι) from their original substantial unity. The text in its next section not cited here but analysed above in Part 4, applies this principle to the entire hierarchy of the rational beings, beginning with the 'virtues on high' and ending up with the human beings and the celestial luminaries, without, however, mentioning the demons.

Our third text, that of QA 122, fills the aforementioned lacuna of QA 3. Now it applies the same principle to the Devil. It emphasises, once again, that this rational being – in its previous state an archangel – became what it is, because it 'had turned toward what is worse', certainly 'not by nature, but by free choice.' It also says that the Devil obtained its name due to its action completed in its previous state – he accused the angels to God before the creation of the visible universe.[79] Of course, one might think that all this was standard Christian theological doctrine – the free fall of the Devil being part of any theodicy – were it not for the identical expressions used in QA 122, in the text of Anathema 2 and in the clearly Origenist passage of QA 3. From the latter's

---

[79] See also the parallel text of QA 44. 12–16: ὅτι δὲ τρεπτοί, ἐναργὴς ἀπόδειξις ὁ ἐπὶ τὸ χεῖρον τραπεὶς ἀρχέκακος διάβολος συναποστήσας ἑαυτῷ ἱκανοὺς τῶν ἀγγέλων οὐ φύσει, ἀλλὰ γνώμῃ τραπέντας τῇ ὑποσπορᾷ τοῦ σφῶν ἡγουμένου κατάλληλον τοῦ δράματος τὴν προσηγορίαν δεξαμένου ἐκ γὰρ τοῦ διαβάλλειν τὸ ὁμόφυλον φερωνύμως κέκληται διάβολος, σατὰν δὲ ἐκ τοῦ θεῷ καὶ ἀνθρώποις ἀντικεῖσθαι. ('That [the angels are] changeable, to this clear demonstration is given by the arch-evil Devil, who turned toward the worse and made to rebel together with him a good number of angels, who changed not according to nature but according to their will because of the instigation of their leader, who received his name corresponding to his deeds; for he is called Devil from the fact of accusing his kin, and Satan from the fact of opposing God and men').

doctrine of subsequent falls there also follows the doctrine of a gradual fall of the Devil: first he was an archangel, before obtaining his present status.

However, the text also says much more than this. It identifies sin, as such, with the Devil, but at the same time denies that evil or sin would have a nature of its own. Thus evil is a rational being, having an originally good nature, who, however, by its free motion, as a result of a series of gradual falls, fills the inherent possibility of evilness; in other words, out of its free choice, not being evil by nature, it identifies with the role of absolute evil. This is equivalent to saying, with the words found in Anathema 4, that the Devil is a rational being who 'has run until the extremity of vice', thus exhausting this possibility, logically inherent in the emanationist theory of the Origenists. This also corresponds to the way Evagrius interpreted Proverbs 2. 17: 'the evil thought' (κακὴ βουλή) is the Devil, who had thought evil to the extent of becoming the evil thought itself, 'abandoning the teaching of his youth' (ἀπέλιπεν διδασκαλίαν νεότητος), that is, its original contemplative state, and 'forgetting about the divine testament' (θείας ἐπελάθετο διαθήκης).[80] The same teaching is also expressed in Evagrius' scholion on Proverbs 30. 10:

> Φυγόντα νοῦν τὴν κακίαν μὴ πάλιν παραδῷς τῇ κακίᾳ, εἴπερ
> 'πᾶς ὁ ποιῶν τὴν ἁμαρτίαν δοῦλός ἐστι τῆς ἁμαρτίας'. Ἁμαρτία
> δὲ νῦν ὀνομάζεται ὁ ἐνεργῶν τὴν ἁμαρτίαν διάβολος.[81]

> Don't give up again to vice the mind that has fled from vice, if it is true that 'everybody who commits sin is a servant of sin' [Ioh. 8. 34]. Here by 'sin' is meant the Devil who is practising sin.

However, in fact, here not only the teaching of Ps.-Caesarius is closely reminiscent of that of Evagrius, but also the vocabulary. Both texts say, although concerning two different Scriptural verses, that at certain places, when Scripture speaks about 'sin', in fact it means the Devil who is the sinner *par excellence*.

QA 122 also illuminates Ps.-Caesarius's criticism of the allegorical interpretation of the original Fall, which he – follow-

---

[80] See Evagrius of Pontus, *In Prov.* 2. 17 (SC 340, p. 116, n. 23).
[81] Evagrius of Pontus, *In Prov.* 30. 10 (SC 340, p. 382, n. 289).

ing Justinian's edict – attributes to 'the most unholy Origen',[82] according to which the story of the Paradise and man's transgression in it would be an allegory of the original Fall from the incorporeal state.

According to the theory that we may reconstruct based on QA 122, by his conscious and free movement, the Devil had become the incorporation of Sin itself. So, he was thrown down from the 'supramundane region' and became dead. Thus he was Sin itself before the creation of the material universe, 'when man, whom he had cheated, did not yet exist', so that he revived only after the creation of the universe and, within the latter, of earth, man and Paradise, and the placement of man in the garden of Eden accompanied by the commandment of not eating from the forbidden fruit. Here we have the story of two Falls, one of the Devil and his angels from the supramundane heights before the creation of the universe and one of man from Paradise. If, once again, we put together the information received from the text of QA 122 with that from the programmatic QA 3, we may understand that the first Fall, preceding the creation of the universe, is also, in one way or another, the cause of its creation. The Devil had apparently at least three states: first that of a pure mind, then, that of an archangel before the Fall immediately preceding the creation of the material universe and that of a demon after the Fall and the creation of the universe. However, there also was an intermediate state after the Fall but before the creation of the universe, when he was not an archangel anymore, nor a demon as yet, but was 'dead'; it was only after the appearance of the new world and his appearance in it as the Enemy and the Tempter to sin, that he 'revived when the commandment came.'

One may ask whether this is also true for man. Did he exist before he arrived in the visible universe, or was his soul created together with the body? Our text contains an odd expression indicating the first thesis, while the 'official' position of Caesarius is a denial of the pre-existence of the human soul. Now let us try to disentangle this question, too. Ps.-Caesarius writes about the Devil that 'he was an enemy by his deeds before the coming to existence of this visible world, when man whom he had cheated

---

[82] QA 166. 24.

[or: dragged down] did not yet exist', the Greek expression μηδὲ ὑπάρχοντος τοῦ παρ' αὐτοῦ ὑπαχθέντος ἀνθρώπου with the aorist participle ὑπαχθέντος, indicating anteriority, logically meaning that the Devil cheated (or dragged down) man before his coming to existence. Had the expression been to indicate a posterior event, Ps.-Caesarius should have written μηδὲ ὑπάρχοντος τοῦ παρ' αὐτοῦ ὑπαχθησομένου ἀνθρώπου. So, logically, this expression seems to indicate, in one way or another, the pre-existence of the subjectivity that was going to become man, although not in a human form, given that man did not exist before the creation of the material universe. This doctrine would fully fit into the framework of our attempt at deciphering Caesarius' doctrine.

7. Conclusions

In this essay I have analysed the structure of Ps.-Caesarius's *Questions and Answers*, containing a brief *Summa Theologiae*. The work starts with the doctrines of the Trinity and of Christology, continues with a detailed exegesis of the creation of the universe, followed by that of the creation of man and of his being created in the image and likeness of God, to end with the theory of divinisation and the last end of humanity. This writing also receives an odd appendix connected to the eschatological part: a rabid attack on the Jewish community, denying the traditional doctrine of the historical salvation, at the end of the times, of the Jewish people. This reinterpretation is based on an Origenist exegesis of St Paul's relevant words promising the salvation of Israel as referring to the final Restoration, or Apokatastasis. I also gave a preliminary analysis of the 'anti-Origenian' part of the *Questions and Answers*, showing that it is verbally based on Justinian's edict of 542/43 condemning Origen, with which the author subtly engages and which he criticises in a cryptic manner. He is happy to endorse the condemnation of the theory of the pre-existence of the souls as proposed by the edict, given that it does not correspond to his own convictions, but establishes another, much more subtle, doctrine of the pre-existence of incorporeal minds in a unitary, precosmic substance, which has as its corollary a doctrine of gradual individuation understood as a series of subsequent and graded falls leading finally to the creation of man on earth as a corporeal being and to a final fall, in which man has lost a more spiritual existence in an earthly Paradise.

This doctrine Ps.-Caesarius inserts in his narrative by means of a number of encoding methods, out of which the present analysis revealed three main techniques, which were called that *of the background texts*, that *of the twisted authorities* and that *of the duplicates*. I believe that the recognition of these encoding methods combined to a fourth one, not corresponding to any encoding, that *of the condemnatory parallels*, has permitted, to a hitherto unprecedented degree, the understanding of this difficult text and to give it the importance it deserves as one of the direct witnesses to the doctrines of the sixth-century Palestinian monks condemned under the label 'Origenism' at the fifth ecumenical council in 553.

Moreover, I believe that the analyses presented here have furnished additional proof for the thesis first proposed in 2006 and, then, further exposed in two recent studies, according to which the Ps.-Caesarius is none else than Theodore, titulary bishop of Caesarea and Justinian's main theological advisor between 536 and 553, the main author of the condemnation of the Three Chapters, the anti-hero of Cyril of Scythopolis's *Life of Sabas* and of Liberatus of Carthage's *Brief history of the cause of the Nestorians and the Eutychians*,[83] the leader of the clandestine Isochrist Origenist party of the New Lavra, one of the most powerful, most controversial and most hated figures of Byzantine politics in the sixth century, being also the main target of the anti-Origenist condemnations of 553. With the restitution of the Ps.-Caesarian *Questions and Answers* to him, we are holding in our hands one of the most important sources of sixth-century political and doctrinal history, which awaits further exploitation.

Bibliography

B. E. Daley (1976), 'The Origenism of Leontius of Byzantium', in *Journal of Theological Studies*, 27, p. 333–369.

B. E. Daley (1995), 'What did "Origenism" Mean in the Sixth Century?', in G. Dorival & A. le Boulluec (eds), *Origeniana Sexta:*

[83] ACO III, p. 98–141.

Origène et la Bible (Actes du Colloquium Origenianum Sextum, Chantilly, 30 août – 3 septembre 1993), Leuven: Peeters, p. 627–638 (Bibliotheca Ephemeridum Theologicarum Lovaniensium, CXVIII).

F. Diekamp (1899), *Die Origenistischen Streitigkeiten im sechsten Jahrhundert und das fünfte allgemeine Concil*, Münster: Aschendorff.

N. de Lange (1999), 'Etudier et prier à Byzance', in *Revue des Etudes Juives*, 158, p. 51–59.

N. de Lange (2016), 'Hebraists and Hellenists in the Sixth-Century Synagogue: A New Reading of Justinian's Novel 146', in C. Cordoni et al. (eds), *"Let the wise listen and add to their learning" (Prov 1:5). Festschrift for Günter Stemberger*, Berlin: de Gruyter, p. 217–226.

G. Dorival (1974), *Les chaînes exégétiques grecques sur le Psaume 118. Recherches sur les filiations des chaînes exégétiques grecques sur les psaumes et publication de fragments inédits*, thèse de doctorat de 3ᵉ cycle, Paris.

L. Doutreleau (ed., 1976), *Origène. Homélies sur la Genèse, nouvelle édition : texte latin, traduction et notes*, Paris: Editions du Cerf.

D. B. Evans (1970), *Leontius of Byzantium: An Origenist Christology*, Washington: Dumbarton Oaks (Dumbarton Oaks Studies, 13).

D. B. Evans (1980), 'Leontius of Byzantium and Dionysius the Areopagite', in *Byzantine Studies / Etudes Byzantines*, 7, p. 1–34.

D. B. Evans (2001), 'The Christology of Pseudo-Dionysios the Areopagite', in *Acta Antiqua Academiae Scientiarum Hungaricae*, 41, p. 147–155.

H. Görgemanns & H. Karpp (eds, 1976), *Origenes. Vier Bücher von den Prinzipien*, Darmstadt: Wissenschaftliche Buchgesellschaft.

A. Grillmeier (1989), *Jesus der Christus im Glauben der Kirche*. Bd. 2/2. *Die Kirche der Konstantinopel im 6. Jahrhundert*, in collaboration with T. Hainthaler, Freiburg – Basel – Vienna: Herder.

M. Harl (1972), *La chaîne palestinienne sur le psaume 118 (Origène, Eusèbe, Didyme, Apollinaire, Athanase, Théodoret)*, in collaboration with G. Dorival, 2 vols, Paris: Cerf (Sources Chrétiennes, 189, 190).

R. E. Heine (tr., 1982), *Origen, Homilies on Genesis and Exodus*, The Fathers of the Church 71, Washington, DC: The Catholic University of America Press.

M. Kertsch (1983), 'Pseudo-Kaisarios als indirekter Textzeuge für Gregor von Nazianz', in *Jahrbuch der Österreichischen Byzantinistik*, 33, p. 17–24.

C. Macé (2015), 'Pseudo-Césaire, Anastase, Pseudo-Athanase : quelques réflexions sur les collections de Questions-et-Réponses dans la littérature grecque chrétienne', in *SHS Web of Conferences*, 22, article 4.

Y. Papadogiannakis (2013), 'Didacticism, Exegesis and Polemics in pseudo-Kaisarios's Erotapokriseis' in M.-P. Bussières (ed.), *La littérature des questions et réponses dans l'Antiquité profane et chrétienne: de l'enseignement à l'exégèse*, Turnhout: Brepols, p. 271–290.

I. Perczel (1999), 'Le pseudo-Denys, lecteur d'Origène', in W. A. Bienert & U. Kühneweg (eds), *Origeniana Septima. Origenes in den Auseinandersetzungen des 4. Jahrhunderts*, Leuven: Leuven University Press – Uitgeverij Peeters, p. 673–710.

I. Perczel (2001), '"Théologiens" et "magiciens" dans le *Corpus Dionysien*', in *Adamantius: Newsletter of the Italian Research Group 'Origen and the Alexandrian Tradition'*, 7, p. 54–75.

I. Perczel (2006–2007), 'Finding a Place for the *Erotapokriseis* of Pseudo-Caesarius: A New Document of Sixth-century Palestinian Origenism', in *Palestinian Christianity: Pilgrimages and Shrines*, *ARAM Periodical*, 18–19, p. 49–83.

I. Perczel (2013), 'The Pseudo-Didymian *De trinitate* and Pseudo-Dionysius the Areopagite: A Preliminary Study', in *Studia Patristica 58/6: Neoplatonism and Patristics*, Leuven – Paris – Walpole, MA: Peeters, p. 83–108.

I. Perczel (2017a), 'Clandestine Heresy and Politics in Sixth-century Constantinople: Theodore of Caesarea at the Court of Justinian', in H. Amirav & F. Celia (eds), *New Themes, New Styles in the Eastern Mediterranean: Christian, Jewish and Islamic Encounters, 5th–8th Centuries*, Leuven – Paris – Bristol, CT: Peeters, p. 137–171.

I. Perczel (2017b), 'Universal Salvation as an Antidote to Apocalyptic Expectations: Origenism in the Service of Justinian's Religious Politics', in H. Amirav, E. Grypeou & G. G. Stroumsa (eds), *Apocalypticism and Eschatology in Late Antiquity: Encounters in the Abrahamic Religions, 6th–8th Centuries*, Leuven – Paris – Bristol, CT: Peeters, p. 125–161.

J. B. Pitra (1883), *Analecta sacra spicilegio Solesmensi parata*, vol. 3, Paris: Tusculum.

U. Riedinger (1964), 'Die Epiphanios-Paraphrase des Pseudo-Kaisarios', in *Miscellanea critica: aus Anlaß des 150-jährigen Bestehens der Verlagsgesellschaft und des Graphischen Betriebes B. G. Teubner, Leipzig*, vol. 1, Leipzig: Teubner, p. 218–239.

R. Riedinger (1969), *Pseudo-Kaisarios, Überlieferungsgeschichte und Verfasserfrage*, München: Beck (Byzantinisches Archiv, 12).

M.-J. Rondeau (1960), 'Le commentaire sur les Psaumes d'Évagre le Pontique', in *Orientalia Christiana Periodica*, 26, p. 307–348.

L. Rutgers (2003), 'Justinian's *Novella 146* between Jews and Christians', in R. Lee Calmin & S. Schwartz (eds), *Jewish Culture and Society under the Christian Empire*, Leuven: Peeters, p. 385–407.

R. Schöll & W. Kroll (eds, 1912), *Corpus Iuris Civilis*, vol. 3, 4th ed., Berlin: Weidmann.

N. Spanu (2014), 'Some initial Remarks on Pseudo-Kaisarios' *Erotapokriseis*', lecture given at the King's College London Patristics Seminar, November 2014, text published at https://www.academia.edu/3320197/Some_initial_Remarks_on_Pseudo-Kaisarios_Erotapokriseis_lecture_given_at_the_Kings_College_London_Patristics_Seminar_November_2014_.

N. Spanu (2016), 'Pseudo-Kaisarios and Cosmas Indicopleustes on Genesis 1–3', in *E-Patrologos*, 2/1, p. 22–46.

C. Stewart (2015), 'Another Cassian?' in *Journal of Ecclesiastical History*, 66, p. 372–376.

B. R. Suchla (ed., 1990), *Dionysius Areopagiticus. Corpus Dionysiacum. I: De Divinis Nominibus*, Berlin: de Gruyter.

E. Schwartz (ed., 1939), *Kyrillos von Skythopolis*, Leipzig: Hinrichs.

P. Tzamalikos (2012a), *A Newly Discovered Greek Father: Cassian the Sabaite Eclipsed by John Cassian of Marseilles*, Leiden – Boston: Brill.

P. Tzamalikos (2012b), *The Real Cassian Revisited: Monastic Life, Greek Paideia, and Origenism in the Sixth Century*, Leiden – Boston: Brill.

G. Veltri (1994), 'Die Novelle 146 περὶ Ἑβραίων. Das Verbot des Targumvortrags in Justinians Politik', in M. Hengel & A. M. Schwemer (eds), *Die Septuaginta zwischen Judentum und Christentum*, Tübingen: Mohr Siebeck, p. 116–130.

Abstract

This study examines the *Erotapokriseis* (*Questions and Answers*) pseudonymously attributed to Caesarius, the brother of Gregory of Nazianzus. In earlier studies the author proposed the hypothesis that the *Erotapokriseis* was written by Theodore of Caesarea, one of the leaders of the secret Isochrist Origenists of Palestine, who became Justinian's all-powerful adviser. He also proposed earlier that Pseudo-Caesarius had used a coded language, for the decoding of which he suggested a methodology. In the present article he is applying this methodology to the question of cosmology and protology, showing that Pseudo-

Caesarius consistently exposed the creation of all the rational beings before the beginning of time in a unitary created substance ('henad'), without any number and corporeal extension, and taught the precosmic fall of these beings and their subsequent incorporation in angelic, human and demonic bodies. This, Pseudo-Caesarius does using several encoding methods, among which the most interesting is that of the 'twisted authorities', in which an ecclesiastic authority is paraphrased so that the resulting text gets a new meaning. Moreover, the present study treats Pseudo-Caesarius' apparent anti-Origenist passages, showing that they are based on Justinian's anti-Origenist edict of 543, so that the meaning of the texts of the edict is subtly twisted through distortions and the inclusions of Origenian and Evagrian texts and doctrines.

PART 4
QUESTIONING GENRE
IN THE MIDDLE-BYZANTINE PERIOD

MICHIEL MEEUSEN

PAGAN GARLANDS AND CHRISTIAN ROSES. PLUTARCH'S *QUAESTIONES CONVIVALES* IN MICHAEL PSELLUS' *DE OMNIFARIA DOCTRINA*

'To reach an understanding in a dialogue is not merely a manner of putting oneself forward and successfully asserting one's own point of view, but being transformed into a communion in which we do not remain what we were.'[1]

1. *For the Love of God, for the Sake of Education*

Michael Psellus (*c.* 1018 – after 1078) lived in a time when open affiliation with Hellenic – that is pagan – philosophy was considered an offensive secession from the Eastern-Orthodox faith.[2] As Chief of the Philosophers (ὕπατος τῶν φιλοσόφων) with clear Neoplatonic aspirations, Psellus was clever enough not to advocate pagan philosophy openly. Yet, the red line between philosophical do and don't was particularly thin, and Psellus very well knew this. The case of his student, John Italus, is there to illustrate this. In the *Synodikon of Orthodoxy* of 1082, two (of the twelve) anathemas apply to John Italus' promotion of Hellenic beliefs in his school curriculum:

> Τοῖς εὐσεβεῖν μὲν ἐπαγγελλομένοις, τὰ τῶν Ἑλλήνων δὲ δυσσεβῆ δόγματα τῇ ὀρθοδόξῳ καὶ καθολικῇ ἐκκλησίᾳ περί τε ψυχῶν ἀνθρωπίνων καὶ οὐρανοῦ καὶ γῆς καὶ τῶν ἄλλων κτισμάτων ἀναιδῶς ἢ μᾶλλον ἀσεβῶς ἐπεισάγουσιν, ἀνάθεμα. [...] Τοῖς τὰ ἑλληνικὰ διεξιοῦσι μαθήματα καὶ μὴ διὰ παίδευσιν μόνον ταῦτα παιδευομένοις, ἀλλὰ καὶ δόξαις αὐτῶν ταῖς ματαίαις ἑπομένοις καὶ ὡς ἀληθέσι πιστεύουσι, καὶ οὕτως αὐταῖς ὡς τὸ βέβαιον ἐχούσαις

---

[1] Gadamer 2003, p. 371.

[2] Cf. the definition in the *Suda* (phi.416.1–3 ed. Adler; trans. Duffy 2002, p. 140): Φιλοσοφία ἐστὶν ἠθῶν κατόρθωσις μετὰ δόξης τῆς περὶ τοῦ ὄντος γνώσεως ἀληθοῦς. ταύτης δὲ ἀπεσφάλησαν Ἰουδαῖοι καὶ Ἕλληνες. ('Philosophy is correct moral practice combined with a doctrine of true knowledge about Being. Jews and Hellenes have fallen short of this knowledge').

Questioning the World, Greek Patristic and Byzantine Question-and-Answer Literature, ed. by Bram Demulder and Peter Van Deun, Turnhout, 2021 (*LECTIO*, 11), pp. 363-378   © BREPOLS❧PUBLISHERS   DOI 10.1484/M.LECTIO-EB.5.121511

ἐγκειμένοις, ὥστε καὶ ἑτέρους ποτὲ μὲν λάθρᾳ, ποτὲ δὲ φανερῶς
ἐνάγειν αὐταῖς καὶ διδάσκειν ἀνενδοιάστως, ἀνάθεμα.[3]

Those who profess to be pious, but who in fact impudently
or rather impiously introduce into the Orthodox and Catholic Church the impious beliefs of the Hellenes concerning
human souls, heaven, earth and other creations, let them be
anathematised! [...] Those who offer courses on Hellenic subjects and do not teach these subjects solely for the sake of education, but who follow the vain opinions of the Hellenes and
believe in them as being true, and thus, considering them to
be correct, induce others – either secretly or even publicly –
to follow them and instruct them without second thoughts,
let them be anathematised![4]

As far as we know, Psellus himself was never anathematised.
Throughout his oeuvre, Psellus walks warily not to overstep the
mark of Christian orthodoxy, while cleverly incorporating Hellenic μαθήματα in his philosophical and theological discourses.
In fact, Psellus conveniently glosses over this heretic practice by
making it absolutely clear that he taught these μαθήματα solely for
the sake of education. He justified this by pointing at the intellectual benefits of comprehensive knowledge and love of learning (πολυμάθεια, φιλομάθεια), and by asserting that his inquiry into
Hellenic matters was no idle curiosity (περιεργασία) but a consequence of his intellectual conviction that 'a philosopher has to
be a man of all sorts' (e.g., *Theol.* 114.2: δεῖ τὸν σοφὸν παντοδαπὸν
εἶναι).

In his *De omnifaria doctrina*, Psellus suits the action to the
word. He offers a philosophical-theological encyclopaedia in the
form of questions and answers, discussing a wide range of topics
that cover the entire span of human knowledge, beginning with
questions concerning the intelligible world (god, intelligence
and the soul), and afterwards delving into the sensible world
(of physics, physiology, astronomy and meteorology).[5] As to Psel-

---

[3] *Synodikon of Orthodoxy* 57.190–192; 59.214–218 ed. Gouillard 1967.

[4] Trans. Agapitos 1998, p. 187 (with further literature). For further commentary, see Gouillard 1967, p. 188–202.

[5] For Psellus' encyclopaedism, cf. Mussini 1990, p. 9. See also more generally
Van Deun & Macé 2011 (p. 18–19 for Psellus' *De omnifaria doctrina* in particular).

lus' sources, for psychology and metaphysics, he mainly relies on Proclus; for physics, physiology, and astronomy it is Plutarch (esp. Ps.-Plutarch's *Placita*); and for matters of meteorology, he relies on Olympiodorus' commentary on Aristotle's *Meteorology* (and on Aristotle directly).[6] The wider framework of the collection is informed by a generic Christian dogma: Psellus starts from a profession of faith in the holy trinity (§ 1.2: πιστεύομεν εἰς ἕνα πατέρα κτλ.) and concludes with a short epilogue (§ 201), where he addresses the reader and admits that (in expounding the concepts about the soul)[7] he not only drew from 'our holy craters' but also from the 'salty Hellenic waters'. Psellus closes the collection by noting that the reader 'should know that the roses of Christian scripture are quite genuine, but those of others also have τὸ φαρμακῶδες hidden in the flower'.[8]

Clearly, it is Psellus' intention with *De omnifaria doctrina* – or in Greek Διδασκαλία παντοδαπή – to contribute to the general education of the implied reader, and it is exactly under this pretext that a great many theories and concepts of Hellenic philosophers pass under review. In the titles of some manuscripts the Διδασκαλία is even qualified as being πάντη ἀναγκαιοτάτη ('very necessary', 'elementary'), presumably for the all-round instruction of the reader – who was none other than the Byzantine emperor.[9] The relationship between encyclopaedic knowledge and imperial power is not without interest, as it provides an understanding of what highly placed Byzantine figures were expected to know, or, at the very least, to have read.

---

[6] For more detail on Psellus' sources, see Westerink 1948, p. 2–3 (with p. 14 for further literature and with Meeusen 2012, p. 121 for a schematic overview). See also Zervos 1973, p. 127.

[7] Westerink 1948, p. 5 is right that '[t]he sections περὶ νοῦ and περὶ ψυχῆς (§§ 21–47) were [...] intended as a separate work, as the epilogue (§ 201) proves, but it cannot be decided whether they were ever published as such'.

[8] Trans. Wilson 1983, p. 158 (adapted). The pun may be on φαρμακῶδες, which can imply both 'poisonous' and 'healing' (see Meeusen 2012, p. 120). However, in *Theol.* 74.147 Psellus opposes τὰς φαρμακῶδεις (βοτάνας) to τὰς θεραπευούσας. For the notion that a drug can turn into poison when given in high dosage, cf., e.g., Ps.-Arist. *Pr.* 1.47.865a7–9.

[9] See MS Bodleianus Roe gr. 18. Alternatively, in MS Athous 103 πάντη ἀναγκαιοτάτη is (perhaps not so remarkably) ruled by ἔκθεσις τῆς ἡμῶν πίστεως.

In his 1948 edition of *De omnifaria doctrina*, Westerink distinguishes four different redactions in the manuscripts.[10] The first one is dated around 1050 and was dedicated to emperor Constantine IX Monomachus (who reigned over the empire from 1042 to 1054).[11] It is entitled Ἐπιλύσεις σύντομοι ἀποριῶν φυσικῶν and contains only sections on physics. In the second redaction (dated around 1075), Psellus adds a number of chapters on theology (§§ 1–14), psychology (§§ 21–47) and ethics (§§ 66–81). He there addresses his pupil Michael VII Ducas (who reigned from 1071 to 1078).[12] The final two redactions 'are the result of a final systematic rearrangement of the whole book'.[13]

As to the first redaction, '[t]he plan was obviously to deal with the subjects treated in [(Ps.-)]Plutarch's *Placita*, from which, however, as a rule only the headings of the sections are taken; in the second half a good deal of other matter is added'. Parts of Plutarch's *Quaestiones convivales* and *Quaestiones naturales* are among these other materials (see above for Psellus' other sources). I have dealt with Psellus' incorporation of Plutarch's *Quaestiones naturales* elsewhere, so will limit myself in this contribution to examining the material drawn from *Quaestiones convivales*.[14]

2. Quaestiones convivales *in* De omnifaria doctrina

Plutarch's *Quaestiones convivales* have attracted much scholarly attention in the last decade.[15] We are dealing with a particularly rich text, that straddles a large variety of questions (and answers) pertaining to ancient history, literature, science, philosophy and so on.[16] Plutarch discusses these questions (προβλήματα, ἀπορίαι,

---

[10] Westerink 1948, p. 2–10.

[11] The titles of MSS Matritensis gr. 51 and Athous 4310 mention Monomachus. An anonymous emperor is named in §§ 127 and 143.

[12] See § 6.4: σύ, ὁ βασιλεὺς Μιχαήλ. See also §§ 3.2; 4.4–5; 12.2; 12.4; 12.37–38; 13.2.

[13] Westerink 1948, p. 6.

[14] The other part of the diptych is Meeusen 2012.

[15] See recently König 2007; Klotz & Oikonomopoulou 2011; Vamvouri Ruffy 2012.

[16] On the miscellaneous nature of *Quaestiones convivales*, see Morgan 2011.

ζητήματα) against the literary decor of the symposia that he says to have attended both in Rome and in Greece (*QC* 1.*Pr.*, 612E). He dedicates the work to Q. Sosius Senecio, a Roman politician and general, and close friend of emperor Hadrian, and stages both himself and his close family, peers and students in the sympotic discussions – thus, in a way, immortalising them in this learned *Festschrift*, this sympotic *liber amicorum*.[17] The work was relatively popular in Late Antiquity and enjoyed a rich reception in even later days.[18]

As can be expected from the focus on ἀπορίαι φυσικαί in the first redaction of *De omnifaria doctrina*, Psellus only draws from Plutarch's discussions on natural philosophy.[19] These depart from particular problems about (often relatively peculiar) natural phenomena but subtly ramify into broader questions of scientific method and world view. Psellus only draws from books five and (especially) six of *Quaestiones convivales*.[20] Issues that attract his attention include the problem of the evil eye and the cause of bulimy, as well as problems related to drinking, eating, fasting and so on (see the table below). Since no clear thematic unity can be distinguished in these chapters, Psellus' choice is probably inspired by motives of general intellectual curiosity about profane natural phenomena.[21] Apparently such marvellous and paradoxical topics were considered useful to the Imperial ear.[22]

---

[17] On Plutarch's authorial self-promotion and self-effacement in this work, see Klotz 2007 and König 2011.

[18] See Hubert 1938 (esp. p. 318–319 for Psellus' role).

[19] This type of (natural) problems covers approximately one third of the source text (see Meeusen 2014, p. 311, n. 3). Notably, Psellus does not incorporate the two problems about the Jews in book four (viz. *QC* 4.5: about their abstention from pork; 4.6: about their God, identifying him with Dionysus).

[20] There is no way of knowing whether Psellus had access to the entire collection or only to those two sections. This is difficult to say, precisely due to the deficient manuscript tradition of *Quaestiones convivales*. According to Hubert 1938, p. 319, 'hatte Psellus, hochstwahrscheinlich einige Jahrzehnte nach der Herstellung des Vindobonensis [gr. 148], eine Handschrift vor sich, die aus der gleichen Überlieferungsbahn stammte'.

[21] Indeed, the concept of wonder occurs at several places: § 109.4: θαυμαστήν; § 191.2: θαυμαστόν; § 192.5: θαυμασιώτατον.

[22] Notably, Psellus also attributed a Περὶ παραδόξων ἀναγνωσμάτων (or ἀκουσμάτων?) to Michael VII Ducas (see Giannini 1965, p. 397, nr. XL).

Quaestiones convivales in *De omnifaria doctrina*[23]

QC	1st redaction	§ Westerink	Content
5.7	131	109	Evil eye
6.1	132	118	Thirst caused by fasting
6.3	133	119	Drinking and hunger
6.5	134	190	Pebbles/lead cool water
6.6	135	191	Straw/cloths protect snow
6.8	136	192	Bulimy
6.10	137	193	Fig tree rots flesh

As I have shown in my previous analysis of the *Quaestiones naturales* material in *De omnifaria doctrina*, Psellus, in transforming Plutarch's natural problems into the Byzantine *capita* format, often makes very literal, though abridged extracts from his source text.[24] At other times, he radically adapts Plutarch's arguments (e.g., when they are difficult to understand), relocates and rephrases chunks of texts, adds new material, and so on. We will see that this is no different in the case of the material drawn from *Quaestiones convivales*. An interesting case to illustrate this is found in § 109, which corresponds to *QC* 5.7 (680C–683B). The discussion at hand concerns people who are said to cast a spell (καταβασκαίνειν) and have an evil eye (βάσκανον ὀφθαλμόν).

3. The Problem of the Evil Eye (§ 109 ~ QC 5.7)

Plutarch treats the problem of the evil eye against the backdrop of a sympotic discussion where he stages himself and a number of his close acquaintances (Florus, Patrocleas, Soclarus and Gaius)

---

[23] To this list can be added two chapters that possibly contain the remnants of two lost *Quaestiones naturales*: viz. § 170 = *QN* 40 ('How does it come that brine bursts forth from the sea when a thunderbolt falls in it?') and § 188 = *QN* 41 ('Why do roses flower better when certain ill-smelling plants have been planted beside them?'). These chapters contain parallels with *QC* 5.10 (cf. also § 180.10–12) and 5.9 respectively. For further detail, see Meeusen 2012, p. 107–110.

[24] Meeusen 2012, p. 110–114. Cf. also Doehner 1859, p. 410.

as participants in the debate. The introduction is seminal for Plutarch's general attitude towards natural *mirabilia* and for his method of raising and solving natural problems.[25] We read that Florus (the host of the symposium), in opposition to those who make fun of the popular belief about the evil eye, ascribes credibility to the phenomenon, noting that 'the facts amazingly support the belief' (τὰ μὲν γινόμενα τῇ φήμῃ θαυμαστῶς βοηθεῖν), but that 'by ignorance of the cause the report is disbelieved' (τῷ δ' αἰτίας ἀπορεῖν ἀπιστεῖσθαι τὴν ἱστορίαν). This is not right, according to Florus, because there are a great many cases that clearly exist, but of which 'an account of the cause escapes us' (ὁ τῆς αἰτίας λόγος ἡμᾶς διαπέφευγεν). He continues that seeking 'a reasonable explanation' (τὸ εὔλογον) destroys wonder, 'for when an account of the cause escapes us we begin to be puzzled, that is to philosophise' (ὅπου γὰρ ὁ τῆς αἰτίας ἐπιλείπει λόγος, ἐκεῖθεν ἄρχεται τὸ ἀπορεῖν, τουτέστι τὸ φιλοσοφεῖν). So, in a way, people destroy philosophy when they disbelieve wonderful phenomena. In fact, so Florus says, it is necessary to seek 'the cause for which something happens by means of reason, but to accept the fact that it happens from history' (τὸ μὲν διὰ τί γίνεται τῷ λόγῳ μετιέναι, τὸ δ' ὅτι γίνεται παρὰ τῆς ἱστορίας λαμβάνειν). This is meant not so much as an incentive to accept the phenomenon without further ado, but to look for plausible explanations while maintaining a zetetic and inquisitive attitude in the debate.[26] This is, indeed, reflected in what follows, as we will see.

After Florus' speech, Plutarch (as a literary character in the debate) tries his hand at an explanation. Finding his inspiration in Empedocles' theory of emanations (ἀπόρροιαι), he argues that 'it is *probable*' (εἰκός ἐστι) that a stream of emanations comes especially from the eyes. The rest of the explanation is synthesised by Psellus as follows (I have underlined which parts are copied verbatim from Plutarch's text):

> Εἰ ἀληθὲς τὸ καταβασκαίνεσθαι τινὰς ὑπὸ τῶν ὁρώντων.
>   Οὐ ψεῦδός ἐστι τὸ καταβασκαίνεσθαι τινὰς καὶ μαραίνεσθαι
> ὑπὸ τῆς τῶν ὁρώντων ὄψεως. <u>πολυκίνητος γὰρ ἡ ὄψις οὖσα μετὰ</u>

---

[25] For more detail about Plutarch's science of natural problems, see Meeusen 2014 and 2016.

[26] Cf. Opsomer 1998, p. 80; Meeusen 2014, p. 325.

πνεύματος αὐγὴν ἀφιέντος πυρώδη θαυμαστήν τινα διασπείρει
δύναμιν, ὥστε πολλὰ καὶ πάσχειν καὶ ποιεῖν δι᾽ αὐτῆς τὸν
ἄνθρωπον. καὶ τῶν ἐρωτικῶν, ἃ δὴ μέγιστα καὶ σφοδρότατα
παθήματα τῆς ψυχῆς ἐστίν, ἀρχὴν ἡ ὄψις ἐνδίδωσιν, ὥστε ῥεῖν καὶ
λείβεσθαι τὸν ἐρωτικόν, ὅταν ἐμβλέπῃ τοῖς ἀγαθοῖς καὶ καλοῖς. τὸ
γὰρ διὰ τῶν ὀμμάτων ἐκπῖπτον εἴτε φῶς εἴτε ῥεῦμα τοὺς ἐρῶντας
ἐντήκει καὶ ἀπόλλυσι, τοιαύτη γίνεται διάδοσις καὶ ἀνάφλεξις
ὑπὸ τῆς ὄψεως. αἱ γὰρ τῶν καλῶν ὄψεις, κἂν πάνυ πόρρωθεν
ἀντιβλέπωσι, πῦρ ἐν ταῖς τῶν ἐρωτικῶν ψυχαῖς ἀνάπτουσι· καὶ τὸ
σῶμα δὲ τῶν ἐρωμένων καὶ ὁρωμένων βλάπτεται ἐν ταῖς τοιαύταις
ἀποφοραῖς.

If it is true that some are bewitched by the evil eye people cast
at them.

It is not a lie that some are bewitched by the evil eye and
waste away by the sight of those staring at them. For, together
with the breath that releases a fiery brilliance, sight, being
full of movement, disperses a wonderful force, so that man
both experiences and effects many things by it. And sight
gives the impulse to matters of love, which are the biggest
and most violent passions of the soul, so that someone who
is in love melts and is dissolved when he puts an eye on good
and beautiful persons. For what departs from the eyes, be it
light or a stream (of particles), melts lovers and destroys them
– such an excretion and inflammation is generated by sight.
For the glances of beautiful people kindle a fire in the soul
of those who are in love, even if they look straight at them
from far away. And the body of those who are loved and seen
is damaged in such effluxes.

Notably, Psellus more often quotes the argument given by Plutarch's literary *alter ego* in the sympotic debates of *Quaestiones
convivales* rather than that of his peers (cf. also §§ 118, 119,
190, 191). In doing so, he condenses the argument drastically and
does not cite Plutarch's name and authority. Of course, concerns
about plagiarism were different in Byzantine times, but one can
very well imagine that Psellus, rather than having the intention
to pocket the explanation as his own, had to be careful not to
show too much open affiliation with pagan philosophy.[27] Simi-

---

[27] However, there are several occasions in Psellus' writings where Plutarch
is quoted by name, albeit in different contexts: *Or.* 7.140 (concerning Plutarch's

larly, in § 180 (concerning the divine character of salt), Psellus copies from *QC* 5.10, 684F (and also from *QN* 3, 912DF), but he only repeats the quote from the ποιητής (Homer, *Il.* 9.214), thus omitting the additional Platonic parallel Plutarch reports in his text (*Tim.* 60e).

A peculiar case to illustrate this is found in another chapter, viz. § 190: 'Why do pebbles and pieces of lead make water cooler when thrown in it?'. Psellus says that this is a very difficult question and that Aristotle left it unsolved in his *Problemata* (*physica*). The same point is made by Plutarch (via his literary *alter ego*) in *QC* 6.5, where the problem is also considered δυσθεώρητος (= fr. 213 Rose). While, apparently, Psellus sees nothing wrong in mentioning Aristotle's authority explicitly, he copies and abridges Plutarch's tentative explanation without tagging his name (in fact, only the tentativeness of Plutarch's explanation disappears in Psellus, the main argument still being that these objects by their density do not let cold air through but reflect it back into the water). What seems to matter more for Psellus is the link with *Aristotle's* causal model of natural scientific research, as displayed in the *Problemata* (*physica*), rather than Plutarch's later contribution to it. The same idea applies to § 170, concerning the problem: 'How does it come that brine bursts forth from the sea when a thunderbolt falls in it?' (= *QN* 40: see n. 23). Psellus there explains that lightning evaporates the drinkable constituent in seawater and solidifies the salty one. At the end, he notes that 'both Aristotle the philosopher and the best physicians approve of this explanation' (fr. 218 Rose: ταύτην τὴν αἰτίαν καὶ Ἀριστοτέλης ὁ φιλόσοφος ἀποδέχεται καὶ οἱ κρείττους τῶν φυσικῶν), thus again emphasising

characterisation of Cato Minor), *Theol.* 49.214 (Plutarch considers atheism more sacrilegious than superstition), *Op.* 63.3 and 66.24 (concerning Plutarch's psychology). Cf. also Ps.-Psell. *Poem.* 68.30 (the author ridicules a haughty monk who thinks himself superior to Plato, Diogenes, Plutarch, Isocrates and other ancient Greek authors). Notably, Plutarch's attitude towards religion so impressed Johannes Mauropus, one of Psellus' teachers, that he mentioned Plato and Plutarch as the two pagans who may be saved from the wrath of Christ, because they were closest to Christian law in doctrine and character. Moreover, an impoverished Johannes Tzetzes chose to keep a copy of Plutarch's works as his only piece of literature. For both, see Pade 2007, I, p. 56–57.

the intellectual link with Aristotle's causal model of scientific inquiry.[28]

To come back to the problem of the evil eye now, Psellus' argument diverges from Plutarch's at one salient point. In order to express the object of love/desire, Plutarch uses καλοῖς, which primarily indicates the *physical* appearance of beautiful *males*. Even if, syntactically speaking, καλοῖς may be neuter (Plutarch thus referring to *both* males and females in a genderless fashion), the context may well be homo-erotic (cf. the parallel discussion about love in Plato's *Symposium*).[29] Whatever may be the case, Plutarch puts main emphasis on the *physical* appearance of the persons that are loved (there is nothing in his natural scientific argument that suggests otherwise). Psellus may have found this problematic, if not offensive. Notably, he tidies up Plutarch's text by means of a simple adaptation. Instead of changing καλοῖς in καλαῖς (which would perhaps have made it sound more 'natural' to Psellus – i.e. heterosexual), he adds ἀγαθοῖς before it (ὅταν ἐμβλέπῃ τοῖς ἀγαθοῖς καὶ καλοῖς), thus lifting the discourse on an *ethical* echelon, which is more suitable for a Christian audience.[30] As such, love is not just engendered by a person's physical appearance, according to Psellus, but also (and more importantly) by his moral beauty. This, however, is of no relevance to Plutarch's natural scientific argument and may even distract from the main point, which is physical, not moralistic.[31]

---

[28] Plutarch often identifies the Stagirite as a φιλόσοφος, perhaps to distinguish him from the historian Aristotle of Chalcis. It is, therefore, 'neither an *epitheton ornans* nor a *cognomen ex virtute*' (Roskam 2011, p. 42). Considering the uncertain origin of this chapter, it is unclear whether Psellus himself would count Plutarch among the 'better physicians'.

[29] The fact that Plato's *Symposium* served as one of Plutarch's models for the composition of *Quaestiones convivales* is clearly stated in *QC* 1.*Pr.*, 612D and 6.*Pr.*, 686CD. The context may also be pederastic, cf. *QC* 6.6, 691C.

[30] Similarly, in § 193 Psellus concludes a chapter ('How does it come that meat hung from a fig tree putrefies easily?' ~ *QC* 6.10) with a quote from Scripture: 'the fig tree produces its fruit' (Cant. 2. 13: ἡ συκῆ ἐξήνεγκεν ὀλύνθους αὐτῆς). In what follows, Psellus interprets this verse in light of psychic catharsis, where he holds that the soul discharges the useless part out of its system, just as a fig tree does by storing useless moisture in its fruits, thus leaving the plant itself sweet.

[31] On the general absence of moral philosophy in Plutarch's natural problems, see Meeusen 2013.

Apart from this peculiar case, the verbatim correspondences with Plutarch's text are, indeed, remarkable.[32] What is perhaps even more remarkable, though, is the persuasion and conviction with which Psellus reformulates it. Without further detail Psellus writes that bewitchment by the evil eye really exists: he first asks if it is true (εἰ ἀληθές) but immediately replies that it is not a lie (ψεῦδος), period. Of course, Florus goes in the same direction, but his point seems to be more methodological: his intention is not only to support the value of traditional ἱστορία in philosophical debate, but also to advocate an inquisitive and zetetic stance in the search for an explanation, as we saw. Indeed, in Plutarch's text the element of plausibility and probability plays a very prominent role, as is marked: 1) by the recurrence of the concept of εἰκός throughout the argumentation, 2) by a number of follow-up questions and objections raised by Plutarch's fellow symposiasts, and 3) by the eventual suspension of the discussion to the other day (i.e. when Plutarch has had a night of rest to recover from his wine-induced splurge of εὑρησιλογία: *QC* 5.7, 682BC). One is inclined to see in this a sign of Plutarch's ἀπορία and persistent inquisitiveness in natural scientific matters, which can be interpreted in light of his Academic ἐποχή and, more broadly, his Platonic view of the world (as inspired by the εἰκὼς μῦθος of the *Timaeus*).

None of this can be traced in Psellus' version, though. To put things sharply, it is exactly by stating the argument so directly and unequivocally that Psellus, in a way, destroys philosophy, since he leaves no room for further discussion and doubt. Clearly, Psellus had different intentions than Plutarch. Whereas Plutarch's *Quaestiones convivales* provide a lively (though, presumably, idealised) picture of the socio-intellectual dimension of philosophical debate in Plutarch's intellectual milieu – showing how problems could be raised in a friendly, sociable setting, and how arguments could be tentatively put forward, evaluated and criticised –

---

[32] Sometimes Psellus uses technical terminology in rephrasing Plutarch's text, but this does not change the meaning. This is the case, e.g., in § 192.9, where Psellus writes ἀντιπεριιστάμενον (said of heat being contracted in the body by surrounding cold), whereas Plutarch simply has συστελλομένην καὶ πλεονάζουσαν (*QC* 6.8, 694E). See Opsomer 1999.

the dialogical aspect of the questions and answers in Psellus' *De omnifaria doctrina* is reduced to a rather lifeless and one-dimensional monologue between a teacher and his student.[33] Obviously, the bite-size format of Psellus' *capita* (which mostly contain approximately 10–15 lines per chapter) promotes memorisation by the implied reader, who is invited to absorb this knowledge rather than to question it. This feature is, so it seems, inherent to Psellus' educational programme: by use of the question and answer format Psellus aims to provide clear-cut information tailored to the needs and authorial preferences of the Imperial reader. As a result, there is not much room for alternative viewpoints, nor for original contributions to the debate.

4. *A Generic Conclusion*

In conclusion, it seems that Psellus' reading of Plutarch's *Quaestiones convivales* was not really the one originally intended or even implied by Plutarch (which, in a way, justifies the fact that the Chaeronean is never named as his source). Whereas Plutarch's choice for the question and answer format of προβλήματα is first and foremost methodically motivated, Psellus rather uses it as an efficient tool to transform and transfer traditional knowledge in a very concise, derivative, depersonalised and dogmatic fashion, thus reducing it to, what some scholars would consider, unpretentious *Gebrauchsliteratur* ideal for the Byzantine classroom and a model of Imperial παιδεία.[34]

But Psellus' case (and with him that of Plutarch) also tells us something about the later reception of the Aristotelian genre of natural problems, as known from the *Problemata physica* (which studies particular natural phenomena in terms of their material-instrumental causes).[35] Indeed, there is a clear discursive distinction between the Aristotelian *Problemata*, after which Plutarch's collections of *quaestiones* are modelled, and Psellus'

---

[33] Yet, the discourse is made more engaging by the use of personal pronouns and imperatives that address the reader directly. See Meeusen 2012, p. 111.

[34] See Garzya 1983, p. 56 and p. 61–62. See also Pecere & Stramaglia 1996 more generally.

[35] See Mayhew 2011, I, p. xxii–xxiii.

erotapocritical approach in *De omnifaria doctrina* (or elsewhere). By its interrogative organisation and inquisitive nature (where the explanations are famously structured as a compound question: πότερον [...]; ἤ [...]; ἤ [...];), the Aristotelian genre of problems creates a virtual dialogue where the reader is invited to participate in the debate by looking for alternative explanations or by selecting the most convincing in case more than one is offered. This can be traced back to the research context of Aristotle's school, the Lyceum, whence the *Problemata* emerged and where the genre must have fostered much discussion and dialectical debate.[36] In the figure of Plutarch we see how the Aristotelian genre of natural problems drew the attention of a Middle-Platonic philosopher, showing how it was reused and appropriated to a new epistemic system. This system involves an aporetic stance in (natural) philosophical debate, which, in turn, is centred around the concept of plausibility (τὸ πιθανόν) and probability (τὸ εἰκός). Interestingly, it is through Plutarch's lens that Psellus looks at, and approves of, Aristotle's causal approach in the *Problemata*. Yet, his approval develops into a mere transformation and canonisation of received 'Aristotelian' knowledge, and does not as such envisage a continuation or adaptation of Aristotle's scientific project (as is the case rather with Plutarch's natural problems). The time simply was not right to revolutionise either of these approaches (as people like Galileo will do much later). It is quite clear that, at this stage, some marginal comments to the science behind Genesis were more requisite. The merit of Psellus' (first redaction of) *De omnifaria doctrina*, therefore, lies in its attempt to create a genuine Christian world view (a nice chapter to illustrate this is provided by the one about earthquakes, § 164.2: τὸν σεισμὸν ποιεῖ μὲν ὁ θεός κτλ.). As to the intended reader, to whom other could Psellus address this book, than to God's regent on earth?

---

[36] On the well-established didactic role of the (Aristotelian) genre of problems, see, e.g., Jacob 2004. For the educational value of question and answer literature more generally, see Papadogiannakis 2013. A similar distinction has recently been drawn between the Byzantine and the Latin *quaestio* by Demetracopoulos 2012, p. 336: 'the traditional Byzantine *quaestio* pertained to teaching, whereas the Latin *quaestio* pertained to research'.

Bibliography

P. A. Agapitos (1998), 'Teachers, Pupils and Imperial Power in Eleventh-Century Byzantium', in Y. L. Too & N. Livingstone (eds), *Pedagogy and Power: Rhetorics of Classical Learning*, Cambridge: Cambridge University Press (Ideas in Context, 50), p. 170–191.

J. A. Demetracopoulos (2012), 'Thomas Aquinas' Impact on Late Byzantine Theology and Philosophy: The Issues of Method or "*Modus Sciendi*" and "*Dignitas Hominis*"', in A. Speer & P. Steinkrüger (eds), *Knotenpunkt Byzanz: Wissensformen und kulturelle Wechselbeziehungen*, Berlin: de Gruyter, p. 333–410.

T. Doehner (1859), 'Zu Michael Psellus und Plutarch', in *Philologus*, 14, p. 407–410.

J. Duffy (2002), 'Hellenic Philosophy in Byzantium and the Lonely Mission of Michael Psellos', in K. Ierodiakonou (ed.), *Byzantine Philosophy and its Ancient Sources*, Oxford: Oxford University Press, p. 139–156.

H.-G. Gadamer (2003), *Truth and Method*, trans. rev. by J. Weinsheimer & D. G. Marshall, New York: Continuum.

A. Garzya (1983), 'Testi letterari d'uso strumentale a Bisanzio', in A. Garzya (ed.), *Il mandarino e il quotidiano: saggi sulla letteratura tardoantica e bizantina*, Napoli: Bibliopolis, p. 35–71.

J. Gouillard (1967), *'Le synodikon de l'orthodoxie': édition et commentaire*, Paris: de Boccard (Collège de France. Centre de recherche d'histoire et civilisation de Byzance. Travaux et mémoires, 2).

A. Giannini (1965), *Paradoxographorum Graecorum Reliquiae*, Milan: Istituto Ed. Italiano (Classici greci e latini. Sezione Testi e commenti, 3).

K. Hubert (1938), 'Zur indirekten Überlieferung der "Tischgespräche" Plutarchs', in *Hermes*, 73, p. 307–328.

C. Jacob (2004), 'Questions sur les questions: archéologie d'une pratique intellectuelle et d'une forme discursive', in A. Volgers & C. Zamagni (eds), *Erotapokriseis. Early Christian Question-and-Answer Literature in Context. Proceedings of the Utrecht Colloquium, 13–14 October 2003*, Leuven: Peeters (Contributions to Biblical Exegesis and Theology, 37), p. 25–54.

F. Klotz (2007), 'Portraits of the Philosopher: Plutarch's Self-Presentation in the "Quaestiones Convivales"', in *Classical Quarterly*, 57, p. 650–667.

F. Klotz & K. Oikonomopoulou (eds, 2011), *The Philosopher's Banquet. Plutarch's 'Table Talk' in the Intellectual Culture of the Roman Empire*, Oxford: Oxford University Press.

J. König (2007), 'Fragmentation and Coherence in Plutarch's "Sympotic Questions"', in J. König & T. Whitmarsh (eds), *Ordering Knowledge in the Roman Empire*, Cambridge: Cambridge University Press, p. 43–68.

J. König (2011), 'Self-Promotion and Self-Effacement in Plutarch's "Table Talk"', in F. Klotz & K. Oikonomopoulou (eds), *The Philosopher's Banquet. Plutarch's 'Table Talk' in the Intellectual Culture of the Roman Empire*, Oxford: Oxford University Press, p. 179–203.

R. Mayhew (2011), *Aristotle, 'Problems'*, 2 vols, Cambridge, Mass. – London: Harvard University Press (The Loeb Classical Library, 317).

M. Meeusen (2012), 'Salt in the Holy Water: Plutarch's "Quaestiones Naturales" in Michael Psellus' "De omnifaria doctrina"', in L. Roig Lanzillotta & I. Muñoz Gallarte (eds), *Plutarch in the Religious and Philosophical Discourse of Late Antiquity*, Leiden: Brill (Studies in Platonism, Neoplatonism, and the Platonic Tradition, 14), p. 101–121.

M. Meeusen (2013), 'How to Treat a Bee-Sting? On the Higher Cause in Plutarch's "Causes of Natural Phenomena": the Case of Q.N. 35–36', in *Quaderni Urbinati di Cultura Classica*, 105, p. 131–157.

M. Meeusen (2014), 'Plutarch and the Wonder of Nature. Preliminaries to Plutarch's Science of Physical Problems', in *Apeiron: a Journal for Ancient Philosophy and Science*, 47, p. 310–341.

M. Meeusen (2016), *Plutarch's Science of Natural Problems. A Study with Commentary on 'Quaestiones Naturales'*, Leuven: Leuven University Press (Plutarchea Hypomnemata).

T. Morgan (2011), 'The Miscellany and Plutarch', in F. Klotz & K. Oikonomopoulou (eds), *The Philosopher's Banquet. Plutarch's 'Table Talk' in the Intellectual Culture of the Roman Empire*, Oxford: Oxford University Press, p. 49–73.

A. Mussini (1990), *Michele Psello, 'Varia Dottrina'*, Firenze: Nardini (Biblioteca medievale).

J. Opsomer (1998), *In Search of the Truth. Academic Tendencies in Middle Platonism*, Brussel: Koninklijke Academie voor Wetenschappen, Letteren en Schone Kunsten van België (Verhandelingen van de KAWLSK, Klasse der Letteren, 163).

J. Opsomer (1999), 'Antiperistasis: A Platonic Theory', in A. Pérez Jiménez, J. Garciá López & R. M. Aguilar (eds), *Plutarco, Platón y Aristóteles. Actas del V Congreso Internacional de la I.P.S. (Madrid – Cuenca, 4–7 de Mayo de 1999)*, Madrid: Ed. Clásicas, p. 417–429.

M. Pade (2007), *The Reception of Plutarch's* Lives *in Fifteenth-century Italy*, 2 vols, Copenhagen: Museum Tusculanum Press (Renaessancestudier, 14).

Y. Papadogiannakis (2013), 'Erotapokriseis', in R. S. Bagnall, K. Brodersen, C. B. Champion, A. Erskine & S. R. Huebner (eds), *The Encyclopedia of Ancient History*, Chichester: Wiley-Blackwell, p. 2491–2493.

O. Pecere & A. Stramaglia (1996), La Letteratura di Consumo nel Mondo Greco-Latino, *Atti del Convegno internazionale, Cassino, 14–17 settembre 1994*, Cassino: Università degli studi di Cassino.

G. Roskam (2011), 'Aristotle in Middle Platonism. The Case of Plutarch of Chaeronea', in T. Bénatouïl, E. Maffi & F. Trabattoni (eds), *Plato, Aristotle, or Both? Dialogues between Platonism and Aristotelianism in Antiquity*, Hildesheim – Zürich – New York: Georg Olms, p. 35–61.

P. Van Deun & C. Macé, (eds, 2011), *Encyclopaedic Trends in Byzantium?*, Leuven: Peeters (Orientalia Lovaniensia Analecta).

M. Vamvouri Ruffy (2012), *Les Vertus thérapeutiques du banquet. Médecine et idéologie dans les 'Propos de Table' de Plutarque*, Paris: Les Belles Lettres (Collection d'études anciennes, Série grecque, 146).

L. G. Westerink (1948), *Michael Psellus, 'De Omnifaria Doctrina'*, Nijmegem: Centrale Drukkerij.

N. G. Wilson (1983), *Scholars of Byzantium*, London: Duckworth.

C. Zervos (1973), *Un philosophe néoplatonicien du XIe siècle. Michel Psellos: sa vie, son œuvre, ses luttes philosophiques, son influence*, New York: Franklin (Burt Franklin research and source works series. Byzantine series, 41).

Abstract

This contribution deals with the reception of Plutarch's *Quaestiones convivales* in the Byzantine era, more precisely by examining how Michael Psellus incorporates a number of its chapters in his encyclopaedic *De omnifaria doctrina*. Questions that will be addressed include which kind of topics are of interest to the Byzantine Chief of Philosophers, how he incorporates them in his work, what is their place in the overarching encyclopaedic organization, and how they are meant to contribute to the general education of the implied reader (the Byzantine emperor). The argument comes in the form of a case-study of the problem of the evil eye (*QC* 5.7 = § 109 Westerink).

REINHART CEULEMANS

COSMOLOGICAL QUESTIONS ANSWERED WITH SEVERIAN OF GABALA IN MS *ATHONENSIS, LAVRAS* B 43 (EUSTRATIADIS 163)

1. *The Florilegium of the Lavra Manuscript*

In the library of the Great Lavra monastery on Mount Athos one can find a manuscript (shelf mark B 43) which contains, among other works, an anthology that has received only limited attention. The overall contents of the codex can be described as miscellaneous.[1] This shows clearly from the catalogue description, which labels the contents as 'διάφορα' and distinguishes within the codex almost fifty different units of diverging nature.[2] Comparison with the actual manuscript[3] reveals that the specific division into those units was introduced by the cataloguers rather randomly: it does not reflect the structure of the document itself, in which decorated lines are used to distinguish sections. Those markers inform us that a section ends in the middle of fol. 153[r] (this is item 31 in the catalogue survey) and that another one starts on fol. 197[r] (item 44 in the description). In between those folia, no dividing line can be found, which implies that the section on fol. 153[r 4]–196[v] forms one single unit (which corresponds to items 32–43 in the catalogue description). This section itself is miscellaneous in terms of content: it is not a continuous text but a com-

---

[1] On this kind of manuscripts, see Ronconi 2007.

[2] Spyridon Lauriotis & Eustratiadis 1925, p. 17–18 (No. 163). The description contains numerous errors.

[3] Accessed through a microfilmed reproduction (which unfortunately lacks photos of fol. 156[v]–157[r]).

[4] See the following note.

Questioning the World, Greek Patristic and Byzantine Question-and-Answer Literature, ed. by Bram Demulder and Peter Van Deun, Turnhout, 2021 (*LECTIO*, 11), pp. 379–422   ©BREPOLS♛PUBLISHERS   DOI 10.1484/M.LECTIO-EB.5.121512

pilation of many smaller units (which explains the misleading description by the cataloguers). The conclusion that imposes itself is that fol. 153ʳ–196ᵛ of MS *Athonensis, Lavras* B 43 (Eustratiadis 163) offer a single anthology.[5]

1.1. General Contents and Structure

Although this florilegium lacks a title, some observations support the idea that within the manuscript it forms a closed and independent unit. Unlike the texts that precede and follow it, the anthology consists of numbered chapters:[6] those numbers

---

[5] At a first glance, one could hypothesize that the florilegium opens on fol. 157ʳ (or on fol. 156ᵛ), which is missing in the microfilm reproduction (compare n. 3). The absence of a title and chapter numbers α΄–β΄ would then be easily explainable by the suggestion that they could be found on the missing page(s) – the first chapter number one runs into is γ΄ on fol. 157ᵛ. However, the content suggests that the anthology already opens before the missing pages, i.e.: on fol. 153ʳ, where it starts with a treatment of heaven (the first chapter is Περὶ οὐρανοῦ) before moving on to a discussion of thunder, lightning, the clouds, etc. (from fol. 157ᵛ onwards). Such an assumption would indeed agree with the overall design of the compilation (compare below). For what it is worth (compare the critical remarks above), one could point out that in the catalogue description, fol. 153ʳ–160ʳ are indeed described as one item, and that no rupture on fol. 156ᵛ or 157ʳ is mentioned. In this regard it can also be observed that with fol. 153 a new quire starts (compare Fernández 2018, p. lxvii–lxviii n. 196). The absence of a title and of chapter numbers α΄–β΄ needs to be explained in another way – see below for a suggestion. (The discussion regarding the starting point of the anthology is pertinent to the topic of this article, since the first excerpt that is edited below can be found on fol. 154ᵛ–155ʳ).

[6] In the microfilm reproduction, several chapters lack a number. To some extent, this could result from the at times poor state of the reproduction, but it would also appear that at least in some cases, no chapter number was ever written. This is particularly annoying in the opening and closing part of the anthology. The last number that can be found is ϟθ΄ on fol. 193ᵛ, for a chapter that contains four excerpts on the ψυχή (a topic that is treated in several chapters throughout the anthology). On fol. 195ʳ a new chapter title is given: Περὶ ψυχῆς ἑρμην<εία> ἐκ τῶν κανόνων, which is followed by a large amount of text that extends to the end of the florilegium. This would seem to be chapter ρ΄, but no number can be found. A similar problem haunts the opening part of the anthology. The first chapter number that can be read on the microfilm is γ΄, which accompanies the chapter Περὶ βροντῶν on fol. 157ᵛ (compare the previous note). Either the numbers of the first two chapters are only invisible on the microfilm (and not in the codex itself), or the scribe only started to number his chapters from the third one onwards. In defense of the second – at first sight implausible – suggestion one might point out that the division of the anthology is in general rather peculiar and that it was probably carried out ad hoc (compare below).

appear[7] to add up to a total of one hundred chapters, a number that is not coincidental and symbolizes perfect completeness.[8]

The contents of the anthology, too, would seem to reflect a composition that is not coincidental but intentional: a quick survey of the chapter titles gives the impression that the structure of at least the first part of the florilegium is deliberate. Opening with chapters on natural phenomena and their creation (heaven, <rain>,[9] thunder, lightning, clouds, snow, the sun and the moon), the collection continues with sections on the creation of man (and on his soul and heart) before moving on to more celestial (angels, eternity), divine (the properties of divine nature, god) and Trinitarian topics (fatherhood, sonship, the ghost), while adding the treatment of subjects that in the course of Greek Christianity have proven controversial (φύσις, ὑπόστασις, θέλημα and ἐνέργεια; chapters περὶ ἑνώσεως and περὶ ὁμοουσίου only follow in later sections). What then follows are some definitions of human properties (talkativeness, speech, sensation). After those, the compiler turned his attention to what happens at the end of a man's life, in the form of chapters on the perishable, the soul and its leaving the body, the underworld and related themes, God's judgments, and the limitedness of human life. A deliberate structure presents itself down to this point, i.e.: from the creation

One could moreover surmise (but nothing more!) that only the number of the very first chapter is really missing, and that that of the second can be found on the pages that are lacking in the microfilm reproduction (fol. 156ᵛ–157ʳ) – see also n. 9.

[7] See the previous note.

[8] See Meyer & Suntrup 1987. Many literary collections consist of 100 units: cf. Hausherr 1953 and Géhin 2013, p. 4–6, 12 and 15.

[9] Spyridon Lauriotis & Eustratiadis 1925, p. 18 describe the section of fol. 153ʳ–160ʳ as 'Περὶ οὐρανοῦ, περὶ βροχῆς, περὶ χιόνος, περὶ ἀστραπῶν, βροντῶν κλπ.' All of these chapters are retrievable in the codex, except for that on rain (βροχή). One could speculate that this is chapter β΄, that it opens on fol. 156ᵛ or fol. 157ʳ (both pages are missing in the microfilm reproduction, see n. 3), and that it ends with an excerpt from the epitome of Menippus's *Periplus of the Inner Sea* composed by Marcian of Heraclea (sixth century: on this text and the Byzantine collections in which it is transmitted, see Diller 1952, p. 3–14 and 19–22 and Marcotte 2000, p. xix–xxi and lxxvii–cix; these references and helpful comments were kindly offered by Gertjan Verhasselt). The first lines of fol. 157ᵛ present the end of the excerpt from Marcian (I, 6 = Müller 1855, p. 520.5–10); they are followed by the beginning of chapter γ΄ Περὶ βροντῶν. So the fragment from Marcian could have been the last one of a chapter β΄ on rain.

of the world down to death, with in between topics important to Christianity. It is only in the last part that the anthology gives a more chaotic impression, with subsequent chapters on topics such as (in this order) the antichrist, the apocalypse, angels, the divine mysteries, baptism, eternal life, good promises, tears, age differences, leprosy and – again – the soul.[10]

The anthology lacks an overall title: it opens immediately with the title of the first chapter and the attribution of the first excerpt in that chapter: Περὶ οὐρανοῦ. Κυρίλλου Ἱεροσολύμων (fol. 153ʳ).[11] Not all of the chapters have a title. Those that do as a rule have one that follows the template περί + genitive case, but some chapters introduce the excerpts in the form of questions and answers.[12] Some but far from all of the excerpts are accompanied by an attribution to their respective author. The occasional pagan writer excepted (Porphyry, Marcian of Heraclea), the authors tend to be Christian (even orthodox: Cyril of Alexandria, John Chrysostom, Maximus the Confessor, John of Damascus, etc.). The oldest writer whose name is cited is Irenaeus of Lyons († *c.* 200).

What the compiler of the florilegium did not mention, is that he took several excerpts not directly from the original texts themselves. For many of the definitions he offered, he must have relied on a collection similar to the ones preserved in the *Guide* of Anastasius of Sinai (*CPG* 7745) and the *Book on Definitions* of a Ps.-Athanasius (*CPG* 2254).[13] We further know that in other sections the compiler relied on the so-called *Coislin Anthology*, a spiritual florilegium from the late ninth or early tenth century which is arranged alphabetically.[14] In fact, editors have made

---

[10] An attempt to explain the seemingly more chaotic structure of this last part of the anthology is made below.

[11] The excerpt is taken from Cyril's sixth catechetical lecture (*CPG* 3585), ed. Reischl 1848, p. 158.6–10 (§ 3).

[12] To encounter this format in an anthology is of course not very exceptional.

[13] On the definitions in the *Guide* and their reception, see Uthemann 2015, I, p. 188–197 and 1981, p. ccxxi–ccxliii. General information on this kind of literature can be retrieved from Furrer-Pilliod 2000. Another example of how such definitions are combined with other excerpts into a single collection is published by Antonopoulou 2015.

[14] So far, the *stoicheia* A–Θ, N–Ξ, P, Υ and Ψ of this florilegium have been edited; an edition of letter Λ is in preparation. References to relevant secondary literature can be retrieved from the most recent edition: Maksimczuk, Van Deun

use of the evidence of the Lavra anthology in their critical reconstruction of the text of the *Florilegium Coislinianum*, assessing it as a valuable if partial witness.[15] The compiler of the Lavra anthology combined excerpts taken from the *Florilegium Coislinianum* with many other ones.[16] It must not be ruled out that some of those other excerpts were taken from compilations other than the ones mentioned here (compare also n. 40). This might in fact explain the variety in terms of presentation[17] (chapters introduced with περί + genitive vs others in Q-and-A form) and the seeming overlap within the florilegium of the Lavra codex (no less than four chapters dispersed over the anthology are entitled Περὶ ψυχῆς: <ι΄>, λε΄, Ͱ ζ΄, <ρ΄>).[18]

What is furthermore noticeable in this regard, is the fact that the presence of the *Coislin Anthology* increases towards the end of the Lavra florilegium: more than half of the text that was taken from the *Florilegium Coislinianum* (15 out of 27 excerpts)[19]

& Venetskov 2019. Dependence of the compilation in the Lavra manuscript on the *Florilegium Coislinianum* was already mentioned by Richard 1962, col. 486.

[15] The evidence of the Lavra manuscript was used (as witness *R*) in the editions of letters Α, Δ, Ζ, Η, Θ, Ρ and Ψ: Fernández 2018; Maksimczuk 2018b (this edition is in press as volume 91 in the Series Graeca of the Corpus Christianorum); Ceulemans, De Vos, Gielen & Van Deun 2011; Ceulemans, Van Deun & Van Pee 2016; Ceulemans, Gazzini, Maksimczuk & Van Deun 2017; and Ceulemans, De Ridder, Levrie & Van Deun 2013. The following editors of isolated fragments of the *Florilegium Coislinianum* also relied on codex *R*: Fernández 2011, p. 638–639 (excerpt from letter Δ); Van Deun 2015, p. 422–423 (excerpt from letter Κ); Van Deun 2017 (excerpt from letter Λ).

[16] There are many manuscripts of this kind (i.e.: codices in which excerpts from the *Florilegium Coislinianum* are combined with material independent from it), as the reader of any of the works mentioned in n. 14–15 (Maksimczuk 2018b and Fernández 2018, in particular) will notice. They witness to the still largely unexplored indirect tradition of the florilegium (on which, see Maksimczuk 2017 and 2018a and Fernández & Maksimczuk 2019, p. 71–75). Publications that, just like the present one, offer the edition of excerpts that accompany the *Florilegium Coislinianum* in this tradition are: Ceulemans, Van Deun & Wildenboer 2014, p. 62–67 and Fernández 2019.

[17] Perhaps this suggestion could also explain the seemingly chaotic use of terminology such as ἑρμηνεία, σχόλιον etc. that accompanies some of the excerpts in the Lavra anthology.

[18] The principle of including various excerpts on the soul reminds us of Michael Psellus's *De omnifaria doctrina*, which contains several chapters Περὶ ψυχῆς (as was kindly pointed out to me by Peter Van Deun).

[19] These numbers can be subject to change as research on both anthologies continues.

can be found in the last forty chapters of the Lavra anthology. Starting from chapter ξα΄, the first chapter on the antichrist, the mark of the *Florilegium Coislinianum* becomes stronger. This could explain the above observation on the contents of the Lavra anthology, namely that the structure that follows a certain plan in the first part of the florilegium is not retrievable from the chapters on the antichrist onwards. The section of the anthology that follows from that point is to a certain extent indebted to the structure of the *Florilegium Coislinianum*, which has a different (i.e.: alphabetical) arrangement. The selection of excerpts from the *Coislin Anthology* that can be found in the Lavra chapters 61–100 as a rule follow the former's alphabetical set-up, with excerpts taken from (in this order) *stoicheia* A, B, Z, Δ (*sic*), H, Λ, P and Ψ.[20] One has the impression that with chapter ξα΄, the compiler of the Lavra anthology returned to the first page of the *Florilegium Coislinianum* and started to consult it for a second time, while borrowing proportionally more material from it and letting himself be guided by its alphabetical set-up.

A general survey of the Lavra anthology can conclude with the observation that several of the one hundred chapters consist of two or more excerpts, while others contain only one. The latter group outweighs the other, especially in the second half of the anthology. In other words: starting with chapters that all tend to contain several excerpts, the compilation gradually proceeds towards chapters that only consist of one excerpt and are much shorter.[21] Along the same line, the division into chapters is not always the one that one would expect. Sometimes a new chapter starts where one feels that the topic does not change, and the other way around. Together with the fact that some chapter numbers appear to be missing (compare n. 6), this results in a rather sloppy outlook. Such an impression is reinforced by the fact that some attributions are given in the margins, and others in the main text, and that some but not all excerpts

---

[20] Down to chapter 61, excerpts from the following letters of the *Florilegium Coislinianum* can be found (in this order): A, K, O, Θ and B.

[21] The first half of the anthology is almost twice as long as the second: fol. 153ʳ–179ᵛ (chapters <α΄>–μθ΄) vs 180ʳ–196ʳ (chapters ν΄–<ρ΄>).

are seemingly randomly accompanied by terms such as 'scholion' or 'explanation'.[22]

1.2. Dating

With no other witnesses being known, the florilegium that is presented in the above paragraphs is inextricably bound to the Lavra manuscript. It would in fact appear that the person who copied the codex was also the one who compiled the anthology for the occasion. Some of the arguments that suggest that we are dealing with an ad hoc compilation have been outlined above: the overall sloppiness in terms of the division into chapters and numbering (there is no consistently applied principle regarding the link between division, attribution and topic); the random position of attributions (in the title, in the running text, in the margin); the imbalance of the compilation and the growing dominance of the *Florilegium Coislinianum* as a source. The reader has the impression of being confronted with a project that was conceived to be more sizeable and ambitious but whose compiler adjusted the scope in the course of executing it. Until proven otherwise, the florilegium can be approached as being compiled at the moment the Lavra manuscript was made.

Such a hypothesis is certainly not contradicted by an analysis of the *terminus post quem*, which is set by the most recent source to have been excerpted by the compiler and turns out to be quite close to the presumed dating of the Lavra codex (on which, see the end of this section). Dependence on the *Florilegium Coislinianum* already shows that the anthology postdates the late ninth or early tenth century.[23] Two other excerpts in the Lavra compilation push the *terminus post quem* even further.

Chapter κζ′ (Περὶ λόγου) contains as the second of two excerpts a fragment introduced with a vague 'ἄλλως'. This excerpt (fol. 170ʳ⁻ᵛ: Διττοῦ δὲ ὄντος τοῦ λόγου ... ἤτοι προφορικός ἐστιν, ἢ ἐνδιάθετος, ἀλλὰ μὴν οὔτε τοῦτο οὔτε ἐκεῖνο ἐστίν[24]) is taken

---

[22] Compare n. 17 and below. It appears that little importance is to be attached to this disparate terminology, as can be deduced from section 2.2 of this article.

[23] On the date of the *Florilegium Coislinianum*, see Fernández 2018, p. xxi and literature cited there.

[24] Accentuation follows the manuscript: compare Noret 2014, p. 131.

from Theophylact of Ohrid's exegesis of John 1.2, as articulated in his *Commentary on John* (*PG* 123, col. 1141.4–22).[25] This author is today believed to have died after 1126.[26] The precise date of redaction of his *Commentary on John* is unknown. Together with his commentaries on the synoptic gospels, Theophylact may have written it at the request of Maria of Alania, empress wife to successively Michael VII Doukas and Nicephorus III Botaneiates. But as she and Theophylact appear to have been in touch for several years, her patronage does not really allow to refine the dating of the text.[27] Today scholars tend to conclude (if hesitantly) that Theophylact authored his commentaries on all four gospels after his nomination as archbishop in Ohrid, which could have taken place *c.* 1090.[28] Since at least one witness of the *Commentary on John* has been dated to as early as the eleventh/twelfth century[29] and some codices of Theophylact's commentaries on the synoptic gospels even to the eleventh century,[30] one could tentatively date his exegesis of the gospels, including that of John, to the last two decades of that century.[31]

[25] In his exegesis, Theophylact relied on earlier commentaries, but in none of those can the fragment in question be found. Compare with the observation that the citation of Porphyry's *Against the Christians* (fr. 86 Harnack) by Theophylact in the very same fragment cannot be found in any other source (at least not in the same form): see Goulet 2010, p. 145–148; Brisson 2011, p. 277–290; Becker 2016, p. 377–380 (fr. 68F).

[26] Confirmation of S.G. Mercati's findings by Gautier 1963, p. 169–170.

[27] See Beck 1959, p. 650 (with literature); Gautier 1980, p. 58–67 and 1986, p. 81–84 (with some critical observations by Mullett 1984, p. 204–210). For a similar problem of dating ran into by editors of another commentary by Theophylact, see Aussedat & Cassin 2010, p. 78 n. 80.

[28] Cf. Saunders 1957 and Lemerle 1977, p. 96 n. 73. An attempt to date the commentaries to an earlier period was criticized by Gautier 1980, p. 66 n. 78.

[29] Cf. Kouroupou & Géhin 2008, I, p. 112–113 (manuscript 23). Another witness was dated to the eleventh century by Lambros 1895–1900, II, p. 4 (entry 4137), but a more critical description overruled this attempt and proposed a twelfth-century dating: Sotiroudis 1998, p. 29–30 (manuscript 18).

[30] See Mioni 1967 (manuscript I, 57). Cf. also Devreesse 1950, p. 64–65 (codex 642 dated to the eleventh/twelfth century). The dating of MS *Athonensis, Vatopedinus* 248 to the tenth (*sic!*) century by Eustratiadis & Arcadius Vatopedinus 1924, p. 54 has not survived the scrutiny of New Testament textual critics: see e.g. Aland et al. 1994, p. 131 (where codex 1437 is dated to the twelfth century; 30/10/19 I found the same dating on https://ntvmr.uni-muenster.de/liste).

[31] Jacob 2006, p. 22–55 showed on the basis of manuscript evidence and citations that Theophylact's exegesis of the four gospels had certainly already

A second excerpt that is of much weight in this discussion is the one that builds the entire chapter οζ´ in the anthology in the Lavra codex. This chapter does not have any title indicating a topic but only an attribution identifying its author: Γρηγορίου Κορινθ<ίου> (fol. 186ᵛ). This attribution is correct: the excerpt (Ὦ Θεοῦ Λόγε Χριστέ ... τὴν πρώτην μεταποιηθῆναι γέννησιν, fol. 186ᵛ–187ʳ) is taken from the *Commentary on the Iambic Pentecostal Canon* written by Gregory Pardos of Corinth.[32] This author's persona and the precise extent of his oeuvre (a substantial part of which is devoted to grammatical topics) were for a long time shrouded in mysteries, but now scholars tend to be quite sure that he lived between *c.* 1070 and 1156, with his episcopacy having started in 1092 at the earliest.[33] His exegetical oeuvre on the liturgical canons (to which the text under discussion belongs) is believed to be a youthful work, composed before 1124/5.[34] A precise *terminus post quem* is not known, but common sense invites the assumption that it would not predate the late 1080s or early 1090s.[35]

made its way to Southern Italy in the second quarter of the twelfth century at the latest.

[32] Ed. Montana 1995, p. 32.9–34.5 (= IX, 3–4). A thorough presentation of this work is that by Cesaretti & Ronchey 2014, p. 57*–63*, where further literature is offered.

[33] Thus Kominis 1960a, p. 23–36, who together with D. Donnet in the 1960s brought research on Gregory to where it is today (see the references offered in the editions mentioned in the previous note). Their conclusions (which are the ones followed here) have been accepted into standard overviews (such as Browning 1963, p. 19–20; Hunger 1978, I, p. 84–85 and II, p. 15; Dickey 2007, p. 82–83) and in recent literature (such as Hörandner 2012, p. 87 and Bianchi 2011, p. 83). Occasionally, one still comes across attempts to date the author earlier (to the tenth century: so Becares 1988) or later (to the thirteenth century: so Robins 1993, p. 163), but they are unsuccessful.

[34] The main argument for this dating is the fact that some of Gregory's commentaries are transmitted in a manuscript from the year 1124/5 (see Kominis 1960b). The specific commentary that is cited in the Lavra florilegium is not included in this manuscript (see Montana 1995, p. xii–xiii), but there is no reason to assume that it would not have been written at the same moment. In any case, it was cited by Theodore Prodromus in a work probably written before 1157 (see Cesaretti & Ronchey 2014, p. 64*–65*), and it is transmitted in manuscripts from the twelfth century (see Montana 1995, p. xiv–xvi; the manuscripts that were added by Mavrommatides 1998 are all younger).

[35] Other texts of Gregory's hand contain references to contemporaries such as John Tzetzes, but his exegesis of the canons does not. (On the side, it can be added that the usefulness of those references to establish a *terminus post quem* is debated. Some scholars find references such as those to Tzetzes difficult to

In other words: the citations from Theophylact's *Commentary on John* and Gregory Pardos's *Commentary on the Iambic Pentecostal Canon* show that the Lavra florilegium cannot have been compiled before *c.* 1090. This brings us quite close to the *terminus ad quem*: the moment when MS *Lavras* B 43 was made. The catalogue description (see n. 2) dates the manuscript to the twelfth century, ignoring the thirteenth-century dating that was suggested earlier (in equally aphoristic terms).[36] The dating proposed by the cataloguers is accepted in scholarly literature,[37] but one is still awaiting critical codicological and paleographical research (carried out preferably on the basis of the actual codex instead of a reproduction), which could refine the twelfth-century dating that is today's common opinion.

On the basis of the data that are available today and relying on the observations formulated in the above paragraphs, one can assume with reasonable certainty that the creation of the florilegium coincides with the confection of the Lavra codex in the twelfth century, and that the anonymous copyist was the compiler.

2. Severian of Gabala on Cosmological Issues

2.1. Setting

In general, the Lavra manuscript has not received very much attention.[38] This does not mean that nothing of its contents has been published: some scholars edited certain sections directly from the

---

reconcile with the *terminus ante quem* of 1124/5 mentioned above, and have therefore suggested that they could be later interpolations: see e.g. Wilson 1996, p. 184–185. In fact there does not need to be a problem: the references in question do not occur in any of the texts transmitted in the manuscript from 1124/5 but only in those that can have been written after the said date.)

[36] See Papadopoulos-Kerameus 1899, p. 67. The twelfth-century dating suggested by Spyridon Lauriotis & Eustratiadis 1925 was tentatively adjusted to a dating to the eleventh century by Tiftixoglu 1974, p. 54 n. 288. Such a thesis (again, clear arguments are lacking) would appear contradicted by the *terminus post quem* defined above.

[37] See, for example, the publications mentioned in n. 14–15 and 40.

[38] Apart from its capacity as a partial witness of the *Coislin Anthology*: see n. 15.

manuscript or used it as one of many witnesses in their edition.[39] As far as the particular section of the codex is concerned that contains the florilegium that is introduced here (fol. 153^r–196^v), expressions of a similar kind of scholarly interest can be found, but they are scarce.[40] As a step towards further disclosure of the florilegium, this article publishes some excerpts from it.

In this regard, the reader's attention might be directed towards the opening sections of the florilegium, which are most pertinent

[39] A case in point is a section of the manuscript (other than the florilegium under discussion) that offers poetical excerpts taken from various sources: see the editions by Papadopoulos-Kerameus 1899, p. 68–70 (edition of the alphabetical poem that the catalogue erroneously describes to start at fol. 67^r and which in fact can be found on fol. 66^v–67^v); Anastasijević 1907, p. 491–492 (edition of another alphabetical poem, transmitted on fol. 65^v–66^v – so not starting at fol. 66^r, as states the catalogue description). Westerink 1992 adduced the evidence of the Lavra manuscript for his edition of poems 3–5 (resp. fol. 63^v–65^r; 76^v–77^v; 77^v–78^v – the information in the catalogue is not entirely correct) and 90 by Michael Psellus (the last poem is only partially preserved in the Lavra manuscript, in which some of its verses are dispersed over poems by John Geometres: fol. 68^v).

[40] Morani 1981, p. 62 pointed out, without further identification, that fol. 180^r contains an excerpt from *On Human Nature* by Nemesius of Emesa (*CPG* 3550). The fragment can in fact be found on fol. 180^{r-v} and builds the complete chapter να´ of the florilegium (entitled: Περὶ προνοίας Νεμεσίου ἐπισκόπου). It corresponds to p. 135.18–136.11 of the edition by Morani 1987 (who understandably did not use the evidence of the florilegium). Note that the exact same excerpt is included in the compilation that is attached to question XVIII of the Ps.-Anastasian collection of 88 ἐρωταποκρίσεις, and which from thereon was included in the so-called 'collection a', edited in *PG* 89 (here col. 505.44–508.13). Information on those modified redactions of the *Questions and Answers* of Anastasius of Sinai (*CPG* 7746) can be retrieved from the introduction to the edition by Richard† & Munitiz 2006 (esp. p. xxi–xxii; on the collection of 88 questions, see also De Groote 2015, p. 64–66). At this point it can be mentioned that Richard† & Munitiz 2006, p. xxv identified the Lavra manuscript – without naming any folio numbers – as a witness to all or some of four particular Ps.-Anastasian questions. I was not able to retrieve any of those four in the florilegium, and it is not clear on whose authority the editors mentioned the Lavra manuscript: it is not cited in the publication by V. N. Beneševič or in any of the other publications listed on their p. xxiv–xxvi. The Lavra florilegium does contain excerpts from the authentic *Questions and Answers* of Anastasius (e.g. its chapters νδ´ and νϚ´–νη´ offer pieces of questions 29, 19 and 21 of Richard† & Munitiz 2006; also outside the florilegium under discussion here, the Lavra manuscript transmits material from the authentic *Questions and Answers*: see Richard 1962, col. 510). Comparison of those excerpts with the edition by Richard† & Munitiz 2006 shows that the Lavra florilegium has some agreements with the version of the 'collection a' but also differs from it regularly (to agree with other strands of the tradition) and lacks several of its distinctive readings.

to the focus of the present volume: they not only offer, as part
of a section on the elements and natural phenomena, excerpts
on cosmological and cosmogonic elements but also present some
of those in the form of questions and answers.

A text that was excerpted in search for answers to such questions, is Severian of Gabala's *Homilies on the Hexaëmeron* (*CPG*
4194).[41] In the opening chapters of the anthology, Severian
is called upon several times in order to answer questions on the
creation of night and day and on the course of the sun and the
moon. Further excerpts from his homilies are also offered in chapters that are not introduced as questions but are presented as
a treatment of particular cosmological topics ('on heaven', etc.).
Severian's role in this particular section of the florilegium catches
the eye: after having been identified as a source seven times in
the opening chapters, either explicitly by name (4×) or with
'τοῦ αὐτοῦ' (3×),[42] his name is never mentioned again once the
treatment of the creation of the world and of man is closed.
From the point where, after the last fragment edited here, a new
topic is addressed through excerpts on the soul (and its creation),
the name of Severian does not recur even a single time.

2.2. The Excerpts from Severian

This particular use to which Severian is put – exclusively as a source
that is called upon for cosmological and cosmogonic issues –
justifies his being singled out in the present contribution. Below,
the text from his *Homilies on the Hexaëmeron*, mentioned in the
previous section, is edited as it can be found in the Lavra florilegium. It consists of ten fragments.

The first fragment is offered in the very first chapter of the florilegium, which starts on fol. 153ʳ and has the title Περὶ οὐρανοῦ.[43]
The excerpt from Severian can be found more or less in the mid-

---

[41] On exegetical methodology in these homilies, see Molinié 2019.

[42] Attributions are offered either in the main text or in the margins (compare also below). The section under discussion furthermore contains anonymous
text that is taken from Severian (and which is included in the edition offered
further on).

[43] On the chapter number <α´>, which is supplemented in the edition, see
above (n. 5).

dle of the chapter, in between pieces attributed to Basil of Caesarea and John Chrysostom (fol. 154ᵛ–155ʳ). The attribution to
Severian is offered in the margin: in the main text the fragment
is only introduced as an 'explanation' (ἑρμη<νεία>). The fragment
consists of two non-consecutive excerpts, taken from the second
and third homily respectively. There is no rupture between them:
the manuscript presents them as one continuous text.

The second fragment, taken from the third homily, is presented
in the codex as the first of two excerpts that make out chapter
Ϛ΄ (fol. 158ᵛ). This is one of those chapters that give the impression that the division of the florilegium does not always reflect
a very sound judgment, or at least that the compilation leaves
room for fine-tuning in terms of presentation (compare above).
The chapter does not have a title (neither has Severian's short fragment, which opens it).⁴⁴ Positioned between chapters on clouds
(<ε΄> Περὶ νέφους) and snow (ζ΄ Περὶ χιόνος), it contains two
excerpts that both treat the subject of rain (and dew).⁴⁵ Either the
title of the chapter was forgotten, or both excerpts were added
to close the chapter on clouds (and the citation of the number Ϛ΄
is incorrect).⁴⁶

The bulk of the material from Severian is found in a cento
that builds the entire chapter η΄ (fol. 158ᵛ–160ʳ). The excerpts
(3–8 in the present edition) are presented one after the other to
explain the course of the sun and the moon. They are all taken
from Severian's third homily, but only some of them (4–6)
are consecutive in his original text. From the second excerpt
onwards (4 in the present edition), the compiler started to use
the format of questions to introduce the fragments: for the formulation of those questions, he relied on Severian's text itself.
In the last two excerpts (7–8) the material is explicitly presented

⁴⁴ The margin next to the fragment from Severian mentions the abbreviation
σχό<λιον>.

⁴⁵ The second fragment of chapter Ϛ΄, which follows that of Severian, is not
attributed to any author. It is taken from a commentary *On the Hexaëmeron*
(fol. 158ᵛ: Συνάγονται περὶ τὸ ὕψος ... τῶν συγκριθέντων πρὸς τὸ κάτω ἐφίενται,
cf. *PG* 18, col. 712.23–27). On the authorship of this work, falsely ascribed to
Eustathius of Antioch (*CPG* 3393), see Declerck 2002, p. ccccxvi–ccccxvii.

⁴⁶ It would appear that the florilegium already contains another chapter on
rain (βροχή): see n. 9 above.

as ἐρωταποκρίσεις through the use of the terms ἐρώτησ<ις> and ἀπόκρ<ισις> to introduce the title resp. fragment.[47]

The last two fragments in the present edition follow each other in the middle of chapter θ' (fol. 160ᵛ; the chapter starts on fol. 160ʳ). The first is taken from the fourth homily, while the bulk of the second excerpt resembles a passage from the fifth homily. The last words (Εἶδες πῶς ταῖς ἀρεταῖς ἐπιγράφει τὸ 'κατ᾽ εἰκόνα';) are immediately followed, without any blank space and without a new line being started, by another text. Despite the absence of any demarcation and despite the fact that the text that follows has so far escaped identification (Τὸ 'κατ᾽ εἰκόνα' ψυχὴν λογικὴν οἶδεν ὁ λόγος Κυρίλλ<ου> κτλ.), it appears to have nothing to do with Severian. In the microfilm reproduction, fol. 160ᵛ is the single most illegible page of the manuscript: this urged me to supplement the text more than once, and my suggestion to read ἑρμη<νεία> in the title is tentative at best.

2.3. The Florilegium and the Textual Tradition of Severian's Homilies

The above overview and the below edition show clearly that Severian's *Homilies on the Hexaëmeron* were a source that was used by the compiler of the Lavra florilegium, if only in the opening section and for one or two specific topics. In that sense, the anthology witnesses to the indirect tradition of the homilies,[48] although it is not included in the standard but outdated surveys by J. Zellinger (1916) and H.-D. Altendorf (1957).

With the exception of the last one, all of the excerpts remain close to the source text.[49] Also the questions that the compiler used

---

[47] It is possible that, just like that of excerpt 8, the title of excerpt 7 is introduced as a 'question', but that the term ἐρώτησ<ις> disappeared in the inner margin in the microfilm reproduction (as did the initial letter of the first word of the question itself: <Π>όθεν). The name of Severian is offered in the outer margin.

[48] Note that the anthology does not attribute any of the excerpts in question to John Chrysostom.

[49] That is: as far as one can tell on the basis of the *PG* text (vol. 56, col. 429–500), which reprints the edition by B. de Montfaucon (1724), which in turn relies on the editio princeps by H. Savile (1612). A critical edition of the *Homilies on the Hexaëmeron* was started in 2013, but abandoned in 2016 before

to introduce fragments 4–5 and 7–8 are quite faithful adaptations of pieces from Severian's homilies.[50] As a rule, differences from the original text of Severian's homilies are minor and restricted to the occasional synonym, transposition, elucidation, etc. Only once would the florilegium's redaction of the excerpts appear to have deliberately avoided Severian's direct address of the audience in front of which he delivered his homilies (see 6.1); this case is contrasted by enough other ones that echo the oral presentation of the original text (1.2–4, 3.11, 4.2 and 10.5).

Variants that alter the meaning of the original text in a significant way or lead to remarkable results are few in number. A rare such reading is the one at the end of the fifth fragment: if the text of the Lavra manuscript would have been followed, winter's nights would have been shorter instead of longer than those of summer (see the apparatus at 5.5).

Some of the readings that the Lavra florilegium offers in disagreement with the *PG* edition of Severian's homilies are attested in the manuscript tradition of that text.[51] Notably MS *Vaticanus gr.* 1641 from the tenth/eleventh century is found to agree several times with the below edition, against the printed version of Severian's text.[52] Such observations could prove useful when trying to connect the anthology of the Lavra codex with the direct tradition of the *Homilies on the Hexaëmeron* in a more

completion, by Sarah Van Pee. For my research, I relied on the *PG* text, while being able to benefit from collation results generously supplied by Van Pee in 2015.

[50] Note that the question that introduces the fifth fragment reccurs in the running text of the sixth.

[51] My access to the manuscript transmission of Severian's homilies is restricted to collations kindly shared by Sarah Van Pee in an early phase of her – now abandoned – research (compare n. 49). Those do not include all of the manuscripts; the observations that are offered here, and for which I assume full responsibility, are therefore expected to be subject to correction and expansion.

[52] A non-exhaustive list of readings that the Lavra codex shares with this manuscript (sometimes also with other ones) includes: στήσας (1.9), δεῖξαι (3.5), λοιπὸν πλεονεκτεῖ (3.15), γενόμενος ἀριθμὸς (3.18), τό γε (4.4), κατὰ (4.12), ἕλκει (4.13) and Βλέπε οὖν (5.1) consecutively, πάντοτε (6.1), μέλλοντες (8.2–3) and ἡμέρᾳ (8.3). In this regard it might be interesting to recall Voicu's statement that MS *Vat. gr.* 1641 is the only manuscript of the homilies that bears an original attribution to Severian (2006, p. 326: compare with our n. 48). On this codex, see furthermore Voicu 2015a.

precise way than can be attempted here by lack of a critical edition.[53]

Next to comparing the fragments in the Lavra florilegium with the direct transmission of Severian's homilies, one might confront them with the rich indirect tradition of that text. Several of the excerpts that were included in the anthology can also be found in the Genesis section of the type III catena on the Octateuch (*CPG* C 2).[54] Among the catenae on the Octateuch, that type was most popular in Byzantium, as can be deduced from the relatively high number of manuscripts in which it is transmitted. Since that 'vulgar' catena incorporated excerpts from both the earlier catena tradition (*CPG* C 1) and from the so-called *Collectio Coisliniana*, one is not surprised to find parallels between each of the latter two compilations and the excerpts in the Lavra florilegium.[55] At first sight, those parallels – which are documented in the below edition – would appear noteworthy, since occasionally the florilegium, on the one hand, and the catena or *Collectio Coisliniana* on Genesis, on the other hand, do not only share their incipit and desinit but also certain readings that cannot be found in Severian's *PG* text. Examples include 1.11 (cf. the absence of ὅτι in the catena tradition of the *Collectio Coisliniana* frg. 42) and 6.7–8 (where curious readings in the Lavra codex can be restored through the catena tradition, to which it is obviously closer than to Severian's *PG* text). Worthy of note in this regard is certainly also the fact that both frg. 1 of the below edition and frg. 42 of the *Collectio Coisliniana* combine the same two non-

---

[53] For example: the abovementioned link between the anthology and MS *Vat. gr.* 1641 can be expected to not be a direct one. The Vatican manuscript is known to have Italo-Greek origins (see e.g. Giannelli 1950, p. 356; Devreesse 1955, p. 19; Lucà 2007, p. 56), which strongly reduces its chances of having been a direct source of the Lavra codex. It would seem more likely that the compiler of the florilegium depended (indirectly, see below) on a witness of Severian's text that is related to MS *Vat. gr.* 1641 but which is lost or not yet documented in the text-critical research on Severian (compare with Ceulemans, Van Deun & Van Pee 2016, p. 102–103).

[54] Although it does not cover Ruth, the catena tradition tends to be described as one 'on the Octateuch' (not: Heptateuch) for ease of reference.

[55] The ancient catena tradition on Genesis is edited by Petit 1991–1996. She also published an edition of the *Collectio Coisliniana* on Genesis: Petit 1986. Information on the way in which these texts were incorporated into the vulgar, type III catena can be gleaned from the introductions to the said editions (and from the numerous articles by the same scholar).

consecutive excerpts from the second and third homily into one continuous fragment.

Nonetheless, one should not suppose any direct dependence on the catena tradition on the florilegium's part: one simply needs to point at the excerpts in the Lavra codex for which no counterpart in the catena tradition can be found (notably 2 and 7), at the fact that some of the other excerpts are longer in the florilegium than in the catena (e.g. the last three words of fragment 3 or the first four lines of fragment 6), or at the readings that the florilegium shares with Severian's *PG* text against the catena tradition (there are several such cases already in the first fragment).

Furthermore, the catena and the *Collectio Coisliniana* on Genesis are not the only forms of indirect tradition of Severian's homilies that exhibit parallels with the excerpts in the Lavra florilegium. The (admittedly often rudimentary) surveys by Zellinger 1916 and Altendorf 1957 show that a number of manuscripts excerpted one or more passages from the *Homilies on the Hexaëmeron* that would seem quite close to some of the excerpts edited here. For example: more than one compiler or epitomator appears to have selected from Severian's homilies passages 'περὶ ἡλίου καὶ σελήνης' (compare the below fragments 3–8). Next to such manuscripts, writers like Ps.-Caesarius (*CPG* 7482) made extensive use of Severian's homilies, and in fact that author at times also agrees with the Lavra florilegium against Severian's *PG* text.[56] Certainly noteworthy in this regard is the tenth book of Cosmas Indicopleustes's *Christian Topography* (*CPG* 7468), which more than once cites the same excerpts from Severian's homilies as does the Lavra florilegium[57] (although meaningful

---

[56] The expression Ἐκ τοῦ πρωτογόνου φωτός is used both by the Lavra florilegium (see 7.1) and by Ps.-Caesarius (§ 92 = Riedinger 1989, p. 71.4) in their citation of Severian's homily III, 2 (a passage which itself does not contain the expression).

[57] See the following passages of Cosmas's text (references to Wolska-Conus 1973): X, 25.3–10 (= frg. 1.1–7); X, 31.1–14 (= frg. 1.8–15); X, 32.1–7 + 33.1–14 (= title of frg. 4 + 4.1–13); X, 33.14–16 (= frg. 5.1–2); X, 38.1–15 (= frg. 3.10–22). One can furthermore compare X, 30.1–2 and 6–7 with frg. 8.3–4 resp. frg. 7 (title and line 1). The excerpt from Severian's third homily that is cited by both Cosmas and the Lavra florilegium (X, 31.1–14 = frg. 1.8–15) has been highlighted by S. Voicu (with reference to Cosmas) as a passage that promotes a common Antiochene view also put forward by John Chrysostom and others. See Voicu 2015b, p. 549–550 (I owe this reference to Peter Van Deun).

agreements between the anthology and Cosmas's text against Severian's are rare and not as strong as in the case of the catena mentioned above).

All of this shows that, in the absence of more recent and critical research on the Greek indirect tradition of the *Homilies on the Hexaëmeron*,[58] one needs to be careful when formulating conclusions about possible sources and dependence. At this point and in view of the apparently numerous parallels in the indirect tradition, one might carefully suggest a scenario according to which certain sections were lifted out from the homilies quite soon after their original publication and gathered in some form of compilation (whether with or without excerpts from other texts). From thereon they made their way into several other texts, including Cosmas's *Topography*, the catena tradition and the Lavra florilegium.[59]

3. *Edition with Translation*

The Greek text as presented below is edited on the basis of the unique witness MS *Athonensis, Lavras* B 43, referred to as codex *R* in the apparatus. As a rule, an attempt was made to alter the text of the manuscript as little as possible, even when it was pushing the limits of good usage: as long as the text was not downright nonsensical,[60] it was kept as it is in the manuscript.

Text left out by the scribe or illegible from the microfilm is supplemented between fishhooks; *nomina sacra*, however (which are always abbreviated in the manuscript), are completed without such signs. Only once do fishhooks reflect a significant modification of the text: the addition of ὅτι in 1.11.[61] The last fragment finds itself on the single most problematic page of the

---

[58] Recent attention is directed more towards oriental versions of the homilies: see Kim 2019 and (with reference to the *Christian Topography*) Sels & Van Pee 2019. For a more general reflection on Severian's indirect tradition, see Uthemann 2000, p. 5 [= 2017, p. 138].

[59] A similar scenario was also suggested by Fernández 2019, p. 215–217 in response to Ceulemans, Van Deun & Wildenboer 2014, p. 62–67.

[60] Cases in point are the phrases δύσας δὲ καὶ πάλιν ... τὴν νύκτα (5.4–5) and Καὶ ὅταν μέντοι ... ἰσομερίαν ποιεῖ (6.7).

[61] This is also the only addition between fishhooks, together with the restitution of the first chapter number, that is accompanied by an entry in the critical apparatus.

manuscript in terms of readability (at least in the microfilm reproduction): in that case the hooks reflect my best attempts at reading the text.

Punctuation takes its starting point from the manuscript but
is adjusted to common usage. Vowel changes and errors due to
iotacism are seldom: cases in which editorial intervention is necessary are therefore rare.[62] The scribe did not write *iota* in sub-
junctive forms and dative cases consistently:[63] in the edition it is
tacitly added when absent from the manuscript. One exception
left aside (see the introductory question of fragment 8), the use
of ephelcystic *nu* in the manuscript follows a consistent pattern
(i.e.: absent when followed by a consonant, present when followed by vowel); no changes were made in the edited version.
The scribe's habit to treat the agglomerates διατί and διατοῦτο as
single words is respected, as is his way of spelling οὐχ with apostro-
phe.[64] His writing of φημί and φησί with their own accent, which
in the cases in question reflects Byzantine common practice,[65]
is retained as well. The forms of εἰμί and τις as they occur in the
section edited here are written without accent in the manuscript,
in a way that corresponds to both classical and Byzantine usage
in such cases; this was obviously retained in the printed version.
In the edition, barytone words are changed into oxytone ones
when directly preceding whichever punctuation, against Byzantine usage[66] (the manuscript is inconsistent in this regard).
The manuscript's accentuation of ἠκρωτηριᾶσθαι (3.3–4), σφρα-
γῖδα (4.3) and κλῖμα (5.3) is retained, as these forms are frequently
attested elsewhere.[67] Although it is not consistent, the scribe's way
of writing numbers is not modified in the edition.

The fragments are presented in the sequence in which they
can be found scattered over the cosmological opening section

---

[62] They are as a rule not noted in the apparatus. Vowel confusion could also
have played along in the more curious reading of 6.7.

[63] When present in the codex, it is always in subscript, never in adscript.

[64] On the ubiquity of the latter phenomenon in Byzantine manuscripts,
see Noret 2014, p. 118–119.

[65] Cf. Noret 2014, p. 124–125.

[66] See Noret 2014, p. 111–112.

[67] So informs us an online *TLG* search. Also the scribe's consistent spelling
of βορρᾶς (with double *rhô*) vs βορινός was kept. On the other hand, the readings
κρύσταλον (1.2) and κρυσταλῶδες (1.6) were silently corrected.

of the florilegium. Their numbering, offered in the margin, is imposed by the editor. The symbol ¦ is used to distinguish two different passages of the source text that were combined into one fragment in the florilegium. The edition does not record if the chapter numbers, attributions and titles of the excerpts can be found in the main text or in the margin, because one can assume – in view of the hypothesis that the florilegium is an ad hoc creation (see above) – that the position of that information does not reflect any meaningful difference.

The edited text is accompanied by four apparatuses:

- an identification of the source to which the excerpt belongs (each time it is Severian's *Homilies on the Hexaëmeron*) and of relevant biblical citations and allusions;

- a critical apparatus;

- a comparison with Severian's text;[68] orthographical differences between the source and the florilegium are ignored;

- an identification of parallel passages in the Genesis section of the type III catena on the Octateuch (*CPG* C 2).[69] This does not imply dependence on the catena on the florilegium's part (compare above): among the numerous forms of indirect tradition of Severian's homilies, the catena is only mentioned because in fragment 6 (l. 7–8) it was used to restore the text of the Lavra codex.[70]

In my English translation I relied on the late R. Hill's (2010), but modified it more than once.[71] Septuagint passages cited by Severian were adopted from the NETS translation[72] (again modified when deemed appropriate).

---

[68] No comparison is offered for fragment 10, which does not offer a literal citation of Severian's text.

[69] Editions: Petit 1991–1996, vol. I (edition of the ancient catena [*CPG* C 1]) and Petit 1986 (edition of the *Collectio Coisliniana*).

[70] A reason for not including in this apparatus references to Cosmas Indicopleustes is adduced above.

[71] I acknowledge the help of my colleague Bram Demulder, without whose invaluable advise I would still be in the dark about the meaning of fragment 3. Of course I alone assume full responsibility for any errors.

[72] Pietersma & Wright 2007.

Excerpts from Severian of Gabala,
Homilies on the Hexaëmeron
in the Florilegium of MS Athonensis, Lavras B 43:
Greek Text and English Translation

f. 153ʳ   <Α΄ > Περὶ οὐρανοῦ

f. 154ᵛ   [...]

1   Σευηριανοῦ

Ἑρμη‹νεία.› Τὸν οὐρανὸν τοῦτον, οὐ τὸν ἐπάνω ἀλλὰ τὸν ὁρώμενον, ἐξ
ὑδάτων ἐποίησεν ὁ Θεὸς πήξας ὡς κρύσταλλον. Βλέπε δύναμιν ἔργων ἵνα
f. 155ʳ   θαυμάσῃς τὸν δημιουργόν. Βούλομαί σοι παραστῆσαι πρᾶγμα· | πολλὰ γὰρ
ὄψει μᾶλλον ἢ λόγῳ παραδίδοται. Τοῦτο τὸ ὕδωρ ὑπερεῖχε, φέρε εἰπεῖν, τῆς
γῆς πήχεις τριάκοντα, ὡς ἐν εἰκόνι λέγω. Εἶπεν ὁ Θεός· Γενηθήτω στερέωμα   5
ἐν μέσῳ τοῦ ὕδατος· εἶτα ἐν μέσῳ τῶν ὑδάτων ἐπάγη πῆγμα κρυσταλλῶδες,
ὁ οὐρανός, ἐκούφισε τὸ ἥμισυ τοῦ ὕδατος ἄνω καὶ κατέλιπε τὸ ἥμισυ κάτω.
¦ Ἐποίησεν οὖν τὸν οὐρανὸν οὐ σφαῖραν ὡς μυθολογοῦσιν οἱ ματαιολόγοι,
ἀλλ᾽ ὡς φησὶν ὁ προφήτ‹ης›· Ὁ στήσας τὸν οὐρανὸν ὡσεὶ καμάραν, καὶ
διατείνας αὐτὸν ὡς σκηνήν. Οὐ δεῖ οὖν ἡμᾶς πείθεσθ‹αι› ματαιολόγοις.   10
Οἱ προφῆται λέγουσιν ‹ὅτι› ἀρχὴν ἔχει καὶ τέλος ὁ οὐρανός, καὶ διατοῦτο
καὶ ὁ ἥλιος οὐκ ἀναβαίνει ἀλλ᾽ ἐξέρχεται. Λ‹έ›γ‹ει› ἡ Γραφή· Ὁ ἥλιος
ἐξῆλθεν ἐπὶ τὴν γῆν, οὐκ ἀνῆλθε. Καὶ πάλιν· Ἀπ᾽ ἄκρου τοῦ οὐρανοῦ ἡ ἔξ-

---

R

1.1–15 Severianus Gabalensis, *In Cosmogoniam* homiliae II, 3 (PG 56, col.
442.2–10) et III, 4 (PG 56, col. 452.29–44)   **5–6** Gen. 1.6   **9–10** Isa. 40.22
12–13 Gen. 19.23   **13–14** Ps. 18.7

Tit. capitis Α΄] addidi; non. hab. R   **1.1** ἐπάνω] ἀπάνω (sic) R   **11** ὅτι] addidi
cum Severiano; non hab. R | ἔχει] scripsi cum Severiano; ἔχειν R

1.1 Ἑρμηνεία] non hab. Sever.   **2** ἐποίησεν ... Θεός] non hab. Sever. (sed vide PG
56, col. 442.1)   **2–3** Βλέπε ... δημιουργόν] non hab. Sever. (sed vide Homiliam III,
3 [PG 56, col. 450.26])   **4** ante ὄψει] τῇ hab. Sever. | post μᾶλλον] ἡμῶν hab.
Sever. | ante λόγῳ] τῷ hab. Sever.   **5** ὡς ... λέγω] εἶτα Sever.   **6** εἶτα] καὶ λοιπὸν
Sever.   **7** ὁ οὐρανός] καὶ Sever. | καὶ] non hab. Sever.   **8** οὖν] non hab. Sever. |
οὐ] οὐχ ὡς Sever. | μυθολογοῦσιν] φιλοσοφοῦσιν Sever. | post ματαιολόγοι] οὐ
γὰρ ἐποίησε σφαῖραν κυλιομένην hab. Sever.   **9** ante Ὁ] ὁ ἥλιος πῶς τρέχει hab.
Sever. | στήσας] στεγάσας Sever. | ὡσεὶ] ὡς Sever.   **10** Οὐ ... πείθεσθαι] οὐδεὶς
ἡμῶν οὕτως ἀσεβὴς ὥστε πεισθῆναι τοῖς Sever.   **11** καὶ²] non hab. Sever.
12 ἐξέρχεται] ἔρχεται Sever.   **13** post γῆν] καὶ Λὼτ εἰσῆλθεν εἰς Σηγὼρ ὥστε δῆλον
ὅτι ἐξῆλθεν ὁ ἥλιος κατὰ τὴν Γραφὴν καὶ hab. Sever.

1.1–15 Cf. *Collectionem Coislinianam in Genesim*, frg. 42 (ed. Petit 1986,
p. 40–42) in *Catena in Genesim* typi III

I On heaven

[...]

1

From Severian

Explanation. God made this heaven – not the one above it but the visible one – out of water, making it solid like crystal. Behold the power of his work so you would admire the creator. I want to depict the arrangement for you, for many things are transmitted by imagining them rather than by speaking of them. To put it as if in an image: this water rose up over the earth, thirty cubits so to say. *God said: 'Let a firmament come into being in the midst of the water'*: then in the middle of the waters a crystal-like fixture – i.e.: heaven – was set, raising half the water on high and leaving half below. And so he did not create heaven as a sphere, as the idle talkers invent in their mythic tales, but in the way the prophet says: *He who has set up heaven like a vault and stretched it out like a tent*. We must indeed not trust idle talkers. The prophets say that heaven has a beginning and an end, and hence that the sun does not climb, but goes forth. Scripture says: *The sun came out* (not: climbed) *on the earth*. And again: *From heaven's*

ὁδος αὐτοῦ, οὐχ᾽ ἡ ἄνοδος. Εἰ σφαῖρα ἐστίν, ἄκρον οὐκ ἔχει. Τὸ γὰρ πανταχόθεν περιφερὲς ποῦ ἔχει τὸ ἄκρον; Τὸ αὐτὸ λ<έ>γ<ει> καὶ ὁ Σωτήρ.   15

f. 158ᵛ   [...]

Ϛ´

2   Σχό<λιον>

Δεῖ γινώσκειν ὅτι ἐποίησεν ὁ Θεὸς νεφέλας *ὡσεὶ ἀσκούς*, καὶ ἀντλεῖ δι᾽
αὐτῶν τὰ τῆς θαλάσσης ἁλμυρὰ ὕδατα, καὶ μεταβάλλει τὸ ὕδωρ εἰς γλυκύ,
καὶ ποτίζει τὴν γῆν.

[...]

Η´ Περὶ ἡλίου καὶ σελήνης

3   Σευηριανοῦ

Ὅτε ὁ ἥλιος ἐπάγη, εἰς ἀνατολὰς ἐπάγη, καὶ ὅτε ἡ σελήνη ἐπάγη, εἰς δύσιν
ἐπάγη· ἐπειδὴ ὁ μὲν τῆς ἡμέρας, ἡ δὲ τῆς νυκτὸς ἄρχειν ἐτάχθησαν. |
f. 159ʳ   Ἐγένετο οὖν ἡ σελήν<η> τῇ δ᾽ ἡμέρ<ᾳ> πανσέληνος. Οὐ γὰρ ἔδει ἠκρωτηριᾶσθαι τὸ ἔργον εὐθέως, ἀλλ᾽ ἔδει δειχθῆναι τὸν φωστῆρα οἷος ἐγένετο,
μετὰ δὲ ταῦτα τῇ ἀλλοιώσει δεῖξαι χρόνους *καὶ καιροὺς καὶ* διαφορὰς   5

R

1.15 Cf. Matth. 24.31; Marc. 13.27   **2.1–3** Severianus Gabalensis, *In Cosmogoniam* homilia III, 6 (PG 56, col. 454.25–28)   **1** Ps. 77.14   **1–3** cf. Exod.
2.16–17.19   **3.1–22** Severianus Gabalensis, *In Cosmogoniam* homilia III, 2 (PG
56, col. 449.30–61)   **2** cf. Gen. 1.17.18   **4** cf. Gen. 1.14.16   **5–6** Gen. 1.15

3.1 σελήνη] lunae imagunculam hab. R

1.14 οὐχ᾽ ἡ] οὐκ Sever.   **15** Τὸ ... λέγει] ἆρα οὖν ὁ Δαυῒδ μόνος λέγει ἢ Sever.
2.1 Δεῖ ... ὅτι] non hab. Sever. | ὁ Θεὸς] τὰς Sever. | ὡσεὶ] ὡς Sever.   **2** ἁλμυρὰ
ὕδατα] ὕδατα ἁλμυρὰ ὄντα καὶ πληροῖ τὰς νεφέλας Sever. | εἰς γλυκύ] non hab.
Sever.   **3.1** ἀνατολὰς] ἀνατολὴν Sever. | καὶ ὅτε] non hab. Sever. | ἐπάγη³] non
hab. Sever.   **2** ἐπάγη] non hab. Sever. | ὁ] ἐκείνη Sever. | τῆς¹ ... ἡ] ἄρχειν τῆς
νυκτὸς ἐκελεύσθη ὁ Sever. | νυκτὸς ... ἐτάχθησαν] ἡμέρας Sever.   **3** ante τῇ] καὶ
γεννᾶται hab. Sever. | δ᾽] πρώτῃ Sever.   **5** δεῖξαι] ἔδειξε Sever.

3.1–22 Cf. *Catenam in Genesim* typi I, frg. 101.1–24 (ed. Petit 1991–1996, vol.
I, p. 79–82) in *Catena in Genesim* typi III

extremity is his emergence (not: his ascent). If heaven were a sphere, it would not have a furthest point: you see, what is the furthest point of something completely circular? Also the Savior says the same.

[...]

VI

2

A scholion

You should know that God made the clouds like wineskins, that through them he draws up the salty seawater, and that he transforms it into fresh water and gives the earth a drink.

[...]

VII On the sun and the moon

3

From Severian

When the sun was set, it was set in the east, and when the moon was set, it was set in the west, since the former was bidden to rule the day and the latter the night. And so the moon was made on the fourth day, as a full moon. It was not appropriate for the new creation to be deprived of its fullness immediately – instead, the light needed to be shown as it was made and later indicate years and seasons and different

ἡμερῶν. Ποιεῖ αὐτὴν ὁ Θεὸς ὡς πεντεκαιδεκαταίαν πεπληρωμένην. Ὁ
ἥλιος ἀνέτελλεν (ὄρθρου γὰρ ἐπάγη), καὶ ἡ σελήνη ἐν τῷ ὄρθρῳ ἐφαίνετο
πρὸς δύσιν. Ὡς οὖν ἔτρεχεν ὁ ἥλιος τὸν ἴδιον δρόμον εἰς δύσιν, ἡ σελήνη
ἤρξατο εὐθέως ἀνατέλλειν, ἵνα πληρωθῇ τὸ Ἀρχέτωσαν τῆς ἡμέρας καὶ τῆς
νυκτός. Λοιπὸν ζήτημα ἐντεῦθεν ἀναφύεται· διατί ὁ Θεὸς πεπληρωμένην   10
ἐποίησε τὴν σελήνην; Πρόσεχε· τὸ γὰρ νόημα βαθύ. Ἐχρῆν αὐτὴν τῇ δ'
γενομένην ἡμέρ<ᾳ> ὡς τεταρταίαν φαίνεσθ<αι>, καὶ πάλιν εἰ οὖν τεταρταία, τὸ ἄκρον τῆς δύσεως οὐ κατεῖχεν. Εὑρέθη οὖν πλεονεκτοῦσα τὸν
ἥλιον ἔνδεκα ἡμέρ<ας>· τεταρταία ἐγένετο καὶ ἐφαίνετο ὡς πεντεκαιδεκα-
ταία. Ἔνδεκα ἡμέρας λοιπὸν πλεονεκτεῖ ἡ σελήνη τὸν ἥλιον, οὐ τῇ ποιήσει,   15
ἀλλὰ τῇ φαύσει· διατοῦτο ἃς τότε ἐπλεονέκτησεν, ἀποδίδωσι τῷ ἡλίῳ. Ὁ
γὰρ κατὰ σελήνην καθ' ἕκαστον μῆνα ἀπὸ εἰκοσιεννέα ἥμισυ ἡμερῶν
γενόμενος ἀριθμὸς ποιεῖ ἐν τοῖς δώδεκα μησὶ τοῦ ἐνιαυτοῦ ἡμέρας τνδ'.
Ἐὰν γὰρ οὕτως ψηφίσῃς ἀπὸ εἰκοσιεννέα ἥμισυ ἡμερῶν τὸν μῆνα,
γίνοντ<αι> τοῦ ἐνιαυτοῦ ἡμέραι τριακόσιαι πεντήκοντ<α> τέσσαρες, ἵνα   20
ἃς ἐπλεονέκτησε τότε ἡμέρας ἡ σελήνη κατ' ἐνιαυτὸν ἀποδῷ τῷ ἡλίῳ. Ὁ
ψηφιστὴς ψηφιζέτω.

R

3.9–10 Gen. 1.18 (et cf. Gen. 1.16) 11–12 Cf. Gen. 1.19

3.6 πεντεκαιδεκαταίαν] πεντεκαιδεκατιαίαν (sic) R 9 εὐθέως ἀνατέλλειν] transp.
Rᵃ·ᶜ· 21 σελήνη] lunae imagunculam hab. R

3.6 post Ποιεῖ] οὖν hab. Sever. 7 ante γὰρ] ὅτε hab. Sever. | καὶ] non hab. Sever.
8 εἰς] πρὸς Sever. 9 ἤρξατο] ἤρχετο Sever. | ante ἀνατέλλειν] τοῦ hab. Sever.
10 ἐντεῦθεν ἀναφύεται] non hab. Sever. 12 γενομένην ἡμέρᾳ] ἡμέρᾳ γεναμένην
Sever. | καὶ] ἀλλὰ Sever. | οὖν] ἣν Sever. 13 οὐ κατεῖχεν] οὐκ ἀντεῖχεν Sever.
13–14 τὸν ἥλιον] non hab. Sever. 15 λοιπὸν πλεονεκτεῖ] ἐπλεόνεκτει λοιπὸν Sever.
16 post ἐπλεονέκτησεν] ἡ σελήνη hab. Sever. 17 post σελήνην] καὶ hab. Sever.
18 γενόμενος ἀριθμὸς] ἀριθμὸς γιγνόμενος Sever. | δώδεκα] δεκαδύο Sever. 19 τὸν
μῆνα] post ψηφίσῃς hab. Sever. 21 ἀποδῷ] ἀποδίδωσι Sever.

weather by its changing shape. God created it as a full moon, like on the fifteenth day <of the normal lunar cycle>. The sun rose (because it was set in the morning), and in the morning the moon appeared in the west. So as the sun ran its proper course towards the west, the moon immediately started to rise so as to fulfill the commandment '*They have to rule the day and the night*'. From these observations a further question comes up: Why did God make the moon full? Pay attention: it is a profound explanation, you see. The moon, which was created on the fourth day, ought to have appeared like on the fourth day <of the normal lunar cycle>; but if it then would have been <the moon> of the fourth day <of the normal lunar cycle>, it would not have reached the furthest point west. It was therefore found to have a surplus of eleven days compared with the sun: it was <the moon> of the fourth day <of creation>, but it gave the appearance of being on the fifteenth day <of the normal lunar cycle>. As a result, the moon had a surplus of eleven days compared with the sun, not in creation but in brightness; therefore, it restored to the sun the extra days it then had. The fact is that the number of days per month that the moon had was twenty-nine and a half, which in twelve months of the year amounts to 354. In other words, if you count twenty-nine and half days as a month, 354 days make a year, so that the moon restores to the sun the days it then had in excess. If you can count, count them.

4   Τοῦ αὐτοῦ· Ποῦ δύνει ὁ ἥλιος καὶ ποῦ τρέχει τὴν νύκτα;

f. 159ᵛ
Ἑρμη<νεία. Κ>ατὰ μὲν τοὺς ἔξω ὑπὸ τὴν γῆν, καθ᾽ ἡμᾶς δὲ τοὺς *σκηνήν*
τὸν οὐρανὸν λέγοντας, οὐχί. | Πρόσεχε, παρακαλῶ, εἰ μὴ διαψεύδεται τὸ
ῥῆμα, ἀλλ᾽ ἔχε σφραγίδα μεμαρτυρημένην ὑπὸ τῆς ἀληθείας, σύντρεχε τῇ
φράσει, καὶ τό γε νόμισον εἶναι *καμάραν* ἐπικειμένην τῇ *ἀνατολῇ*. Ἐκεῖ
ἐστι κατὰ τὸν τόπον ἄρκτος, ὧδε μεσημβρία, ἐκεῖ δύσις· ἐκεῖθεν ὁ ἥλιος   5
ἀνατέλλων καὶ μέλλων δύνειν, οὐχ᾽ ὑπὸ γῆν δύνει, ἀλλ᾽ ἐξελθὼν τὰ πέρατα
τοῦ οὐρανοῦ τρέχει εἰς τὰ βορινὰ μέρη, ὥσπερ ὑπό τινα τοῖχον
κρυπτόμενος, μὴ συγχωρούντων τῶν ὑδάτων φανῆναι αὐτοῦ τὸν δρόμον,
λοιπὸν τρέχων τὰ βορινὰ μέρη καταλαμβάνει τὴν ἀνατολήν. Καὶ πόθεν
τοῦτο δῆλον; Ὁ μακάριος Σολομὼν ἐν τῷ Ἐκκλησιαστῇ (γραφῇ   10
μεμαρτυρημένη, οὐ παραγραφομένη) *Ἀνατέλλει* φησὶ *ὁ ἥλιος καὶ δύνει ὁ*
ἥλιος· ἀνατέλλων πορεύεται κατὰ δύσιν, καὶ κυκλοῖ πρὸς βορρᾶν· κυκλοῖ
κύκλον, καὶ εἰς τὸν τόπον αὐτοῦ ἕλκει.

5   Πῶς οὖν γίνονται μικραὶ αἱ ἡμέραι;

Βλέπε οὖν αὐτὸν κατὰ μεσημβρίαν τρέχοντα, καὶ τὸν βορρᾶν κυκλοῦντα
τὸ λοιπὸν μάθε ἐν τῇ τοῦ χειμῶνος καταστάσει. Ἐπειδὴ οὐκ ἀπὸ μέσης τῆς
ἀνατολῆς ἀνατέλλει, ἀλλὰ περὶ τὸ κλῖμα τῆς μεσημβρίας πλαγιάζει καὶ

R

Tit. frg. 4 Severianus Gabalensis, *In Cosmogoniam* homilia III, 5 (PG 56, col.
452.50–51) **4.1–13** Severianus Gabalensis, *In Cosmogoniam* homilia III, 5 (PG
56, col. 452.51 – 453.7) **1–2** Isa. 40.22 **4** Isa. 40.22 **11–13** Eccl. 1.5a.6a–c.5b
Tit. frg. 5 Severianus Gabalensis, *In Cosmogoniam* homilia III, 5 (PG 56, col.
453.15) **5.1–5** Severianus Gabalensis, *In Cosmogoniam* homilia III, 5 (PG 56,
col. 453.7–13)

4.1 Ἑρμηνεία] non hab. Sever. | μὲν] non hab. Sever. **2** τὸν οὐρανὸν] αὐτὸν Sever.
(sed vide app. crit.) | οὐχί] τί Sever. **3** ἔχε] εἰ ἔχεις Sever. | σύντρεχε] συντρέχει
Sever. **4** τό γε] ὁ τόπος Sever. | τῇ ἀνατολῇ] ἡ ἀνατολὴ Sever. **5** τόπον] τύπον
Sever. | ἐκεῖθεν ὁ] ἐκεῖ Sever. **9** λοιπὸν ... τὰ] καὶ τρέχει κατὰ Sever. | post μέρη]
καὶ hab. Sever. **10** ante Ὁ] λέγει hab. Sever. **10–11** γραφῇ ... παραγραφομένη]
γραφὴ δέ ἐστι μεμαρτυρημένη οὐ παραγραφομένη Sever. **12** κατὰ] εἰς Sever. **13** κύ-
κλον] κυκλῶν Sever. (et textus biblicus) | ἕλκει] ἀνατέλλει Sever. **5.1** Βλέπε ...
αὐτὸν] non hab. Sever. **2** τὸ] non hab. Sever.

Tit. frg. 4 Cf. *Catenam in Genesim* typi I, frg. 101.25 (ed. Petit 1991–1996, vol.
I, p. 79–82) in *Catena in Genesim* typi III **4.1–13** Cf. *Catenam in Genesim*
typi I, frg. 101.26–36 (ed. Petit 1991–1996, vol. I, p. 79–82) in *Catena in*
Genesim typi III **5.1–5** Cf. *Catenam in Genesim* typi I, frg. 101.36–42 (ed.
Petit 1991–1996, vol. I, p. 79–82) in *Catena in Genesim* typi III

4 From the same author: Where does the sun set and where does it travel
at night?

Explanation. According to the pagans: under the earth; but not
according to us, who claim that heaven is a tent. Pay attention, I beg
you, as to whether that view is not false, but do have a guarantee
confirmed by the truth, concur with the expression, and think of it as
follows: in terms of a curved roof lying over the east. At that position,
north is in one direction, south another, west another. When the sun
rises from there and is destined to set, it does not set under the earth,
but while proceeding to the ends of heaven it travels to the northern
regions, concealed as it were by a wall since the waters prevent its
course being visible, and while traversing the northern regions it
finally reaches the east. In Ecclesiastes – a text that is authentic, not
spurious – blessed Solomon says: *The sun rises, and the sun sets; upon
rising, it goes to its setting and circles to the north; it completes a circle
and draws along to its place.*

5 How are the days briefer?

Observe the sun's traveling south and note finally its turning north in
the period of winter. Since it does not rise due east but verges to the
quarter of the south and follows a shorter route, it produces a briefer

ὀλίγον τεμὼν διάστημα, ποιεῖ μικρὰν τὴν ἡμέραν· δύσας δὲ καὶ πάλιν
κύκλῳ τρέχων, ποιεῖ μακρὰν τὴν νύκτα.   5

6   Καὶ πάλιν·

Ἰστέον ὅτι ὁ ἥλιος οὐ πάντοτε ἀπὸ τοῦ αὐτοῦ κέντρου προέρχεται. Πῶς
οὖν γίνονται μικραὶ αἱ ἡμέραι; Πλησιάζει αὐτοῦ ἡ ἀνατολὴ τῷ κλίματι τῆς
μεσημβρίας· εἶτα οὐ τὴν ὑψηλὴν ἐλθὼν ἀλλὰ τὴν πλαγίαν συντεμὼν τὰς
f. 160ʳ   ἡμέρας ποιεῖ μικράς. | Δύσας δὲ εἰς τὸ ἄκρον τῆς δύσεως, ἀνάγκην ἔχει
κυκλεῦσαι διὰ τῆς νυκτὸς δύσιν ὅλην καὶ ἄρκτον καὶ ἀνατολήν, καὶ φθάσαι   5
ἐπὶ τὸ ἄκρον τῆς μεσημβρίας· καὶ ἀνάγκη μεγάλην γενέσθαι τὴν νύκτα.
Καὶ ὅταν μέντοι ἐξισῶται καὶ διάστημά τι ἴσον ἔχον, ἰσομερίαν ποιεῖ.
Θέρους δὲ πάλιν ἐκκλίνας κατὰ τὸν βορρᾶν, ὥσπερ χειμῶνος εἰς μεσημβρίαν, καὶ τὰ ἄκρα τοῦ βορρᾶ ἀναβαίνων, ὑψοῦται καὶ μεγάλην ποιεῖ τὴν
ἡμέραν· ὀλίγον δὲ ἔχων τὸν κύκλον, μικρὰν ποιεῖ τὴν νύκτα.   10

R

6.1–10 Severianus Gabalensis, *In Cosmogoniam* homilia III, 5 (PG 56, col.
453.13–27)

5.4 καὶ] om. Rᵃ·ᶜ· 5 μακρὰν] scripsi cum Severiano; μικρὰν R   6.2 τῷ κλίματι]
scripsi cum Severiano; τῶν κλιμάτων R   7 ἐξισῶται ... ἴσον] scripsi (cf. etiam
Catenam in Genesim typi I, frg. 101.45 [ed. Petit 1991–1996, vol. I, p. 80] in
Catena in Genesim typi III); ἐξ ἴσου τέμη διάστημα τι ἴσον Rᵛⁱᵈ· 8 Θέρους] scripsi
(cf. etiam *Catenam in Genesim* typi I, frg. 101.46 [ed. Petit 1991–1996, vol. I,
p. 80] in *Catena in Genesim* typi III); θέρος R

5.4 τὴν] non hab. Sever.   5 κύκλῳ] κύκλον Sever. | τὴν] non hab. Sever.
6.1 Ἰστέον] Ἴσμεν, ἀδελφοὶ Sever. | πάντοτε] πάντως Sever.   5 post ἄρκτον] ὅλην
hab. Sever. | post ἀνατολήν] ὅλην hab. Sever.   7 Καὶ] non hab. Sever. | ἐξισῶται]
ἐξισοῦται τῷ μήκει Sever. | διάστημά ... ἰσομερίαν] ἴσον βῆμα ἔχῃ ἰσημερίαν Sever.
8 Θέρους δὲ] non hab. Sever. | ἐκκλίνας] κλίνας Sever.   9 ante τὰ] εἰς hab. Sever.
10 ante ἔχων] μικρὸν hab. Sever.

6.4–10 Cf. *Catenam in Genesim* typi I, frg. 101.42–49 (ed. Petit 1991–1996,
vol. I, p. 79–82) in *Catena in Genesim* typi III

day; and on setting in due course it travels in a circle and produces a longer night.

6 And again:

It should be known that the sun does not always emerge at the same point. So how are the days briefer? Its rising verges towards the southerly quarter; then, instead of going to the heights, it reduces its course and makes the days short. On setting at the furthest point of the west, conversely, it has to cover all the west and north and east in its circle through the night to reach the furthest point of the south, the inevitable result being a long night. And when, by contrast, the course is of equal length, with any interval of the same length, it makes for the same share. Likewise, when during summer it turns away towards the north – as in winter it turns towards the south – and mounts to the furthest points of the north, it is elevated and produces a day of great length. When on the other hand its circle is limited, it produces a night that is brief.

7 Σευηριανοῦ. <Π>όθεν ἐποίησε τὸν ἥλιον καὶ τὴν σελήνην καὶ τὰ ἄστρα ὁ Θεός;
Ἀπόκρ<ισις.> Ἐκ τοῦ πρωτογόνου φωτ<ὸς> ὡς αὐτὸς ἠθέλησεν.

8 Τοῦ αὐτοῦ. Ἐρώτησ<ις.> Διατί τῇ πρώτῃ ἡμέρ<ᾳ> οὐκ ἐποίησεν τὸν ἥλιον καὶ τὴν σελήνην ὁ Θεός;
Ἀπόκρ<ισις.> Ἐπειδὴ οὐδέπω ἦν τὸ στερέωμα γενόμενον ἐν ᾧ ἔμελλον πεπῆχθαι, καὶ οὐ διατοῦτο μόνον, ἀλλ' ἐπειδὴ οὐδέπω ἦσαν οἱ καρποὶ οἱ μέλλοντες θάλπεσθ<αι> (τῇ γὰρ τρίτ<ῃ> ἡμέρᾳ ἐβλάστησαν οἱ καρποί), καὶ ἵνα μὴ νομισθῶσι πάλιν, ὅτι τῇ φύσει τοῦ ἡλίου ἐβλάστησαν, τότε ὁ ἥλιος ἐγένετο.   5

R

Tit. frg. 7.1–2 Severianus Gabalensis, *In Cosmogoniam* homilia III, 2 (PG 56, col. 449.4–5) **7.1** cf. Gen. 1.3.14 | Severianus Gabalensis, *In Cosmogoniam* homilia III, 2 (PG 56, col. 449.7–8) **Tit. frg. 8.**1–2 Severianus Gabalensis, *In Cosmogoniam* homilia III, 2 (PG 56, col. 448.55–56) **8.1–5** Severianus Gabalensis, *In Cosmogoniam* homilia III, 2 (PG 56, col. 448.56 – 449.4) **1** Gen. 1.6 (et 1.7–8) **2** Gen. 1.11–12 **3** Gen. 1.13 | Gen. 1.11–12 **4–5** Cf. Gen. 1.16

8.4 φύσει] φυσικῇ R[a.c.]

Tit. frg. 7.1 ante ἐποίησε] τὰ αὐτὰ hab. Sever. **1–2** τὸν ... Θεός] non hab. Sever. (sed vide PG 56, col. 449.4) **7.1** Ἀπόκρισις] non hab. Sever. | πρωτογόνου φωτός] γενομένου φωτὸς τῇ πρώτῃ ἡμέρᾳ ὃ μετέβαλεν Sever. | αὐτὸς] non hab. Sever. **Tit. frg. 8.1** Διατί] post ἡμέρᾳ hab. Sever. | τὸν] non hab. Sever. **2** τὴν] non hab. Sever. | ὁ Θεός] non hab. Sever. **8.1** Ἀπόκρισις] non hab. Sever. | ἔμελλον] ἔμελλε Sever. **2** οἱ[1]] non hab. Sever. **2–3** μέλλοντες] ὀφείλοντες Sever. **3** ἡμέρᾳ] non hab. Sever. **4** νομισθῶσι] νομισθῇ Sever. **4–5** τότε ... ἐγένετο] ὅτε ἀπηρτίσθη ἡ δημιουργία τότε λοιπὸν ποιεῖ ὁ Θεὸς ἥλιον σελήνην ἄστρα Sever.

Tit. frg. 8.1–2 Cf. *Collectionem Coislinianam in Genesim*, frg. 50.4–5 (ed. Petit 1986, p. 47–48) in *Catena in Genesim* typi III **8.1–4** Cf. *Collectionem Coislinianam in Genesim*, frg. 50.5–11 (ed. Petit 1986, p. 40–42) in *Catena in Genesim* typi III

7   From Severian. From what did God make the sun and the moon and
        the stars?
     Answer: From his first-created light, as he himself wished.

8   From the same author. Question: Why did God not make the sun and
        the moon on the first day?
     Answer: Because at that stage there was no firmament in which they
     were meant to be fixed. And not only for that reason, but also because
     at that stage there was no fruit yet that was meant to be cherished by
     the heat (the fruit being produced on the third day). And lest people
     should think, then, that they were produced naturally by the sun, the
     sun was finally made at that time.

Θ΄ Περὶ τῆς τοῦ ἀνθρώπου κατασκευῆς

f. 160ᵛ [...]

9   Σευηριανοῦ. *Ποιήσωμεν ἄνθρωπον κατ᾽ εἰκόνα*
'*Ποιήσωμεν*' εἶπεν, ἵνα τὸ πληθυντικὸν τῶν ὑποστάσεων δείξῃ· '*κατ᾽*
εἰκόνα δὲ ἡμετέραν', ἵνα τὸ ὁμο<ούσ>ιον ἑρμηνεύσῃ.

10   Ἑρμη<νεία> τοῦ αὐτοῦ
Τίνι εἶπεν ὁ Θεός· *Ποιήσωμεν ἄνθρωπον κατ᾽ εἰκόνα ἡμετέρ<αν*; Τῷ> Υἱῷ
δηλονότι, κατὰ τὸν Ἡσαΐαν· θαυμαστὸς σύμβουλος. <Τὸ> δὲ '*κατ᾽ εἰκόνα*',
κατὰ τὴν ἀρετήν. Φησὶ γάρ· *γίνεσθ<ε> ἅγι<οι καθ>ὼς ἐγὼ ἅγιός εἰμι*, καὶ
τοῦ ἀποστόλ<ου> *Ἐνδύσασθ<ε> τ<ὸν> νέον ἄνθρωπον τὸν κατ᾽ εἰκόνα
κτισθέντα τοῦ κτίσαντος <αὐ>τόν*. Εἶδες πῶς ταῖς ἀρεταῖς ἐπιγράφει τὸ   5
'*κατ᾽ εἰκόνα*';

R

Tit. frg. 9 Gen. 1.26   **9.1** Gen. 1.26   **1–2** Severianus Gabalensis, *In Cosmo-
goniam* homilia IV, 6 (PG 56, col. 465.19–21) | Gen. 1.26   **10.1–2** Cf.
Severianum Gabalensem, *In Cosmogoniam* homilia IV, 7 (PG 56, col. 465.27–37)
1 Gen. 1.26   **2** Cf. Is. 3.3   **2–6** Cf. Severianum Gabalensem, *In Cosmogoniam*
homilia V, 4 (PG 56, col. 475.23–37)   **3** Lev. 11.44–45; 19.2; 20.7.26; I Petr.
1.16   **4–5** Col. 3.10

Tit. frg. 10 Ἑρμηνεία] dubia restitutio mea; R illeg.

9.1 εἶπεν] non hab. Sever.   **2** εἰκόνα δὲ] non hab. Sever.

10.1–6 Cf. *Collectionem Coislinianam in Genesim*, frg. 61.1–22 (ed. Petit 1986,
p. 57–58) in *Catena in Genesim* typi III

IX On the creation of man

[...]

9   From Severian. *Let us make a human in image*
He said '*Let us make*' in order to bring out the plurality of persons [i.e.: *hypostaseis*], and '*according to our image*' in order to explain the oneness of being [i.e.: *homoousion*].

10   Explanation from the same author
To whom did God say '*Let us make a human according to our image*'? To his Son of course, in accordance with Isaiah's designation of him as *wonderful counselor*. The words '*according to our image*' mean 'in virtue'. For it is said: *Become holy in the way that I am holy*. And the apostle said: *Put on the new self, created according to the image of his creator*. Did you see how the expression '*according to our image*' refers to the virtues?

Bibliography

K. Aland et al. (1994), *Kurzgefasste Liste der griechischen Handschriften des Neuen Testaments. Zweite, neubearbeitete und ergänzte Auflage*, Berlin: de Gruyter (Arbeiten zur neutestamentlichen Textforschung, 1).

H.-D. Altendorf (1957), *Untersuchungen zu Severian von Gabala* (unpublished doctoral thesis, Eberhard-Karls-Universität Tübingen).

D. N. Anastasijewić (1907), 'Alphabete', in *Byzantinische Zeitschrift*, 16, p. 479–501.

Th. Antonopoulou (2015), 'A Theological *Opusculum* Allegedly by Emperor Leo VI the Wise', in —, S. Kotzabassi & M. Loukaki (eds), *Myriobiblos. Essays on Byzantine Literature and Culture*, Berlin: de Gruyter (Byzantinisches Archiv, 29), p. 39–54.

M. Aussedat & M. Cassin (2010), 'Le prologue du *Commentaire sur les petits prophètes* de Théophylacte d'Achrida', in *Revue des Études Byzantines*, 68, p. 61–93.

V. Becares (1988), 'Ein unbekanntes Werk des Gregorios von Korinth und seine Lebenszeit', in *Byzantinische Zeitschrift*, 81, p. 247–248.

H.-G. Beck (1959), *Kirche und theologische Literatur im byzantinischen Reich*, Munich: Beck (Handbuch der Altertumswissenschaft, 12.2.1).

M. Becker (2016), *Porphyrios, Contra Christianos*. Neue Sammlung der Fragmente, Testimonien und Dubia mit Einleitung, Übersetzung und Anmerkungen von —, Berlin: de Gruyter (Texte und Kommentare, 52).

N. Bianchi (2011), 'A Neglected Testimonium on Xenophon of Ephesus: Gregory Pardos', in M. P. Futre Pinheir & S. J. Harrison (eds), *Fictional Traces. Receptions of the Ancient Novel. Volume I*, Groningen: Barkhuis – Groningen University Library (Ancient Narrative, Supplementum, 14), p. 83–92.

L. Brisson (2011), 'Le Christ comme *Lógos* suivant Porphyre dans *Contre les chrétiens* (fragment 86 von Harnack = Théophylacte, *Enarr. in Joh.*, PG 123, col. 1141)', in S. Morlet (ed.), *Le traité de Porphyre contre les chrétiens. Un siècle de recherches, nouvelles questions. Actes du colloque international organisé les 8 et 9 septembre 2009 à l'Université de Paris IV-Sorbonne*, Paris: Institut d'Études Augustiniennes (Collection des Études Augustiniennes, Série Antiquité, 190), p. 277–290.

R. Browning (1963), 'The Patriarchal School at Constantinople in the Twelfth Century (part 2)', in *Byzantion*, 33, p. 11–40.

P. Cesaretti & S. Ronchey (2014), *Eustathii Thessalonicensis Exegesis in canonem iambicum pentecostalem*. Recensuerunt indicibusque instruxerunt —, Berlin: de Gruyter (Supplementa byzantina, Texte und Untersuchungen, 10).

R. Ceulemans, E. De Ridder, K. Levrie & P. Van Deun (2013), 'Sur le mensonge, l'âme et les faux prophètes : la Lettre Ψ du *Florilège Coislin*', in *Byzantion*, 83, p. 49–82.

R. Ceulemans, I. De Vos, E. Gielen & P. Van Deun (2011), 'La continuation de l'exploration du *Florilegium Coislinianum* : la Lettre Èta', in *Byzantion*, 81, p. 74–126.

R. Ceulemans, Ch. Gazzini, J. P. Maksimczuk & P. Van Deun (2017), 'La Lettre Rhô du *Florilège Coislin*', in *Byzantion*, 87, p. 143–158.

R. Ceulemans, P. Van Deun & F. A. Wildenboer (2014), 'Questions sur les deux arbres du paradis : la Lettre Ξ du *Florilège Coislin*', in *Byzantion*, 84, p. 49–79.

R. Ceulemans, P. Van Deun & S. Van Pee (2016), 'La vision des quatre bêtes, la *Theotokos*, les douze trônes et d'autres thèmes : la Lettre Θ du *Florilège Coislin*', in *Byzantion*, 86, p. 91–128.

J. H. Declerck (2002), *Eustathii Antiocheni, patris Nicaeni, Opera quae supersunt omnia*. Edidit —, Turnhout: Brepols; Leuven: University Press (Corpus Christianorum, Series Graeca, 51).

M. De Groote (2015), 'The Soterios Project Revisited: Status Quaestionis and the Future Edition', in *Byzantinische Zeitschrift*, 108, p. 63–78.

R. Devreesse (1950), *Codices Vaticani graeci. Tomus III. Codices 604–866*, Vatican: Bibliotheca Vaticana (Bibliothecae Apostolicae Vaticanae codices manu scripti recensiti).

— (1955), *Les manuscrits grecs de l'Italie méridionale (histoire, classement, paléographie)*, Vatican: Biblioteca Apostolica Vaticana (Studi e testi, 183) [repr. 1968].

E. Dickey (2007), *Ancient Greek Scholarship. A Guide to Finding, Reading, and Understanding Scholia, Commentaries, Lexica and Grammatical Treatises, from Their Beginnings to the Byzantine Period*, Oxford: University Press (American Philological Association, Classical Resources Series).

A. Diller (1952), *The Tradition of the Minor Greek Geographers*, Oxford: American Philological Association (Philological Monographs Published by the American Philological Association, 14).

S. Eustratiadis (1931), 'Συμεὼν Λογοθέτης ὁ Μεταφραστής', in Ἐπετηρὶς Ἑταιρείας Βυζαντινῶν Σπουδῶν, 8, p. 47–65.

— & Arcadius Vatopedinus (1924), Κατάλογος τῶν ἐν τῇ Ἱερᾷ Μονῇ Βατοπεδίου ἀποκειμένων κωδίκων, Paris: Champion (Ἁγιορειτικὴ Βιβλιοθήκη, 1) [repr. *Catalogue of the Greek Manuscripts in the Library of the Monastery of Vatopedi on Mt. Athos*, Cambridge, MA: Harvard University Press (Harvard Theological Studies, 11), 1969].

T. Fernández (2011), 'Cosmas Vestitor's Ascetic-Physiological Fragment (*CPG* 8163)', in *Byzantinische Zeitschrift*, 104, p. 633–640.

— (2018), *Florilegium Coislinianum A*. Edidit —, Turnhout: Brepols (Corpus Christianorum, Series Graeca, 66).

— (2019), 'El florilegio de los mss. *F H* en la letra Alfa del *Florilegio Coisliniano*', in B. Roosen & P. Van Deun (eds), *The Literary Legacy of Byzantium. Editions, Translations, and Studies in Honour of J. A. Munitiz SJ*, Turnhout: Brepols (Studies in Byzantine History and Civilization, 15), p. 213–237.

— & J. P. Maksimczuk (2019), 'On the Oldest Witnesses of the Second Recension of the Florilegium Coislinianum: Par. gr. 924 model of Athen., EBE 464 (with an Appendix on the Athon., Laura K 113)', in *Byzantinoslavica*, 77, p. 61–75.

Ch. Furrer-Pilliod (2000), Ὅροι καὶ ὑπογραφαί. *Collections alphabétiques de définitions profanes et sacrées*, Vatican: Biblioteca Apostolica Vaticana (Studi e testi, 395).

P. Gautier (1963), 'L'épiscopat de Théophylacte Héphaistos archevêque de Bulgarie. Notes chronologiques et biographiques', in *Revue des Études Byzantines*, 21, p. 159–178.

— (1980), *Théophylacte d'Achrida, Discours, traités, poésies*. Introduction, texte, traduction et notes par —, Thessaloniki: Association de Recherches Byzantines (Corpus Fontium Historiae Byzantinae, 16.1).

— (1986), *Théophylacte d'Achrida, Lettres*. Introduction, texte, traduction et notes par —, Thessaloniki: Association de Recherches Byzantines (Corpus Fontium Historiae Byzantinae, 16.2).

P. Géhin (2013), 'Les collections de *kephalaia* monastiques : naissance et succès d'un genre entre création originale, plagiat et florilège', in A. Rigo, P. Ermilov & M. Trizio (eds), *Theologica minora. The Minor Genres of Byzantine Theological Literature*, Turnhout: Brepols (Studies in Byzantine History and Civilization, 8), p. 1–50.

C. Giannelli (1950), *Codices Vaticani graeci. Codices 1485–1683*, Vatican: In Bybliotheca Vaticana (Bibliothecae Apostolicae Vaticanae codices manu scripti recensiti).

R. Goulet (2010), 'Cinq nouveaux fragments nominaux du traité de Porphyre "Contre les chrétiens"', in *Vigiliae Christianae*, 64, p. 140–159.

I. Hausherr (1953), 'Centuries', in *Dictionnaire de spiritualité : ascétique et mystique, doctrine et histoire*, 2, col. 416–418.

R. C. Hill (†) (2010), 'Severian of Gabala, Homilies on Creation and Fall, Translated with an Introduction and Notes by —', in M. Glerup (ed.), *Commentaries on Genesis 1–3*, Downers Grove, IL: InterVarsity Press (Ancient Christian Texts), p. 1–93.

W. Hörandner (2012), 'Pseudo-Gregorios Korinthios, *Über die vier Teile der perfekten Rede*', in *Medioevo Greco*, 12, p. 87–131.

H. Hunger (1978), *Die hochsprachliche profane Literatur der Byzantiner*, Munich: Beck (Handbuch der Altertumswissenschaft, 12.5.1–2), 2 vols.

A. Jacob (2006), 'La réception de la littérature byzantine dans l'Italie méridionale après la conquête normande. Les exemples de Théophylacte de Bulgarie et de Michel Psellos', in A. Jacob, J.-M. Martin & Gh. Noyé (eds), *Histoire et culture dans l'Italie byzantine. Acquis et nouvelles recherches*, Rome: École française de Rome (Collection de l'École française de Rome, 363), p. 21–67.

S. Kim (2019), 'Un passage inédit du *De mundi creatione* (*CPG* 4194) de Sévérien de Gabala conservé dans sa version géorgienne', in J. Leemans, G. Roskam & J. Segers (eds), *John Chrysostom and Severian of Gabala: Homilists, Exegetes and Theologians*, Leuven: Peeters (Bibliothèque de Byzantion, 20; Orientalia Lovaniensia Analecta, 282), p. 87–101.

A. D. Kominis (1960a), Γρηγόριος Πάρδος μητροπολίτης Κορίνθου καὶ τὸ ἔργον αὐτοῦ, Rome – Athens: Σπουδαστήριον Βυζαντινῶν καὶ Νεοελληνικῶν Σπουδῶν τοῦ Πανεπιστημίου τῆς Ρώμης (Βυζαντινὰ καὶ νεοελληνικὰ κείμενα καὶ μελέται, 2).

— (1960b), 'Γρηγορίου τοῦ Κορινθίου ἐξηγήσεις εἰς τοὺς ἱερoὺς λειτουργικοὺς κανόνας Ἰωάννου τοῦ Δαμασκηνοῦ καὶ Κοσμᾶ τοῦ Μελῳδοῦ', in F. Dölger & H.-G. Beck (eds), *Akten des XI. internationalen Byzantinistenkongress, München 1958*, Munich: Beck, p. 248–253.

M. Kouroupou & P. Géhin (2008), *Catalogue des manuscrits conservés dans la Bibliothèque du Patriarcat Œcuménique. Les manuscrits du monastère de la Panaghia de Chalki*, Turnhout: Brepols, 2 vols.

S. P. Lambros (1895–1900), Κατάλογος τῶν ἐν ταῖς βιβλιοθήκαις τοῦ Ἁγίου Ὄρους ἑλληνικῶν κωδίκων. *Catalogue of the Greek Manuscripts on Mount Athos*, Cambridge: University Press, 2 vols.

P. Lemerle (1977), 'La diataxis de Michel Attaliate (mars 1077)', in —, *Cinq études sur le XIᵉ siècle byzantin*, Paris: CNRS (Le monde byzantin), p. 65–112.

S. Lucà (2007), 'Dalle collezioni manoscritte di Spagna: libri originari o provenienti dall'Italia greca medievale', in *Rivista di studi bizantini e neoellenici*, 44, p. 39–96.

J. P. Maksimczuk (2017), 'The Textual Tradition of the Florilegium Hierosolymitanum (and its Relations with the Florilegium Coislinianum)', in *Jahrbuch der Österreichischen Byzantinistik* 67, p. 81–101.

— (2018a), 'The Anthology of *Parisinus gr.* 852 and *Vatopediou* 36 and its Relation to the *Florilegium Coislinianum*', in *Revue des Études Byzantines*, 76, p. 99–136.

— (2018b), *Books Δ–Z of the Florilegium Coislinianum* (unpublished doctoral thesis, KU Leuven).

—, P. Van Deun & M. Venetskov (2019), 'La Lettre Upsilon du *Florilège Coislin*', in *Byzantion*, 89, p. 359–395.

D. Marcotte (2000), *Géographes grecs. Tome I. Introduction générale. Ps.-Scymnos : Circuit de la Terre*. Texte établi et traduit par —, Paris: Les Belles Lettres (Collection des Universités de France).

P. Mavrommatides (1998), 'Unbekannte Handschriften des Kommentars von Gregorios Pardos zum *Canon Pentecostalis* von [Iohannes Damaskenos]', in I. Vassis, G. S. Henrich & D. R. Reinsch (eds), *Lesarten. Festschrift für Athanasios Kambylis zum 70. Geburtstag dargebracht von Schülern, Kollegen und Freunden*, Berlin: de Gruyter, p. 110–118.

H. Meyer & R. Suntrup (1987), *Lexikon der mittelalterlichen Zahlenbedeutungen*, Munich: Fink (Münstersche Mittelalter-Schriften, 56).

E. Mioni (1967), *Bibliothecae Divi Marci Venetiarum codices graeci manuscripti. Volumen I: Codices in classes a prima usque ad quintam inclusi. Pars prior: Classis I – classis II, codd. 1–120*, Rome: Istituto poligrafico e zecca dello stato (Ministero per i beni culturali e ambientali, Indici e Cataloghi, Nuova Serie, 6).

P. Molinié (2019), 'Un exemple d'actualisation exégétique : le motif du soir et du matin dans les homélies de Sévérien sur la *Genèse* (*CPG* 4194)', in J. Leemans, G. Roskam & J. Segers (eds), *John Chrysostom and Severian of Gabala: Homilists, Exegetes and Theologians*, Leuven: Peeters (Bibliothèque de Byzantion, 20; Orientalia Lovaniensia Analecta, 282), p. 137–166.

F. Montana (1995), *Gregorio di Corinto, Esegesi al canone giambico per la Pentecoste attribuito a Giovanni Damasceno.* Introduzione, edizione critica, traduzione a cura di —, Pisa: Giardini (Biblioteca di studi antichi, 76).

M. Morani (1981), *La tradizione manoscritta del "De natura hominis" di Nemesio*, Milan: Vita e Pensiero (Scienze filologiche e letteratura, 18).

— (1987), *Nemesii Emeseni De natura hominis.* Edidit —, Leipzig: Teubner (Bibliotheca Scriptorum Graecorum et Romanorum Teubneriana).

K. Müller (1855), *Geographi Graeci minores. Volumen primum.* E codicibus recognovit, prolegomenis annotatione indicibus instruxit, tabulis aeri incisis illustravit —, Paris: Didot [repr. Hildesheim: Olms, 1965].

M. Mullett (1984), 'The "Disgrace" of the Ex-Basilissa Maria', in *Byzantinoslavica*, 45, p. 202–211.

J. Noret (2014), 'L'accentuation byzantine : en quoi et pourquoi elle diffère de l'accentuation "savante" actuelle, parfois absurde', in M. Hinterberger (ed.), *The Language of Byzantine Learned Literature*, Turnhout: Brepols (Studies in Byzantine History and Civilization, 9), p. 96–146.

A. Papadopoulos-Kerameus (1899), 'Βυζαντινὰ Ἀνάλεκτα', in *Byzantinische Zeitschrift*, 8, p. 66–81.

F. Petit (1986), *Catenae Graecae in Genesim et in Exodum. II. Collectio Coisliniana in Genesim*, edita a —, Turnhout: Brepols; Leuven, University Press (Corpus Christianorum, Series Graeca, 15).

— (1991–1996), *La chaîne sur la Genèse. Édition intégrale.* Texte établi par —, Leuven: Peeters (Traditio Exegetica Graeca, 1–4), 4 vols.

A. Pietersma & B. G. Wright (eds, 2007), *A New English Translation of the Septuagint and the Other Greek Translations Traditionally Included Under That Title*, New York – Oxford: University Press.

W. K. Reischl (1848), *S. Patris nostri Cyrilli Hierosolymorum archiepiscopi opera quae supersunt omnia. Volumen I.* Recensuit —, Munich: Lentner [repr. Hildesheim: Olms, 1967].

M. Richard (1962), 'Florilèges spirituels grecs', in *Dictionnaire de spiritualité : ascétique et mystique, doctrine et histoire*, 5, col. 475–512 [repr. *Opera minora*, I, Turnhout: Brepols; Leuven: University Press, 1976, No. 1].

— (†) & J. A. Munitiz (2006), *Anastasii Sinaitae Quaestiones et responsiones.* Ediderunt —, Turnhout: Brepols; Leuven: University Press (Corpus Christianorum, Series Graeca, 59).

R. Riedinger (1989), *Pseudo-Kaisarios, Die Erotapokriseis*. Erstmals vollständig herausgegeben von —, Berlin: Akademie-Verlag (Die griechischen christlichen Schriftsteller der ersten Jahrhunderte).

R. H. Robins (1993), *The Byzantine Grammarians. Their Place in History*, Berlin – New York: Mouton de Gruyter (Trends in Linguistics, Studies and Monographs, 70).

F. Ronconi (2007), *I manoscritti greci miscellanei. Ricerche su esemplari dei secoli IX–XII*, Spoleto: Centro Italiano di studi sull'alto medioevo (Testi, Studi, Strumenti, 21).

E. W. Saunders (1957), 'Theophylact of Bulgaria as Writer and Biblical Interpreter', in *Biblical Research*, 2, p. 31–44.

L. Sels & S. Van Pee (2019), 'The Slavonic Tradition of Severian of Gabala's *De mundi creatione orationes* (*CPG* 4194)', in J. Leemans, G. Roskam & J. Segers (eds), *John Chrysostom and Severian of Gabala: Homilists, Exegetes and Theologians*, Leuven: Peeters (Bibliothèque de Byzantion, 20; Orientalia Lovaniensia Analecta, 282), p. 225–244.

P. Sotiroudis (1998), Ἱερὰ Μονὴ Ἰβήρων. Κατάλογος ἑλληνικῶν χειρογραφῶν. Τόμος Α' (1–100), Holy Mountain: Ἱερὰ Μονὴ Ἰβήρων.

Spyridon Lauriotis & S. Eustratiadis (1925), Κατάλογος τῶν κωδίκων τῆς Μεγίστης Λαύρας (τῆς ἐν Ἁγίῳ Ὄρει). Ἐπλουτίσθη καὶ διὰ τῶν ἐν τέλει δύο παραρτημάτων καὶ τῶν ἀναγκαιούντων εὑρετηρίων πινάκων. *Catalogue of the Greek Manuscripts in the Library of the Laura on Mount Athos, with Notices from other Libraries*, Cambridge, MA: Harvard University Press; Paris: Champion (Harvard Theological Studies, 12).

V. Tiftixoglu (1974), 'Digenes, das "Sophrosyne"-Gedicht des Meliteniotes und der byzantinische Fünfzehnsilber', in *Byzantinische Zeitschrift*, 67, p. 1–63.

K.-H. Uthemann (1981), *Anastasii Sinaitae Viae dux*. Edidit —, Turnhout: Brepols; Leuven: University Press (Corpus Christianorum, Series Graeca, 8).

— (2000), 'Severian von Gabala in Florilegien zum Bilderkult', in *Orientalia Christiana Periodica*, 66, p. 5–47 [repr. *Studien zu Anastasios Sinaites. Mit einem Anhang zu Anastasios I. von Antiochien*, Berlin: de Gruyter, 2017 (Texte und Untersuchungen zur Geschichte der altchristlichen Literatur, 174), p. 138–174].

— (2015), *Anastasios Sinaites. Byzantinisches Christentum in den ersten Jahrzehnten unter arabischer Herrschaft*, Berlin: de Gruyter (Arbeiten zur Kirchengeschichte, 125.1–2), 2 vols.

P. Van Deun (2015), 'Lire en extraits à Byzance : le *Florilegium Coislinianum* et ses sections païennes', in S. Morlet (ed.), *Lire en extraits. Lecture et production des textes de l'Antiquité à la fin du Moyen Âge*, Paris: PUPS (Cultures et civilisations médiévales, 63), p. 415–423.

— (2017), 'Un extrait pseudo-chrysostomien sur l'intempérance et la lèpre (*CPG* 4878)', in F. P. Barone, C. Macé & P. Ubierna (eds), *Philologie, herméneutique et histoire des textes entre Orient et Occident. Mélanges en hommage à S. J. Voicu*, Turnhout: Brepols (Instrumenta Patristica et Mediaevalia, 73), p. 1037–1052.

S. J. Voicu (2006), 'Il nome cancellato: la trasmissione delle omelie di Severiano di Gabala', in *Revue d'histoire des textes*, n.s. 1, p. 317–333.

— (2015a), 'Roma e l'ultimo manoscritto del corpus omiletico di Severiano di Gabala', in C. Carbonetti, S. Lucà & M. Signorini (eds), *Roma e il suo territorio nel medioevo. Le fonti scritte fra tradizione e innovazione. Atti del Convegno internazionale di studio dell'Associazione italiana dei Paleografi e Diplomatisti (Roma, 25–29 ottobre 2012)*, Spoleto: Fondazione Centro Italiano per lo Studio dell'Alto Medioevo (Studi e ricerche, 6), p. 73–87.

— (2015b), 'Due antiocheni periferici: le *Quaestiones et responsiones ad orthodoxos* (CPG 6285) e Severiano di Gabala', in *Augustinianum*, 55, p. 543–557.

L. G. Westerink (1992), *Michaelis Pselli Poemata*. Recensuit —, Stuttgart – Leipzig: Teubner (Bibliotheca Scriptorum Graecorum et Romanorum Teubneriana).

W. Wolska-Conus (1973), *Cosmas Indicopleustès, Topographie chrétienne. Tome III (Livres VI–XII. Index)*. Introduction, texte critique, illustration, traduction et notes par —, Paris: Cerf (Sources Chrétiennes, 197).

N. Wilson (1996), *Scholars of Byzantium. Revised Edition*, London: Duckworth; Cambridge, MA: The Medieval Academy of America.

J. Zellinger (1916), *Die Genesishomilien des Bischofs Severian von Gabala*, Münster: Aschendorff (Alttestamentliche Abhandlungen, 7.1).

Abstract

In the first part of this article I argue that MS B 43 of the Great Lavra monastery on Mount Athos is the unique witness of an untitled anthology of one hundred chapters (fol. 153^r–196^v). It was in all likelihood compiled ad hoc by the anonymous copyist in the twelfth century. The florilegium opens and closes with chapters on the creation of the world and on death, but is as a whole rather chaotic. It is composed of excerpts from (mostly Christian) authors from the second to the late eleventh century; some of them were accessed through earlier anthologies. A number of excerpts are introduced in the form of questions and answers. In the second part of the article, I offer an edition with English translation of the excerpts that were taken from Severian of Gabala's *Homilies on the Hexaëmeron* and which occur in the opening section of the florilegium (on cosmological topics). Most of the ten fragments in question remain close to Severian's text. Occasional parallels with the catena tradition and other indirect witnesses of the *Homilies* might imply that the anonymous anthologist did not access Severian's original text but a reduced version or compilation.

PETER VAN DEUN

LE *DE OECONOMIA DEI* DE NIL DOXAPATRÈS. QUELQUES OBSERVATIONS SUR LE GENRE LITTÉRAIRE DE L'ŒUVRE ET SUR SA TRANSMISSION MANUSCRITE

Depuis des années, mon équipe louvaniste a travaillé sur des florilèges byzantins en général et sur une anthologie en particulier, qui circule sous le titre de *De oeconomia Dei* et est attribuée à un certain Nil Doxapatrès. À Leuven, on a préparé un bon nombre de publications sur ce sujet, parmi lesquelles on relèvera tout particulièrement l'édition critique du premier livre du florilège, préparée grâce à deux thèses de doctorat[1], ainsi que plusieurs études de détail[2]. On notera encore que le projet sur Doxapatrès s'est parfaitement rapproché d'un programme international lancé à l'École française de Rome, intitulé 'La mémoire des Pères grecs (V[e]–XVe siècles)', et dirigé par Camille Rouxpetel, Annick Peters-Custot et Bernadette Cabouret ; ce programme était couronné d'un colloque, qui a eu lieu à Rome du 13 au 15 octobre 2016, et d'un volume collectif paru en 2020, sous le titre *La réception des Pères grecs et orientaux en Italie au Moyen Âge (V[e]–XVe siècle)*[3].

Résumons ce qu'on sait sur ce dossier. L'identité du compilateur ou de l'auteur de cette œuvre constitue un premier problème, assez difficile[4]. Parmi les chercheurs, il y a toutefois un consentement très large pour dire que l'anthologie revient à Nil

---

[1] Neirynck 2014a ; De Vos 2010.

[2] De Vos 2011 ; Neirynck 2009 ; 2010 ; 2011 ; 2012 ; 2014b ; Van Deun 2020 et Van Deun sous presse.

[3] Cabouret e.a. 2020.

[4] L'état de la question le plus récent sur l'auteur et son œuvre se lit dans Neirynck 2014a, p. IX–XXI, ainsi que dans Van Deun 2020.

Questioning the World, Greek Patristic and Byzantine Question-and-Answer Literature, ed. by Bram Demulder and Peter Van Deun, Turnhout, 2021 (*LECTIO*, 11), pp. 423-441 © BREPOLS PUBLISHERS DOI 10.1484/M.LECTIO-EB.5.121513

Doxapatrès, qui ne peut pas être confondu avec un autre membre de la même famille, Jean Doxapatrès, ce rhéteur bien connu du XIᵉ siècle qui a écrit des commentaires sur Aphthonius et Hermogène. Il est possible que le nom de baptême de Nil ait été Nicolas et qu'à un certain moment, il ait embrassé la vie monastique, en prenant un nouveau nom, Nil. Mais il n'y a pas d'arguments vraiment probants pour étayer cette thèse. Malheureusement, la même constatation s'impose pour l'hypothèse que Nil aurait été appelé aux fonctions les plus hautes dans l'administration patriarcale à Constantinople (diacre de Sainte Sophie, nomophylax, notaire et πρωτόεδρος τῶν πρωτοσυγκέλλων), et, tombé en disgrâce, aurait pris la fuite en Sicile.

La seule chose qu'on puisse en dire de certain, est le fait que Nil fut un moine, lié très clairement à la Sicile et à la ville de Palerme en particulier. En effet, on sait qu'il a écrit la Τάξις τῶν πατριαρχικῶν θρόνων, un ouvrage de géographie ecclésiastique achevé à Palerme entre le 1ᵉʳ septembre 1142 et le 31ᵉ août 1143, sur la demande explicite du roi normand Roger II de Sicile (1095–1154)[5] ; le titre de l'œuvre nous apprend que Nil Doxapatrès fut effectivement un moine. À cette information très précieuse, on adjoindra un document de vente daté entre septembre et décembre 1146, pour lequel un des signataires fut Nil Doxapatrès ; il s'agit de la vente de quelques maisons à l'église de Santa Maria dell'Ammiraglio, dite la Martorana, à Palerme[6]. Ce document nous permet de conclure que Nil faisait partie de l'entourage de l'amiral Georges d'Antioche, ce personnage-clef à la cour du roi Roger II[7].

Passons maintenant au *De oeconomia Dei*. Il y a plusieurs éléments permettant de conclure que cette œuvre est liée à la Sicile et revient à Nil Doxapatrès. Tout d'abord, on notera que trois des cinq témoins de l'ouvrage proviennent de la Sicile, et, plus

---

[5] Jusqu'ici, on ne dispose pas d'une édition critique de cette œuvre qui est mieux connue sous son nom latin *Notitia patriarchatuum* ; en effet, elle ne peut être consultée que dans les éditions, peu fiables, de la *PG* 132, col. 1083–1114, ou de Parthey 1866. À propos de cet ouvrage, on consultera avec profit Laurent 1937.

[6] Sur ce document, lire Perria 1981, p. 1–24 ; Neirynck 2014a, p. XIV.

[7] C'est à Augusta Acconcia Longo que revient cette conclusion importante ; voir Acconcia Longo 2014, plus particulièrement p. 119–124.

particulièrement, de Messine, et descendent d'un modèle vénérable, perdu aujourd'hui et achevé, lui aussi, à l'archimandritat
de Messine (en 1213), ce qui permet de formuler l'hypothèse que
Messine serait également l'endroit de confection de l'anthologie et que Nil aurait été moine au monastère de Saint-Sauveur
de Messine. De plus, on dispose d'un inventaire de la bibliothèque grecque du monastère de San Salvatore *in lingua phari*
à Messine (siège de l'archimandritat), dressé en 1563 par Francesco Antonio Napoli : là, l'œuvre est mentionnée sous le nom
de Nil Doxapatrès. On a également constaté[8] que, pour quelques
sources citées, le compilateur semble avoir puisé à des familles
italo-grecques du texte-source et plus particulièrement à des
manuscrits copiés à Messine. Finalement – et cela constitue un
élément décisif nous semble-t-il –, on a découvert[9] qu'à l'intérieur d'une citation de Némésius d'Émèse, Nil a inséré, entre
les villes de Rome et d'Alexandrie, le nom de la Sicile, ce qui est
absent du texte de Némésius ; cette insertion se lit dans toutes les
branches de la tradition du *De oeconomia Dei*.

Le *De oeconomia Dei* est une anthologie, d'envergure monu-
mentale, qui était composée jadis de cinq livres, un fait qui ne
nous est connu que par un chapitre du second livre (II, 41)[10] ;
malheureusement, aujourd'hui, seulement deux livres sont conservés. Dans la tradition manuscrite, l'œuvre est attribuée à un
Doxapatrès, sans nommer de prénom. Le titre général qu'on lit
dans tous les témoins manuscrits (Περὶ τῆς ἐξ ἀρχῆς καὶ μέχρι
τέλους οἰκονομίας τοῦ Θεοῦ εἰς τὸν ἄνθρωπον ἱστορία ἐπωφελής, καὶ
περὶ τῆς χριστιανικῆς πολιτείας ὅπως συνέστη, καὶ κατὰ πάντων τῶν
αἱρετικῶν), montre que l'anthologie est centrée sur la bienveil-
lance de Dieu envers les hommes ; de là le titre sous lequel elle
est connue : *De oeconomia Dei*. Le premier livre insiste longuement sur la création et sur l'état original du premier Adam, tandis
que le deuxième livre se concentre sur le nouvel Adam, le Christ,
et sur son travail rédempteur. De manière exemplaire, le compi-

---

[8] Voir De Vos 2010, p. 9–16, ainsi que Neirynck 2014a, p. xvi–xvii.

[9] Pour cette découverte très importante, on consultera Caruso 1986–1987,
p. 250–283, plus particulièrement p. 271 ; De Vos 2010, p. 16 et 234 (où on lira
le texte du passage en question) ; Neirynck 2014a, p. xv–xvi.

[10] On trouve le texte de ce chapitre dans Neirynck 2014a, p. xxiv–xxv.

lateur y montre sa profonde connaissance de la théologie et de la littérature patristique et byzantine ; en effet, pour une grande partie, l'œuvre enchaîne des extraits d'un bon nombre d'auteurs ; on relèvera ici, à titre d'exemples, l'omniprésent *De opificio hominis* de Grégoire de Nysse, le *De oratione dominica* du même auteur, les *Homiliae in Hexaemeron* de Sévérien de Gabala, le *Commentaire sur la Genèse* de Jean Chrysostome, le *De natura hominis* de Némésius d'Émèse, les *Quaestiones ad Thalassium* de Maxime le Confesseur et l'*Expositio fidei* de Jean Damascène ; à ces champions de la littérature patristique, on ajoutera des extraits tirés d'ouvrages de Théophylacte de Bulgarie, de Michel Psellus et de Nicétas d'Héraclée, l'auteur le plus récent cité dans le florilège (fin du XIe, début du XIIe siècle)[11].

La tradition manuscrite du *De oeconomia Dei* n'est pas abondante ; en effet, jusqu'ici, on n'en connaissait que cinq témoins directs que nous présenterons très brièvement[12] : le *Parisinus gr. 1277*, probablement de la seconde moitié du XIIIe siècle, qui contient l'intégralité du livre I, ainsi qu'une partie du deuxième livre (sigle *P*) ; le *Vaticanus gr. 696*, du XIIe siècle, achevé à Messine en 'style de Reggio' (sigle *R*) ; le *Vaticanus gr. 1426*, manuscrit de papier qui revient au scribe sicilien Ἰωακεὶμ Τούμβουτα, dont on connaît un manuscrit daté de l'année 1534 et qui, très probablement, fut moine au monastère de San Salvatore de Messine (sigle *V*)[13] ; le *Matritensis gr. 4591*, manuscrit frère de *V*, achevé par Georges Basilikos vers 1547, dans l'archimandritat de Messine (sigle *M*)[14] ; finalement le *Parisinus gr. 1945*, apographe du manuscrit *R*, de la main du scribe Francesco Gozzadino, scriptor à la Vaticane, vers le milieu du XVIe siècle (sigle *G*).

---

[11] Pour un bon nombre des chapitres du florilège, Stefaan Neyrinck a relevé des lieux parallèles avec les *Annales* et les *Quaestiones in sacram Scripturam* de Michel Glykas, contemporain de Nil Doxapatrès ; à ce propos, lire surtout Neirynck 2010, p. XLV–XLVII ; 2014b, p. 181–182 ; voir également, ci-dessous, n. 22.

[12] On trouvera une discussion, très détaillée, de la tradition manuscrite et des liens qui unissent tous ces codex, dans les thèses de De Vos 2010, p. 49–123, et de Neirynck 2014a, p. XLIX–XCI.

[13] Comme on l'a déjà relevé ci-dessus, ce manuscrit est copié d'un modèle perdu aujourd'hui, achevé le 2 août 1213 au monastère de San Salvatore de Messine.

[14] Également copié sur le mystérieux *Messanensis*, perdu aujourd'hui.

À cette tradition manuscrite directe, qui s'avère être très pauvre, on ajoutera le cas spécial du *Vaticanus gr. 1768*, œuvre de Nicéphore Chartophylax, scribe bien connu, higoumène du monastère S. Jean de Patmos et métropolite de Laodicée ; c'est un des manuscrits qu'Alvise Lollino (circa 1552–1625), futur évêque de Belluno, a commandités entre les années 1583 et 1585, sur base de manuscrits de Patmos (sigle *L*). Le *Vaticanus* ne contient pas l'intégralité du florilège, mais seulement des parties du texte, en respectant, pour la plus grande partie, l'ordre du texte transmis dans la tradition directe ; il s'agit donc d'un épitomé fait sur base d'un manuscrit de Patmos, qui, à son tour, est apparenté au manuscrit *P* que nous avons cité ci-dessus.

Les éditeurs du premier livre de l'anthologie ont visualisé les relations qui unissent tous ces témoins, de la manière suivante[15] :

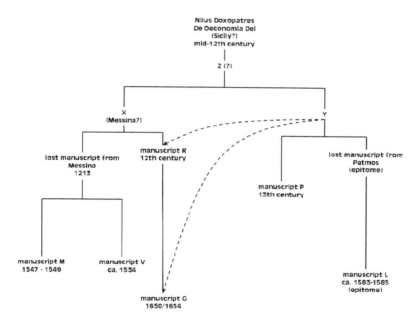

En appendice, on trouvera la discussion d'un nouveau témoin du texte, partiel il est vrai, que nous avons découvert tout récemment.

---

[15] On reprend ici le *stemma codicum* tel qu'on le trouve dans De Vos 2010, p. 103.

Puisque le premier livre de l'œuvre se concentre sur la création du monde, et, plus particulièrement, sur la création de l'homme, ainsi que sur l'état originel et la chute du premier Adam, il n'y a rien d'étonnant à ce que cette partie du florilège suive de tout près le texte du livre de la Genèse[16]. Ainsi, les chapitres 1 à 30 sont centrés sur le verset 7 du deuxième chapitre de la Genèse et plus particulièrement sur le thème de l'insufflation de l'esprit (Gen. 2. 7 : καὶ ἔπλασεν ὁ Θεὸς τὸν ἄνθρωπον χοῦν ἀπὸ τῆς γῆς καὶ ἐνεφύσησεν εἰς τὸ πρόσωπον αὐτοῦ πνοὴν ζωῆς, καὶ ἐγένετο ὁ ἄνθρωπος εἰς ψυχὴν ζῶσαν). Une section très large (chapitres 31–87) traite longuement de l'arbre de la connaissance du bien et du mal, ainsi que de l'arbre de vie, tels qu'on les trouve dans Gen. 2. 9 (καὶ ἐξανέτειλεν ὁ Θεὸς ἔτι ἐκ τῆς γῆς πᾶν ξύλον ὡραῖον εἰς ὅρασιν καὶ καλὸν εἰς βρῶσιν καὶ τὸ ξύλον τῆς ζωῆς ἐν μέσῳ τῷ παραδείσῳ καὶ τὸ ξύλον τοῦ εἰδέναι γνωστὸν καλοῦ καὶ πονηροῦ) et 2. 16–17 (καὶ ἐνετείλατο κύριος ὁ Θεὸς τῷ Ἀδὰμ λέγων· Ἀπὸ παντὸς ξύλου τοῦ ἐν τῷ παραδείσῳ βρώσει φάγῃ, ἀπὸ δὲ τοῦ ξύλου τοῦ γινώσκειν καλὸν καὶ πονηρόν, οὐ φάγεσθε ἀπ'αὐτοῦ· ᾗ δ'ἂν ἡμέρᾳ φάγητε ἀπ'αὐτοῦ, θανάτῳ ἀποθανεῖσθε). Le péché, la chute et la punition de l'homme et de la femme, ainsi que du serpent constituent les thèmes majeurs des chapitres 88–163, donnant ainsi l'exégèse de Gen. 3. 1–21, une place spéciale étant réservée à Dieu qui habille Adam et Eve de vêtements de peaux (Gen. 3. 21 : Καὶ ἐποίησεν κύριος ὁ Θεὸς τῷ Ἀδὰμ καὶ τῇ γυναικὶ αὐτοῦ χιτῶνας δερματίνους καὶ ἐνέδυσεν αὐτούς). Inspirée par ce même passage (Gen. 3. 21), suit une longue partie (chapitres 164–254) contemplant la condition humaine, physique et spirituelle, affectée par le péché et la chute. Tout à la fin du premier livre (chapitres 255–263), Nil revient au commentaire proprement dit de la Genèse, plus particulièrement de Gen. 3. 22–24, racontant l'histoire de l'expulsion du Paradis (καὶ εἶπεν ὁ Θεός· Ἰδοὺ Ἀδὰμ γέγονεν ὡς εἷς ἐξ ἡμῶν τοῦ γινώσκειν καλὸν καὶ πονηρόν, καὶ νῦν μήποτε ἐκτείνῃ τὴν χεῖρα καὶ λάβῃ τοῦ ξύλου τῆς ζωῆς καὶ φάγῃ καὶ ζήσεται εἰς τὸν αἰῶνα. Καὶ ἐξαπέστειλεν αὐτὸν κύριος ὁ Θεὸς ἐκ τοῦ παραδείσου τῆς τρυφῆς ἐργάζεσθαι τὴν γῆν, ἐξ ἧς ἐλήμφθη. Καὶ ἐξέβαλεν τὸν Ἀδὰμ καὶ κατῴκισεν αὐτὸν ἀπέναντι τοῦ

---

[16] Ce paragraphe résume les belles pages que Stefaan Neirynck a consacrées à ce sujet, principalement dans Neirynck 2014a, p. XXVI–XXVII et XXIX–XXXVII.

παραδείσου τῆς τρυφῆς καὶ ἔταξεν τὰ Χερουβὶμ καὶ τὴν φλογίνην ῥομφαίαν τὴν στρεφομένην φυλάσσειν τὴν ὁδὸν τοῦ ξύλου τῆς ζωῆς).

Évidemment, on connaît bien les grands commentaires sur la Genèse et, plus particulièrement, sur le récit de la création des six jours (Hexaéméron) ; on ne citera ici que les *Homiliae in Hexaemeron* de Basile de Césarée, le *De opificio hominis* de Grégoire de Nysse, les *Homiliae in Genesim* de Jean Chrysostome, les *Commentaires sur l'Hexaéméron* de Sévérien de Gabala et d'Anastase le Sinaïte, l'*In Hexaemeron*, en vers, de Georges de Pisidie, et les différentes chaînes sur la Genèse et sur l'Octateuque. Après l'âge patristique, de telles œuvres de grande envergure ont disparu[17], mais cela n'empêche pas que des développements exégétiques, plus modestes, se cachent dans un bon nombre de collections et de florilèges byzantins. L'ouvrage de Nil Doxapatrès en est un bon exemple, nous semble-t-il.

Abordons maintenant la question à quel genre littéraire le *De oeconomia Dei* appartient[18]. À première vue, la réponse à cette question semble être assez claire : il s'agit ici d'un florilège typiquement byzantin, qui, en citant un nombre inouï d'extraits tirés de Pères de l'Église et de théologiens byzantins, joue un rôle important dans la transmission du savoir du passé. Mais, cette première impression est troublée par le fait qu'un nombre de chapitres, assez élevé, ont résisté à toute identification et ont toutes les chances d'être sortis de la plume de Nil Doxapatrès, ce qui donne un cachet original à l'œuvre, bien qu'il s'agisse principalement d'une anthologie.

Concentrons-nous de nouveau sur les 263 chapitres du premier livre, pour lequel on dispose d'un texte critique fiable ; le matériel y est structuré de façons différentes.

Une manière importante d'organiser l'anthologie a été d'introduire le contenu des chapitres par le mot περί suivi d'un génitif. Dans la compilation de Nil, les exemples abondent (à peu pres un quart de tous les chapitres) ; citons, à titre d'exemples, les cas suivants qui donneront une bonne impression de la grande diversité des sujets traités : Περὶ τῆς ἑνώσεως τῆς ψυχῆς

---

[17] À ce propos, on lira par exemple Gouillard 1973.

[18] Nous élaborons ce que S. Neirynck a écrit à ce propos : Neirynck 2011, p. 262–268.

καὶ τοῦ σώματος (chapitre 14) ; Περὶ τοῦ νοός (28) ; Ἔτι περὶ ἐνυπνίων (33) ; Περὶ διαφόρων ὀνείρων (35) ; Περὶ τῶν τριῶν καταστάσεων καὶ προαιρέσεων κατὰ τὸν Ἀπόστολον καὶ τῷ Εὐαγγελίῳ (40) ; Περὶ δοθέντος νόμου τῷ Ἀδάμ (54) ; Περὶ φθορᾶς, διαφθορᾶς καὶ θανάτου (57) ; Περὶ τοῦ παντὸς ξύλου καὶ τοῦ τῆς ζωῆς (60) ; Περὶ τοῦ ξύλου τῆς γνώσεως (61) ; Περὶ τῆς γνώσεως ξύλου ἕτερον (63) ; Περὶ τοῦ περιζώματος τῶν φύλλων τῆς συκῆς (65) ; Ἔτι περὶ τοῦ παραδείσου, τῶν ἐν αὐτῷ ξύλων, καὶ τοῦ παντὸς ξύλου (73) ; Ἔτι περὶ τοῦ ξύλου τῆς γνώσεως, καὶ τῆς ἀπὸ τοῦ Θεοῦ κρύψεως, καὶ τῆς ἀνοίξεως τῶν ὀφθαλμῶν καὶ τῆς αἰσχύνης καὶ τοῦ περιζώματος (84) ; Τοῦ ἁγίου Μαξίμου, περὶ τοῦ ξύλου τῆς ζωῆς καὶ τοῦ τῆς γνώσεως (85) ; Περὶ τοῦ παραδείσου καὶ τῶν ξύλων καὶ τῆς γυμνώσεως, καὶ τῆς τοῦ σώματος καὶ τῆς ψυχῆς πλάσεως τοῦ Ἀδάμ, καὶ τῆς διανοίξεως τῶν ὀφθαλμῶν αὐτῶν, καὶ περὶ τοῦ ὁποῖος ἐπλάσθη, εἴτε θνητὸς εἴτε ἀθάνατος ἐξ ἀρχῆς, καὶ περὶ τοῦ κατ'εἰκόνα καὶ καθ'ὁμοίωσιν, κατὰ τὸν Χρυσόστομον (91) ; Τοῦ Γαβαλῶν Σεβηριανοῦ, περὶ τοῦ ἀνθρώπου καὶ τῆς Ἀδὰμ προσηγορίας (105) ; Περὶ τῆς ἔχθρας τῆς ἀναμέσον τεθείσης ἡμῶν καὶ τοῦ ὄφεως ἤτοι τοῦ διάβολου (130) ; Περὶ τῆς κατὰ τὸ ἄρσεν καὶ θῆλυ διαφορᾶς τῆς εἰκόνος τοῦ Θεοῦ ἤτοι τοῦ ἀνθρώπου (143) ; Περὶ τοῦ ῥήματος τοῦ *Πορεύσῃ ἐπὶ τῷ στήθει* (152) ; Περὶ τῆς τηρήσεως τῆς κεφαλῆς τοῦ νοητοῦ ὄφεως, καὶ τῆς τηρήσεως τοῦ ἀνθρώπου, ἑτέρως (153) ; Περὶ τῆς τοῦ Ἀδὰμ καταδίκης ἱστορικῶς (166) ; Περὶ τῶν δερματίνων χιτώνων ἱστορικῶς (172) ; Περὶ τοῦ ἐγκεφάλου καὶ τοῦ κατ'αὐτὸν ὑμένος (167) ; Περὶ τοῦ πόρου δι'οὗ εἴσεισιν ἡ τροφὴ καὶ τοῦ ἄλλου δι'οὗ τὸ πνεῦμα εἰσέρχεται (175) ; Περὶ τοῦ θυμικοῦ καὶ ἐπιθυμητικοῦ (193) ; Περὶ τοῦ ἐνδιαθέτου λόγου καὶ τοῦ προφορικοῦ (222) ; Περὶ τοῦ δυνάμει καὶ τοῦ ἐνεργείᾳ (239) ; Περὶ τῶν ἀρετῶν καὶ κακιῶν τῶν τριῶν μερῶν τῆς ψυχῆς (240) ; Περὶ τοῦ κατὰ ἄγνοιαν ἀκουσίου (243) ; Περὶ τοῦ αὐτεξουσίου ἤτοι τοῦ ἐφ'ἡμῖν (245) ; Ἔτι περὶ τοῦ Ἀδὰμ (263).

À peu près dans un cas sur six, le sujet du chapitre est simplement introduit par le mot ὅτι ; en voici quelques exemples de cet usage : Ὅτι τὸ σῶμα ἐκ τοῦ ἀλόγου μέρους εἴληπται παρὰ τοῦ Θεοῦ (chapitre 9) ; Ὅτι ἄγνωστος παντελῶς ἡ ἕνωσις τῆς ψυχῆς καὶ τοῦ σώματος (12) ; Ὅτι οὔτε προΰπαρξιν δεῖ λέγειν τῆς ψυχῆς, οὔτε συνύπαρξιν, οὔτε μεθύπαρξιν, ἀλλὰ κατὰ τὸν χρόνον ἅμα καταστῆναι τῆς νοερᾶς ψυχῆς ἔξωθεν ἐπεισκρινομένης (15) ; Ὅτι ἐπὶ μόνης τῆς τοῦ ἀνθρώπου κτίσεως βουλὴ προηγήσατο (21) ; Ὅτι αὐτεξούσιος ἐπλά

σθη ὁ ἄνθρωπος (22) ; Ὅτι γυμνὸς ἐπλάσθη ὁ ἄνθρωπος πανταχόθεν
(25) ; Ὅτι ἁπλῶς καὶ τὸ ὅλον τοῦ ἀνθρώπου σχῆμα ὀργανικὸν κατε-
σκευάσθη διὰ τὸ ἐπιτηδείως πρὸς τὸ λέγειν ἔχειν (27) ; Ὅτι ὁ νοῦς ἐν
πᾶσιν τοῖς σωματικοῖς μέρεσιν ἐπίσης καὶ διὰ πάντων διήει, οὔτε ἐντὸς
κρατούμενος, οὔτε ἐκτὸς περιλαμβανόμενος (30) ; Ὅτι κυρίως ψυχὴ
ἡ λογική, αἱ δὲ ἄλλαι καταχρηστικῶς καὶ κατὰ ὁμωνυμίαν λέγονται
(38) ; Ὅτι οὔτε θνητός, οὐδὲ ἀθάνατος ἐπλάσθη ὁ Ἀδάμ (55) ; Ὅτι
μείζων τοῦ παραδείσου ἡ τῶν οὐρανῶν βασιλεία (56) ; Ὅτι διττὸν τὸ
τῆς γνώσεως ὄνομα (69) ; Ὅτι ἡ εἴδησις διττή (70) ; Ὅτι πάλιν ἡ πρὸ
τῶν πραγμάτων εἴδησις διττή (71) ; Ὅτι κατὰ τὸν Χρυσόστομον ἀθάνατος ἐπλάσθη ὁ ἄνθρωπος (92) ; Ὅτι κατὰ τὸν Χρυσόστομον ἐπι-
γέγονεν ἡ ψυχὴ τῷ σώματι (96) ; Τοῦ αὐτοῦ (= Jean Chrysostome),
ὅτι ἀθάνατοι οἱ πρωτόπλαστοι πρὸ τῆς παραβάσεως (103) ; Ὅτι
προηγήσατο τὸ σῶμα τῆς ψυχῆς, τοῦ αὐτοῦ (= Sévérien de Gabala)
(107) ; Τοῦ αὐτοῦ (= toujours Sévérien de Gabala), ὅτι ὁ Ἀδὰμ ἔξω
τοῦ παραδείσου ἐπλάσθη (109) ; Ὅτι εὐστοχώτερον νοοῦσιν οἱ λέγοντες τὰ τοῦ παραδείσου ξύλα ἢ πάντα νοητά, ἢ τὰ μὲν νοητά, τὰ δὲ
αἰσθητά (115) ; Ὅτι καλῶς τῷ ἁγίῳ Μαξίμῳ καὶ τῷ Νύσσης εἴρηται
μὴ συνεκτίσθαι τὰ πάθη τῷ ἀνθρώπῳ· τῇ μὲν γὰρ κατ᾽εἰκόνα φύσει
τοῦ ἀνθρώπου οὐ συνεκτίσθη, τῷ δὲ Ἀδὰμ τῷ χοϊκῷ ᾧ συνεκτίσθη
καὶ ἡ κατὰ τὸ ἄρρεν καὶ θῆλυ διαφορά, συνεκτίσθη καὶ τὰ πάθη – οὐ
πάθη ἀλλὰ δυνάμεις τῆς ψυχῆς, ἐπιπειθεῖς τῇ λογικῇ δυνάμει καὶ ὑπεί-
κουσαι (144) ; Ὅτι ἄλλο σῶμα καὶ ἄλλο σάρξ (164) ; Ὅτι τρεῖς εἰσιν
αἱ διοικοῦσαι τὸ σῶμα ἡμῶν δυνάμεις (166) ; Ὅτι μόνη ἐστὶν ἀληθινὴ
ψυχὴ καὶ τελεία ἡ ἀνθρωπίνη (187) ; Ὅτι οἱ νοοῦντες τοὺς δερματίνους χιτῶνας τὴν πλάσιν εἶναι τοῦ ὀργανικοῦ τούτου σχήματος τοῦ
ἀνθρωπίνου σώματος, εἰς πολλὰ ἐμπίπτουσιν ἄτοπα (197) ; Ὅτι ἐκ
τοῦ οὕτω νοεῖν κακῶς τοὺς δερματίνους χιτῶνας συνάγεται τὸ δόγμα
τὸ ὠριγενιακὸν τὸ λέγον σφαιροειδῆ μέλλειν ἀνίστασθαι τὰ σώματα
(198) ; Ὅτι ἐκεῖνοι ἀπὸ τοῦ περὶ ἀναστάσεως λόγου κακῶς πιστοῦν-
ται τὸν ἑαυτῶν λόγον, ἡμεῖς δὲ μᾶλλον ἐκ τούτου πείσομεν αὐτοὺς ὅτι
ὀργανικὸν ἐξαρχῆς ἐπλάσθη τὸ σῶμα, διὸ καὶ τοιοῦτον ἀναστήσεται
(199) ; Ὅτι καινοτάτη ἐστὶν ἡ ἕνωσις τοῦ σώματος καὶ τῆς ψυχῆς
καὶ τῶν δυνάμεων αὐτῆς (213) ; Ὅτι ὁ Θεὸς οὐκ ἐβούλετο τὴν τοῦ
ἀλόγου μέρους δύναμιν ψυχικὴν ἐνθεῖναι τῷ ἀνθρώπῳ ἀλλὰ γνοὺς ποῦ
ῥέπει ὁ ἄνθρωπος, μᾶλλον δὲ προγινώσκων, δέδωκε τῇ ψυχῇ καὶ τὸ
ἄλογον μέρος (215) ; Ὅτι ἄλλος ὁ νοῦς καὶ ἄλλη ἡ ψυχή, εἰ καὶ μὴ
ἀλλοία (217) ; Ὅτι ἐν τῇ ἀναστάσει παυθήσεται τὸ ἄλογον τῆς ψυχῆς
μέρος, ἐπεὶ καὶ τὸ θῆλυ (219).

Dans quelques cas, on rencontre une formule hybride qui combine celle introduite par περί avec celle par ὅτι ; ce sont : Γρηγορίου Νυσσαέως, περὶ ψυχῆς καὶ τοῦ σώματος, ὅτι οὐ προτερεύει τοῦ ἑτέρου τὸ ἕτερον (chapitre 2) ; Ἔτι περὶ τοῦ διπλοῦ ξύλου τῆς προγραφείσης ἄλλης ἐννοίας, ὅτι ὁ αἰσθητὸς κόσμος ἐστὶ τοῦτο τὸ ξύλον, καὶ πρὸς τὴν χρῆσιν αὐτοῦ ἢ καλός ἐστιν ἢ κακός (79) ; Περὶ τῶν ἐκ τοῦ θυμοῦ, καὶ τῆς ἐπιθυμίας κακίας ἕξ παθῶν, ὅτι οὐ συνεκτίσθησαν τῷ ἀνθρώπῳ, καὶ παράθεσις τῶν ἐκ τοῦ ἁγίου Μαξίμου καὶ τοῦ Νύσσης ῥητῶν (140) ; Ἔτι περὶ τῶν δερματίνων χιτώνων, ὅτι καὶ πρὸ τῆς παραβάσεως ὀργανικὸν ἦν τὸ τοῦ ἀνθρώπου σχῆμα (184) ; Περὶ τοῦ ὅτι ὡς ἀνέστη ὁ κύριος, οὕτω καὶ ἡμεῖς ἀναστησόμεθα (210).

Dans presque la moitié des cas, le sujet des chapitres est formulé sous la forme d'une question, à laquelle est donnée la réponse dans les lignes ou les pages qui suivent. Ce procédé se rapproche parfaitement du format littéraire des *quaestiones et responsiones*. Voici un nombre d'exemples : Διατί ἐφθόνησεν ὁ διάβολος τὸν ἄνθρωπον (5) ; Διατί ἐν τῇ ἕκτῃ ἡμέρᾳ ἐπλάσθη ὁ ἄνθρωπος (6) ; Πῶς νοητέον τὸ *Ποιήσωμεν ἄνθρωπον καὶ τὸ κατ'εἰκόνα ἡμετέραν καὶ καθ'ὁμοίωσιν* (7) ; Διατί ὄρθιον τὸ σχῆμα τοῦ ἀνθρώπου (23) ; Τί ἑρμηνεύεται Ἀδάμ (43) ; Πῶς δυνατὸν πλασθῆναι τὸν ἄνθρωπον κατ'εἰκόνα Θεοῦ (44) ; Διατί γυμνὸς ἐνδυμάτων φυσικῶν καὶ τεχνικῶν ἐπλάσθη ὁ ἄνθρωπος (90) ; Τί δηλοῖ, κατὰ τὸν Χρυσόστομον, τὸ *Ἐργάζεσθαι καὶ φυλάττειν τὸν παράδεισον* (97) ; Τί τὸ *Ἐπὶ τῷ στήθει καὶ τῇ κοιλίᾳ πορεύσῃ, καὶ τί τὸ *Χοῦν ἐσθίειν* (117) ; Διατί ψεύστης λέγεται ὁ διάβολος ἀπ'ἀρχῆς (122) ; Τί τὸ ἀξίωμα τοῦ διαβόλου, καὶ τίς ὁ τόπος τῆς ἀρχῆς αὐτοῦ (126) ; Διατί λέγεται ἄρχων τοῦ κόσμου τούτου (127) ; Πῶς παρεικάζεται τῷ ὄφει ὁ διάβολος (147) ; Πῶς ἦν ὁ διάβολος συνήθης τῇ Εὔᾳ (149) ; Διατί τοὺς ἀνθρώπους πρῶτον ἐρώτησεν ὁ Θεὸς καὶ οὐκ αὐτίκα ἐκόλασεν, ἀλλὰ τὸν ὄφιν πρῶτον ἐτιμωρήσατο, εἶτα ἐκείνους, καὶ πῶς πάλιν πρὸ τοῦ Ἀδὰμ τὴν γυναῖκα ἐκόλασεν (158) ; Πῶς τρεφόμεθα (172) ; Διατί ἐπλάσθη ἄρρεν καὶ θῆλυ (191) ; Πῶς εἰκὼν καὶ ὁμοίωμα τοῦ Θεοῦ ὁ ἄνθρωπος, ἐν ᾧ ἐστι τὸ ἄρρεν καὶ θῆλυ (192) ; Τί δηλοῖ τὸ *Αὐξάνεσθε καὶ πληθύνεσθε* (194) ; Διατί ἀνώνυμος ὁ πλούσιος, ὁ δὲ πτωχὸς μετὰ τοῦ ὀνόματος ἐκπεφώνηται (207) ; Τί ἐστιν αἴσθησις (226) ; Πῶς γίνεται ἡ ὅρασις (233) ; Τί νόησις καὶ τί ἔννοια καὶ τί ἐνθύμησις καὶ τί φρόνησις καὶ τί λόγος ἐνδιάθετος (235) ; Τί ἐστι τὸ *Ἰδοὺ γέγονεν*

Ἀδὰμ ὡς εἷς ἐξ ἡμῶν (255) ; Τί ἐστὶ τὸ Ἀπέναντι τοῦ παραδείσου (262).

Il y a quelques cas dans lesquels une telle question se combine avec la formule introduite par περί ; en voici un nombre d'exemples : Γρηγορίου Νύσσης, ἔτι περὶ τῆς ψυχῆς καὶ τοῦ σώματος, πῶς ἐγένοντο (chapitre 3) ; Περὶ τοῦ πῶς εἰκὼν τοῦ Θεοῦ ὁ ἄνθρωπος, καὶ διατί ἀκατανόητος ὁ νοῦς (29) ; Πόθεν σύγκειται τὰ τῶν ἀψύχων σωμάτων, καὶ περὶ τῶν στοιχείων τῶν χυμῶν (52) ; Κατὰ τὸν αὐτόν (c'est-à-dire de Jean Chrysostome), περὶ τοῦ τί ἐστι Τοῦτο νῦν ὀστοῦν ἐκ τῶν ὀστῶν μου (98) ; Τοῦ αὐτοῦ (= Sévérien de Gabala), περὶ τοῦ τί δηλοῖ ἡ τοῦ ἔπλασεν λέξις (106) ; Ἐκ τοῦ αὐτοῦ (= Sévérien de Gabala), περὶ τῶν ξύλων, διατί εἶπεν ὅτι Ἐφυτεύθη πᾶν ξύλον ὡραῖον εἰς ὅρασιν καὶ καλὸν εἰς βρῶσιν (111) ; Περὶ ὀρέξεως· τί ἐστι καὶ πῶς συμβαίνει (176) ; Ἔτι περὶ τοῦ ἥπατος· πῶς ἐξαιματοῖ τὴν τροφὴν καὶ ἀλλοιοῖ (177) ; Περὶ τῆς ἐπιθυμίας· πῶς συνίσταται καὶ πῶς ἡ ἡδονὴ καὶ πῶς ὁ φόβος καὶ πῶς ἡ λύπη (221) ; Περὶ τοῦ φυτοῦ τοῦ ἀπηγορευμένου· διατί ὅλως ἐφυτεύθη ἐν τῷ παραδείσῳ (258).

La combinaison d'une question et de ὅτι se rencontre une seule fois : le chapitre 104 (Ἔτι διατί ξύλον τὸ διπλοῦν οὕτως ἐκλήθη, καὶ ὅτι οὐκ ἐκ τούτου ἔσχε τὴν γνῶσιν ὁ ἄνθρωπος).

Mais ce qui est plus important, c'est que, par endroits, le cachet du genre des questions et réponses est encore beaucoup plus visible, lorsque Nil ajoute aux titres les mots techniques tels ἐρώτημα, ἐρώτησις, ἀπορία et ἄπορον (ἀπορέω), ζήτημα, ἀπόκρισις (ἀποκρίνομαι), λύσις (λύω et διαλύω), ἀνατροπή et ἀντίρρησις ou ἀντιλογία. On citera ici les exemples les plus importants. Le titre du chapitre 49, lequel est tiré du *De opificio hominis* de Grégoire de Nysse – ouvrage qui ne se compose pas d'ἐρωταποκρίσεις –, se lit : Λύσις τοῦ προτεθέντος ζητήματος πῶς ὁ ἄθλιος ἄνθρωπος εἰκὼν εἴη τοῦ μακαρίου Θεοῦ. Le chapitre 141, pris également au *De opificio hominis*, est intitulé Ἀπόκρισις πρὸς τοὺς ἀποροῦντας εἰ μὴ παιδοποιΐα, πῶς ἂν ἐγένοντο αἱ ψυχαί, εἰ μὴ ἥμαρτον οἱ πρωτόπλαστοι ; le texte lui-même débute avec les mots suivants, qui ne sont pas tirés de Grégoire de Nysse et reviennent donc à Nil Doxapatrès (l. 1–6) :

> Δεῖ τοίνυν ἄρτι πληρῶσαι ἡμᾶς τὴν ὑπόσχεσιν καὶ πρῶτον πρὸς τοὺς ἀποροῦντας περὶ τοῦ πληθυσμοῦ ἀποκρίνασθαι, καὶ τότε τὴν λύσιν τῆς ἀπορίας τῆς περὶ τῆς εἰκόνος ἐπαγαγεῖν, πῶς ὕστερον ἐπετεχνάσθη αὐτῇ ἡ κατὰ τὸ ἄρσεν καὶ θῆλυ διαφορά.

Un peu plus loin dans le texte, Nil ajoute encore les mots Πρὸς οὓς ἀποκρινόμεθα (l. 18). La source du chapitre 142 est également le *De opificio hominis* grégorien ; Nil y a introduit le titre :

Λύσις τῆς προτέρας ἀπορίας διατί τῇ εἰκόνι τοῦ Θεοῦ ἐπετεχνά-
σθη ἡ κατὰ τὸ ἄρσεν καὶ θῆλυ διάφυσις· τοίνυν οὕτω λυθέντος,
καιρὸς ἂν εἴη ἀκολούθως διαλύσασθαι καὶ τὸ ἐρώτημα ἐκεῖνο τὸ
περὶ τῆς ἐπιτεχνασθείσης ὕστερον τῇ εἰκόνι τοῦ Θεοῦ διαφορᾶς
κατὰ τὸ ἄρσεν καὶ θῆλυ.

Les chapitres 167 et 168, tirés des *Quaestiones ad Thalassium* de Maxime le Confesseur, sont introduits par ἐρώτησις et ἀπόκρισις respectivement, mais ces deux mots proviendraient très probablement du texte-source. Le titre du chapitre 205, pour une bonne partie inspiré du *De opificio hominis* de Grégoire de Nysse, se lit Ἀντίρρησις πρὸς τοὺς ἀντιλέγοντας περὶ τῆς ἀναστάσεως διὰ τοὺς ἰχθυοβρώτους ἢ θηριοβρώτους ἢ πυρικαύστους ἢ πρὸ πολλοῦ φθαρέντας ; plus loin dans le chapitre, on reconnaît le format de question-réponse, plus particulièrement aux l. 1 (Ἀλλὰ καὶ πάλιν τινὲς ...), 8–9 (οἱ μὴ τοιοῦτον λέγοντες) et 15 (πρὸς οὓς φαμὲν ὅτι ...). Le *caput* 206, tiré encore une fois du *De opificio hominis*, est intitulé Ἑτέρα ἀντίρρησις τῆς ἀναστάσεως καὶ ἀνατροπὴ αὐτῆς τῆς ἀντιρρήσεως. Le titre du chapitre 214, tiré du *De natura hominis* de Némésius d'Émèse, se lit : Λύσις τῆς ἀπορίας πῶς ἥνωται ἡ ψυχὴ καὶ τὸ σῶμα, ὡς εἶναι ἓν τὸν ἄνθρωπον ; Nil introduit la citation de Némésius de la manière suivante : Ἀλλὰ τὸ τοιοῦτον ἄπορον οὕτως λυθήσεται (l. 1). Le *caput* 257 revient à Nil Doxapatrès lui-même et a reçu comme titre Ἀντιλογία πρὸς τοὺς λέγοντας κακὸν εἶναι τὸν θάνατον καὶ διατί οὐ συνεχώρησε τὸν ἄνθρωπον ὁ Θεός, ἅπαξ πταίσαντα ; ce chapitre assez long s'ouvre avec les mots Πρὸς οὓς φαμὲν ὅτι ... (l. 1). Le titre du chapitre 259, pour lequel nous n'avons pas identifié de source, se lit Πρὸς τοὺς λέγοντας διατί ὁ Θεὸς προειδὼς τὴν ἀνθρωπίνην συμφορὰν ἔπλασεν αὐτόν ; le texte du chapitre s'articule sous la forme de question et réponse : Εἰ δὲ πάλιν ἀποροῦσι διατί ... (l. 1) et Πρὸς αὐτοὺς φαμὲν ὅτι ... (l. 8). La même constatation vaut pour le chapitre suivant (260), intitulé Πρὸς τοὺς λέγοντας διατί ὁ Θεὸς ὡς δυνατὸς οὐκ ἐκώλυσε τὸν Ἀδὰμ καὶ ἄκοντα τοῦ μεταλαβεῖν τοῦ ἀπηγορευμένου ξύλου, suivi de la réponse à cette question ou à cette objection ; la formule question-réponse se retrouve dans le texte même du chapitre : Ἀλλ' ἴσως πάλιν ἐροῦσιν ὅτι ... (l. 1) et Πρὸς οὓς ἀρκεῖ τὰ ὄπισθεν εἰρημένα ἐν τῷ περὶ αὐτεξουσίου λόγῳ ... (l. 3–4).

De toutes ces observations, il ressort encore une fois qu'il est très difficile de bien distinguer les genres littéraires byzantins les uns des autres et d'attribuer tel ou tel texte byzantin à un seul format littéraire. Ainsi, le *De oeconomia Dei* appartient évidemment à la littérature anthologique, mais renferme également des éléments qui sont caractéristiques des textes organisés par question et réponse[19]. Par endroits, le florilège prend la forme d'un vrai commentaire biblique.

Appendice :
découverte d'un nouveau témoin, partiel,
de l'anthologie de Nil Doxapatrès

Ci-dessus, nous avons décrit très sommairement les cinq manuscrits de la tradition directe, ainsi que la version abrégée conservée dans le codex *L*. Jusqu'ici, on avait vraiment l'impression d'avoir retrouvé tous les témoins du texte qui nous sont parvenus. Tout récemment, nous avons toutefois découvert un nouveau témoin de l'anthologie. Avouons-le tout de suite : nous aurions dû le connaître, car il est étudié dans un article de Bart Janssens[20] qui a préparé sa dissertation de doctorat sur Maxime le Confesseur sous notre direction. Notre seule excuse est que Monsieur Janssens n'avait pas mis en rapport ces quelques morceaux de texte cités dans le manuscrit qu'il étudie, avec l'anthologie de Doxapatrès ; en effet, en se basant sur le titre qu'on lit dans le manuscrit (voir ci-dessous), il les attribue à un 'anonymous scholiast on Genesis'.

Il s'agit d'un manuscrit qui se trouvait jadis à Istanbul, dans la bibliothèque du Μετόχιον τοῦ Παναγίου Τάφου, et est conservé actuellement à la Bibliothèque Nationale d'Athènes : l'*Atheniensis, Ἐθνικὴ Βιβλιοθήκη τῆς Ἑλλάδος, Μετόχιον τοῦ Παναγίου Τάφου 37*. C'est un volume factice rassemblant deux manuscrits indépendants. On ne se concentre ici que sur la première partie, composée de 28

---

[19] Finalement, on notera que, dans le *De oeconomia Dei*, les titres sont parfois accompagnés de termes techniques comme ἀναγωγή (chapitres 116, 133, 136, 139, 146, 154, 163, 167 et 196), ἀπόδειξις (182, 183, 200, 201, 202, 203 et 209), ἔκληψις (81), ἐπανάληψις (42, 47 et 190), ἐπιβολή (72, 74 et 75), θεωρία (93 et 165), κατασκευή (208), παράδειγμα (185), στηλογραφία (77) et σύνοψις (87).

[20] Janssens 2000 ; voir également Janssens 2002, p. LVIII.

folios seulement, transcrits par un scribe resté anonyme, dont l'écriture est attribuée au XVIIIe siècle. Il contient, respectivement, les extraits suivants : un fragment tiré d'un traité anti-latin de Matthieu Angelos Panaretos (auteur de la seconde moitié du XIVe siècle) ; des extraits recueillis à partir des *Ambigua ad Thomam*, des *Ambigua ad Ioannem* et des *Quaestiones et Dubia* de Maxime le Confesseur ; des fragments de différents *paenitentialia* et *canonaria* byzantins (par exemple celui mis sous le nom de Jean le Jeûneur) ; des extraits sur la Genèse (voir ci-dessous) ; des extraits pris, de nouveau, aux *Ambigua ad Ioannem* de Maxime le Confesseur.

Concentrons-nous maintenant sur les fol. 13^v–14 de l'*Atheniensis*, où on lit les extraits expliquant quelques passages du livre de la Genèse[21]. Cette section porte comme titre : ἔκ τινος ἀνωνύμου (ἴσως Γενναδίου ἢ Κορεσσίου), en suggérant que ces pages reviendraient peut-être à Georges Gennade Scholarios (vers 1400 – vers 1473) ou à Georges Koressios (vers 1570–1659/1660), une conjecture qui s'avère être fautive, comme on le constatera tout de suite. Le scribe conclut cette section du manuscrit, en soulignant qu'il s'agissait ici d'un petit choix qu'il avait fait (ταῦτα ἐκ πολλῶν ὀλίγα).

Les fragments qu'on y lit, donnent l'explication de ξύλον τῆς ζωῆς (Gen. 2. 9), de ξύλον τοῦ εἰδέναι γνωστὸν καλοῦ καὶ πονηροῦ ou de ξύλον τοῦ γινώσκειν καλὸν καὶ πονηρόν (Gen. 2. 9 et 17), de ἔσεσθε ὡς θεοί, γινώσκοντες καλὸν καὶ πονηρόν (Gen. 3. 5), de εἶδεν ἡ γυνὴ ὅτι καλὸν τὸ ξύλον εἰς βρῶσιν ... ἔφαγεν (Gen. 3. 6), de καὶ διηνοίχθησαν οἱ ὀφθαλμοὶ τῶν δύο, καὶ ἔγνωσαν ὅτι γυμνοὶ ἦσαν (Gen. 3. 7), et de καὶ ἐκρύβησαν ... ἀπὸ προσώπου κυρίου τοῦ Θεοῦ (Gen. 3. 8). Un peu par hasard, nous avons découvert qu'il s'agit ici de morceaux choisis pris au *De oeconomia Dei* de Nil Doxapatrès. Ce qu'on lit dans l'*Atheniensis*, correspond plus particulièrement aux chapitres suivants faisant partie de la première section du premier livre de l'anthologie (éd. Neirynck) : l'intégralité du chapitre 83, l. 1 (Ἔστι δὲ καὶ ἄλλως νοῆσαι τὰ ξύλα ταῦτα) – 36 (ξύλου τῆς ζωῆς ἐξωρίσθησαν καὶ θνητοὶ γεγόνασιν) ; les premières lignes du chapitre 84 (sans titre), l. 1 (Ἐπεὶ γὰρ γνώσεως ἦν τὸ ξύλον, πρῶτον τὴν ἑαυτῶν γύμνωσιν) – 5 (καὶ ἐκρύβησαν ἀπὸ προσώπου τοῦ Θεοῦ) ; des parties du chapitre 85 : l. 7 (ὅτι τὸ ξύλον τῆς ζωῆς καὶ μὴ τὸ τοιοῦτον ἐξ αὐτοῦ) – 30 (ἄνθρωπος ἐνετάλθη, κἂν οὐκ ἐφύλαξε) et l. 38 (Ἄμφω γὰρ τὰ ξύλα ἤτοι ὁ νοῦς καὶ ἡ αἴσθησις) – 67 (ἧς τοῦ χείρονος τὸ κρεῖττον προετίμησε) ; des parties du chapitre 86 (sans titre) : l. 1 (Δεῖ τοίνυν νοεῖν ὅτι τὸ ἁπλῶς λεγόμενον κακὸν) – 11 (κατὰ στέρησιν ταύτης ἐπιγινομένη διάθεσις) ; l'intégralité du chapitre 87 (sans titre et

---

[21] Dans Janssens 2000, p. 259–262, Monsieur Janssens avait l'heureuse idée de donner, en appendice à sa contribution, une transcription de cette section.

remaniée) : l. 1 (Μανθάνομεν τοίνυν ὡς οἱ μὲν πάντα νοητὰ) – 14 (τῶν νεωτέρων πνευματοφόρων διδασκάλων) ; une partie du chapire 88 (sans titre) : l. 1 (Εὑρίσκομεν δὲ καὶ τὸν οὐρανοβάμονα καὶ μέγαν Βασίλειον) – 7 (ὅτι οὐκ αἴτιος τῶν κακῶν ὁ Θεὸς ἦν) ; une partie du chapitre 91 (sans titre et remaniée) : l. 8 (Ὁ δὲ κοινὸς φωστὴρ τῆς οἰκουμένης καὶ διδάσκαλος) – 11 (ἐκ τῶν ὑψηλοτέρων καὶ ἀναγωγικοτέρων) ; et, finalement, une partie du chapitre 115 (sans titre) : l. 1 (Πλὴν οὔ μοι δοκεῖ εὐστόχως λέγεσθαι) – 21 (εἰς διάφορα μεριζόμενον πρὸς τὴν χρῆσιν).

Est-ce qu'on connaît la source de ces extraits cités dans l'*Atheniensis* ? Au fol. 10 (à propos de l'extrait pris aux *Ambigua ad Thomam* maximiens), le scribe du manuscrit a laissé une note très intéressante, qui se lit : ἐκ τῆς χειρογράφου βίβλου τῆς ἐν βεμβράναις (*sic*) τοῦ ὁμολογητοῦ μαξίμου ἣν εὗρον ἐν τῷ σινᾷ. Il est bien probable qu'également pour d'autres extraits présents dans le manuscrit, le scribe ait utilisé un manuscrit faisant partie de la bibliothèque du monastère de S. Cathérine au Mont Sinaï. Mais jusqu'ici, on ne dispose d'aucun témoin du *De oeconomia Dei* appartenant à cette bibliothèque, mais puisqu'on connaît très mal cette collection tellement riche, il est possible qu'un tel manuscrit se cache encore au Mont Sinaï ; la chasse est ouverte ...

Est-il possible de rapprocher l'*Atheniensis* d'un des témoins de la tradition directe que nous avons énumérés ci-dessus ?

Voici d'abord toutes les fautes et variantes qui isolent ce manuscrit d'Athènes de tout le reste de la tradition : 83, 1–2 (un début très remanié : Ξύλον μὲν ζωῆς καὶ πᾶν ξύλον ἐστὶν ἐννοῆσαι au lieu de Ἔστι δὲ καὶ ἄλλως νοῆσαι τὰ ξύλα ταῦτα. Ξύλον μὲν ζωῆς καὶ πᾶν ξύλον) ; 83, 7 (ἐλθεῖν au lieu de ἦλθε) ; 83, 10 (πονηρόν au lieu de κακόν) ; 83, 17 (l'addition de θεωρεῖται après ἐν οἷς) ; 83, 19 (l'omission de αὐτοῦ) ; 83, 19–20 (la transposition de ὁ Θεὸς après αὐτῷ) ; 83, 31 (οἱ σωματικοὶ αὐτῶν ὀφθαλμοί au lieu de αὐτῶν ὀφθαλμοί) ; 85, 10 (l'addition de δῆλον après διαφοράν) ; 85, 22 (l'omission de ἕξεως) ; 85, 24 (συνεστῶτος au lieu de συνεστὼς) ; 85, 38 (γοῦν au lieu de γὰρ) ; 85, 44 (αἰσθητῶν au lieu de αἰσθητικῶν) ; 85, 49 (l'addition de καὶ après αἰσθητικῆς) ; 85, 65–66 (la transposition de ἔχων après μόνην) ; 86, 1 (οὐχ᾽ au lieu de ὅτι τὸ) ; 86, 2 (τὸ καλὸν καὶ κακὸν au lieu de κακόν) ; les multiples modifications qu'on a relevées pour le chapitre 87 : 87, 1 (Εἰδέναι τοίνυν δέον au lieu de Μανθάνομεν τοίνυν) ; 87, 1 (οἱ μὲν τῶν πατέρων au lieu de οἱ μὲν) ; 87, 4 (l'omission de l'article τὸν devant Θεολόγον) ; 87, 5–6 (τὸν ὑψηλόνουν Μάξιμον au lieu de τὸν σοφὸν καὶ ὑψηλόφρονα Μάξιμον) ; 87, 6–7 (Νεῖλον τὸν θεῖον au lieu de τὸν χρυσορρόαν Νεῖλον) ; 87, 14 (πατέρων au lieu de διδασκάλων) ; 88, 3 (ἐκλαμβανόμενον au lieu de ἐκλαβόμενον) ; 88, 5–6 (un remaniement considérable : ὡς ἔστιν εἰδεῖν [*sic*] ἐν τῷ ἐπιγεγραμμένῳ αὐτοῦ λόγῳ au lieu de φησὶ γάρ που ἐν τῷ θεοπνεύστῳ λόγῳ αὐτοῦ τῷ ἐπιγεγραμμένῳ) ; 91, 1–3 (un début totale ment remanié : τῆς ἐκκλησίας φωστὴρ Ἰωάννης ὁ χρυσορρήμων au lieu de κοινὸς φωστὴρ τῆς οἰκουμένης καὶ διδάσκαλος ὁ δαψιλέστατος ποταμὸς καὶ ἀέννaος ὁ χρυσορρήμων Ἰωάννης) ; 115, 4 (l'addition de γὰρ après ἐπεὶ) ; 115, 4 (δι'οὗ au lieu de δι'ὃν) ; 115, 6 (l'omission du premier καὶ) ; 115, 9 (ἑαυτὸ au lieu de ἑαυτὸν) ; 115, 11 (l'omission du verbe ἦν) ; 115, 11 (la transposition de ἀμφότερα après εἶναι) ; 115, 11 (αὐτοῦ ἔνδον au lieu de μέσον) ; 115, 12 (ἦν au lieu de ἐστίν) ; 115, 14 (κατὰ τὸ μέρος au lieu de κατά τι μέρος) ; 115, 15 (τὸν κύκλον au lieu de κύκλον) ; 115, 16 et 19 (l'omission des articles τῷ et τῆς) ; 115, 20 (l'addition de ἢ après ἀνάπαλιν)[22].

Quant au modèle de l'*Atheniensis*, il est difficile à repérer. Mais ce qui est sûr, c'est qu'il ne contient aucune leçon qui caractérise le manuscrit *P* seul et ne coïncide nulle part avec la version de l'épitomé conservé en *L*.

Heureusement, nous avons découvert plusieurs cas où l'*Atheniensis* se rattache à la famille dite de Messine, qui unit les témoins *M V* et *R* (et *G*, l'apographe de *R*) ; en voici la liste : 84, 2 (ὅτι au lieu de ἥτις, tout comme dans les manuscrits *M V R G*) ; 85, 12–13 (la transposition de δῆλον après ποιητικόν, comme en *M V R G*) ; 85, 23 (ἐπεὶ au lieu de ἐπειδὴ, tout comme en *M V R G*) ; 85, 41 (transposition de ἀντέχεσθαι après πείθει, comme en *M V R G*) ; 85, 42 (l'addition de πείθει devant ὑπεραίρεσθαι, comme en *M V R G*) ; 87, 10 (οὐ νοητήν, ἀλλὰ αἰσθητὴν au lieu de αἰσθητὴν καὶ οὐ νοητὴν, tout comme en *M*[23] *R G*) ; 87, 12–13 (τὸν πολὺν τὰ θεῖα Δαμασκηνὸν Ἰωάννην au lieu de τὸν σοφώτατον καὶ τὰ θεῖα πεπαιδευμένον πολὺν Ἰωάννην τὸν Δαμασκηνὸν, ce qui se rapproche de ce qu'on lit dans les manuscrits *M*[24] *R G* : τὸν σοφώτατον καὶ τὰ θεῖα πολὺν Ἰωάννην τὸν Δαμασκηνὸν, donc avec l'omission de πεπαιδευμένον) ; 88, 7 (οὐκ ἔστιν αἴτιος τῶν κακῶν ὁ Θεὸς au lieu de οὐκ αἴτιος τῶν κακῶν ὁ Θεὸς ἦν, ce qui se rapproche de la leçon de *M V R G* [οὐκ ἔστιν ὁ Θεὸς αἴτιος τῶν κακῶν]) ; 91, 5 (ἐκλαμβάνεται καὶ αἰσθητῶς au lieu de αἰσθητὸν ἐκλαμβάνεται, tout comme en *M V R G*) ; 115, 12 (ἀληθῶς au lieu de ἀληθὲς, tout comme en *M V R G*). Mais, à d'autres endroits, l'*Atheniensis* rejoint le codex *P*, contre *M V R G* ; autrement dit, dans ces cas, le manuscrit d'Athènes ne contient pas les fautes et

---

[22] Dans la marge de l'*Atheniensis*, à propos de *De oeconomia Dei* 115, 1–5, on lit la note ὅρα περὶ τούτου καὶ Μιχαὴλ τὸν Γλυκᾶ ; Janssens 2000, p. 261 n. 51, donne un renvoi à Michel Glykas, *Annales*, *PG* 158, col. 177B–221D ; ci-dessus (n. 11), nous avons déjà noté qu'un nombre de fois, Nil Doxapatrès et Michel Glykas se sont inspirés de la même source ou de la même tradition.

[23] On notera que le manuscrit *V*, frère du codex *M*, a omis presque l'intégralité du chapitre 87.

[24] Voir la note précédente.

variantes qui isolent *M V R G*. Il semble donc que l'*Atheniensis* remonte plus haut dans le *stemma codicum* que le modèle commun de *M V R G*.

Bibliographie

A. Acconcia Longo (2014), 'La letteratura italogreca nell'XI e XII secolo', dans R. Lavagnini & C. Rognoni (éd.), *Byzantino-Sicula, VI, La Sicilia e Bisanzio nei secoli XI e XII. Atti delle X Giornate di Studio della Associazione Italiana di Studi Bizantini (Palermo, 27–28 Maggio 2011)*, Palermo : Istituto Siciliano di Studi Bizantini e Neoellenici "Bruno Lavagnini" (Istituto Siciliano di Studi Bizantini e Neoellenici "Bruno Lavagnini". Quaderni, 18), p. 107–130.

B. Cabouret, A. Peters-Custot & C. Rouxpetel (éd., 2020), *La réception des Pères grecs et orientaux en Italie au Moyen Âge (V^e–XVe siècle)*, Paris : Les Éditions du Cerf.

S. Caruso (1986–1987), 'Per l'edizione del De oeconomia Dei di Nilo Doxapatres', dans *Δίπτυχα*, 4, p. 250–283.

I. De Vos (2010), *Good Counsel Never Comes Amiss. Nilus Doxapatres and the* De oeconomia Dei : *critical edition of book I, 164–263* (dissertation de doctorat non publiée, KU Leuven).

I. De Vos (2011), 'East or West, Home is Best. Where to Situate the Cradle of the *De Oeconomia Dei* ?', dans C. Macé & P. Van Deun (éd.), *Encyclopedic Trends in Byzantium ? Proceedings of the International Conference held in Leuven, 6–8 May 2009*, Leuven – Paris – Walpole (MA) : Peeters (Orientalia Lovaniensia Analecta, 212), p. 245–255.

J. Gouillard (1973), 'L'interprétation de Genèse 1, 1–3 à l'époque byzantine', dans *In principio. Interprétations des premiers versets de la Genèse*, Paris : Études augustiniennes (École pratique des Hautes Études. Section des Sciences religieuses. Centre d'études des religions du livre, 152), p. 133–152.

B. Janssens (2000), 'An Unnoticed Witness of Some Works of Maximus the Confessor : *Atheniensis, EBE, Μετόχιον τοῦ Παναγίου Τάφου* 37', dans *Byzantion*, 70, p. 242–262.

B. Janssens (2002), *Maximi Confessoris Ambigua ad Thomam una cum Epistula secunda ad eundem*, Turnhout – Leuven : Brepols (Corpus Christianorum. Series Graeca, 48).

V. Laurent (1937), 'L'œuvre géographique du moine sicilien Nil Doxapatris', dans *Échos d'Orient*, 36, p. 5–30.

S. Neirynck (2009), 'Nilus Doxapatres's *De oeconomia Dei*. In Search of the Author Behind the Compilation', dans A. Rigo & P. Ermilov (éd.), *Byzantine Theologians. The Systematization of their Own Doctrine and the Perception of Foreign Doctrines*, Rome : Università degli Studi di Roma "Tor Vergata" (Quaderni di Νέα 'Ρώμη, 3), p. 51–69.

S. Neirynck (2010), 'The *De Oeconomia Dei* by Nilus Doxapatres : Some Introductory Remarks to the Work and its Edition & Chapter I, 40 : Edition, Translation and Commentary', dans *Byzantion*, 80, p. 265–307.

S. Neirynck (2011), 'The *De Oeconomia Dei* by Nilus Doxapatres : a Tentative Definition', dans C. Macé & P. Van Deun (éd.), *Encyclopedic Trends in Byzantium ? Proceedings of the International Conference held in Leuven, 6–8 May 2009*, Leuven – Paris – Walpole (MA) : Peeters (Orientalia Lovaniensia Analecta, 212), p. 257–268.

S. Neirynck (2012), 'Le *De Oeconomia Dei* de Nil Doxapatres. La théologie entre Constantinople et la Sicile, du XIIème siècle à la modernité', dans A. Speer & P. Steinkrüger (éd.), *Knotenpunkt Byzanz. Wissensformen und kulturelle Wechselbeziehungen*, Berlin – Boston : de Gruyter (Miscellanea Mediaevalia, 36), p. 274–287.

S. Neirynck (2014a), *La théologie byzantine en Sicile normande. Nil Doxapatres (XIIe siècle). De oeconomia Dei, Livre I, 1–163. Édition critique et introduction* (dissertation de doctorat non publiée, KU Leuven).

S. Neirynck (2014b), 'Nil Doxapatres et son *De Oeconomia Dei*. La théologie byzantine en terre sicilienne au XIIe siècle', dans R. Lavagnini & C. Rognoni (éd.), *Byzantino-Sicula, VI, La Sicilia e Bisanzio nei secoli XI e XII. Atti delle X Giornate di Studio della Associazione Italiana di Studi Bizantini (Palermo, 27–28 Maggio 2011)*, Palermo : Istituto Siciliano di Studi Bizantini e Neoellenici "Bruno Lavagnini" (Istituto Siciliano di Studi Bizantini e Neoellenici "Bruno Lavagnini". Quaderni, 18), p. 175–186.

G. Parthey (1866), *Hieroclis Synecdemus et notitiae graecae episcopatuum. Accedunt Nili Doxapatrii Notitia patriarchatuum et locorum nomina immutata*, Berlin : In aedibus Friderici Nicolai [réimpr. Amsterdam : Hakkert, 1967].

L. Perria (1981), 'Una pergamena greca dell'anno 1146 per la chiesa di S. Maria dell'Ammiraglio', dans *Quellen und Forschungen aus italienischen Archiven und Bibliotheken*, 61, p. 1–24.

P. Van Deun (2020), 'Lire les Pères grecs en Sicile normande: le cas du *De oeconomia Dei* de Nil Doxapatrès', dans B. Cabouret,

A. Peters-Custot & C. Rouxpetel (éd., 2020), *La réception des Pères grecs et orientaux en Italie au Moyen Âge (V^e–XVe siècle)*, Paris : Les Éditions du Cerf, p. 161–179.

P. Van Deun (sous presse), 'Neilos (Nikolaos) Doxapatres (fl. 12th c.)', dans M. Grünbart & A. Riehle, *Lexikon byzantinischer Autoren*.

Abstract

This present article reflects on the literary format of a Byzantine anthology, the *De oeconomia Dei*, compiled by the monk Nilus Doxapatres, probably in Sicily by order of king Roger II (1095–1154). Many chapters of the text echo the question and answer genre ; very often the focus is upon the creation of the world and of mankind. Until now only six manuscripts were known preserving the first two books of the florilegium. In appendix a new partial witness will be presented (*Athens, Metochion Panagiou Taphou 37*, from the 18th c.).

LIST OF ABBREVIATIONS

ACO	*Acta conciliorum oecumenicorum* (Berlin)
CAG	*Commentaria in Aristotelem Graeca* (Berlin)
CAp	*Corpus apologetarum christianorum saeculi secundi* (Jena)
CCSG	*Corpus Christianorum Series Graeca* (Turnhout)
CPG	*Clavis patrum graecorum* (Turnhout)
CSCO	*Corpus scriptorum christianorum orientalium* (Louvain)
CSEL	*Corpus scriptorum ecclesiasticorum latinorum* (Wien)
DK	*Die Fragmente der Vorsokratiker*, eds H. Diels & W. Kranz
GCS	*Griechische Christliche Schriftsteller* (Berlin)
GNO	*Gregorii Nysseni Opera* (Leiden)
NPNF	*Nicene and Post-Nicene Fathers*, eds P. Schaff & H. Wace
PG	*Patrologia Graeca* (Paris)
SC	*Sources chrétiennes* (Lyon)
TLG	*Thesaurus Linguae Graecae*

INDICES

INDEX BIBLICVS

Prepared by
Maxim VENETSKOV

INDEX FONTIVM

Prepared by
Maxim VENETSKOV

449